THE PROBATE RECORDS

OF

LINCOLN COUNTY,

MAINE.

1760 TO 1800.

COMPILED AND EDITED
FOR THE
MAINE GENEALOGICAL SOCIETY,
BY
WILLIAM D. PATTERSON,
WISCASSET, ME.

Southern Historical Press, Inc.
Greenville, South Carolina

This volume was reproduced
from a personal copy located in
the Publishers private library

All rights reserved. No part of this publication may be reproduced,
stored in a retrieval system, transmitted in any form, posted
on the web in any form or by any means without the
prior written permission of the publisher.

Please direct all correspondence and book orders to:
SOUTHERN HISTORICAL PRESS, Inc.
1071 Park West Blvd.
Greenville, SC 29611

Published 1895:
   Portland, ME.
ISBN #978-1-63914-665-9
Printed in the United States of America

CONTENTS.

PREFACE	Pages 5—11
INTRODUCTION	Pages iii—xxi
ERRATA	Page xxiii
LINCOLN PROBATE RECORDS	Pages 1—368
INDEX OF NAMES	Pages 1—48
INDEX OF PLACES	Pages 49—53

PREFACE.

This book contains copies of the wills filed in the Probate Court for Lincoln County from the year 1760 to the year 1800 and brief abstracts of the records of the proceedings of that court during the same period.

Perhaps the earliest existing record of probate proceedings had in this section of Maine is that found in the record* made

> At a court held at Pemaquid 22 July 1674 by Major Tho: clarke Humphry Dauie: Richd Collicut, and Left Thomas Gardner according to commission and order of the Generall Courte of the Massatusetts collony, Dated in Boston in N: E: 27 day of May 1674,

which record is in the following words:

Administration to the estate of John Walter a fisherman somtymes Resident at Monheghen & sometymes at Damerells coue who dyed about four yeares since is granted to Geo: Burnett Resident at Monheghen who is to dispose of the same according to the cleerest testimony of, and to whome ye Estate doeth belong & to bring in an Inventory of the same to ye next comission Court, heere, & himselfe as principall & Richd Oliver as Suerty doe bind themselves in fifty pounds a peece that this Order shall bee attended & p'formed.

In this instance the General Court appears to have delegated its functions as a court of probate, a custom that was subsequently adopted by the Governor and Council who under the Province charter of 1691 had power to " doe execute or performe all that is necessary for the Probate of Wills, Granting of Administracons for, touching or concerning any Interest or Estate which any person or persons shall

---

*Printed entire in M. H. S. coll. "Baxter MSS.," pp. 343-348.

NOTE. This was probably the only County Court established under the Massachusetts Colony charter within the territory subsequently known as Lincoln County. At that court the region between the Sagadahoc and Georges rivers seems to have been first called and known as the County of Devon.

have within our said Province or Territory ". Soon, however, after the charter become operative judges of probate were commissioned, inferior probate tribunals were established and suitable persons were designated as registers thereof in the several counties; and in probate matters the Governor and Council reserved to themselves and exercised only the powers of a Supreme Court of Probate to which appeals from the probate courts could be had. Finally, near the close of the administration of Governor Pownall, in 1760, they became duly organized as the Supreme Court of Probate for the province and adopted a seal therefor.

The act of the General Court of the Province of Massachusetts Bay for erecting and establishing two new counties in the easterly part of the county of York provided that from and after the first of November, 1760, the most eastern county, bounded on the west by the county of Cumberland, on the east by the province of Nova Scotia, on the south and southeast by the sea or western ocean, and on the north by the utmost northern limits of the province, should be called and known as the County of Lincoln. This act established the town of Pownalborough, which then included the territory now embraced in the towns of Wiscasset, Dresden, Alna and Perkins, as the shire or county town. This town had been incorporated on the 13th of February, 1760, and named in honor of that able colonial statesman, Thomas Pownall, who was then governor of Massachusetts, and this town, the name of which was changed to Wiscasset in 1802, has ever since been the principal shire town of Lincoln County.

The Lincoln Probate Court was constituted by the appointment of William Cushing as judge and Jonathan Bowman as register. The earliest act of the court as found in its records granted letters of administration upon the estate of Humphry Purrington, late of Georgetown, under date of the 14th of November, 1760. The record does not disclose whether the court upon that occasion was held at Georgetown or Pownalborough: the letters were dated at Georgetown; the warrant to appraisers at Pownalborough; both bear the same date. At that date and for several years afterwards there seems to have been no regularly established time and place for holding the court and it was probably held at either Pownalborough or Georgetown, as was most for the convenience of parties having business before it, and but little formality observed. The wills of Nathaniel Donnell and Patrick Drummond, two old time residents of Georgetown, were probated at that place. On two or three occasions the court appears to have sat at Richmond.

William Cushing, the first judge of the court, was of a distinguished Massachusetts family residing at Scituate, where he was born on the first day of March, 1732, third son of the Hon. John Cushing. He graduated from Harvard College in 1751 and after studying for a time with Jeremy Gridley he established himself in the practice of the law. Upon receiving his appointment as judge of probate he removed to Pownalborough where, until the arrival of Timothy Langdon, in 1769, he was the only educated lawyer and as such he appeared as counsel in the most important cases brought before the common law courts of the county. If one can judge by documents drawn by him, now extant, it may safely be concluded that he was methodical in his affairs and careful in all his undertakings. In the work of transcribing these records it has been a pleasure to take in hand a will or other instrument in his beautiful handwriting and elegant arrangement of paragraphs. He filled the office of judge of this court until 1772 when he was appointed a justice of the Superior Court of Judicature. He then returned to Massachusetts where he ever after made his home. Judge Cushing continued as a justice of the Superior Court until several years after it came to be known as the Supreme Judicial Court, a title which it retains to this day. At Pownalborough, on the 11th of July, 1786, Cushing, then chief justice, opened the first term of the Supreme Judicial Court that was held in this county. Associate Justices Sargent, Sewall and Sumner presided with him at that term of court. Upon the establishment of the Supreme Court of the United States, in 1789, Judge Cushing was selected by Washington as chief justice. Cushing declined the honor, but accepted a seat as associate justice and continued to occupy the same until his death, 7 September, 1810, ended a long and honorable career.

The name of Jonathan Bowman is found in the records of this court for a period of more than forty years: first as register and afterwards as judge. Born at Dorchester, Massachusetts, 8 December, 1735, he was graduated from Harvard College in 1755. When the first officers of this court were selected one William Bryant, whose appointment appears to have been desired by certain of the proprietors of the Kennebec Purchase, was a candidate for the office of register and it seems to have been understood by some of his friends that he would be appointed, but the influence in favor of Bowman carried the day. At about the same time the governor of Massachusetts, agreeably to the act incorporating Lincoln County, appointed a register of deeds for the county for the term of five years from February, 1761. Bowman received that appointment. Upon the organization of the Inferior Court of Common Pleas and the Court of General Sessions of the Peace a few months later he was appointed clerk for those courts and continued as such for upwards of thirty years and until he relinquished the offices to his son and successor, Jonathan Bowman, Jr. He appears to have entered upon the duties of register of probate at the time when Cushing became judge and he served in that capacity until he succeeded to the judgeship which position he filled during the Revolutionary period and under the government of the Commonwealth, having been recommissioned therein by his relative, Governor Hancock. The first instrument signed by him as judge found in these records bears date the tenth of June, 1772. In the Revolutionary days the records of the court were swollen by proceedings involving the care and disposition of the confiscated estates of absentee loyalists and at these "tory trials," as the hearings were commonly called, Judge Bowman presided. He continued in the performance of the duties of this responsible position during the remainder of the period covered by this book and until his decease, 4 September, 1804. The comfortable and spacious two-storied mansion in which Judge Bowman made his home still stands near the bank of the Kennebec river in Dresden. It is a well-preserved house having a broad, roomy hall and staircase and in each of its high-wainscoted rooms a capacious open fire-place. With its traditions of the Hancocks, of John Adams and Increase Sumner, and of Bowdoin and the Gardiners it is an interesting relic of the provincial days in the eastern country and one of the notable houses of the county.

Roland Cushing, the youngest brother of Judge Cushing and himself a lawyer, succeeded Bowman as register of probate. Roland Cushing was born at Scituate, 26 February, 1750, and was educated at Harvard College which he left in 1768 and entered upon the study of law with his brother William at Pownalborough. He held the office of register of this court for fifteen years. His death occured in 1788 at Waldoborough where he was then a resident. The personal recollections of those who knew him have been preserved and show that endowed by nature with a graceful and manly form, possessing brilliant mental parts cultivated and enriched by study, eloquent and forceful in argument, he enjoyed a popularity that was long remembered. His untimely death and the indulgence of habits that led to it were much deplored by his friends and associates.

On the 29th of January, 1787, Judge Bowman designated Nathaniel Thwing, of Woolwich, as register of the court *pro tempore*. Thwing's home was at Hutchinson's Point, now known as Thwing's Point, on the bank of the Kennebec and a few miles from the residence of Judge Bowman. Thwing was long time an upright magistrate and well-known office-holder in this county. He was an admirable recording officer and the records made by him are unequalled for legibility, neatness and precision. He appears to have discharged the duties of register of this court until 1792, a period of about five years. Portions of the second and third volumes, the whole of the fourth volume and the first fifty-eight folios of the fifth volume are in his handwriting. A portion of the records in volume III are attested by Thomas Tileston, register *pro tempore*, of whom nothing further is here known at this time.

The next regularly appointed register of the court after Roland Cushing was Jonathan Bowman, Jr., eldest son of Judge Bowman. At the date of his appointment, young Bowman was barely twenty-one years of age. He was born 17 April, 1771, and was graduated at Harvard College in 1791. He made records that are models of neatness and legibility. He held the office of register of probate for about ten years, and during a part of that time he was clerk of the common law courts for the county. He resided for some years at Wiscasset. His death occurred at the early age of thirty-seven years.

These short personal sketches may serve to revive in some degree the *personnel* of the court for the first forty years of its existence. The careful student of these records will not overlook their importance, but will find in them that which will suggest pictures of the economical and social life of this section of Maine during the last half of the eighteenth century in a manner that no other records now extant can revive. In them will be found evidences of the religious beliefs of the last century inhabitants of this anciently settled county, testimony of their patriotism, traces of their loves, their hates and their family feuds and strifes; their standard of comparative wealth and station and their customs and modes of life. There is not room to particularize within the limits of this brief note. The pages of this book contain many of those details in which, to use the words of John Adams, posterity delights.

It has been seen that the earliest sittings of this court were at Pownalborough, Georgetown and Richmond. The records indicate that the court was most frequently held at Pownalborough, usually in the west precinct of the town and at Pownalborough court house which historic building, erected by the Proprietors of the Kennebec Purchase in accordance with a vote passed by them on the 13th of April, 1761, for the purpose of providing a suitable place for holding the courts, still stands within the limits of the former parade ground of old Fort Shirley in the town of Dresden. It is a substantial frame structure, three stories high. The court room, situate on the second floor overlooking the Kennebec, was an apartment forty-five feet long and nineteen and a half feet wide. It is rich with memories of John Adams and the Cushings, the Sewalls and the Sullivans; of Robert Auchmuty, the younger, of Chipman and Wyer, Bradbury and Paine; and of Gardiner and Bridge, Lithgow and Langdon. It is not famous alone for having been the temple of justice. The service of the church of England was often held within its walls by the Rev. Jacob Bailey, rector of the ancient St. John's parish before his church structure was erected; and there the preachers of other religious denominations from time to time gathered their hearers.

A few years after the Revolution the population of the county had increased to such an extent that the inhabitants of the eastern part, desirous of being no longer subject to the necessity of making the long and tiresome journey which was involved in attending to probate business and visiting the registry of deeds at Pownalborough, succeeded in procuring the passage on the 6th of November, 1784, of "An Act empowering the Inhabitants of the County of Lincoln Eastward of Union River to choose a Register of Deeds, and for the establishing of a Court of Probate to be holden within and for all that part of the said County which lies to the Eastward of said River." From and after the date when that act went into effect and until the incorporation of Hancock and Washington counties this court was known as that of the "west district" of the county. The establishment of the eastern district foreshadowed the separation that soon followed. After the area of the county was reduced and as population multiplied and the business of the court increased it became customary to hold the several terms during the year in different towns, usually at the houses of innholders, when held outside of the shire town. In the year 1790, the court sat at Pownalborough court house in May, August, September and October; at the house of Lazarus Goodwin, in Hallowell, and at the house of Joseph Lambard, in Bath, in May; at the house of Samuel Nickels, in Newcastle, and at the house of Cornelius Turner, in Waldoborough, in September; and in the year 1791 : at Pownalborough court house in January, April, June and August; at the house of Amos Pollard, in Hallowell, in January; at Lambard's, Bath, in June; at the house of Charles Samson and at Turner's, both in Waldoborough, in September, and at the house of Ebenezer Whittier, in Pownalborough, in December. For many years and until the establishment of the eastern district the jurisdiction of this court extended throughout all that part of Maine eastward of the then eastern boundary of Cumberland county and in its records are found traces of those who lived as far east as Bangor, Mount Desert and Machias and northward to Farmington and Norridgewock. Its territory was first reduced by the act creating the eastern district and that was rapidly followed by the incorporation of Hancock county, in 1789, and Kennebec, in 1799.

It is hoped that the scope of this volume and the arrangement of its contents will commend it to the student of genealogy. Full copies of the wills are given in the order in which they are found of record. The abstracts from the records of proceedings relating to the estates of intestates are given in like order and contain mention of every act of the court and of the representatives of the estates found of record, together with reference to the volumes and folios where such are recorded, thus forming in connection with the index of names an index to the first eight volumes of the probate records of Lincoln County.

The cordial thanks of the Society are hereby extended to that learned antiquary, Rufus K. Sewall, Esq., for the timely and comprehensive sketch of the early history of English common law proceedings in Maine that is embodied in the introduction, so generously furnished by him for this book, the value of which is best attested in the following note here printed by the kind permission of the Hon. John A. Peters, chief justice of the Supreme Judicial Court of the State of Maine.

Wiscasset, May 6, 1895.

HON. R. K. SEWALL,
 Dear Sir:

I have read with exceeding interest the paper which you have prepared as an introduction to the book, to be published, of the Probate Records of the County of Lincoln (or Cornwall) up to the year inclusive, of 1800. Your paper very finely illustrates, in brief form, the principles and practice of the Common Law of England, during that ancient period, to be found in the probate records to be published. There will be seen in them clear pictures of the civilization of that period, which an American citizen will readily appreciate and much enjoy.

Very sincerely yours,

JOHN A. PETERS.

The *indices* to this volume have been prepared by Joseph P. Thompson, Esq., who has thus rendered invaluable aid.

Wiscasset, 1 November, 1895.

WILLIAM D. PATTERSON.

INTRODUCTION.

These mortuary records of Lincoln County are matter of public interest and importance. In them we have an epitome of the thrift of the generations past of this ancient part of our state as a culmination of the English common law, where first applied in the beginnings of New England, to shape and develop the life forms of society and Christian civilization in its civil relations.

The record also discloses, in clear and precise features, the religious and Christian sentiments of the fathers of Lincoln County to have been eminently biblical in all phases of man's mortuary relations to the pregnant future of human life. The facts of this record, in this respect, we deem quite remarkable.

As an outgrowth of pre-existing legal conditions of the history of this county, where first was applied in New England the forces of the English common law as a colonizing agency, I propose to make the facts of such application and the incidents of development a supplement to the legal records herein published; which had origin in the charter of April 10, A. D., 1606; practically enforced on the peninsula of Sabino, now Sagadahoc, in seizen and possession, under the English theories of valid land title in A. D. 1607; and further developed at Pemaquid and Sheepscot, when Lincoln County was an integrant part of Ducal Territory to 1689; and the organization of Lincoln Bar.

COLONIAL CHARTER. April 10, A. D., 1606.

Expansion and application of the English common law as a colonizing force and antecedents.

UNDERLYING FACTS. A. D. 1492.

The fact of the existence of a continent in the west had been revived and certified to the nations of Europe by Columbus.

The next year, 1493, the newly discovered lands were partitioned to

Spain and Portugal in virtue of alleged Divine vice-geral domination in a dotal act of Pope Alexander VI. These facts startled and excited Europe. The legal soundness of land title so acquired was questioned, as matter of international law. France wanted to find Adam's will and see the clause warranting its exclusion to a share of the new world.

England protested: appealed to natural right and justice: declared there was no good title in land without possession in newly discovered countries.

It was her common law doctrine of "seizen and possession," as applied to her popular homestead holdings.

The international conflict raised grave questions of right. England pressed the issue with incisive diplomacy.

The British Lion shook his mane; and bristling with resentment at the wrong of Papal presumption, roared,—*"prescriptio sine possessione, haud valeat"* and made preparation to force her common law postulate of homestead holdings into the international code and have it applied to trans-atlantic interests in defiance of the Pope's authority and in derogation of his assumed right in giving away the lands of the newly discovered world.

The English doctrine was novel. It was also revolutionary. The conflict deepened. Spain was supreme in prestige and power on sea and land, and also a petted child of the Church of that day. The issue of trans-atlantic titles had become national. England was resolute. The issue narrowed. Spain led off, the champion, not only of her dotal title, but also of Divine vice-geral authority in the Pope. More than a century* had passed the Papal grant, when the English Parliament declared, that by law of nature and nations, seizen and possession were sole grounds of good title to newly discovered lands. In 1580,† this postulate of her common law was officially declared. The doctrine of possession, as the ground of perfected right in lands abroad, as well as at home, had become a battle ground of statesmanship and diplomacy in the legal arena.

CRISIS. A. D. 1588.

The argument was ended. Spain resolved to cut the Gordian knot with the sword. She marshalled an "Armada,"—arrogantly called, "the invincible",—entered the English Channel, with all the pomp and pride of a Divine mission, the 19th of July. England gathered her ships of

---

*Holmes' Annals, vol. 1, p. 1.
†Poor's Vindication, p. 9.

war, and massed her guns to meet the issue. Battle was joined the 21st day of July. Drake led the English manœuvres. Fifteen different* engagements were fought. The conflict continued to the 27th of July, and Spain lost five thousand men and seventeen ships of war. England burned and sunk, and storms scattered, the Armada of Spain; and her naval supremacy went with it; and England became herself mistress of the sea.

Spain, to crush England in her presumption, had failed and fallen in the struggle. The Pope's dictum and dotal, heretofore regarded and respected as the end of all law, went down with the "Great Armada." The issue gave force and effect to the doctrine of English "seizen and possession," as a guarantee of title to an American foothold in the new world.

The ancient doctrine of Papal Divine right, as an element of international law, was thus over-ruled. Possession now became the ground of right to valid title in North America.

Thereupon the maritime nations pushed for discovery of eligible sites for possession and the English common law of seizen and possession became a great colonizing force.

RESULTS. 1602.

Maritime restlessness in the west of England took shape in a voyage of discovery, by a new and untried route, to the American shores, direct in course west, as the winds would allow. The vessel was the "Concord," Bartholomew Gosnold, master. The result was that he made and touched the new world in a land full of hillocks, an "outpoint of tall grown trees ahead, a rock-bound coast and shores of white sand in Lat. 40° N."

It was a sunrise view. A Spanish sloop with mast and sail and iron grapnel came along-side; and the Indian seamen, some clad in European costume, came on board and chalked a map of the country on deck which they called "Ma-voo-shan."

Its attractions were noted, and reported in England; and the landfall marked, for further examination.

In 1605, a "new survey" was projected, and executed, by Captain George Weymouth, and returned before autumn. This survey resulted in the discovery of a magnificient harbor, the little River of Pemaquid, and the Saga-da-hock, the notable river of the Ma-voo-shan land-fall of the Concord's voyage of 1602.

---

*Teig's Chronology.

These rivers, of this land-fall, at once became coveted points of commercial value to England, for seizure and possession, where the forms and forces of English common law, should be applied, in planting homesteads of the English race, in New England.

The report of Gosnold, the survey of Weymouth, fixed the English idea of desirable locality, for eminent domain, in a national act of "Seizen and possession," for a "great state project."

Spacious harbors, grand river tributaries, magnificent woods, abounding in sea-shore fisheries and beaver haunts, were the appreciated features of commercial promise, in the panorama, of the Mavooshan land-fall, for places "fit and convenient, for hopeful plantations."

Sagadahoc, the notable river of the Gosnold land-fall of Mavooshan, was the magnet of subsequent colonial and commercial activity, to the west of England communities.

Gosnold's "wooded out-point" of the Mavooshan land-fall, the beaver haunts of Pemaquid dependencies, Sheepscot and Muscongus, with Sagadahoc, environed with waters, "the strangest fish-pond of the western seas," land-marked by Monhegan and highlands of Penobscot in the east and the twinkling mountains of "Au-co-cisco," west, in 1606, had become a land of promise, to the commercial industries of England, as a seat of English Empire in North America.

CHARTER OF APRIL 10, 1606 A. D.

Public interest and enterprise, took definite shape, 10 of April 1606.

English purposes of seizen and possession then took form and expression, in legal muniments of contract.

A corporation was organized under a crown grant composed of eminent subjects of England.

The grant covered agreements. "We do grant and agree," were the words of compact. In tenor, it was a Royal license, hedged about with conditions precedent to future and further concessions.

The grantees, were government contractors. The transaction, was a conception, legal and formal, of valid title and permanent possession, covering a purpose of enduring foot-hold of the English race, at the points of seizen and possession, made.

The Christian nobility of England, joined the commercial agencies of her great seaports, in pressing government to participate in the enterprise. "The wings of man's life are plumed with the feathers of death," was cried in the ears of Elizabeth, in urgency of national colonization in the New World.

The Lord Chief Justice of the English Bench, Sir John Popham, headed the west of England movement, who is described as eminently* honorable and patriotic, and by the jealous Spaniards, a *"Great Puritan."* He manipulated the contract. The conditions were the making of habitations, leading out colonies of volunteer subjects of Great Britain, and planting them in "fit and convenient places." The contractors were required to "build and fortify" where they should inhabit, and could lawfully colonize only those of English citizenship, who would emigrate as volunteers.

The salient points of the contract of April 10, 1606, for seizing and holding actual and permanent possession of the American coast at and near the 44° N. E. are full and clear in purpose and plan. Gosnold's land-fall, the out-point of fair tall trees, little green round hills inland with the rockey shores of white sand, in the country of the Mavooshans was the contemplated *"locus in quo,"* of the colonial undertakings.

English voluntary colonization, domiciliation of the race, military occupancy of fit and convenient places herein and about the latitude described, were the avowed purposes of both the government and its grantees, the adventurers, of the charter license.

George Popham and Rawley Gilbert with other eminent men of English nobility, their heirs, assigns and successors, were executive agents, under the grant.

Such a colonization by them accomplished under royal stipulations, insured, a future endowment of plenary rights to the fruits of their undertaking in a crown deed, or patent to the section of country by them discovered and so seized and possessed, on their petition therefor.

The contract of the 10th, April, 1606, pregnant with the forces of English common law at once began to unfold in starting effective English colonization at two eligible points in the Temperate Zone of North America, north of Florida, in English cartography, marked "Virginia." Two* colonial adventures were organized under the contracts of April 10, 1606, known as "the first and second colonies."

DUAL COLONIAL EXODUS.

The first sailed for Chesapeake Bay and seized the peninsula of Jamestown, on James River, May 12, 1607. (O. S.)

The second sailed May 31st, 1607, for Mavooshan, landing at and

---

*Genesis of U. S. p. 45, Vol. 1.

seizing the peninsula of Sabino, Sagadahoc, 20th August, 1607 "the place to which it was directed."*

The first act of possession, was a formal solemn consecration, in the public worship of Almighty God, with prayer, praise and a sermon on the spot chosen for a town.

One hundred and twenty colonies landed and stood there together, under the English flag.

The church of England, in canonical robes with hallowed endowments of state, in support of law, stood among them.

The sermon endorsed the transactions of state in progress; with the bible in her right hand and in her left, the cross, symbolic of Christian faith, the church of England, by holy invocation, consecrated the place and sanctified the occasion; and so set up the pillars of the new state on English constitutional grounds in religion and law, for a new English Commonwealth.

A civil polity was duly organized. A body of laws promulged. George Popham was nominated and inaugurated by oath of office not as a governor, or vice-roy, but as *"President,"* to hold and to wield the great function of sovereignty, as chief magistrate. Subordinate officers were sworn in.

Then the President took a spade† and "Set the first† spit of ground unto it;" turning the sod, as a formal act of seizen and possession perfected by the formularies of English land title in "turf and twig," under the common law of England.

Of this colonial planting the first material fruits, were realized in an English village homestead of fifty houses, a ware house, a fort entrenched and fortified with mounted cannon, a church with a steeple, shipyard and thirty ton vessel on the stocks. These were the adornments of the shore margins, of the sheltering head-lands of Sagadahoc, at its mouth, where a permanent foot-hold was contemplated, and all the elements of English civilization in law and religion, the great civilizing forces of humanity were first combined and took organic form on the soil of New England.

---

*Two plantations, in virtue of Chief Justice Popham's agency were undertaken to be settled on the coasts of America, called the first and second colonies. The first was in the interest of London men and the second, the west of England. The second colony sailed on the 31st of May, 1607, under Capt. Geo. Popham and Rawley Gilbert, for "Seizing" the place to which they were directed.—Holmes' Annals, Vol. 1, p. 155.

†Lambeth Palace Papers.

FIRST COURT OF LAW IN NEW ENGLAND.

The President and his sworn assistants constituted the first organized court of law. It had a seal. "*Sigellum Regis Magnae Britaniae Franciae et Hiberniae,*" was the legend on one face. On the reverse, it ran: "*Pro Concillio Secundae Coloniae Virginae,*" and this court was within the ancient Lincoln County bounds.

LAWS.

"Tumults, rebellion, conspiracy, mutiny, sedition, man-slaughter, incest, rape and murder, were capital offences. Adultry, drunkenness, and vagrancy were punishable offences.

They all must be tried within the colonial precintsc. Magistrates were required to hold in suspense judgment on crime in aid of application to the king for pardon.

Records of judgments, were required to be set forth fully, as basis for appeals. Christian teaching and civilization of the Indians were ordained of law, which also demanded, preaching of Christian religion as established by the English Constitution.

CHARTER RIGHTS.

Nucleus of American Polity.

All the rights of home-born English citizenship, were guaranteed to the residents of the Sagadahoc Town of Fort St. George. The writ* of habeas corpus trial by jury and the elective franchise, were assured rights. "These my loving subjects, shall have the right *annually* to elect a *President* and *other officers, possess and enjoy forever, the right to make all needful laws for their own government*" were the precious words, of their constitutional charter.

In its expansion, *perpetual self-governing power, was an endowmeut of the Sagadahoc free-hold*:—a boon of English constitutional law; an organic element in the civil life, of English Colonization, here first planted in New England. With these facts before us, it is no matter of surprise, that under President Popham's beneficient administration the Sabbath at Sagadahoc, was duly observed to God's honor in prayers and religious services,"morning and evening;"and without doubt according to the venerable, reverential, decorous and exact formularies of the church of England:—whose solemn and devout forms of worship of the true God here first awed the savage mind and touched the savage heart. The fear and worship of God were marked features of that ad-

---

*Chartet 1606. Menoval, p. 94.

ministration. Sunday* Oct. 5th, Nahanada and wife of Pemaquid, and the Indian Pilot of the Popham colony, a member of the Royal house of Mavooshan, and one Amenquin, a sagamore, went with President Popham, to the place of public prayers, both morning and evening, attending with great veneration, reverence and silence."

This scheme of civil polity pregnant with the seeds of our subsequent free institutions of the United States sown in it by force of English common law, first applied here in Maine to New England homestead life, was thus set to work out natural results, with the machinery of law and religion, into which the civilizing forces of Christian ethics fully entered to shape the embryo of out growing states.

Beneficient progress was made during the administration of Pres't Popham. The 15th of December a dispatch was penned, in Mavooshan at Fort St George and sent to the King of England, announcing present success with sketching of incidents of promise in these beginnings of English homesteads at Sagadahoc.

It is in Latin and now extant, the usual language of State-papers of that day.

President Popham was an aged, but God-fearing man, "stout † built, honest, discrete, careful: somewhat timid, but conciliatory in demeanor. Popham was the life of the colony. Seymour, the colonial chaplain was eminent for his industry and honest endeavors. The same is recorded of Turner, the surgeon.

But Rawley Gilbert official representative of the London Element in the adventure, is described to have been of a jealous, ambitious turn, a sensual man of loose life, head strong, little religious zeal, poor judgment, little experience, though valiant. Sinister and selfish, he was a mischievous factor, in the colonial development. More or less friction appeared; but President Popham calmed and reconciled differences, during his rule.‡

On the 5th of Feb., 1608, Popham, whose conduct had impressed even the savages with his virtues died, probably the victim of a climatic convulsion. The last of January for seven hours, thunder, lightning, fearful and frequent rain, snow, hail and frost in excessive and and awful succession, over whelmed with cyclonic and winter rigors, the little village of English free-holders at Sagadahoc.

But the hamlet survived the dire calamities of the season, to encoun-

---

*L. P, Mss. Journal, Mass. Hist. Col., p. 109, Vol. 18.
†Gorges to Cecil, p. 286. Maine Hist. Quarterly, July, 1891.
‡Brown's Genesis United. States.

ter the caprice, irresolution and selfishness of succession in Gilbert.

The catastrophe of climate presaged not only the demise of the good president at Sagahahoc, but further fatalities. Though captain Davis declared on his arrival with new supplies in the spring he found "all things in good condition in the colony, many furs stored and the New Virginia—a pretty vessel launched, ready for sea, Gilbert, now in command had become restless and inclined to abandon the enterprise.

Notwithstanding the good condition of affairs at Sagadahoc, Gilbert proposed to leave Fort St. George and return to London.

The proposal met the sympathies, at least of the London people in the colony; and the London ship Mary and John and the pretty Virginia, whose master builder was Digby of London, were laden with colonists in sympathy with their chief, and sailed away homeward bound about Oct. 8, 1608, and the settlement on the River of Sagadahoc was broken up.

The corporation dissolved. Its president Popham, buried within the precincts of Fort St. George, was left, where no doubt his ashes remain, mingled with the soil of Maine—at the mouth of the Kennebec—the ashes of the first dead president, as a chief Magistrate in the United States.

The colonial life at Sagadahoc lasted a little over a year, or to October 8, 1608. Lord Chief Justice Popham, had also died. His son and heir Sir Francis, succeeded to his father's estate and interest in the colonial undertakings.

The Popham families, especially Sir Francis, son of the Chief Justice, who had contrived the scheme of English homestead possession in the New World, valued the legal advantages gained at so much cost, and determined not to lose the legal benefits, that by seizen and possession of the continent he had taken, had been acquired.

The Popham ship and her tender (the fly-boat,) Gift of God (whose log has not been recovered) was in at the colonial debarkation and aided in the colonial transactions taken at Sagadahoc. There is no clear record of her return, on the sailing of the Mary and John.

Sir Francis protested the Sagadahoc abandonment. The record is "he would not so give over the design of the undertaking abandoned;" but withdrew the ships and provisions remaining in his possession, and did, diverse times after, send* to the *same coast* for trade and fishing.

---

*2d series, Vol. 5, Mass. His. Coll. p. 37. Gorges.

POPHAM AT PEMAQUID.

The Popham ships, were therefore kept employed within the precints of the colonial posessesion, after Sagadahoc had been evacuated. *But where?* Here starts the thread of the legal continuity of the life of the Popham colonization, its expansion and holdings, as recorded by Strachey and Hackluit and Gorges.

"To the* north in the height of 44° lyeth the country of Pemaquid :— the Kingdom wherein our western colony upon the Sagadahoc, was *sometime settled.*"

"The first† place ever possessed by the English in hopes of making a plantation, was a place on the west side of the Kennebec, called Sagadahoc :—*other places adjoining, were soon after seized and improved in trading and fishing.*" The French‡ reported (*Pemcuit*) Pemaquid, was the *first point which was occupied by the English.*" Eight years after the abandonment of Sagadahoc and the Popham protest, history lifts its curtain on further Popham transactions, in holding possession of the colonial seizings.

A. D. 1614.

The Popham ship in the interest of Sir Francis, son of the Lord Chief Justice and heir of his estates is found in an established business, on the east shore of Pemaquid under Monhegan Island where a port had grown up, out of the fur trade and fisheries, which for many years before 1614, had been used by the Pophams alone.

The Earl of Southampton was concerned with the Pophams in the business enterprises here.

PEMAQUID. *Land Titles.* A. D. 1625.

Brown's purchase opens the next view of legal procedure within the limits of the Popham *establishments* on the coast of Maine. The tide of English emigration had already covered the environings of "Popham's Port," and attracted the commercial enterprise of the commercial centers of England. The lands had acquired marketable value.

The Mayor of Bristol, England, and the mercantile house he represented bought up the lands at and about the mouth of Pemaquid River, on the Sagadahoc side of Pemaquid. The Bristol firm of "Aldworth & Elbridge" laid out a fishing plantation on their purchase at Pemaquid

---
*Strachey Trav. in Va. Hacklint Papers.
†Hubbard Indian Wars, 1676, p. 246.
‡Mons. Cadillac, 1671. M. His. Soc Coll., vol 1, p. 282.

Harbor; and Abraham Shurt, their agent, represented the firm in their business and was a civil magistrate. With an eye to the thrift and progress of the Popham Pemaquid settlements, the extent and growth and permanency of agricultural industries, then and there, Brown's purchase, suggested legal confirmation; and on the 24th of July, 1626, Brown's Deed was duly executed by acknowledgement and record in the exact formularies of the English common law, before and by Abraham Shurt, at Pemaquid :—the first transaction of the kind in New England if not in all North America.

The Pemaquid settlements, says Thornton, in 1629, "were larger and more important than Quebec."

Abraham Shurt stands eminent as a man and magistrate. His integrity was incorruptible. On his word the Indians relied with filial faith. East and west and in the Bay settlements, mid rivalries and competition, he conducted a native and foreign trade with skill and success. History has left neither touch or shade of taint on any of his transactions.

A. D. 1631.

A proprietor's court replaced the Shurt magistracy at Pemaquid under seal of patent authority of the crown; and Thomas Elbridge, a man of small stature, presided; and to it the residents of Monhegan and Damariscove resorted for legal redress to about 1647.

The charter powers of the Pemaquid civil organization were granted with a view to replenish the deserts with a people governed by laws and magistrates," as expressed in the grant.

The administration of civil affairs contemplated a nearly pure democracy. The laws and ordinances were required to be executed by such officer and officers as should be chosen by the majority of the popular voice. The principle of a majority rule was the governing element of the civil polity. It prevailed up to the 5th of Sept., 1665.

The 12th of March, 1664, the Pemaquid Country and dependencies were assigned to James Duke of York by Royal grant. The Ducal Province was erected into a civil organization as the county of "Cornwall" appurtenant to New York by a Royal commission, Sept. 5, 1665, at the house of John Mason, Sheepscot Farms; and Sheepscot Farms were organized into a shire town named, "New Dartmouth." Col. Richard Nicols had been designated governor of the Ducal Province, but before he could enter on his duties was killed in a naval battle with the Dutch, 1672. The civil affairs of Pemaquid, meanwhile fell into confusion, till Governor Lovelace assumed command.

Pemaquid, Muscongus, and Sagadahoc, now consolidated into a county, justice was administrated by a duly organized Court of record, called the court of "General Sessions", whose sittings were held the last Wednesday of June and the first Wednesday of November at Jamestown of Pemaquid and by circuit at New Dartmouth. Henry Jocelyn, Esq., was Chief Justice and Rev. Robert Jordan, Thomas Gardiner of Pemaquid, William Dyer of Sheepscot, Nicholas Raynal, associates.

Sullivan says this court had jurisdiction in matters ecclesiastical; and in the event of disagreement, Justice Jocelyn decided the issue.

Walter Philips was Clerk of Courts at New Dartmouth, and William Short for the Sessions at Pemaquid. Books of Record were duly kept at both places, entitled: "Rolls of acts and orders passed at sessions holden in the territories of the Duke of York." John Allen of Sheepscot was High Sheriff.

Precepts ran, to Constables or Sheriffs, as follows, viz:

Greeting: "By virtue hereof you are required in his majesty's name and under authority of his Highness, Duke of York, to apprehend the body or goods of Deft. and take bond for value of——with sufficient surety or sureties, for his personal appearance at court, &c., &c., then and there to answer unto complaint of A. B. for not yielding a debt or due-bill, bearing date, &c., * * *. Hereof fail not as you will answer it at your peril, &c." *Return.* "I have attached the body of A. B. and taken bail for his appearance at next court to answer to the complaint of B. C. in an action of the case. This is a true return." (Signed C. D. official.)

Walter Philips, clerk of the New Dartmouth sessions, first appears a resident at the mouth of Damariscotta River on a place called "Winnegance," (Indian carrying place to Pemaquid) in March, 1660. Thence he moved to the "oyster banks" above the site of Newcastle, near lower falls and purchased a large landed estate of the Indians embracing their Ped-auk-gowack (place of thunder) and made large improvements. His orchards yielded apples to the fugitives of King Philip's war in 1676, on their flight to Pemaquid. His book of Records are lost. He fled to Massachusetts, resided in Charlestown and died there in 1680.

Chief Justice Jocelyn originally came to Black Point, Scarboro, 1635; from England, 1634, as agent for John Mason, then resident on the Piscataqua, of Gorges' Province of Maine.

He was son of Sir Thomas Jocelyn of Kent, Knight, and of noble blood. He made an incomplete survey of interior wilds, then married the widow of Captain Cammock of Scarboro. The marshes of Scarboro made it attractive to early immigration for settlement, as did the marshes of Sheepscot farms in the Ducal Province of Pemaquid. These marshes stimulated the earliest agriculture.

Commissioned by Sir Ferdinando Gorges, Jocelyn first sat as Judge at Saco, 25 March, 1636, under the administration of Sir William, son (Governor) of Sir Ferdinando, of his Province of Maine. One of his first judicial orders was made in the interests of temperance. "Any man that doth sell strong liquor, Wine, &c., shall suffer his neighbor, laborer or servant to continue drinking in the house, said offences being seen by one Justice of the Peace or constable, or proved by two witnesses before a Justice of the Peace, such seller of strong drink, or wine, shall forfeit for every such offence, ten shillings."

In 1639, Jocelyn was nominated Counsellor of the Province of Maine and authorized to try all causes coming before him; and also to act as Deputy Governor, under Gorges, in exigencies requiring the exercise of such office. This eminence in public affairs and in the confidence of Gorges made him an object of special surveillance with the Bay state authorities.

MASSACHUSETTS USURPATION.

In 1668, a crisis was reached in a conflict of jurisdiction between Gorges and the Massachusetts administration in Maine. Issue was made at York on the 6th of July and turned on the exercise of judicial authority in Gorges Province of Maine, then limited in its boundaries to the east shores of Casco and Merrymeeting bays.

The day before court sat at York, men from Massachusetts, heralded and escorted by a troop of horse, entered the town, announced as "Massachusetts Commissioners."

Jocelyn and his associates met the new-comers with courtesy. The Massachusetts men, thereupon, warned the Maine Judges not to oppose their proceedings, and repaired to the meeting-house to open their court.

Jocelyn and the King's Judges thereupon seized the meeting-house steps, and had proclamation made to hear the King's commands.

The Commission within, hearing the crier's call, "bade all persons having his Majesty's commands and showing them in court, the court would be ready to hear the same." Nevertheless, on account of the pressure of business, the reading thereof could not be heard before the afternoon.

An adjournment for dinner followed. While the Massachusetts intruders were eating, Jocelyn and the associate Maine Judges entered the meeting-house and sat on the benches, holding the judicial seats.

Informed of this, the foreign commission left their dining tables, rushed into the church and took seats beside the King's Magistrates; and now refused to read or hear the King's commissions.

Jocelyn and the* Maine Judges thereupon, in the interests of peace withdrew and abandoned the ground, making the record: "Massachusetts entered the Province of Maine in hostile array; turned the Judges of the King and Gorges off the bench; imprisoned the commander of the militia; threatened the judges and friends of Gorges, and usurped the judicial authority of Maine."

Jocelyn left Maine and took residence in the Ducal Province of Pemaquid; and in August, A. D., 1677, we find him there holding court as Chief Justice.

He was respected, honored and trusted by royal authority. Government assigned to his choice any lot at Pemaquid he might desire for building himself a house and £10 out of the public treasury, with provisions out of the public supplies, and orders, further, "that his rent should be paid if he elected to hire a house." These provisions were made for his support in June, 1680.

Three years after, 1683, his demise at Pemaquid is reported to the public authorities with regret.

Eminent for loyalty to the crown, for peace and good order, fidelity to his public trusts, clearness and uprightness, Chief Justice Henry Jocelyn died in his judicial robes, unsullied, and was buried at Pemaquid between the 24th of August, 1682 and May 10, 1683, where his ashes repose to this day.

The restraints of law were loosened in his death.

A commercial town had grown up around Fort Charles called James town, at Pemaquid Harbor, from the Aldworth and Elbridge Plantation, and the trade of Popham's port, now a suburb.

Public necessity required filling the vacant seat of Justice, and Thomas Giles was thereupon commissioned as Chief Justice of the Ducal Province, appointed, among others, 28th April, 1684.

---

*Mass. purchased Maine, May 6, 1677.

Thomas Giles seems to have been a land holder at Pemaquid, residing near the Fort, a strict observer of the Sabbath, and otherwise a conscientious, God-fearing man and officer of the law. He had much difficulty in correcting abuses at the Fort. During his administration the Revolution of William and Mary in England set in, ending the Stuart Dynasty and the jurisdiction of the Duke of York, in Maine, 1689.

The French were on the alert to defeat the accession of William and Mary to the English throne, and stirred up their Indian allies to improve the opportunity of the public confusion and consequent anarchy.

Combined, they planned an invasion to overthrow British rule and seize English strong-holds in the Ducal, Province and subdue the old County of Cornwall.

Judge Giles, on the 12th of Aug., 1689, had gone to his farms at the Falls of Pemaquid with his little boys to superintend finishing his harvest of hay and the hoeing of his corn-fields. It was noon. Dinner had been served to his workmen. Giles and the boys were still at the farm-house, the workmen having dispersed to their labor.

Suddenly the guns of Fort Charles boomed an alarm. All were startled. The Judge hoped it heralded good news of re-inforcements at the Fort—return of the soldiers, who had been drawn off. The next moment savage yells and the war-whoop, with volleys of musketry from hills in the rear, broke on the ear.

This din of war brought the Judge to his feet, crying, "What now—what now?"

It is the story of a child, his youngest boy, an eyewitness. His father seemed to be handling a gun.

Moxus, Sachem of the Kennebec, led the fray. The child fled. Pursued by a painted brave, with gun and cutlass in hand, the glitter of which dazzled the child, who fell, was seized and pinioned. Led back to his father, he saw him, walking slowly, pale and bloody. The men at harvest were shot down where they stood, or on the flats with others, tomahawked, crying, "O Lord! O Lord!" The captives were made to sit down till the slaughter was ended and then were taken towards the fort on the east side of the river, a mile and a half distant. Smoke and crash of fire-arms were, on all sides, seen and heard. The old Fort, in loud roar of its cannon added to the din and dismay of the captives.

Judge Giles was brought in. Moxus expressed regrets saying strange Indians did the mischief. Giles replied:—"I am a dying man. I ask no favor but a chance to pray with my boys." It was granted. Earnestly commending them to the care of God with calmness of assuring faith he took leave of his children with a blessing and counsel, encouraging them to hope for a meeting hereafter in the better land. Pale with the loss of blood now gushing from his shoes and tottering in step he was led aside. We heard the blows of the hatchet but neither shriek or groan added the child. Seven bullets had pierced his body, which was buried in a brush heap where he fell.

The captives were taken into a swamp in view of the Fort where the smoke and thunder of battle raged till surrender was made and the town fired and some twenty houses burned. The French record of these transactions is: "that at the first tidings of the sudden attack, the Fort opened fire with all its cannon but it did not deter the Canabis (Kennebec Indians) from getting possession of ten or twelve stonehouses forming a street from the village square to the Fort." They then entrenched themselves, partly at a cellar door of the house next the Fort, partly behind a rock on the sea shore and from these two points kept up such terrible fire of musketry on the Fort from noon till evening of the 14th no one* durst appear openly."

This catastrophe ended the civil, religious and industrial existence of old Cornwall of Pemaquid and dependencies, and of the communities of Popham's Port, Aldworth and Elbridge's Plantation and the Sheepscot farms of near seventy years standing and growth. Thus the ancient aristocratic organizations, social and civil, all passed away in old Cornwall.

The people were all killed, captured or scattered; their flocks of cattle and stores of grain left to plunder and waste.

More than† one hundred miles of sea coast adorned with flourishing settlements, improved estates and comfortable homes were made waste and became desolate. Title deeds, town and court records were burned and lost, and even the sites of ancient plantations soon turned to original solitudes.

REVIVAL.

A. D. 1713 the success of the British arms led to the treaty of Utrecht and the acquisition of Acadia. Peace followed.

The fugitives in Massachusetts from the ancient dominions of Maine combined for return to their war-wasted possessions.

---

*Shea's Charlevoix, vol. 4, p. 41.
†Will. Hist., vol. 2, p. 80.

Government of Massachusetts determined to aid the re-settlement, of Maine, the restoration of ancient homesteads and to quiet conflicting claims.

Maine, with the Ducal Province of Pemaquid, had become the property, of the Bay State and were merged in one jurisdisction. The plan of concentrated population on three or four acre lots at the seaside in families, with outlying pasture ground, was recommended.

This village system developed the defensive architectural device of "Garrison houses," as places of refuge in time of peril. Sagadahoc retained its ancient influence and attraction as a re-peopling center. Its sandy and rocky shores, as of old, were magnets to popular resort, and Government would permit a return of inhabitants to no other point, initial, to re-occupancy of the "Eastern parts."

A. D. 1714.

The heirs of Clark and Lake of old Arrowsick, at the head of a cove opposite Drummore of Phipsburgh Centre, started re-settlements to recover the ancient island possessions.

John Watts of Boston built there a garrison of bricks brought from Medford, Mass., with flankers mounted with cannon, a refuge for families, gathered, under cover of the guns of the garrison.

It became the nucleus of an organized township and was named Georgetown, incorporated 1716.

Land-holders and government stimulated re-peopling the new town.

Capt. John Penhallow was assigned to command the garrison. Old Georgetown fostered thus, continued to grow, and was made the shire, east, of the newly organized York-Shire County, into which Maine was converted. It was the capital of the valley of the Kennebec; and the seat of legal authority, to the resettled wastes of the "Ancient Dominions of Maine."

A. D. 1728.

Samuel Denny, an English emigrant, built himself a block house, near Butler's Cove, and the Watts' Garrison; and acted as a civil magistrate. Denny was a man of education, of industrious habits and decision of character. He sat as Judge and acted as his own bailiff, at court. It was currently reported, that the stocks, as late as 1833, were remembered, wherein the sentences of his own court were executed by his own hand. John Stinson of Arrowsic, was also a Magistrate of Yorkshire: and Jonathan Williamson of Wiscasset, sheriff, whose precepts and record of service, survive to this day.

Justice Stinson was a staunch loyalist in Revolutionary times.

Cushing of Pownalborough sent officers to make his arrest. The charge* was treasonable acts; for which orders were issued to bring him before the court.

Stinson armed himself, and resisted effectually the officer's attempt to make his arrest. His wife, ready to be confined, was so shocked at the assault and resistance made by her husband, she fell sick and died.

For more than a quarter of a century, "Old Georgetown" stood the capital of Eastern Maine, and the center of the administration of the law and justice, as a shire of old Yorkshire.

Land-holders of the old Plymouth, Kennebec purchase, were active in bringing their lands into notice for settlement, and agitated, a division of Yorkshire, and the erection of its eastern fragment into a new county. On the 19 of June, 1760, the agitation bore fruit. The General Court organized a new county, and called it Lincoln; and incorporated Wiscasset Point, New Milford and Dresden, into a town called Pownalborough for its shire.

A court-house and jail of hewn timber were built, in the west precinct of the New Shire; and so Lincoln, succeeded to Old Cornwall County of the Ducal Province of Pemaquid and dependencies.

A legal organization of higher jurisdiction and forms of procedure was created and organized into Lincoln Bar. It retained the Old Cornwall style, a court of sessions; and held its sittings second Tuesdays of June and September. Samuel Denny, William Lithgow, Aaron Hinkley and John North, were Justices presiding. William Cushing, Jonathan Bowman, Joseph Patten, James Howard and John Stinson, Esqrs., were also Magistrates.

A. D. 1762.

Organization.

"Lincoln ss, Anno Regni Regis Georgii Tertii, Magnae Britanniae, Franciae et Hiberniae Primo" was the opening record of the first session; and the first order designated Jonathan Bowman, clerk.

At His Majesty's Court of General Sessions of the Peace held at Pownalborough, within and for the County of Lincoln, on the first Tuesday of June, being the first day of the month A. D. 1762, it was further "Ordered (at said session) that a Seal presented by Samuel Denny, Esqr. the Motto whereof being a Cup and three Mullets, being the lawful Coat of Arms of the said Denny's Family with said Denny's

---

*Fron. Miss, p. 265.

name at large in the Verge thereof, be accepted and that it be established to be the common Seal of this Court."

A. D. 1786.

Lincoln county had grown in importance and its necessities in matters of law required an enlargement of judicial facilities.

By act of legislation, the courts for Lincoln County were extended and enlarged in jurisdiction, by sessions of the Supreme Court of Massachusetts directed to be holden at Pownalborough, this year, Chief Justice Cushing, Judges Sargent, Sewall and Sumner, presiding.

AT WISCASSET POINT.

In 1794, further changes were made; and the court ordered to hold alternate sessions at Wiscasset Point and at Hallowell. The change was inaugurated, and its first session held under Judges Paine, Sumner and Dawes. The inauguration of the above change, in incidents of ancient judicial formularies, we give from the late Chief Justice Weston.

Three sheriffs in cocked hats, girt with swords, holding long white staves, guarded the court and led the way in procession followed by the bar, and at Hallowell, marched to court at the beat of a drum. Its formularies of procedure were imposing and dignified. From that day to this, Wiscasset Point, has been the seat of legal administration of Justice for the communities, (except lately Sagadahoc,) occupying the territories, of the ancient aristocratic Jurisdiction of Cornwall, of the Ducal Province of Pemaquid and dependencies.

Thus we have sketched the leading facts and incidents, of the beginnings of jurisprudence out of which has grown the mortuary record now published to the world.

RUFUS KING SEWALL.

Wiscasset, March 16, 1895.

NOTE. The landfall of Gosnold in the "Concord" in 1602 was in latitude 43° 44' N. See p. v where it is erroneously printed 40° N.

ERRATA.

Page	line		Page	line	
3	35	after Disallow omit &.	136	7	after And insert I
11	14	for 72 read 92.	141	28	for Heyard read Heywood.
14	32	after she insert may.			
16	29	for 74 read 174.	142	19	for Cod read God.
25	3	for 42 read 142.	145	28	for Eightenth read Eighten.
26	35	for and read all.			
28	38	for 1767 read 1768.	147	35	for IV read V.
29	33	after third insert part.	160	31	for 2786 read 1786.
35	12	after by insert my.	162	24	for Mary read Sarah.
38	19	for 1766 read 1769.	163	32	for 427 read 247.
38	21	for 28 Sep. read 20 Ap.	168	26	for in read an.
40	23	before arrive omit shall.	175	20	for so read as.
41	15	before sound insert a.	176	16	after Gave insert it.
47	7	before as insert free.	176	36	for Jabex read Jabez.
56	4	for into read unto.	181	18	after I insert now.
57	10	at end of line add frying pan.	183	39	for Kiver read River.
			188	19	for VI read VII.
65	17	for Carlton read Clark.	190	1	for constute read constitute.
69	39	for 269 read 262.			
71	29	before mortality insert the.	190	34	for Consttute read Constute.
71	37	omit any.	190	36	after Dissannul omit and.
72	9	for the read all			
73	4	for James Fulton read John Fulton.	198	12	after my insert beloved.
			206	28	for 1794 read 1791.
74	13	after that insert my.	207	4	for 1891 read 1791.
77	7	for G read &.	212	4	for except read excepting.
84	20	for 3 read 30.			
86	25	for eighteenth read eighth.	213	40	for Daughter read Daughters.
88	31	omit that.	215	5	for in read of.
91	25	for reocking read revocking.	216	25	after law insert is.
			221	2	for VII read VIII.
94		between lines 26 and 27 insert Item I give and bequeath to my beloved Son Uriah the Sixth part of all my Real Estate after my wifes Decease Item I give and bequeath to my beloved Son Peter the Sixth part of all my Real Estate after my wifes Decease	226	33	for 1795 read 1792.
			227	16,	for 1795 read 1796.
			229	21	omit all after [V, 197.]
			238	9	after £200 : 1 : 2 insert [VIII, 121-122.]
			240	22	after time insert then.
			251	27	after 1795 insert [VI, 42.]
95	20	for Mary read Jerusha.	264	39	for 1790 read 1796.
97	37	for know read known.	298	30	for $13.92 read $139.92.
99	25	after County insert of.	336	34	for And read Ann.
99	31	for Lots read Lott.	337	4	for 1810 read 1800.
104	2	after same insert sum.	337	34	omit real.
107	37	omit all after sureties.	339	28	for Samuel read Daniel.
107	38	omit all before Inventory.			
			343	38	for 1800 read 1804.
110	12	for 1782 read 1781.	349	25	for $824.75 read $624.75.
110	19	for Nov. read Oct.			
115	16	after other insert said.			
125	9	for 1774 read 1784.	354	24	for votes read notes.

LINCOLN PROBATE RECORDS.

ABSTRACTS

FROM THE

Records of the Probate Court at Wiscasset,

LINCOLN COUNTY, MAINE.

County Incorporated June 19, 1760.

The numeral letters and figures enclosed in brackets refer to volumes and folios of records.

Humphry Purrington, late of Georgetown. Nathaniel Purrington, of Georgetown, Adm'r, 14 Nov., 1760. William Philbrook, blacksmith, of Georgetown, and Philip Aubens, of Brunswick, sureties. [I, 1.] Inventory by James Thompson, Isaac Snow and Nathaniel Larrabee, all of Georgetown, 16 Mar., 1761, £124 : 18 : 7½. [I, 2.]

Louis Cavelear, late of Pownalborough. Mary Cavelear, of Pownalborough, widow, Adm'x, 10 June, 1761. [I, 2.] Inventory by Jonas Fitch, James Bugnon, and Francis Ridley, [Rittal] all of Pownalborough, 10 June, 1761, £48 : 9 : 1. [I, 3.]

James Fredrick Jacquins, late of Pownalborough. Margaret Jacquins, of Pownalborough, widow, Adm'x, 10 June, 1761. [I, 3.] Jonas Fitch and Abner Marson, sureties on bond. Inventory by Jonas Fitch, Jacques Bugnon and Francis Rittal, 10 June, 1761, £67 : 10 : 6. [I, 4.] Accounts filed 26 Apr., 1763. [I, 32.] Christopher Jakin chose Margaret Jakin to be his guardian, 3 Apr., 1764. [I, 52.]

John Blithen, late of Georgetown. Hannah Blithen, of Georgetown, widow, Adm'x, 8 June, 1761. [I, 4.] Inventory by John Parker and Joseph Mackentier, both of Georgetown, 7 Aug., 1761, £128 : 5 : 11. [I, 14.] John Parker and Joseph McIntire, commissioners to examine claims. [I, 16.] Accounts filed 22 Feb., 1763, [I, 30,] and 1 Oct., 1763, at which latter date the administratrix had become the wife of David Curtis, of Harpswell. [I, 38.]

William Robinson, late of Topsham. Margaret Robinson, of Topsham, widow, Adm'x, 16 June, 1761. Ezra Randal and Richard Knowles, sureties. [I, 5.] Inventory by Ezra Randall and Richard Knowles, 16 June, 1761, £176 : 9 : 5½. [I, 6.]

Solomon Hopkins, late of Newcastle. David Hopkins, of Newcastle, Adm'r, 11 Sept., 1761. [I, 7.] Inventory by Benjamin Woodbridge, John Cunningham and Samuel Nickels, all of Newcastle, 11 Nov., 1761, £150 : 2 : 6. [I, 15.] Account filed 4 Oct., 1763. [I, 41.] Order regarding real estate, 4 Sept., 1765. Grandchildren : Solomon Hopkins, Mary Hopkins, Martha Hopkins, Agnes Hopkins, Jennet Hopkins, children of eldest son, William; David Hopkins, and Mary Wood, children of Solomon. [I, 112-113.]

William Huston, late of Walpole. Ann Huston, of Walpole, widow, Adm'x, 27 Aug., 1761. [I, 7.] John Stinson, of Georgetown, and James Huston, of Walpole, sureties. Inventory by William Millar and Robert Huston, both of Walpole, and James Brown, of Newcastle, 19 Oct., 1761, £346 : 15 : 11. [I, 19-20.] Account filed 5 Sept., 1764. [I, 61.]

William Hopkins, late of Newcastle. Mary Hopkins, of Newcastle, widow, Adm'x, 22 Sept., 1761. Peter Paterson, of Newcastle, and Robert Cocheran, of the East side of Wiscasset Bay, sureties. [I, 8.] Mary Hopkins, widow of William Hopkins, appointed Guardian to Solomon, Mary, Agnes, Jane, and Martha, children of said William; Robert Hodge and David Given, both of Newcastle, sureties. [I, 10.] Inventory by Robert Hodge, David Given and John Cunningham, all of Newcastle, 18 Nov., 1761. £261 : 9 : 3. [I,13.] Account filed 4 Oct., 1763, at which time the widow had become wife of Hugh Holmes, of Newcastle. [I, 39.] Partition of real estate by Benjamin Woodbridge, David Given and Alexander Campbell, committee, 15 Oct., 1771, [II, 68 to 70,] at which time Jennet or Jane had become the wife of David Somes.

In The Name of God Amen : the Twenty Ninth Day of May 1761, I Nath'll Donnell of George Town, Gentleman In the County of Lincoln, Being very Sick & Week In body butt of Perfect Mind & Memory Thanks be to God therefore Calling Unto Mind the Mortality of my Body & Knowing that it is Appointed for all Men Once to Dye Do Make & Ordain This my Last Will & Testement that is for to say Principally & first of All I Give and Recomend my Soul Into the

Hands of God that Gave it & for my body I Recomend it to The Earth to be Buried In a Christian Like manner at the Discreation of my Executor Nothing Doubting but at the Generall Resurrection I shall Receive the same by the Mighty Power of God—& as Touching Such Worldly Estate Wherewith it has Pleased to Bless me In this Life I Give Devise and Dispose of the same In the following Manner & form

Imprimis It is my will & I Do Order that In the first Place all My Just Debts & Funerall Charges be paid & satisfied

Item I Give To my well Beloved wife Elizabeth the Income of all My Estate During Her Life & After Her Decease she is for To Give Unto my Daughter Elizabeth all the Housold Stuff—& Likewise I Give Unto my Wife all my Cattle sheep & stock for To be at Her Dispoasall as She shall think proper—& Likewise I Do Appoint my Wife Elizabeth my Sole Executor.

Item I Give & Bequeath Unto my Well Beloved Sons Benjamin & Thomas All my Lands Where I Now Dwell Bounded on Long Reach & Runing Over to New Meadow River & for the same for to be Devided Between them: Each One Half & for them Two. I Appoint that they Choose a Committee for to Devide the Same if they Cannot Agree them Selves—

Item I Order & Appoint that my Two Sons Benjamin & Thomas pay Unto my Son Nathanell thirteen pounds six shillings & Eight Pence Lawfull Money: & Likewise Unto my Daughter Elizabeth Six pounds thirteen & four Pence Lawfull Money to be paid by Them after the Decease of my Wife—& Furthermore I Give & Bequeath Unto my Son Benjamin all my Right Title & Interest In an Island Lying & Known By the Name of Jewells Island In Casco bay So Called—

Item I Give & Bequeath Unto my Son Thomas an Island Lying In Sheepscoot River Where my Son Thomas build a House Lying Near to Resqueaghean Island or Parkers Island so Called—

Item I Doe Hereby make a Reserve out of the Lands I have Bequeathed Unto my Two sons Benjamin & Thomas a Certain Piece of Land Where the Meeting House Now stands for the Use & Service of said Parrish, the Same Containing about Three Quarters of one Acre or thereabouts

I Do Hereby Uterly Disallow & revoke & Disannull all & Every Other former Testaments, Wills Legaces & Executors by Me In Any Ways Before this And No Other to be my Last will & Testament

In Witness Whereof I have Hereunto Sett my hand & Seal the Day & Year Above Written

         Nathaniel Donnell (Seal)

Signed Sealed Published
Pronounced & Declared By the
said Nath'll Donnell as his
Last Will & Testament In
the Presence of Us the Subscribers,
  Sam'll Todd
  Meecres Carr
      His
James J M Mickels
    Mark

Probated 8 Dec., 1761. [I, 9.]

Inventory by John Shaw, Elisha Shaw and James Michaels, 14 June 1762, £222 : 15 : 10. [I, 23.]

Hezekiah Purinton, late of Georgetown. Isabella Purinton, of Georgetown, widow, Adm'x, 7 Dec., 1761 ; Charles Cushing and Joshua Purinton, sureties. [I, 13.] Inventory by Aaron Hinkley, James Thompson and Isaac Snow, all of Brunswick, 15 Jan., 1762. [I, 25.]

In the name of God amen I Patrick Drummond of Georgetown within the county of York and province of the Masachusets bay in new-Ingland gentelman being very weke of body but of sound minde and memory thanks be to God for it and knowing that it is appointed for all men onse to die do therefore take this opertunity to make this my larst will and testament in maner and form following in tne first plase I give and bequeth my precious and Emortal soul into the hands of God who gave it me and my body I Recomend to the Earth to be buried in desient christial burial at the discretion of my dear wife and my dear son Elijah and to be born by them in Equal halves by them out of what I shal hereafter herein bequethed unto them and as to such worldly Estate as God have ben pleased to give me I will bequeth and give after the following manner

Itam I give and bequeth unto my dearly beloved wife Susanah the hous barn and other buildings where I now dwell in Georgetown aforesaid with the tract of land hereafter described on which said buildings stand viz—begining at a large hemlock tree marked on fower sids standing on the Edg of Winigance marshes thense runing south a cros my tract or farm to John lemonts land—thence on the line betwen said lemont and me to the westward to Wineganse salt crick thense over the crick to a point below what is called Prebles landing thense along the shore to the Eastward to a sartain bridg thense to run to the Eastward on the nothward side of a ledg that lyeth next to the northward of my said dwelling hous until it comes to what is called the new country road and from thense to Winigance crick East and by south half south—thense by the Edge of Winiganse marsh to the first mentioned hemlock tree together with all the marsh belonging to me in said Winiganse marshes during hir natural life and after her deceas to be divided as followeth viz that part of my said marsh that lyeth to the Estward of the main crick I give to my son Elijah and to his heirs forever the remainder of the said tract the one half of it I give unto my son John and the other half to be Equally divided between my daughter Lutitia and my daughter Ann and to their heirs and assigns for Ever and I further give unto my said wife all my household furniture together with one half of my Impliments of husbandry together with one yoak of oxen two cows two calves one hefer one bole one mare six shepe and one half of the lambs together with the swine to hir for Ever only it is to be understood that John Lutitia and Ann is to be maintained out of the incum of what is above given unto my said wife untill they severally arive at lawful age—

Itam I give further to my son Elijah all that part of my land or farm that ly to the Estward of that tract before bequethed unto my wife as also an other tract begining at the point below Prebels landing and bounded on that tract given to my said wife untill it Extend in width fifty five pearch noth and by East half East and thense thense runing west and by noth half noth to Stephens River all my land that lyeth to the southward and westward of the two above mentioned lines this tract I give to him to inabel him to discharge my Just debts to the amount of twenty six pounds thirteen shillings and fower pence and if my debts should Exced that sum then I will that my legetes pay in proportion according to the legesies in this will bequethed unto them—

And I further give unto my said son Elijah one yoak of oxen one cow one calf one coult three Ews and one lamb and one half of my utensals of husbandry—

Itam I unto my daughter Ann the wife of the Revd Mr William Mclanaken one hundred and sixty akers of land to be laid out as nere as maybe in a square body in that part of my farm called birch point—

Itam I give unto my daughter frances one hundred and Eight akers of land on the nothern side of my farme bounded notherly by my brother Alexander Campbell begining on the western side of Winigance crick and Extending west and by noath half noath at the width of forty two pearch untill the said 108 akers be completed together with one heffer—

Itam I give the remainder of all my real Estate to be Equally divided between my daughter Margaret and my daughter Jane and I further give unto my daughter Jane two cows and what I have hereby given unto my said children I do hereby give unto them their heirs and assigns forever and if there is any part of my Estate not perticulerly bequethed I do hereby give and bequeth that unto my loving wife and I do hereby constitute and appoint my loving brother James Drummond gentelman and my brother by law Alexander Campbell yeoman and both of Georgetown aforesaid my Exectrs of this my larst will and testement hereby revoking all other wills and bequests I do hereby acknowledg and declare this and no other to be my larst will and testement in witnis whereof I have hereunto set my hand and seal this twenty second day of August *anno domini* 1758 and in the thirty second year of his majestys Reign—

signed sealed published
pronounced and declared
by the said Patrick Drummond to be his larst will
and testament in
presants of us
George Rodgers   Patrick Drummond   (Seal)
Benjamin Kendall
     his
James 8 Mikels
    marke

                         Probated 10 Mar., 1762. [I, 17-18.]

James Drummond and Alexander Campbell disclaimed executorship 10 Mar., 1762. [I, 17.] Susannah Drummond and Elijah Drummond, Adm'rs *cum Testamento Annexo*, 10 Mar., 1762. [I, 17.] Alexander Campbell, of Georgetown, surety. Inventory by William Butler, James McCobb and James Drummond, all of Georgetown, 11 Sep., 1762, £491 : 19 : 4. [I, 24.]

John Ballantine, late of Newcastle. Mary Ballantine, widow, and John Cunningham, both of Newcastle, Adm'rs, 14 Apr., 1762. [I, 19.] Inventory by Benjamin Woodbridge, Jonathan Laiten and Samuel Nickels, all of Newcastle, 8 June, 1762, £288 : 5 : 11. [I, 21.] Account filed 12 Feb., 1767. [I, 117.] Return of Benjamin Woodbridge, Robert Hodge and John McNear, all of Newcastle, of partition of real estate, 17 Apr., 1767. To Mary Ballantine, widow of deceased, her dower, being one third. Of the remainder: one half to Sarah Cunningham, a daughter of deceased; one half to John McClelan, William McClelan, James McClelan, Samuel McClelan, Alexander McClelan, Elizabeth Murray, Margaret McClelan, Sarah McClelan, Mary McClelan and Martha McClelan, children and heirs of Mary McClelan, deceased, the only other daughter and child of said John Ballantine. [I, 216 to 219.]

Thomas Tenney, late of Newcastle. Jonathan Laiten, of Newcastle, Adm'r, 2 June, 1762. [I, 20.] Inventory by James Cargill, John Cunningham and Samuel Nickels, all of Newcastle, 8 June, 1762, £33 : 9 : 3. [I, 22.]

George Gray, late of Wiscasset, now Pownalborough. John Fairfield, of Pownalborough, Adm'r, 27 Sep., 1762. [I, 26.] Jonathan Williamson and Michael Sevey, both of Pownalborough, sureties and appraisers. Inventory 30 Sep., 1762. [I, 33.]

Findley Kelley, (or Kellock) late of St. Georges. Alexander Kelley, (or Kellock) of St Georges, Adm'r, 29 Sep., 1762. [I, 28.] Hugh McLean and John McCarter, both of St. Georges, sureties. Inventory by Alexander Larmond, Samuel Creaton and Samuel Bogs, all of St. Georges, 8 Oct., 1762, £40 : 18 : 4. [I, 33.] Alexander Larmond, Samuel Creaton and Samuel Bogs, commissioners to examine claims. [I, 29.] Alexander Larmond, Samuel Creaton and Samuel Bogs, committee to set off widow's dower, made their return 20 Jan., 1764. [I, 46.] Account filed 11 Sep., 1764. [I, 62 dna 70.] Distribution of estate ordered 29 May, 1765. [I, 70.]

John Sally, late of Georgetown. John Sally, of Georgetown, Adm'r, 20 Oct., 1762. [I, 29.] William Malcom and Daniel Mcfaddin, both of Georgetown, sureties. [I, 28.] Inventory by John Stinson, Jonathan Preble and Charles Snipe, all of Georgetown, 2 Nov., 1762, £66 : 13 : 4. [I, 30 and 107.] Daniel McFadden appointed Guardian to Daniel Sally, minor son, 24 July, 1764. Account filed 24 July, 1764. [I, 54.] Elizabeth Sally, minor daughter, chose Daniel McFadden to be her guardian, 24 July, 1764. [I, 71.] Order regarding real estate, 13 Aug., 1766. [I, 107-8.]

Christopher Hembly, (or Handbury or Hanbery) late of St. Georges. Hugh McLean, of St. Georges, Adm'r, 18 Dec., 1762. [I, 29.] Inventory by Alexander Larmond, Samuel Creaton and David Patterson, all of St. Georges, 17 Jan., 1763, £45 : 6 : 8. [I, 36.] Moses Copeland, Samuel Gillchrist and Alexander Kellock, all of St. Georges, commissioners to examine claims. [I, 36.] Account filed 22 July, 1766. Distribution of estate ordered 13 Aug., 1766. [I, 91.]

In the Name of God Amen I William Rodgers of Georgetown in the County of York and Province of the Massachusets Bay in New England Husbandman being Weak in Body but Sound and perfect in Mind and Memory thanks be to God and calling to mind the Mortality of this my Body and knowing that it is appointed for all Men once of Die Do make and ordain this to be My last will and Testament that is to say Principaly and first of all I Recomend my Soul to God who gave it and as for my Body I Recomend it unto the Earth to be Buried in a Christian Manner at the Discretion of my Executors Nothing Doubting but at the General Resurection I shall Receive the same again by the Mighty Power of God And as for what wordly Goods it hath pleased God to bestow on me I shall dispose of them in the following manner and form my Will is in the first Place that there be sold and disposed of by my Executors as much of my Goods and Chattels as will pay my Just Debts.—

Item   I give and bequeath to my well beloved Wife Ruth one third of the Remainder of my personal Estate and one third of all my Meadows and Marshes and one third part of all my farm whereon I live with housing and fences During her Natural Life whom I Constitute and ordain one of my Executors.—

Item   I Give and bequeath to my beloved Son George Rodgers whom I Constitute one of my Executors my lot of Land in the westward Side of winey gants Marshes Containing seventy four Acres and a half and Seventeen Rods as will appear by a plan taken by Samuel Denny Esqr. Now in the hands of Brother McCobb and likewise I give said Son George the one third of all my Marshes.—

Item   I give and bequeath to my beloved Son Thomas Rodgers twenty shillings Lawful Money to be paid him by my Executors and his Equal Share with other Children of my personal Estate.—

Item   I Give and bequeath to my beloved Son Hugh who has been the staf of my old Age the one full Moiety or half part of all that Lot of Land whereon I now Live in the Eastern Side of winey gants Marshes with the half of all the Buildings and fences and the one third of all my Meadow or Marsh ground I likewise Constitute and ordain said Son Hugh one of my Executors.

Item I Give and bequeath to my other three Sons William Rodgers John Rodgers and Robert Rodgers twenty shillings each to be paid them by my said Executors out of my personal Estate and at my Wife her Decease my will is that they have the half of my homestead farm whereon I Now live with one third of all my Marshes to be Equaly Divided among them together with a point of Land in the Middle of winey gants Marshes Containing about twelve Acres.—

Item I Give and bequeath to my beloved Daughter Jean Kendall twenty shillings to be paid by my said Executors out of my personal Estate and likewise her Equal share with the other Children of the household furniture.

Item I Give and bequeath to my beloved Daughter Margrat Rodger twenty shillings to be paid her by my said Executors out of my personal Estate with her share of the household Stuff.—

Item I Give and bequeath to my beloved Daughter Ann Read twenty shillings to be paid her by my said Executors out of my personal Estate with her Equal Share of the Household furniture with the other Children.—

I do hereby Disanul and Revoak all former Wills by me made Ratifying and Confirming this and No other to be my Last will and Testament In Witness whereof I have set my hand and seal the fifteenth Day of March one Thousand Seven hundred and Sixty in the Thirty third year of his Majestys Reign—

Signed sealed and published in
the presence of us by William
Rodgers as his Last Will and
Testament   William Rodgers   (Seal)
John Parker
James McCobb
George Rodgers

Probated 11 May, 1763.   [I, 3.]

Ruth Rodgers disclaimed executorship, 11 May, 1763.   [I, 32.]

In the Name of God Amen.—I John North of St. Georges in the County of York and Province of the Massachusetts Bay in New England Esq; do make this my Last Will and Testament—

Imprimis—When it shall please God to take me from this Life, I do most Humbly recommend my Soul to God who gave it. And my Body I commit to the Dust for decent Burial at the Discretion of my

Executrix hereafter named in Hope and Expectation of the Forgiveness of all my Sins, and the Resurrection of my Body to Life Eternal Thro' Jesus Christ my Lord and Saviour.

As to such outward and Worldly Estate as God has blessed me with, I will and dispose thereof in manner following. After my Just Debts and funeral Charges are paid and discharged, I give and bequeath unto my Loving and Dutifull Wife Elizabeth the one half of all my personal Estate, To have the Same to her, her Execut'rs Adm'rs and assigns forever.

Item, I Give and bequeath unto my Eldest Son Joseph, one quarter part of my personal Estate To him his Execut'rs Adm'rs and assigns forever.

Item, I Give to my Youngest Son William, the other quarter part of my personal Estate, To him his Execut'rs Adm'rs and assigns forever.

Item, I give to my Daughter Mary, now call'd Mary McKachnie, the sum of Ten pounds sterling To be paid Equally by my Wife and two Sons before named, out of what I have before in this my will given to them.

And I give my Daughter no More of my Estate by reason of her undutifullness in contracting marriage with a Man who is Not to my good liking.

The Reason of my making No Mention of Real Estate in this my will is, that I have already by Deed given, to my Eldest Son, the Real Estate I had at Harrington and the Real Estate at North-yarmouth I have only my Life in it, and as my Youngest Son is the only Child of my wife Elizabeth, I presume the whole of that Estate will descend to him, or his Mother will give the same to him and my Desire is that she would do so whereby my Sons will Inherit from their Parents, Near equally alike.

Lastly I do hereby Constitute My Loving Wife Elizabeth the Sole Executrix of this my Last Will and Testament.

Signed, Sealed, published and declared by me the said Testator this twenty sixth day of May *Annoque Domini* Seventeen hundred and Sixty.

In presence of   John North   (Seal)
Benj. Kent
Gideon Thayer
Andw. Cazneau

                                                    Probated 6 July, 1763.   [I, 33-4.]

Inventory by James Boies, Alexander Lermond and Hugh McLean, 27 June, 1763, £1948 : 6 : 7. [I, 43 to 45.]

Benjamin Burton, late of St. Georges. Alice Burton, of St. Georges, widow, Adm'x, 24 Aug., 1763. [I, 34.] Inventory by Samuel Gillchrist, Boyce Cooper and Patrick Porterfield, all of St. Georges, 18 July, 1763, £414 : 2 : 9 : 3 : 3. [I, 47-8.] Account filed 20 Feb., 1782. [II, 260.]

William Allen, late of St. Georges. Hugh McLean, of St. Georges, Adm'r, 24 Aug., 1763. [I, 35.] Inventory by Moses Copeland, Alexander Kellock and Samuel Gillchrist, all of St. Georges, 24 Sep., 1763, £50. [I, 37.] Alexander Kellock, Moses Copeland and Alexander Larmond, all of St. Georges, commissioners to examine claims. [I, 37.] Account filed 22 July, 1766. Distribution of estate ordered 13 Aug., 1766. [1, 72.]

(John) Ulerick Mier, [Mayers], late of Pownalborough. Molly Mier, of Pownalborough, widow, Adm'x, 17 Sep., 1763. [I, 35.] Inventory by Francis Ridley, [Rittal], John Stain and George Lilly, all of Pownalborough, 4 Oct., 1763, £140 : 0 : 1 : 2 : 6 : [I, 42.] Account filed 21 Mar., 1764. [I, 49.] Catharine Miers chose Abiel Lovejoy, of Pownalborough, to be her guardian, 23 Mar., 1764. [I, 50.] Charles Cushing, Francis Rittal and John, Stain, committee to divide real estate, made report 5 Apr., 1764. Children named : PhilipM ayers, Catharine Mayers, Cassimier Mayers, GeorgeM ayers. [I,55-6.] Division of real estate by Obadiah Call, Jr., Christopher Jackins and John McGown, 25 Sep., 1779. [II, 111.]

William McCleland, late of Newcastle. Elizabeth McCleland, simpster, and John Cunningham, both of Newcastle, Adm'rs, 4 Oct. 1763. David Hopkins and Hugh Holmes, both of Newcastle, sureties. [I, 39.] Inventory by Benjamin Woodbridge, Robert Hodge and Samuel Nickels, all of Newcastle, 1 Jan., 1764, £600 : 13 : 6½. [I, 59.] William, minor son, Mary and Sarah, minor daughters, chose John Cunningham to be their guardian 8 Oct., 1765. [I, 81-82.] John McClelan appointed guardian unto James, Samuel and Alexander, minor sons, and Martha, minor daughter, 8 Oct., 1765. [I, 83-85.] Account filed 12 Feb., 1767. [I, 118.] Return of partition of real estate by Benjamin Woodbridge, Robert Hodge and John McNear, all of Newcastle, 17 Apr., 1767, mentions John, the eldest son, and William, James, Samuel, Alexander, Elizabeth, Margaret, Sarah, Mary and Martha, children of deceased. [I, 219.]

Daniel Anderson, late of Newcastle. Samuel Anderson, of Newcastle, Adm'r, 4 Oct., 1763. [I, 40.] Inventory by John Cunningham, Robert Hodge and John McNear, all of Newcastle, 15 Dec., 1763, £116 : 2 : 4. Account filed 12 Jan., 1764. [I, 43.]

John Malcom, late of St. Georges. David Patterson, Junr., of St. Georges, Adm'r, 4 Jan., 1764. [I, 41.] Inventory by Alexander Larmond, Alexander Kellock and Moses Copeland, all of St. Georges, 14 Jan., 1764, £56 : 13 : 4. [I, 46.]

James Hilton, of a place called Broad Cove, appointed guardian unto Mary Matchloffe, minor daughter of Mathias Matchloffe, late of said Broad Cove. [I, 53.]

In the Name of God, Amen. The Twenty fifth Day of March 1758 I Robert Montgomery of Townsend in the County of York and province of the Massachusetts Bay in New England Gentleman, being very sick & weak in Body, but of perfect mind and memory, Thanks be given unto God, therefore calling unto mind the mortality of my Body, and knowing that it is appointed unto all men Once to die, do make and ordain this my last Will and testament, that is to say, first of all I give and Recommend my soul into the hands of God, that gave it; and my body I recommend to the Earth to be buried in decent Christian Burial at the discretion of my Executors, nothing doubting but at the general Resurrection I shall receive the same again by the mighty Power of God. And as touching such worldly Estate wherewith it hath pleased God to bless me in this life, I give, demise and dispose of the same in the following manner and form.

Imprimis—I ordain, Order and direct, that all the lawful Debts I owe or stand indebted for, shall be punctually paid to my respective Creditors out of my Estate ; and the remainder, if any be, to be disposed of as follows,

Item—I give and bequeath to my beloved Wife Sarah One third part of all my personal and Real Estate, that remains when my Debts is paid.

Item—And out of the Remainder I give and bequeath to my son James Montgomery five shillings lawful money

Item. I give to my son Robert Montgomery five shillings lawful money.

Item. I give and bequeath to my Daughter Anna Montgomery One half of the Remainder of my whole Estate Real and personal.

Item I give and Bequeath to my Sons John Montgomery and Samuel Montgomery the Remainder of my whole Estate to be equally divided between them

I do likewise Constitute and appoint my beloved Wife Sarah, and my beloved Brother Capt. William Miller and my trusty friend Ensign Samuel McCobb my sole Executors and Executrix of this my last Will and Testament, all and singular my lands, Tenements and personal Estate to be taken into their Charge & Care. And I do hereby utterly disallow & Revoke all and every other former Testaments, Wills and Bequests and Executors by me in any ways before named, Confirming this and no other to be my last Will and Testament. In Witness whereof I have hereunto set my hand and seal the Day & Year above written.

Robert Montgomery   (Seal)

Signed, Sealed, pronounced and declared by the said Robert Montgomery as his last will & Testament in the presence of us,
John North
Walter Baker
John Montgomery

Probated 27 Sep., 1763. [I, 48-9.]

William Miller disclaimed executorship 21 Mar., 1764. [I, 49.] Inventory by Robert Wyley, John Orr, and William Fullerton, all of Townsend, 19 July, 1764. [I, 58.]

In the Name of God Amen—April 25th, 1763 I Moses Robinson senr. of St. Georges being full of Bodily Pains but sound in my senses and Judgment thanks to Almighty God for all his gifts and benefits to unworthy me in continuing and preserving me by his providential Care through many dangers of life, to fill up so many years as by the Course of Nature I must be near to my dissolution, and yield to death when it shall please God to Call me. I do hereby Ordain & declare this to be my last Will and Testament in manner & Form following, and by these presents revoking & annulling all other Testaments or Wills, either in Writing or Words, and this to be taken only for my last Will and Testament and none other. And first being by Grace and Mercy to me made sensible of my Original Sin and my actual transgressions I most humbly beg forgiveness for the same. I humbly bequeath and Commit my Soul to Almighty God my Saviour and Redeemer in whom, and by the Merits of Jesus Christ I trust and believe Assuredly by Assisting Grace I shall be saved. My Body I commit to the Earth to be decently buried in any Place where my Children shall see proper, which Body I believe shall arise again at the general Resurrection & be reunited to my soul, and through the Merits of Christs Death and Passion, possess & inherit those Mansions of Glory in the Kingdom of Heaven prepared for The Elect and Chosen Ones—& now for settling my temporal affairs, such as my real and personal Estate, as it hath pleased God far above my deserts, to bestow upon me, I do order, give and dispose of the same in the following manner viz First I will That all Debts as I owe in Right of Conscience to any One, shall be hastily paid, as soon as possible, after my decease by my Executors

Item—I leave and bequeath to my beloved Wife Mary Robinson, if she outlives me, to have the sole command of all that I now possess, only my real Estate she is not to dispose of to any other, which I bequeath to my youngest son William Robinson, which I Constitute and ordain to be my sole heir, to inherit my estate so long as he lives and his sons after him, if he shall have any lawfully begotten, but in Case he never marry or have no male heir to enjoy the said Estate, then it shall descend to my oldest son Joseph's son Moses Robinson to enjoy, but neither of them shall sell their Right of Inheritance to any Stranger whilest there is so many of the Name and relations to enjoy the same.

Item. To Son Archibald what assistance can be afforded of hay and provisions for two years or three at the beginning of his own place, as also One Cow and Calf.

Item. To Son John I leave the cutting of One load of English hay, yearly and every year during his lifetime.

Item I leave to any One of my Nine Children, that is not contented with what I have done but thinks themselves wronged, I Order my Executors Mary and William Robinson to pay unto the discontented person he or she, the sum of five Shillings Sterling which I leave to them or any of them, for the preventing debates or Trouble which otherwise might arise. And further be it known That as I leave my well beloved Wife, sole Executor over all my personal Estate that I now possess to have the full Command and Ordering of the same, with the advice of her Children, That she may have a Comfortable way of living, during her lifetime here, and if she cannot enjoy a satisfying easy way of a Contented life with her son William, I desire that she have her proportionable Share out of the Estate laid out to her self for her Maintenance according as the law directs, and if any Debate or Misunderstanding should Arise with any Neighbour or among themselves, I desire that it may not go to law, but let it be done away by an Arbitration or Reference of two or three Judicious, honest Neighbours.

Item. To Mary Rivers, One Cow aud a Calf when she shall stand in Need of them and to be wintered free the first year if she desires it.

Item—I leave to my son Moses Robinson all my right and Title, which I received by Will from Daniel FitzGerald, deceased of that lot which he now enjoys.

Furthermore I constitute and Ordain my beloved Friends, Mr Boyce Cooper, Joseph Robinson and Moses Robinson Junr. to be my sole Executors in seeing Justice done, and oversight of the whole, especially concerning my dear beloved Wife, and leave this as my last Will and Testament

As Witness my hand & Seal this twenty fifth day of April One thousand Seven hundred and sixty three

Moses Robinson   (Seal)

Witness present
Boyce Cooper
Joseph Robinson
Moses Robinson Junr.

Probated 4 Mar., 1764. [I. 50-52.]

Mary Robinson disclaimed executorship 6 Mar., 1764. [I, 50.]

Ebenezer Greenleaf, late of Woolwich. John Kingsbury, of Pownalborough, Adm'r, 27 June, 1764. [I, 53.]

Robert Montgomery, late of Townsend. John Montgomery, of Townsend, Adm'r, 5 Sept., 1764. [I, 56.] Samuel McCobb and Tobias Glidden, sureties. Inventory by Samuel McCobb and Robert Wiley, both of Townsend, and John Orr, of Walpole, 3 Nov., 1754, £35 : 15 : 10. [I, 99.]

James Montgomery, late of Townsend. Sarah Montgomery, of Townsend, widow, Adm'x, 5 Sep., 1764. [I, 57.] John Montgomery and Jonas Fitch, sureties. Inventory by Robert Wiley and Samuel McCobb, both of Townsend, and John Orr, of Walpole 3 Nov., 1764, £5 : 13 : 5. [I, 98.] Account filed 23 Sep., 1769. [I, 195.]

In the Name of God Amen I James Miller of Walpole So Caled in the Countey of Lincol and Provence of the Massachisets Bay in New England Husbandman Being Senceable of the Mortalety of my Body and at the Presant Time Infirem as to helth yet of Sound Mind and Perfect Memory Blised be God for it Do hearby Make and Confirm this as my Last Will and Testament Wherein I Do in the first Place Recomend my Soul to God and my Body to Deasont Cristain Buriel and as Touching my Wordly Substance with which God has Blised me with I Do Hearby Dispose thereof In forem and Maner Ass Foloweth—

Item I Give and Bequeth To my Beloved Wife Annas Miller an Equel Part or Porshen with Each of my Childer and my Childer an Equel part with my Wife to wite Jeannet Miller Ann Marey John Sarah Robert Miller of my Real Esteat that I ame Posesed of at my Death and as to my movables I Give and Bequeth to my Beloved Wife that is the Howle of them and my Will is that my Wife Pay the Dets Dew out of the Real Estat and that my Wife Dispos of Such a Part of the Real Estat as Shall Pay all my Dets Dew at my Deces and my Will is that my Wife have the Improvment of my Estat During hir Widowhood and my Will is that She and my Childer Be Conted Therewith Further more I Do hereby Constitute my Beloved Wife Annas Miller Sole Executor of this my Last Will and Testament Delivring this to be my Last Will and Testamente made and ordained this Second Day of July *anna Domini* 1764

Subscribed Sealed & Declared

In Presence of us

John McNear

Tobias Glidden James Millar (Seal)

Arch'd Robinson

Probated 5 Sep., 1764. [I, 60.]

John Kingsbury, late of Pownalborough. Patience Kingsbury, of Pownalborough, widow, Adm'x, 7 Sep., 1764. [I, 61.] Michael Sevey and Jonathan Williamson, sureties. Inventory by Benjamin Woodbridge, of Newcastle, Michal Sevey and Jonathan Williamson, both of Pownalborough, 21 Nov., 1764, £966 : 16 : 10. [I, 73 to 75.] Charles Cushing and Abiel Wood, both of Pownalborough, commissioners to examine claims. [I, 168.] Account filed 12 Oct., 1769. [I, 74.] Distribution of estate ordered 12 Sep., 1770. [I, 175.]

Walter Cane, late of Pownalborough. James Flagg, of Cobbiseconte, Adm'r, 25 Feb., 1765. [I, 62] Charles Cushing and Edmund Bridge, sureties. Inventory by Jonas Fitch, Adino Nye and Francis Rittal, all of Powalborough, 1767, £54 : 11 : 10. [I,129.] Charles Cushing and Thomas Allen, both of Pownalborough commissioners to examine claims. [I, 144.] Account filed and distribution ordered 7 Oct., 1769. [I, 172-173.]

James Elder, lately residing at Georgetown. James Springer, of

Georgetown, Adm'r, 11 Mar., 1765. [I, 63.] Jacob Bailey and Adino Nye, sureties.

Paul Ricker, late of a place called Cobbiseconte. Abiel Lovejoy, of Pownalborough, Adm'r, 17 Sep., 1764. [I, 64.] Thomas Allen and George Gray, sureties. Charles Cushing and Thomas Allen, commissioners to examine claims. [I, 97.] Inventory by Thomas Allen and George Gray, both of Pownalborough, 14 Nov., 1763, £43 : 1 : 8 : 12. [I, 116.]

Thomas Leiton, of a place called Gouldsbury. Josiah Tucker, of a place called Gouldsbury, coaster, Adm'r, 30 Mar., 1765. [I, 64.] Robert Gould and Francis Shaw, both of Boston, sureties.

Elias Cheney, late of Pownalborough. Sybyl Cheney, of Pownalborough, Adm'x, 24 Ap., 1765. [I, 65.] Jonas Fitch and Abner Marson, sureties. Inventory by Jonas Fitch, John Barker and Stephen Marson, all of Pownalborough, 2 May, 1765, £64 : 10 : 4. [I, 88.]

Samuel Tolman, late of Kennebeck river. Mary Tolman, of Kennebeck River, near Fort Western, so called, Adm'x, 29 Ap., 1765. [I, 65.] Levi Powers and Mathew Hastings, sureties. Inventory by Mathew Hastings, Edward Savage and Levi Powers, all of Kennebeck River, 27 Sep., 1765, £192 : 18 : 6. [I, 110-111.]

Kennebeck River March 15th 1765. This is to certifie whomsoever it may concern, That this the Will of Mr. Daniel Day And We do think, that he is in his Right mind; but if God should take him out of the World this is his Mind and Will That his Wife Mary Day should heir all what is left, all my Lands and———and all the household furniture and all the Debts and Notes, only said Mary Day is to give my Sister Sarah Day Ten Dollars, which is my mind & will; and all the Rest is Mary Day's my Wife, free from all Fathers or Mothers, Sisters or Brothers or any body in the World Besides, but what Sarah Day has—It is my Will that David Standley should have Two pounds, thirteen Shillings & four Pence lawful money This is my Desire and all that I shall dispose of—   his
Witness present,   Daniel V Day
    his   mark
James X Sally
    mark
David Standley

Probated 29 Ap., 1765, to apply to personal Estate. [I, 66.]

Mathew Hastings and Levi Powers, both of a place in Kennebeck River above Fort Western, sureties.

James Grant, late of Woolwich. Catharine Grant, of Woolwich, widow, Adm'x, 30 Ap., 1765. [I, 66.] Isaac Savage and Samuel Stinson, sureties. Inventory by Thomas Stinson, Samuel Harnden and John Curtis, all of Woolwich. 29 July, 1765, £53 : 7 : 10. [I, 76-7.] Charles Cushing, of Pownalborough, and Benjamin Trott, of Woolwich, commissioners to examine claims. [I, 96.] Account filed 4 May, 1767. [I, 114.] Distribution of estate ordered 6 May, 1767. [I, 115.]

Mathew Hastings, of a place in Kennebeck River above Fort Western, so called, appointed guardian unto Lovel Fairbrother, minor son of Thomas Fairbrother, late of Attleborough, in the County of Bristol, 7 May, 1765. [I, 67.]

In the Name of God amen the thirtieth first day of December one thousand seven Hundred and sixty four I Benjamin Thompson of Georgetown and County of Lincoln &c yeoman being very sick & weak in Body but of perfect mind and memory thanks be given to God for it, therefore Calling unto Mind the Mortality of My Body and Knowing that it is appointed for all Men once to dye, do make and ordain this my last will and testament that is to say principally and first of all I Give and Recommend My soul into the Hands of God yt gave it, and My Body I recommend to the Earth to be buried in decent Christian Burial at the discretion of My Executrix nothing doubting but at the General Resurection I shall Receive the same again by the Mighty power of God, and as touching such wordly Estate wherewith it hath pleased God to Bless Me in this life I Give Demise and dispose of the same in the following Manner and form

Imprimis I give and bequeath to Abigail My dearly beloved wife all My Moveables and personal Estate togeather with the Income of my real Estate for the decent bring up of my Cheildren as well her own Comfortable subsistance whom likewise I Constitute, make and appoint My sole Executrix of all this My last will and testement all and singular my lands Messuages and tenements by her freely to be possesed and Injoyed untill My Children shall arive at the age of twenty one years old or be given in Maraige and in Case any one of My Children or al of them shall or do arive of the age as above or are Marryed in Every such Case they Each receive out of My real Estate that part

Each of them would by law have received had not this My last will bin Made I likewise hereby Giving unto my said Executrix full power to sel and dispose of so much of my real Estate as shall be sufficient to pay My Just Debts and I do hereby uterly disalow and revoke and disanal all and every other former testement wills lagaces and bequests and Executors by me in any ways before named willed and bequeathed reatifying and Confirming this and no other to be My last will and testament In Witness whereof I have hereunto set my hand and seal the day and year first above written

Signed sealed published
pronounced and Declared
by the said Benjamin   Benjamin Thompson   (Seal)
Thompson as his last
will and testment in
the presents of us
  Tobias Ham
  James Hinkley
  Benjamin Ham
  Aaron Hinkley

Probated 7 May, 1765. [I, 68.] Inventory by Dummer Sewall, Moses Hodgkins and Elisha Shaw, all of Georgetown, 15 Aug., 1765, £401 : 1. [I, 87-88.]

Daniel Goodwin, late of Pownalborough. Charles Cushing, of Pownalborough, Adm'r, 10 May, 1765. [I, 69.] Samuel Goodwin, Jr., and Edmund Bridge sureties. Inventory by Adino Nye, Edmund Bridge and Samuel Goodwin, Jun., all of Pownalborough, 28 Sep., 1767, £4 : 12 : 4. [I, 127.]

Amos Goudrey, or Goudey, late of Harrington. Mercy Goudrey, of Harrington, widow, Adm'x, 21 May, 1765. [I, 70.] Ephraim McFarland and Thomas Humphreys, sureties. Mercy Goudey appointed guardian unto Betty, minor daughter, 18 Sep., 1765. [I, 78.] Inventory by Ephraim McFarland and Paul Reed, both of Boothbay and Thomas Humphrys, of Newcastle, 16 July, 1765, £420 : 3 : 4. [I, 79 to 81.] Account filed 28 Sep., 1765. [I, 81.]

Stevens Chase, late of Kennebeck River. Roger Chase, of Pownalborough, Adm'r, 13 June, 1765. [I, 72.] Edmund Bridge and Samuel Goodwin, Jr., sureties. Inventory by Samuel Goodwin, Jun., and Edmund Bridge, both of Pownalborough, and John Hankerson, of Kennebeck River, 26 June, 1765, £106 : 14 : 5. [I, 75-76.]

Charles Cushing and Thomas Allen, both of Pownalborough, commissioners to examine claims. [I, 132.] Account filed 5 Aug., 1768. [I, 132.] Distribution of estate ordered 26 Aug., 1768. [I, 133.]

Zacheus Trafton, late of Georgetown. William Marshall, of Georgetown, Adm'r, 17 June, 1765. [I, 72.] Bryant Roberson and James Thornton, sureties. Inventory by Bryant Roberson, James Thornton and David Trufant, 15 July, 1765, Old Tenor £203 : 12 : 0. [I, 86.] Account filed 17 June, 1767. [I, 142.]

Robert Burns, late of Cobbiseconte. Joseph Burns, of Cobbiseconte, Adm'r, 8 July, 1765. [I, 76.] James Burns and Edmund Bridge, sureties. Inventory by James Flagg, William Bacon and Abram Wyman, £23 : 19 : 11. [I, 86.] Charles Cushing, of Pownalborough, and William Bacon, of Cobbiseconte, commissioners to examine claims. [I, 103.] Account filed 3 Sep., 1768. [I, 150.]

Samuel Collamore, late of Georgetown. Sarah Collamore, of Georgetown, widow, Adm'x, 13 May, 1766. [I, 89.] James Lemont and Jonas Fitch, sureties. Inventory by Samuel Watts, Isaiah Crooker and Elisha Shaw, all of Georgetown, 10 July, 1766, £309 : 10 : 0. [I, 101.] Christopher Mitchel, of Georgetown, appointed Guardian unto Susannah and Deborah, minor daughters, 21 Jan., 1767. [I, 113-114.]

Richard Falle, late of St Georges. Samuel Bogs, of St Georges, Adm'r, 24 Sep., 1765. [I, 90.] Andrew Malcom and James Cargill, sureties. Inventory by Alexander Kellock, Andrew Malcom and Moses Copeland, all of St. Georges, 10 Mar., 1766, £40. [I, 100.] Henry Hendley, of Boston, Adm'r, *de bonis non*, 26 Nov., 1770. [I, 226.] Reuben Hall, of St Georges, and Richard Young and William Henley, both of Boston, appraisers, 27 Dec., 1770. [I, 211.]

In the Name of God Amen— The Sixth Day of March One Thousand Seven Hundred & Sixty Six I Joseph Gould of GeorgeTown in the County of Lincoln Housewright being Very Sick and Weak in Body but of perfect Mind & Memory Thanks be given unto God : Therefore Calling unto Mind the Mortallity of my Body and knowing that it is Appointed for all men Once to die do Make and Ordain this my Last Will and Testament that is to Say, Principally, and first of all I give and Recommend my Soul into the Hands of God that gave it and my Body I Recommend to the Earth to be Buried in decent Christian Burial at the Discretion of my Executors Nothing Doubting but at the General Resurrection I shall receive the Same again by the Mighty Power of God And as touching Such Worldly Estate Wherewith it hath Pleased God to Bless me in this Life I give Demise and Dispose of the Same in the following Manner and Form

Imprimis I give and bequeath to Hanah my Dearly beloved Wife Whom I likewise Constitute Make and Ordain my Sole Executrix of this my Last Will and Testament all and Singular my Lands Messuages and Tenement by her freely to be Possessed and enjoyed During her Life & to be Disposed of as She Sall think meet before or at her Death with all my Household goods and moveable Effects & Debts— Excepting What I give to my Son Joseph & the Rest of my Children Item I give and bequeath to my Son Joseph Gould One hand Saw One Pannel Ditto & One fine Ditto One quarter Round One paring Chisle One pannel Plain Sash plain groveing Plough One astikle two Oges One Joynter fore plain & Smoothing plain One Ax One adds One Old Mall two Rabbit Plains to be delivered to him by my Said Executrix Out of What tools that I leave behind and unto Each of my Other Children I do leave Ten Shillings a Peice to be paid unto them out of my Estate and I do hereby utterly Dissallow revoke and Disannul all and every other Former Testament Wills Legacies and Bequests and Executors by me in any ways before Named Willed and Bequeathed Ratifying and Confirming this and no Other to be my Last Will and Testament in Witness Whereof I have hereunto Set my hand and Seal the Day and Year above Written

Signed Sealed Published Pronounced
and Declared by the said Joseph
Gould as his last Will and Testament
in the Presence of us the Subscribers   Joseph Goold   (Seal)
   Isaac Harding
   Francis Smally
   Josiah Harding

Probated 14 May, 1766. [I, 93.]

Inventory by Joseph Berrey, Abiezer Holbrook and Philip Higgins 30 May, 1766. [I, 227-8.]

In the Name of God Amen the Twenty first Day of October 1762 I William Wilson of Topsham in the County of Lincoln Husbandman being Very Sick and Weak in Body but of Perfect Mind and Memory Thanks be Given to God: Therefore Calling unto mind The Mortality of my Body and knowing that it is appointed for all men once to Die

Do make and ordain this my Last Will and Testament That is to say. Principally and first of all I Give and Recommend my soul into the Hands of God that Gave it and my Body I Recommend to the Earth To be Buried in Decent Christian Burial at the Discretion of my Executors nothing Doubting but at the General Resurrection I shall Receive the Same again by the Mighty Power of God: and as Touching such Worldly Estate wherewith it hath pleased God to bless me in this Life I Give Demise and Dispose of the same in the following Manner and form

Imprimis. I give and bequeath to my well beloved sons Viz, William Wilson John Wilson & Samuel Wilson all and Singular my Lands Messuages and Tenements with all the Right I Have in any Saw Mill or Mills Together with all my Household Goods Chattles Debts and Moveable Effects by Them and Each of them freely to be possesed and Enjoyed I Likewise Give and bequeath to my well beloved Daughters Mary and Isabella Wilson So much Money to be raised and Levyed out of my Estate by the afforsaid William John and Samuel Wilson to pay to the afforsaid Daughters as shall make all my Children to have an Equal Share—

Item. I Constitute make and ordain Isabella my Dearly and Well beloved wife my Sole Executrix of this my Last will and Testament and She the said Isabella to have the Income of Said Estate till the Heirs Come of age unless She Should Marry before that Time and I Do hereby utterly Disalow Revoke and Disannul all and Every other former Testaments Wills Legacies and Bequeasts and Executors by me in Any ways before Named willed and Bequeathed Ratifying and Confirming this and no other to be my Last will and Testament In Witness whereof I have hereunto Set my Hand and Seal the Day and Year above Written

Signed Sealed Published
Pronounced and Declared   William Willson   (Seal)
by the Said William
Wilson as his Last will
and Testament in the
Presence of us the
Subscribers
  Thos Willson
  James Potter
  Samll Moody
  William Alexander

Probated 13 Aug., 1766. [I, 94.]
Inventory by Thomas Willson, William Alexander and John Merrill, 1 Sep., 1766, £297 : 12 : 6. [III, 195.] Account filed 17 Sep., 1787. [III, 196.]

John Sheen, late of Topsham. Nicholas FitzGerald, of Topsham, Adm'r, 9 May, 1766. [I, 95.] Samuel Winchell and John Winchell, sureties. Inventory by Samuel Winchell, John Winchell and James Hunter, all of Topsham, 31 May, 1766, £5 : 3 : 9. [I, 111.] Account filed 17 June, 1767. [I, 143.]

David Gusten, late of Topsham. Samuel Winchell, of Topsham, Adm'r, 11 June, 1766. [I, 101.] John Winchell and Nicholas Fitz-Gerald, sureties. Inventory by John Winchell, Samuel Graves and Joseph Graves, all of Topsham, 16 June, 1766, £62 : 4 : 7. [I, 105.]

In the Name of God, Amen. The Sixteenth Day of July in the Year of our Lord 1766 I James Clark Late of the Town of NewCastle, but at present of The Town of Bristol in the County of Lincoln Yeoman, Being weak in Body, but of perfect mind & memory, Thanks be given unto God for the Same ; And calling to mind the Mortality of my Body, and knowing, that is appointed for all men once to Die, do make and ordain this my Last will and Testament : That is, to Say Principally and first of all, I give and Recommend my Soul into the hands of God that gave it ; And for my Body I recomend it to the Earth to be buried in a Christian like and decent manner, at the Discretion of my Executor nothing Doubting but at the Generall Resurrection, I shall receive the same a gain by the mighty power of God ; And as Touching such worldly Estate wherewith it hath pleased God to Bless me in this Life, I Give, Devise, and Dispose of the Same in manner and form following :

That is to Say

In the first place, I Give and Bequeath to My Dearly beloved wife the one third part of all that I poses, as also one third of the Income of my Lands The same to have and Enjoy During her naturall Life

Also I give to My Son William Clark of Pownalborough The Sum of Ten Shillings Lawful Money to be paid by my Executor—

Also I give to My Son James Clark of Pownalborough The Sum of Ten Shillings Lawfull Money to be paid by my Executor—

Also I give to my Son Thomas Clark of NewCastle the Sum of twenty Six pounds thirteen shillings and four pence Lawfull which I have already paid him and have no Receipt for the Same—

Also I give To my Daughter Hannah Fling a Cow and a Heifer Calf that She hath now in possesion as also a pair of Steeres a Year old Last Spring

Also I give To my Son in Law John Randell of Bristol aforesd and Jane his wife All and Singular what may be found Appertaining to Me Excepting what is before Mentioned in this present will & Testament as also the one half of a Mare of three Years old which is now at New-Castle by him freely to be possesed and The aforesaid John Randell I Likewise Constitute make and ordain my only and Sole Executor of this my Last Will and Testament

And I doe hereby Utterly Disallow, Revoke and Disannul all and Every Other former Testaments, Wills, and Legacies bequests & Executors by me in any ways before this time Named Willed and Bequeathed, Ratifying and Confirming this and no other to be my Last Will and Testament In Wittness whereof I have hereunto Set my hand & Seal the Day and Year above written   Jam's Clark   (Seal)

Sign'd Seal'd Publish'd Pronounc'd and Declar'd by the Said Jam's Clark as his Last Will & Testament in presence of us the Subscribers, That is to Say

    Wm Loud
    James Baily
    Nathaniel Bishop

                                Probated 10 Sep., 1766. [I, 103.]

Inventory by John Cunningham, James Cargill and David Given, all of NewCastle, 30 Sep., 1766, £189 : 7 : 9¾. [I, 106.]

Hezekiah Cloutman, late of Kennebeck River. Abiel Lovejoy, of Pownalborough, Adm'r, 18 Aug., 1766. [I, 106.] Adino Nye and James Flagg, sureties. Inventory by Bennet Woods and Isaac Spencer, of Kennebeck River, 7 Nov., 1766, £14 : 12 : 2. [I, 143.]

James Springer, Jun., late of Georgetown. Rachel Springer, of Georgetown, widow, Adm'x, 19 Aug., 1766. [I, 108.] Joseph White and William Sylvester, sureties. Inventory by Elisha Shaw, Joshua Philbrook and Dummer Sewall, all of Georgetown, 18 Sep., 1766, £271 : 18 : 10. [I, 109.]

William Huston, minor son of John Huston, late of Dunstable, N. H., chose Seth Greeley, of Kennebeck River, to be his guardian, 17 June, 1766. [I, 119.]

Lazarus Noble, late of Pownalborough. Benjamin Noble, of Pownalborough, Adm'r, 27 Feb., 1767. [I, 119.] Samuel Goodwin and John Noble, sureties. Inventory by Jonathan Bryant and William Wyman, both of Pownalborough,—Ap., 1767, £21 : 12 : 4. [I, 42.] Francis Noble, minor daughter, chose Abiel Lovejoy to be her guardian, 18 Jan., 1764. [I, 50]

David Trufant, late of Georgetown. David Trufant, and Mary Trufant, widow, Adm'rs, 11 May, 1767. [I, 120.] John Springer and Edward Pettingill, sureties. Inventory by Isaiah Crooker, Joshua Philbrook and Moses Hodgkins, all of Georgetown, 19 May, 1767, £102 : 5 : 9. [I, 128.] Account filed 14 July, 1768. [I, 229.]

John Wolfe Rupert, late of Pownalborough. Samuel Goodwin, of Pownalborough, Adm'r, 11 Feb., 1767. [I, 121.] Samuel Goodwin, Jr., and James Hodge, sureties. Inventory by Charles Cushing, Thomas Allen and Adino Nye, all of Pownalborough, 12 June, 1767, £42 : 0 : 0. [I, 145.] Charles Cushing and Roger Chase, both of Pownalborough, commissioners to examine claims. [I, 222.]

John Henry Kier, late of Pownalborough. Samuel Goodwin, of Pownalborough, Adm'r, 11 Feb., 1767. [I, 121.] Samuel Goodwin, Jr., and James Hodge, sureties. Inventory by Charles Cushing, Thomas Allen and Adino Nye, all of Pownalborough, 12 June, 1767, £47 : 6 : 8. [I, 146] Charles Cushing and Roger Chase, both of Pownalborough, commissioners to examine claims. [I, 221.]

Zachariah Narden, late of Pownalborough. Samuel Goodwin, of Pownalborough, Adm'r, 27 May, 1767. [I, 122.] Thomas Allen and Samuel Goodwin, Jr., sureties. Inventory by Charles Cushing, Thomas Allen and Adino Nye, all of Pownalborough, 12 June, 1767, £42 : 0 : 0. [I, 145.] Charles Cushing and Roger Chase both of Pownalborough, commissioners to examine claims. [I, 222.]

In the name of God Amen the thirtieth day of October *Anno Domini* 1766 I David Olover of Georgetown in the County of Lincoln yeoman being sick and weak in body but of perfict mind and memory thanks be to God for it therefore Knowing that it is appointed for all men onse to dye do make and ordain this my Larst will and Testament that is to say primarily and in the first plase I give and Recomend my soul into the hands of God that gave it and my body I Recomend to the Earth to be buried in desent Christian burial at the discretion of my Executor nothing doubting but to Receive the same again by the mighty power of God at the general Resurrection and as to such worldly Estate which I am the owner of I give and demise and dispose of in the following manner and form

Imprimis I give and bequeth unto hanah my dearly beloved wife all my household firnituer and all my stock of cattel shep and swine together with the whole of my intrist in a sawmill at robinhoods cove in said town To hir and hir heirs and assigns forever out of the Ishews and profits thereof my will and plesure is that she discharge all my Just debts and funaral Expenses and further I give and bequeth unto hir during hir natural Life the use and improvement of the Low Rom and chamber in the notherly End of my dwelling hous in which I now dwell and one half of the siller in said hous together with barnrome for hay and housing for fower or five head of cattel

Itum I give unto my son Thomas Olover the western half of my farm or Lott ot Land where he now dwell and one third part of all my solt marsh during the nateral Life of his mother and after hir desease one half of said marsh said upland and marsh To him his Heirs and assigns forever

Itum I give unto my son Ephriem Olover the sum of twenty six shillings and Eight pence

Itum I give unto my daughter Hanah Hinkley the sum of fower pound

Itum I give unto hanah curtis the daughter of my son Henery Olover the sum of thirten shillings and fower pence and unto Henery Olover the son of my said son Henery Olover the sum of twentysix shillings and Eight pence

Itum I give unto my son Jacob Olover the sum of six pounds thirten shillings and fower pence

The above sums To be paid to my above mentioned childrin and grand children by my son John Olover out of what I give and bequeth to him and that at the deseas of his mother and not before and the above sums together with what I have done for them in my Lifetime is a Just proportion of my Estate to Each of them

Itum I give unto my son John Olover whom I Likewise constitute and make and ordain my sole Executor of this my Larst will and testament and and singular the Residue and Remainder of all and singuler of my Estate both real and personal of what name or nature soever to him his Heirs and assigns for Ever he paying the above mentioned Legases and that he also give and deliver unto his honered mother yearly and Every year during hir natteral Life towards hir confertable support one forth part of all the grain and corn and Roots and Inglish hay that he shel rais upon the farm that hereby I give and bequeth unto him and three Load of solt hay yearly during said Tearm and I do hereby utterly dissalow Revoke and disanul all other and former will and Testament and Executors by me named Ratifying and confirming this and no other to be my Larst will and Testament In witnis whereof I have hereunto set my hand and seal the day and year above written

Signed sealed published pronounsed
and declared by the said David
Olover as his larst will and
Testament in the presants of
us the subscribers   David Olover   (Seal)
George Rodgers
John Rodgers
Tobias Hill

Probated 13 May, 1767.   [I, 123-4.]

In the name of God Amen on the fourteenth Day of March A. D. 1764 I John Lemont of Georgetown In the County of Lincoln and Province of the Massachusetts Bay In New England Gentleman Being week in body but of Perfect mind & memory Thanks be Given to God : Therefore Calling to mind the mortallity of my body and Knowing that it is appointed for all men once to Die Do make and ordain this my Last will and Testament that is to say Principlely and first of all I Give and Recomend my soul Into the Hands of God that gave it and my body I Recomend to the Earth to be buried in decent Christian Burial at the Discretion of my Executors Nothing Doubting but at the General Resurrection I shall Receive the same again by the Mighty Power of God and Touching such worldly Estate wherewith it Hath Pleased God to Bless me with in this Life I give demise and Dispose of the same in the following maner and form—

Imprimise   I Give and bequeath to Elisebeth my Dearly beloved wife the use and Improvement of my Dwelling House and barn and the whole of my farm whereon the buildings stand withe all my Cattles stock and moveables within Doors & without till my son David Lemont arives to sixten years of age and afterwards Duringher widdowhood at the Expiration of which Time the said Elisebeth is to Deliver ye use and Improvment of the s'd artickels with all the artickels to my surviving Hiers in as good Repare as when she Receved them

Item—as I have already Given to my sons Benjamin and James Lemont Eighty acres of Land to Each of them I further Give to my sons Benjn & James one third Part of a Saw mill standing on wisgig Creek with one third Part of all Privilidgs thereunto Belonging—

Item—the Remainder of my Estate after my honest Debts are Paid to be Eaquelly Devided Between my five Youngest sons viz: John Thomas Robert Samuel & David Lemont there Paying to my Daughters Mary Woodside thirten Pounds six shillings & Eight Pence Lawfull money Likwise Paying the sixtenth Part of the whole of my Estate to Each of my four Youngest Daughters viz Nancy Sarah Elisebeth and hanah Lemont—

I do appoint and ordain James McCobb & John Parker of Georgetown aboves'd Gentlemen my sole Executors of this my Last will and Testement and I do hereby utterly Disallow Revoke and Disanul all and Every other former Testements wills Legases and bequests & Executors by me in any ways before Named willed and bequeathed Ratifiing and Confirming this and no other to be my Last will and Testement In witness whereof I have hereunto set my hand and seal the Day and Yeare above written—

Signed sealed Published Pronounced
and Declared by the said John
Lemont as his Last will and
Testement in the Presence of
us the subscribers   John Lemont   (Seal)
   Phinehas Nevers
   Samuell Nevers
   John Tebbits
   Jams. McHonane
   James Mckibb

Probated 13 May, 1767. [I, 125.]

John Parker disclaimed executorship 4 Feb., 1767. [I, 124.] Inventory by Samuel Watts, Isaiah Crooker and Moses Hodgkins, all of Georgetown, 23 June, 1767. [I, 129-130.] Thomas Lemont, minor son, Elizabeth Lemont and Hannah Lemont, minor daughters, chose their brother Benjamin Lemont to be their guardian 16 Feb., 1767. [I, 150-1.] John Lemont of Bath, Adm'r *de bonis non*, 15 Ap., 1791. [V, 29.] Samuel Lemont and David Lemont, both of Bath, sureties.

John Moore, late of Pownalborough. Sarah Moore, of Pownalborough, widow, Adm'x, 25 Ap., 1767. [I, 126.] Inventory by Thomas Rice, Jonathan Williamson and Michal Sevey, all of Pownalborough, 30 Ap., 1768, £301 : 16 : 3¾. [I, 151-2.] Consent of Stephen and Mary Sevey, John and Sarah Cunningham, Samuel Marrow and Sarah Day, heirs for division of real estate, 20 Ap., 1786 ; warrant for such division issued to Thomas Boyd, of Boothbay, Daniel Webster and Thomas Ring, of Edgecomb, 15 Nov., 1785. [II, 237.] Return of division, 21 Ap., 1786. [II, 238.] Account of Sarah Day, Adm'x, filed 17 June, 1783. [IV, 3-4.]

Henry Miller, late of Broad Bay. George Light, Jun., of Broad Bay, Adm'r, 17 Feb., 1768. [I, 131.] George Light and Francis Rittal, sureties. Inventory by Jacob Ludwig, Mathias Hofesess and Henry Keyler, all of Broad Bay, 14 Mar., 1768, £40 : 02 : 10½. Account filed 5 June, 1769. [I, 172.]

Robert Rankin, late of the River Kennebeck. Mathew Hastings, resident at the River Kennebeck, Adm'r, 16 Sep., 1767. [I, 131.] Charles Webber and Josiah Butterfield, sureties. Inventory by John Marsh, James Bacon and Thomas Clark, all of Kennebeck River,—Jan., 1766, £24 : 19 : 9. [I, 133-4.]

In the name of God Amen
I Jonathan Preble of Georgetown In the Countey of Lincoln and Province of Masschusetts Bay In New Englen Gentelman Beaing very Sick and weak In Body But of perfect mind and memorey thanks be given to God therefor Calling unto mind the mortality of my Body and knowing that It Is appointed for all men once to die do make and ordain this my Last will and testament that Is to say Principalley and first of all I give and Recommend my Soul Into the hands of God that Give It and my Body I Recommend to the Earth to be Buried In decent Christian Burial at the discretion of my Executors nothing doubting But at the Generall Resurrection I shall Recive the same again By the mighty Power of God and as touching Such worldly Estate wherewith God hath Been pleased to Bless me In this Life I give demise and dispose of the Same In the following manner & forom my Just Debts and funnarel Expences Being first paid

Item   I give unto my Loving wife Mehitable Preble on third of all my Real Estate on the Island of Arrowsick In said Georgetown during hir nateral Life and on third part of my Personall during said term

Item   I give unto my Loving Son Jonnathan Preble and to his Heirs and assings forever two hundred akers of Land situated on the nothern side of Merimetting Bay In said Countey of Lincoln at a plase Called

Abiggedusat and Bounded Southwardly By said Bay and Extending northwardly or northward according as It Is described By the Instrumint of Convaince of said tract of Land unto me untill two Hundred akers be Compleat as also my Best fowling pice

Item I give unto the Hairs of my Dearly Beloved Son Ebenezer Preble deseased and unto ther Heirs and assings for Ever fiftey akers of said Land ajoyning to the northen part of that tract as Henrafter given to my Son Abraham and this with what I have formerly given to my said Son Ebenezer In his Life time and alowing him to Shair In the produse of a tract of Land on Cusens Island In North yarmouth to the value of on houndred pounds to be said Hairs part of my Real Estate

Item I give unto my Son Abraham Preble his Heirs or assings for Ever fiftey akers of Land ajoyning to the north part of that tract as above given to my Son Jonnathan and to Extend northward from Saied tract and Southward on a tract of fiftey akers given to the Heairs of my Son Ebenezer deseased till said fiftey akers Is Completed and this with what I have formerly done for him In allowing him to Share a part of the Sale of a tract of land Lying on Cusenses Island in Northyarmouth to the valu of on hundred pounds to be his Share of my Real Estate

Item I give unto my Son Joseph Preble whom with my Son Abraham preble I Constitute and appoint to be my Executors of this my Last will and testament and to his Hairs and assigns for Ever that third part of my Real Estate on Arrowsick Island ter   d th of my wife which I have as above given unto hir during   r L tog er with all and Every part of my Real Estate L ig   dea g on aid Island

Item I give the Remainder of all my personall Estate not Before disposed of after the folowing manner viz on fourth part thereof to my Son Abraham Preble on fourth part to the heirs of my desesed Son Ebenezer and on forth p   to my   Ton t   e ar   f   part ot my Son Josep prebl   I ch   d ver of e   irs and asigns forever But   e   th La l   mther above to my Son Jonnathan Preble Is not Such But that ther Is a posability of his failing In holding the Land I have will to him as above and mor probell that he may be put to som Expences By Law or otherwise to Secure his title to sead Lands at Abagdusect It therfor Is my will and order that my Son Abraham my Son Joseph and the Heirs of my Son Ebenezer pribell Each and Everey of them and the heirs pay unto my Son Jonnathan Preble or his heirs on fourth part of all such Charges arising By Law Suits or otherwise that Is to Say my Son Abraham or his heirs pay on fourth part and the Heirs of my Son Ebenezer dessed pay on fourth part and the Heirs of my Son Joseph prible on fourth part of all the Charges that may arise on defenden the title to said track on Abageduset that I have willed to my Son Jonnathan In this my Last will and furder It Is my will & pleasure that Before my Son Abraham preble the heirs of my Son Ebenezer preble and my Son Joseph Preble have and Receive ther Share or part of my personal Estate that they Saverley Becom Bound to my Son Jonnathan prebie that If he Cannot Injoy said tract By virtu of this my will By the failuer of my title to the Saim that then my Son Abraham preble pay to my Son Jonathan preble twentey pounds Lafull money and the Heirs of my Son Ebenezer preble pay thirteen pounds Six Shillings and Eght pence and my Son Joseph prible pay twintey six pounds thirteen Shillings and fower pen Lafull money the above Sums to be pay'd to my Son Jonnathan or his Heirs

Revoking all other wills and Bequethments I do Ratify allow and Confirm this and no other to be my Last will and testament In witnes wherof I do Hereunto Sett my hand and Seal 24 day of October *anno* 1763 ye 3 year of His Majesteys Reign
N B the 2 words By & the In the 30 Line the word Son In the 90 Line Enterlined Befor Signed ye word pound In 40 Line Enterlined Befor Signed

Signed Sealed published   Jonathan Preble   (Seal)
and pronounced and declamed
By the Said Jonathan preble
to be his Last will and
testament In presants of us
   John Trott
   Benja Trott Juner
   Lemuel Trott
Before Sigen nine words In twintey fifth Line and five words In twintey Sixth Line Both In the Second page Rased Befor Signed

                     Probated 13 Ap., 1768. [I, 134-5.]
Inventory by Samuel Denny and John Stinson, both of Georgetown, and John Patten, of Topsham. 3 May, 1768, £901 : 15 : 9. [I, 136-7.] Samuel Preble and Ebenezer Preble, minor sons of Ebenezer

Preble, late of Woolwich, deceased, chose Samuel Harnden, of Woolwich, to be their guardian, 1768. [I, 151.] Samuel Harden appointed guardian unto Mary Preble, minor daughter of Ebenezer Preble, late of Woolwich, deceased, 27 Sep., 1768. [I, 154.]

Meddunkcooke July ye 26th 1767

To all people to whome these presents shall come Greeting: Know ye that I Samuel Jameson of Meeddunkcooke in the county of Lincoln in the province of the Massachusetts-bay in New-england husband-man being sick and weak of body and Judging the time of my death is nigh yet bing by the mercy of God in ye use of my reason & perfect in my understanding, do make my last will & testament as follows,

Imprimis I do Constitute and appoint my loving Wife Sarah and my Son Martin Jameson to be my Joint executors to this my last will & testament. Item I do give unto my eldest daughter Jane Jameson of falmouth one half of my land which I bought of Yardly Lewis which lyeth on Georges river to her her heirs and assigns forever, and the other half of s'd lot of land I give to my eldest Son Martin Jameson to him his heirs and assigns forever he to have ye back part

Item my homestead on which I now dwell I give to my five Sons namely Martin Jameson Joseph Jameson Samuel Jameson brice Jameson and George Jameson to be equaly divided among them when the youngest comes to lawful age they paying to each of my two daughters namely Mary Jameson & Rachel Jameson the sum of two pounds thirteen shillings and four pence when the land is divided that is to be in lawfun money: and to my wife Sarah Jameson I give the improvement of my land & moveables for the payment of my Just debts & bringing up of my children till they come of age & then one third part of the moveables to belong to her as long as she lives & then to be equally divided among the children & the other two thirds to be equally divided among the children: & if any of the children die before they come of age then their part to be divided equally among the Sons and upon mature consideration I declare this to be my last will & testament hereby disowning all other things of this nature in witness whereof I have hereunto set my hand & seal the day & date first mentioned

Signed & sealed in   Samuel Jameson (Seal)
presence of
   Paul Jameson
   Ebenezer Davis
   Abiah Wadsworth

Probated 10 Aug., 1768. [I, 137-8.]

Inventory by Samuel Gilchrist, Patrick Porterfield and Paul Jameson, of Meduncook, 9 Aug., 1768. [I, 199.]

In the Name of GOD, Amen

The twenty thard Day of April *Anno Domini* one Thousand Seven hundred and Sixty four I Samuel Bogs of St Georges in the County of Lincoln and province of the Massachusetts Bay in New England Husbandman being weak in Body but of perfect Mind and Memory Thanks be given to GOD;

Therefore Calling to mind the mortality of my Body, and knowing that it is appointed for all Men to Die, Do Make and Ordain this my Last Will and Testament That is to say principally and first of all I give and recommend my Soul into the hands of GOD who gave it and my Body I recommend to the Earth to be buried in decent Christian Burial at the Discretion of my Executors, nothing Doubting but the General Resurrection I shall receive the same a gain by the Mighty Powar of GOD. And as touching Such Worldly Estate wherewith it hath pleased GOD to Bless me in this Life I give, demise, and Dispose of the Same in the following Manner & Form.

Imprimis I give and bequeath to my well Beloved Daughter Jane Motley five Shillings to be paid her by my Executors out of my Estate which with what She has all ready Received is her full protion or Share out of my Estate

Imprimis I give and bequeath to my well Beloved Son John Bogs one Straitboded Coat of Broad Cloath one great Bibble one Large loin pott, one pair of Larg Stillerds one pair of Larg Andioin with SunDries of outher Smal things twanty Six pounds thirdteen and four peance for my Bord and twanty pounds from those Deats that Shall be Call in which with what he has allredy Received is his full protion or share of my Estate

Imprimis I give And bequeath to my well beloved Daughter Anne Rax Six pounds thirdteen Shillings and four pence paid her by my Executors Out of my Estate which with what She has allready Received is her full protion or Share out of my Estate

Imprimis I give and bequeath to my well beloved Son Samuel Bogs one great Coat of Myen one Not that I had of Chusen one Not that I had of Bickmore which with what he has Received is his full protion or Shear out of my Estate

Imprimis I give and bequeath to my well belove Son William Bogs a Fathers Bead that I know Lie on and all that belongs to the Bead which with what he has had or Received is his full protion or Shear out of my Estate

Imprimis I give and bequeath to my well belove Daughter Mary Burns five Shilling which with what She has allrady Receive is her full protion or Shear out of my Estate

Imprimis I give and bequeath to my well beloved Grand Daughter Ann mcDaniel Six pounds thardteen Shilling and four pence to be left in the Trusuery tel She Shall Com of Eage by the order of the Executors

Imprimis I give and bequeath to my well beloveed Grand Son Samuel Bogs three pounds Six Shilling and Eaght pence to be Left in the hands of the Executors tel he Shall Com of Eage with Lawfull Intress tel then and if God Shall take away his Breath this Sum is to go to his Sister Anne.

I Do hearby apint John and William Bogs my Sons to be my Executors of this my Last Will and Testiment Whereof I have hereunto Set my hand and Seal—

Witness Preseant   Samuel Bogs (Seal)
John Crawford   I Declar this to be
John Millar   my Last will and
Andrew Storer   Testament

Probated 15 June, 1768. [I, 139.]
John Bogs disclaimed executorship 19 May, 1768. [I, 138.] Inventories by Patrick Porterfield, Alexander Lermond and Samuel Creighton, all of St Georges. [I, 140 & 223.] Account filed 3 Oct., 1770. [I, 223.]

Adino Nye, late of a place upon Kennebeck River without the Bounds of any Town. Mary Nye, of said place, widow. Adm'x, 30 Jan., 1768. [I, 141.] Charles Cushing and Edmund Bridge, sureties. Inventory by Charles Cushing, Edmund Bridge and William Silvester, all of Pownaborough, 23 June, 1768, £211 : 10 : 5¾. [I, 146-7.]

Samuel Hinkley, late of Georgetown. Sarah Hinkley, of Georgetown, widow, Adm'x, 18 June, 1767. [I, 148.] Edmund Hinkley and Abiel Lovejoy, sureties. Inventory by George Rodgers, Joseph Harford and Mathew Mckenny, all of Georgetown, 1 July, 1767. [I, 148-9.]

Henry Fosset, late of Pemaquid. George Caldwell, of Bristol, Adm'r, 30 July, 1765. [I, 152.] Samuel Goodwin and Jonas Fitch, sureties. Inventory by Patrick Rodgers, William Sproul and Francis Young, all of Bristol. 5 Aug., 1765, £100 : 0 : 0. [I, 153.]

In the name of God Amen, the fourth day of April A. D. 1766, I James Wyman of Pownalborough in the County of Lincoln yeoman being aged & infirm of body, but of sound mind, after commending my Soul into the hands of Almighty God, & my body to the Earth to decent burial, do make this my last will & testament & dispose of my worldly estate in manner following That is to say—

Imps I give & bequeath to my beloved Wife Bethiah one Cow & all my household stuff & furniture, besides her Dower in my real estate—

Item, I give to my Daughter Elizabeth McCausland the sum of Five shillings to be paid with a year & an half after my decease by Son William which with what I heretofore gave her at Marriage or since is in full of her portion of my estate—

Item I give to my Daughter Bethiah Small the sum of five shillings to be paid her in a year & an half after my decease by my Son William, which with what I heretofore gave her at Marriage & since is in full of her portion of my estate—

Item I give to my Daughter Abigail Bickford the sum of five shillings to be paid her by my Son William in a year & an half after my decease, which with what I heretofore gave her at Marriage & since is in full of her portion of my estate—

Item I give to my Daughter Prudence Goodwin the sum of Fourty shillings to be paid her in a year & an half after my decease by my son William which with what I gave her at Marriage & since is in full of her portion of my estate—

Item I give to my Daughter Deliverance Call the sum of Two pounds Thirteen shillings & Four pence to be paid her by my Son William in a year & an half after my decease, which what I gave her at Marriage & since is in full of her portion of my estate—

Item I give to my Daughter Olive Goodwin the sum of Six pounds Thirteen shillings & four pence to be paid her in a year & an half after my decease by my son William which with what I gave her at Marriage & since is in full of her portion of my estate—

Item I give to my Daughter Molly the sum of Twenty pounds to be paid her when she arrives at the age of Eighteen years by my Son Daniel.

Item I give to my Grand Daughter Hannah Daughter of my son James deceased the sum of five shillings to be paid her by my son William in a year & an half after my decease—

Item I give & devise to my son Daniel his heirs & assigns forever my half of the land & real estate at Bowdoinham in said County of Lincoln, which was conveyed to me & my son William by Deed by Agreen Crabtree, the whole being about Fourty acres, also Twenty acres of Land on the northerly part of my Land on Swan Island in said Pownalborough, at the West End of the Eighty acres of Land Lazarus Noble lived upon, he the said Daniel paying the said Legacy of Twenty pounds to my Daughter Molly as aforementioned—

Item, All the rest & residue of my estate real & personal upon said Swan Island, in s'd Pownalborough, & at Falmouth in the County of Cumberland, or wheresoever else lying situate or being, of what name or nature soever I give & devise to my son William his heirs & assigns forever he the said William paying all my debts & funeral Charges, & all the Legacies herein severally given to my Daughters except said Twenty pound Legacy he also upon demand making executing & delivering to my son Daniel & his heirs a good & sufficient deed in the Law of all the Estate right title & Interest which he the said William shall then have in & to the the said half of said Fourty acres of Land at said Bowdoinham herein devised to the said Daniel

Lastly I appoint my son William Exec'r of this my Will—In witness whereof I have hereto set my hand & seal the day first aforewritten—

Memo. the words (my) (with) (William) (& his heirs) were interlined before sign'g &c.

signed sealed published &
declared by the said James
the Testator to be his last   James Wyman   (Seal)
Will & testament in pre-
sence of
   Wm Cushing
   Abiel Lovejoy
   Samuel Reed

Probated 23 Ap., 1766. [I, 154.] Abiel Lovejoy and Obadiah Call, sureties.

Samuel Harnden, late of Woolwich. Mary Harnden, widow, and Samuel Harnden, both of Woolwich, Adm'rs, 19 Aug., 1768. [I, 155.] Abraham Preble and Joseph Preble, sureties. Inventory by Aaron Hinkley, John Stinson and David Gilmor, 17 Nov., 1768. [I, 229.]

In the Name of God Amen
The Second Day of July, 1767. I Morgan McCaffry of the Town of

Bristol, husbandman, being very Sick and weak in Body, But of perfect mind and Memory, Thanks be Given unto God:—

Therefore Calling unto mind the Mortality of my Body, and Knowing that it is appointed for all men once to Dye, Do make and ordain this my Last will and Testament, That is to Say

Principally and first of all, I give and Recommend my Soul into the hands of God that Gave it, and my Body I Recommend to the Earth, to be Buried in Decent Christian Burial at the Discretion of my Executor; Nothing Doubting but at the General Resurrection I shall Receive the Same by the Mighty power of God. And as Touching Such worldly Estate wherewith it hath pleased God to Bless me in this Life I Give Demise and Dispose of the Same in the following manner and form

Imprimis I will that my Estate Both personal and Real be Disposed of after my Decease according to the Method and Discretion of my Executor and Executrix as they Shall think most Convenient and that my Just Debts should be paid to my Creditors out of the Same.

Item I give to my well Beloved wife Ann McCaffry one Third of the whole of my Estate after it shall be Disposed of as before mentioned for her sole and proper use to be Raised and Levied out of my Estate

Item, and whatever Else shall Remain of my Said Estate after it be Disposed of in manner aforesaid I Give to my Children To W my Sons James, John, my Daughters, Frances, Jane, Mary & Margarett

I Do hereby utterly Dissalow, revoke and Disannull all and every other former Testaments, wills Legacies, by me in any wayes before named Ratyfying and Confirming this and no other to be my Last will and Testament. Likewise I make Constitute and ordain James Little of New Castle to be my Executor and Ann McCaffry my Beloved wife to be my Executrix to this my Last will and Testament In whittness whereof I have hereunto Sett my hand and Seal The Day and Year above written

Signed Sealed published pronounced
and Declared by the Said Morgan McCaffry
as his Last will and Testament in the presence
of us the Subscribers   Morgan McCaffry   (Seal)
    David Drowne
    Patr'k Rodgers
    John Mcfarland

                      Probated 15 June, 1768. [I, 156.]

Ann McCaffry and James Little disclaimed executorship 21 Aug.,

1767. [I, 156.] Joseph Henshaw, of Boston, and Robert Sproul, of Bristol, Adm'rs *cum Testamento annexo*, 14 June, 1768. [I, 157.] Robert Sproul, William Burns and William McClain, sureties. Inventory by Alexander Nickels, Samuel Boyd and Alexander Fosset, all of Bristol, 8 Dec., 1768, £182 : 0 : 2. [I, 208.] Alexander Nickels and Samuel Boyd, both of Bristol, commissioners to examine claims, 13 June, 1768. [I, 209.] Account filed 27 Nov., 1770. [I, 210.]

John Louis Cavalear, late of Pownalborough. Mary Cavalear, of Boston, widow, Adm'x, 28 Oct., 1768. [I, 157.] Rudolph Frederick Geyer and Christian Franckfort, both of Boston, sureties. Inventory by Charles Cushing, Francis Rittal and John Stein, all of Pownalborough, 26 June, 1770, £100 : 13 : 4. [I, 214.]

Ralph Chapman, late of Pownalborough. Prudence Chapman, of Pownalborough, widow, Adm'x, 26 Dec., 1768. [I, 158.] Samuel Goodwin, Jr., and Edmund Bridge, sureties. Inventory by Samuel Emerson, Richard Kidder and Edmund Bridge, 26 Jan., 1769, £558 : 17 : 3½. [I, 204.] Account filed 24 May, 1771. [I, 207.]

Thomas Patridge, late of Bristol. Alexander Nickels, of Bristol, Adm'r, 10 Jan., 1766. [I, 158.] Alexander McGlathry and Charles Cushing, sureties. Inventory by John McFarland, Patrick Rodgers and Alexander McGlathry, 28 Sep., 1769, £11 : 6 : 8. [I, 169.]

Robert McGlathry, late of Bristol. Alexander McGlathry, of Bristol, Adm'r, 10 Jan., 1769. [I, 158.] Alexander Nickels and Charles Cushing, sureties. Inventory by Alexander Nickels, Patrick Rodgers and John McFarland, all of Bristol 23 Mar., 1769, £169 : 8 : 0. [I, 190.] Account filed 1 Mar., 1770. [I, 190.] William McGlathry, of Bristol, guardian unto Margaret and Sarah, minor daughters, 1 Feb., 1774. [II, 170.]

Samuel Hodge, late of Newcastle. Henry Hodge, of Newcastle, Adm'r, 13 Jan., 1769. [I, 159.] Inventory by John McNear, James Cargill and Benjamin Woodbridge, all of Newcastle, 23 Jan., 1769, £213 : 4 : 9. [I, 170.] Arthur Noble, of a place called Walpole, and Samuel Nickels, of Newcastle, commissioners to examine claims. [I, 267.] Account filed 29 Oct., 1774. [I, 268.]

Charles Leissner, late of Broad Bay. Mary Leissner, of Broad Bay, widow, Adm'x, 22 Feb., 1769. [I, 159.] Inventory by John Martin, Jun., John Ulmer and Mathias Rameley, 27 Feb., 1769, £3433 : 16 : 1, Old Tenor. [I, 192-3.]

Jacob Hearsy, late of Pownalborough. John Andrews, of Pownalborough, Adm'r, 24 Feb., 1769. [I, 160.] John McGown and George Goud, sureties. Inventory by John McGown, George Goud and Edmund Bridge, all of Pownalborough, 19 Mar., 1770, £12 : 7 : 8. [I, 198.] Charles Cushing and Samuel Goodwin, both of Pownalborough, commissioners to examine claims, 27 Aug., 1769. [I, 231.]

Philip Rominger, late of Broad Bay. Caleb Howard, of Broad Bay, Adm'r, 3 Mar., 1769. [I, 160.] George Dalheim and Michael Sides, sureties. Inventory by George Dalheim, Michael Sides and Mathias Remely, all of Broad Bay, 30 Mar., 1769, £592 : 5 : 0, Old Tenor. [I, 184.] Account filed 9 May, 1769. [I, 185.]

In the Name of GOD, Amen
I William Watson of a place called St Georges in the County of Lincoln and Province of Massachusetts Bay in New-England yeoman. Being Sick and Weak of Body, but of perfect Mind and Memory, Thanks be given to God therefor calling to mind the mortality of my Body and knowing that it is appointed unto all men once to Die, do make and ordain this my last Will and Testament, that is to say principally and first of all I give and reccommend my Soul into the Hand of Almighty God that gave it, and my Body I reccommend to the Earth to be buried in decent Christian Burial at the Discretion of my Executors nothing Doubting but at the general Resurrection I shall receive the Same again by the Mighty Power of God. And as touching such worldly Estate wherewith it hath pleased God to bless me in this life, I give demise and dispose of the same in the following Manner and Form

Imprimis I give and Bequeath unto my well beloved Son William Watson the full two third parts of all my Lands and Real Estate namely the westerly part of my Farm to be divided by a Strait Line from St Georges River to the opposite Line, together with all my personal, or movable Estate of what name or nature soever

Item I give unto my well beloved Son James Watson one third part of my Real Estate namely the Easterly part of my said Farm to be divided in manner aforesaid, but if my said Son James shall not in his own proper person come and settle on the said Lands and improve the same, then my will is that the aforesaid one third part of the Land be equally divided between my Sons David, & Matthew, or to the longest liver of them if either of them shall Die without Children

Item I give unto my well beloved Son David Watson one Yoke of

Oxen and one Cow, to be delivered unto him in one year after my decease or when he shall arrive at the age of twenty & one years, he to be suitably instructed in Reading writing and Cyphering suitable for a person of his Station to be levied and paid for out of the whole of my Estate

Item. I give unto my well beloved Son Matthew Watson one Yoke of Oxen and one Cow to be delivered unto him in one year after my decease or when he shall arrive at the Age of twenty and one years he also to be instructed in Reading writing & Cyphering suitable for a person of his Station to be levied and paid for out of the whole of my Estate

Item. I give unto my well beloved Daughters namely Jane Libbee, Margaret Robinson, and Elizabeth Watson & to each of them a Bible each to be delivered in one year after my decease to be levied and paid out of my whole Estate which together with what they have already had is their full portion out of my Estate

Item. I give unto my Grandson John Watson son of my son John Watson deceased one Yoke of Oxen, in one year after my decease or when he shall arrive at the Age of twenty and one years if he shall live thereunto, to be levied out of my whole Estate

Item. I give unto my Grandson Jeremiah Gore son of my Daughter Mary Gore deceased, one Cow, in one year after my Decease or when he shall arrive at the age of twenty & one years, if he shall live so long to be levied out of the whole of my Estate. My further will is concerning my Sons David & Matthew that they be instructed in the Art of making Shoes

And I do constitute make and ordain David Fales Esqr Joseph Robinson & Samuel Creighton Gentlemen all of St Georges aforesaid to be the Executors of this my last Will and Testament. And I do hereby utterly disallow, revoke and disannul all and every other former Testaments, Wills, Legacies, Bequests, and Executors, by me in any ways before-named willed and Bequeathed, ratifying and confirming this and no other to be my last Will and Testament. In Witness whereof I have hereunto set my Hand and Seal, this twentieth Day of November in the eighth year of the Reign of our Sovereign Lord George the third King &c *Annoque Domini* One Thousand Seven Hundred and Sixty Seven

             Willm Watson (Seal)

Signed, Sealed, published, pronounced
 and declared by the said William

Watson to be his last, Will, &
Testament, in presence of us
who have hereunto subscribed
our Names
Jonathan Nutting
Mason Wheaton
John McCarter

Probated 8 Feb., 1769. [I, 161-2.]

Joseph Robinson and Samuel Creighton disclaimed executorship 8 Feb., 1769. [I, 162-3] Inventory by Mason Wheaton, John McCarter and Alexander Lermond, all of St Georges, 16 Feb., 1769, £191 : 13 : 6. [I, 186.]

In the Name of God Amen

This is the will and testement of Me the Subscriber James Patterson of Pownalboro in the County of Lincoln Being of sound mind & perfect Reason

Item I Give My Soul to all mighty God from whome I Received it and My Body to the Earth to be Deasently Buried in sure & Certain Hoops of a Glorious Reserrection to life Earearnell

Item I Give unto My Dear beloved wife Margrett Patterson all my whole Easteate Reall & personall after My lawful Debts are paid and my funeral Charges paid and my three Children viz two sons & one Daughter is to be Hansomly Brough up to Lawfull age out of my Eastate and allso to pay to My son William ten pounds lawfull mony and to my Daughter Abigill ten pounds Lawfull money & allso to my son James Howard Patterson ten pounds Lawfull mony out of my Easteate as the Come of Lawfull Age to be paid to them by my beloved wife Margrett whome I hereby make & orda'n My Soul Executrix to this my Last will & testement maid this sixth Day of May 1764

Signed Sealled Sealed & Delly'd

In presents of   James Patterson (Seal)
  Mary Bryant
  James Howard
  Jona. Bryant

Probated 12 Ap., 1769. [I, 163-4.]

In the Name of God amen the twelth day of January *Anno Domini* 1769 I James Work of Topsham in the County of Lincoln yeoman being very sick and weak in body but of perfect mind and Memory, thanks be given unto God,—therefore Calling to mind the Mortality of

My body and that it is appointed unto all Men once to dye, do make and ordain this My Last Will and testament. that is to say, principally and first of all I Give and recommend my soul into the hands of God that gave it: and my body I recommend to the Earth to be buried in decent Christian burial at the discretion of my Executor nothing doubting but at the General Resurrection I shall receive the same again by the Mighty power of God. and as touching such worldly Estate wherewith it hath pleased God to bless me in this Life I Give demise and dispose of the same in the following manner and form—

Imprimis I give and bequeath to Margret my dearly beloved Wife all my household furniture with the one half of My Cattle and Sheep (Except, one Cow and Calf, and five Sheep out of her half which I give to my son William or is hereafter Mentioned) to be at her disposal forever, as also one third of all My Lands with one third of My House and barn with one half of all My farming tools during her natrual Life

Item I give to my well beloved son Ebenezer Work whom I likewise Constitute make and ordain my sole Executor of this my Last Will and testament all and singular My Lands Meassuags and tenements by him freely to be disposed of (after my said wifes desease) the two thirds of which to be freely possessed and Injoyed by him during her life togeather with the one half of all My Cattle and sheep with one half of all my farming tooles

Item I give to my well beloved son William Work one Cow and Calf and five sheep

Item I give to my well beloved Daughter Janne Dunlop ten shillings to be paid her out of my Estate by my Executor within twelve Months after my Death

Item I give to my well beloved Daughter Elizebath Orr ten shillings to be paid to her out of my Estate by my said Executor within twelve Months after my Death

And I do hereby utterly disalow revok and disannul all and evry other former Testament Wills Legacies and bequests and Executors by Me in any ways before named willed and bequeathed Rattifying and Confirming this and no other to be My Last Will and testament In witness whereof I have hereunto set my hand and seal the day and year first above written

Signed sealed published
pronounced and declared by
the said James Work as his
Last Will and testament

his
James O Work (Seal)
Mark

in the presents of us the
subscribers
    William Thorne
    Prince Rose
    Willliam Thorne Junior

Probated 12 Ap., 1769. [I, 164.]

In the Name of God Amen. on the 31st Day of March in the Year of our Lord 1767 I John Reed of Boothbay in the County of Lincoln and Province of Massachusetts-bay in New England, being very sick and weak in body, but of perfect mind and memory, calling to mind the Mortality of my nature and expecting soon to go the way of all living do, with deliberation, and of my own free Choice, make and ordain this my last will and testament, that is to say

first of all I commit my Soul unto God thro' the hands of my only Advocate, the Lord Jesus Christ, on whose perfect righteousness alone I depend for Justification, thro that everlasting Covenant of Grace which I desire to die embracing as the only plan of my redemption; and my body to the dust to be interred, with decent Christian burial at the discretion of my Executors; hoping to receive the same again at the resurrection of the Just; and touching the Family and worldly substance with which it hath pleased God to bless me in this life, I dispose of them in the manner following.

Item Secondly I do constitute and appoint my trusty friends the Revd John Murray Mr Robert Murray and Mr David Reed all of Boothbay to be the Executors of this my last Will and testament and Guardians of my beloved Wife and all my Children until they shall legally choose other Guardians for themselves; and I do authorize them to oversee, direct, and dispose of my said family as faithful Guardians, in such a manner, in all their affairs, as shall appear to them, in their best Judgment, to be most for the advantage of my said family.

Item Thirdly I do especially require my said Executors to take care that all my children be educated in the fear of God, in the Protestant reformed Religion, agreeable to the Westminster Confession of Faith and Catechisms, according to their Circumstances in life, at the expense of my Estate.

Item fourthly I ordain that all my Debts shall be paid out of my whole estate :

Item fifthly I allow my whole estate to be kept undivided until my eldest son Andrew arrive at years of maturity, or until such time as a majority of my said Executors shall think a division necessary or expedient; until then it shall be improved by my Widow and Children, (or such of them as shall be thought fittest by my Executors,) for the benefit of the whole, and shall be liable to pay all the debts justly contracted for the education or Maintainance of my children until they arrive at the years of maturity; and I ordain that if they or any of them shall be charged as debtors to my Estate for their needful maintainance of food and raiment until their arrival at said mature age, then my said estate shall be liable to pay to such child or children for his, hers, or their service, work, or labour before said age such wages as shall be judged right, by my said Executors with three other Judicious men chosen by consent of my widow & such child or children; which six shall also determine what shall be paid to the whole estate for such provision.

Item I ordain that whenever a division shall be agreed on, my beloved wife shall have over and above her share, one yoke of steers given off the whole; and then all my moveable goods and chattles shall be equally divided amongst all my dear children;

Item whereas, at the death of my hon'd Mother, there will fall to me an equal share with her other Children, out of her estate, I ordain that it be equally divided as my other goods.

Item seventhly I ordain that my real estate, inclosed within my fence, bounded by Mr Slosses, Mr McCulloch's, and Rev'd Mr Murray's lots be, at the discretion of my said Executors, divided into equal shares amongst my Children as my other goods: Andrew to have his share next to Campbell's pond, John to have his share next to him, and so my other children, my Dear Wife to have that part next the shore with the house &c in hers: and if with the consent of my said Executors, they or any of them shall choose to sell their shares, then I do ordain that my Son Andrew shall have the first right of purchase of all such shares as shall be sold, my Son John the next, my Son Henry the next, my Son David the next right and then my Daughters according to their age, and I do hereby ratifie and confirm this as my last Will and testament the day and time first above written

Signed sealed published pronounced
and declared by John Reed to be
his last Will in the presence of
 Andw McFarland
 Samuel Adams
 William Reed

        mark
      John O Reed (Seal)
        his

Probated 14 June, 1769. [I, 165-6.]
Inventory by Andrew McFarland and Edward Emerson, of Boothbay, and Thomas Boyd, of Bristol, 24 Mar., 1770, £55 : 6 : 8. [I, 243.]

Andrew Willard, late of Broad Bay. George Demuth, of Broad Bay, Adm'r, 14 June, 1769. [I, 167.] John Warner and Peter Bracht, sureties. Christopher Kline, of Broad Bay, guardian unto Margaret, minor daughter, 5 June, 1770. [I, 182.] Inventory by John Hoettenheim, John Warner and Joanne Peter Broest, all of Broad Bay, 15 June, 1769, £82 : 12 : 9. [I, 187.] Account filed 15 June, 1770. [I, 188.]

Gawen Wilson, late of Falmouth. Jeremiah Pote, of Falmouth, Adm'r. 26 Sep., 1769. [I, 167.] Stephen Longfellow and James McCobb, sureties. Inventories : personal estate by Noah Michell, Daniel Merit and Moses Wostar, all of Pleasant River, 2 May, 1769, £22 : 10 : 5½ ; real estate in Berwick, York County, by Peter Morrell, Jedidiah Morrell and Nathan Lord, 4 Oct., 1771, £15 ; real estate in Falmouth by William Bucknam, Nathaniel Carll and Benjamin Ingersoll, all of Falmouth, 1 June, 1770, £216. [Unrecorded]

Hugh Wilson, late of Topsham. Elizabeth Wilson, of Topsham, widow, Adm'x, 30 Aug., 1769. [I, 173.] Thomas Willson and Samuel Wilson, sureties. Inventory by Thomas Wilson, Robert Gower and Actor Patten, all of Topsham, 3 Oct., 1769, £649 : 11 : 0. [I, 191.] Account of Elizabeth Weymouth, Adm'x, 9 Mar., 1787. [III, 137 and 245.] Samuel Thompson, of Brunswick, guardian unto William, minor son, 17 Sep., 1787. [III, 160.]

Henry Little. late of Newcastle. James Little, of Newcastle, Adm'r, 25 Ap., 1769. [I, 174.] Alexander Campbell and Edmund Lieson, sureties. Inventory by Benjamin Woodbridge, Alexander Campbell and James Cargill, 12 July, 1769. [I, 196.]

Lochran McLean, late of Penobscot. Hugh McLean, of Milton, Adm'r, 30 June, 1769. [I, 176.] Richard Codman and John Kent, both of Falmouth, sureties.

In the nam of God Amen this tenth Day of November *Anno Dominie* one thousand saven Houndred and sixty nine and In the tenth year of his majsteys Rign I William Stinson of Georgetown within the County Lincoln and Province of the Masscutsset Bay In NewEngland yeoman Beanig much Indisposed In Boodey But of Parfet mind and

memorey thanks be to God for His Goodness to me Calling to mind
the frealety of my Bodey and knowing that It Is apointed for for all
men to die do mak this my Last will and Testment that Is to Say Prinsably
and In the first Plaes I Give and Bequeth my Soul to God that
Gave It and my Bodey I Reconmend to the Earth to be Buried In a Cristen
and Deesent manar at the Discration of my of my Executors nothing
Doubting But I Shall Rec It agean at ye Genarell Resurection By the
Infinet Powr of God and as to such wordley Goods and Esteat as God
heas Bestoed on me In this wordal I Give Demise and Dispose of In
the fowling maner and foram *Imprimis* I Give and Bequath to my
Beloved Dughter Sarah five Shillings Itam I Bequeth to my Beloved
Daughter Jean five Shillings and Six Sheepe

Iatem I Bequath to my Beloved Dughter Margrat one yok of young
oxon of threa years old and five Shillings

Itam I Bequath to my Beloved Daughtar Marcy Six Shillings and Six
Sheepe Iatem I Bequath to my Bloved Son John Stinson on Sarten
track or pearsell of Land on Arowsick Island Butted and Bounded as
folloeth viz villes march on the west on the South By Lott No'r ninteen
& on the Est by the Back Riverr Beaing part of Lott nomber
twintey twintey on & Lott nobr twintey two now In his Posetion I furder
Give unto my Son John another Sarten track or Parsell of Land
Bounded as folloeth viz Bouned on the Est By villes march on the
South By Lot noumber ninteen on the north By Lott nombr twentey
one Runing west towards Kenabek River as far as the Senter of the
Great Lage on the East Side of the fresh water pond on Arowsick Island
the above money Bequethed to Be payd In Six months after my
Desses Item I Bequeth unto my Beloved Son James Stinson one
milch Cow and Six pounds Six and Eght Lawfull money to pe payd to
him out of my Esteat that I Bequeth to my Son William Stinson

Itam I Bequath to my Beloved Daughter Ann twintey Six pounds
thirteen Shillins and Eght Pene Lawfull money to be payd unto hir in
three years from the Day of my Barell out of my Esteat that I Leave
to my Son William Stinson Item I Leave and Bequath to my Beloved
wife Elizeabeth Stinson on half of all my Chatels and all my Sheepe
not disposed of Befor Lickwise all my houshold furniter my Beeds
and Beiden Itam I Bequeath to my Beloved Son John Stinson on
Lott of march at a plies Called Bokers point In the Bak River on
Arowsick Island which Lott of March Blongs to Lott numbr twintey
of up Land on said Island Itam I Bequeth to my Beloved Son

William Stinson all all the Remeander of of my Reall and personall Esteat on a Rowsick Island not Disposed of Before viz my Intrist In three Lotts of Land upland viz Lot No twintey twintey one & twintey two with on Lott of march at Bokers point In the Back River Beaing the westermost Lott of two Laieng ther & one half Lott of march In the mill Creek with on half of my Chatels not Disposed of Befor to him his hairs and assigns forEver as a Esteat of Inherintenc I Bequath and Give unto my said Son William my fishing Sconer now Laieng In Kenbeck River It furder Is my will and plesuer that my Seaid Son William Stinson pay may Daughter Ann the above twintey Six pounds thirteen Shillings 8d willed to her as above out of my Esteat Left to him and all the Depts that I ow It Is my furder will and Plesuer that my Sead Son William Stinson and my Brother John Stinson Esq whom I apoint and ordean my Sole Executors of this my Last will and testment and I do hearbey Disanule and Revok all former wills and tistments or Bequathments By me In Eneys ways mead By me Before this Ractificing and Confirming this and no other to be my Last will and testmint In witness whereof I have Sett my hand and Sell this tinth Day of November *Anno Domina* on thousand Saven hundred and Sixtey nine and In the tenth year of his majsteys Rign

           William Stinson (Seal)

Charles Snipe
James Drummond
William Sullivan

the fifth sixth seventh and part of the Eght Lines In the Seond page was Rased Befor Singen and Selling this will
Lincoln Sis Georgetown November 10 1769 William Stinson acknowlidg this his Last will and Testment to be his ack and Deed Before me John Stinson Justies Peaes-

         Probated 8 Aug., 1770. [I, 177-8.]
Inventory by Charles Snipe, Daniel Mcfaden and James Drummond, Jr., all of Georgetown, 29 Oct., 1770, £515 : 7 : 4. [I, 213.]

Amos Pinkham, late of Bristol. William McClain, of Bristol, Adm'r. 13 Sep., 1769. [I. 179.] William Martin and Jacob Dockendorf, sureties. Inventory by William Martin, Jacob Dockendorf and Thomas Johnston, all of Bristol, 5 Ap., 1770, £98 : 3 : 10. [I, 189.]

Samuel Davis, late of a place called Freetown. Moses Davis, of Newbury Port, Adm'r, 20 June, 1769. [I, 176.] Nathan Gove and Samuel Goodwin, sureties.

Thomas Perrin, late of Pownalborough. Mathias Smith, of Tisbury, Adm'r, 14 Aug., 1769. [I, 180.] Samuel Goodwin and Samuel Goodwin, Jr., sureties Inventory by Samuel Goodwin, Robert Twycross and William Silvester, 21 Aug., 1769. £173 : 16 : 1 : 0. [I, 193-5.] Charles Cushing and Robert Twycross, commissioners to examine claims. [III, 3.] Account filed May, 1773. [III, 4.]

Moses Grele, late of the River Kennebeck. Moses Grele, residing at the River Kennebeck, Adm'r, 12 May, 1769. [I, 180.] Roger Chase and Mathew Chase, sureties.

Philip Call, late of Pownalborough. John Call, of Pownalborough, Adm'r, 18 Aug., 1769. [I, 181.] Inventory by Samuel Goodwin, Robert Twycross and Mathias Smith, 24 Aug., 1770, £264 : 5 : 2. [I, 224.] Account filed 12 Feb., 1772. [I, 232.]

In the Name of God Amen The twenty Eight day of Ocr one thousand Seven Hundred & Sixty Six I Joseph Young of Pownalborough in the County of Lincoln & Province of the Massachusetts bay in New England Yeoman Weak in Body but of Perfect mind & memory thanks be given unto God therefore Calling unto mind the Mortality of my Body and knowing that it is appointed for all Men once to die do make and Ordain this my last will and Testament that is to Say Principaly and first of all I Give and Recomend my Soul into the Hands of God that gave it & as for my Body I Recomend it to the Erth to Buried in a Christian like & Decent Manner at the Discration of my Executors nothing Doubting but at the General Resurection I shall Recive the same again by the Mighty Power of God—And as touching such Worldly goods & Estate wherewith it hath Pleased God to bless me in this life I Give Devise and Dispose of the Same in the following Manner and form—

Imprimus I make Constitute & Ordain my Sons Isaac & Joshua Young Executors of this my last will & Testament which I Confirm & no Other

2ly I give and bequeath unto my Eldest son Joseph Young of s'd Pownalborough all that tract of Land in s'd Town that he hath now in Posation whare he now lives

3ly I give and Devise unto Isaac & Joshua Young my Sons & Executors as aforesaid all the Remaining Part of my land in Pownalborough aforesaid to be Equally Divided betwixt them after my Discese

4ly I give and Devise unto Thomas Young Son of my Son Thomas

Young late of Pownalborough Dec's'd twenty Shillings to be Paid out of my Personal Estate by my Executors & as to the Rest of my Personal Estate I give & Devise unto my two Daughters Viz Sarah Holbrook the Wife of Rich'd Holbrook & Anna Pearce the Wife of John Perce both of the Town aforesaid to be Equally Divided betwixt them

In Witness Whereof I have hereunto set my hand & Seal the day & Year above Written
Witnes Present
Jona. Williamson
Lucy Silvester   Joseph Young   (Seal)
Jane Silvester
                    Probated 13 June, 1770. [I, 181.]

Jacques Bugnon, late of Pownalborough. Charles Cushing, of Pownalborough, Adm'r, 1 June, 1769. [I, 183.] Edmund Bridge and James Flagg, sureties. Inventory by James Flagg, Robert Twycross and Edmund Bridge 3 June, 1769, £251 : 0 : 5. [I, 184.] Account filed 10 Nov., 1774. [I, 271.] Division of real estate by Philip Theobald, William Lewis and Asa Dinsmore, all of Pownalborough, 22 Dec., 1788 : dower to Margaret, wife of Michael Stilfinn, and late widow of deceased ; remainder to James, only son, by consent of Margread, Jane and Susanna, daughters. Order regarding same, 24 Dec., 1789. [IV, 98 to 101.]

In the Name of God, Amen—The Twenty seventh Day of April A. D. One thousand seven hundred and sixty seven, I Daniel Goud of Pownalborough in the County of Lincoln, yeoman, being of perfect mind and Memory, & knowing that it is appointed to all men once to die & thinking it my Duty to set my house in Order, before that awful last hour overtakes me, do hereby make and ordain my Last Will and Testament ; that is to say, principally and first of all I commend my Soul into the hands of God that gave it, trusting in the Merits of his Dear Son My Lord and Saviour, for the pardon of all my Sins and Acceptance with him—My Body I commit to the Earth to be buried at the Discretion of my Executor, nothing doubting but that I shall receive the same by the mighty power of God at the General Resurrection. And as to my worldly Estate wherewith it hath pleased God to bless me in this Life, I give, devise and dispose of in manner and form following that is to say

Imps I give to my Daughter Elizabeth Clancey the sum of six shillings to be paid her in one year after my Decease which, with what I gave her in my Life Time is in full of her portion of my Estate

Item   I give to my Daughter Susannah Carney the sum of six shillings which with what I gave her in my Life Time is in full of her portion of my Estate

lastly All the Rest and Residue of my Estate Real, personal or mixed, wheresoever the same is, I give and devise to my Son George Goud, to hold to him, and his heirs forever, he the said George paying to my two Daughters aforesaid the said sum of six shillings apiece, also he paying all my Just Debts and funeral Charges.

And I do hereby constitute and appoint my said Son George Goud sole Executor of this my last Will and Testament revoking and disannulling all other and former Testaments by me heretofore made; declaring this and no other to be my last Will & Testament—

In Witness whereof I the said Daniel Goud do hereto set my hand & seal the Day & year aforewritten.

Signed, Sealed & Deliver'd,   Daniel Goud   (Seal)
& declared by the said
Testator to be his last
Will & Testament in presence of
  Chas. Cushing
  Mary Nye
  Jona. Bowman

Probated 12 Ap., 1769. [I, 196-7.] Inventory by Samuel Emerson, Richard Kidder and George Lilly, all of Pownalborough, 7 Ap., 1770, £31 : 16 : 4. [I, 198.]

John Shaw, late of Georgetown. Elisha Shaw, of Georgetown, Adm'r, 28 Jan., 1771. [I, 200.] John Shaw and Ebenezer Hovey, sureties. Inventory by Isaiah Crooker, John Shaw and Ebenezer Hovey, all of Georgetown, 9 May, 1771. [I, 215.]

John Lermond, late of Bristol. Alexander Lermond, of St. Georges, Adm'r, 27 Sep., 1770. [I, 200.] Moses Copeland and Bryan Ryan, sureties. Inventory by James Brown, of Newcastle, and William Jones and James Huston, both of Bristol, 2 Dec., 1770. [I, 212.]

Robert Wiley, late of Boothbay. Martha Wiley, of Boothbay, widow, Adm'x, 26 Sep., 1770. [I, 201.] John Wiley and Thomas Boyd, sureties. Inventory by Israel Davis and Andrew McFarland, both of Boothbay, and Thomas Hodgdon, of Jerremy Island, 18 Ap., 1772, £307 : 8 : 9. [I, 236.] Account filed, 9 June, 1772. [I, 237.]

David Reed, Elizabeth Reed and Joseph Reed, all of Boothbay, grandchildren, chose Joseph Reed, of Boothbay, to be their guardian, 25 Oct., 1792. Division of estate by Henry Hunter, of Bristol, John Borland and William McCobb, both of Boothbay, 21 Oct., 1794, in which the heirs named were Robart, son of Neal Wylie, Easther, wife of Abijah Kenney, Jane, wife of Joseph Lewis, Robart Wylie, the heirs of Samuel Wylie, Mary Reed, the children of Joseph Reed, Martha, wife of David Reed, the heirs of William Wylie, Alexander Wylie, John Wylie, Katharine, wife of Thomas Boyd. [Unrecorded.]

Robert Dunlap, late of Topsham. John Dunlap, of Topsham, Adm'r, 29 Ap., 1771. [I, 201.] Ebenezer Work and Robert Dunlap, sureties. Inventory by Thomas Wilson, Prince Rose and John Merrill, all of Topsham, 10 May, 1771, £246: 12: 7. [I, 214.] Account filed 10 Mar., 1773. [I, 247.] Return of partition of real estate by Thomas Wilson, John Merrill and Prince Rose, all of Topsham, 31 Mar., 1773, mentions Mary Dunlap, widow of deceased, John Dunlap, Margaret Potter and Jane Eaton, children of deceased. [II, 2.]

Andrew Reed, late of Boothbay. David Reed, of Boothbay, Adm'r, 4 June, 1771. [I, 203.] William Reed and John Stinson, sureties. Inventory by John Stinson, of Georgetown, Israel Davis, of Boothbay, and Thomas Hodgdon, of a place called Jerymisquam, 28 Sep., 1773, £149: 9: 4. [II, 14.]

David Patterson, Jr., late of St. Georges. Nancy Patterson, of St. Georges, widow, Adm'x, 6 Ap., 1771. [I, 203.] David Patterson, Alexander Lermond and William James, sureties. Inventory by Alexander Lermond, Samuel Creighton and William Watson, all of St. Georges, 27 May, 1771, £115: 9: 8½. [I, 228.] Benjamin Packard, of St. Georges, guardian of David, minor son, 30 Sep., 1776. [II, 72.] David Fales and Mason Wheaton, both of St. Georges, commissioners to examine claims. [III, 31.] Benjamin Packard, of St. Georges, Adm'r *de bonis non*, 23 Sep., 1776. [III, 31.] Moses Copeland, of St. Georges, and Jacob Eichorn, of Waldoborough, sureties. Account filed 24 Sep., 1776. [III, 32.]

John Brewer, of Boothbay, minor son of James Brewer, late of Boothbay, chose Israel Davis, of Boothbay, to be his guardian, 4 June, 1771. [I, 225.]

John Barker, Jr., late of Pownalborough. Susannah Barker, of Pownalborough, widow, Adm'x, 26 Feb., 1771. [I, 226.] Edmund

Bridge and Samuel Goodwin, Jr., sureties. Inventory by Edmund Bridge and Richard Kidder, both of Pownalborough, 1 May, 1771, £10 : 11 : 0. [I, 231.]

Westbrook Berry, late of Mechias. John Crocker, of Mechias, Adm'r, 23 Sep., 1771. [I, 227.] Jonathan Longfellow and Nathaniel Sinkler, sureties. Inventory by Japhet Hill, Joseph Libbee and William Curtis, all of Mechias, 17 Sep., 1772, £102 : 2 : 9. [I, 247.] Jonathan Longfellow and Nathaniel Sinkler, commissioners to examine claims. [I, 248.] Distribution ordered 1 Oct., 1774. Account filed 30 Sep., 1774. [I, 263.]

George High, of a place called Broadbay, guardian unto Lehn Weller, minor daughter of Andrew Weller, 31 May, 1771. [I, 227.]

John All, late of Boothbay. Samuel McCobb, of Boothbay, Adm'r, 24 Sep., 1771. [I, 233.] Israel Davis and John Murray, sureties. Inventory by Jeremiah Beath, Thomas Boyd and William Fuller, all of Boothbay, 8 Oct., 1771, £770 : 16 : 9. William McCobb and Andrew McFarland, commissioners to examine claims. [I, 253.]

In the Name of God Amen, the twenty ninth day of July 1771 I Charles Robartson of Topsham &c yeoman being sick and Weak of Body, but of perfect mind & memory, thanks be given to God for it : therefore Calling unto mind the mortality of my Body and Knowing that it is appointed unto all men once to dye, do make and ordain this my last will and testament that is to say principaly and first of all I give & recomend my soul into the Hands of God who gave it ; and my Body I recomend to the Earth to be Buried in decent Christian burial at the discretion of my Executrix nothing Doubting but at the general Resurection I shall receive the same again by the mighty power of God : and as touching such worldly Estate wherewith it hath pleased God to bless me in this life I give, demise and dispose of the same in the following manner and form

Imprimis I give and bequeath to Martha my Dearly beloved wife one yoak of my best oxen, one Cow, all my sheep togeather with all my Houshold Goods, debts, and moveable effects whom I likewise Constitute, make & ordain my sole Executrix of this my last will and testament

Item I give to my beloved grandson William Robartson (only son to my Eldest son William Robartson decess'd) one Cow at my Deces

Item I give to my beloved Daughter Elezebath Savage one Cow to be delivered at my Deceass

Item I give to my beloved Daughter Mary Stinson one yoak of young Oxen to be delivered at my Decease

Item I give to my beloved Daughter Jane Stinson four pounds Lawfull Money at my Decease

Item I give to my yongest son David Robartson ten shillings

Item I give to my youngest Daughter Charity Robartson thirteen pounds six shillings & Eight pence and likewise one Colt two years old, & one Case of Draws and one Cow to be paid her when she shall arive at the age of Eighteen years, or on her Mariage day. and I do hereby utterly disalow, revok and disannul all and every other former testaments Wills legacies and bequestes and Executors by me in any ways before named, willed and bequeathed, Ratifying and Confirming this and no other to be my last will and testament. In Witness whereof I have hereunto set my hand and seal the day and year first above written

Signed sealed published, pronounced
and Declared by the said Charles
Robartson as his Last will and
testament in the presents of us
the subscribers   his
   Aaron Hinkley   Charles X Robartson
   Ezra Randall   Mark
   Joseph Foster
   Joseph Randall

Probated 23 Jan., 1772. [I, 233-4.]

Joseph Decker, late of a place called Jerrymisquam Island. John Decker, Jr., of Pownalborough, Adm'r, 26 Aug., 1772. [I, 234.] Joseph Decker and Samuel Goodwin, Jr., sureties. Inventory by Thomas Rice, Jonathan Williamson and Michael Sevey, 17 Sep., 1772, £245 : 3 : 3. [I, 272.] Account filed 28 Oct., 1773. [II, 2.]

John Burton, late of St. Georges. Benjamin Burton, of St. Georges, Adm'r, 10 June, 1772. [I, 235.] Joseph North and William Young, sureties.

Nathaniel Bryant, late of Newcastle, shipwright Hannah Bryant, of Newcastle, widow, Adm'x, 20 Aug., 1772. [I, 235.] David Reed and Samuel Goodwin, Jr., sureties. Inventory by Arthur Noble, of a place called Walpole, Samuel Nickels, of Newcastle, and David Reed, of Boothbay, 8 Sep., 1772, £1965: 17 : 3. [I, 245.] Inventory by Abijah White and John Cushing, Jr., of Scituate, and Peleg Rogers, of Marshfield, of real estate in Plymouth County, 28 Mar., 1774, £29: 19: 4. [II, 63.] Account filed 15 Oct., 1777. [II, 63.] Jeremiah Barker, of Barnstable, guardian to Patience and Hannah, minor daughters, and Nathaniel, minor son, 25 Oct., 1776. [II, 80-1.] List of sundry articles omitted from inventory, £100 : 5 : 2. [II, 98.] Guardian's account filed 4 Oct., 1786. [III, 178-9.] Division of real estate by Arthur Noble and Jesse Flint, both of a place called Walpole, and John Farley, of Newcastle, 13 June, 1787. [V, 4 to 6.] Account of guardian of Hannah Barker Bryant filed 29 Ap., 1794, and appeal from decree of allowance thereof by Enos Clap, of Hallowell, and Hannah Barker Clap, his wife, 26 May, 1794. [V, 244 to 246.] Account of guardian of Patience Bryant filed 29 Ap., 1794, and appeal from decree of allowance thereof by William Waters, of Newcastle, husband of Patience, 19 May, 1794. [V, 246 to 248.]

Nathaniel Webb, late of Woolwich. Jane Webb, of Woolwich, widow, Adm'x, 2 Sep., 1772. [I, 237.] Joseph Wade and Joshua Bailey, sureties. Inventory by Joseph Wade, Samuel Harnden and David Gilmore, Jr., all of Woolwich, 13 Oct., 1772. [II, 29-30.] Account filed 15 Jan., 1777. [II, 72.] Israel Smith, guardian of Sarah and Lydia, minor daughters, and Luther, minor son. [II, 72 to 74.] Widow's dower set off 18 June, 1781, by Joseph Wade, Jonathan Fuller and Thomas Snell, all of Woolwich. [III, 231.]

In the name of God Amen, This 13th day of August A. D. 1768, I Zaccheus Beal of Bowdoinham in the County of Lincoln yeoman, being Sensible of my own mortality, but being of sound mind, after commending my Soul into the hands of Almighty God, & my body to the Earth to decent burial, do hereby make this my last will & testament & therein dispose of my worldly estate in manner following, that is to say,

Imprimis, I give bequeath & devise to my beloved Wife Mary the use & improvement of all my Estate real & personal situate or being in said Bowdoinham, or Elsewhere, during her natural life, Saving a right & priviledge to my Daughters Abigail and Eleanor, severally of living in my dwelling house during the times they shall severally remain unmarried with their Mother

Item At my said Wife's decease & when her said Use & improvement expires in my Estate, I give & devise to my said Daughters

Abigail & Eleanor their heirs & Assigns forever Five acres of Land in the Front of my Land in Bowdoinham where I dwell, said Five acres to be next Abbagadasset river, & to be divided from the rest of my Land there, by a back line running across My Land at right angles with the side lines thereof & all the buildings upon said Five acres of Land, equally to be divided between them, also I give them severally the priviledge aforementioned of living with their mother as afore expressed—Also I give them each one Third part of my personal Estate forever after my Wife's use therein ceases, & the remaining Third part of said personal Estate I give them after said Use expires, the use of, during the joint Lives of my Daughter Dorcas & her husband David Wilson

Item, In Case said Dorcas survives her said husband I give her forever the said remaining Third part of said personal Estate to take effect at & after the decease of both my said Wife & said David & not before also I give her said Dorcas the sum of Five shillings to be paid her by my Executrix in six months after my Decease, but if said Dorcas should not survive her said husband I give said Abigail & Eleanor said remaining Third part of the personal Estate forever equally to be divided.

Item I give & devise to my Three Sons Zaccheus Josiah & Joshua, all the rest & residue of my real Estate in said Bowdoinham & Elsewhere except said Five acres & said buildings to them their heirs & assigns forever after my said Wife's Use therein expires

Lastly, I appoint my said Wife Executrix of this my Will. In Witness whereof I hereto set my hand & seal the day first herein aforewritten.

Memo. ye Words, "all" "heirs" "forever" "Estate" were interlin'd before Signing &c

Signed, sealed & Declar'd by s'd Zaccheus to be his
last Will & Testam't. In presence of

 Wm. Cushing   Zacheus Beal (seal)
 David Bailey
 Nathaniel Bailey

      Probated 16 Sep., 1772. [I, 238- 239 & 251.]

In the name of God amen this tenth day of September *Anno Domini* 1771, I Samuell Denny of Georgetown within the County of Lincoln in New Ingland Esqr being weak in body, but of sound minde and memory through mercy do make this my larst will and testament in

manner folowing viz in the first and chief plase I give and biqueth my
pretious and Emortal soul into the hand of that God who gave it me
praying throw the merits and Intersession of the glorious Redemer I
may Receive the sam again at the Resurrection of the Just into Eternal Life and as to my temporal Intrest I give and dispose of the same
after the folowing maner

Itum I give unto my loving wife Catherin Denny fower good milch
cows one yoak of oxen yoak and chain ten sheep the best bed underbed and bedstead together with an Equal share of all that belong
unto beds both of lining and wooling with the rest of my fether beds
that may be in my hous at my deseace both for quantity and quality
the looking glars with the black frame tabel and smorl trunck in my
Rome in the grate Rome and Elseware the chist of drawers the best
tea tabel and that of my make 6 tea cups and sarsers 1 teapot 1 Tea
Kittel shuger dish crempot all these of the best together with the best
tongs shovel and belows three large and thre smorl silver spons six best
puter plates and three puter dishes six best Earthin plat fower best
candelsticks the belmettel and brass scilit a pair of Iron dogs 2 flat
Irons the boxiron and 2 heters warming pan toster the grate bibel
2 bras chafendishes one large and one smorl spining wheale 2 puter
basins 3 puter poringers 3 brkfas basins 3 wine glarsses 2 bekers
2 bowls all the provision that may be in the hous of meal pork
bief flower butter chese talu candels molases shuger cofey tea rise
spises chocolet corn and other grain together with all the woole
yarn flax lining or wooling not made up sope tabellining all the
tin ware all the dairey vessels pails tubs and barels hay in the barn
1 spade 1 how 1 ax the silver can 6 comon puter plats as also what
time I may have in Ebeneser Kelly by Indentor together with the sute
of curtains

The above mentioned artacels and Every of them I give unto my said
wife for hir to use or dispose of according unto to hir own will and
plesure and not to be accountable to any furthermore for and towards
hir comfortable support during hir natural Life I give the use and Improvement of my now dwelling hous with all the other buildings contigus together with the land and marsh to the southward of the stone
worl nere the meting-hous and the hither dam which Includ Lotts No.
4, 5, 6, 7 together with what Land I own on borld head and the marsh
to the southward of Newtown bay and crick and night pasture for said
cows and oxen in that pasture betwen the road and the marsh to be
improved by hir living on the plase and not by a tennant together with

a Right to cut firewood on other of my land on Arrowsick Iland and
that on the Easterd side of the country road and that for hir own fire
only and to be burnt on the premises together with the use and improvement of tobias and Susanah two of my negros she maintaining
of them in sickness and helth together with the crane hooks grate
tongs shovel citchin table and clock all the Iron holow ware and all
the chairs together with the smorl bras Kittel and cofey mill with the
sum of tenn pounds Lawful money to be paid out my other Estate
yearly and Every year during her natural Life and to be paid quarterly
if she chuise it that is £2 : 10 : 0 per quarter the use of the pew the
the word ten is so made by me and the figurs £2 : 10 : 0 the nesary
charge of repairing the premises from time to time to be done at the
charge of other of my Estate

Itum I give unto my son by law John White all all my appariel that I
Ever wore both of Lining and wooling the Looking glars in the grate
rom the desk the square table the grate trunck and grate chist

The Residue and Remainder of all my Estate both Real and personal
I give unto my Dear and only Daughter Rachal McCobb and unto hir
Heirs and assigns forever and I do hereby constitute and appoint my
son by law Samuell McCobb and the within named John White to be
my Executors to this my Larst will and testament

In witnis whereof I hereunto set my hand and seal the day and
year above written

Signed sealed published
pronounsed and declared
by the said Samuell Denny
to be his larst will and
testament in presants
of us
Benjamin Pattee Junior
Jeremiah Tozer   Samuell Denny   (seal)
Elisabeth Pattee

be it Known to all men by these presants that whereas I Samuell
Denny of Georgetown within the County of Lincoln and province of
the Masachusets bay in Newingland Esqr have made and declared my
Larst will and testament in wrighting baring date the tenth day of
September 1771 I the said Samuell Denny by this presant codicil do
ratify and confirm my said larst will and testament and do will and
bequeth unto my loving wife Cathrin Denny the sum of Eight pounds
Lawful money in addition to ten pounds given unto my said will and

to be paid unto hir in the same maner as is prescribed in said will for the payment of the said ten pounds during hir natural life by my residuary legete or Executors out of my Estate and my will and mening is that this codacel or schdule to be and aiudged to be part and parsel of my larst will and testament and all things mentioned and contained in this codasel to be faithfully and truely performed and as fully and trewly performed and as fully and amply In Every Respect as if the same ware so declared and set down in my said larst will and and Testament in witnis whereof I have set my hand and seal this twenty ninth day of May *Anno Domini* 1772 and in the twelfth year of his majestys reign

Signed sealed published and Declared
and Declared by the said Samuell
Denny to be a codasel to my larst
will and testament
and part and parsel
of the sam in
presants of us   Samuell Denny   (seal)
Benja Pattee Junr.
Jeremiah Tozer
Elisabeth Pattee

                        Probated 17 June, 1772. [I, 239 to 241.]

Moses Rogers, late of a place called Dyers River. Elisha Rogers, of Marblehead, Adm'r, 1 Oct., 1772. [I, 241.] William Clifford and Ebenezer Gray, sureties.

In the Name of God, Amen. I Thomas Killpatrick of a place called St Georges in the County of Lincoln and Province of Massachusetts Bay in New England Gentleman being Sick and Weak in Body, but of perfect Mind & Memory Thanks be given to God; calling to Mind the Mortality of my Body, and knowing that it appointed for all Men once to die do make and ordain this my last Will and Testament; That is to say, principally and first of all, I give and recommend my Soul into the Hand of Almighty God that gave it, and my Body I recommend to the Earth to be buried in decent Christian Burial, at the Discretion of my Executors; nothing doubting but at the general Resurrection I shall receive the same again by the mighty Power of God. And as touching such worldly Estate wherewith it has pleased God to bless me in this Life I give, demise, and dispose of the same in the following Manner and Form

Imprimis I give and Bequeath unto my well beloved Sister Elizabeth Killpatrick all my House Hold Furnature of what name or nature (except my Bed and Bedding)

Item   I give unto my Cousin James McCordy the Sum of Six Shillings and Eight Lawful Money to be paid him or his legal Representative in one year after my decease

Item   I give unto my Cousin Elizabeth Calderwood the Sum of Six Shillings and eight pence Lawful Money to be paid to her or her legal Representative in one year after my decease

Item   I give unto my Cousin Martha McCordy the Sum of twelve pounds Lawful Money to be paid her, or her legal Representative in one year after my decease; Or the Value of the aforesaid Sum of twelve pounds to be delivered to her in Cows and Sheep at the market price

Item   I give unto Thomas Shibles, son of My Friend John Shibles, my Bed & Bedding, together with all my wearing Apparel, and a Gun.

Item,   I give unto Robert Killpatrick Shibles (another Son of the said John Shibles) a Gun.

Itim   I give unto John Shibles junr (another Son of the said John Shibles) a Gun.

And lastly I give unto my True and trusty Friend John Shibles of St Georges aforesaid Yeoman, whom I likewise constitute make and ordain the Sole Executor of this my last Will and Testament, The whole Remainder of my Estate both Real, personal and mixt of what name or nature soever, by him freely to be possed and enjoyed, he paying my just Debts, and Funeral Charges. And I do hereby utterly disallow, revoke and disannul all and every other former Testaments, Wills, Legacies, Bequests, and Executors, by me in any ways beforenamed, willed, and bequeathed; ratifying and confirming this and no other to be my last Will and Testament.

In Witness whereof I have hereunto set my Hand, and Seal, this twenty Second Day of June in the Year of Our Lord One Thousand Seven Hundred and Seventy two

Signed, Sealed, published,
pronounced, and declared
by the said Thomas   Tho. Killpatrick   (seal)
Killpatrick, as his last
Will & Testament, in the
Presence of us
Patrick porterfield

Jonathan Spear
David Fales

Probated 16 Dec., 1772. [I, 241-2.]
Inventory by David Fales, Patrick Porterfield and Alexander Lermond, all of St. Georges, 11 Mar., 1773, £138 : 9 : 6. [II, 12.]

In the Name of God Amen. I Jonathan Laiten of Newcastle in the County of Lincoln and Provinc of the Masecutis Bay in Newegland Being in Perfict helth (Praised be God) do mack this My Last will and testament as followth. *Imprimis* I Give to my bloved wife Mary Laiten fifteen acors of Up Land and Marsh on the southerly Part of My farm with one half of the Dweling hous and one third Part of the Barn and two milce kows and six shep with one third Part of the houshold Goods so long as she Contineus My widdow and no Longer &c Iteam I Give to My son John Laiten ten Pounds to Be pay'd in one year After My deceas By My Executor Item I Give to My son Moses Laiten Eight Pounds— Itiam. I Give to My son Richard Laiten thirty Pounds. Itiam Itiam I Give to my dafter Mary three Pounds to Be paid in two years after My deceas Itiam I Give to My dafter Martha six Pounds and I give to My dafter Jean seven Pounds & to My dafter Sarah I Give six Pounds and I Give to My dafter Rebecka five Pounds in fower years after My deceas Itiam I Give to My dafter Hannah five Pounds to Bee Paid in five years after My deceas and I Give to My son Ezekiel Laiten whome I Mack sole Executor of this My Last will and testament I Give and demise and Bequeath to him and his heirs all and Evry of My Messuages Lands and Parsonal Estat with all my husbandderey tols Hereditament whatsoever and wheirsoever which I allso Charge with the Payment of all My said Legacis and honest debts and Decont Burail : in witnes wheir of I have hereunto seit My hand and seeal the 15th day of May and in the year of Ower Lord 1772 Seal'd Published and Declare by the above named Jonathan Laiten for and as his Last will and testament in the Presents of us
witness Joshua fuller

Jeremiah Bran   Jonathan Laiten   (seal)
Nathanael Chapman

Probated 7 Sep., 1772. [I, 243.]
Inventory by James Cargill, Robert Hodge and David Hopkins, all of Newcastle, 2 Dec., 1772, £471 : 13 : 6. [I, 252.]

Reuben Pitcher, late of Penobscott River. Thomas Goldthwait, of

Fort Pownall, Adm'r, 7 June, 1773. [I, 248.] William Gardiner and Moses Copeland, sureties. [II, 214.]

Jonathan Winn, late of Woolwich. Joseph Winn, of Wilmington, Adm'r, 20 Sep., 1773. [I, 249.] Nathan Weston and Francis Ford, sureties. Inventory by Jonathan Reed, Samuel Ford and John Hathorn, all of Woolwich, 22 Sep., 1773, £141 : 13 : 0. [I, 255.]

In the Name of God Amen The Twenty Seventh Day of April 1772 I Sarrah Mountgomray of the Town of Booth Bay in the County of Lincoln and Province of the Massachusetts Bay New England Wedow being very sick & weak in Body but of perfet mind and memory Thanks be given unto God Therefore Caling unto mind the Mortality of my Body and Knowing That it is appointed for all men Once to Die Do make and Ordain This my Last will and Testament That is to Say first of all I Give and recommend my soul into the hands of God That gave it and my Body I Recomend to the Earth To be buried in a desant Christian Burial at the Discation of my Executors nothing doubting but at the Genral Reserrection I shall recive the same again by the Mighty powr of God and as Touching such worldly Estate wherewith it hath pleased God to bless me with in this Life I give demis and Dispose of the Same in the following mennor and form—

Imprimis I ordain Oarder and deract that all the Lawfull Debts I ow or stand indebted for Shall be punctuely payead to my respective Creditiors out of my Estate and the Remender if any be to be Disposed of as follows—

Item I give and bequeath to my beloved Son John Mountgomray out of my personal Estate Two hefers Three years old five Sheep & one mear one Barrow hog one Bed & clos now in the west Chamber one grat whell & one Small whell one pot that houlds Two pelfulls Four Delf pleats & four putter pleats one per of andirns one Small Ovel Table Three Cheers with Cloth Baks Two putter Dishes my great Bibel & Him Book & all the Remender of my Books of Devenitey & all my farming youTenchels—& I give unto my grand Daufter Sarrah Mountgomray Johns Dafter my Tee Kitel one per of flat Irns and one pere of andirns one Tramel—

Item I give to my beloved Son Samul Mountgomray all that part of my Real Estate of Land that Lays between his Land and the Linecans Land be it more or Lese only the wood Cut on Said Lands I reserve I Likways give to my Son Samul a note of hand payeble to him in Six years after my Deth & with out Intrest Tel Then of Thirteen pound

Six & Eight pence Lawfull Money and out of my personal Estate I give him one hefer Two years olde one bed & one pot one Shovel & Tongs four Delfe plats & four putter plats Two putter platers I give to Samul the plase and Spot of Land Caled the Shep yeard for the Tarm of six years after my Death and no Longer—

Itim I give & bequeath to my beloved Dafter Anne Murrey my Lume and all the Tackling of said Lume & all my Parsonal Estate now In my house not yet menchoned in the above & within writing & one Cow of Ride color & five sheep to the Care use of her Housban by the halfs & to be acountable for the Same & one yok of oxin for four years to the Care of John Murry hir housban & then to be sold & the money put to yous & to be in the Care of my Executiors for her Cheldran

Itim I give & bequeath to my beloved grandchild Robart Mountgomray Murray a note of hand payable to him at forteen years old from my Son John Mountgomray of Thirteen pounds six & Eight pence Lawfull money & without Intrest Til That Time & then to Draw Intrest tel payed & the bove named Rid Cow & five Sheep and the one half of the Incress when the said Robart coms of age to be given him then & one yok of oxin to be in the Care of his father four years and then to be Sold and the money put to yous til he is of age the above named Cow & shep the said John Murrey is to be Acountable to the Executiors of this will for the Same—

Itim I give and bequeth to my beloved Grandchild John Murrey a note of hand payeable to him at fourteen years of age of Thirteen pound Six and Eight pence Lawfull money from my Son John Mountgomray and not to Draw Intrest til then and then to Draw Intrest til payed—

I give to the within Named Anne Murray Sarrah Bards Time That She has to Sarve til She arives to the age of Eighteen and if my Dafter Anne Should Die before that Time the said Sarah is to be free the said Sarah Beard is to have my Two Gowns & my stais & all my petecots and the above gowns & stais & petecots to be in the Care of my Dafter Anne Murrays Care & to be given her acording to her behaver and the said Sarah is to have one year old Calf & to be Capt on my homstade til said Calf is Three years old and then to be Sold & the money put to use & given to hir when She is out of hir Time—there is yet Three Cows not yet Disposed of which I alow towards Setling my Estate after my Death to be in the Care of my Executiors—

I Do Likwise Constitute and appount my Trustey Friends Alex'r:

Nickels Esqur. & Willam McCob & my well beloved John Mountgomray My sole Executiors & Executrin of this Will my Last Will & Testament all & singler my Lands & Tenements & personal Estate to be Taken into Thir Charge & Care and I Do hereby utterly Disalow and revoke all and Every other former Testaments Wills and Bequests & Executiors by me in any ways before named Confirming this & no other to be my Last will & Testement in Witness whereof I have herunto set my hand & seal the Day & year above written.

Siegned sealed prounced & Delevered by the Said Sarrah Mountgomray as her Last Will & Testament in presants of
  Alexr. Nickels
  Nathaniel Winslow
      hir
  Martha z Winslow
      mark

         hir
Sarah ⊃ Mountgomray (seal)
    mark

the above nots menchonad is Leveft in the hands of Alxr Nickels Esqr.
Probated 17 June, 1772. [I, 249-250.]

Joseph Young, late of Pownalborough. Abihail Young, of Pownalborough, widow, Adm'x, 18 Dec., 1772. Richard Holbrook and Alexander Gray, sureties. Inventory by Thomas Rice, Michael Sevey and Moses Hilton, 19 Feb., 1773. [I, 256.]

John Drummond, late of Georgetown. Mary Drummond, of Georgetown, widow, Adm'x, 16 June, 1773. [I, 257.] Daniel McFaden and James McFaden, sureties.

John McFarland, late of Boothbay. Lydia McFarland, of Boothbay, widow, Adm'x, 18 Sep., 1773. [J, 257.] Nathaniel Tibbetts and John Daws, sureties. Inventory by John Stinson, of Georgetown, and Samuel McCobb and William McCobb, both of Boothbay, 2 Nov., 1773, £67 : 9 : 8. [J, 263.] Stinson and McCobb, commissioners to examine claims. [II, 66.] Account filed 13 June, 1773. [II, 67.]

James Springer, late of Georgetown. Nathaniel Springer, of Georgetown, Adm'r, 28 Dec., 1772. [I, 258.] Moses Hodgkins and Joseph White, sureties. Inventory by Isaiah Crooker, Dummer Sewall and John Wood, all of Georgetown, £668 : 11 : 12. [I, 244.] Adm'r adds to inventory 29 June, 1774, £1 : 17 : 4. [II, 29.] Account filed 18 Aug., 1774. [II, 124.] Isaiah Crooker and Dummer Sewall, both of Georgetown, commissioners to examine claims, 4 Oct., 1773, [II, 125.] Order regarding real estate 1 May, 1782, mentions Edward, eldest son; John, residing at Frenchman's Bay, second son; Mary Sylvester, Martha Norcross, daughters; James Springer, son; Rachel and Anna, daughters of James, Jr., deceased, grandchildren; Abigail Digby, daughter of Abigail Gleason, late of Boston, deceased, grand-daughter; Sarah Lemont, wife of James Lemont and late widow of Nathaniel Springer, a son of deceased: Nathaniel Bracket, Anthony Bracket, James Bracket, Mary Hodgkins, Eunice, wife of Simeon Paine, Susanna, wife of James Jewell, Joanna, wife of Philip Norcross, Elizabeth, wife of George Andrews, Sarah Bracket, Hannah, wife of James Springer, Abraham Bracket, Jr., all children of Joanna, deceased, late wife of Abraham Bracket, and a daughter of intestate. [II, 179-180.] Joseph Lambard, of Bath, appointed guardian unto Rachel Springer, granddaughter, 2 May, 1782. [II, 180.] Joshua Raynes, of Bath, appointed guardian unto James Springer, grandson, 1 May, 1782. [II, 181.] John Springer, of Frenchman's Bay, so called, Adm'r *de bonis non*, 26 Aug., 1780. [II, 181.] William Swanton and David Trufant, both of Georgetown, sureties. Inventory by Isaiah Crooker, Hatherly Foster and Joshua Philbrook, all of Bath, 7 Mar., 1782. [II, 185.] Account filed 29 Sep., 1781. [III, 43.]

John Dickey, late of Bristol, mariner. Alexander Erskins, of Bristol, Adm'r, 27 Sep., 1773. [I, 258.] Thomas Drowne and Samuel Goodwin, sureties. Inventories by Robert McKown and James Sprowl, of Bristol, and Samuel Nickels, of Newcastle, 6 and 28 Oct., 1773, £199 : 16 : 8, to which Adm'r added sundry small articles and "one half the Sloop Susanna sold Col. Lee before the apprizement made £206 : 13 : 4." [II, 57-8.] John Thomson and Samuel Patterson, both of Bristol, commissioners to examine claims, 27 Oct., 1773. [II, 58.] Account filed 8 Sep., 1774. [II, 59.]

Samuel Borland, late of Bristol. John Borland, of Bristol, Adm'r, 6 Oct., 1773. [I, 259.] Henry Hunter and Joseph Clark, sureties. Inventory by John Thomson, Samuel Patterson and Ninyin Erskins, all of Bristol, 15 Nov., 1773, £57 : 1 : 8. [I, 262.]

William Reed, late of Topsham. David Reed, of Topsham, Adm'r, 19 Oct., 1773. [I, 260.] Israel Davis and Andrew McFarland, sureties.

James Brown, of Newcastle. Jane Brown, of Newcastle, widow, Adm'x, 17 Nov., 1773. [I, 260.] Samuel Calley and John Hussey, sureties. Inventory by Benjamin Woodbridge and John Ward, both of Newcastle, and Thomas Flint, of a place called Walpole. 26 Feb., 1774. [II, 15.] Account filed 14 Aug., 1780. [III, 20.] Division of estate by Jonathan Jones and Samuel Waters, of Newcastle, and Thomas Boyd, of Boothbay, 22 Sep., 1781. Children mentioned: John Brown, James Brown and Martha Brown. [III, 21-3.] James chose Jane Brown, widow, to be his guardian 14 Aug., 1780. Martha Brown chose John Farley, of Newcastle, to be her guardian 14 Aug., 1780. [III, 23.]

John Hilton, late of Pownalborough. Rebecca Hilton, of Pownalborough, widow, Adm'x, 18 Dec., 1773. [I, 261.] Samuel Goodwin and Asa Smith, sureties. Inventory by Asa Smith, William Carlton and David Plumer, all of Pownalborough, 23 Dec., 1773, £152 : 19 : 4. [III, 33.]

In the name of God Amen
the tenth Day of October in the year of our Lord 1771 William Millar of Bristol In the County of Lincoln Gentm being in perfect hailth of Bodey and mind and memory thanks be Given to God for the same and Calling to mind the mortality of my Body and Knowing that it is appointed for all men once to die do make and ordain this my Last Will & Testament that is to say principally & first first of all I give and Recommend my Soul Into the the Hands of God that Give it : and for my Body I recomend it to the Eairth to be Buried in a Christon lick and Deecreit manner at the Discretion of my Executors nothing doubting but at the General Resurection I Shall Receive the Same again by the Mighty Power of God : and as touching such Worldly Estate Wherewith it hath Pleased God to Bless me in this Life I Give Devise and Dispose of the Same in Manner and Form following that is to Say—
In the fairst place I give and bequath to Hannah my dearly beloved Wife one third part of all my Reail Estate Exepteing my Estat in Bouthbaie Which I ordain to pay my Juist Dabets and my Bacick Laind Which is more than thre Houndred acres With my medow To mening Said Land to my Well beloved Sons William Millar & Robert

Millar Said Traeick of Laind to be Equally divided betwein thim Liakweis I Will and bequeath to the said Hannah all my personeil Estat that is to say one third of my Dwelling House and all my Housel fourentor & all hir Life teeim and at hir Dath I Will that the above mantioned Estattes Shall be only to hir Chaldren and myinn and to no others that is to Say: to Alexander Nickels Millar & James Millar & John Millar & Nancey Millar & Thomeis Millar & Samuil Millar & Hannah Millar to be Equally Divided:— Lickwyus I Will that the Whole Estate Should be in the hands of the above Said Hannah in her Widdowhoud butt if She marries the two thirds to go to our Chaldrin to give thim Education: I Will that my Juist Dabets be payed out of my Estates the Bouthebe to be sold and to pay: I Bequith to my Daughtir Mariy five shillings Lawfull monney & to my Daugehtr Jain twenty shillings Lawfull monney & my Son Robeirt Millar thirteen pouinds six shillings above his Deveishon With his Brother William: I Lickwyes do Constute make & ordaein my Well bloved Wief Hannah Millar and my Good and Trousty frainds William Burns and James Huston to be my only & Sole Executors of this my Last Will and teastment: and I do hear by utterly Disalow Revoke & Disanul all and Every other Testa Wills & Legacys Bequests Executors by me in any ways Before this Named Willed & Bequeathed Ratifying and Confirmed this & no other to be my Laist Will and Teastmant in Wittness Were of I have hereto Set my Hand and Seal the Day and year above Written

Willm Millar (seal)

Signed Sealed published prouounsed & Declared by the Said William Millar as his Laist Will and testament in the presenc of us the Subscribers that is to Say

John Holland

Robert Thompson

Her

Rachel X Dodge

mark

Probated 15 June, 1773. [I, 264.] William Burns and James Huston disclaimed executorship 14 June, 1773. Inventory by Arthur Noble, of a place called Walpole, Robert Hodge and Samuel Calley, both of Newcastle, 24 Sep., 1773, £728: 3: 4. [III, 213.]

Daniel Locke, late of St. Georges, surgeon. Abraham Locke, of St. Georges, Adm'r: Alexander Lermond and Thomas Starrett, sureties,

15 Mar., 1774. Inventory by Samuel Creighton, Hatevil Libby and John McIntyer, all of St. Georges, 6 Ap., 1774, £105 : 15 : 6. [I, 264.] Account filed 2 Ap., 1777; David Fales and Alexander Lermond, Jun'r, commissioners to examine claims 17 June, 1774. [II, 48.]

John Godwin, late of St. Georges. James Watson, of St. Georges, Adm'r, 1 Feb., 1774. Andrew Malcom and Samuel Creighton, sureties. Inventory by Edward Killeran, Moses Copeland, and Samuel Gragg, 8 Feb., 1774, £198 : 7 : 2½. [I, 266.]

Stephen Marson, late of Pownalborough. Elizabeth Marson, of Pownalborough, widow, Adm'x, 5 Jan., 1775. [I, 267.] Edmund Bridge and Samuel Goodwin, Jr., sureties. George Marson, minor son, chose Charles Cushing to be his guardian 8 Mar., 1776. [II, 230.] Inventory by Samuel Goodwin, Jr., Edmund Bridge and Carr Barker, all of Pownalborough, 31 Aug., 1775, £255 : 6 : 1. [II, 232.] Elizabeth Harris Marson, minor daughter, chose Elizabeth Marson to be her guardian 23 Nov., 1780. Elizabeth Marson, guardian unto Sarah and Susanna, minor daughters, and Stephen, minor son, 1 Sep., 1783. [II, 233.] Account filed 13 Sep., 1781. [II, 234.]

In the name of God Amen I Joel Crosby of Winslow in the county of Lincoln and province of the Masechusets Bay yeoman being infirm in body but being of sound and disposing mind and memory do make and ordain this my last will and testament in manner and form following that is to say, I give and recommend my soul into the hand of allmighty God that gave it, and my body I recommend to the earth to be decently interred at the discretion of my executrix, and touching such worldly estate which it hath pleased God to bless me with I will and bequeath in the following manner and form.

I bequeath to Hannah Crosby my dearly beloved wife whome I likewise constitute make and ordain the sole executrix of this my last will and testament the one half of what remains of all my Estate both Real and parsonal after my lawfull debtes are paid and my children brought up to the age of Eighteen years the other half to be Equelly devided between my four well beloved Daughters namely Ruth Right Crosby, Hannah Crosby, Joanna Crosby and Rebeckah Crosby likewise I will that Hannah Crosby my well beloved wife have full power to make sale of any part or all of my aforesaid Estate for the payment of my debts or for hir own maintainence or for the maintainence of my children and that shee have power to portion of my Daughters as they arive to the age of Eighteen years or at such time as my above mentioned executrix shall think proper.

In witness whereof I have hereunto set my hand and seal this thirteenth day of February and in the fifteenth year of his majestyes Reaign A. D. 1775

                              Joel Crosby (seal)

Signed Sealed published and pronounced by the said Joel Crosby as his last will and testament in the presents of us who in his presents and the presents of each other have hereunto subscribed our names

    Jonathan Whiting
    Zimri Heywood
    Daniel Smith
    Obadiah Parker

                      Probated 19 Ap., 1775. [I, 269.]

Inventory by William Richardson, Zimri Heywood and John Tozier, all of Winslow, 20 June, 1775. [II, 6-7.]

Daniel Fogg, late of Mechias. Samuel Rich, of Mechias, Adm'r, 26 June, 1775. [I, 270.] Samuel Goodwin, Jr., and John Johnson, sureties. Inventory by Stephen Jones, Samuel Libbee and James Noble Shannon, 28 July, 1775, £65 : 13 : 5. [Unrecorded.]

Cornelius Clouse, late of Waldoborough. Daniel Beckler, of Waldoborough, Adm'r, 10 June, 1775. [I, 271.] Daniel Beckler, guardian unto Mary, minor daughter, 19 Nov. 1776. [II, 33.] Inventory by Andrew Schancks, Jacob Wingebow and Jacob Winchereback, all of Waldoborough, 22 June, 1775, £106 : 19 : 10½. [II, 37-8.] Account filed 30 May, 1776. [II, 38.] Peter Hilt, of Waldoborough, guardian unto Mary Clouse, 18 June, 1777. [II, 189.]

In the Name of God Amen The twenty fifth day of Aprill in the Year of our Lord 1766 I Christan Boyinton of Pownalborough in the County of Lincoln Widow being weak in Body but of Perfect minde and Memory thanks be given unto God therefore Calling unto minde the Mortality of my body and Knowing that it is Appointed for all men once to die do make and ordain this my last will and Testament That is to say Principaly and first of all I give and Recomend my Soul into the Hands of God that gave it and for my Body I Recomend it to the Earth to be Buried in a Christen like and Decent manner at the descretion of my Executor. Nothing doubting but at the General Resurrection I Shall recive the same again by the Mighty Power of God and as touching such worldly Estate wherewith it hath Pleased God to bless me in this life I give devise and dispose of the same in the following manner and form.

Imprimus. I give and bequeath to my Grand Children the Children of my Son John Boyinton Decsd Viz to Joshua Boyinton of Falmouth in the County of Cumberland Marriner the Sum of three Shillings to John Boyinton of Pownalboro. aforesd. the Sum of three Shillings to Bety Gray the wife of John Gray of Pownalboro' aforesd. the sum of three Shillings and to Sarah Boyinton of Fallmouth aforesd. the Sum of three Shillings

Itam I give and bequeath to my Son William Boyinton one Quarter part of all the Remaining Part of my Personal Estate that shall be left after my Funeral Charges and other nesesary charges shall be Paid

Item I give and bequeath to my Grand Children the Children of my Daughter Rachel Decker Decesd. an Other Quarter Part of my Personal Estate to be equaly Divided amongst them.

Itam I give and bequeath to my Daughter Anna Delano the Wife of Amasa Delano one Quarter part of my Real Estate

Itam I give and bequeath to my Daughter Hepsebah Hilton the wife of William Hilton the Other Quarter Part of my Remaining Personal Estate

Also I Constitute make and Ordain Jona. Williamson of Pownalborough in the County aforesd. Gent. my Only and Sole Executor of this my last will and Testament and I do Hereby utterly disallow revoke and disanul all and every other former Testaments wills and legacies Bequests and Executors by me in any ways before this time named willed and bequethed Ratifying and Confirming this and no Other to be my last will and Testament In Witness whereof I have hereunto set my hand and Seal the day and Year above Written Signed Sealed published Pronounced and Declared by the said Christaen Boyinton as her last will and Testament in the Presence of us the Subscribers
Viz.
  Thomas Williamson
  Mary Silvester   Christan boynton   (seal)
  Jane Silvester

[Unrecorded.]

Elisha Shaw, late of Georgetown. Susanna Shaw, of Georgetown, widow, Adm'x, 2 May, 1776. [II, 1.] Luke Lambard and David Trufant, sureties. Inventory by Dummer Sewall, David Lemont and David Trufant, Ap., 1779. [II, 269.]

In the name of God Amen. I Josiah Bradbury of Pownalborough

in the County of Lincoln Inholder being weak of body, but of sound & disposing mind & memory do make publish and declare this to be my last will & testament.

Imprimis. I give my soul to God who gave it hopeing for Salvation thro' a blessed redeamer, and my body to the grave.

Item. I give & bequeath to my beloved wife Anna my farm on Jeremy-Squam-Island to have & to hold the same to her, her heirs & assigns as an Estate in fee simple forever.

Item. All the residue of my Estate, real, personal, or mixed I give & bequeath to my said Wife Anna so long as she shall remain my Widow.

Item. After the death or marriage of my said Wife Anna I give devise & bequeath to my daughter Anna Decker one third part of all my Estate to have & to hold the same to her, her heirs & assigns forever as an Estate in fee simple,

Item. After the death or marriage of my said Wife Anna I give devise & bequeath to my daughter Meriah Sevey one third part of all my Estate, to have & to hold the same to her, her heirs & assigns forever as an Estate in fee simple.

Item. To my Grand daughter Catharine Bradbury I demise & bequeath one sixth part of all my Estate that shall remain after the death or marriage of my wife Anna to have & to hold the same to her, her heirs & assigns forever as an Estate in fee simple provided she shall arrive to the age of twenty one years.

Item. I give & bequeath to my Grandson Josiah Bradbury one Sixth part of my Estate that shall remain after the death or marriage of my wife Anna to have and to hold the same to him his heirs & assigns as an Estate in fee simple provided he arrives at the age of twenty one years.

Item. My Will is that in case the said Catharine Bradbury shall die before she arrives to the age of twenty one years that her part shall go to her brother Josiah in fee simple & In case the said Josiah dies before he arrives to the age of twenty one years his part shall go to his sister Catharine in fee simple & in case the said Josiah & Catharine shall both die before they arrive to the age of twenty one years that the said two sixth parts of my estate be equally divided between my Daughter Anna & Meriah as an Estate in fee Simple.

Item. My Will is, that the two sixth parts of my Estate devised to Catharine & Josiah Bradbury remain in the hands of my Executors till they arrive to the age of twenty one years or till their death, my Executors laying out the profits for them as they sha'l see proper for Education & necessaries.

Item My Will is that, in case my said wife Anna should marry again she shou'd have set off to her one third part of all my Real Estate instead of the whole of my Estate & that the residue of the Estate I shall leave, be divided according to the before mentioned legacies & after her decease the residue of the Real estate I shall leave to be divided according to the within mentioned legacies.

Lastly. I do constitute and appoint my beloved wife Anna & my son in law John Decker my executors to this my last will and testament to see that the same is faithfully performed. In Witness whereof I have hereunto set my hand & seal the eighth day of October A D seventeen hundred & seventy four.

Signed sealed published & declared
to be the last will & testament of the
said Josiah Bradbury before us—
The words "I devise & bequeath" in
the space between the third and forth
lines from the bottom of the first
page being first interlined.

           Josiah Bradbury   [seal]

John Page
Thos. Rice
Mary Silvester
  Probated 13 June, 1775. [Il, 3.]

  In the name of God Amen; I Daniel McCurdy of Boothbay in the County of Lincoln & Province of Massachusetts bay yeoman, being very sick in body, but of sound disposing memory & judgment from a sense of mortality of my state & danger of my disease do make & ordain this my last will & Testament.

Imprimis I give up my soul to Almighty God who gave it, thro the the hands of my Lord Jesus Christ by whose merit & righteousness alone I expect to be justified at the great tribunal, and my body to the dust from whence it came to be interred by decent Christian burial at the discretion of my Executors, nothing doubting that I shall again receive the same at the resurrection of the dead :

  And touching any such worldly goods wherewith it has pleased God to bless me in this life I do dispose thereof in the following manner viz.

2   Item, I ordain that all my just debts & funeral charges be in the first place paid out of my personal estate.

Item 3dly I give & bequeath to my beloved sister in law Dorothy Tully in token of friendship, & also in consideration of the trouble she has had with me & my dear deceased wife, one red heifer—& one cow, named flower, of my live stock—to her & her heirs for ever.

Item 4thly to my little niece Margaret Magwyer & her heirs forever I give and bequeath my cow called Bloss.

Item 5thly all my other estate real & personal—with the debts justly owing to me by any person, I give & bequeath to my dearly beloved nephew Daniel McCurdy, whom I had adopted as my own, and to his heirs for ever ;

Item 6thly I constitute & appoint William McCobb--Patrick Magwyer and John Leishman to be the executors of this my last will & testament and guardians of my said nephew Daniel McCurdy until he shall come of age.

And finally I do hereby ratify and confirm this and no other to be my last will and testament :   In Wittness of all which I have hereunto set my hand and seal this eighth day of July in the fifteenth year of the reign of George the third, and in the year of our Lord one thousand seven hundred and seventy five

Signed, sealed, published
pronounced and declared   his
by Daniel McCurdy to be his   Daniel ⋊ McCurdy
last Will and testament   mark   [seal]
in presence of us
Jno Murray
Thomas Boyd
Thomas Bradlee

Probated 6 Sep., 1775. [II, 4.]

Inventory by Samuel McCobb, James Auld and Jeremiah Beath. all of Boothbay, 9 Sep., 1775, £126 : 15 : 8½. [II, 5-6.]

William Lancey, late of Hallowell. William Howard, of Hallowell, Adm'r, 13 June, 1776. [II, 8.] Abiel Lovejoy and John Marsh, sureties.

Nathan Moore, late of Vassalborough. Sarah Moore, of Vassalborough, widow, Adm'x, 13 June, 1776. [II, 8.] Ebenezer Moore, Levi Moore and John Marsh, sureties. Inventory by Abiel Lovejoy, John Marsh and Mathew Hastings, all of Vassalborough, 15 Oct., 1776,

£193 :17 :0. [II, 70.] Account filed 25 Sep., 1778. [II, 149.]

Adam Hunter, late of Topsham. Arthur Hunter, of Topsham, Adm'r, 10 Ap., 1776. [II, 9.] John Fulton and William Randall, sureties. Inventory by James Fulton, James Mustard and William Randall, all of Topsham, 24 May, 1776. [II, 9-10-147.] Account filed 5 Mar., 1777. [II, 146.] Joseph Berry, of Topsham, guardian unto his son Adam, grandson of Adam Hunter, deceased, 15 Oct., 1778. [II, 154.] Order setttling estate 11 Mar., 1779, mentions children, James, eldest son; Robert; Elizabeth, wife of William Woodside; Susanna, wife of Benjamin Lemont; Mary, wife of James Lemont; Margaret, wife of Robert Patten; Arthur, youngest son; John, deceased; Jane, deceased wife of Joseph Berry. [III, 228-9.]

Joseph McIntire, late of Georgetown. Sarah McIntire, of Georgetown, widow, Adm'x, 4 June, 1776. [II, 12.] Francis Wyman and Nathaniel Wyman, sureties. Inventory by Nathaniel Wyman, Francis Wyman and William Sprague, all of Georgetown, 4 June, 1776, £708 : 5 :6. [II, 13-14.] Nathaniel Wyman, guardian of Joseph and William, minor sons, 1 Sep., 1784. Account filed 1 June, 1779. [II, 132.] Inventory by Francis Wyman, William Sprague and John Soule, 15 Sep. 1784, £625 :0 :4. [III, 236.] Account filed 2 June, 1786. [III, 237.] David Morse, of Georgetown, Adm'r *de bonis non*, 27 Sep., 1784, [IV, 17] Henry, minor son, chose Francis Wyman, of Georgetown, to be his guardian, 28 May, 1790. [IV, 132.]

Baltas Cnaster, [Casner] late of Waldoborough. Ludwig Cnaster, of Waldoborough, Adm'r, 29 July, 1774. [II, 16.] Joseph Cole and John Newbit, sureties. Ustana Casner, widow. Ludwig Casner, son. Inventory by Nathaniel Simmons, Christopher Newbit and John Shuman, all of Waldoborough, 19 Sep., 1774, £110 : 13 : 3. [II, 153.] Account filed 6 June, 1775. [II, 154.]

In the Name of God Amen, I Jonas Jones of Georgetown In the County of Lincoln & Province of the Massachusetts Bay In New England, Serveyor, Being Week In Body but of sound Memory Blessed be God for itt, Do this third Day of May One thousand Seven Hundred & Seventy three Do make & Publish this my Last Will & Testament In Manner following that is to say: First: I Will that all those Debts As I Due Owe In Right or Conscienes to Any Manner of Person Or Persons Whatsoever shall be Well & Truly Contented & Paid or Ordained to be paid In Convenient time after my Decease by my Executor hereafter Named.

Item   I give & Bequeath to Hannah my Beloved Wife One Half of the Income or Profitts of all my Lands: houses Barn or Any Income What so Ever of Every Name & Nature, What so Ever During her Naturall Life & to my Daughter Lydia the Other half Part for to be Equally Devided Between them—& as to the Moveables, Housold: Goods: One Half part Is to be Equally Devided Between them, Only my Daughter is for to have but One bed & Beding out of them & if In Case my Daughter Dies With out Isue the Above Named Housold Goods is at my wife's Disposall & for to have the Bennefitt of the Whole of the Income of Every Part During her Life of said Lands, Houses & Barn or other Incomes What so Ever.

I-Tem: I order that part of the Saw mill be sold if Not sold In my Life Time & as much of my Out Lands as my Executor shall think proper.

I Tem: I Give to James Seals Purrinton Junr. One Calf: Now & the Privilidge of Keeping the same on the Farm Untill the same be three Years Old: & One sheep During his Liveing With his Grandmother— & Likewise if said James Scales Purrinton Lives: With: his Grandmother: Untill he Comes to the Age of Twenty One Years: he shall have Two steers of Two Years Old, the spring: before he is Twenty One Years of Age & One Hiafer of the same Age of Two Years Old & my Serveyors Tools & a book Called Loves art & I order that said said James be Learnt to Read & Write & Cypher as far as Thee Rule of three & the Sirveyors Art: & Further I Order that if said James Leaves his Grandmother before he is Twenty One if she Lives he is Not for to have any of the above Articles but if she Dies: When he is Eighteen Years old or Nineteen he shall be Intitled to Each & Every Article as above Discribed—& Further I Order that if said James: Lives: but Two or three Years & his Grand Mother Dies he shall have the Above Articles but he must Take them of of said Farm & Likewise he shall have Two suits of Apperall suitable for him.

I Tem.   I Order if In Case said James Leaves his Grandmother With Out Her Consent, He shall have Only his Wearing Apperill.

I Tem.   I Likewise Constitute make & Ordain my Dearly Beloved Wife Hannah to be my Only & Sole Executor of this my Last Will & Testament & I Doe hereby Utterly Disallow, Revoke & Disannull all & Every Other Former Testements, Wills & Legaces Bequests & Executors by me In Any Ways Before this Time Named: Furthermore I

Doe Constitute & Desire that my Brother Jabez Jones would be Aiding
& Assisting as a Guarden : to my Daughter Lydia : Untell she shall
Arrive to full Age or by Law is Capable to Act for her self : & Upon
his Refusall I Doe Intreat my Good friend Mr. Isaac Snow of Harps-
well to a Guarden : to my Daughter Lydia.
& Furthermore I Do Confirm this & No Other to be My Last Will &
Testement. In Witness Whereof I Have here Unto sett my hand &
seal the Day & Year Above Written
Note the Word but was Interlined before signing In Twentieth Line
& also In ye 29 Line Word Scales & In ye 38 Line the Words, &
Sypher—& Furthermore I Appoint my brother Jabez Jones As Assitance
With my Wife In her Executorship
Signed Sealed Published
Pronounced & Declared by the
said Jonas Jones as his Last Will
& Testement In the Presence of
John Lowell   Jonas Jones   (seal)
Samuel Lumbar(t?)
Sam Brown

Probated 23 Feb., 1774.   [II, 16-17.]
Inventory by Elisha Shaw, Dummer Sewall and John Burrel, all of
Georgetown, 18 Oct., 1774, £230 : 1 : 2. [II, 18.]

Benjamin Howland, Jun'r, late of Bowdoinham. Benjamin Howland,
of Bowdoinham, Adm'r, 25 May, 1774. [II, 18.] Jonas Fitch and
Francis Rittal, sureties.

John Hunter, late of Topsham. Margaret Hunter, of Topsham,
widow, Adm'x, 6 June, 1776. [II, 19.] James Hunter and David
Reed, sureties. Inventory by David Reed, John Fulton and James
Fulton, all of Topsham, 2 July, 1776, £697 : 10 : 7. [II, 36-7.]
Margaret Hunter, widow, guardian of Thomas, William and John,
minor sons, and Ann, minor daughter, 15 Oct., 1778. [II, 85 to 87.]

John Ingraham, late of Boothbay. Catharine Ingraham, of Boothbay, widow, Adm'x. 16 June, 1774. [II, 19.] Joseph Harford and
Jonas Fitch, sureties. Inventory by Thomas Stevens, Arad Powers
and Samuel Harris, all of Boothbay, 23 July, 1774, £23 : 18 : 9. [II,
20.]

In the Name of God, Amen. I Martha Campbell of New Castle
in the County of Lincoln Province of the Massachusets Bay Widow—
being in an infirm State of Health but of sound & disposing Memory,

do make this my last Will & Testament: in manner & form following, (that is to say,) First and Principally I resign my Soul into the Hands of Almighty God, hoping for Salvation through the alone Merits of Jesus Christ, and my Body I desire may be buried at the Discretion of my Executors & Executrixes herein after mentioned. And as for such Worldly Goods & Temporal Estate, which God has been pleased to give me: I give devise, and dispose thereof as follows—I will order & appoint that all such just Debts as I shall owe at the time of my Decease, shall be paid & satisfied out of my personal Estate And whereas Mr. William Vaughan late of Dammiscotty; did in & by his last Will & Testament bearing Date the Twenty third Day of June in the Year of our Lord One thousand Seven hundred and forty four (amongst other things give and devise unto Mr. John Campbell my late Husband, and unto me the Sum of Fifty pounds per Annum, the same to be paid out of the produc of the said Testators Mills at Damiscotty of and both of them—and whereas the said Sum of Fifty pounds, hath been hitherto unpaid and is now due and owing by Virtue of the said Testators Will—I give devise & bequeath one equal Third, of all the said Annuity of Fifty pounds per Annum now owing, or which shall or may be due & owing at the time of my Decease, or was due at the time of the Decease of my late Husband Mr. John Campbell, unto each of my three Daughters that is to say unto Jane Brown the Wife of Mr. James Brown of NewCastle in the s'd County of Lincoln, and unto Mary Cawley Wife of Mr. Samuel Cawley of the Town of Newcastle in the said County of Lincoln, and unto Elizabeth Fitts the Wife of Mark Fitts of Newbery Port in the County of Essex to them & their Heirs forever. And whereas the said Mr. William Vaughan did in and by his said last Will & Testament appoint Mr. Eliot Vaughan & my late Husband Mr. John Campbell to be his Executors, (who are both deceased) and Mrs. Jane Vaughan late Jane Noble (who is also deceased) & myself to be his Executrixes of his last Will & Testament, to whom if there should be any Residue of his Estate, he gave the same—And whereas I am the only surviving Executrix of the said Testator, I appoint Mr. James Brown and Mr. Samuel Cawley aforementioned to be my Executors, and my two Daughters Mrs. Jane Brown & Mrs. Mary Cawley to be my Executrixes of this my last Will and Testament, as well in regard to my own Estates, as also in regard to my Right as Executrix to the Will of the said Testator Mr. William Vaughan lastly I give devise & bequeath all the Rest & Residue of all my Real & personal Estates to my three Daughters one equal third to Jane

Brown, one third to Mary Cawley & one third to Elizabeth Fitts to them & their Heirs forever. In Witness whereof I have hereunto set my Hand & Seal this twenty-Ninth day of February in the Year of our Lord One thousand Seven hundred and Seventy two.

Martha Campbell (seal)

Signed, Sealed, published and declared by the said Testator Martha Campbell to be her last Will & Testamt. in the presence of us who subscribed our Names as Witnesses thereunto in her Presence.
John Ward
John Hussey
Kenelm Winslow

Probated 23 Sep., 1776. [II, 21-2.] Inventory of personal estate by John Ward, John Hussey and Kenelm Winslow, all of Newcastle, 24 Sep., 1776, £60 : 2 : 11¾. [Unrecorded.]

Alexander Gray, late of Woolwich. Abihail Gray, of Woolwich, widow, Adm'x, 10 Oct., 1776. [II, 22.] Jonathan Colburn and Gabriel Hamilton, sureties. Inventory by Moses Hilton, Joshua Young and John Pierce, all of Pownalborough, 25 Oct., 1776, £105 : 12 : 8. [II, 25-6.]

Joseph Oakman, late residing at a place called Gardinerston, mariner. Samuel Oakman, residing at said Gardinerston, mariner, Adm'r, 6 June, 1776. [II, 23.] Samuel Doggett, of Boston, surety. Inventory by John Wood, Isaiah Crooker and Joseph Lambard, 3 Aug., 1776, £573 : 13. [III, 46.] Account filed 31 Aug., 1779. [III, 47.]

[John] Peter Cool, late of Winslow. Hannah Cool, of Winslow, widow, Adm'x, 26 Sep., 1773. [II, 24.] John Tozer and James Howard, sureties. Inventory by John McKecnie, Nathaniel Carter and Joseph Carter, 28 Oct., 1773, £95 : 10 : 0. [II, 215.] Account filed 22 July, 1774. [II, 215.]

In the Name of GOD Amen. I John Rogers of Vassalborough in the County of Lincoln and Province of the Massachusetts Bay in New England, Trader, being weak in Body, but of sound Mind and understanding; knowing that I must shortly leave this earthly Tabernacle, do commit my Soul into the Hands of the Almighty Creator thereof, relying on the Merits of my Lord and Saviour Jesus Christ for it's eternal Salvation, and resign my Body to be decently inter'd in it's Mother Earth. And, with Respect to the worldly Estate wherewith it hath pleased my albountiful Benefactor to endow me, I will that first. all my just Debts be paid and discharged.

Secondly For the Love and Affection I bear to Kata, my Wife, I give and bequeath unto her all my Houshold Furniture and wearing apparel, all my Carpenter's Tools; my Watch, my Silver Shoe-Buckles & Neck-Buckle, together with all the Provisions that shall be in my possession at the Time of my Death.

Thirdly I give and Bequeath all the Residue of my Estate unto her the said Kata, unto Mary Rogers, my eldest Daughter and unto Elizabeth Rogers my youngest Daughter, to be divided between the said Kata, Mary and Elizabeth, in equal Thirds.

Fourthly, I desire that the said Kata, my Wife and Abiel Lovejoy of Pownalborough, in s'd County of Lincoln, Gent. may be appointed joint Guardians of my said Daughters Mary Rogers and Elizabeth Rogers. And

Lastly I ordain, make and appoint William Howard of Hallowell, in said County of Lincoln, Gentleman, Sole Executor of this my last Will and Testament, hereby revoking and making void all Wills by me heretofore made. In Testimony whereof I the said John Rogers have hereunto set my Hand and Seal this sixth Day of October, *Anno Domini* One Thousand, Seven Hundred and Seventy four, and in the fourteenth year of his Majesty's Reign

John Rogers (seal)

Signed, sealed and declared
by the said John Rogers to
be his last Will and Testament in Presence of us-
The Word my "Horse" on the other
side being first erased.
John Marsh
Sam'l Devens
W. Wilkins

Probated 11 Nov., 1776. [II, 24.] Kata Rogers, of Vassalborough, widow, Adm'x, *cum testamento annexo*, 11 Nov., 1776. Moses Hastings, Mathew Hastings and Aaron Healy, all of Vassalborough, sureties. Mathew Hastings, of Vassalborough, Adm'r *de bonis non*, 11 June, 1781. Samuel Basset and Ebenezer Moore, both of Vassalborough, sureties. [II, 234.]

Nathaniel Winslow, late of Bristol. Anna Winslow, of Bristol, widow, Adm'x, 23 May, 1776. [II, 26.] John Borland and Joseph Clark, both of Bristol, sureties. Inventory by Robert Sproul, Samuel Clark and Elisha Clark, all of Bristol, 1 June, 1779, £23 : 13 : 3. [II, 128.]

John Spinney, late of Georgetown. Joanna Spinney, of Georgetown, widow, Adm'x, 27 Feb., 1776. [II, 27.] John Hinkley and Nathaniel Wyman, both of Georgetown, sureties.

Joseph Wesson, late residing at a place called Canaan. Eunice Wesson, residing at Canaan, widow, and Jonah Crosby, of Winslow, husbandman, Adm'rs, 7 Feb., 1776. [II, 27.] Timothy Heald and Joseph Cragin, sureties. Inventory by Ezekiel Pattee and Timothy Heald, both of Winslow, and John White, of Canaan, 15 Mar., 1776. [II, 28-29-138.] Account filed 4 Sep., 1778. [II, 139.]

In the Name of God, Amen. I John Bogs of a place called St Georges in the County of Lincoln & Province of Massachusetts Bay in New England yeoman being very Sick and Weak in Body but of perfect Mind and Memory Thanks be given unto God; calling unto mind the Mortality of my Body, and knowing that it is appointed for all Men once to die, do make and ordain this my last Will and Testament; That is to say, principally and first of all, I give and recommend my Soul into the Hand of Almighty God that gave it, and my Body I recommend to the Earth to be buried in decent Christian Burial, at the Discretion of my Executors; nothing doubting but at the general Resurrection I shall receive the same again by the mighty Power of God. And as touching such worldly Estate wherewith it has pleased God to bless me in this Life, I give demise, & dispose of the same in the following Manner and Form.

Imprimis, I give and bequeath to Mary my dearly beloved Wife the free and uninterrupted use, occupation, Possession and Enjoyment of one Third part of all my Real Estate, during her natural Life, with one third part of all my personal Estate to be entirely at her own disposal together with the free Use, Occupation & improvement of the other two Third parts of my Estate both real and personal until the youngest of my surviving Children (as well those that are now unborn, if any such there shall be, as those that are born) arrive at the Age of twenty one Years for the bringing up of my said Children; if she shall continue my Widow until that time; but if she shall marry at any time before that, then each Child by it self, or it's Guardian to come into the Possession of it's own part or Share and I do likewise constitute make and ordain my said Wife the sole Executrix of this my last Will and Testament.

Item I give and bequeath unto my well beloved Children (born and unborn as aforesaid) the whole Remainder of my Estate of what Name or Nature soever, to be divided to and amongst them and each of them, or their legal Representatives, in the following manner and Form, to wit, My Sons each one of them to have two parts or Shares in all my Lands and Real Estate, and my Daughters each to have part or Share; the Sons to have Liberty of Redemption; And my Personal Estate to be equally divided to and amongst all my said Children. And I do hereby utterly disallow, revoke and disannul all and every other former Testaments, Wills, Legacies, Bequests, and Executors, by me in any ways before-named willed and bequeathed: rattifying & confirming this and no other to be my last Will and Testament. In witness whereof I the said John Bogs have hereunto set my Hand and Seal this twenty Second Day of September, in the Year of our Lord One Thousand Seven Hundred and Seventy three.

The Words "for the bringing up of my children" were interlined before Signing and Sealing, as also the words, "& confirming"

Signed, Sealed, published, pronounced,
and declared by the said John Bogs,   John Bogs (seal)
as his last Will and Testament in
the presence of us, who in his presence, and in the presence of each
other, have hereunto subscribed
our Names
    David Fales
    William Bogs
    Nathanael Fales junr.

Probated 17 June, 1774. [II. 30-1.] Inventory by Alexander Lermond, Samuel Creighton and Thomas Starret, all of St. Georges, 30 Sep., 1776, £254 : 9 : 8. [II, 49.]

Robert McKown, late of Bristol. Margaret McKown, of Bristol, widow, Adm'x, 2 Sep., 1776. [II, 32.] Alexander Nickels and Samuel Nickels, sureties. Inventory by Robert Given, George Rodgers and James Sprowl, 19 July, 1777, £454 : 1 : 10. [II, 51.]

Thomas Smart, late of a place called Penobscot. Elizabeth Smart, residing at a place called Penobscot, widow, Adm'x, 25 June, 1776. [II. 33.] John Smart and Robert Stinson, sureties. Inventory by Samuel Kidder, Andrew Webster, Jr., and Ebenezer Haynes, all of said Penobscot, 29 July, 1776. £123 : 2 : 8. [II, 34.]

In the Name of God Amen The Twenty Eight of August 1774 I Hannah Gould of Georgetown in the County of Lincoln Spinster Being Very Sick and Weak in Body But of perfect Mind and Memory Thanks Be Given To God : Therefore Calling unto Mind the Mortality of My Body and Knowing it is appointed For all Men Once to die do Make and Ordain this My Last Will and Testament That is to Say Principaly and First of All I give and recommend my Soul into The hands of God who gave it : and my Body I recommend To The Earth to Be buried in Decent Christian Burial at The discretion of my Executors nothing Doubting but at The General Resurrection I Shall receive the Same Again by ye Mighty Power of God. and as Touching Such Worldly Estate wherewith it hath Pleased God To Bless me in this Life I Give demise and Dispose of ye Same in the Following Manner and Form &c

Item I give to my well Beloved Daughter Mercy Gould Ten Shilling Lawful Money as also To my Well Beloved Daughter Hannah Ten Shillings Lawful Money also I Give To my Well Beloved Son Joseph Gould Ten Shillings Lawful.

Item I Give and Bequeath to my Well Beloved Daughter Mary Gould Ten Shillings Lawful Money

Item I Give and Bequeath To Stephen Gould my Well Beloved Son Twenty Shillings Lawful Money

Item I Give and Bequeath To my Well Beloved Daughter Anstis Gould all the Moveables Belonging To The house.

Item I Give and Bequeath To my Well Beloved Son Moses Gould and To My Well Beloved Daughter Anstis Gould after All my Honest Debts are Paid All My Lands and Buildings Together with all My Stock To Be by Them Equally Divided For their own Proper Use and Benefit

Item I Make Constitute and Ordain Philip Higgins of Georgetown in ye. County of Lincoln Merchant my Sole Executrix To this my Last Will and Testament

And I do Hereby Utterly disallow revoke and disannul all and every other former Testaments Wills Legacies and Bequests and Executors by me in any Ways before Named Willed and Bequeathed Ratifying and Confirming This and No other to Be my Last will and Testament. In Witness Whereof I have hereunto Set my Hand and Seal The Day and Year Above Written.

            Hannah Goold (seal)

Signed Sealed Published

Pronounced and declared
By the Said Hannah Gould
as her Last Will and Testament
In Presence of
  John Williams
        his
  Abel X Eaton Juner
       mark
  John Farrin

Probated 22 Ap., 1777. [II, 35.] Inventory by Benjamin Brown, Abiezer Holbrook and James Lemont, all of Georgetown, 2 June, 1777. [II, 68.]

Abel Burnham, late of Topsham. John Merrill, of Topsham, Adm'r, 14 Mar., 1777. [II, 39.] John Fulton and James Fulton, sureties. Inventory of goods and chattels by Actor Patten, John Whitten and Pelathiah Haly, all of Topsham, 26 May, 1777, £101 : 11 : 2. Inventory of real estate in Royalsborough, County of Cumberland, by Charles Gerrish, Charles Hill and Benjamin Vining, 23 May, 1777, £24 : 16 : 0. [II, 47.] Account filed 1 Dec., 1777. [II, 62.]

Jacob Lash, late of Waldoborough. Mary Lash, of Waldoborough, widow, Adm'x, 19 Nov., 1776 [II, 39.] Andrew Shenk and Jacob Ludwig, sureties. Inventory by George Demuth, John Ulmer and Jabez Cole, all of Waldoborough, 1 Jan., 1777, £97 : 6 : 3. [II, 45-6.]

William Simpson, late of Newcastle. Elizabeth Simpson, of Newcastle, widow, Adm'x, 10 June, 1776. [II, 40.] David Hopkins and David Given, sureties. Inventory by David Given, David Hopkins and Samuel Anderson, all of Newcastle, 26 Sep., 1777, £255 : 2 : 8. [II, 71.]

William Thorn, Jun'r, late of Topsham. Lucy Thorn, of Topsham, widow, Adm'x, 19 July, 1777. [II, 40.] William Malcom and Joseph Malcom, sureties. Inventory by James Hunter, William Malcom and Joseph Malcom, all of Topsham, 30 Sep., 1777. [II,61.] Lucy Thorn, guardian unto Sarah, Thomas, Elizabeth and Martha, minor children, 20 Jan., 1792. [V, 49.] Account filed 9 Sep., 1791. [V, 49-50.] Advertisement of sale of real estate, 15 Mar., 1792. [V, 57.]

Jacob Elwell, late of Meduncook. James Morton, of Meduncook,

Adm'r, 11 Dec., 1776. [II, 41.] Cornelius Bradford and Joshua Morton, sureties. Inventory by Cornelius Bradford, Alexander Jameson and John Davis, all of Medumcook, 22 Ap., 1777, £42 : 4 : 0. [II, 57.] Joshua Collamore, of Medumcook, guardian of William, minor son, 19 June, 1778. [II, 78.] Account filed 26 Nov., 1779. [II, 116.]

In the Name of God Amen.
I William Armstrong of Winthrop in the County of Lincoln yeoman being in a weak State of Body but of Sound mind and memory make and ordain this my last Will and Testament first I Recommend my Soul into the hands of a Gracious Redeemer whoe by his Sufferings upon Earth has mad Satisfaction for the Sins of the whole world.. my Body I committ to the dust to be Buried in decent Christian Burial at the discretion of my Executrix hearafter Named my Worldly Goods I dispose of in maner following viz.
I Give and Bequeath unto Hannah Armstrong my Well beloved Wife all and Singular my Goods and Chattles House and Lands and all my Estate Real and Personal after my Just Debts are Discharged to be at her own Disposeing and Sole use for ever Committing to her care all my dear Children to be brought up as She Shall See fit whoe are all Small and Young at present
Lastly I Constitute and appoint the above Said Hannah Armstrong my well Beloved Wife the Sole Executrix of this my last will and Testament Ratifeing and Confirming this and no other to be my last Will and Testament in Testimony whereof I have hereunto Set my hand and Seal this ninth day of April 1777
Signed and Sealed in Presence of
John Chandler

his
William o Armstrong (seal)
Ichabod How   mark

Disallowed 25 Ap., 1777. [Unrecorded.] Hannah Armstrong, of Winthrop, widow, Adm'x, 25 Ap., 1777. [II, 41.] John Chandler and Ichabod How, sureties. Inventory by John Chandler, Ichabod How and Stephen Pullen, all of Winthrop, 7 May, 1777, £125 : 19 : 4. [II, 50.]

Moses Gould, late of Georgetown. Joseph Gould, of Georgetown, Adm'r. 22 Ap., 1777. [II, 42.] Philip Higgins and John Williams, sureties. Inventory by Abiezer Holbrook, James Lemont and Benjamin Brown, all of Georgetown, 29 Ap., 1777. [II, 217.]

John Mehany, late of Georgetown. Jane Clary, of Georgetown, widow, Adm'x, 18 Ap., 1777. [II, 42.] Benjamin Pattee, Jr., and Robert Power, sureties. Inventory by William Butler, Benjamin Pattee and Bryant Lennan, all of Georgetown, 23 June, 1777. [II, 62.]

Mathias Eichorn, late of Waldoborough. Margaret Eichorn, of Waldoborough, widow, Adm'x, 29 Ap., 1777. [II, 43.] Frank Miller and Michael Reed, sureties. Inventory by Jacob Ludwig, Frank Miller and John Miller, all of Waldoborough, 29 Ap., 1777, £280. [II, 65.] Account filed 27 June, 1777. [II, 66.]

Robert Fulton, late of Bowdoinham. John Fulton, of Topsham, Adm'r, 14 Mar., 1777. [II, 43.] James Fulton and John Merrill, sureties. Inventory by Benjamin Gardiner and Abraham Whittemore, both of Bowdoinham, and William Randall, of Topsham, 19 Mar., 1777, £501 : 15 : 1½. [II, 150.] Account filed 27 Mar., 1778. [II, 151.] Receipts of Jonathan Ellis as attorney to Jenny and Sally Fulton, and in the right of Mrs. Ellis, heirs, 21 June, 1794. [VI, 86.] Receipt of John Fulton, Jr., son, 12 July, 1794. [VI, 86.]

Thomas Clark, late of Vassalborough. Joseph Clark, of Vassalborough, Adm'r, 3 Dec., 1774. [II, 44.] James Burns and Simeon Wyman, sureties. Inventory by Mathew Hastings, John Marsh and Aaron Healy, all of Vassalborough, 2 Feb., 1775. [II, 45.] Lois Clark, of Vassalborough, widow, Adm'x *de bonis non*, 11 Mar., 1783 ; Mathew Hastings and Jonathan Dyer, both of Vassalborough, sureties. [III, 230.]

David Purrington, late of Bowdoinham. Mary Purrington, of Bowdoinham, widow, Adm'x, 8 Dec., 1774. [II, 44.] George Thomas and James Buker, sureties. Inventory by James Bowker, Benjamin Gardner and Richard Temple, all of Bowdoinham, 7 Feb., 1775. [II, 228.]

In the Name of GOD Amen

The Twentifirst Day of May *Anno Domini* one Thousand Seven Hundred and Sixty four I William James of St Georges in the County of Lincoln and province of the Massachusetts Bay in New England genttelman being weak in Body but of perfect mind and memory thanks be given to God, Therefore calling to mind the mortality of my Body, and knowing that it is appointed for all men once to Die, Do make and ordain this my Last will and Testament That is to say Principally and first of all I give and Recommand my Soul into the hands of God who gave it and and my Body I Recommend to the Earth to be buried in decent Christian Burial at the Discretion of my Executors, nothing Doubting but at the General Resurrection I shall receive the Same again by the mighty powar of GOD. And as touching Such Worldly Estate wherewith it hath pleased God to Bless me in this Life I give demise, and Dispose of the Same in the following maner & form

Imprimis I give And bequeath to my well beloved wife a Comforttabel maintanence out of my Estate as Long as she Shall Live my house and Cattel and William my Son to fine fodder for the Cattel with all my househool moveabeles Effects in the Low of Dowre out out of my Estate

Item I give and bequeath to my well beloved Son Pattrick James Chillren five pounds to be paid at my Deseas out of my Estate by my Executors

Item I give and bequeath to my well beloved Dafter Febby Parcey five pounds to be paid her at my Deseas by my Executors out of my Estate

Item I give and bequeath to my well beloved Dafter Frances James to be Capt and maintain out of my Estate by my Executors

Item I give and bequeath to my well beloved Son William James my Lands and all out a Dore moveabeles whom I Likewise Constitute make and ordain my Sole Executrix of this my Last Will and Testament.

Item I give and bequeath to my well be Loved Dafter Catran Treast five pounds to be paid her at my Deseas out of my Estate by my Executors

Item I give and bequeath to my well be Loved Dafter Anne James five pounds to be paid her out of my Estate at my Deseas by my Executors

Item The said William James is not to Sell or Morggage the Land or any part there of in the Life time of his Mother or if he Should Die without a heir of his one body or Child Less for the Estate to Com Back to my proper heirs and I Do hearby utterly Disallow Revoke and Disanul all and every other will or testament and Declear this to be my Last will & Testament

in witness whereof I have hear unto set my hand and Seal the Day and year above Written.

Singed Sealed published pro-

nounced and Declared by the
Said William James as his
Last will and Testament in the
presentce of us the Subscribers. William James (seal)
Alexander Lermond
Robert Griffin
Samuel Counce

Probated Sep., 1771. [II, 52.] The executor named in the will having deceased, Sarah James, of St. Georges, widow, was appointed Adm'x *cum testamento annexo*, 30 Sep., 1776. [II, 52.] Moses Copeland and Reuben Hall, sureties. Inventory by Patrick Porterfield, Samuel Creighton and John Watt, all of St. Georges, 30 Sep., 1776, £148 : 18 : 1. [II, 55-6.] Patrick Porterfield and Samuel Brown, both of Thomaston, commissioners to examine claims, 11 Oct., 1787. [V, 78-79.] Advertisement of sale of real estate, 9 June, 1792. Account filed, 18 Sep., 1792. [V, 79-80.]

William James, late of St. Georges. Sarah James, of St. Georges, widow, Adm'x, 23 Sep., 1774. [II, 53.] Patrick Porterfield and Reuben Hall, sureties. Inventory by Patrick Porterfield, Samuel Creighton and John Watt, all of St. Georges, 30 Sep., 1776, £167 : 9 : 0. [II, 54-5.]

In the Name of God Amen—I William Crawford of Fort Pownall being of sound mind and memory, (for which it is reasonable that every one should be thankful) do this eighteenth day of march, one thousand seven hundred & seventy five, make and publish this my last will and Testament; in the manner following, viz. First, I pray god, that I may alway be a fit subject for Happiness in the world to come; —I bequeath to my loving wife Mary Crawford one third part of my Estate during her Lifetime. Item that my son James Crawford & Josiah Brewer Crawford have two Shares or Parts of my s'd Estate each & my Daughters Mary & Margaret have each one share, or part, upon an equal division, with this reserve, that if I should have other Sons or Daughters that they come in, in the same manner & proportion as the others : Debts I owe none, & funeral charges, to be no more than decent. I order that a Small Tomb of Stone or Brick may be erected, in which I may be deposited, when dead, in such place as may then be Judged most convenient; this I expect perform'd.—

I appoint my wife Mary Crawford executrix & my Brother Josiah

Brewer Executor of this my last will & Testament.
This done, in presence W Crawford. (seal)
of us
Joseph Chadwick
Benja. Shute
Fra's Archibald, Junr.

Probated 29 Sep., 1777. [II, 53-4.]

Charles Callahan, late of Pownalborough, gent., absentee. Nathaniel Thwing, of Woolwich, Esq., agent, 17 Nov., 1777. [II, 60.] Accounts filed 9 Ap., 1779; 2 Mar., 1780; 7 Ap., 1780. [II, 79,96, and 117.] Inventory by Samuel Emerson, Richard Kidder and Philip Call, all of Pownalborough, 20 Dec., 1777, £1021 : 4 : 8. [II, 118.] Charles Cushing, Roland Cushing and William Wilkins, all of Pownalborough, commissioners to examine claims, 1 Dec., 1778. [II, 119.] Accounts filed 2 Mar., 1781 ; 6 Jan., 1783 ; 25 Mar., 1784. [IV, 1-2.] Edmund Bridge, Jonathan Reed and Richard Kidder, all of Pownalborough, commissioners to examine claims. [IV, 3.]

John Wheeler, late of Boothbay. Elizabeth Wheeler, of Boothbay, widow, Adm'x, 7 Nov., 1777. [II, 74.] Daniel Knight, of Boothbay, and Samuel Goodwin, sureties.

John Lee, late residing at a place called Gardinerston, absentee. Joseph North, of said Gardinerston, agent, 4 July, 1777. [II, 75.] Account filed 1 Jan., 1782. [II, 182.] Inventory by Reuben Colburn, Thomas Agry and Seth Soper, 27 Mar., 1778. [II, 248.] Charles Cushing and Edmund Bridge, commissioners to examine claims. [II, 249.] Accounts filed 12 Ap., 1779 ; 1 Ap., 1780 ; 17 Jan., 1784. [II, 250-1.] Account filed 4 July, 1781. [Unrecorded.]

Elias Tailor, late of Winthrop. Mary Tailor, of Winthrop, widow, Adm'x, 20 Jan., 1778. [II, 75.] Peter Hopkins and Abiah Coye, both of Hallowell, sureties. Inventory by Abiah Coye, John Shaw and Abisha Cowin, all of Hallowell, 7 Ap., 1778, £127 : 0 : 2. [II, 218.] Account filed 11 Sep., 1783. [II, 218.]

Samuel Trask, late of Hallowell. William Trask, of Hallowell, Adm'r, 7 Ap., 1778. [II, 76.] Samuel Badcock and Henry Badcock, both of Hallowell, sureties. Inventory by David Thomas, Samuel Badcock and Daniel Savage, all of Hallowell, 11 July, 1778, £54 : 7 : 8. [II, 138.]

David Hancock, late of Hallowell, housewright. Susanna Hancock, of Hallowell, widow, Adm'x, 1 Ap., 1778. [II, 76.] Thomas Hinkley and David Clark, both of Hallowell, sureties. Inventory by Daniel Savage, James Robinson and Thomas Hinkley, all of Hallowell, 15 June, 1778, £82 : 18 : 2. [II, 95.] Account filed 29 May, 1779. [II, 96.]

Samuel Plumer, late of Hallowell, son of Samuel Plummer, of Almsbury. John Plumer, of Almsbury, Essex County, Adm'r, 9 June, 1778. [II, 77.] Jonas Clark and Isaac Clark, both of Hallowell, sureties. Inventory by Uriah Clark, Daniel Savage and David Thomas, 22 Nov., 1784, £393 : 3 : 0. [III, 41.]

Jonah Gay, late of Medumcook. Wellington Gay, of Medumcook, Adm'r, 19 June, 1778. [II, 78.] Joshua Collamore and William Elwell, Jr., both of Medumcook, sureties. Account filed 6 July, 1779. [II, 132.] Inventory by Jesse Thomas, Paul Jameson and Richard Adams, all of Medumcook, 24 June, 1778, £617 : 4 : 0. [II, 145-6.]

John Moody, late residing at Damariscotta pond. Amos Moody, of Damariscotta pond, Adm'r, 24 Ap., 1778. [II, 79.] John Moody and Nathan Jewett, both of Damariscotta Pond, sureties. Inventory by Elisha Clark, Nathan Jewett and John Weeks, all of Damariscotta Pond, 15 May, 1778. [II, 127.]

In the name of God Amen; the thirteenth day of January in the year of our Lord one thousand seven hundred and seventy nine : I Patrick McKown of Boothbay in the County of Lincoln & State of Massachusetts bay yeoman, being very sick and weak in body but of sound & perfect memory, calling to mind the mortality of my state & apprehending myself to be drawing nigh to my great and last change do make and ordain this my last will and testament

Imprimis I commit my soul to God thro' the hands of Jesus Christ my redeemer, by whose merit alone I expect everlasting life ; & my body to the dust to be interred by decent Christian burial at the discretion of my executors nothing doubting but that I shall receive the same again at the resurrection of the just.

Item as touching such worldly goods wherewith it has pleased God to bless me in life I dispose of the same after the following manner.

Item thirdly I appoint John Murray Clerk, William McCobb Esq'r & John Dawse yeoman all of Boothbay to be the Executors of this my last Will & testament and the Guardians of all my children.

Item fourthly I ordain that all my just debts & funeral charges be first paid out of my personal estate: & the remainder I devise as follows.

Item fifthly I ordain that my beloved wife & dear children live together on my real estate as long as they can without sinking their property; but when that can no longer be done I order that my Executors place out and dispose of my children as they shall judge most for their advantage:—excepting that it is my desire that my sister Mary Dawse take my youngest son John & my daughter Nancy as her own, immediately, or as soon as my Executors with the consent of my wife shall order.

Item sixthly when my Executors shall find it necessary to break up my family, then & not till then I order that partition should be made by them of all my estate real & personal as follows viz.

Item seventhly. I order that my dear & beloved wife possess & enjoy the third part of my real estate during her widowhood; and at the end thereof I give & bequeath to her & her heirs for ever all her own clothes, also her bed & bedding, & two cows if my Executors in their discretion shall judge all circumstances to admit of it.

Item eighthly I order all the remainder of my estate real and personal to be divided in equal shares among all my children:

Item ninthly if any child should choose to sell his or her part of the real estate then I settle the first right to purchase the same first on my sons & next on my daughters severally according to their age.

Item tenthly my own wearing apparel, sword, & gun I order my Executors to divide among my sons at their discretion over & above their shares.

Item eleventhly my estate or house & garden in Taberwyne street in Glenarm in the County of Antrim, Ireland, adjoining to the house formerly possessed by George Eaton I give & bequeath to my eldest son Robert if he shall go there for it, if not then to my second son William on the same condition, & in his default to my youngest son John on the same terms, & to their heirs forever: hereby revoking all other wills & ratifying this & no other as my last will & testament. In testimony whereof I have hereunto set my hand & seal the day & year first above written.

Signed sealed & delivered before us.   Patrick McKown   (seal)
Jno. Murray   Joseph Beath   Ebenezer Fullerton.
              Probated 5 May, 1779.   [II, 81.]
Inventory by John Montgomery and Samuel Brier, 22 June, 1779, £947 : 1 : 0.   [II, 223.)

Jonathan Nutting, late of St. Georges, mariner. Waterman Thomas, of Waldoborough, Adm'r, 19 May, 1779. [II, 83.] Moses Copeland, of Warren, and Micah Packard, of St. Georges, sureties. Inventory by Moses Copeland and Hopestill Sumner, both of Warren, and Haunce Robinson, of St. Georges, 21 May, 1779, £3727 : 4 : 5. [II, 143-4.] Waterman Thomas, guardian unto Oliver, George and Ebenezer, minor sons, 9 June, 1785. [IV, 18.] Yearly income of estate estimated at £6. [IV, 234.] Account filed 20 Sep., 1791. [IV, 235-6.] Moses Copeland and William Farnsworth, commissioners to examine claims. [V, 57.] Distribution of estate, 25 May, 1792. [V, 58.]

John Hodge, late of Newcastle, mariner. Mary Hodge, of Newcastle, Adm'x, 25 Dec., 1778. [II, 83.] James Little and Henry Little, both of Newcastle, sureties. Inventory by James Cargill and Samuel Waters, of Newcastle, and David Hopkins, of a place called Dyer's River, 7 Jan., 1779. [II, 133.]

Jonathan Ballard, late of Vassalborough. Alice Ballard, of Vassalborough, widow, Adm'x, 21 Sep., 1778. [II, 84.] Thomas Town, of Vassalborough, and Ephraim Ballard, of Hallowell, sureties. Inventory by Abiel Lovejoy, Nehemiah Gatchel and Levi Moore, all of Vassalborough, 9 Dec., 1778. [II, 148.] Darius and Calvin, minor sons, and Alice, minor daughter, chose Charles Webber, of Vassalborough, to be their guardian, June, 1789. [IV, 54-55.] Account of Alice Williams, Adm'x, filed 30 June, 1789. [IV, 56.]

In the name of God Amen, the Eighteenth day of October, A. D. 1768, I David Bailey residing at Richmond in the County of Lincoln yeoman, being sensible of my own Mortality, but being of sound mind, after recommending my Soul into the hands of Almighty God, & my body to the Earth for decent burial, do hereby make this my last will and testament & dispose of my worldly Estate in manner following, viz.—

Imps. I give & devise to my beloved Wife Hannah her heirs & assigns forever my Lot of Land situate in Pownalborough in said County of Lincoln, which I purchased of Philip Fought, lying on the East side of Kennebeck river, containing Thirty Acres more or less, also my Lot of Land containing about one hundred acres situate on the East side of said river above Pownalborough in said County, not in any Town, & also all my other Estate real & personal wheresoever lying or being of what name or nature soever—said Lot of one hundred acres was granted to me by the proprietors of the Common & undivided Lands in the Kennebeck purchase (in the Counties of Lincoln & Cumberland) from the late Colony of Newplimouth.

Lastly, I hereby appoint my said Wife Sole Executrix to this my Will—
In Witness whereof I have hereunto set my hand & seal the day & year first above written—

Signed, sealed, published, pronounced & declared by said David Bailey to be his last Will & Testament in presence of David Bailey (seal)

  test Eph'm Cowen
  Jonathan Emery
      hur
  Easter X Kindel
     mark

Probated 6 Oct., 1779. [II, 85.]

Inventory by Samuel Goodwin, Thomas Dinsmore and Philip Call, all of Pownalborough, 16 Sep., 1779, £8785 : 5 : 10. [II, 141-2.]

In the Name of God. Amen.—

I Samuel Webb, of Woolwich in the County of Lincoln, Tailer, being very sick & weak in body but of perfect Mind & Memory, calling to mind mortality of my body, knowing it is appointed for man once to die, do make this my last Will & Testament; reocking all former Wills & Testaments whenever or howsomever made by me.

I give & commit my Soul into the hands of God, who gave it.

And for my Body, I recommend it to the Earth, to be buried in a deasent & a Christian-like manner. And as for my *Worldly Estate*, I give, devise, and dispose of in the following manner.

Imprimis. It is my will & I do order that all my just debts & funeral charges be paid & Satisfied, in the first place.

Itim. I give & bequeath unto Sarah my dearly beloved Wife, my whole Estate, real & personal, to be intirely at her dispose, wheresoever, & in whose hands-somever it may be found.

Itim. I also appoint & constitute Sarah my dearly beloved Wife my only & Sole Executrix, of this my last Will & Testament, which I declare to be my last, revocking all former Wills &c :

And as for my well beloved Children, I pray God to be their portion; I think it proper & prudent not to give them any of my Estate, because I have so little, their *Mother* being old, Stands in need of the Whole I leave In Witness Whereof, I hereunto Set my hand & Seal this twenty third day of August one thousand seven hundred & seventy three.

Sam'l Webb   (seal)

Signed and Sealed, by the
above named Samuel Webb,
in the presence of us the
Subscribers.
  Joseph Lankaster
  Elihu Lancester
  John Carlton   [Unrecorded]

Sarah Webb, widow, Adm'x, 27 Nov., 1778. [II, 116.] John Carlton and Joel Reed, both of Woolwich, sureties. Inventory by Joseph Wade, Samuel Harnden and John Carlton, all of Woolwich, 4 Jan., 1774. [II, 87.] Account filed 31 May, 1779. [II, 88.] Nathaniel Thwing and Joseph Wade, both of Woolwich, commissioners to examine claims. Dividend from estate 31 May, 1779. [II, 89.] Widow's dower set off by Samuel Ford, John Carlton and David Gilmore, Jr., all of Woolwich, 1779. [III, 232.]

Israel Averell, late of Pownalborough. Enoch Averell, of a place called Ball-town, Adm'r, 7 Aug., 1778. [II, 90.] Job Averell and Samuel Averell, both of Pownalborough, sureties. Inventory by Daniel Scott, James Ayer and Henry Hodge, all of Pownalborongh, 25 Sep., 1778, £1006 : 12, added by Adm'r, £24 : 11. [II, 91.]

Mecrus Carr, late residing at Dyer's River. Elizabeth Carr, of the same place, widow, Adm'x, 2 Oct., 1779. [II, 92.] Enoch Averell, of a place called Dyer's Pond, and John Sleeper, of Hallowell, sureties.

Ebenezer Gray, late of Pownalborough. Reuben Gray, of Pownalborough, Adm'r, 28 Jan., 1778. [II, 92.] Jonathan Williamson and Isaac Young, both of Pownalborough, sureties. Inventory by Thomas Rice, Jonathan Williamson and Michael Sevey, all of Pownalborough, 18 Feb., 1778; inventory of wearing apparel of Mary Gray, wife of deceased, by same apprizers, 24 June, 1779; account filed 19 Jan., 1779. [II, 99.] Account filed 22 Sep., 1779. [II, 100.] Reuben Gray, of Pownalborough, guardian of Jemima, minor daughter, and Levi and Ebenezer, minor sons, 22 Sep., 1779; John Huse, of Pownalborough, guardian of Thomas, minor son, 22 Ap., 1779. [II, 130-1.] Mary and Elizabeth, minor daughters, chose Azariah Pottle, of Pownalborough, to be their guardian, Jan. 1779. [III, 255.] Account of Reuben Gray, guardian of Jemima and Ebenezer, filed 1 May, 1790. [Unrecorded.]

James Clark, late of Pownalborough. Margaret Clark, of Pownalborough, widow, Adm'x, 7 Aug., 1778. [II, 93.] John Averell, of Pownalborough, and Enoch Averell, of a place called Ball Town, sureties. Inventory by Daniel Scott, Samuel Averell and George Erskin, all of Pownalborough, 3 Nov., 1778, £325 : 3 : 0. [III, 127.] Widow's dower set off by David Murray and James Cooper, both of Newcastle, and Asa Smith, of Pownalborough, 13 Aug., 1785. [III, 233.]

Oliver Allen, late of Winthrop. Levina Allen, of Winthrop, widow, Adm'x, 20 Jan., 1778. [II, 93.] Peter Hopkins and Abiah Coye, both of Hallowell, sureties.

Amos Moody, late of Damariscotta pond. Amos Moody, of Damariscotta pond, Adm'r, 24 Ap., 1778. [II, 94.]

In the Name of God Amen I John Mustard of Topsham in the County of Lincoln &c marener being weak in Body but of sound mind and memory (blessed be God for it) do this fourth day of february in the year of our Lord Christ one thousand seven Hundred & seventy nine make & publish this my last will & testament in the maner following (that is to say) *Imprimis* I Give & bequath to my loving wife Abigal Mustard one Hundred pounds lawful Money togather with all her waring aparel and also all the Household furneture she brought with Her, likewise half dusen puter plaits, one set Chiney one Iron pott, Item I Give to my Brother James Mustard one bever Hatt. Item and to my other Brothers & Sisters I Give Each twenty shillings lawfull, and the remainder of my Estate I Give to my Honored father James Mustard, whom I make Constitute and ordain my Executor to pay my Debts and my funeral Charges In witness hereof I the said Jhon Mustard have set my Hand and seal the day and year first above written

Signed sealed published &
Declared by the testator as and
for his last will and testament   John Mustard   (seal)
in the presents of us who at
his request, in his presents and
in the presents of Each other

Have subscribed our names thereto
   Aaron Hinkley
   George Heddean
      his
   John O Orr
      mark

Probated 2 June, 1779. [II, 97.]
Inventory by James Hunter, George Heddean and Robert Hunter, all of Topsham, 19 Mar., 1779. [II, 135-6.]

In the Name of GOD amen the Seventh Day of December *anno Domini* 1772.
I. Pease Clark of Hallowell in the County of Lincoln and in the Province of the Massachutts Bay in New-England Gent, Calling to mind the mortallity of my Body and Knowing that it is appointed unto man once to Dye do make and ordain this my Last will and Testiment.

That is to Say First of all I Give and Recommend my Soul into the Hands of GOD who Gave it, and my Body to the Earth to be Buried in a decent manner at the Decretion of my Executor not doubting but I Shall Receive the same again by the powr of GOD and as to Such worly Estate wherewith it hath plesed GOD to Bless me in this Life I Give demis and dispose of in Form following viz I will and order my Funeral Charges and my Just debts to be payed out of my Personal Estate by my Executor hereafter named

Imprimus I give and bequeath to my dearly beloved Wife Abigail the Improvement of all my Estate Borth Real and Personal during Her Natural Life

Item I Give and bequeath to my beloved Son David one sixth part of my Real Estate after my wief's Decease

Item I Give and beqeath to my beloved Son Isaac one sixth part of my Real Estate after my wife's Decease

Item, I Give and bequeath to my beloved Son Jonas one sixth part of my Real Estate after my wife's Decease

Item I Give and bequeath to my beloved Son Simeon one sixth part of my Real Estate after my wief's Decase

Item, I give to my beloved daughter Abigail the wife of Benjamin Follet, one halfe of my Indoore moveables after my wif's Decase

Item I Give unto my beloved daughter Susanna the wife of david Hancock one halfe of my Indoor moveables after my wif's Decease

Furthermore I Give the Rest of my Personal Estate (after the Funeral

Charges and Debts are Paid), to be Equally divided amoung all my Children both Sons and daughters

I do hereby Constitute and appoint my Son Peter Clark to be my Sole Executor of this my Last will and Testament, and do hereby Revoke and Utterly disanul all and Every other former Will Legasies and Bequeaths by me heretofore made : Ratifying and Confirming this and no other to be my Last Will and Testament in Witness where of I have hereunto Set my hand and Seal the day and year afores'd.

    Signed Sealed Published Pronounced
    Declared and delivered by the s'd
    Testator as his Last will and
    Testament in Presence of us

John Whiting
Thurston Whiting   Pease Clark   (seal)
Jonathan Whiting

Probated 5 Ap., 1780. [II, 101.] Inventory by Levi Robinson, Benjamin White and Robert Kennedy, all of Hallowell, 30 Mar., 1780. [II, 103.] Account filed 2 May, 1781. [II, 104.]

Andrew Lepear, late of Georgetown. Mary Lepear, of Georgetown, widow, Adm'x, 21 June, 1780. [II, 102.] Jonathan Davis, of Boston, and Joseph White, of Georgetown, sureties.

Thomas Sloman, late of Woolwich. Lydia Sloman, of Woolwich, widow, Adm'x, 22 Sep., 1780. [II, 105.] Nathaniel Tibbetts and Thomas Snell, both of Woolwich, sureties. Inventory by Joseph Wade, Jonathan Fuller and Thomas Snell, all of Woolwich, 25 Sep., 1780. [II, 106.] Joseph Wade and Thomas Snell, both of Woolwich, commissioners to examine claims 30 Sep., 1788. [II, 226.] Account filed 14 June, 1783. [II, 227.]

I Thomas Stinson of Woolwich in the County of Lincoln, Gentleman being under Indisposition of Body but of sound Mind and Memory, do make this my last Will and Testament, viz. In the first place I recommend my Soul to the hands of God who gave it, and my Body to the Earth, to be buried in a decent Manner at the Discretion of my Executor herein after named, not doubting but that I shall receive the same again at the Resurrection of the just.

And as to such worldly Estate as it hath pleased God to bestow upon me in this Life, I give, devise & dispose of the same in Manner and form following

Imprimis I give unto my Son James Stinson the sum of twenty four Pounds eleven shillings, to be paid him immediately after my Decease by my Executor; I also give unto my said Son three Cows, to be delivered him in three years after my Decease; which with what I gave him in my Life Time is in full of his Portion out of my Estate.

Item I give unto my Son Thomas Stinson the sum of Ten shillings, to be paid him by my Executor immediately after my Decease; the same sum, with what I have already given him at the Time of his Marriage, being in full of his Portion of my Estate.

Item I give unto my Son Robert Stinson the sum of seven Pounds sixteen shillings to be paid him by my Executor immediately after my Decease; the same sum, with what I have already given him in my Life Time, being in full of his Portion of my Estate.

Item I give unto my Daughter Isabella Paine fourteen Pounds seventeen shillings & one penny to be paid her by my Executor immediately after my Decease—I also give unto my said Daughter three Cows, to be deliver'd her by my said Executor within three years after my Decease; the same with what I gave her in my Life Time, being in full of her Portion of my Estate.

Item: I give to my Daughter Mary Hourd two Cows, to be delivered her by my Executor within three years after my Decease; the same, with what I have given her in my Life Time being in full of her Portion of my Estate.

Item It is my will and pleasure That my son John be maintained out of my Estate, and I do order that my Son Samuel provide for him & support him comfortably out of my Estate during the Term of his the said John's natural Life.

Item. All the Rest and Residue of my Estate real and personal wheresoever the same is or May be found, I give & devise unto my Son Samuel Stinson, he paying all my just Debts & funeral Expenses, and all & every of the aforemention'd Legacies, & maintaining my said Son John as aforesaid—To hold to him & his heirs forever.

Lastly. I do hereby constitute & appoint my said Son Samuel sole Executor of this my last Will & Testament: hereby revoking any former Testament by me heretofore made, I declare this to be my last Will & Testament. Witness my Hand and Seal this thirtieth day of Septem'r A. D. 1779.

Signed Seal'd and declared by the said Thomas Stinson the Testator to be his last Will & Testament in presence of

(seal)

Thomas Stinson

John White
Hop still Delano
Eben'r Hasey Jun

Probated 3 May, 1780. [II, 106.]
Inventory by Hopestill Delano, Joshua Farnham and William Chalmers, all of Woolwich, 21 June, 1780. [II, 108.]

In the Name of God Amen this Sixteenth day of July A D 1779 I Mary Magdalene Mayer residing at Woolwich in the County of Lincoln Widow being weak & infirm in body but of sound mind do make & ordain this my last Will & Testament

Impri's I Commit my Soul to God & my Body to the Dust to be decently interred.

Item—It is my Will that my Daughter Catharine Reed (with whom I intend to spend the remainder of my days) be generously paid for her care & trouble during my illness & infirmity, out of my Estate, Exclusive of the bequests herein after made her.

Item I bequeath to my said Daughter all my wearing apparrel & a piece of Linnen I now have by me over & above her dividend of one fourth part of my Estate herein after mentioned.

Item The residue of my Estate after payment of my Just debts & funeral Charges I ordain to be divided into four Equal shares or parts & distributed Equally among my three Sons & my said Daughter Catharine.

Lastly I Constitute & appoint Lewis Houdelette of Pownalborough in said County Yeoman Executor to this my last Will & Testament In Witness whereof I have hereunto set my hand & seal the day & year aforesaid

Signed Sealed publish'd
pronounced & declared by the
said Mary as her last Will & Testament   her
In presence of   Mary Magdalene X Mayer   (seal)
   Jos. Winship   mark
   Jonathan Reed

Probated 6 Oct., 1779. [II, 109.]
Inventory by Obadiah Call, Jr., Francis Rittal and Christopher Jackin, all of Pownalborough, 25 Sep., 1779, £407 : 18 : 0. [11, 112.]

Be it know to all men by these Presents that I Peserved Hall of

Hallowell in the County of Lincoln being very Sick and weak but of Perfect mind and memory thanks be Given unto God Calling unto mind the mortality of my body and knowing that it is appointed for all men once to die do make and ordain this my Last will and testament that is to Say Principally and first of all I give and recommend my Soul into the hand of God that gave it and my body I recommend to the Earth to be buried in decent Christian burial at the discretion of my Executor, and as touching such worldly Estate wherewith it has Pleased God to bless me in this Life I give, demise and dispose of the same in the following manner and form.

First. I give and bequeath to Abigal Hall my beloved wife all my Estate real and personal, Except two heffers, full Power and Lawfull othority to Sell and Convey by the advice of my Executor hereafter named, the interest of the money or the use of the Estate to Her own benefit and behofe. if them two heffers are not anuff to pay the debts there shall be an Equal Poportion takeing out of the Real and Personal Estate to Pay the debts and to Seport the aged widow if neded, and after the decase of Abigal my beloved wife if there be any of my Estate, I give and bequeath to my son Timothy Hall and my son Jeremiah Hall, and to the heirs of Nathan Hall the deces'd the one tweneth Part Each of them in makin the heirs before mentond Equal with one my sons and to my son Jonathan Hall I give and bequeath the one tenth Part of my Real and Personal Estate and the Remainder of my Real Estate if there be any I give and bequeath to my son Josiah Hall and I appoint him my soul Executor of this my Last will and testment. and my Personal Estate if there be any I give and bequeath to my dafter Abigal Standly.

I Do Publish and declare this will to be my Last will and Testment in witness whereof I have hereunto set my hand and seal this 20 the day of July in the year of our Lord one thousand seven hundred and Eighty.

Signed Sealed Published Prononced
and declared by the said Preserved
Hall as his Last will and testament,   Preserved Hall (seal)
in the presence of us, who, in his
Presence, and in the presence of Each
other have hereto subscribed our
        Names
  Ebenezer Tyler

Natnaniel Floyd
Reuben Brainerd

Probated 6 Sep., 1780. [II, 113.]
Inventory by Solomon Whiting, Samuel Dutton and Benjamin Brainerd, 9 Dec., 1780, £77 : 4 : 9. [III, 34.]

In the Name of God Amen this Twenty third of August *Anno Domini* one Thousand Seven hundred and Sixty Nine I Francis Wyman of Georgetown in the County of Lincoln and Province of the Massachusetts Bay in New England being infirm of Body but of perfect mind & memory blessed be God & Calling to mind my Mortallity & knowing that Ere long I must put off this Earthly Tabernacle do make & Appoint this to be my last will & Testament.

And first at my Decease I commit my Soul to God who Gave it hopeing Thro' the Merrits of Jesus Christ to receive A free & full Remission of All my Sins I also commit my body to the Grave by A Decent Burial According to the Decretion of my Executors here after Named Nothing doubting but at the General Resurrection I shall receive the Same Again by the Almighty power of God.

And Secondly that all my Just Debts & dues be paid in Convenient time after my decease by my s'd Executors & Thirdly as Touching such Worldly Estate as the Lord has Lent me I give & bequeath in Manner & form following That is to Say I give unto my Daughter Hester Byonton besides what she has Already receiv'd one third part of the three following Lotts or Rights in the Common & undivided Lands in the Town of North Yarmouth & County Cumberland & Province Afores'd Bought from John Powel & Ammi Ruhama Cutter of said Town Viz. Lotts No. Twenty Seven Twenty Nine & Thirty Two lying in A place Called the Gore at ye Upper End of s'd Town I give unto my Son Franciss Wyman besides what he has Already Rec'd my homeStead Aboout fifteen Acres more or less where my house stood in s'd North Yarmouth & one hundred Acre Lots No. Twenty Seven Range C East side of Royals River. I give unto my Daughter Jane Sweetser the Sum of fifty pounds besides what She has Already Receiv'd I give unto my Son Nathaniel Wyman besides what he has already Rec'd one hundred Acres of upland & Six Acres of Salt marsh Lying at Small point in Georgetown Afors'd Also one hundred & Twenty Acres lying Undivided being part of three Lotts Nos. Eleven Twelve & Thirteen in the one hundred & Twenty Acre division in Gidneys Claim.

I give unto my Daughter Sarah Rogers besides what She has Already

Rec'd four Acres of Salt Marsh 1 Bought of Cornelius Soul & Two Acres of Do. I bought from Phineas Jones which is To remain in the hands of my Son Nath'l Wyman Till the decease of me & my Wife

Also one Right in the Common & undivided lands belonging to house lott No. Eleven & one Right in the Islands belonging To s'd house lott No. Eleven

N B The Above lands that are left To Sarah Rogers is to remain in the hands of my Executors for her Childern if it Shou'd please God She Should have any Who Shou'd live to Come of Age then To be given to them or in Case she Shou'd live to become A Widow then She herSelf to Receive them or Otherwise they are to be Equally divided Among the Rest of my Childern

Lastly I make my Sons Francis Wyman & Nath'l Wyman my Executors of this my last Will & Testament

In Testimony Whereof I have hereunto Sett my hand & Seal the Day & Year Above Written.

Signed Seal'd &
Declar'd in presence of
 Jethro Sprague   Francis Wyman (seal)
 William Sprague
 Jno. Wilson

              A Codicile to the Aforegoing Will Sayes:

I would let the Executors to my Will know that I have a Mortgage Deed from Stephen Mitchell at North Yarmouth, for one hundred Pounds Lawful Money & if I do not receive the Money in my life time I desire that they would reserve Eighty Dollars of it for my Wife, & to her use while she lives as her Occasion may require.

I desire also that the Sum of Fifty Pounds of the said Sum of One Hundred Pounds shall be paid to my Daughter Jane Sweetcher, which will be agreeable to the Sum bequeath to her in the foregoing Will. And the Remainder I desire my Executors to divide between themselves, & the rest of my Children. I conclude as in the Close of my Will setting hereunto my hand & Seal this Twenty Seventh Day of June One Thousand Seven hundred and Seventy.

Signed sealed & declared   Francis Wyman
in the Presence of
 James Mchonane
 Welthey Blethen

          Probated 6 Jan., 1779. [II, 114-5.]

John Crocket, late of Fox Islands. Zebulon Howland, of Fox Islands, Adm'r, 16 Dec., 1772. [II, 119.] Jonathan Crockit and Nathaniel Crockit, both of the Fox Islands, sureties. Inventory by Ebenezer Robbins, Joseph Waterman and James Cooper, of Fox Islands, 13 Sep., 1773, £15 : 13 : 10. [II, 120.]

Solomon Hewet, late of Waldoborough. Deborah Hewet, of Waldoborough, widow, Adm'x, 18 Jan., 1779. [II, 121.] Charles Sampson and Abijah Waterman, both of Waldoborough, sureties. Inventory by Waterman Thomas and Nathan Soule, of Waldoborough, and Thomas Johnston, of Bristol, Oct., 1778, £4631 : 16 : 3. [II, 240-1.] Deborah, minor daughter, chose Oliver Nash, of Bristol, to be her guardian, 19 Feb., 1787. [III, 167.] Account filed 20 Feb., 1787. [III, 179 to 181.]

Joseph Floyd, late of Boothbay. William McCobb, of Boothbay, Adm'r, 5 Ap., 1780. [II, 121.] Joseph Carlisle and Benjamin McFarland, both of Boothbay, sureties. Inventory by John Daws, Joseph Carlisle and John Mathews, all of Boothbay, 2 June and 28 Oct., 1780, £1550 : 10 : 8. [III, 28.] Thomas Boyd, Jr., and John Daws, commissioners to examine claims. [III, 28.] Account filed 26 Mar., 1782. [III, 29.] Account filed 8 Sep., 1794. [V, 202.] Distribution ordered 10 Dec., 1794. [V, 203.] Dower set off to Mary Rollings, late widow, 13 Ap., 1782, by Thomas Boyd, Jr., John Daws and John Holten, all of Boothbay. [Unrecorded.]

Andrew Bird, late of St. Georges. Alexander Hathhorn, of St. Georges, Adm'r, 28 Sep., 1779. [II, 122.] Samuel Hathhorn, of St. Georges, and Joshua Collamore, of Medumcook, sureties. Inventory by Joshua Collamore and Paul Jameson, both of Medumcook, and Moses Robinson, of St. Georges, 14 Dec., 1779, £512 : 14 : 0. [II, 123.] Account filed 31 Jan., 1787. [III, 140.]

Joseph Starling, late of Bristol. Moses Starling, of Bristol, Adm'r, 2 Feb., 1780. [II, 123.] Thomas Johnston and William McClain, both of Bristol, sureties.

In the Name of God Amen

The Ninth Day of May in the year of our Lord 1778

I John Gross of Waldoborough in the County of Lincoln, Black Smith : Being Vary Sick and Weak in Body : but of Perfect Mind and Memory, Thanks be unto God for the Same : and Calling to Mind the Mortality of My Body, and knowing, That it is appointed

for all men once to Die, Do Make and Ordain this my Last Will and Testament, That is to Say, Principally, and first of all, I Give and Recommend my Soul into the Hands of God That Gave it, and as Concerning my Body: I Recommend it To the Earth, to be Buried in a Decent Manner: at the Discretion of my Executors, nothing Doubting, but at the General Resurrection, to obtain Everlasting Happiness in the Life to Come: Through the Merits and mediation of my Blessed Redeemer Jesus Christ, And as Touching Such Worldly Estate wherewith it hath Pleased God to Bless me in in this Life, I Give Devise and Dispose of the Same in Manner and form following that is to Say:—
in the first Place, I Give and bequeath to Anna Catharinah my Dearly Beloved Wife all my Estate both Real and Personal Turing Life Excepting my Black Smiths Tools.

Also I Give to my well beloved Son Peter Gross all the Black Smiths Tools and my well beloved Son Peter Gross is to Give to my well beloved Daughter Mari Elizabeth a Haffer at 1½ or 2 years old.

Also I Give to my well beloved Daughter Mary My Bible.

Also I Give to my well beloved Son Peter Gross aforSaid, after my Dearly beloved wifes Decease all my Land and Real Estate for which he is to Pay to my well beloved Daughters namly Mary and Mari Elizabeth; Each Thirten Pounds Six Shillings and Eight Pence Lawful money, afther the Decease of my wifes: further: My Barsonal Estate is to be Devidet amonge my Childeren, ofthe Decease of my wifes if thar anny bee further more: My well beloved Son Peter is to have the first offer: for working the Land for the Halfs for my well beloved wife: or to Hired the Land of my wife

And I Do hereby: utterly Disallow: Revoke: and Disannul: all and Every other former Testaments: wills and Legacies Bequests and Executors, by me in any ways before this time Named: willed and Bequeathed: Ratifying and Confirming This: and no Other to be my Last will and Testament in Witness whearof I have here unto Set my Hand and Seal the Day and year first above written

               his
             John X Gross (seal)
               mark

Signed Sealed Published Pronounced and Declared by the Said John Gross as his Last will and Testament in Presence of us the Subscribers that is to Say
 Jacob Winchenbach
 Godfrid bornheimer
 Jacob Ludwig

Probated 26 June, 1781. [II, 126.] Inventory by Joseph Weaver, Godfried Burnheimer and Francis Miller, all of Waldoborough, 7 Sep., 1781, £98 : 10 : 1. [II, 212.] Receipts for legacies by Mary Newbert, wife of Christopher Newbert and Mary Lissabot Mink, wife of Peter Mink, 1795. [VI, 189.]

In the Name of God Amen, I Daniel Knights of Boothbay in the County of Lincoln & State of Massachusetts Bay yeoman, being Very weak in body but of sound disposing memory, & Judgment, from a Sence of the Mortality of my State, & danger of my disease do make & ordain this My last Will & Testament :

Imprimis I Give up my soul to Almighty God who gave it, thro' the hands of my Lord Jesus Christ, by whose Merit & Righteousness alone I expect to be Justified at the great Tribunal; and my body to the Dust, from whence it came ; to be interred by decent Christian burial, at the discration of my Executors nothing doubting but I shall again receive the same at the Resurrection of the Dead ; and Toutching such worldly Goods wherewith it has pleased God to bless me in this Life; 1 do Dispose thereof in the following manner, Viz.

2 Item. I ordain that all my Just debts & funeral Charges be in the first place paid out of my personal Estate ;—

Itam 3rdly I give & bequeath unto my Beloved Daughter Susana Williams one cow out of my live stock to hir & hir heirs for ever,

Itam 4ly I Give & bequath to my Beloved Daughter Judeth Knights also one cow of my live stock to hir & hir heirs for Ever,—

Itam 5tly I Give and bequath to my Beloved Son Daniel Knights the one half of Damerescove Island Said Daniel paying therefor unto my Beloved Daughter Elizabeth Wheeler, twenty pounds Lawfull Money within two months after my Decese ; also s'd Daniel to pay to my Beloved Daughters Mary Burnom & Marthue Day thirteen pounds six shillings & Eight pence Each, within one year after my Decese ; the above said Legiesies to be made Equal in Value of what the said sums would purchase in provisions in the year 1775.

Itam 6tly I Give & bequeath unto my Beloved youngest Son Patishel Knights the whole of my Real Estate at pleasent Cove which I now live upon unto him & his heirs forever as also all my personal Estate (Except the above two cows) together with all outstanding Debts Due to me He the said Patishel Knights to pay unto my Beloved Daughters Susanah Williams and Judath Knights twenty Pounds Lawfull Money Each within two years after my Deceas and the said twenty pounds to be made good in Value in purchasing provisions as the same would have done in the year 1775—

Item 7thly I constitute & appoint William McCobb Esqr Solomon Burnom & Joseph Carlile to be the Executors of this my last Will & Testement.

And finally I do hereby ratify & confirm this & no other to be my last Will & Testement In Wittness of all which I have hereunto set my hand & seal this tenth Day of January and in the year of our Lord seventeen hundred & Eighty

Signed Sealed published
pronounced & Declared by
Daniel Knights to be his
last will & Testement In
presence of us
  Wm. McCobb
      his
  Joseph X Pirkens
      his
  Benjm. X McFarland
     mark

            his
Daniel H Knights (seal)
       mark

Probated 5 Ap., 1780. [II, 129.] Inventory by Thomas Boyd, Samuel Brier and John Montgomery, all of Boothbay, 15 Ap., 1780, £27471 : 3 : 10. [III, 27.]

Robert Spear, late of Winslow. Roger Chase, residing at Kennebeck, Adm'r, 1 Oct., 1778. Ezekiel Chase, of Hallowell, and Matthew Chase, of Kennebeck River, sureties. Inventory by Jonathan Emery, Ephraim Wilson and Silas Warner, all residing at Kennebeck River, 10 Nov., 1778, (at which date the widow of deceased had become Mrs. Chase), £32 : 12 : 1. [II, 134.]

Ludowick Cassemire Mayer, of Pownalborough, physician, absentee. Edmund Bridge, of Pownalborough, agent, 20 Mar., 1780. [II, 137.]

Josiah Bradbury, Jun., late of Pownalborough. Benjamin Gray, Adm'r. Inventory by Thomas Rice, Jonathan Williamson and Michall Sevey, all of Pownalborough, 17 Dec., 1777, £303 : 17 : 7½. [II, 140.]

Cornelius Bradford, of Medumcook, appointed guardian unto Cornelius Morton, minor son of Cornelius Morton, late of Medumcook, 11 Dec., 1776. [II, 140.]

To All people Whome it may Concern Know ye that I Benjamin Gardner of Bowdoinham in the County of Lincoln in the State of Massachusetts Bay in New England; Being Somthing Indisposed in Body but of Sound mind & Memory do make this my Last will in manner following; first I will that all my just Debts be paid by my Executor & Executrix here After Named; I give to my Beloved Wife Ruth All my Estate Both Real & personal during her Widowhood And at ye end of ye s'd Term Whether by Death or Marriage s'd Estatate to be divided Among my Children in Manner as followeth I Give to my four Sons namely Abdial Benjamin Richard & Daniel All my Estate Both Real & personal Except my House-hold Stuff And wearing Apparrel; I give to My Son Abdial my best Sute of Wearing Apparrel; & the rest of my wearing Apparrel i give to My other three Sones namely Benjamin Richard & Daniel to be Divided Equaly Between them My Silver Cup i give to my Daughter Mary My Looking Glass i give to my Daughter Hannah; And the Rest of My House-hold furniture i give to all my Daughters namely Hannah Parthena Sabrina Rebeckah & Mary to be divided Equaly Between them; My Clock i meant as a part of my house hold Stuf—

And i do finily Appoint my Beloved Wife Ruth My Executrix and With her Prince Coffin of Pownalborough my Executor of this my Last will & Testament; In witteness whereof I have here unto Set my hand & Seal this Twenty Seventh day of ye 10 m 1778.

Sined & Sealed in presence of us
Abrm. Preble
Barnabas Paddock
William Barnard

(The alteration in ye fifteenth line was made Before Signing)
mark
Benjamin X Gardner
his

Probated 6 Jan., 1779. [II, 152.]

William Kahler, of a place called Broad Bay, appointed guardian unto John Weller, minor son of Andrew Weller, late of said Broad Bay, 5 June, 1772. [II, 154.]

Thomas McCobb, late of Georgetown, merchant. James McCobb, of Georgetown, Esq., Adm'r, 10 June, 1782. [II, 155.] William Lithgow, of Georgetown, and Briggs Hallowell, of Hallowell, sureties.

In the neam of God Amean this ninth Day of feburey *Anno Domini* one thousand saven hundred and Saventy two and In the twevlth year of the Rigen of his magstey George the third I Charls Snipe of Georgetown within Countey of Lincoln and Province of the Masseschuset Bay

In new England yeman Bearing under Som Bodley InDispotion But of perfet mind and memary thanks Be to God therfor Calling to mind the mortaletey of Bodey knowing that It Is apointed for all men to Die Do mak and ordane this my Last will and testement that Is to Say Prinsabley and In first Plaes I Give and Bequath my Soul Into God that Gave It and my Body I Recommend to the Earth to be Buried In a Cristen Desant Burall at Discration of my Executors nothing Doupting But at the Genneral Resuration I Shall Recive the Same agean By the mightey Powar of God and as to Such things and wordley Estate as It hath Plesed God to Bliss me with In this Life I Give and Demise and Dispose the Same In the fowling menner and form *Imprimis* I Give and Bequath to my Beloved wife Ann Snipe During hir naturell Life one third part of my Reall Estat on Arowsick Island with one third part of all my Chattels with my Best Beed and Beeding and all my Houshold furniture Itim I Do Give unto my Beloved Dughter Sarah Potter teen Shillings Itim I Do Give unto my Beloved Dughter Hannah Drumond teen Shillings Itim I Do Give unto my Beloved Dughter Ann Potter two milch Cows one heffer and Six Sheepe Item I Give unto my Beloved Dughter Jean two milch Cows one heffer Six Sheepe and saven pounds Lawfull money one Beed and Beding Item I Give unto my Beloved Dughter Marthow Snipe two milch Cows one heffer Six Sheepe and Saven pounds Lawfull money one Beed and Beeding Item I Do Give unto my Beloved Sons John Charls and Gordon Snipe all my Esteat Both Reall and Parsonall Layeing and Bearing on Arowsick Island or Elswhear not Given Before and as I have Given my Beloved wife Ann Snipe the Emprovment of one third of my Reall Estate During hir Lif and one third of my Chatols It Is my furder will and Plesuer that at hir Desses my Sons John Charls and Gordon Shall Inherret have and poses the Said third and the Chattols that my Said wife Shall Leave at hir Deses I will that they be Equley Devided Betwen my five Dughters Sarah Hannah Ann Jean and Marthow the money to be payd By my Executors within two years after my Desses I Do Constuet mak and ordean John Stinson Esqr and my Beloved Son John Snipe my Sole Executors of this my Last will and testament and I Do hearbey utterly Disalow Revoke and and Disanule all and Evrey formar will testment or bequathment and Executors By me are Enewise Before named Raitifieng and Confirming this and no other to be my Last will and testement In witnes wherof I have Sett my hand and Seall the Day and year above writen

Signed Sealed Pubshled Pronounced and Declard By the Sead Charls Snipe as his Last will and testement In the presances us
Daniel Mcfaden
Joseph Preble   Charles Snipe (seal)
Daniel Mcfaden Junr
Probated first Wed. of Mar., 1782. [II, 156.] Inventory by Daniel Mcfaden, Joseph Preble and William Stinson, all of Georgetown, 26 Feb., 1783, £1276 : 1 : 6. [Unrecorded.]

William Patten, late of Bowdoinham. Hannah Patten, of Bowdoinham, widow, Adm'x, 1 June, 1780. [II, 159.] John Patten, of Bowdoinham, and David Fowler, of Vassalborough, sureties. Robert, minor son, chose Mathew Patten to be his guardian 23 Mar., 1782. [II, 159.] Mathew Patten appointed guardian unto Charles, minor son, 21 Feb., 1785. [II, 158.] Inventory by Thomas Wilson and John Fulton, both of Topsham, and Abraham Whittemore, of Bowdoinham, 25 June, 1780. [III, 221-2.] Account filed 31 May, 1781. [III, 223.[Widow's dower set off by John Fulton, of Topsham, Abraham Whittemore and Samuel Jameson, both of Bowdoinham, 5 Sep., 1782. [III, 224.] Hannah Patten appointed guardian unto Sarah, minor daughter, 15 Sep., 1783. [III, 225.] Appraisal of real estate by Jonathan Perry and James Fulton, of Topsham, and Samuel Jameson, of Bowdoinham, 15 Jan., 1784. [III, 225-6.] Order settling estate 10 Feb., 1784, mentions children, James the eldest son, Mathew, John, (deceased,) William, Robert, Charles and Sarah. [III, 227.]

Daniel Townsend, late of Vassalborough. Sarah Townsend, of Vassalborough, widow, Adm'x, 15 June, 1779. [II, 160.] Ephraim Butterfield, of Hallowell, and Samuel Goodwin, Jun., of Pownalborough, sureties. Inventory by Daniel Savage and David McNight, both of Hallowell, and James Cowan, of Vassalborough, 17 July, 1779, £240 : 13 : 0. [II, 245.] William Howard and Daniel Savage, both of Hallowell, commissioners to examine claims. Account filed 19 June, 1782, at which date the administratrix had become the wife of Nathan Sartell. [II, 246.]

John Decker, late of Pownalborough. Anna Decker, of Pownalborough, widow, Adm'x, 12 May, 1780. [II, 160.] Thomas Rice and John Hues, both of Pownalborough, sureties. Distribution of estate to creditors ordered 22 Jan., 1784. [II, 193.] Inventory by Thomas

Rice, Jonathan Williamson and John Huse, all of Pownalborough, 8 Oct., 1781. [II, 255.]

Benjamin Howland, late of Bowdoinham. Obadiah Call, of Pownalborough, Adm'r, 17 Oct., 1777. [II, 161.] Philip Call and Stephen Call, both of Pownalborough, sureties. Inventory by Edmund Bridge, Philip Call and William Lewis, all of Pownalborough, 25 Oct., 1777, £17 : 7 : 6. [II, 220.]

John Shibles, late of Thomaston. Mary Shibles, of Thomaston, widow, Adm'x, 26 Sep., 1777. [II. 161.] James Watson, of Warren, and Haunce Robinson, of St. Georges lower Town, sureties. John Dillaway, of Thomaston, guardian unto James and David, minor sons, 31 Jan., 1787. [III, 142.] Moses Copeland, of Warren, guardian unto John, minor son, 31 Jan, 1787, [III, 142.] Alexander Lermond, junr., of Warren, guardian unto Robert Kilpatrick, minor son, 31 Jan., 1787. [III, 143.] Division of real estate by David Fales, of Thomaston, Thomas Starret and William Lermond, both of Warren, 8 May, 1790 : dower to Mary Dillaway, late widow; remainder to sons Thomas, Robert, John, James and David. [IV, 236 to 241.] Accounts filed, 26 July, 1791. [IV, 241-2.] Inventory by Hatevil Libbey, Alexander Lermond and William Watson, 7 Oct., 1777, £673 : 0 : 6. [Unrecorded.]

Abram [or Abraham] Preble, late of Pownalborough. Solomon Hearsey, of Pownalborough, Adm'r, 16 Jan., 1779. [II, 162.] Inventory by Thomas Rice, David Boynton and Jacob Lowell, all of Pownalborough, 20 May, 1782. [II, 175.] Adm'r having deceased, Mary, widow, Ebenezer Greenleaf, Mary Greenleaf, James Preble, Ezekiel Peaslee, Anna Peaslee, Oliver Peaslee, Sarah Peaslee, Jedediah Preble and Betsey Hearsey, next of kin, declined adm'n, 18 May, 1791. [IV, 223.] Jacob Lowell, of Pownalborough, Adm'r, *de bonis non*, 26 May, 1791. [IV, 224.] Widow's petition for dower. [V, 17.] Jonathan Spafford and Daniel Scott, both of Pownalborough, commissioners to examine claims, 29 June, 1782. [V, 108.] Advertisement of sale of real estate, 10 Sep., 1792. [V, 109.] Account filed and distribution ordered 4 Jan., 1793. [V, 111-112.] Appeal of Thomas Rice et als. from decree of distribution, 12 May, 1794. [VI, 249-50.]

In the name of God Amen the 27nth Day of July 1782 I Roger Chase on Kenebec River about ten Miles above Fort halifax being Considerably advanced in years but of sound mind and memory Calling to mind the mortality of ye body and knowing it is appointed unto all men once to die Do therefore make and ordain this my Last Will and testament—

And in the first place I recommend my Soul to God who gave it and my Body to ye Earth to be buried at the Discretion of my Executor in a decent Christian manner Nothing Doubting that I shall Recive the same again by ye hand and power of God, at ye general Resuration and as touching Such worldly Estate as God has bles'd me with in this life I give and Dispose of the Same in the following manner *Imprimis* I give to my So in Law asa Prat all my Real and Personal Estate with all my Cattle & Sheep with all my utensils and husbandry tools he paying to his Children the heirs of my Daughter Sarah Deceast being the Lawful heirs of her bodie viz to James, and to David thirty Pound Each and to Sarah and to Elizabeth, fifteen pound Each out of the Estate which I have given him when they arive to the age of Twenty one years old and my Will further is that my Son in Law Asa Prat shall be my Sole Executor this my Last will and testament

Secondly I give to my Beloved wife Abigail During her Remaining my Widow out of my *Estate the west End of my Dweling house & ye produce of a Quarter* of my Farm to be found and broat to her with a Sufficiency of fire wood Cut and broat home to her with all my house hold Stuff. I give to my Son Mathew to be Endorsed on a note I have against him So much as to answer a note which Squire Howard has against him in Case s'd Mathew discharges me and my Estate from paying all or any part of the Same.

3 I give to my daughters Mary powers and tamor Noble Each Seven Pounds I give to my Son Ezekiel and Mathew Each five pounds to be paid in 3 years from my Decease and the Legacies to the Daughters afore mentioned to be paid in Two years after my decease.

I give to my grand Children Vernum and Abigail Chase Three pounds Each to be paid in four years from my Decease.

My Will further is that when my wife Shall decease She Shall be buried by my Son Prat as afors'd in a decent Christian manner my will further is that and I and my wife Shall Comfortably be Supported by my Son Prat during our natural Lives. I hereby Disalow and Revoke all other wills and bequests by me made and Ratifie to be my last will and testament

Sighd Seald publisht and to pronounc'd In presence of us
Nymphas Bodfish

Robt. Hood   Roger Chase   (seal)
Ezek'l Chase
              Probated 4 Dec., 1782. [II, 164.]
Inventory by Peter Heywood, John White and Solomon Steward, all residing at a place called Canaan, 15 Oct., 1782. [II, 247.]

William Clifford, late of of Edgecomb. Samuel Clifford, of Edgecomb, Adm'r, 30 Nov., 1782. [II, 165.] William Clifford and Solomon Gove, both of Edgecomb, sureties. Inventory by James Patterson, Joseph Decker and William Cunningham, all of Edgecomb, 11 Dec., 1782, £198 : 4 : 6. [II, 263.]

Robert Cochran, late of Newcastle. Robert Cochran, of Newcastle, Adm'r, 7 June, 1782. [II, 165.] James Cargill and Samuel Kennedy, Jr., both of Newcastle, sureties. Inventory by Samuel Nickels, Robert Hodge, Jr., and David Murray, all of Newcastle, 27 Aug., 1781. [II, 221.] Account filed 8 Nov., 1782. [II, 222.]

Archibald Gamble, late of Warren. Nathan Bucklen, of Warren, Adm'r, 7 Sep., 1780. [II, 166.] Hatevil Libbey and Moses Copeland, both of Warren, sureties. Inventory by Hatevil Libbey, Reuben Hall and Moses Copeland, 30 Nov., 1780, £89 : 7 : 11. [II, 259.] Account filed 21 Feb., 1782. [II, 260.]

William Potter, late of Bowdoinham. Prince Rose, of West Bowdoinham, so called, Adm'r, 22 Feb., 1780. [II, 167.] Abijah Richardson, of West Bowdoinham, and James Potter, of Topsham, sureties. Inventory by Abijah Richardson, Benjamin Jaques and John Farnam, all of West Bowdoinham, 1 Mar., 1780, £2066 : 16 : 0, "allowing Eighteen pence old Tenor as money went at in the year 1774 for one dollar or six shill'gs now." [II, 225.]

Abijah Waterman, late of Waldoborough. Mary Waterman, of Waldoborough, widow, Adm'x, 20 Feb., 1782. [II, 167.] Charles Samson and Andrew Schenck, both of Waldoborough, sureties. Zebedee Simmons, of Waldoborough, guardian unto Thomas, minor son, Deborah and Mary, minor daughters, 1 June, 1785. [II, 238.] Account filed 1 June, 1785. [III, 58.] Inventory by William Farnsworth, Charles Sampson and Andrew Schenck, all of Waldoborough, 17 July, 1782. [IV, 6-8.] Deborah chose Charles Samson, of Waldoborough, to be her guardian, 26 Ap., 1794. [VI, 26.] Thomas chose Charles Samson to be his guardian, 27 Oct., 1794. [VI, 27.]

Samuel Creighton, late of Warren. Lucretia Creighton, of Warren, widow, Adm'x, 7 Feb., 1782. [II, 168.] Thomas Starret and Hatevil Libbey, both of Warren, sureties. Inventory by Moses Copeland, Thomas Starret and Hatevil Libbey, all of Warren, 21 Feb., 1782, £578 : 12 : 5. [III, 240-1.] Account filed 30 Jan., 1787. [III, 141.] Hatevil Libbey, of Warren, guardian unto Jane, minor daughter, 30 Jan., 1787. [III, 142.] Account filed 11 Oct., 1787. [III, 241-2.] James, minor son, chose Hatevil Libbey to be his guardian, 31 Jan., 1787. [IV, 128.]

William Palmer, late residing at St. Georges. Reuben Hall, of Warren, Adm'r, 1 Sep., 1782. [II, 168.] Moses Copeland and Hopestill Sumner, both of Warren, sureties. Lawrence Parsons, of St. Georges, guardian unto Mary, minor daughter, 24 Feb., 1782. [II, 157.] Inventory by Moses Copeland, William Watson and Seth Vose, all of Warren, 20 Feb., 1782, £218 : 17 : 2. [III, 238.] Account filed 29 May, 1786. [III, 239.] Lawrence Parsons, of Cushing, guardian unto Nancy, minor daughter, 26 July, 1791. [IV, 213.]

Samuel Bogs, late of Warren. Mary Bogs, of Warren, widow, Adm'x, 26 May, 1781. [II, 169.] William Bogs, of Warren, and Philip Robbins, of a place called Sterlington, sureties.

John Reed, late of Boothbay. Sarah Reed, of Boothbay, widow, Adm'x, 5 Ap., 1782. [II, 170.] John Murray and Daniel Herrin, both of Boothbay, sureties. Inventory by William McCobb, John Dawes and John Murray, all of Boothbay, 12 Ap., 1782, £99 : 6 : 10, to which Adm'x, added cash £18 : 9 : 8, and sundry small articles. [II, 264.]

Samuel Coney, late of Hallowell. Susanna Coney, of Hallowell, widow, Adm'x, 3 Jan., 1781. [II, 170.] James Howard and Daniel Coney, both of Hallowell, sureties. Inventory by Benjamin Pettingill, Ephraim Ballard and Robert Kennedy, all of Hallowell, 5 Jan., 1781. [II, 206.] Account filed 28 Feb., 1781. [II, 207.] Heartson and Jason, minor sons, chose William Brooks, of Hallowell, to be their guardian, 9 Mar., 1789; William Brooks guardian unto Samuel, minor son, and Susanna, minor daughter, 9 Mar., 1789. [IV, 32 to 36.] Guardian's petition for division. [IV, 159.] Division of real estate by Henry Sewall, Benjamin Pettingill and Ephraim Ballard, all of Hallowell, 28 Dec., 1790 : dower to Susanna Brooks, widow; remainder to Heartson, Samuel and Jason, sons, and Sukey, daughter. [IV, 224 to 226.]

In the name of God Amen. I Joseph Malcom of Topsham in the County of Lincoln and State of the Massachusetts Bay, Blacksmith, being weak of body but of Sound mind and Memory (blessed be God) do this Seventeenth day of January in the year of our Lord one thousand Seven hundred and eighty-one, make and publish this my last will and Testament; in manner following (that is to say) *Imprimis*, I give to my loving wife Sarah Malcom the whole of all my Estate real and personal Goods and Chattels until my yongest Child if a Son Shall arive to the age of twenty one years, or if a daughter to the age of eighteen years and to my Said wife I Commit the Care of all my Children and after my said yongest Child Shall arive to the age above mentioned; and after that time to my said wife one third part of all my estate real and personal during her natural life, allowing her my Said wife to pay all my Lawfull debts.

Item, I give to each of my Sons that Shall be living at the time above mentioned an equal Share of all my Estate both real and personal; not before disposed of to my Said wife.

Item, I give to my daughter or daughters if I should have more than one, twenty pounds Lawful money each, to be paid in Silver or Gold or other money equivalent thereto in one year after my youngest Child Shall arive to the age above mentioned, to be paid by my surviving Son or Sons who Shall possess the Said estate and I make and ordain her my Said Wife Sole Executrix of this my will. in witness whereof I the Said Joseph Malcom have to this my last will and testament, Set my hand and Seal the day and year above written.

Signed Sealed published and
declared by the Said Joseph   Joseph Malcom   (seal)
Malcom as and for his last will
and Testament, in presence of
us whose names are hereunto
under written, who did each of
us Subscribe our names as
witnesses at his request and in
his presence in the room where
he then was.
James Hunter
William Bourk
John Merrill

Probated 4 July, 1781.   [II, 172.]

In the Name of God Amen. I Samuel Hutchinson of Woolwich of the County Linclon & Common-wealth of Massachusetts yeoman: Being very weak in Body, but of perfect Mind & Memory blessed be God: Calling to mind the mortality of my Body & Knowing that it is appointed for all men once to die: Do make & ordain this my last Will & Testament.

That is to Say principally & first of all, I give & recommend my Soul into the Hands of God who gave it, & for my Body, I commit it to the Earth to be buried in a decent Christian like manner at the discretion of my Executors, hoping in the mercy of God thro' Christ to receive the Same made like unto Christs glorious Body at the last Day.

And as to my Worldly Estate which God hath blessed me with in this life, I give, Demise, & Dispose of the Same in manner following.

imprimis. It is my will & I order, that first of all, my just debts & funeral charges be paid & Satisfied.

item. I Give & Bequeath unto Sarah my dearly beloved Wife the free use & improvement of the whole of my Estate both real & personal during her natural life.

item. I give to my beloved Daughter Elizabeth Turner (besides what I have already given her) & to her Heirs the Sum of one pound lawful money to be paied out of my Estate at the Death of my said Wife.

item. I give to my beloved Daughter Susannah Six pounds thirteen Shillings & four pence lawful money to be paied out of my Estate immediately after the Decease of my said Wife.

item. I give to my beloved Daughter Hannah Meloey Six pounds thirteen Shillings & four pence lawful money to be paied out of my Estate immediately after the Decease of my Saied Wife.

item. I give unto my Six Daughters (after named) Ruth Hopkins, Sarah Bridgdon, Mary Avery, Susannah, Hannah Meloey, Martha Fullington to them, their Heirs & asigns forever, all the remainder of my Estate both Real & Personal of whatever nature or kind: or where-ever found, to be Equally divided betwen them & their Heirs upon my Said Wifs Decease.—Excepting to my Daughter Mary Avery to her & her Heirs I give in this Division but one half as much as to one of the Six of my Daughters above named, because She the Said Mary hath already received of me, so much more than the other five of my Daughters personaly have;

I Do also Constitute Timothy Bridgdon of Charlstown in the County

of Middlesex & James Fullington of Woolwich in the County of Lincoln, both in the Commonwealth of the Massachusetts my Executors of this my last Will & Testament & hereby revoke all former Wills or Testaments by me made, & Confirm this & no other to be my last Will & Testament, in confirmation whereof I do hereunto Set my hand & Seal this first day of March, A: D: one thousand Seven hundred & Eighty one : & in the fifth year of the American independence.
Signed, Sealed, Published, Pronounced and
Declared by the Said Samuel Hutchinson
to be his last Will & testament in presence

of Jos : Winship
John Gray } N. B. Samuel Hutchinson (seal)
Benjamin Shaw } the Word
                God was
                interlined
                before Seigning
                & Sealing

Probated first Wed. of July, 1781. [II, 174.] Inventory by Samuel Ford, Robert Stinson and David Gilmore, all of Woolwich, 2 Dec., 1781, £40 : 4 : 10. [III, 181.] Inventory by John Hay, Benjamin Goodwin and Isaac Mallet, all of Charlestown, 12 Ap., 1783. [III, 182.] Account filed 30 May, 1794. [VI, 77 to 79.]

In the Name of God, Amen. I Andrew McFarland of Boothbay in the County of Lincoln and Commonwealth of Massachusetts Esquire being weak and pained in body, but of sound disposing memory & judgment, apprehending myself near to the period of this mortal life, do make & ordain this MY LAST WILL & TESTAMENT.

Imprimis, I give up my immortal Spirit to God who made it, thro' the hands of the Lord Jesus Christ ; and my body to the dust from which it came, to be interred by decent Christian burial, in assurance of its rising again at the general resurrection of the dead.

And, touching such worldly goods or estate wherewith it hath pleased God to bless me in this life, I do dispose thereof in the manner following viz.

Item secondly, I ordain that all my just debts & funeral charges be in the first place paid out of my personal estate

Item thirdly, I do constitute & appoint my dearly beloved wife Elizabeth, my beloved son Andrew McFarland & my trusty friend William

McCobb Esquire all of Boothbay aforesaid to be the Executors & Executrix of this my last will and Testament.

Item fourthly, I appoint & ordain that my dearly beloved wife aforesaid still endeavour to keep my young children under her own eye, & in my family; & with the consent of my other Executors, that she take care to furnish each of them, my said children, with a good education suitable to their circumstances; and I further ordain that all the expence & cost of the maintenance & education of all my said young children until they shall severally have arrived at the age of maturity, be defrayed out of the income of my house & farm whereon I dwell in said Boothbay, & out of the profits arising from the live-stock kept on said farm; & also out of the earnings of the sloop now a building for me by Charles Bryant of Newcastle; But if all these resources shall be found not to suffice for this purpose, the remaining demands which cannot be answered by them I order to be paid out of such parts of my personal estate, not hereafter otherwise devised, as she and my other Executors shall think proper.

Item fifthly, I order to enable my said wife faithfully to fulfill this trust, & for the sake & behoof thereof I do give & bequeath unto her the possession & improvement of my said mansion house with all the buildings thereunto belonging; likewise of the farm on which it stands; & of the live stock kept on said farm; together with the use & improvement of said sloop & of every part of my personal estate not herein specially devised, in trust for the above use, & for the uses hereinafter mentioned: of all which she is to continue possessed until my beloved Son John McFarland shall have arrived at the age of maturity.

Item sixthly when the period last mentioned shall have been completed, I appoint & ordain that my beloved wife shall declare before my other executors whether she doth choose to have a full & honorable maintenance for herself secured & furnished to her by my said Son John, out of his part or inheritance hereinafter bequeathed to him; or in lieu thereof to appropriate to herself, the possession, use, & improvement of one third part of my said houses, farm & live stock; & if she shall make choice of the former I do hereby give & bequeath the same to her, out of the portion of said John, during her widowhood; if the latter is her choice I give & bequeath the same to her during her natural life.

Item seventhly, I give & bequeath unto my beloved son Andrew

McFarland & to his heirs for ever, all my lot of land lying on the East side of the meeting house in said Boothbay; also one half of my estate of land on Spruce-point, so called, in said town; also one half of a lot of land of two hundred acres on Barter's island, so called, in said town, now possessed by the family of Samuel Barter junior; or in lieu of said lot, one half of the debt due thereon; if it shall be redeemed by said family; also one half of my part of little Green island, so called, in Penobscut-bay; also one half of a pew in the diamond of the Meeting house in Boothbay aforesaid, which pew I bought of my brother Ephraim McFarland; also one half of my pew in the gallery in said Meeting house, next to the singer's pew; also one quarter part of the sails, rigging, & iron formerly belonging to the sloop I lately lost; likewise one pair of steers of three years old, & one colt of one year old; as the whole of his inheritance in my estate real & personal.

Item eighthly, I give & bequeath to my beloved son Ephraim McFarland, & to his heirs for ever, all my right in the real estate of my father John McFarland; together with the lot of land adjoining to said estate, which I bought of John McKechnie; also my lot of land bounding on the north part of said estate; likewise one half of the two hundred acre lot above mentioned on Barter's island, so called, in said Boothbay, or in lieu thereof, one half of the debt due thereon, if it should be redeemed by the family of Samuel Barter junior now possessing the same; also one half of my estate of land on Spruce-point aforesaid; also one half of my right in little Green island already mentioned, & one half of each of the pews aforesaid; also one quarter of the sails rigging & iron formerly belonging to the lost sloop last mentioned, or the just value thereof in money to be paid him out of the earnings of the of the new sloop now building for me by the above mentioned Charles Bryant, at such times and proportions as the exigencies of my family shall, in the judgment of my said Executors & Executrix, admit, also one pair of steers of three years old; one colt of one year old, & one good new silver watch or money sufficient to purchase the same, as the whole of his inheritance in my estate real & personal.

Item ninthly, I give & bequeath unto my beloved son John Murray McFarland and to his heirs for ever, under the conditions and incumbrances mentioned in favor of my beloved wife & minor children, in the fourth, fifth, & sixth articles in this my last will & testament, all and singular estate and estates real & personal belonging, or in any wise appertaining to me, that shall be remaining over and above the estates and legacies herein already devised and bequeathed, or that shall be bequeathed in the articles following.

Item tenthly, I give and bequeath unto the lawful heir of my late beloved daughter Jane Reed twelve shillings in lieu of all inheritance, she the said Jane having received her full portion of my estate in her life time.

Item eleventhly, To my daughter Mary Reed, & to my daughter Elizabeth McFarland, also to my other daughters Sarah, Rosanna, Margaret, & Susannah McFarland I give & bequeath & to the heirs of of each of them, respectively forever, one feather bed & bedding each, as the whole portion of my estate of right belonging to them; & further I do hereby empower my said Executors & Executrix if they shall think it fit, & also shall find, when the above articles are executed, that the circumstances of my family & estate will justly afford it, to give to each of my daughters mentioned in this article one cow or heifer when they shall all have arrived at the age of maturity.

Item twelfthly, if one of my said sons should die in minority, or without lawful heirs then my will is and I do hereby ordain, that in that case all the estate & legacies herein bequeathed or devised to him shall be divided in equal shares between my two surviving sons or their heirs; to be by them & their heirs respectively enjoyed as their own proper patrimony: If two of my said sons should die as aforesaid, then I ordain that all the estate real & personal herein bequeathed to them shall go, without any deduction, to the one surviving son & his heirs forever; & if all my sons should decease in the case above mentioned, I order the whole of their inhertance to be divided in equal shares amongst all my daughters and their heirs as their proper patrimony for ever.

Item 13thly if my said Executors & Executrix shall be unanimously of opinion, when my said son John shall have arrived at the age of maturity, that after bearing all the burdens above laid on his patrimony, there does still remain so much out standing debt due to my estate, in good hands, & easily recoverable, as shall make the inheritance of the said John greatly to exceed in value the inheritance of either of his said brothers, then & in that case I ordain that so much of said debts as that overplus shall amount to, shall be divided, in equal shares, amongst my three sons aforesaid, as part of their patrimony respectively: & if it shall appear to my said Executors at that time, that the inheritance of my said son John is not equal to that of either of his brothers, then I ordain that so much shall be paid to him by each of my other sons out of his respective patrimony as my said Executors shall judge necessary to make the inheritance of the three equal.

And finally, hereby dissannulling & revoking all other testaments, I do hereby ratify & confirm this & no other to be my last will & testament: In wittness whereof I have hereunto set my hand & seal, this tenth day of November in the year of our Lord one thousand seven hundred & eighty.

Andw. Mc,Farland (seal)

Signed, sealed, published, pronounced
and declared by Andrew McFarland
to be his last will and testament,
in presence of us
  Jno Murray
  Paul Reed
  John Reed

Probated 1st Wed. of Oct., 1781. [II, 176-8.] Inventories by John Leishman, Samuel McCobb and John Holten, all of Boothbay, 31 July, 1781, £814 : 0 : 8. [II, 229;] 26 Sep., 1782, £41 : 16 : 8. [II, 230.]

William McClintock, late of Boothbay. Margaret McClintock, of Boothbay, widow, Adm'x, 26 Sep., 1781. [II, 182.] William Lithgow and James McCobb, both of Georgetown, sureties. Inventory by Edward Emerson, of Boothbay, David Gilmore and James Fullerton, both of Woolwich, 26 Oct., 1781. [II, 257.]

John Hinkley, late of Georgetown. Hannah Hinkley, of Georgetown, widow, Adm'x, 31 May, 1781. [II, 183] Jordan Parker and Samuel Hinkley, both of Georgetown, sureties. Inventory by Jordan Parker, David Oliver and Nathaniel Wyman, 21 Sep., 1781, £141 : 3 : 11. [III, 59.] Jordan Parker and Nathaniel Wyman, commissioners to examine claims. [III, 60.] Account filed 4 May, 1786. [III, 108.]

Charles Stuart, late of Penobscott River, mariner. Abigail Stuart, of St. Georges, widow, Adm'x, 30 Nov., 1780. [II, 183.] George McCobb, of St. Georges, and William Farnsworth, of Waldoborough, sureties. Inventory by George McCobb, Joseph Robinson and Isaac Wiley, all of St. Georges, 12 Dec., 1780, £19 : 12 : 5. [III, 80.]

William Farnsworth, of Waldoborough, and Moses Copeland, of Warren, commissioners to examine claims. [III, 81.] Account of Abigail Farnsworth, Adm'x, filed 30 May, 1786. [III, 82.]

In the name of God Amen. I Huldah Randall of Topsham in the County Lincoln and Common Wealh of Massachusetts; Single woman, being weak in body, but of sound mind and memory (blessed be God) do this tenth day of September in the year of our LORD one thousand Seven hundred and Eighty two, make and publish this my last will and testament, in manner following, (that is to Say) *Imprimis* I give and bequeath unto my well beloved Brothers William Randall and Daniel Randall in equal halves all my Goods Chattles and Estate to them the Said William Randall and Daniel Randall their Heirs and Assigns forever, and I do Constitute and appoint the Said William Randall and Daniel Randall to be my Executors of this my last will and Testement in witness whereof I have hereunto Set my hand and Seal the day and year above mentioned.—

Signed Sealed published
and declared by the Said   huldah Randall   (seal)
Testator as and for her last
will and testament, in the presence
of us who at her request and in
her presence in the presence of
each other, have Subscribed our
names as witnesses thereto
John Merrill
David Robertson
        her
Hannah X Allen
        mark

Probated 1st Wed. of Jan., 1782. [II, 184.]

James Archibald, late residing at Machias, trader. Jonas Farnsworth, of Machias, Adm'r, 1 Nov., 1783. [II, 186.] James Avery and Benjamin Coolidge, both of Boston, sureties.

Prince Barker, late of Newcastle, mariner. Hannah Barker, of Newcastle, widow, Adm'x, 23 Jan., 1783. [II, 186.] John Hussey and Joseph Taylor, both of Newcastle, sureties. Inventory by Benjamin Woodbridge, John Ward and Kenelm Winslow, all of Newcastle, 20 Feb., 1783, £17 : 7 : 4. [III, 220.] Account filed 17 Sep., 1788. [Unrecorded.]

In the Name of God, Amen. The third Day of October in the Year of our Lord 1782. I Rachael Joyce on the Island Muscongus, in the County of Lincoln and State of the Massachusetts, Spinster, being in perfect mind and memory thanks be given to God for the Same; and Calling to mind the Mortality of my Body, and knowing, that it is appointed for all once to Dye, Do make and ordain this my last Will and Testament: That is to Say, Principally and first of All I Give and Recomend my Soul into the hands of God that gave it; and for my Body I recomend it to the Earth to be buried at the Discretion of my Survivors nothing Doubting, but at the Generall Resurection, I Shall receive the Same again by the Mighty power of God; and as Touching Such Worldly Estate wherewith it hath Pleased God to bless me in this life I give and Dispose of the Same in manner and form following; That is to Say.

In the first place, I Give my Great Chair which is in Marshfeild my Great Chair to my Son Seth Joyce.

Item I Give to his oldest Daughter Margarett a Chest with one Drawer and Square Table which is at Jonathan Joyces. As also all the house hold Goods I left at her fathers.

Item as I have given my Son Jonathan a Trade to Support him That is his part

Item I give to Jonathan's Daughter Rachael a feather bed I left with her father.

Item I give to my Son in Law Barney Fountain a Great Chair.

Item I give my Grandson Jacob Fountain my land att Foxhole in Marshfeild.

Item I give to my grand Daughters Elizabeth and Rachael Fountain all my household Goods that I Leave here to be Equally Divided

Item I Give to my Daughter Elizabeth Fountain my Weaving Loom and Tackling.

Item I Give to my Grandaughters Elizabeth and Rachael Fountain fiveteen pounds old Tenour which their father Barney Fountain owed me for takeing up his note for that Sum of Carpous White to be Equally Divided as also a Johannes in Gold I lent him the sd Barney Fountain to get his Chimneys Built to be Divided between his Daughters Elizabeth and Rachael.

Item As I have Given my Son Isaac Joyce a Trade to Support him that is his part.

I also appoint my Grandson Jacob Fountain to see this my will to be

Settled as I have given, and I Do revoke all or any other Will Ratifying this and no other to be my Last Will and Testament.
In Wittness Whereof I have hereunto Set my hand and Seal, the Day and Year above written.

Sign'd Seal'd and publish'd
pronounc'd and Declar'd
by the S'd Rachael Joyce as her
Last Will & Testament in
presence of us the Subscribers
Wm Loud
Nathaniel Hupper
    her
Susanna X Hupper
    mark

       her
Rachael X Joyce (seal)
      mark

Probated 12 Ap., 1783. [II. 187.]

Robert Wilson, late of Topsham. Samuel Wilson, residing at little River, so called, Adm'r, 4 June, 1783. [II, 188.] David Reed, of Topsham, and Enoch Danford, of Brunswick, sureties. Inventory by Andrew Dunning, of Brunswick, Actor Patten and James Wilson, both of Topsham, 12 Aug., 1783, £36 : 0 : 0. [III, 113.] John Merrill and Actor Patten, both of Topsham, commissioners to examine claims. [III, 113.] Account filed 4 Jan., 1787. [III, 129.]

John Springer, late of Frenchman's Bay, shipwright. Hannah Springer, of Frenchman's Bay, widow, Adm'x, 12 June, 1783. [II, 190.] John Johnson, of Frenchman's Bay, and William Springer, of Bath, sureties. Inventory by Thomas Hill, of Gouldsborough, Moses Butler and Paul Simpson, both of Frenchman's Bay, 8 Aug., 1783, £284 : 14. [II, 208.]

Samuel Winchell, late of Topsham. Sarah Winchell, of Topsham, widow, Adm'x, 29 May, 1783. [II, 191.] James Fulton and Arthur Hunter, both of Topsham, sureties. Arthur Hunter, of Topsham, Adm'r *de bonis non*, 15 Ap., 1786; James Fulton and James Henry, both of Topsham, sureties. [III, 158.] Account filed 15 Mar., 1787. [III, 244-5.] Inventory by John Patten, of Bowdoinham, Samuel Graves and John Rogers, both of Topsham, 1783. [IV, 4-6.]

Hezekiah Sautell, late of Vassalborough. Nehemiah Longley, of Vassalborough, Adm'r, 16 Sep., 1783. [II, 191.] Joseph North, of Hallowell, and Samuel Goodwin, Jr., of Pownalborough, sureties.

William Howard and Joseph North, both of Hallowell, commissioners to examine claims. [III, 129.] Account filed 6 Feb., 1787. [III, 130.] Inventory by Obadiah Sawtell, Asa Holden and Jonas Page, all of Shirley, Middlesex County, 9 Sep., 1783, £14 : 18 : 6. [IV, 10.] Inventory by Moses Sawtell, Thomas Smiley and Isaac Cowen, all of Vassalborough, 4 Oct., 1783, £28 : 0 : 1. [IV, 10-11.]

In the Name of God Amen the Twenty Seventh day of July *Anno dominy* 1783. I David Clark of Hallowell in the County of Lincoln and in the province of the Massachusets Bay In New England.
Calling to mind the mortality of my Body and knowing that it is appointed unto man once to Dye Do make and ordain this my last Will and Testament.
That is to say First of all I Give and Recommend my Soul into the hands of God who gave it and my Body to the Earth to be Buried in a Decent manner at the discretion of my Executor not doubting but I shall Receive the same again by the Power of God and as to such Worldly Estate wherewith it hath Pleased God to Bless me in this life I Give demise and Dispose of in form Following (viz)
I will and order my Real Estate to be Sold at the Discretion of my Executor here after named and my Just Debts to be paid out of my Real Estate by my Executor if there be Enough if not to be made up out of my Personal Estate.
after my Funeral Charges are paid and my Just Debts Paid—*Imprimis* I Give and bequeath to my Executor one Half of all my Estate Real and Personal that Is left
Item the Other Half I Give and Bequeath to my three Children David. John. and Polly. to be Fqually Divided amongst them by my Executor.
Item I Give and Bequeath my wareing Apperil to my Executor
Sarah that was once my wife I utterly Refuse having any part in my Estate or being my Heir or havind any Right of Heirship in my Estate

I Do hereby Constitute and appoint my Beloved Brother Simeon Clark to be my Sole Executor of this my last Will and Testament and do hereby Revoke and utterly disannul all and Every other former Will legasies and bequeaths by me heretofore made Ratifying and Confirming this and no other to be my last Will and Testament. In witness whereof I have hereunto set my hand and seal the Day and year afore said
Signd and Seald in Presents

of us
Thomas Hinkley   David Clark   (seal)
James Hinkley
Jonas Dutton

Probated 15 Sep., 1783. [II, 192.]
Inventory by Thomas Hinkley, Jonas Dutton and Paul Blake, all of Hallowell, 17 Dec., 1783. [IV, 14.]

In the Name of God Amen.
I Christian Cline of a place called Waldoborough In the County of Lincoln and province of Massachusetts Bay in Newengland yeoman being in healh of Body and of perfect mind & memory
thanks be given to god. Calling to mind the Mortality of my Body and knowing that it is appointed for all men once to Die do make and ordain this my last will & testament: that is to say principally and first of all I give and recommend my Soul into the hand of almighty God that gave it and my body I recommend to the Earth to be buried at the discresion of my Executors: nothing doubting but at the general Resurrection I shall receive the same again by the mighty power of God and as touching such worley Estate wherewith it has pleased God to Bless me in this life I give demise and dispose of the same in the following manner and form—

I give and Bequeath to Elibeath my dearly beloved wife whoume I likewise constitute make and ordain the Soul Executrix of this my Last will and Testament one yoake of oxen one horse one Cow & young Calfe one heffer given to her.

I give unto my well beloved son George Cline the one Cow & one hefer & one hefer Calf one year old one young Calf.

I give and Bequeath to Elibeath my Daughter one Cow one Iron Stow and one Brace Kittle holds four pails of warter the wife of the said Cline is to Keep the Stow and Brace Kittle her Life time.

I give to John milk Cline one pear of yearlin Sears and one Sheep I give one Sheep to Mary Veerz one Sheep

and I do hareby utterly disllow revoke and disannull all & Every other former testament will Legacie Bequaest & Executions by me in any ways before named willed and bequethed Reatfing and Confirming this to Be my Last will and testament in witness whereof I have sett my hand & seal this twenty Day of March in the year of our Lord one thousand seven hundred and Eighty three

Signed sealed published and delivered by the said Christian Cline as

his last will and testament in the presence of
test John Hunt   Christian Cline   (seal)
  Nathan Sprague
Probated 1 Oct., 1783. [II, 194.] Inventory by Jacob Umbehind, Daniel Feilheur and John |Hunt, all of Waldoborough, 18 Nov., 1783, £65 : 17 : 5. [III, 35.] Account filed 29 Nov., 1783. [III, 36.]

Joseph Swasey, late of Vassalborough. Judith Coye, of Hallowell, widow, Adm'x, 24 June, 1783. [II, 195.] Jeremiah Hall, of Winthrop, and Oliver Hall, of a place called Washington, sureties.

Abiah Coye, late of Hallowell. Judith Coye, of Hallowell, widow, Adm'x, 24 June, 1783. [II, 196.] Jeremiah Hall, of Hallowell, and Oliver Hall, of Washington, sureties. Daniel, minor son, chose Squire Bishop, of Winthrop, to be his guardian 6 Jan., 1783. [II, 201.]

William Simpson, late of Newcastle. Elizabeth Simpson, of Newcastle, widow, Adm'x, 10 June, 1776. [II, 196.]

Richard Temple, late of Bowdoinham. Elizabeth Temple, of Bowdoinham, widow, Adm'x, 24 Sep., 1783. [II, 197.] Zacheus Beal and Zebulon Preble, both of Bowdoinham, sureties. Inventory by Abraham Preble, James Bowker and Nathaniel Jellison all of Bowdoinham, 14 Oct., 1783, £86 : 15 : 8. [II, 209.] Zacheus Beal and George Thomas, both of Bowdoinham, commissioners to examine claims, 27 Jan., 1786. [III, 183.] Account filed and distribution ordered, 3 Oct., 1786. [III, 184-5.]

Jacob Stevens, late of Edgecomb. John Ryan, of Edgecomb, Adm'r, 11 Sep., 1783. [II, 198.] William Cunningham and Samuel Hall, both of Edgecomb, sureties. Account filed 9 Sep., 1784. [III, 128.] Inventory by Asa Gove, Samuel Webber and William Cunningham, all of Edgecomb, £97 : 14 : 2. [IV, 15.]

James Thornton, late of Bath. Susanna Thornton, of Bath, widow, Adm'x, 17 Oct., 1783. [II, 198.] John McFarland and Samuel Beal, both of Bath, sureties. Inventory by Henry Sewall, Hatherly Foster and Joseph Lambard, all of Bath, 16 Jan., 1784, £464 : 17 : 4. [II, 210.] Account filed 5 Sep., 1794. [V, 251-1.] Division of estate by Dummer Sewall, Simeon Turner and Joseph Lambard, all of Bath, 1 July, 1796, among John Thornton, William Thornton, Joshua Thornton and James Thornton. [VI, 222.] James and Joshua, minor sons, chose Susanna, widow, to be their guardian, 27 May, 1796. Susanna, widow, guardian unto William, minor son, 27 May, 1797. [VII, 52.53.]

Elizabeth Ellison, late of Topsham, widow. William Malcom, of Topsham, Adm'r, 22 Jan., 1784. [II, 199.] John Reed, Jr., and John Umphrize, both of Topsham, sureties. Inventory by George White, John Reed and William Randall, all of Topsham. [IV, 12.]

Jonathan Spafford, of Pownalborough, guardian unto Mary and Martha, minor daughters of Samuel Cochran, late of Newcastle, deceased, 20 Mar., 1774. [II, 200.] Mary Cochran chose Robert Cochran. of Newcastle, to be her guardian, 7 Oct., 1789. Robert Cochran, guardian unto Martha, 7 Oct., 1789. [IV, 89.]

In the Name of God amen—

The 21st Day of April in ye Year of our Lord 1775, I John Molloy of Pownalborough in ye County of Lincoln in ye Province of ye Massachuset Bay in New England, Cord winder, being of perfect Mind & Memory thanks to almighty G'd calling to mind the uncertainty of this frail Life, & knowing that it is appointed unto all Men once to die, do make Constitute & declare this my last will & Testament,—viz first of all I give & recommend my soul into ye hands of God that gave it, & my Body I recommend to ye Earth to be buried in a decent Christian Burial at ye discression of my Executor hereafter named nothing doubting but at ye Resurection I shall receive ye same again by ye Almighty Power of God—and as touching such worly Estate with which it has pleased almighty God to bless me in this Life, I give demise & dispose of all ye same in ye following manner, viz my Mind & will is that my just Debts I owe to any Person or Persons whatsoever shall be paid by my Executrix hereafter named in Convenient Time after my Death.

Imprimis- I give & bequeath to my well beloved & intended Wife Hannah Hutchinson ye whole of my Estate both real & Personal & household goods & Every thing I die possessed of, to enable her to pay my just Debts & Funeral Charges, & for her Comfort & soport, for her Use & improvement, & disposal for Ever—I do hereby Nominate & Constitute & ordain my well Beloved & intended Wife Hannah Hutchinson above named my Sole Executrix of this my last will & Testament, & I do hereby utterly Disannul, revoke & disallow all & Every other former will & Testament, ratifying & Confirming this, & this only to be my last will & Testament, in witness whereof I have hereunto set my Hand & Seal ye Day & Year first above mentioned, In present of

Thos. Moore
Seth Hammon
Susannah Crosby

John Molloy (seal)

Probated 4 Feb., 1784. [II, 202.]

In the Name of God Amen I Godfry filler of Waldoborough in the County of Linclon in ye Massachusetts State being Very Sick in body but of perfect Sences and Knowing that I must die and how Sone I Know not I have thought fit to make this my Last Will and testament viz in the first place I give my Soul into ye hands of God who Gave itt and my body to the Earth to be decently buried att ye Discresion of my Executor whome my will is should be my Loving son John filler and I doe here will and appoint ye said John filler to Execute upon this my will in all Respects. and as to what Worldly goods itt hath pleas'd God to bless me with I Give and Dispose of in the following maner viz I Give unto my Loving wife Regine filler all my Estate both Real and personal after my Just depts are paid as her own to use occupye and Improve dureing Her Life and upon her deth I Give and Dipose of the Same to my Children to be Equelly Divided betwene them in Equel shares both for Quanetee and Qualety and I doe hereby Disanul and make Void all other wills or testaments of what name or Nature whatsoever holding good and Vallied this my Last will and testement in witness whereof I the above said Godfry filler doe hereunto set my hand and seal this third day of March in the year 1784 Signed seal'd and Deliv'd att Waldoborough
in the Pressents of us
Jabesh Cole
Christopher Newbert
Andrew Storer

his
Godfry X Filler (seal)
mark

Probated 5 May, 1784. [II, 203.]

Inventory by Jabesh Cole, Christopher Newbert and Andrew Storer, all of Waldoborough, 15 Ap., 1784. [IV, 16-17.]

Benjamin Wheeler, late of Penobscott river. Elizabeth Wheeler, of Penobscott River, widow, Adm'x, 5 July, 1784. [II, 205.] Elisha Grant and John Patten, both of Penobscott River, sureties. Inventory by Andrew Grant, Robert McCordey and Elihu Hewes, all of Penobscot River, 1 July, 1785, £429 : 18 : 0. [Unrecorded.] Simeon Fowler, of Orrington, and Reuben Newcomb, of Frankfort commissioners to examine claims, 11 July, 1793.

In the Name of God Amen this second day of July A : D : 1784 I Elizabeth Milliner of Vassalborough in the Connty of Lincoln and Commonwealth of the Massachusetts being weak in body but of sound mind and memory thanks be Given to God therefor calling to mind the Mortallity of my body and Knowing that it is appointed for all Men once to die first and Principally Recommend my Soul into the hands of God that Gave it and my body to the Earth to be buried in a decent manner at the discretion of my Executor : Do make and ordain this my last Will and Testament and as touching such worly Estate wherewith it hath Pleased Allmighty God to Bless me with first
I Give and bequeath to Nathaniel Lovejoy of Vassalborough thirteen Pounds Six shillings and Eight pence out of the money that is due to me which now in the Island of Antego if said money shall be recovered
2ly I Give unto Stephen Lovejoy forty Pounds to be layed out in scoling him at the discression of my Executor.
3ly I Give to Sarah Lovejoy my Green Damas Gown and Pettecote and Read Quilted Pettecote and one pare of Stays
And all the Remainder of my Estate Real and Personal I Give and bequeath to Abial Lovejoy Esqr whome I make and ordain my sole Heir and Executor of this my last will and testament hereby disannuling any former wills made by me Rattifiing this my last Will and testiment in witness whereof I have hereunto sett my hand and Seal the day and year abovesaid
Signed sealed and declared by the said Elizabeth Milliner to be her last will and testiment in Presents of
 Samuel Dinsmore   Elizabeth Millner (seal)
 Abiel Lovejoy Jr
 Polley Lovejoy
         Probated 27 Jan., 1785. [II, 211.]

 In the Name of God amen
I James Morton of Bristol in the County of Lincoln yeoman being in perfect Helth of Body and of perfect mind and memory thanks be gavien unto God ; Calling unto mind the mortality of my body and Knowing that it is appointed for all men once to Die Do make and ordain this my last will and testament ; that is to say principally and first of all I gave and recommend my soul to God that gave it and my body to the Earth to be buried in Decent Christian burial at the Discration of my Executors ; nothing Doubting but att the General Resurection I sall receive the same agin by the mighty power of God. And

as toching such worldly Estate wherewith it has pleased God to bliss me in this life, I gave and Demise & Dispose of the same in the following manner and form : first I gave and bequeth to Sarah my Dearly beloved wife the manadgement of my whole Estate both real and personal Duering her life whom I likewise Constatute ordain and appoint the sole Executerix of this my last will and testament and all and singuler the aforesaid Estate by her freely to be possesed and enjoyed. and after the Decess of my beloved wife I lave to my son William two ponnd lawfull money out of my Estate liwise unto James my second son I lave two pound lawfull money to be paid out of said Estate unto my third son Robert I lave & bequeath to him the point on which he raised his house allowing him Eighty acres of land and the remander of my homestead farm and stock I leave to my forth son John him paying out of said Estate to each of my Daughters viz Sarrah Margret & Jean one hundred pound lawfull money to each of them likwise the back land in my possion I leave amongest the whole of my Children each Drawing a equal share it being one hundred acres of land.

ratifying and Confirming this and no other to be my last Will and testament. in Wittness whereof I have heareunto set my hand and seal this twenty seventh of feberuary one thousand seven hundred and eighty one

Signed sealed published and pronounced and Declared by the said James Morton as his last Will and testament in the presence of us Who in his presence
and in the presence of
eath other have hearto
subscribed our names   James Morton   (seal)
William McClain
Samuel McClain
Fergus McClain

Probated 12 May, 1784. [II, 213.]

Inventory by William Burns, David Bryant, Jr., and Lemuel Bryant, all of Bristol, 1 June, 1793, £343 : 18 : 0. [V, 250-1.]

Seth Webb, late of a place called Holt's Island. Solomon Kimball, of Bigwaduce, trader, Adm'r, 10 Jan., 1787. [II, 214.] Nathan Jones, of Frenchman's Bay, and Oliver Mann, of Bigwaduce, sureties. Inventory by Richard Hunnewell, Jr., Jonathan Lowder and Thomas Phillips, all of a place called MajaBigwaduce, 28 Mar., 1787, £73 : 9 : 0. [III, 239-40.] Thomas Phillips and Richard Hunnewell, commissioners to examine claims. [II, 261.]

Nathan Hall, late of Winthrop. Elizabeth Hall, of Winthrop, widow, Adm'x, 27 Feb., 1776. Jonathan Whiting and Stephen Pullen, both of Winthrop, sureties. Inventory by Jonathan Whiting, Stephen Pullen and John Chandler, all of Winthrop, 18 June, 1777, £293 : 11 : 6. [II, 224.] Assignment of estate to Abijah Hall, the son, 8 Jan., 1796, mentions Mary, daughter, wife of Daniel Hemmenway, and Elizabeth, "the other daughter." [VI, 130-1.] Appraisement of estate by Nathaniel Fairbanks, Stephen Pullen and Squire Bishop, all of Winthrop, 23 Dec., 1795, $572. VI, 202.] Receipts of daughters to Abijah, for their shares, 27 Oct., 1795. [VI, 202.]

Silas Hathorn, late of Penobscot River. Silas Hathorn, of Penobscot River, Adm'r.[e] Inventory by Andrew Webster, James Budge and Isaac Freeze, all of Penobscot River, 17 Aug., 1787, £389 : 2 : 0 ; 22 Aug., 1788, £18 : 5 : 0. Jonathan Lowder and James Ginn, both of Penobscot River, commissioners to examine claims, 12 Sep., 1787. [II, 236.]

Levi Soule, late of Waldoborough. Abigail Soule, of Waldoborough, widow, Adm'x, 4 June, 1782. Cornelius Turner and Moses Copeland, sureties. [II, 241.] Inventory by Moses Copeland, of Warren, and Nathaniel Simmons and David Vinall, both of Waldoborough, 3 July, 1783. [III, 132-3.] Account filed 2 Mar., 1796, at which date the administratrix had become the wife of Cornelius Turner. [VII, 223.] Widow's dower set off by Waterman Thomas, Charles Samson and Michael Sprague, all of Waldoborough, 1798. [VIII, 5.] Division of personal estate among widow, Levi, and Abigail, wife of Joshua Howard, Jr., 19 Sep., 1797. [VIII, 6.]

Nathan Soule, late of Waldoborough. Sarah Soule, of Waldoborough, widow, Adm'x, 23 May, 1783. Andrew Schenck and Charles Sampson, both of Waldoborough, sureties. [II, 242.] Inventory by Charles Samson, Andrew Schenck and Zebedee Simmons, 28 Jan., 1784. [III, 134-5.] Inventory of real estate in Plymouth County by Briggs Alden, Levi Loring and Perez Loring, all of Duxborough, 11 Ap., 1788, £500 :0 :0. [III, 261.] Heirs: John Trowbridge, Sarah Trowbridge, Alexander Turner, and Anna Soule. Account filed 2 Mar., 1796. [III, 262.]

Joseph Stevens, late of Winthrop. Rachel Stevens, of Winthrop, widow, Adm'x, 27 July, 1784. [II, 242.] Timothy Foster, of Winthrop, and Jonathan Low, of Vassalborough, sureties. Inventory by Moses Chandler, John Blunt and Gideon Lambert, 7 Sep., 1784, £111 :3 :0. [Unrecorded.]

Eliphalet Foster, late of Winthrop. Timothy Foster, of Winthrop, Adm'r, 11 Mar., 1784. [II, 242.]

Amos Pearson, late of Newcastle. Marcy Pearson, of Newcastle, widow, Adm'x, 17 May, 1784. [II, 243.] Inventory by Samuel Waters, David Murray and Robert Hodge, all of Newcastle, 13 Dec., 1784, £379 :2 :4. [III, 104.] David Plummer, Jr., of New Milford, guardian into Amos, minor son, 2 June, 1800. [IX, 193.] Maria and Elizabeth, minor daughters, chose David Plummer, Jr., to be their guardian, 2 June, 1800. [IX, 248-9.] Widow's dower set off by Samuel Waters, of Balltown, David Murray, of Newcastle, and Jonathan Morrison, of New Milford, 6 Nov., 1798, at which date the widow had become the wife of Peter Gilman. [Unrecorded.]

Jacob Davis, late of Medumcook. Samuel Davis, of Medumcook, Adm'r, 14 July, 1784. Paul Jameson, of Medumcook, and William Solomon Loud, of Muscongus Island, sureties. [II, 244.] Inventory by Robert Jameson, Jesse Thomas and John Demoss, 14 Aug., 1784, £101 :9 :3. [III, 29.] Account filed 28 Sep., 1785. [III, 30.]

Richard Humphrey, late of Winthrop. Peter Hopkins, of Wales, Adm'r, 25 Mar., 1784. [II, 244.] Abner Marson and Edward Fuller, both of Pittston, sureties. Inventory by Philip Allen, Thomas Curtis and Solomon Stanley, all of Winthrop, 29 Mar. 1784, £126 :14 : 9. [III, 233-4.] Philip Allen, of Winthrop, guardian unto Samuel and William minor sons, 21 June, 1785. [III, 256.]

In the Name of God. Amen.

I Philip White of Woolwich in the County of Lincoln, & State of Massachusetts Bay, being of sound & disposing mind & memory Blessed be God therefor, & considering that it is appointed for all Men once to die, do make & ordain this my last Will and testament in manner following. *Imprimis*, I commend my soul into the hands of Almighty God, who gave it, and my body to the Earth from whence it came, in hopes of a joyful Resurrection, through the merits of my Saviour Jesus-Christ; And as for that Worldly Estate wherewith it has pleased God to bless me, I give & bequeath as follows, First, Whereas I have given to my son Robert White one half of my Lands on which I now live, with one half of the buildings thereon, & one half of the priviledges thereto belonging, it is my Will that the same be consider as his full Right, or

Share of my Real Estate, except as hereafter.

Item, I give & bequeath to my daughters, Sarah White & Mary White the other half of my Land together with the other half of the buildings standing on the same also the priviledges of the fishery belonging to the same, to be equally enjoy'd by them for and towards their comfortable support & maintainance during their Natural lives, unless they should Marry, in which case it shall go to my son Robert upon his paying them the sum of Fifty three pounds, six shillings & Eight pence each, in Silver, Equal to six shillings & eight pence p ounce, and in case either of my said daughters should die before the other, then her part shall be enjoy'd by the surviving daughter during her life, or untill marriage as aforesaid, & on the marriage of the said surviving daughter then the whole shall go to my sd son Robert as aforesaid, upon his paying her the aforesaid sum of Fifty three pounds six shillings & eight pence, as aforesaid, and in Case my son Robert should die before my said daughters, then my will is that my said daughters, shall hold & enjoy the aforesaid Other half of my Lands & buildings with the priviledges aforesaid, equally to them and their heirs forever.

Item I give & bequeath to my son Robert White, all my farming Utensils, saving the one half of the use of them to my said daughters Sarah & Mary for & towards their support as aforesaid, during their lives or untill marriage as aforesaid, & in case of death of either my son or daughters then the same to be disposed of in the same manner as the Land & buildings aforemention'd. Also I give to my sd: Son Robert all my Wearing Apparel, also the following books, Vizt: Dodriges ten sermons, Baileys dictionary, and Cockers Arithmetick.

Item, I give to my Grandson Philip White, when he shall arive at the age of twenty one years, my black Ox, and my small firelock, also my feather bed on which I ly, with one pillow, one blew and white Coverlid, and one sheet, and in case my said Grandson should die before he arrives at the age of twenty one years, then what I have given him shall go to my sd: daughters and their heirs forever.

Item, I give to my sd: daughters, Sarrah & Mary, all my household furniture, & Indoor movables of every kind, also my Great Bible, & all my other books except what I have given to my son Robert, to be equally enjoy'd by them and their heirs forever. Also I give to my sd: daughters, all my Stock of Cattle, Swine, Sheep &c except my black Ox aforesaid, to be Equally enjoy'd by them & their heirs forever.

Item, Whereas I am possess'd of a pew in the meeting house in Woolwich, for which when said pew is finish'd there will be due to the Committee of sd: House the sum of forty eight shillings, equall to silver at six shillings & eight pence p oz, and on my sd. Son Roberts paying sd. sum of forty eight shillings to sd: Committee or their order, then my Will is that my said son Robert shall hold & enjoy one half of sd. Pew, and my sd. Daughters Sarah & Mary shall hold & enjoy the other half, & in case my sd. Son Robert shall refuse or Neglect to pay sd. sum when demanded then my sd daughters are to pay the same & shall hold & enjoy the whole of sd Pew to them & their Heirs forever.

Also it is my Will that my Funeral Expences be paid by my sd. Daughters, Sarah & Mary, out of what I have given them. Item all the rest & residue of my Personal Estate that may not have been mention'd herein I give to my sd. Daughters Sarah & Mary equally to them & their Heirs for Ever. And I do make & appoint Nathaniel Thwing of Woolwich aforesd: Esqr: sole Executor of this my last Will & Testament. In Witness whereof I the said Philip White have to this my last Will & Testament set my hand & seal this seventeenth day of October, in the Year of our Lord, one thousand seven hundred & Eighty, & in the fifth year of American Independence.

Philip White   (seal)

Signed, sealed, Published, & declared
by the said Testator, as & for his last Will
& Testament, in the presence of us, who, at
his Request, in his presence, and in presence
of each other, have subscribed our Names as Witnesses thereto.
John Trott
Robert Reed
Seth Hathorne

Probated 1st Wed. of Ap., 1782. [II, 252.] Inventory by Samuel Harnden, Joseph Wade and Samuel Ford, all of Woolwich, 17 Ap., 1781, £223 : 12 : 2. [II, 254.] Account filed, 17 Jan., 1783. [II, 255.]

Thomas Clark, late of St. Georges. Elisha Snow, of Thomaston, Adm'r, 29 May, 1782; John Bridges and James Stacpole both of Thomaston, sureties. [II, 258.] Inventory by Moses Copeland, of Warren, Hezekiah Batchelder and Jonathan Orbeton, both of Thomaston, 28 July, 1782, £96 : 5 : 1. [II, 265.]

In the Name of God Amen. I Ambrose Colby of Pownalborough in the County of Lincoln Blacksmith, being in sound Mind & Memory for which I thank God, but calling to mind the Frailty of Life & certainty of Death, & being desirous that the worldly Estate with which God hath blessed me should be disposed of agreeable to my Mind after my Decease, do make this my last Will & Testament in manner following, viz. I bequeath my Soul into the Hand of God who gave it and my Body to the Earth, to be decently buried at the Discretion of My Executrix, hoping at the last Day it will have a joyfull Resurrection· As to my worldly Goods, 'tis my Will

Imprimis, That my Executrix pay my just Debts out of the Estate I leave.

Item. I give & bequeathe to my beloved Daughter Annah Hoyt my Looking Glass.

Item. I give & bequeath to my beloved Grandson Ambros Colby my Great Bible.

Item. I give & bequeath to my beloved Wife Betty Colby All the rest & residue of my Estate both real & personal, to be absolutely hers forever, and hereby appoint her sole Executrix of this my last Will & Testament, hereby revoking and disannulling all former Wills & Testaments.

In witness whereof I hereto set my hand & Seal the second Day of March A D 1778 ·
Signed Sealed published &
declared to be the last Will
& Testament of the Testator   Ambros Colby   (seal)
in presence of
Tho. Rice
Jacob Pressey
John Kingsbury

[Unrecorded.]

Courtney Babbage late of Deer Island. Courtney Babbage, of Deer Island, Adm'r. Inventory by Joseph Whitmore, Belcher Tyler and George Frees, 7 June, 1784, £94 : 16 : 0. Mark Haskell and Theophilus Eaton, commissioners to examine claims. Account filed 28 Nov., 1785. Distribution of estate 29 Nov., 1785. [III, 1-3.]

In the Name of God Amen I Joseph Carlile of Boothbay in the County of Lincoln & Common Walth of Massachusetts Bay Gentelman being very sick in body but of sound disposing memory and Judgment, from the sence of the Mortallity of my state & danger of my disease do make & ordain this my last Will & Testament—

Imprimis I Give up my Soul to Almighty God who gave it through the hands of my Lord Jesus Christ, by whose Merit & Righteousness alone I expect to be Justifyed at the great Tribunal, and my body to the Dust from whence it came to be intarred by decent Christian Burial, nothing doubting but I shall again receive the same at the Resurrection of the Dead. And Touching such worldly Goods or Estate wherewith it has pleased God to bless me in this Life, I do dispose thereof in the following manner Viz—

2 Item I ordain that all my Just debts & funeral Charges be in the first place paid out of my personal Estate—

Item 3dly—I give and bequeath unto my beloved Wife Elizebath Carlile one Cow of my live stock in Considration of a Cow which I Received with hir at our marradge, also unto my beloved Wife the use & Improvement of the one third of my Real & personal Estate so long as shee (my said beloved Wife) Remains a Widow, or shall think proper to live upon the said Estate also the whole of the housal Funiture which I had with hir at our marradge to hir & heirs forever.

Item 4thly To my well beloved son Joseph Carlile I give & bequeath the whole of my Homestad one Dameracoty so as take sixty six acers & one half out of my whole Tract, most convenant to the homestad, with the whole of the buildings and all other Appurteninces to the same belonging (except the use & Improvement of one third unto my Beloved Wife as above) to him & his heirs forever—also the use & benefit of the Remaining sixty six acers & one half untill my beloved youngest son James Carlile arives at twenty one years of age=also the whole of my personal Estate with all out standing Debts Except as above ordred and disposed off, to him the said Joseph & his heirs forever—

Item 5thly I give & bequeath unto my beloved youngest son James Carlile when he arives at twenty one years of age sixty six acers & one half of my unimproved Land to him and his heirs forever

Item 6thly I also order & bequeath unto my beloved eldest Daughter Abigal Carlile to be Delivered by my son Joseph Carlile within two years after my Death one good Cow or the Value thereof—

Item 7thly I bequeath and order unto my beloved Daughter Mirriam

Carlile to be Delivered also by my son Joseph within three years after my Death one good Cow or the value thereof.

Item 8thly and I also bequeath and order unto my beloved youngest Daughter Mary Carlile to be Delivered by my son Joseph two good Cows or the Value thereof within four years after my Death—

Item 9thly I constitute and appoint William McCobb Esquire to be my Sole Executor of this my last Will and Testament

And finally I do hereby ratify & Confirm this and no other to be my last Will and Testament, In Witness of all which I have hereunto set my hand & seal this first Day of March in the year of our Lord one Thousand seven hundred & Eighty one and in the fifth year of Amarecan Independance—

Signed Sealed published
pronounced & declared by
Joseph Carlile to be his last Will
and Testament in presence of us
Wm. McCobb					Joseph Carlile (seal)
Henry Williams
    his
Benjm x McFarland
    mark

Probated 5 June, 1781. [III, 5-6.] Inventory by Samuel Briar, John Davis and Benjamin McFarland, all of Boothbay, 9 July, 1781, £336 : 14 : 0. [III, 107.]

In the Name of God Amen. I John Groves of Pownalboro' in the County of Lincoln yeoman, calling to Mind the brevity of Life, and labouring under great Bodily Infirmities, tho' of sound & disposing Mind & Memory for which I thank God, do make & ordain this my last Will and Testament in manner following. In the first Place, when I shall die, I will & bequeath my Soul into the Hands of God from whom I received it; and my Body to the Earth to be decently buried at the Discretion of my Executors, hoping hereafter they will be reunited & enter into eternal Life And as to my worldly Estate with which God hath blessed me, I will & dispose of it in the following manner, *Imprimis* My Will is that my Executors pay all my just Debts out of my Personal Estate, and what of it after paying such Debts may be left, if any, I give to my beloved Wife Mary to be absolutely her own forever.

I also give & bequeath to my said Wife the Use & improvement of all my real Estate during her continuing my Widow, and if she should again marry my Will is that she have the Use & improvement of one third part only of my real Estate during Life.

Item. I give & bequeath to my beloved Children Samuel, Alice, William, Hannah, John & Rebecca, all my real Estate to be equally divided amongst them, after the Estate my said Wife has in it ceases. And do hereby constitute & appoint my beloved Wife Mary & my Son Samuel my Executors of this my last Will & Testament, hereby revoking & disannulling all other & former Wills & devises & declare this to be my last Will & Testament.

In Witness whereof I hereto set my hand & seal the twentyseventh Day of Novr. A D 1777
Signed sealed published & declared
by the Testator to be his last Will
& Testament in presence of
Ebenezer Whittier his
Ebenezer Whittier Jr. John S Groves (seal)
Thos Rice mark

Probated 17 Mar., 1785. [III, 7.]
Inventory by Ebenezer Whittier, David Silvester and John Sevey, all of Pownalborough, 12 Oct., 1785, £11 : 17 : 0. [Unrecorded.]

Thomas Agry, late of Pittston, shipwright. Anna Agry, widow, and Thomas Agry, shipwright, both of Pittston, Adm'rs, 21 Mar., 1785. [III, 9.] Samuel Oakman, of Pittston, and Joseph North, of Hallowell, sureties. Inventory by Reuben Colburn, Seth Soper and Henry Smith, 1786. [III, 253-4.] Inventory of real estate in Pearsontown, Cumberland County, 4 July, 1785. [III, 255.]

Nicholas Kennedy, late of Edgecomb. Joseph Merry, of Edgecomb, Adm'r, 26 Ap., 1785. [III, 9.] Nathaniel Winslow, of Edgecomb, and Benjamin Dodge, of Newcastle, sureties. Inventory by Moses Davis, William Cunningham and Zachariah Dodge, all of Edgecomb, 3 Nov., 1785, £83 : 2 : 8. [III, 49.] Account filed 28 Mar., 1786. [III, 110.]

Joshua Sawyer, late of Edgecomb, shipwright. Benjamin Sawyer, of Boothbay, Adm'r, 20 Sep., 1785. [III, 10.] Aaron Sawyer, of Boothbay, and Solomon Gove, of Edgecomb, sureties. Inventory by Moses Davis, David Trask and Solomon Gove, all of Edgecomb, 24 Sep., 1785, £196 : 5 : 10. [III, 99.]

Nathaniel Springer, late of Georgetown. Sarah Springer, of Georgetown, widow, Adm'x, 25 Nov., 1779. [III, 11.] John Wood, of Georgetown, and Nathaniel Thwing, of Woolwich, sureties. Inventory by Dummer Sewall, Joshua Philbrook and Isaiah Crooker, 22 Feb., 1780, £8214 : 3. [III, 51-52.] Account filed 20 Sep., 1785. [III, 52.] Joseph White, of Bath, guardian unto Lucy and Betsey, minor daughters, Samuel and Nathaniel, minor sons, 25 May, 1789. [IV, 41-43.]

Daniel Gent Tuckerman, late of Pownalbrough, tailor. Job Averell, of Pownalborough, Adm'r, 25 Mar., 1785. [III, 12.] James Hodge and Asa Andrews, both of Pownalborough, sureties. Inventory by Ebenezer Whittier, Asa Andrews and Calvin Graves, all of Pownalborough, 26 Mar., 1785, £49 : 18 : 1, to which administrator added sundry articles, £3 : 6 : 0. [III, 62.] Account filed 29 June, 1786. [III, 105.] Asa Andrews and China Smith, both of Pownalborough, commissioners to examine claims, 28 Mar., 1785. [III, 194.] Widow's dower set off by David Silvester, Ebenezer Whittier and Jacob Woodman, all of Pownalborough, 30 June, 1796. [VII, 218.]

Benjamin Lemont, late of Bath. Susanna Lemont, of Bath, widow, Adm'x, 27 Sep., 1784. [III, 12.] James Lemont and Thomas Lemont, both of Bath, sureties. Inventory by Dummer Sewall, Benjamin Ham and John Foot, all of Bath, 2 Feb., 1785, £506 : 8 : 7. [III, 115.] Francis Winter and Dummer Sewall, commissioners to examine claims. [III, 116.] Widow's dower set off 8 Dec., 1788. [IV, 121.] Account filed 28 May, 1790. [IV, 133.]

Nathaniel Whittier, late of Winthrop. Thomas Whittier, of Winthrop, Adm'r, 24 Nov., 1784. [III, 13.] Philip Theobald and Richard Kidder, both of Pownalborough, sureties. Inventory by Joseph Hutchins, Francis Fuller and John Evans, 15 Dec., 1784, £41 : 2 : 4, to which administrator added two notes of hand, £97 : 16 : 0. [III, 61.] Account filed 11 Mar., 1786. [III, 127.] Ichabod How and John Hubbard, both of Winthrop, commissioners to examine claims, 15 Mar., 1785. [III, 193.]

John Carlton, late of Woolwich. Jane Carlton, of Woolwich, widow, Adm'x, 17 June, 1785. [III, 14.] James Fullerton, of Woolwich, and Philip Theobald, of Pownalborough, sureties. Inventory by Samuel Ford, James Fullerton and James Blen, all of Woolwich, 20 May, 1786, £74 : 4 : 6. [III, 101.] Samuel Stinson and Thomas Snell, both of Woolwich, commissioners to examine claims. [III, 175.] Account filed and distribution ordered 20 Aug., 1788. [III, 176 to 178.] Zebediah Farnham, of Woolwich, mariner, Adm'r *de bonis non*, 6 May, 1805. [IX, 49.] Inventory by Ebenezer Smith, Abner Wade and Josiah Brookins, Jr., all of Woolwich, 1803, $404.61. [X, 85.] Advertisement of sale of real estate 25 May, 1804. [X, 217.] Account filed 9 June, 1805. [X, 218-219.]

Joseph Hutchins, late of Pownalborough. Hollis Hutchins, of a place called Sheepscutt Great pond, Adm'r, 28 June, 1785. [III, 15.] Samuel Emerson and David Plumer, both of Pownalborough, sureties. Inventory by John Plumer, Christopher Erskine and Joseph Wood, all of Pownalborough, 27 Sep., 1785. [IV, 60-61.] Samuel Waters and Christopher Erskine, commissioners to examine claims. [IV, 245-6.] Account filed 26 May, 1791. [IV, 246-7.] Distribution ordered 6 Jan., 1792. [IV, 247.]

William Foster, late of Winthrop. Timothy Foster, of Winthrop, Adm'r, 4 Aug., 1785. [III, 15.] Joseph Rice, of Winthrop, and Daniel Allen, of Wales, sureties. Inventory by Josiah French, Stephen Pullen and Nathaniel Fairbanks, all of Winthrop, 11 Aug., 1785, £654 : 15 : 9. 1. [III, 64.]

Nathaniel Perkins, late of Newcastle, mariner, Eunice Perkins, of Salem in the County of Essex, widow, Adm'x, 2 Sep., 1785. [III, 16.] Hugh Smith and Thomas Sanford, both of Salem, sureties.

James Hutchinson, late of Vassalborough. Benjamin Branch, and Abigail Branch, his wife, of Vassalborough, Adm'rs, 31 May, 1785. [III, 17.] Daniel Townsend and John Ward, both of Vassalborough, sureties. Inventory by Abiel Lovejoy, Mathew Hastings and John Ward, all of Vassalborough, 7 June, 1785, £118 : 6 : 6. [III, 42.]

Jesse Crossman, late of Pownalborough. Sarah Crossman, of Pownalborough, widow, Adm'x, 1 Oct., 1774. [III, 18.] Obadiah Call and Philip Call, both Pownalborough, sureties. Inventory by Obadiah Call, Robert Barker and Philip Call, all of Pownalborough, 8 Oct., 1774, £384 : 15 : 11. [III, 18-19.]

In the Name of GOD Amen. I David Jewett Minister of the Gosple in Winthrop in the county of Lincoln and commonwealth of the Massechutts Being very Sick and weak but of Sound Mind and memory blessed be God therefore—Do this 30th Day of January 1783 and in the 7th year of amaricies Independency; make and publish this my last Will and Testament in manner and Forme following (that is to Say) *Imprimis*, I commend my Soul into the hands of almity God who gave it me. and my Body to the Earth From whence it came in hopes of a Joyfull Resurrection through the Merits of my Saviour Jesus Christ; and as for that worldly Estate wherewith it hath pleased God to Bless me with, I dispose thereof as follows, First I give to my loving wife Phebe Jewett whilst she Remains my widow all my Estate both in Town and out of Town, both Real and Personal Including Mills, Notes of hand, books Accompts and Stock with Ful Liberty to Sel and dispose of them at her own Discretion and her Deeds and Conveyances Shall be Lawfull and authentick and if the above said Phebe Should marry aGain I Give unto the said Phebe one third of all my Estate Both Real and personal at her own Dispose forever; and my Doctring, Funeral Charges and Just Debts to Be paid by my Executrix hereafter named out of the other two thirds that remains.

Item, I Give to my Sons David and John Winthrop Jewett, (they Paying out to the Daughters Fifty Spanish Mil'd Dollars Each when they arive to The age of Eighteen that is to Phebe, Eunice and Sarah) the other Two Thirds after the above Accounts are sittled to be Eqilly Divided betweene the S'd David and John Winthrop Jewett.

Furthermore it is my Will that if the above s'd David or John Winthrop Dies before they arive to lawfull age or Ither of them, then and in that case thir potion Shall be divided amoung the Other children as the Laws of this Commonwealth Divides Intest Estates.

And I make and ordain Phebe Jewett my Said wife Sole Executrix of this my last will and Testament.

In witnes whereof I have hereunto Set my Hand and Seale to this my Last will and Testament the Day and year above written.
Signed, Sealed, published and declared by the s'd
David Jewett as and for his last will and testament
in the presence of us whose names are here under
written who did Each of us Subscribe our names as
witnesses at his request and in his presence in
the rome where he then was
Josiah French, David Jewett (seal)
Benjamin Brainerd,
Jonathan Whiting.

Probated 2 Ap., 1783. [III, 14.] Inventory by Benjamin Brainerd, Jonathan Whiting and Josiah French, 23 Sep., 1783, £648 : 2 : 2. [III, 26.] Account of Phebe Spafford, Executrix, filed 27 July, 1789. [IV, 61-62.]

William Sylvester, late of Bath. Mary Sylvester, of Bath, widow, Adm'x, 25 June, 1781. [III, 37.] John Springer, residing at a place called Frenchman's Bay, and George Andrew, of Bath, sureties. Inventory by Hatherly Foster, Isaiah Crooker and James Owen, 23 Ap., 1783. [III, 38.] Isaiah Crooker and Wensly Hobby, commissioners to examine claims. Account filed 20 Aug., 1785. [III, 39.]

Benjamin Gooch, late of Machias. Benjamin Gooch, of Machias, Adm'r, 22 Sep., 1783. David Longfellow and Jacob Townsley, both of Machias, sureties. Inventory by Amos Boyinton, Joseph Libbey and Daniel Ston, 31 Aug., 1784, £172 : 15 : 0. [III, 40.] William Tupper and Amos Boyinton, commissioners to examine claims. [III, 109.]

Thomas Humphrys, late of Newcastle. Sarah Humphrys, widow, and Joseph Humphrys, both of Newcastle, Adm'rs, 14 Aug., 1780. Christopher Hopkins and Kenelm Winslow, both of Newcastle, sureties. Inventory by James Little, John Dodge and Zachariah Dodge, 19 Aug., 1780, £452 : 18 : 2. [III, 43-44.] Account filed 22 June, 1781. [III, 45.]

Caleb Cressey, late of a place called Ball Town. Meribah Cressey, of Pownalborough, widow, Adm'x, 23 Aug., 1784. [III, 47.] Samuel Emerson and Joseph McFarland, both of Pownalborough, sureties. Inventory by Obadiah Call, Jr., Richard Kidder and Joseph McFarland, Jr., 23 Aug., 1784, £5 : 1 : 0. [III, 48.]

Amos Paris, late of Pownalborough. Margaret Paris, of Pownalborough, widow, Adm'x, 14 June, 1773. [III, 50.] Jonathan Reed, Jr., and Francis Rittal, both of Pownalborough, sureties. Inventory by Jonathan Reed, Jr., Philip Call, Jr., and Francis Rittal, all of Pownalborough, 14 June, 1773, £56 : 15 : 4. [III, 51.]

John Fullerton, late of St. Georges. William McCobb, of Boothbay, Adm'r, 13 Aug., 1785. [III, 53.] John Johnson and George Lilly, both of Pownalborough, sureties. Inventory by Archibald Robinson, Alexander Hathorn and Moses Rivers, all of St. Georges, 24 Aug., 1784, £140. [III, 54.] Account filed 12 Feb., 1789. [IV, 28.]

John McKechnie, late of Winslow. Mary McKechnie, of Winslow, widow, Adm'x, 6 Mar., 1783. [III, 54.] Ezekiel Pattee, of Winslow, and Joseph North, of Hallowell, sureties. Inventory by Ezekiel Pattee, Asa Phillips and Solomon Parker, all of Winslow, 10 July, 1783, £1049 : 11 : 0. [III, 55-56.] Inventory of land in Bowdoinham by Abraham Preble, Zacheus Beal and George Thomas, all of Bowdoinham, 8 Ap., 1784. [III, 57.] Mary McKechnie, widow, appointed guardian unto Alexander, Joseph, and William, minor sons, Lydia, Jane and Mary, minor daughters, 1 Aug., 1784. [III, 64 to 66.] Josiah Hayden and George Warren, both of Winslow, commissioners to examine claims, 30 May, 1793. [VII, 201-2.] Widow's dower set off by Josiah Hayden and George Warren, both of Winslow, and Nehemiah Getchel, of Vassalborough, 1792. [VII, 202-3.] Division of estate by Ezekiel Pattee, Josiah Hayden and Jacob Diman, all of Winslow, 12 Jan., 1795, among Thomas McKechnie, Rebecca, wife of Simon Tozer, Mary, wife of James Stackpole, Jr., John McKechnie, Sarah, wife of Abraham Steward, Jane McKechnie, Lydia McKechnie, Elizabeth, wife of Samuel McFarland, Joseph McKechnie, Alexander McKechnie, William McKechnie, Mary Pattee, and the heirs of Hannah Craig, deceased. [VII, 203 to 205.] Advertisement of sale of real estate, 1794, at which date the administratrix had become the wife of David Pattee. [VII, 205.] Account filed 29 May, 1794. [VII, 206-7.]

William Wyman, late of Winslow. Love Wyman, of Winslow, widow, Adm'x, 10 Mar., 1783. [III, 57.] Benjamin Runels and Ephraim Osburn, both of Winslow, sureties. Inventory by Josiah Brewer, Ephraim Osburn and Benjamin Runels, all of Winslow, Mar., 1783, £87 : 12 : 4. [III, 95.] Josiah Brewer and Zimri Heyard, both of Winslow, commissioners to examine claims. [III, 96.] Account filed 26 Sep., 1785. [III, 97.]

James Mustard, late of West Bowdoinham. John Alexander, of West Bowdoinham, Adm'r, 25 May, 1785. [III, 66.] James Alexander, of West Bowdoinham, and John Small, of Topsham, sureties. Inventory by Benjamin Jaques, Prince Rose and Humphrey Purinton, 11 June, 1785. [III, 107.] Priscilla Alexander, of Bowdoin, widow, Adm'x *de bonis non*, 10 Sep., 1806. [IX, 108.] Account filed 4 Oct., 1808. [XIII, 134-5.]

Timothy Heald, late of Norridgewalk. Elizabeth Heald, widow, and Josiah Heald, both of Norridgewalk, Adm'rs, 22 June, 1786. [III, 67.] Josiah Warren, of Norridgewalk, and John Moore, of Seven Mile Brook, sureties. Inventory by Josiah Warren, Obadiah Witherell and John Moore, 13 Dec., 1786. [IV, 25-26.]

James Henry, late of Topsham. James Henry, of Topsham, Adm'r, 5 Ap., 1786. [III, 68.] James Fulton and Arthur Hunter, both of Topsham, sureties. Inventory by James Fulton, Actor Patten and William Randall, all of Topsham, 26 May, 1788, £368:0:0. [V, 171-2.]

In the Name of God Amen.

I Fredrick Swatz of Waldoborough in the County of Lincoln, yeoman being in good health of Body and of Sound mind and memory, and being forthwith, to depart, A Soilder in the Continental Army, And Considering the uncertainty of this transitory life, do make Publish and Declare, this my last will and Testament, in manner and form following, (to wit.)

First I desire a Decant and Christian Burial, If I should not be killed in an Ingaigement, Then & in that case I commit my Body to the Dust, and my Soul unto Cod who gave it.

Also, I give and bequeath unto my Dear beloved Wife Lucy Swatz all my Estate, which I shall die Seized of, for to bring up my Sons & Dafters to, the Age of Twenty One years, Provided she should so Long remain my Widow, but at the time of her Marrying of A nother Husband I give and bequeath, to all my Sons & Daughters all my Estate, at the time of my Wife's marage to be equally sheard & divided amongst my Children, Viz—Anna Castner, Wife of Ludwig Castner, Peter Swatz, Catharine Swatz, Mary Swatz. Jacob Swatz, Fredrick Swatz, Christehana Swatz, Margrate Swatz, Susannah Swatz, and all other of my children which shall hereafter be born, of the body of my wife, and in case ary a one of my said children should, die, his or her share to be equally, dived amongst the other Brothers & Sisters, in witness whareof I have hereunto set my Hand and Seal this Sixteenth Day of June In the year of our Lord, One Thousand Seven Hundred & Sevinty Seven.

Also I appoint my Wife Lucy Swatz my Executrix.

Signed Sealed published and declared
by the said Testator Fredrick Swatz   Fredrick Swatz   (Seal)
as a_ _ _ _r his last will and Testament
in t_ _ _ _nce of us who in his presence

and at his request have Subscribed our Names
as Witnesses thereto
George Demuth
Waterman Thomas [Unrecorded]

Lucy Swatz, of Waldoborongh, widow, Adm'x, 13 May, 1786. [III, 68.] John Benner and Lawrence Sides, both of Waldoborough, sureties. Inventory by John Benner, Lawrence Sides and Jabesh Cole, all of Waldoborough, 7 July, 1786, £200 : 18 : 8. [V, 165-6.] Account filed, 16 Sep., 1788. [V, 166.]

Mathias Sidenparker, late of Waldoborough. Susanna Sidenparker, of Waldoborough, widow, Adm'x, 30 May, 1786. [III, 69.] John Martin Schaffer and Andrew Schenck, both of Waldoborough, sureties. Mathias and Michael, minor sons, chose Susanna to be their guardian, 15 Sep., 1789. [IV, 63 to 65.] Inventory by John Ulmer, Jabesh Cole and Lawrence Sides, all of Waldoborough, 19 Aug., 1786, £246 : 6 : 2. [V, 167-8.] Account filed, 18 Sep., 1788. [V, 168.]

Joseph Davis, late of Medumcook. Ezra Sumner, of Warren, Adm'r, 29 May, 1786. [III, 70.] Moses Copeland and Reuben Hall, both of Warren, sureties. Inventory by Hatevil Libby, Reuben Hall and Moses Copeland, all of Warren, 24 Jan., 1787, £7 : 11 : 3. [III, 137.] Ezra Sumner guardian unto Mark and Israel, minor sons, and Mary, minor daughter, 29 May, 1786. [III, 159.] Mark, minor son, chose John Demorse, Junr, of Medumcook, to be his guardian, 15 Sep., 1789. [IV, 66.]

John Robinson, late of St. Georges. Sarah Robinson, of St. Georges, widow, Adm'x, 29 May, 1786. [III, 71.] Moses Copeland, of Warren, and Joshua Collamore, of Medumcook, sureties. Inventory by Joshua Collamore and James Thompson, both of Medumcook, and Archibald Robinson, of St. Georges, 8 Sep., 1786, £168 : 3 : 6. [III, 131.]

William Hodge, late of Edgecomb. Mary Hodge, of Edgecomb, widow, Adm'x, 29 May, 1786. [III, 72.] Nathaniel Leeman, of Edgecomb, and Robert Cochran, of Newcastle, sureties. Inventory by Ebenezer Gove and Moses Davis, both of Edgecomb, and Samuel Waters, of Newcastle, 30 June, 1786, £779 : 16 : 9. [III, 111.] Account filed 4 Oct., 1786. [III, 131.] William, minor son, chose Samuel Waters, of Newcastle, to be his guardian, 4 Oct., 1786. [III, 167.] Division of real estate by Moses Davis and Ebenezer Gove, both of Edgecomb, and Samuel Waters, of Newcastle, 19 July, 1788: dower to Mary, widow; remainder to Jane, William, Jennet Osborn, Allis Trask, Sarah Kennedy, Elizabeth Trask, James and Anna Woodbridge, children. John, a son, was "absent, out of this Common Wealth, in Parts beyond Sea." [IV, 103 to 105.]

John Furneld, late of Medumcook. Moses Copeland, of Warren, Adm'r, 29 May, 1786. [III, 73.] Reuben Hall and Ezra Sumner, both of Warren, sureties. Account filed 26 July, 1791. [IV, 258.]

Ebenezer Thompson, late of St. Georges. William Thompson, of Thomaston, Adm'r, 29 May, 1786. [III, 74.] Moses Copeland, of Warren, and James Malcom, of St. Georges, sureties. Inventory by Samuel Crane, of St. Georges, Samuel Counce, and Moses Copeland, both of Warren, 24 Jan., 1787, £28 : 6 : 4. [III, 243-4.] Moses Copeland and Samuel Counce, both of Warren, commissioners to examine claims. [III, 244.] Account filed 26 July, 1791. [IV, 207.] Distribution ordered 27 Dec., 1791. [IV, 208.]

Eliphalet Foster, late of Winthrop. David Foster, of Winthrop, Adm'r, 14 Mar., 1786. [III, 74.] William Lewis, of Pownalborough, and Jonathan How, of a place called Pocasset, sureties. Inventory by Josiah French, Stephen Pullen and Benjamin Fairbanks, all of Winthrop, 27 Mar., 1784, £323 : 17 : 6. [IV, 13.]

John Brown, late of Newcastle. Mary Brown, of Newcastle, widow, Adm'x, 27 June, 1786. [III, 75.] Paul Dodge and Christopher Hopkins, both of Newcastle, sureties. Inventory by John Farley, Paul Dodge and Benjamin Jones, all of Newcastle, 21 Aug., 1786, £127 : 12 : 11. [III, 106.] Benjamin Jones and Jonathan Jones, commissioners to examine claims. [V, 190.] Account filed 30 May, 1793, at which date the administratrix had become the wife of Israel Leavit. [V, 191.] Nathaniel Bryant, of Newcastle, guardian unto Martha, James, and Jane, minor children, 1 Nov., 1794. [VI, 82-83.] Widow's dower set off by John Farley, Benjamin Lincoln and Solomon Dunbar, all of Newcastle, 6 Jan., 1796. [VII, 74.] Guardian's accounts filed 8 Dec., 1795. [VII, 74-75.]

Samuel Patterson, late of Bristol. John Patterson, of Bristol, Adm'r, 13 Ap., 1785. [III, 76.] Amos Goudey and Zebulon Howland, both of Bristol, sureties. Inventory by Henry Hunter, Jonas Fitch and John Trask, all of Bristol, 20 June, 1785. [III, 78.] Account filed 7 Feb., 1787. [III, 126.]

Enoch Averell, late of Balltown. Ruth Averell, of Balltown, widow, Adm'x, 1 Feb., 1786. [III, 83.] Samuel Waters and Benjamin Glidden, both of Newcastle, sureties. Inventory by David Hopkins and Jacob Rowell, both of Balltown, and Samuel Waters, of Newcastle, 12 Ap., 1786, £263 : 7 : 0. [III, 84.] David Hopkins and John Weeks, both of Balltown, commissioners to examine claims, 4 Jan., 1787. [III, 188.] Account filed 17 Mar., 1788. [III, 189.] Distribution ordered 14 Ap., 1788. [III, 190.]

Nathaniel Dole, late of Pownalborough, mariner. Moses Davis, of Edgecomb, Adm'r, 21 June, 1786. [III, 85.] Samuel Goodwin and Nymphas Bodfish, both of Pownalborough, sureties. Ebenezer Whittier and David Silvester, both of Pownalborough, commissioners to examine claims. [IV, 149.] Account filed 13 Sep., 1790. [IV, 150.] Distribution ordered 20 Sep., 1790. [IV, 153.]

John Montgomery, late of Boothbay. Lydia Montgomery, of Boothbay, widow, Adm'x, 13 Aug., 1784. [III, 86.] John Murray and James Auld, both of Boothbay, sureties. Inventory by John Leishman, James Auld and John McCobb, all of Boothbay, 20 Sep., 1785, £331 : 19 : 4. [III, 87.]

Samuel Gragg, late of Waldoborough, mariner. Sarah Gragg, of Waldoborough, widow, Adm'x, 22 May, 1786. [III, 88.] William Farnsworth and Waterman Thomas, both of Waldoborough, sureties. Inventory by Nathaniel Pitcher, Barnabas Simmons and Samuel Sweetland, all of Waldoborough, 30 May, 1786. [III, 90 & 185.] Barnabas Simmons and Nathaniel Pitcher, both of Waldoborough, commissioners to examine claims, 30 May, 1786. [III, 186.] Account filed 1 Feb., 1787. [III, 187.]

In The Name of God Amen The Eightenth Day of November *Anno Domino* one Thousand Seven Hundred and Sixtey Seven, I William Groves New Endland Yomman being Aged and Weack In body but of Sound Disposeing Mind and Memorey Thanks, be given unto God therefore, Calling Unto Mind The Mortality of my body, and Knowing That it is Appinted for all Men once to Dye, Do Mak and Ordaine This my Last will & Tesiament, That is to say Principally, & first of all, I Give & Committ my Soul into The hands of God That Gave it & my body, I Recommend to the Earth to Be Buried In a Deacint & Christian Manner, at The Descretion of my Executor hereafter Named. And as Touching Such Worldly Estate Wherewith it hath Pleased God to bless me in this Life, I Give Demise & Dispose, of The Same in the Followeing Manner and Form

Imprimis. My will is that all my Jusst & Lawfull Debts, & my Funeral Charges be Raised & paid out of my Estate as Soon as may be Conveniently, after my Decease.

Item. I Give & bequeath unto Annarh my well be Loved wife The whole & Sole use & Improvement of all my Estate Both Real & Personall During my Widow & what of Estate that shall be remaining after her Decease my will is that my Son John Groves Shall have all as Above wrighten

Item I Do hereby make & ordain hannh my Wife and sd John Sole Executr. & Adminsr of This my Last my Last will and Testament And I Do hereby Utterly Dissallow Revoke and Disannul all & Every other former wills Leagacies & Bequests by me any ways before named willed & Bequeathed Ratifying and Confirming This & no other to be my Last will and Testament In Wittness Whereof I have Hereunto Sett my hand And Seal The Day and Year above wrighten

Willm. Groves (seal)

Signed Sealed Published
Pronounceed & Declared by
The Sd William Groves
as his Last will & Testament
  Wittness David Silvester
        John Sevey
        Joshua Fowle

Probated 17 Mar., 1785. [III, 90.] Inventory by Ebenezer Whittier, David Silvester and John Sevey, all of Pownalborough, 12 Oct., 1785, £419 : 10 : 0. [Unrecorded.]

In the Name of God Amen. I Gardner Williams of Pittston and in the County of Lincorn Being Very sick and weak in Body, But of perfect Mind and Memory, Thanks be given unto God, Calling unto Mind the Mortality of my Body and knowing That it is Appointed for all Men once to die, do make and Ordain this my Last Will and Testament, That is to say, Principally and first of all, I Give and recommend my Soule into the hand of Almighty God that Gave it, and my Body I Recommend to the Earth, to be Buried in decent Christian Burial, at the Discretion of my Executors; Nothing doubting but at the general Resurrection I shall receive the same again, by the Mighty power of God, and as Touching such Worldly Estate wherewith it has pleased God to Bless me in This Life, I Give devise, and dispose of the same in the following Manner and form :

First, I give and bequeathe to Polley my dearley beloved Wife ; after my debts is paid, the whole of My Estate that I now have, or shall fall to Me hereafter by Heirship Whome I likewise Constitute, Make, and Ordain the Sole Executrix of this my Last Will and Testament and I do hereby utterly disallow, Revock and disannul all and Every other former Testaments, Wills, Legacis, Bequests, and Executors by me in any wais before Named willed and Bequeathed, Ratifying and Confirming this, and no Other, to be my Last will and Testament. In witness whereof I have hereunto set my hand and seale, This twenty second day of April in the yeare of our Lord one thousand seven hundred and Eighty six.

Gardiner Williams (seal)

Signed sealed published pronounced
and declared by the said Gardner
Williams as his Last Will and Testament in his presents
and in the Presents of Each other have hereunto subscribed
our names

   Joseph Hammatt
   Seth Gay
   Isaac Barnard

Probated 24 May, 1786. [III, 93.] Inventory by Henry Dearborn, Jedediah Jewett and William Barker, 7 Feb., 1787, £285 : 10 : 2. [IV, 154-5.] Jedediah Jewett and William Barker, commissioners to examine claims. [IV, 155.] Account filed 10 Sep., 1790. [IV, 156 to 158.] Distribution ordered 18 Oct., 1790. [IV, 158-9.]

John Graffam, late of Bristol. Lydia Graffam, of Bristol, widow, Adm'x, 14 Mar., 1786. [III, 97.] Inventory by Thomas Johnston, Ezekiel Farrow and Moses Starling, all of Bristol, 18 Mar., 1786, £189 : 15 : 10. [III, 99.] Thomas Johnston and John Paine, both of Bristol, commissioners to examine claims. [V, 232.] Account filed 17 Sep., 1793, at which date the administratrix had become the wife of Daniel McCurdy. [IV, 233-4.] Distribution ordered 20 Sep., 1793. [V, 234-5.]

John Kirkpatrick, late of Warren. Ann Kirkpatrick, of Warren, widow, Adm'x, 29 May, 1786. [III, 102.] Moses Copeland and William Killpatrick, both of Warren, and James Malcom, of St. Georges, sureties. Inventory by William Bogs, Joseph Copeland and Archibald Crawford, 6 Jan., 1786, £140 : 2 : 0. [III, 102.] Thomas Starret and Joseph Copeland, both of Warren, commissioners to examine claims. [V, 59.] Account filed and distribution ordered, 18 Sep., 1792. [V, 60 to 62.]

Ebenezer Hovey, late of Hallowell. Daniel Bolton and Benjamin Brown, Jr., both of Hallowell, Adm'rs, 28 Feb., 1785. [III, 112.] Benjamin Brown, of Bath, and Isaac Savage, Jr., of Hallowell, sureties. Inventory by Joseph North, Noah Woodward and Abisha Cowen, 1786, £106 : 6 : 6. [III, 263.] Samuel Colman and James Page, both of Hallowell, commissioners to examine claims. [III, 264.] Account filed 19 Jan., 1796; dividend ordered 9 Sep., 1796. [III, 265-6.] Samuel, minor son, chose Beriah Ingraham, of Hallowell, to be his guardian 16 Jan., 1789; Beriah Ingraham, guardian of Ebenezer, minor son, 16 Jan., 1789. [IV, 25.] Ebenezer, minor son, chose Beriah Ingraham to be his guardian 18 Jan., 1791. [IV, 188.]

Samuel Wing, late of Winthrop. Daniel Wing, of Winthrop, Adm'r, 5 Sep., 1785. [III, 114.] Matthias Smith and Joseph Baker, both of Winthrop, sureties. Inventory by Joshua Bean, Robert Page and Matthias Smith, 8 June, 1786, £220 : 13 : 0. [Unrecorded.]

In the Name of God AMen the fourth Day of April *anno Domini* one thousand Seven Hundred and Eighty six I William Bonny of Winthrop in the County of Lincoln and Common Wealth of Massachusetts Yeoman being Sick and indiposed in Body but of Sound mind and Memory do make and ordain this my Last Will and Testament and First I Give and Recommend my Soul into the hands of God whoe Gave it my Body I Commit to the Dust to be Buried at the Discresion of my Executor heafter named in a Christian decent manner and my worldly goods that God has blessed me with I dispose of in the following manner viz first I will that all my Just Debts and Funeral Charges shall be paid out of my Estate by my Executor in one year after my Deceas and that my wareing apperrill be Sold and applyed to that use as far as it will go.

Imprimmis. I Give and Bequeath unto Lucy Bonny my well beloved Wife the use of my Dwelling House and Land and all my Household goods of every kind, and two Swine So long as She Shall remain my Widow or till my Daughter Silva shall Come of age and at the arrival of my Daughter at age my Widow to have the improvment of one half of my Dwelling house and half the land and half the houshold goods Except a red Chest dureing her Natural Life or Marraige.

Item. I make my Beloved Daughter Silva Bonny my only Child my Legatee and Give and bequeath unto her all my Estate Real and Personal and all and Singuler my goods and Chattles of Ever sort and kind except what I have before disposed of in this Will to be Delivered to her by my Executor when she Comes of age and in Case of the Deceas of her mother or marraig before that time So much of my Estate as is Necesary to be used by my Executor in bringing up and providing for said Silvy Bonny the Residue of my Estate Real and Personal to be the said Silva Bonny's at her own disposing for ever.

Lastly I Constitute and appoint Mr. John Chandler Junr of Winthrop in the County of Lincoln & Common Wealth of Massachusetts Yeoman Sole Executor of this my Last Will and testament and hearby Ratifying and Confirming this and no other to be my last will and Testament made and pronounced the Day and Year first above written in Testimony whereof I have hearunto Sett my hand and Seal

atest

 Isaac Bonney   William Bonney   [seal]
 Simeon Boney
 Ichabod Howe

Probated 9 Sep., 1786. [III, 119.] Inventory by Ichabod How, Gideon Lambard and William Pullen, all of Winthrop, 2 Oct., 1786, £124 : 14 : 9. [III, 195.]

In the Name of God Aman I Jonathan Oaks of Canaan in the County of Lincoln: Being through the Abundant Goodness of God, tho; Week in Body, Yet of a sound and perfect understanding and Memory, do Constitute this My Last Will and testament, and Desire it may be Received by All as Such: first I most humbly Bequeath My Soul to God My Maker, beseeching his Most Gracious Acceptance of it, through the All-sufficient Merits and Mediation of my most Compassionate Redeemor Jesus Christ, Who Gave himself to Be an Atonement for My Sins. And is Able to Save to the Uttermost all that Come Unto God by him, Seeing he ever Liveth to Make Intercession for them, and who, I trust, will not reject Me, a returning penitent Sinner, when I Come to him for Mercy in this hope and Confidence I render up My Soul With Comfort, humbly beseeching the most Blessed and Glorious Trinity, one God, Most holy, Most Mercifull and Gracious to prepair Me for the time of my Dissolution, and then to take me to himself into that peace and Rest, which he has prepared for them, that Love and fear his holy Name. Amen. Blessed be God. I Give my Body to the Earth, from whence it was taken in full Assurance of its Resurrection from thence at the Last Day, as for my Burial I desire it May Be decent, at the Discretion of my Dear Wife and my Executors hearafter Named, who, I doubt not will Manage it with prudence as to my Worldly Estate I will and positively order that all my Debts be paid first I Give to my Dear and Loving Wife, I will and order that She have a Cumfortable Maintainance in Sickness and helth So long as She remains My Widdow togeather with all my household Moveables So Long as She Remains with her Children; And unto My Eldest Daughter Mary I Give five Shilling. She haveing had her part & more out of My Estate Before: and to my Daughter Lydda I Give five Shillings, She haveing had her full part out of my Estate Before: and to My Daughter Elizabeth I Give five Shillings, She haveing had her part out of my Estate Before And to my Daughter Sarah I Give five Shillings out of my Estate: And to my Eldest Son Jonathan Oaks I Give ten Shillings to Be paid him out of My Estate if he Ever Comes to this place again And to My Daughter Rebeckah, I Give five Shillings She having had her part out of my Estate Before: And to My Son John Oaks I Give five Shillings he haveing had his part out of my Estate Before And to my Son Daniel Oaks I Give five Shillings to be paid him out of My Estate: And to my daughter Lois I Give five Shillings She haveing had her part out of My Estate before And to my Two Beloved Sons Levi Oaks & Solomon Oaks I Give and bequeath to to them Jointly & Severly My home Lot on which I Live togeather with all My Improvements adjoining togeather with My Island which Lyeth a Little to the South of my Lot, with all the Improvements and Appertinances there to Belonging with all My Moveable stock and farming touls and Carpenders tools to them there Heirs and Assigns forever: And I do positively order that they pay my funarel Charges, and pay All My Just Debts, and provide their Mother a Comfortable Maintainance in Sickness & helth So Long as She Remains My Widdow and if She Remains so through Life, a Decent Buriel after Death, and pay the Several Legises to their Brothers & Sisters Before above mentioned And to their three Youngest Sisters Mille, Sibbel & Lucy four pounds Each Mille to have her Dowrey at Ninteen years of Age & Sibbel & Lucy to have their Shear at Eighteen Years of Age, And to their two Youngest Brothers I positively order that they Be att the

Cost of procuring a title to the Lot of Land I had of Daniel Lamberd, from the proprietors for them it being the third Lot from Wesserunsett up the main River   And Likewise that they Give teen Bushels of Corn yearly each from the time they are Eightteen Years of Age two years I Likewise order that they Live with their Brothers, to wit: Abel with Levi and William with Solomon untill they are Eightteen Years of Age and that they provid for them decently in Victuls and Cloths and Larn to read wright and Cypher and give them a freedom Suite   I Likewise order that my two Sons Levi & Solomon Colect All Debts Due to my Estate   And to my three Youngest Daughters Mille Sibbel & Lucy I Give four pounds Each as I have ordered them paid by their Brothers Above.   And to my two youngest Son Abel and William I give Jointly & Severally My right and title which I purchased of Daniel Lamberd to a Lot of Land it being the third Lot from Wesserumseet together with what I have above order'd paid to and procured for them, by their two Brothers: Levi & Solomon

finally I do Constitute My Son Solomon Oaks togeather with Solomon Clark Executors of this My Last will and testament, and trustees to see this my Last will performed agreeable to my Mind as I have above Expresed, in Witness whareof I have hearunto Set my hand and Seal the Second Day of December in the year of our Lord one thousand seven Hundred & Eighty four

Witnesses   Jonathan Oaks   (seal)   hear I take
                                                                                              of my Seal and
Peter Heywood   do Declear this
Peter Heywood Jr   to be my Last Will
John Fowler   and testement

Probated 12 Mar., 1785. [III, 121-2.] Inventory by Peter Heywood, James Turner and Joseph Weston, all residing at Howardston, 15 Mar., 1785, £219 : 11 : 10. [III, 235.] Peter Heywood and Joseph Weston, both of Howardston, commissioners to examine claims. [III, 235.]

In the name of God amen.

I Simeon Bonny of Winthrop in the County Lincoln and Common Wealh of Massachusetts Bay yeoman being in a weak and low Estate of Body but of Sound mind and memory make and ordain my Last Will and Testament first I bequeath my Spirit to God in and through a Redeemer my Body to the Dust in Sure and Certain hope &c.

My worldly Goods and Estate I dispose of in the following manner viz Firstly I will that all my Just Debts and Funeral Charges shall be Paid by my Executors hearafter named out of my Estate.

Imprimis I Give and bequeath unto my Beloved wife Thankful Bonny all my within Doors moveables at her Disposal for ever and two Cows

Item   I Give and bequeath unto my Son William Bonny and my Son Simeon Bonny one Hundred acres of Land Situate in Winthrop aforesaid viz one half of the Lot No. 47 the Easterly end of Said lot and one Hundred and twenty five acres of Land in Silvester being the Lot No. 10

Item   my Son James Bonny, I Give and bequeath my Gun

Item   I Give and bequeath to my Son Isaac Bonny a Syth and an ox

Item   I Give and bequeath to my Son Joseph Bonny two Bushels of Indian Corn.

Item   I Give and bequeath to my Son Daniel Forty Bushels of Indian Corn when he arives at twenty one years of age.

Item   I Give and bequeath unto my Sons Bariah Bonny Solomon Bony Andrew Bonny, and my Daughters Rebecca Bonny Deborah Bonny and Silva Bonny one Silver Dollar each to be paid them when they Come of age.

Item   I Give and bequeath to my Son Simeon Bonny all my Farming Tools not before mentioned

Lastly I Constitute and appoint my Sons William Bonny and Simeon Bonny the Executors of this my last Will and Testament and Legatees of all my Estate and goods of every kind not before mentioned

I testimony wherof I hearof I have hearunto Set my hand and Seal this 18 day of September A D 1781

Moses Chandler   Simeon Bonny' (seal)
Jacob Chandler
Ichabod Howe

[Howe sworn 9 Sep., 1786; unrecorded.]

George Light, Jr., late of Waldoborough. Jacob Ludwig, of Waldoborough, Adm'r, 3 Oct., 1786. [III, 124.] Joseph Ludwig and Godfry Bornheimer, both of Waldoborough, sureties. Inventory by Joseph Ludwig, George Dolheim and Charles Kaler, all of Waldoborough, 26 Oct., 1786, £39 : 11 : 0. [III, 139.] Thomas McGuire and Joseph Ludwig, both of Waldoborough, commissioners to examine claims. [III, 152.] Account filed 17 Sep., 1788. [III, 154.] Distribution ordered 24 Nov., 1788. [III, 156.] Account filed, 22

Nov., 1790. [IV, 186.]

Peter Hilt, late of Waldoborough. Mary Hilt, of Waldoborough, widow, Adm'x, 13 Sep., 1786. [III, 125.] George Clowes and George Heibner, both of Waldoborough, sureties. Inventory by Jacob Ludwig, Peter Gross and Daniel Feiltren, all of Waldoborough, 14 Sep., 1786, £31 : 18 : 4. [III, 138.] Jacob Ludwig, of Waldoborough, and Nathan Jewett, of a place called Walpole, commissioners to examine claims. [III, 157.] Account filed 17 Sep., 1788. [III, 158.]

Sarah Williamson, of Pownalborough, widow, guardian unto Ruth, Abigail, Lucy, Anna and Hannah, minor daughters of Thomas Williamson, late of Pownalborough, deceased, 3 Feb., 1787. [III, 143.]

Hannah Boyinton, of Pownalborough, guardian unto John, Joshua, Daniel, Caleb and Joseph, minor sons, and Hannah, Susanna and Sarah, minor daughters of John Boyinton, late of Pownalborough, deceased, 3 Feb., 1787. [III, 143.]

In the Name of God, Amen.

I Zebulun Baker, of Pownalborough, in the County of Lincoln and State of the Massachusetts-Bay, in New-England, Mariner, being of sound disposing Mind & Memory, and also, in good Health of Body; but mind ful of my Frailty and Mortality, do make & publish this my Last Will & Testament, in manner and Form following, Viz :
In the first Place, I commend my Soul to the mercy of God, my Savior Whenever It shall be separated from my Body, which I commit to the Earth or Sea, as shall seem best to a Wise & Good Providence to dispose of the same; And as for such worldly Estate It hath pleased God to bestow upon Me, I give to each of my beloved Children, five pounds thereof, Viz : to my Son Thomas Baker five pounds & no more, to my Son Zebulun Baker, five pounds & no more, and to my Son George Baker, five pounds & no more : All the rest of my Estate I give to my good & well-beloved Wife, Susanna Baker, Viz : All such Wages, Debts, and Sums of Money, as are now or may hereafter be due or owing to me by or from any person or persons whatsoever, together with all such Share or Shares of prizes or prize-money that I may have a legal claim to; and also all my Goods & Chattels, and whatever Estate I may die possessed of, or be any Ways interested in, (as well Real Estate as Personal Estate,) at the Time of my Decease, whereever such Estate may be found, or I may have a Title to in Re-

version, I hereby freely give and bequeath, all & every part of the same to my said Wife Susanna and to her Heirs and assigns, to and for Her & Their sole Use & Benefit for Ever; And I do constitute & appoint Her, the said Susanna Baker my beloved Wife, Sole Executrix of this my last Will & Testament; hereby absolutely revoking any Will or Wills, heretofore by me made.

In Witness whereof, I the said Zebulun Baker, have hereunto, as to my Last Will and Testament, set my Hand & Seal this eighteenth Day of August In the Year of OUR LORD, One Thousand, Seven Hundred & Seventy Eight.

Signed, Sealed, Published and   Zebulon Baker   (seal)
Declared, by the said Testator,
as & for his Last Will & Testament,
in Presence of Us, who in his Presence,
and at his request, signed our Names, as
Witnesses to the Same.
    James Hughes
    Joseph Billings
    Tho's Russell

                            Probated 4 Oct., 1786.   [III, 143.]

    In the Name of God, Amen.

The twelfth day of May 1787, I Jonathan Spafford of Pownalborough in the County of Lincoln and in the State of Massachusetts farmer, being very sick and Weak in Body but of perfect mind and memory, thanks be given to God. Therefore calling to mind the Mortality of my Body and knowing that it is appointed for all men once to die, do make and ordain this my last Will and Testament, that is to say, principally and first of all I give and recommend my Soul into the hands of God that gave it; and my Body I recommend to the Earth to be buried in decent christian Burial at the Discretion of my Executors, nothing doubting but at the general Resurrection, I shall receive the same again, by the mighty power of God— And as touching such worldly estate wherewith it hath pleased God to bless me in this Life, I give, demise, and dispose of the same in the following manner and form—first my funeral Charges be paid and my lawful Debts.

Imprimis. I give and bequeath to my Daughter Martha Rogers one half of my houshold Goods, except my bed for the Use of the young Children, and the remainder part of my houshell Goods I give to my Daughter Mary.

    Item. I give to my Son Jacob five pounds lawful money to be

raised and levied out of my personal Estate and to be paid when he comes to lawful Age for himself.

I give to my Son William five Pounds when he comes of lawful Age, it is to be raised & levied out of my personal Estate.

I give to my Son Robert five pounds when he comes of lawful Age; it is to be raised and levied out of my personal Estate.

I give unto my Son John five pounds when he comes of lawful Age, it is to be raised & levied out of my personal Estate.

I give unto my Son Samuel five pounds when he comes of lawful Age; it is to be raised and levied out of my personal Estate.

I give to my Son James five pounds when he comes of lawful Age, it to be raised & levied out of my personal Estate; all which Sum to be paid to each of my heirs when they come of Age, to be prised and raised and levied out of my personal Estate by my Executors. Also my farming tools to be kept on the farm, and that my farm be improved together with all my real Estate for the support of my heirs till they come of lawful Age to take Care of themselves, and when the youngest heir comes of age then the real Estate to be prised, together with all the Remains of my personal Estate, and to be equally divided between the whole named heirs—that Martha and Mary be paid in Cash their proportion

I likewise constitute make and ordain Major John Huse and Rogers Smith my sole Executrix of this my last Will and Testament, all by them freely to be possessed and improved for the support of my heirs till they come of Age. And I do hereby utterly disallow, revoke & disanul all and every other former Testaments Wills Legacies and Bequests & Executors by me in any way before named, willed and bequeathed, ratifying and confirming this and no other to be my last Will & Testament.

In Witness whereof I have hereunto set my hand and seal this day and year above written.

                                        Jon Spafford   (seal)

Signed sealed, published, pronounced and declared by the said Jonathan Spafford his last Will and Testament in the presence of us the subscribers

    William Decker
    William Clark
        her
    Sary 1 1 1 1 Clark
        Mark

Probated 3 July, 1787. [III, 145-6.] Inventory by Ebenezer Whittier, Daniel Scott and Nymphas Stacy, all of Pownalborough, 1787, £506 : 12 : 0. [III, 246.] Account filed 8 Aug., 1803. [X, 70-1.] Advertisement of sale of real estate 17 Feb., 1806. [XI, 191-2.] Account filed 4 Oct., 1809. [XIII, 520.]

In the Name of God, Amen.
I Samuel Ford of Woolwich in the County of Lincoln and Common Wealth of Massachusetts; Gentleman, being weak & infirm in body, but of a Sound and disposing mind & memory for which I desire to bless God and considering the shortness and uncertainty of Life, and that it is appointed for all Men once to die, do make & ordain this my last Will and Testament in manner following, First I give and bequeath my Soul into the hands of Almighty God who gave it, and my body to the Earth to be buried with a decent Christian burial (at the discretion of my Executrix) in hopes of a joyfull Resurrection, through the merits & mediation of my Saviour Jesus-Christ. And as to that Worldly Estate with which it has pleased God to bless me. I give and bequeath in manner following.
Imprimis. I give and bequeath unto my Nephew John Perkins a lott of Land Containing about eighty eight acres more or less lying in Woolwich and is lott No. 18 in the second division of lotts in said Woolwich, to him & his heirs forever.
Item I give & bequeath unto my Neice Hannah Blair the wife of John Blair the one half of a lott of Land being Lott No. 48 in the second division of Lotts in s'd Woolwich, to her & her heirs forever.
Item. All the rest and residue of my Estate both Real and personal of every kind (after the discharge of my just debts) I give and bequeath unto my beloved Wife Mary Ford to her and her heirs forever. And I do appoint and ordain my beloved Wife Mary Ford, Sole Executrix of this my last Will & Testament. In Testimony whereof I have hereunto set my hand & seal this twenty second day of January *Anno Domini* 1782, and in the sixth year of American Independence.

NB. the word "with" on the other side & the words "rest and" above were interlin'd before signing.
Signed, sealed, published & declar'd
by the Testator as & for his last Will
& Testament, in presence of us, who   Samll. Ford (seal)
at his request, in his presence,
and in presence of each other

have Subscribed our Names
as Witnesses thereto.
  Nathl. Thwing
  John Hathorn
  Robert Cushman

Probated 5 Sep., 1787. [III, 147.]
Inventory by David Gilmore, Samuel Stinson and Seth Hathorn, all of Woolwich, 28 Sep., 1787, £897 : 11 : 8. [IV, 23-24.]

I James Howard of Hallowell in the County of Lincoln, and Commonwealth of Massachusetts, being now in Health of Body and of a sound Mind, and calling to Mind the Certainty of Death and the Uncertainty of the Time thereof, do make this my last Will and Testament that is to say, first and principally I commend my Soul into the Hands of God who gave it, and my Body to the Earth to be decently interr'd at the Discretion of my Executors hereafter named. And as to such Worldly Estate as it hath pleased God to bestow upon me in this Life, I give, devise and dispose of the same in the following Manner and form—that is to say,

Imprimis I will and order that all my just Debts & funeral Expences be paid out of my Estate as soon as conveniently may be after my Decease.

Item I give unto my beloved Wife Susanna two hundred & fifty Pounds to be paid her out of my Estate. I also give unto my said Wife one third part of all my household funiture of every sort & kind, to dispose of as she thinks proper; I also give to her my said Wife the Use and Improvement of one third part of all my real Estate during the Term of her natural Life.

Item I give unto my Son John Howard the sum of Twenty shillings, to be paid him, or to his Guardian, by my Executors out of my Estate immediately after my Decease.

Item I give unto my Son Samuel Howard, the sum of twenty shillings to be paid him by My Executors out of my Estate immediately after my Decease.

Item I give unto my Son William Howard the sum of Twenty shillings to be paid him by my Executors out of my Estate immediately after my Decease.

Item I give unto my Daughter Margaret Patterson the sum of twenty shillings, to be paid her out of my Estate by my Executors immediately after my Decease.

Item All the rest and Residue of my Estate real, personal & mixed wheresoever the same is or may be found, I give & devise unto my two Children Isabella and James, (the Children which I had by my present Wife Susanna) to be equally divided between them, and to hold to them and their respective heirs for ever— And in Case that either of my said two last mentioned Children shall die without Issue then my Will is that the share of such deceased Child shall be and accrue to the survivor of the said two Children and his Or her heirs for ever— And in Case both the said last mentioned Children should die without Issue then it is my Will that the whole Estate real & personal given & devised to the said Isabella & James shall accrue to and be equally divided among all my Grand Children, to wit, the Children of my Son Samuel, William, & Margaret; to hold unto my said Grand Children & their heirs for ever.

Lastly I do hereby appoint my said Wife and my Son William Howard Executors of this my last Will and Testament and I do hereby revoke all other & former Wills by me heretofore made, and declare this & no other to be my last Will and Testament.

In Testimony whereof I the said James Howard do hereunto set my hand and seal this thirteenth Day of January in the Year of our Lord one thousand seven hundred & Eighty six.

Signed Sealed and declared by the Testator to be his last Will and Testament in presence of us—

Mem'o The words *"real & personal* given & were interlined before sealing &c

I James Howard declair this (seal) Instrument to be my last will and testment

H : Sewall
Elisha Bisbe
William Howard Junr

Probated 14 Jan., 1788. [III, 148-149.] William Brooks of Hallowell, guardian of James, minor son, 9 Mar., 1789. [IV, 36.] Inventory by Nathaniel Thwing, of Woolwich, Joseph North and Benjamin Pettingill, both of Hallowell, 5 Nov., 1788, £3785 : 12 : 8. [IV, 72 to 75.] Account filed 16 Aug., 1804. [X, 296 to 300.]

In the Name of God amen this Instrument made the third day of April AD one thousand seven hundred & eighty seven, I Solomon Page of Bath in the County of Lincoln & in the Commonwealth of Massachusetts, being of sound Mind & good memory (blessed be God for it) calling to mind the Mortallity of my Body & knowing that it appointed unto all Men once to die Do make & ordain this my last will & Testament that is to say principly & first of all I give & commend my Soul into the hands of Him who gave it and my Body I recommend to the dust out of which it was formed not doubting but at the general resurrection I shall be raised the same again by the mighty power of God. and as touching my worly Estate of what nature or kind soever, after my Just Debts & funiral Charges are paid, I do hereby give & bequeath in the following manner Viz—

Imprimis I give & bequeath to my true & beloved Wife Judith the free use & improvement of one half of my Farm I now live on in the Town of Bath aforesaid so long as she remains my Widow, & the improvement of one half of my dwelling House & Barn also one third part of the live stock & all the houseel stuff in my house that belongs to me & all my Books & all my Notes against one Abner Clough—and one half of what Mr. Ephraim Fitts owes me—

Item I give & bequeath to the lawfull heirs of of my son Nathan Page deceast thirteen pounds six shillings & eight pence to be paid in five Years after the decease of myself & my aforesaid Wife to be paid by my Executor in such articels as he, my Execu't & said heirs shall agree on—

Item I give & bequeath to the Children of my Daughter Ruth deceast thirteen pounds six shillings & eight pence to be paid in five years af- the decease of myself & my aforesaid Wife, by my Executor in such articels as he, my said Execu't & said Children shall agree on—

Item I give & bequeath to my son Simon Page thirteen pounds six shillings & eight pence to be paid in one year after the decease of myself & my Wife aforesaid by my Executor in such articels as he, my Execu't & said Simon shall agree on—

Item—I give & bequeath to my son Dudly Page five shillings—

Item—I give & bequeath to my Daugter Owen six pounds to be paid in one year after the decease of myself & my aforesaid Wife—

Item—I give & bequeath to my son Edward Hall Page one half of the Farm I now live on in Bath aforesaid, one half of my dwelling House & Barn & the other half of said Farm, house & Barn at my aforesaid Wifes decease with two thirds of the live stock upon it at my decease also I give to said Hall half the Money which Mr. Ephraim Fitts owes me also all my husbandry tools & utensials, also all my wearing Cloaths—

Item I give & bequeath to my Daughter Dorcas Shurtlef six pounds to be paid in one year after my decease—

I Do appoint my Wife Judith & my son Edward Hall Page to be the Executors of this my last Will & Testament & my son Edward Hall Page to pay all the above mentioned Legacies—

And I give & bequeath all my Estate Real & Personal that is not before bequeath & mentioned to my said Executors—

In witness whereof I have hereunto set my hand & seal the third day of April AD one thousand seven hundred & eighty seven—

Signed Sealed & Declared by the Testator to be his last Will & Testament in Presents of us who subscribed the same in presents of the said Testator—
    Solomon Page   (seal)

  Ephraim Fitts
  Moses Brown
  Dumr. Sewall

Probated 25 Ap., 1788. [III, 150-151.] Inventory by Dummer Sewall, John Berry and Joseph White, all of Bath, 21 May, 1788, £422 : 17 : 8. [V, 169.]

William Wescutt, late of Majabaggaduce. Elizabeth Wescutt, of Majabaggaduce, widow, Adm'x, 13 Sep., 1786 ; Jonathan Lowder, of Penobscot River, and William Thompson, of Thomaston, sureties. [III, 159.] Inventory by Joseph Perkins, William Webber and Jonathan Lowder, all of Penobscott, 1 Nov., 1786, £133 : 11 : 0, and £151 : 11 : 0. [V, 64.] Oliver Parker and Joseph Perkins, commissioners to examine claims. [V, 65.] Account filed and distribution ordered, 18 Sep., 1792. [V, 67 to 69.] Widow's dower set off by Jacob Sherburne, David Moore and Joseph Hibbert, all of Penobscot, 19 Sep., 1791. [V, 84.] Account filed and distribution ordered, 30 May, 1793. [V, 143-4.]

William Wilson, late of Topsham. Gideon Owen, of Topsham, Adm'r, 4 Dec., 2786 ; Nicholas Gaubert, of Bowdoinham, and Nymphas Bodfish, of Pownalborough, sureties. [III, 160.] Account filed 1 Sep., 1789. [IV, 57.] Philip Hoyt and John Fulton, commissioners to examine claims. [IV, 57.] Distribution ordered 29 Sep., 1789. [IV, 58.] Inventory by William Randall, John Rogers and Philip Hoyt, all of Topsham, 6 Nov., 1787. [V, 173.]

Jerusha Taylor, late of Newcastle, widow. Joseph Taylor, of Newcastle, Adm'r, 15 Feb., 1787 ; Nathaniel Bryant and Ephraim Taylor, both of Newcastle, sureties. [III, 160.]

Abner Shepard, late of Hallowell. Jonathan Clark, of Winthrop, Adm'r, 7 Mar., 1787; Josiah Mitchell and Daniel Wyman, both of Winthrop, sureties. [III, 160.] Inventory by Samuel Grant and Nehemiah Getchel, both of Vassalborough, and Enoch Page, of Hallowell, 20 Ap., 1787, £76: 2: 6. [V, 11-12.] Robert Page and William Whittier, both of Winthrop, commissioners to examine claims. [V, 12.] Account filed 17 Jan., 1792. [V, 13.] Distribution ordered 31 May, 1792. [V, 14.]

William Gardiner, late of Pittston. John Gardiner, of Pownalbo-ough, Adm'r, 16 June, 1787; John Silvester John Gardiner and James Tupper, both of Pownalborough, sureties. [III, 160.] Inventory by Edmund Bridge, Richard Kidder and Nymphas Bodfish, 17 June, 1788, £37: 19: 3. [IV, 114.] Schedule of notes of hand filed by administrator. [IV, 115 to 117.] William Gardiner, of Pownalborough, Adm'r *de bonis non*, 1 May, 1794. [VI, 69.] Account filed 9 Sep., 1806. [XII, 44.]

Phineas Nevers, late of Penobscot River. John Nevers, of Penobscot River, Adm'r, 20 June, 1787; Jonathan Preble and Ebenezer Preble, both of Woolwich, sureties. [III, 160.] Inventory by John Brewer, Jonathan Eddy and John Crosby, all of Penobscot River, 12 July, 1787, £169: 5: 0. [III, 249.] Jonathan Lowder and James Ginn, both of Penobscot River, commissioners to examine claims. [III, 250.]

Obadiah Call, late of Pownalborough. Experience Call, of Pownalborough, widow, Adm'x, 22 June, 1787; Edmund Bridge and Caleb Barker, both of Pownalborough, sureties. [III, 160.] Inventory by William Lewis, Asa Dinsmore and Richard Kidder, all of Pownalborough, 29 June, 1787. [III, 247 to 249.]

Silas Hathorne, late of Penobscot River. Silas Hathorne, of Penobscot River, Adm'r, 5 July, 1787; Archibald McPhetress and Elisha Grant, both of Penobscot River, sureties. [III, 161.]

Ebenezer Coombes, late of Topsham. Abagail Coombes, of Topsham, widow, Adm'x, 5 Sep., 1787; Samuel Wilson, of a place called little River and James Crawford, of Brunswick, sureties. [III, 161.] Inventory by Samuel Thompson, Philip Hoyt and Gideon Owen, all of Topsham, 11 Sep., 1787. [III, 191.] Philip Hoyt and Gideon Owen, both of Topsham, commissioners to examine claims, 12 Nov., 1787. [III, 192.] Account filed 26 May, 1788. [III, 192.]

Samuel Demorse, late of Long Island in Penobscot Bay. John Demorse, of Medumcook, Adm'r, 13 Sep., 1787; Thomas Henderson, of St. Georges, and Samuel Sweetland, of Waldoborough, sureties. [III, 162.]

Philip Call, late of Pownalborough. Deliverance Call, of Pownalborough, widow, Adm'x, 24 Sep., 1787; Edmund Bridge and William Patterson, both of Pownalborough, sureties. [III, 162.] Inventory by Richard Kidder, Samuel Emerson and George Lilly, all of Pownalborough, 4 Sep., 1787, £340 : 16 : 0. [III, 251.] Deliverance Call, guardian unto John, William and Philip, minor sons, Deliverance and Bethiah, minor daughters, 19 Mar., 1789. [IV, 30-31-39.] Account filed 19 Mar., 1789. [IV, 31.] Obadiah, minor son, chose William Lewis to be his guardian, 19 Mar., 1789. Margaret, minor daughter, chose William Lewis to be her guardian, 20 Mar., 1789. [IV, 31-32.] Division of real estate by Jonathan Reed, James Goud and Louis Houdlette, all of Pownalborough, 7 Mar., 1789 : dower to Deliverance, widow; remainder to Philip and Charles, two of the sons, by consent of other heirs, James, Olive Allen, Elizabeth Patterson, Hannah, Lydia. Order of distribution, 2 Ap., 1789. [IV, 109 to 113.]

Nathaniel Jellison, late of Bowdoinham. Hannah Jellison, of Bowdoinham, widow, Adm'x, 4 Oct., 1787; Elisha Pratt and Abraham Malcom, both of Bowdoinham, sureties. [III, 162.]

John Askins, late of Bristol, mariner. Mary Askins, of Bristol, widow, Adm'x, 23 Oct., 1787; Jonas Fitch and Daniel Herren, both of Bristol, sureties. [III, 162.]

Lot Curtis, late of Deer Island. Nathan Johnson, of Deer Island, Adm'r, 26 Oct., 1787; Benjamin Rea and Cornelius Bramhall, both of Deer Island, sureties. [III, 162.] Inventory by Ignatius Haskell, John Hooper and Ezekiel Morey, 10 Nov., 1787, £29 : 14 : 3. [III, 252.] Proceedings discontinued 22 Nov., 1787. [III, 252.]

Daniel Fairfield, Jr., late of Vassalborough. Elizabeth Fairfield, widow, and Samuel Grant, both of Vassalborough, Adm'rs, 24 Dec., 1787; Nehemiah Gatchel and Charles Jackson, both of Vassalborough, sureties. [III, 162.] Inventory by Remington Hobby, Flint Barton and Asa Redington, all of Vassalborough, 22 Ap., 1788, £198 : 12 : 6. [IV, 27.] Widow's dower set off by Dennis Getchell, Flint Barton and Asa Reddington, all of Vassalborough, 13 Aug., 1790. [IV, 268.]

Ezra King, late of Pownalborough, shipwright. Prudence King, of Pownalborough, widow, Adm'x, 29 Dec., 1787; Obadiah Call and Joseph McFarland, both of Pownalborough, sureties. [III, 163.] Inventory by Richard Kidder, William Patterson and Joseph McFarland, 3 Jan., 1788, £13 : 14 : 10. [III, 257.] Account filed 24 Mar., 1788, [III, 258.]

Timothy Kimball, late of Bristol, mariner. Eleanor Kimball, of Bristol, widow, Adm'x, 16 Jan. 1788; Arunah Weston and Thomas Arnold, both of Bristol, sureties. [III, 163.] Inventory by Thomas Johnston, William Burns and Joseph Burns, all of Bristol, 21 Jan., 1788, £33 : 10 : 2. [IV, 203.] Moses Copeland, of Warren, and William Burns, of Bristol, commissioners to examine claims. Account filed by Samuel Bartlet and Eleanor Bartlet, Adm'rs, 26 July, 1791. [IV, 204-5.] Distribution ordered 27 Dec., 1791. [IV, 205.]

David Averell, late of Pownalborough. Joseph Hilton, of Pownalborough, Adm'r, 24 Jan., 1788; George Erskin and Stuart Hunt, both of Pownalborough, sureties. [III, 163.] Daniel, minor son, chose William Averell to be his guardian 18 Aug., 1788. [III, 165.] Simeon, minor son, chose John Averell to be his guardian 18 Aug., 1788. [III, 166.] Account filed 10 Sep., 1890. [IV, 177.]

John Chase, late of Newcastle. Rachel Chase, of Newcastle, widow, Adm'x, 18 Mar., 1788; Charles Chase and Briggs Turner, both of Newcastle, sureties. [III, 163.] Inventory by Briggs Turner, Benjamin Woodbridge, Jun'r, and Samuel Waters, all of Newcastle, 4 Ap., 1788, £22 : 1 : 8. [IV, 162.] Benjamin Woodbridge, Jun'r, and Thomas Kennedy, both of Newcastle, commissioners to examine claims. [IV, 162.] Account filed 13 Sep., 1790. [IV, 163-4.]

Michael Clary, late of Bristol. John Costelow, of Pownalborough, Adm'r, 27 Mar., 1788; William Lewis and John McGown, both of Pownalborough, sureties. [III, 163.] Account filed 5 June, 1797. [VII, 218-219.] Advertisement of sale of real estate, 10 Aug., 1797. [VII, 246-427.]

Adam Cogswell, late of Township No. four, mariner. David Carlton, of Township No. four, Adm'r, 15 Ap., 1788; Theophilus Eaton, of Deer Island, and Benjamin Friend, of Township No. four, sureties. [III, 164.] Inventory by Jonathan Lowder, of Penobscot, Ebenezer Herrick and Benjamin Friend, both of Township No. four, 7 May, 1788, £242 : 7 : 2. [V, 163.] Enoch Blasdel, of Township No. four, and Joseph Wood, of Township No. five, commissioners to examine claims. [V, 164.]

George Couch, late of Pownalborough. Anna Couch, of Pownalborough, widow, Adm'x, 24 May, 1788; Jonathan Reed and Nathaniel Hathorne, both of Pownalborough, sureties. [III, 164.] Inventory by Lemuel Trott, Jacob Eames and Seth Hathorn, all of Woolwich, 14 June, 1788, £51 : 11 : 2. [VII, 224-5.] Lazarus Goodwin and Samuel Woodward, both of Pownalborough, commissioners to examine claims. [VII, 225.] Widow's dower set off by Lemuel Trott and Jacob Eames, both of Woolwich, and James Atkins, of Pownalborough, 31 May, 1793. [VII, 226.]

John Laiten, late of Norridgewalk. Jean Laughton, of Norridgewalk, widow, Adm'x, 2 June, 1788; Eleazer Spaulding and Amos Adams, both of Norridgewalk, sureties. [III, 164.] Inventory by James Waugh, John Moore and William Spaulding, all of Norridgewalk, 1788, £248 : 11 : 8. [IV, 262-3.] Widow's dower set off by Eleazer Spaulding, Obadiah Witherell and John Clark, all of Norridgewalk, 27 Ap., 1789. [IV, 264.] John Clark and Josiah Spaulding, both of Norridgewalk, commissioners to examine claims. [IV, 265.] Account filed 9 Sep., 1791. [IV, 265-6.]

Hezekiah Colby, late of Deer Island. Joshua Colby, of New Rowley in the County of Essex, Adm'r, 17 July, 1788; Charles Walker and William Arnold, both of Pownalborough, sureties. [III, 164.]

Hatherly Foster, late of Bath. Mary Foster, of Bath, widow, Adm'x, 28 July, 1788; Dummer Sewall and Edward Hall Page both of Bath, sureties. [III, 164.]

Jonah Dodge, late of Bluehill bay. Sarah Dodge, of Bluehill bay, widow, Adm'x, 12 Aug., 1788; Daniel Osgood and Jedediah Holt, both of Bluehill bay, sureties. [III, 164.]

In the Name of God Amen, I Jonah Dodge of Blue hill Bay in the County of Lincolon and Common-wealth of Massachusetts in New England, Yeoman: Being through the abundant Goodness and Mercy of God of a sound disposing Mind and Memory; yet calling to Mind the frailty of my Nature, my continual exposedness to the Stroke of Death, Knowing that it is appointed for man once to Die; Do therefore make and Constitute this my last Will and Testament, desiring that it may be received by all as such; First I most humbly recommend my Soul to God its Maker, earnestly intreating his most gracious Acceptance of it through Jesus Christ my ever blessed Redeemer, who gave himself a Propitiation for Sin and is able to save all who come unto God through him; who I hope and trust will not reject, but own me, in the Day when he shall make up his Jewels; in hope and Confidence of which, I chearfully resign my Spirit into his hands; most earnestly Imploring the divine Aids, that I may be found ready, and prepared for Deatth, whenever it shall come, That my Soul may wing its way, under the convoy of Angelic Hosts, to the Mansions of Eternal Bliss—My Body I commit to the Dust, whence it was taken in full Assurance of its Resurrection at the last Day. My Burial I desire may be decent and leave it to the Discretion of my Executrix, who I doubt not will manage it with all Requisite Prudence. As to my worldly Estate, with which it has Pleased Almighty to bless me, I Will and positively order, that all my Debts, and funeral Charges be first paid, by my Executrix hereafter named; and then to be disposed of in Manner and form following, That is to Say.

Imprimis I give to my beloved Wife Sarah: The Improvement of one half of all my Estate both Real and Personal so long as she remains my widow.

Item I give and bequeath to my son Jonah Dodge and to his Heirs forever Thirteen pounds Six Shillings & Eight pence to be payed him by my two Sons viz John and Reuben they each paying their Proportionable part of said Money to their Brother, in one year after my Decease provided, I do live till Reuben comes to Be Twenty one years of Age but if I should Die before Reuben comes to be Twenty one years of Age then it is to be paid in one years after Reuben comes of Age. Item I give and bequeath to my Three Sons viz Abner Dodge Benjamen Dodge & Abraham Dodge, Each Son, the Sum of Thirteen pounds Six Shillings & Eight lawful Money to be pay'd them by my two Sons viz John and Reuben one third part of Said Money to be paid them in two years after my Decease another third in Three Years and the Remaining part in four years after my Decease provided 1 do live till my Son Reuben comes to be Twenty one years of Age. but if I should Die before Reuben arives to the afores'd Age then the Respectives Sums afores'd are to be paid to them Yearly as before Expressed in four years after Reuben come to the Age of Twenty one.

Item I Give to my Daughter Abigail Wife of Simon Dodge fifteen shillings which together with what She has had is her full Share.

Item I Give & Bequeath to my two Sons viz John Dodge and Reuben Dodge they paying the afores'd Legaces to their Brothers & Sister, the whole of the Remainder of all my Estate both Real and Personal which I shall Die Possessed off, and further It is my Will, If it should please the Allrighteous Ruler of the Universe, in whose hand their Breath is to take one or both of them away by Death before they shall have any lawful Heirs begotten, that his, or their Proportion of my Estate, Should Revert to, and be Equally Divided among the Surviving Brothers.

Lastly, I make and Constitute my Wife the Executrix to this my last Will and Testament:

In Witness whereof I have hereunto Set my hand and Seal this Seventeenth Day of June in the Year of our Lord, one thousand, seven Hundred and Eighty four.

Jonah Dodge (seal)

Signed, Sealed, published,
Ratified and declared, to be
my last Will and Testament,
In Presence off us,
    John Peters
    Daniel Osgood
    Jedidiah Holt

Probated on the first Wednesday in September, 1788. [IV, 90-91.] Inventory by Joseph Wood, Jr., Robert Parker and Jonathan Darling, all of Blue Hill Bay, 1 Sep., 1788, £326 : 5 : 10. [V, 160-1.] John and Reuben, minor sons, chose Sarah, widow, to be their guardian, 27 Aug., 1788. [V, 161-2.]

Nathaniel Jellison, late of Bowdoinham. Job Jellison, of Bowdoinham, Adm'r, 1 Sep., 1788; Zacheus Beal and Elisha Pratt, both of Bowdoinham, sureties. [III, 164.]

Joseph Potter, late of a place on Penobscot River called Sunbury. Margaret Potter, of Sunbury, widow, Adm'x, 9 Sep., 1788; Silas Hathorne and Crowell Cook, both of Sunbury, sureties. [III, 165.] Inventory by Jonathan Lowder, of Penobscott, Andrew Webster and Archibald McPhetres, both of Sunbury on Penobscott River, 29 Oct., 1789, £165 : 18 : 0. [IV, 97.]

James Duning, late of Sunbury. Jean Duning, of Sunbury, widow, Adm'x, 9 Sep., 1788; Silas Hathorne, of Sunbury, and Cornelius Bradford, of Medumcook, sureties. [III, 165.]

Thomas Murphy, Jr., late of Pownalborough. Priscilla Murphy, of Waldoborough, widow, Adm'x, 10 Sep., 1788; Cornelius Turner, of Waldoborough, and George Ulmer, of Duck Trap, sureties. [III, 165.]

Briggs Hallowell, late of Hallowell, merchant. Eunice Hallowell, of Boston, widow, Adm'x, 10 July, 1786; Samuel Vaughan, Jr., of Philadelphia, surety. Joseph North, William Howard and Lazarus Goodwin, all of Hallowell, commissioners to examine claims. [III, 168.] Account filed 22 Mar., 1788. [III, 171-2.] Distribution ordered 29 July, 1788. [III, 173 to 175.]

Jane Brown, of Newcastle, widow, a person *non compos*. James Brown, of Newcastle, guardian, 27 June, 1786. [III, 195.] Inventory by John Farley, Christopher Hopkins and George Barstow, all of Newcastle, 4 Sep., 1786, £93 : 7 : 4. [V, 17-18.] Account filed 6 Jan., 1792. [V, 18-19.]

In the Name of God, Amen. I John George Reed of Waldoborough in the County of Lincoln Yeoman being of perfect Mind & Memory, and knowing that it is appointed for all men once to die, do make and ordain this my last Will & Testament—That is to say, in the first place I recommend my Soul to the Hands of God who gave it, and my Body I commit to the Earth to be buried at the Discretion of my Executrix hereafter named, not Doubting but that I shall receive the same again by the Mighty Power of God—And as to my Worldy Estate, I give devise & dispose of the same in manner following, that is to say—

Imprimis I will and order That all my just Debts & funeral Expences be paid assoon as may after my Decease—

Item, I give unto my Wife Mary Magdalene the Improvement of all my Estate real & personal during the Term of her Natural Life—

Item I give to my Son Michael Reed the Sum of one Pound six shillings & Eight pence to be paid him by my Executrix hereafter named, after the Decease of my said Wife— I also give unto my said Son all my wearing Apparel & Cloathing.

Item I give to my Daughter Eve Christine Margaret Reed an Iron Stow & Cloaths Chest.

Item. All the Rest & Residue of my Estate real & personal wheresoever the same is or may be found I give & devise unto my four Children Jacob Reed Sevilla Magdalene Kilbert, Margaret Catharine Bave Eichorn, & Eve Christine Margaret Reed equally to be divided between then after the Death of my said Wife, & to hold to them & their heirs in severalty for ever—

Lastly. I do hereby constitute and appoint my said Daughter Eve Christine Margaret Reed to be sole Executrix of this my last Will & Testament. And I do hereby revoke all other & former Testaments

by me heretofore made, declaring this & no other to be my last Will and Testament. In Testimony whereof I the said John George Reed do hereunto set my hand & seal this first Day of June A. D. 1776.
Signed Sealed published   John George Reed
& declared by the Testator
to be his last Will and
Testament in presence of
Stephen Brown
Francis Rittal
Mary Bowman

Probated 5 Oct., 1787. [III, 197.]

In the Name of GOD Amen I Quash Winchell of Topsham in the County of Lincoln Labourer being Sick & Week in bodily Health but Perfect in Mind & Memory thanks be to God for the Same Calling to mind the Uncertainty of Life & the certainty of Death Do make and Ordain this my last will & Testament Recommending my soul into the hands of God who Gave it And my body to the Earth to be decently buried according to the Descretion of My Executor whom I Shall hereafter Appoint An as to What of this worlds goods it has Pleased God to Bless me with I dispose of in the following Manner (Viz)

Imprimis I Give & Bequeath to my Benevolent Friends Silence Purrenton Sarah Hunter Mary Given Anne Winchell & Hannah Winchell all & Singular the Goods & Chattells to me in any Manner belonging being at Presant one Horse & Tackling two Cows & one three Year old Heiffer with 20 Sheep allowing the said Hannah one third more then Either of the Oathers and then in Equal Divison among them With a Certain Number of Notes of hand Some payable in my Name & Sum in my Late Masters Samuel Winchells Deceased being Given to me When I Was a Slave & so Wrote in his Name Furthermore I Appoint Mr. Arthur Hunter to be my Sole & Lawfull Executor of this my Last Will & Testament in Witness Whereof I have hereunto put my hand & Seal this third day of March AD 1788

                         his
                  Quash X Winchell   (seal)
                        mark

Signed Sealed Pronounc'd
to be the Last Will & Testament
in the Presance of us Witneses
by the said Quash Winchell

Samuel Stapel
Philip Hoyt
Joshua Smart

Probated 26 June, 1788. [III, 198.]
Inventory by John Sanford, Samuel Stapel and Joseph Groves, all of Topsham, 26 June, 1788. [V, 170-1.]

In the Name of God Amen. I Robert Hodge Junr. of Newcastle in the County of Lincoln, calling to mind the uncertainty of Life, and feeling my Health declining, tho' of sound & disposing mind & memory, do make and ordain this my last Will & Testament as follows. In the first place I bequeath my Soul into the Hands of God who gave it, and my Body to the Earth to be decently buryed at the discretion of my Executors hereafter named. And as to my earthly Substance with which Providence hath blessed me I will and dispose of it in manner following. *Imprimis*, my Will & desire is that my Executors hereafter named, pay all my just Debts out of such part of my Estate as in their Judgment will least injure the Estate, then after, this is done, I give & bequeath to my Executors two hundred and sixty five Pounds to be by them, laid out upon my six youngest Children for their further bringing up & Education in the following proportion viz, to my oldest Son Robert, fifteen Pounds, to my Daughter Hannah, twenty Pounds, to my Daughter Sally thirty five Pounds, to my Daughter Sarah fifty Pounds, to my Son Henry sixty five Pounds, and to my Daughter Jane Nickels, eighty Pounds, the aforesaid Sums to be disposed of and laid out on said six Children, at the discretion of my Executors, for the purposes aforesaid.

I further give & bequeath to William Hodge Son of my Brother Henry Hodge, Ninety Pounds to be paid to him when he shall arrive at the Age of twenty one years.

All the rest and residue of my Estate both real and personal I give and bequeath to all my beloved Children to be equally divided between them, and the Share of each Child to be paid to him or her as they arrive at the Age of twenty one years. And I do hereby constitute and appoint Henry Hodge of Pownalboro' Samuel Nickels Esqr. of Newcastle & John McKown of Bristol Executors to this my last Will & Testament, and hereby revoke & disannul all former Wills by me made, and declare this to be my last Will & Testament. In witness whereof I hereto set my hand & Seal this ninth Day of June in the year of our Lord one thousand seven hundred and eighty eight.

Robt. Hodge   (seal)

Signed sealed published
& declared by the Testator
to be his last Will & Testament in presence of
  William Kennedy
  John Farley
  Seth Pratt

Probated 23 July, 1788. [III, 199.] Thomas Rice and Abiel Wood, both of Pownalborough, sureties. [III, 201.] Inventory by Thomas Rice, Abiel Wood and Francis Cook, all of Pownalborough, 15 Oct., 1788, £3895 : 4 : 10 [IV, 248 to 254.] Henry Hodge, of Pownalborough, guardian unto Sarah, Henry and Robert, minor children, 27 Dec., 1791. [IV, 272.] Samuel Nickels, of Newcastle, guardian unto Jenny, minor daughter, 27 Dec., 1791. [IV, 273.] Hannah, minor daughter, chose Spencer Tinkham, of Pownalborough to be her gardian, 27 Dec., 1791. [IV, 273-4.] Sally, minor daughter, chose John McKown, of Bristol, to be her guardian, 24 Feb., 1792. Division of estate by Thomas Rice and Abiel Wood, both of Pownalborough, and Dummer Sewall, of Bath, 1 Oct., 1793, among Robert Hodge, Polly Tinkham, wife of Spencer Tinkham, Jane Hodge, Sarah Hodge, Hannah Hodge, Margaret Roby, wife of Henry Roby, Henry Hodge and Sally Hodge. [VI, 247-8.] Henry, minor son, chose Henry Hodge, of Pownalborough, to be his guardian, 11 Sep., 1797. [VII, 160-1.] Distribution of estate among Mary, wife of Spencer Tinkham; Margaret, wife of Henry Roby; Hannan, wife of Abiel Wood, Jr., Sally, wife of Henry Hodge; Sarah and Jane Hodge, minors; Robert Hodge, and Henry Hodge, minor, 25 Nov., 1800. [VIII, 126-7.] Sarah, minor daughter, chose Silas Lee, of Pownalborough, to be her guardian, 5 Ap., 1799. [IX, 229.]

George Kline, late of Waldoborough, an Absentee. Moses Copeland, of Warren, agent, 6 Jan., 1781; Nathan Bucklen and Joseph Copeland, both of Warren, sureties. [III, 201.] William Farnsworth and Jabez Cole, both of Waldoborough, and Joshua Collamore, of Medumcook, appraisers and commissioners to examine claims. Inventory 28 June, 1781, £100 : 0 : 0. [III, 201-2.] Account filed 15 June, 1784. [III, 204.]

Jacob Young, late of Waldoborough, an Absentee. Moses Copeland, of Warren, agent, 6 Jan., 1781; Nathan Bucklen and Joseph Copeland, both of Warren, sureties. [III, 204.] William Farnsworth and Jabez Cole, both of Waldoborough, and Joshua Collamore, of Medumcook, appraisers and commissioners to examine claims. Inventory 29 Mar., 1781, £130 : 0 : 0. [III, 204-5.] Account filed 15 June, 1784. [III, 206.]

John Smouse, late of Waldoborough, an Absentee. Moses Copeland, of Warren, agent, 6 Jan., 1781; Nathan Bucklen and Joseph Copeland, both of Warren, sureties. [III, 206.] William Farnsworth and Jabez Cole, both of Waldoborough, and Joshua Collamore of Medumcook, appraisers and commissioners to examine claims. [III, 206-7.] Inventory 29 Mar., 1781, £103 : 0 : 0. [III, 206.] Account filed 15 June, 1784. [III, 208.]

James Meloney, late of St. Georges, an Absentee. Moses Copeland, of Warren, agent, 20 June, 1781; Joshua Collamore, of Medumcook, and Hugh McLean, of Milton, Suffolk County, sureties. Inventory by Archibald Robinson, Owen Maddin and Lawrance Parsons, all of St. Georges, 12 June, 1781, £26 : 0 : 0. [III, 208.] Andrew Malcom, John McCarty and Seth Vose, all of St. Georges, commissioners to examine claims. Account filed 15 June, 1784. [III, 209.]

John Fullerton, late of St. Georges, an Absentee. Moses Copeland, of Warren, agent, 2 Oct., 1780; Hopestill Sumner, of Warren, and Andrew Malcom, of St. Georges, sureties. [III, 209.] Inventory by Archibald Robinson, Lawrance Parsons and Owen Madden, all of St. Georges, 1 Jan., 1781, £208 : 4 : 3. [III, 210.] Micah Packard, Andrew Malcom and John McKelly, all of St. Georges, commissioners to examine claims. [III, 211.] Account filed 15 June, 1784 [III, 212.]

In the Name of God Amen The Twenty third Day of January 1776 I Ceasar Barron of Vassalboro' in the County of Lincoln and province of the Massachusets Bay in New England Tanner Being in perfect mind and memory and as I am about to Repair to the American Camp So Called att Cambridge &c with an Intent to tarry One year in Defence of America Therefore Calling to mind the mortaility of my Body and that it is appointed for all men Once to Die do make and Ordain this my Last Will and Testament that is to Say Pricipally and first of all I give and Recommend my Soul into the Hands of God that gave it and my Body I Recommend to the Earth to be Buried

in Decent Christian Burial at the Descretion of my Executor Nothing Doubting but at the General Resurection I shall Receive the same again by the Mighty Power of God— And as Touching Such worldly Estate wherewith it hath Pleased God to Bless me in this Life I Give Demise and Dispose of the same in The following manner and form *Imprimus* After the payment of all my Just Debts and funeral Charges I Give and bequeath to my Good Friend Asa Phillips of Vassalboro In the County and Province Aforesaid Cordwainer whom I Likewise Constitute make and Ordain my soul Executor of this my Last will and Testament all and singular my Lands messuages and Tennements Together with all my Household Goods Debts and moveable Effects whatsoever By him freely to be possesed and Enjoyed and I do hereby utterly Disallow Revoke and Disannul all and Every other former Testaments Wills Legacies and Bequests and Executors by me in any wise before named willed and Bequeathed Rattifying and Confirming this and no other to be my Last will and Testament In Case I should not marry nor Live to Return again but if I should Either marry or Return this will to be Void otherwise to Remain In full force and Vertue— In Witness whereof I have hearunto Set my hand and Seal The Day and Year Above Written
Signed Sealed Published and
Pronounced and Declared by the
said Ceasar Barron as his Last
will and Testament in the Presence
of us the Subscribers

    Thomas Gullefer   Cesar Barron   (seal)
    Thomas Evans
    Stephen Barton

                        Probated 16 Sep., 1777   [III, 213-14.]

            In the Name of God Amen.

I Edward Blanchard of Vassallborough in the County of Lincoln and State of Massachusetts-Bay Yeoman being weak of Body but of Sound Mind & Memory blessed be God therefor do make and Publish this my last Will & Testament in Manner Following Vizt—

Imprimis I Commend my Soul into the hands of Allmighty God who gave it me and my Body to the Earth from whence it Came in hopes of a Joyfull Resurrection through the Merits of my Saviour Jesus Christ and as for the Worldly Estate wherewith it hath pleased God to Bless me, I Dispose thereof as Follows Vizt—

First. I give to my son Edward the sum of Five shillings.

Item. I give my Daughter Sarah the sum of Five shillings.

Item. I give to my Daughter Rachell the sum of five shillings.

Item. I give to my Daughters, Mary, Sybill & Anna, the Front Lott of Land I now Dwell upon being lott No 87 Containing one hundred acres, with the Buildings thereon to Have & to Hold to them & their Heirs forever, together with all my Goods, Chattles, Real & Personal Estate whatsoever that I possess to be Equally Divided amongst them, On Condition that they Maintain in a Decent & Comfortable Manner my loving Wife & Daughter Ellena during their Lives and paying all my Debts.

I appoint Joseph Stephens of Winthrop Executor to this my last Will & Testament, praying Him to Accept of the Trust & Execute the same according to my true Intent & Meaning. In Witness whereof I the said Edward Blanchard have to this my last Will & Testament set my hand & seal this Twenty Sixth day of March *Anno Domini* One thousand seven hundred & seventy Eight. N B The words "being Lott 87" was wrote before sign'g sealing &c

Sign'd, Seal'd, & Deliver'd
by the Testator, as, & for his
last Will & Testament in
Presence of
Remington Hobby
John Gatchel

          his
Eliab   X Smith
          Mark.

         his
Edward X Blanchard (seal)
         Mark

Probated 9 Oct., 1778. [III, 215.] Inventory by Remington Hobby, Samuel Grant and Solomon Parker, 19 June, 1784, £141 : 8 : 8. [III, 216.] Rachel Blanchard, Adm'x *de bonis non*. [III, 217.] Solomon Parker and Jonathan Low, both of Winslow, sureties. [IV, 17.]

In the Name of God Amen this Sixth Day of January A: D: 1781 I Phillip Fought of Vassalborough in the county of Lincoln and State of the Massachusetts yeoman Sick and week in body but of Sound mind and memory thanks be given to God therefor Calling to mind the Mortallity of my body and Knowing that it is appointed for all men once to Die Do make and ordain this my last Will and Testament that is to say Principaily and first of all I give and Recommend my Soul into the hands of God that gave it and my body I recommend to the earth to be buried in a Decent Christian manner at the Discression of my Executor and as touching such worldly Estate wherewith it hath pleased God to bless me in this life I Give Demise and Dispose of the same in the following manner—

I give and bequeath to Hannah my beloved wife all my indoor moveables and all the moneys that are Due to Me what Soever and two cows and Six Sheep and one Rume in my house and Half the garden and fire wood all ways cut at the Door suffitiant for her fire and her cows and Sheep Keept on the place summer and winter and to find her twenty bushels of corn ten of Rye and Wheat and thirty bushels of petators and twenty Pounds of Flax anually Dureing her life or so long as She Remains my widdow

I give unto my Son Jacob fifty pounds lawfull money to be paid in Spanish mill'd Dollars at Six Shillings pr Dollar said money to be paid in one year after my widdows Decease

I give unto my Son Frederick fifty pounds lawfull money in Spanish mill'd Dollars to be paid as above said in one year after my widdows Decease

I give unto my Daughter Rachel one cow and fifty pounds lawfull money in Spanish mill'd Dollars to be paid as above said in one year after my Decease

I give unto my Daughter Marget fifty pounds lawfull money in in Spanish mill'd Dollars as above said to be paid in one year after my Decease

I give unto my Son Anthoney all my lands, buildings, Stock and farming utentials Except what is willed as above said to be by him freely possessed and Injoyed he paying all the leagacy as above said and providing for my widdow as above said he allso paying all my Just Debts and funeral Charges

And I do likewise Constitue make and ordain Mathew Hasting of Vassalborough Gent my Executor of this my last will and Testimant and I Do hereby Disallow & Revoke all other wills and Testiments by me made before this time Rattifiing this my last will and Testiment

In Witness Whereof I have hereunto set my hand and seal the Day and year above written

            his
         Phillip X Fought (seal)
            mark

Signed Sealed Published Pronounced and Declared by the said Phillip

fought as his last Will and Testiment in Presence of us the Subscribers
Ebenezer Moore
Samuel Basset
Nath'll Davis

Probated 11 June, 1781. [III, 217-18.]

Samuel Harnden, late of Woolwich. Inventory by Samuel Ford, Francis Ford and John Hathorn, all of Woolwich, 21 Jan., 1778, £240:0:0. [III, 219.]

In the Name of God Amen this Second Day of September A: D: 1782 I Joseph Clarke of Vassalborough in the county of Lincoln and Commonwealth of the Massachusetts yeoman being Sick and week in body but of Sound mind and memeroy thanks be Given to God therefore Calling to mind the mortallity of my body and Knowing that it is appointed for all men once to die do make and ordain this my last Will and Testiment: That is to say—Principally and first of all I Give and Recommend my Soul into the hands of God that Gave it. And my body I commend to the earth to be buried in Christian like manner at the Discretion of my Executor nothing doubting but at the General Resurrection I shall Receive the Same again by the mighty Power of God: And so touching Such worldly Estate wherewith it hath Pleased God to Bless me in this life I Give and Dispose of the Same in the following manner after paying my Just Debts and funeral Charges

I Give and bequeath to my well beloved Cusen Joseph Clarke of Vassalborough a minor all my Estate Real and Personal all and Singular my lands messuages and tenements to be by him freely Possessed and enjoyed: And I likewise make and ordain Loes Clarke of Vassalboro widow and Rellick of Thomas Clarke late of Vassalborough Deceas'd my only and Sole Executor of this my last will and testament and I do hereby Disanul and Revoke all other former Wills by me made Ratifing and Conferiming this my last will and Testiment In Witness whereof I have hereunto Set my hand and Seal the Day and year above said Signed Sealed Published and Declared by the said Joseph Clarke as his last will and Testiment in Presence of

   Mathew Hastings   his
   Hugh Smiley   Joseph X Clarke   (seal)
   Jonathan Dyer   marke

Probated 11 Mar., 1783. [III, 229.]

Ebenezer Cox, of Bristol, *non compos*. Israel Cox, of Bristol, guardian, 15 Ap., 1786; Thomas Bracket and Jonas Fitch, both of Bristol, sureties. Inventory by Henry Fosset, James Drummond and Joseph Boyd, all of Bristol, 1786, £76 : 2 : 0. [III, 242.] Account filed 2 June, 1787. [III, 243.] Guardian licensed to sell real estate, 20 Sep., 1791. [IV, 261.]

Stephen Foster, of Winthrop, minor son of Timothy Foster, late of Winthrop, deceased, chose Jonathan Whiting, of Winthrop, to be his guardian, 3 May, 1786. [III, 256.]

In the Name of God Amen this Sixth day of Febuary 1787 I Jabez Crowel of Vassalborough in the county of Lincoln and Commonwealth of the Massachusetts yeoman being Sick and weak in body but of Sound mind and memory thanks be Given to God therefor and Calling to mind the mortality of my body and Knowing that it is appointed for all men once to die do make and ordain this my last Will and testament that is to Say first and Principally I Give and recommend my Soul in to the hands of God that Gave and my body I commit to the earth to be buried in a decent manner at the discretion of my Executor; and as touching Such worly Estate as it hath Pleased God to bless me with in this life I Give Demise and Dispose of it in the following manner viz

first I Give and bequeath to my Granson Barna Basset all my Carpenters tools and my Gun and Sword

the Remainder of my Estate Real and Parsonal after paying my Just Debts I Give to thankfull my well beloved wife to be at her disposal dureing her life or so long as She Shall Remain my wido and at her Decease all that Shall Remain I Give to my Daughter thankfull Crowel She Paying to her two Sisters Samuel Bassets wife and James Mathas wife Six Shillings each to be paid at her mothers Decease

I likewise make and appoint Mathew Hastings of Vassalborough aforeSaid Gentn Executor of this my last will and testament and I do hereby Disanul and make void every other will and testament by me made before this time Rattifiing and Confeirming this and no other to be my last will and testament In witness whereof I have hereunto Set my hand and Seal the Day and year above Said

his
Jabex X Crowell (seal)
mark

Signed Sealed Published Pronounced and Declared

by the Said Jabez Crowel as his last will and
testament in the Presence of us the Subscribers viz
  James Bacon Senr
  Winthrop Robinson
      his
  James X Bacon Jr
     mark

    Probated 5 June, 1787. [III, 258.] Inventories by Thomas Hawes, James Bacon and Winthrop Robinson, all of Vassalborough, and Josiah Thatcher, Abner Crowell and Jabez Lewis, all of Yarmouth, 1788, £19 : 15 : 6. [III, 259.]

    David Averell, late of Pownalborough. Joseph Hilton, of Pownalborough, Adm'r, 24 Jan., 1788; George Erskine and Stuart Hunt, both of Pownalborough, sureties. Inventory by Samuel Waters and Daniel Quigg, both of Newcastle, 21 Ap., 1788, £40 : 0 : 0. Account filed 19 May, 1788. [III, 260.]

In the Name of God Amen I Henry Benner of Waldoborough in ye County of Linclon in the Massachusetts State being weak in body and Knowing tis appointed for all men to die and how sone I Know not and being now in my Perfect Sences I have thought fit to make this my Last Will and testament in ye following manner viz. in the first place I Give my Soul into ye hands of God whoe gave itt and my body to ye Earth to be Decently Buried att the Discresion of my Executor whome my will is and I appoint to be my Loving wife Margret benner. And as to what worldly goods God has ben pleased to bless me with I give and dispose of in the following manner in the first place I Give unto my Loving wife all my whole Estate both Real and personel to use occupie in all Respects as She Shall think proper as Long as She Shall Continue in this Life and as to what depts Shall be found due from me my will is She Should Sell Stock Enough to pay them and as to what depts Shall be due to me I Give to her to doe with as She Shall think proper and upon her deth the Real Estate which I am posesed with. I Give to my youngest Son Henry benner that is to Say my farm House and all other Buildings meadows and all appurtances belonging there unto. and as to my moveabels or personel Estate I Give in the manner following. there is sum of my Childer have had sum things all Ready and sum have had nothing and my will is they should be made Equel : all but John Benner, Matice Benner and Elizebeth Newbit they have had as much as I Ever purposed to Give them and as to the Rest. My Son Jacob I gave him a Cow: Keaty I Give a Cow; Sedony I Gave a Cow=and Sally I gave a Cow=Charles and John and Molly and Henry I have Gave Nothing to none of them and my will is they all should be Equel and if any thing should Remain of my Personel or moveable Estate that itt should be Divided Equelly amongst them. and now I doe Disanul and make void all other wills and testaments of all Kinds and all Naturs whatsoever. I doe hold good and Vallid this my Last will and testament: and in testimony hereof I doe hereunto set my hand and Seal this 23-day of June in ye year-1783

Sign'd seal'd and deliv'd in presence of us   Henri Benner   (seal)
  Johannes Kesler
  Math Rameley
  Jabesh Cole

Probated 9 June, 1784. [IV, 8-9.]

Peter Heald, late of Georgetown. Richard Poor, of Balltown, Adm'r, 10 Aug., 1784; Ebenezer Grover and Jonathan Peasley, both of Balltown, sureties. [IV, 17.]

Alexander Askins, late of Bristol. Robert Askins, of Bristol, Adm'r, 15 June, 1785; Richard Jones, of Bristol, and Nathaniel Winslow, of Edgecomb, sureties. [IV, 17.]

William Elliot, late of Boothbay, physician. Sarah Elliot, of Boothbay, widow, Adm'x, 16 June, 1785; John Huse and Nymphas Stacy, both of Pownalborough, sureties. [IV, 18.]

George Harward, late of Bowdoinham. Thomas Harward, of Bowdoinham, mariner, Adm'r, 15 June, 1786; Edmund Bridge, of Pownalborough, and James Maxwell, of Bowdoinham, sureties. [IV, 18.]

In the Name of God Amen I Michal McClary of Bristol in the County of Lincoln Husbandman Being Now in health and of a Sound mind make this my last Will & Testament as Follows that is to say I Recomend my Sole to god and my Body to the Earth to be Decently buried at the Discretion of my Executor and for such worldly Estate with which his providence Hath entrusted me I dispose thereof as Follows Vizt—

Imprimis I will that my House Barn & the hole of the land that I bought of John Savage is I Give unto his Son Thomas Savage for him or his Heirs after my Deceased—

Item I give to him the said Thomas Savage the hole of the land I Bought of his Father I order my Executor to Deliver it to him the said Thomas free & Clear of Debt hereby Revoking and Disannulling all Former Wills by me made declaring this and no other to be my last— In Witness whereof I hereunto set my hand & Seal this fourteenth day of June *Anno Domini* one Thousand Seven hundred and Eighty four—

Michael Clary (seal)

Signed Sealed & Deliverd in
  Presence of us—
  David Pottle
  James McDaniel
  John Savage

Probated 6 Sep., 1788. [IV, 19.] John Costelow, of Pownalborough, Adm'r, 27 Mar., 1788; William Lewis and John McGown, both of Pownalborough, sureties. Inventory by Robert Given, Henry Fosset and James Sproul, all of Bristol, 31 Mar., 1788, £218 : 2 : 9. [V, 170.]

In the Name of God amen this Seventh Day of April one Thousand Seven Hundred and Seventy Nine I William Woodcock of the Town of Attleborough in the County of Bristol in the State of the Massachusets Bay in New England yeoman being in helth and of a Sound Disposing mind and memory, Thanks be Given to God, but Calling to minde the Mortality of my Bodey and knowing that it is appointed for all men once to Die do make and ordain this my Last will and Testement that is to Say Princpaly and first of all I Give and Recomend my Soul into the hands of God that Gave it and my Bodey I Recomend to the Eairth to be Buried in Deacent Christian Burial at the Descresion of my Executor hearafter Named nothing Doubting but I Shall Recive the Same again at the General Resurection by the mighty Power of God—and as Touching Such Worldly Estate as it hath pleased God to Bless me with in this Life I Give Demise and Dispose of the Same in the maner and form following

Imprimis I Give to my true and well Beloved wife Submit Woodcock the one thurd part of all my Estate.

I Give to my Daughter Mary Fields the wife of Jams Fields the Sum of five Shilling Lawful mony to be paid to her or her heirs by my Executor hearafter Named Imedatly after my Decease if Demanded

I Give to my Daughter Phebe Rogers the Sum of five Shillings Lawful mony to be paid to her by my Said Executor at my Deceas if Demanded

I Give to my Daughter Lucey Drown the wife of John Drown the Sum of five Shillings Lawful mony to be paid her or her heirs by my Said Executor at my Decease if Demanded

I Give to my Daughter Submit the Sum of five Shillings Lawful mony to be paid her by my Said Executor at my Decease if Demanded

I Give to my Son Benjmin Woodcock the Sum of five Shillings Lawful mony to be paid to him by my Said Executor at my Decease if Demanded

And I hearby appoint make and Constitute my Son David Woodcock the Sole Executor to this my Last Will and Testemen hearby ordring him to pay all my Just Debts funaral Charges and the Legecyes which I have Given and Bequethed by this my Will and I Do hearby Give to my Said Son David all the Remainder of my Estate Except what I have Given as is Described in this my will that is to Say all the Remaing part of my Estate (after he has Paid my Just Debts and Leagecies as afor Said) to him or to his heirs or asigns for Ever and I Do hearby utterly Disalow Revoke and Disanul all and Every other former Testement wills Leagecis and Bequests and Executors by me in any wise before Named willed and bequethed Ratifieng and Confairming this and no Other to be my Last Will and Testement In Wittness wharof I have hearunto Set my hand and Seal the Day and year above Written

Signed Sealed Published   his
Pronounced and Declaired   William X Woodcock (seal)
by the Said Willim Woodcock as his Last will and   Mark
Testement in the Presence of us the Subscribers
    John Daggett
    Thomas Starkey
    Jesse Daggett

[Received 16 Nov., 1788; unrecorded.]

Roland Cushing, late of Waldoborough. Edmund Bridge, of Pownalborough, Adm'r, 24 Nov., 1788. [IV, 20.] Joseph North and William Lithgow, Jun., both of Hallowell, sureties. Inventory by Nathaniel Thwing, of Woolwich, Richard Kidder and Samuel Emerson, both of Pownalborough, 1789, £362 : 12 : 2. [IV, 51-52.] Nathaniel Thwing, of Woolwich, and James Tupper, of Pownalborough, commissioners to examine claims. [V, 27.] Account filed and distribution ordered, 31 May, 1792. [V, 37 to 39.] Advertisement of sale of real estate, 9 Nov., 1791. [V, 46.]

In the Name of God Amen : I Nathanael Simmons of Waldoborough

in the County of Lincoln in the State of Massachusetts Bay in America
Husbandman Calling to mind the Shortness of my Life and Being in
Perfect mind and memory think fit to Ordain and appoint these Presents to be my Last Will and Testament I therefore in the first Place
give my soul to God in Jesus Christ and my Body to be Buried Decently according to the Discresion of my Executors herein after named
Believing that at the grate and General Resurection to Receive the
Same again=and I Do Hereby Dispose of the Estate which Almigty
God has Bles'ed me with in manner as followeth. Itim first I give
to my True and Loving Wife the one half of all my Real Estate together with the Improvement of all my House-movables
and I here further give to my wife Mrs Marcy Simmons the Improvement of three Cows and five Sheep=What is here ment is the Improvement of all the Real and Personal Estate here given to my wife
so Long as She the sd Marcy Simmons shall Remain my Widow=Itim
I hereby Give too my two oldest Sones viz Joseph Simmons and Zebedee Simmons the whole of that my Farme it Being the Homestead
Farme on which I Dwell after their mothers Improvement as above to
them and their Heirs forever Equally : further I give to s'd Joseph and
Zebedee my four best oxen together with my Horse and two thirds of
all my tools of all sorts : further I give Joseph and Zebedee the two
Gunes that they now Improve and my two Swoards —Item I here-
by give to my Son Steven Simmons the Long Island farme which
I bought of Benjamin Bradford Lying on Long Island near a
Place Called the midle narrows further I give to my son Steven my
Half of the farme on which he the s'd Steven now Does now Dwells on—
further I give Steven the gun that he Improves Itim I here-
by Give to my four Daughters viz Mary the wife of John
Hunt Dorothy wife of John Winslow Sarah Simmons Rachel Sim-
mons all that my Farme which I bought of Mrs Jane Cleveland and
Contains one Hundred Acres and lyeth on the Southerly side of Jacob
Wades farme all which farmes or Tracts of Land Laying within the
Township of Waldoborough above s'd Except the Long Island Lot
further I hereby give to Mary and Dorothy four Pounds a Piece to be
Paid to them in one year after my Deceas further I give Mary
and Dorothy Each of them one Cow a piece itim I hereby
give to my three Children now Living at home viz Zebedee
Sarah and Rachel after my wifes Improvement as above the three
Cows and five Sheep together with all the House movables to be Equally
divided among them further I give to Zebedee Six Sheep and what

Remains after my Debts and funaral Charge are paid Equally to be Divided among my Seven Children I hereby appoint my two Sones Joseph and Zebedee to be my sole and only Executors to this my Last will and Testament in Consideration of the Love that I bare to my Loving wife and Dutiful Children I give as above s'd to them and their heirs forever In witness and Confirmation whereof I hereunto set my hand and Seal this Twenty Second Day of January in the year of our Lord one Thousand Seven Hundred and Eighty Seven

Signed Sealed and Declared to be my Last Will and Testament In Presence of these Witnesses

Peleg Oldham
John Haupt   Nathanael Simmons   (seal)
Andrew Storer

Probated 22 Jan., 1789. [IV, 21.] Inventory by Nathaniel Pitcher, Jabesh Cole and Peleg Oldham, all of Waldoborough, 2 Feb., 1789. [IV, 85 to 87.] Cornelius Turner and Peleg Oldham, both of Waldoborough, sureties. Account filed 18 Sep., 1792. [V, 91-92.]

In the Name of God. Amen. I Zachariah Dodge of Edgecombe in the County of Lincoln, & Common Wealth of Massachusetts, Yeoman, being of sound mind and memory, knowing the frailty of human Nature, and the Uncertainty of the time when I shall die, do make publish and declare this to be my last Will and Testament.— *Imprimis.* I resign my soul to him who is the supreme Governor of the Universe, hoping for Salvation through the Blood of the Redeemer, and my Body to the Dust, hoping for a glorious Resurrection. As to my Worldly Estate, I dispose of it in the following manner, Vizt. After my just Debts & funeral Charges are paid, which I hereby order to be paid out of my Personal Estate, I give unto my Wife Sarah, my whole Estate both Real & Personall, for her to enjoy and improve as she shall think Proper, so long as she shall remain my Widow, but in case my said Wife should marry, Then and in that Case my Will is that she shall Relinquish & give up all her Right & Title to said Estate, without receiving any Dower whatever.

Item, and in Case my said Wife should marry or die and leave one or more of my Children uncapable of maintaining themselves then & in that Case my Will is that all my children shall be equally maintained out of the whole of said Estate untill they are able to maintain themselves and further my Will is that at the marriage or death of my said

Wife, my whole Estate shall be divided equally amongst all my Children to one as much as another, without any Exception, only as is before Provided for the Uncapable Children. Lastly, I make constitute and appoint Moses Davis Esquire Executor to this my last Will & Testament, hereby revoking all Wills, by me heretofore made. In Witness whereof I have hereunto set my hand & seal this Ninth day of February in the Year of our Lord, one thousand seven hundred & Eighty seven. Signed, sealed Published and declared to be the last Will & Testament of the above named Zachariah Dodge.

Zachariah Dodge   (seal)

in presence of us
Barnabas Sears
Thomas Ring
William Cunningham

Probated 19 Mar., 1789. [IV, 28-29.] Inventory by Barnabas Sears, Thomas Ring and William Cunningham, all of Edgecomb, 20 Ap., 1789, £330 : 8 : 8. [IV, 45-46.]

Joshua Coombs, late of Bath. Jacob Coombs, of Bath, Adm'r, 28 Ap., 1789. William Brown and George Fields Coombs, both of Bath, sureties. [IV, 41.] Inventory by Benjamin Higgins, Benjamin Brown and William Brown, all of Bath, 13 June, 1789, £150 : 12 : 0. [IV, 48.]

Jonathan Fly, late of Union River. Sarah Fly, of Union River, widow, Adm'x, 3 June, 1789. [IV, 43-44.] Christopher Bartlet and David Bartlet, both of Mount Desert, sureties. Inventory by Joseph Wood, Nathan Parker and Robert Parker, all of Blue-hill-bay, 26 Aug., 1789, £98 : 17 : 7. [IV, 62-63.]

Nathaniel Wyman, late of Georgetown. Martha Wyman, widow, and Isaiah Wyman, both of Georgetown, Adm'rs, 10 June, 1789. [IV, 44.] Inventory by Dummer Sewall, of Bath, John White and Jordan Parker, both of Georgetown, 16 July, 1789, £668 : 15 : 2. [IV, 134.] Inventory of land in Cumberland County by John Lewis, Andrew Gray and John Hayes, all of North Yarmouth, 22 June, 1789, £54. [IV, 135.] Account filed 28 May, 1790. [IV, 135-6.]

Thomas Cook, late of Norridgewalk. James Waugh, of a Place called Sandy River, Adm'r, 20 Mar., 1789. [IV, 47.] Robert Crosby, of Sandy River, and John Moor, of Norridgewalk, sureties. Inventory by Moriah Gould and Nathan Parlin, both of Norridgewalk, and Robert Crosby, of Sandy River, 4 Ap., 1789, £94 : 5 : 6. [IV,

45-47.] Anna Cook, John Cook and Joseph Cook refusal to administer. [IV, 87.] Account filed 17 Jan., 1792. [V, 24.] Widow's dower set off by Robert Crosby, Moriah Gould and Nathan Parlin, 18 Ap., 1792. [VI, 84.]

Alexander Murphy, late of Bristol. Thomas Murphy, of Sandy River, Adm'r, 3 July, 1789. [IV, 49.]

Be it Remembered that I Moses Kimball of Vassalborough in the County of Lincoln and State of Massachusets Bay yeoman being in a Decline, but through Divine mercy of a Sound mind and memory, Do make and ordain this my Last will and testament in manner following Viz

1st I will that all my Just Debts and funeral Charges be paid out of my Estate by my Excrutix hereafter named

2d I give and Bequeath unto my Beloved Wife Hannah and my three Children, namely Molly, Ruth, and Anna, all the Rest of My Estate Intrust and property whatsoever and wharesoever I Die posessed of in the manner following, that my wife for herselfe and on behalfe and in trust for my said Children be in full possession of the Rest of my Estate, and to Bring up my Children tharewith untill my youngest Child Living Shall arive to the age of Eightteen years olde or be Married; (Except giving my Daughter Molly at the age of Eightteen years olde one good Cow and two good Sheep I give them to her because that She is of a Weakly Constitution and being the Eldist having more Cair put upon her then her other Sisters) giving them an Education Sutable to to her Curcumstances and when my youngest Daughter Living arives to the age of Eightteen years olde, or be married I will that Distribution be made of what Shall Remain in My wifes hands the one half of the Moveable Estate with the One Hundred Acre Lot of mine, a part of which is in the town of Winslow to be Eaqually Devided betwen my Daughters to be by them posessed and Enjoyed as thare own Propperty and Right: and the other half of the Moveable Estate with the farm I now Live upon to my wife During her Life, and at her Decease to be Eaqually Devided Between my Daughters, to be by them posessed as thare own property

3ly I Nominat and appoint my Beloved wife Hannah a gardean for my Children

4ly I hereby Nominat and appoint my Beloved wife Hannah Sole Executrix to this my Last will and testament Disallowing and Disannulling all other Wills by me Made In witness whareof I have hereunto Set my hand and Seal this Twelfth Day of the Fifth Month one Thousand Seven hundred and Eighty nine.

Signed Seal'd and published by the Testator as and for his Last will and Testament in presence of us the Subscribers
  David Bowerman
  Moses Sleeper
  Remington Hobby

N. B. the words "*One Hundred Acre*" were wrote, before Signing Sealing &c—

Moses Kimball   (seal)

Probated 1 July, 1789. [IV, 50.] Inventory by Joseph Thomas, Asa Soule and Timothy Robinson, all of Vassalborough, Aug., 1789, £207 : 2 : 10. [V, 45.] Account filed 12 Mar., 1805, at which date the executrix had become the wife of Philip Emerson. [X, 342-3.]

Nathaniel Jellison, late of Bowdoinham. Nathaniel Jellison, of Bowdoinham, Adm'r, 6 July, 1789. [IV, 52.] Joseph Wheeler, of Bowdoin, and Elisha Pratt, of Bowdoinham, sureties. Inventory by Nathaniel Thwing, of Woolwich, Zacheus Beal and Elnathan Raymond, both of Bowdoinham, 7 Oct., 1788, £178 : 18 : 2. [IV, 90.] Account filed 7 Jan., 1791. [IV, 189.]

John Gillingham, late of Georgetown. Elijah Drummond, of Georgetown, Adm'r, 8 July, 1789. [IV, 53.] William Lee, Junr., and John Rogers, both of Georgetown, sureties. Inventory by Benjamin Pattee, John Rogers and Thomas Butler, 5 Nov., 1789, £10 : 12 : 8. [IV, 101.]

In the name of God amen, I James McCobb Esqr of Georgetown in the County of Lincoln, and province of the Massachusetts Bay in new England, being sound in mind and memory, but advanced in Age, and calling to mind my mortality, do make this my last will and Testament in the manner following—

Imprimis, I recommend my soul to God and my Body to the dust in hopes of a future resurrection to eternal life through the merits of Christ my Saviour

And as touching such Estate as it hath pleased God to bestow upon me, I dispose of the same as follows

1st. I give unto my well beloved wife Mary for her extraordinary kindness & attention to me in my old Age, the One half of all the improved, Cultivated, or uncultivated upland, and the One half of all the salt marsh, which my Farm contains on Honeywells point, so called, laying on the west-side of Kenebeck River, together with all the Building which belong to said Farm which Farm I bought of Samuel Waterhouse as by his deed to me will appear; which half of said Farm and all the buildings as above I freely give & bequeath to the said Mary my wife to be hers forever, and to do with the same as she may think best—this being my free gift exclusively of her right to the One third part of all my Real & personal Estate, after the above—and also Six Milch Cows with Calves, One pair of Oxen—together with my oldest black mare and Six Sheep to be hers forever in the same way and manner and for the same reasons as the land and buildings above mentioned are—

2d I give to my Son Samuel McCobb, One hundred Acres of uncultivated land which does not Join or lay adjacent to this Farm called the Homestead, or any other of my Farms which are any way or in any manner cultivated or improved this to take place after my decease.

3d I give to my four daughters, now married viz- Isabele Parker, Elizabeth Mains, Francis Cushing and Margaret Lee, One hundred Acres of Uncultivated land each which does not Join or lay adjacent to this Farm called the Homestead or any other of my Farms which are any ways, or in any manner cultivated or improved.—this to take place after my decease

4th I give and bequeath to my Daughter Nancy now unmarried One hundred and Fifty Acres of uncultivated land which does not belong to this Farm or adjacent thereto being the Homestead so called, or any other of my Farms which are any ways or in any manner cultivated or improv'd—(this to take place after *my decease*

5th I give to my Son in law, *Mark Langdon Hill*, for his kindness and particular attention to me in my *Old Age* Fifty Acres of Land bounding on the North & west side of the mill pond so called near my present dwelling House, forty Rods on the front and continuing the same width and running back about a Westerly Course until the said Fifty Acres of said land is compleated to have and to hold the said land, to him, his heirs & assigns forever—*this to take place after my decease.*

6th I give and bequeath to my three youngest Children who are not of age to act for themselves—viz Thomas my son & Polly—and Jenny my two daughters, for their maintenance, educating and bringing them up, the whole and every part of my estate both Real & Personal, which shall remain after my disease,—excepting what I have given to my other

Children agreable to the foregoing Will, and also to my well beloved wife Mary & to my son in law Mark,—as is before expressed and reserving at the same to my well beloved wife Mary One third part of all and every thing appertaining and belonging to my Real & personal Estate by which she is entitled by law,—meaning for her dowry exclusively of what I have given her in the foregoing will—and I do hereby revoke all former wills & Testaments by me heretofore made and declare this & this Only to be my last will & testament—in witness whereof I have hereunto set my hand and seal this tenth day of September in the year of our lord One thousand seven hundred & Eighty seven

NB. The Fifty Acres as enterlined was done
before the signing hereof   James McCobb   [seal]

 The foregoing will is signed sealed published pronounced and declared by said Testator as and for his last will and Testament in presence of us who in his presence and in ye presence of each other have hereunto set our names as witnesses—

 Eli Perry   Ebenezer Storer
 Martha Perry

 Lastly I do hereby appoint my said wife Mary Execrutix and Captn. Samuel Nicols of Newcastle in the County of Lincoln Executor of this my last Will and Testament as is written in the foregoing Instrument—hereby revoking and disanulling all former Wills and Testaments by me in any manner made confirming this foregoing will and no other to be my last Will and Testament—In witness whereof I have hereunto set my hand & seal the tenth day of September *Anno Domini* One thousand seven hundred & Eighty seven—and further I do hereby appoint the said Mary my Wife & said Samuell Nicols as above to take the particular charge of my three youngest Children as heretofore mentioned viz Thomas my Son & Polly and Jenney my daughters educating & brining them up in such a manner as to enable them to act and do for themselves—

NB the alteration Samuel &
enterlineation witness as above was   James McCobb   [seal]
made before the signing hereof
Signed sealed published and
declared by the said Testator to
be his last will in presence of us
all who have subscribed hereto

as witnesses in presence of the
Testator and of each other
Ebenezer Storer
Eli Perry
Martha Perry

Disallowed 28 Jan., 1789, from which decision executors appealed 20 Feb., 1789. [IV. 59.] Decision affirmed by Supreme Court 7 July, 1789. Mary McCobb of Georgetown, widow, Adm'x, 15 Sep., 1789, [IV. 77-78.] Samuel Nickels, of Newcastle, guardian unto Thomas, minor son, Mary and Jenny, minor daughters, 7 Sep.,1789. [IV, 78 to 80.] Inventory by Thomas Rice, of Pownalborough, Dummer Sewall, of Bath, and Joseph Booker, of Georgetown, 28 Sep., 1789. [IV, 136 to 142.] Widow's dower set off 30 Ap., 1790. [IV, 143.] Petition of heirs for a division. [IV, 144.] Division of estate by Thomas Rice, of Pownalborough, Dummer Sewall, of Bath, and Henry Totman, of Georgetown, 7 Aug., 1792. Heirs mentioned: Rachel McCobb, Isabella Parker, Beatrice Mains, Margaret Lee, Frances Cushing, Nancy McCobb, Mary McCobb, Jane McCobb, Thomas McCobb. [V, 103 to 106.] Account filed 31 May, 1796. [VI, 34 to 45.]

Job Stanwood, late of Mount Desert. Robert Young, of Mount Desert, Adm'r, 3 June, 1788. Samuel Cousens and Thomas Cousens, both of Nasskeeg, sureties. Thomas Paine and Ezra Young, both of Mount Desert, commissioners to examine claims, 26 Nov., 1788. [IV, 65.] Inventory by Thomas Paine, Cornelius Thompson and Ezra Young, all of Mount Desert, 5 Aug., 1788, £34 : 9 : 9. [Unrecorded.]

John Allen, late of Georges Island. Keturah Allen, of Georges Island, widow, Adm'x, 8 Sep., 1790. [IV, 67.] Cornelius Turner, of Waldoborough, and Robert Henderson, of Cushing, sureties. Inventory by Dunbar Henderson, Eleazer Gay and John Barter, all of Cushing, 17 Oct., 1789, £39 : 14 : 4. [IV, 182.] Eleazer Gay and Dunbar Henderson, commissioners to examine claims. [IV, 236.] Account filed 18 Sep., 1792. [V, 74-75.]

John George Stilkey, late of Waldoborough. George Ulmer, of a Place called Ducktrap, Adm'r, 15 Sep., 1789. [IV, 68.] Cornelius Turner, of Waldoborough, and Moses Copeland, of Warren, sureties.

John Obrian, late a Resident of Waldoborough. George Ulmer, of a Place called Ducktrap, Adm'r, 15 Sep., 1789. [IV, 68.] Cornelius Turner, of Waldoborough, and Moses Copeland, of Warren, sureties.

Zenas Cook, late of Medumcook, mariner. Hannah Cook, of Medumcook, widow, Adm'x, 15 Sep., 1789. [IV, 69.] John Demorse and Wellington Gay, both of Medumcook, sureties. Inventory by Paul Jameson, Eleazer Gay and Richard Adams, 23 Dec., 1789, £3037 : 7 : 2. [IV, 184-5.] Inventory of real estate in Dighton, Bristol County, by Samuel Talbut, Thomas B. Richmond and William Brown, 14 July, 1790, £70 : 4 : 0. [IV, 186.] Account filed 16 Jan., 1801, at which date the administratrix had become the wife of William Jameson. [XIII, 338-9.] Real estate divided and set off from that of James Cook, deceased, (with which it lay in common), by James Malcom and Edward Killeran, both of Cushing, and Moses Copeland, of Warren, 26 June, 1801. [XIII, 446 to 450.]

David Pierce, late of Boothbay. Jane Peirce, of Boothbay, widow, Adm'x, 17 Sep., 1789. [IV, 70.] Edward Bird, of Boothbay, and John Tucker, of Pownalborough, sureties. Inventory by Jonathan Sawyer, John Murray and Robert Reed, all of Boothbay, Oct., 1789, £234 : 4 : 6. [IV, 88.]

In the Name of God Amen. I Thomas Story of Bristol, in the County of Lincoln, State of Massachusetts Bay, Yeoman : being thro' the abundant Goodness of God, tho' weak in Body, yet of a sound Understanding & Memory ; do constitute this my last Will & Testament, and desire it may be received by all as such.

First. I bequeath my Soul to God who gave it, hoping for eternal life and Glory thro' the allsufficient Merits and Mediation of my Saviour the Lord Jesus Christ ; & I give my Body to the Earth of which it was made, in full assurance of its Resurrection from thence at the last day : I desire I may be buried in the same Grave with my first wife decently, without any Pomp, at the discretion of my wife & Executors hereafter mentioned, & that a Stone with an Inscription be plac'd at the Head of the Grave.

As to my worldly Estate, I will that all my Debts be paid.—I give & bequeath to my Grandson Story Thompson all my land that I Occupy, with all my goods and Chattels and personal Estate whatever : my loving Wife to have a Room in my House during her life, with the profits of the third part of the Land, & one third of the goods during her life ; But if the aforesaid Story Thompson should die without Issue, then the Land to descend to my Daughter Jane, & the Heirs of her Body :—I also give to my Daughter Jane, the sum of thirteen pounds six shillings and eight pence Lawful money, to be paid her

after my decease, by the aforesaid Story Thompson: And I constute William Jones & Henry Hunter, both of the aforesaid Bristol Gentlemen, my Executors of this my last Will and Testament, & Trustees for my Wife and Grandson. In witness whereof, I have hereunto set my hand and Seal this twenty fifth day of February, in the Year of our Lord, one thousand Seven Hundred and Eighty four.
In presence of
 Henry Hunter   Thomas Story (seal)
 John Patterson   His ෆ mark
 John Hunter

           Probated 15 Sep., 1789. [IV, 70-71.]
William McClain and John Patterson, both of Bristol, sureties. Inventory by John Huston, Richard Hitchcock and Thomas McClure, all of Bristol, 25 Sep., 1789, £407 : 5 : 10. [Unrecorded.]

In the Name of God Amen. I Jean Claveland of the town of Waldowbourgh in the County of Lincoln widow being sick and weak in helth of Body but of perfect mind and memory thanks be gaven unto god, Calling Calling unto mind the mortallty of my body and knowing that appointed for all men once to Die, do make and ordain this my last Will and testament that to say, principally and first of all I gave and recommend my soul into the Hand of allmighty God that gave it, and my body I recommend to the Earth, to be buried in Deacent Christian Burial at the Decretion of my Executor, nothing Doubting but att the general resurrection I shall receive the same again by the mighty power of God, as touching such worldly Estate wherwith it has pleased God to Bliss me in this life I gave, Dismiss and Dispose of in the same in the following manner and form.—
first I gave and bequeath to my Daughter Rebeckah's Child Rebeckah if liveing one hallf of my land and three gouns one skirt one quilt A Coat and if any money is laft after all Debts & other Expences that may arise is paid my said grand daughter is to have the whole and allso to my other Daughter Sarrah McMoullin the other half of my land and all my other moveables and houshold stuff
Captn James Hillton of Bristol and County aforesaid I allso Constute and ordain the sole Executor of this my last Will and testament and I Do hereby utterly Dissanull and revouk and Disalow all and every otheher former testament will legecies and Executors by me in any wise before Named willed and bequeathed ratifying and Confirming this and no other to be my last will and testament. in Wittness Where-

of I have hereunto set my Hand and seal, this first Day of augst in the year of our Lord one thousand seven hundred and eighty nine.

Singed sealed pubished pronounced & Declared by the said Jenney Claveland as her last will and testament in the presence of us who in her presence and in the presence of each other have hereunto subscribed our nams

Willm: McClain   Jean Cleveland   (seal)
Elizabeth Rhods
Joshua Hillton

Probated 15 Sep., 1789. [IV, 76.] Inventories by Thomas Johnston, Oliver Nash and Joseph Burns, all of Bristol, 18 and 26 Sep., 1789, £196 : 19 : 6. [IV, 84-85.]

I Nathan Sherburne of Hallowell in the County of Lincoln, Yeoman, being sick in Body but of perfect mind and Memory, and knowing that the Time approaches and is near at hand when I must put off this earthly Tabernacle, depart hence and be here no more, do make & ordain this my last Will and Testament, that is to say.

In the first place I commend my Soul into the Hands of God that gave it, humbly beseeching him to pardon all my Sins thro the Merits of Jesus Christ my only Saviour, who died for Sinners.

My Body I commit to the Earth there to see Corruption, but in full Assurance of a Resurrection to Life again, by the Mighty power of God.

My Worldly Estate I give devise and dispose of in the following manner & form-viz-

Imprimis. I give and devise unto my beloved Wife Abiel the whole of my real Estate in the said Town of Hallowell, consisting of about half an Acre of Land with a dwelling house thereon, where I now live, to hold to her the said Abiel and her heirs for ever. I also give unto my said Wife all my personal Estate of every sort and kind, to dispose of as she thinks proper; she to take Care of my Daughter and to bring her up and educate her in the best manner she shall be able, and paying her what is herein after given her—

Item I give unto my said Daughter Polly, the Sum of Twenty shillings to be paid her by my Executrix hereafter named when she shall arrive to the Age of Eighteen Years.

And I do hereby appoint my said Wife Executrix of this my last Will and Testament.

In Testimony whereof I the said Nathan do hereto set my hand and seal the twenty fifth day of December in the year of our Lord 1789.

           Nathan Sherburne (seal)

Signed sealed, published & declared }
by the Testator to be his last Will }
and Testament in presence of us }

 Joseph Metcalf
 Benjamin Walker
 Thomas Metcalf

Probated 20 Jan., 1790. [IV, 81.] James Page and Joseph Metcalf, both of Hallowell, sureties. Inventory by Lazarus Goodwin, Nathaniel Shaw and James Page, all of Hallowell, 25 Jan., 1790, £179 : 14 : 1. [IV, 123-4.]

Thomas Gerrish, late of Camden. Joanna Gerrish, of Cushing, widow, Adm'x, 9 July, 1789. [IV, 82.] John McKellar and Andrew Malcom, Jr., both of Cushing, sureties.

Thomas McFarland, late of Boothbay, mariner. Lydia McFarland, of Woolwich, widow, Adm'x, 12 Oct., 1789. [IV, 83.] Nathaniel Tibbetts and Jones Mitchel, both of Woolwich, sureties. Inventory by William McCobb, John Leishman and Joseph Reed, all of Boothbay, 26 Oct., 1789, £38 : 16 : 0. [IV, 160.] Account filed 13 Sep., 1790. [IV, 161.]

Prince Coffin, late of Pownalborough. Mary Coffin, of Pownalborough, widow, Adm'x, 11 Feb., 1790. [IV, 92.] Jacob Brown and William Dinsmore, both of Pownalborough, sureties. Inventory by Elihu Getchel, of Bowdoinham, Jacob Brown, of Pownalborough, and Seth Hathorn, of Woolwich, 19 Feb., 1790. [IV, 190.]

Paul Jones, late of Fairfield Plantation. Agreement of heirs not to prove will of deceased and division of estate by Apollos Jones, of Fairfield Plantation, only surviving son ; Rosanna, wife of Joseph Jones, of Barnstable, County of Barnstable, a daughter; Avis, wife of Daniel Shepherd, of Fairfield Plantation, a daughter; Meribah Allen Jones, of Barnstable, a daughter ; Pamelia, wife of Zacheus Bowerman, of Fairfield Plantation, a daughter; 8 Jan., 1788. [IV, 93 to 96.]

Martin Hayley, late of Pittston. William Hayley, of Pittston, Adm'r, 30 May, 1789. [IV, 102.] Philip Theobald, of Pownalborough, and John Haley, of Pittston, sureties. Inventory by Philip Theobald, Samuel Woodward and Carr Barker, all of Pownalborough, 25 Sep., 1789, £178 : 3 : 0. [IV, 130.] Widow's dower set off by Philip Theobald, Samuel Woodward and Carr Barker, all of Pownalborough, 10 Dec., 1791. [V, 1-2.] Account filed 9 Sep., 1791. [V, 3.]

Elisha Partridge, late of Union. Sarah Partridge, of Union, widow, Adm'x, 30 Jan., 1787; James Stackpole and Israel Loveit, both of Thomaston, sureties. Inventory by Philip Robbins, Moses Hawes and Joel Adams, all of Union, Ap., 1787, £300 : 6 : 2. Moses Copeland, of Warren, and Samuel Brown, of Thomaston, commissioners to examine claims. [IV, 106 to 108.] Moses Hawes, of Union, guardian unto Elisha, minor son, 31 Jan., 1787. [III, 142.] Account filed 15 Sep., 1789. [IV, 109.] Distribution ordered, 27 Dec., 1791. [IV, 206.] Account filed 26 July, 1791. [IV, 206-7.]

Ebenezer Webb, late of Woolwich. Joel Reed, of Woolwich, Adm'r, 14 Ap., 1790. Heirs: Sarah, John, Benjamin, Nathan, Bersheba Gahan, Anne Reed, Sarah Bayley. [IV, 113.] Jonathan Reed and Samuel Reed, both of Woolwich, sureties. Inventory and account filed by Adm'r, 30 May, 1793. [VI, 120.]

I Gideon Parkman of Canaan in the County of Lincoln & State of Massachusetts. Sensible that I am mortal & must Soon leave this world & appear before God my final judge, to receive of him according to the Deeds done in the body, & being of Sound mind & memory, I make this my last will & testament;

And first I commit my Soul to God as my only portion & refuge thro' the merits of Jesus Christ his Son my only redeemer, on whose merits alone I depend for justification & acceptance before God now & in the day of judgment; & my body I commit to the dust to be decently, but not Sumptuously buried, in a firm belief that it Shall be raised again by the virtue & power of my head Jesus Christ who is the resurrection & the life

And as to the Small temporal interest God hath blessed me with I dispose of it in the following manner, viz

First, I give to Mary my beloved wife all my household goods & furniture for her use during her life, & after her decease to be equally divided (except a bed Noah Parkman lodges on & a bible, Which I give to said Noah) among my Daughters Betty Clark, Rhode Whitman & Mary Prat.

Item I give to my Son Daniel Parkman one pound to be paid by Noah Parkman when he shall be twenty two years old.

Item I give to Noah Parkman my grandson my Cow & calf & all my farming utensils & also all my sheep

Item I give him the said Noah Parkman & to his heirs & assigns all that tract of land lying in Canaan afores'd which I bought of Lieutenant Isaac Smith of Canaan togather with the house & barn & all the appurtanances thereunto belonging for his & their use forever, after the death of Mary my wife; but I will & bequeath to her the s'd Mary my wife, the sole use & benefit of the afores'd land & buildings during her life

This I declare to be my last will & testament given under my hand & seal this twenty eighth Day of May 1788.

Signed Sealed & declared in presence of   Gideon Parkman (seal)

  Nathl. Whitaker
  John White
    Peter Heywood Jr
    Joseph Weston

Schedule: Before the Sealing & delivery of these presents I appoint Mr Brice McCleland to be my Sole Executor to this my last will & testament, which appointment was forgot, till the above was finished.

Probated 15 Sep., 1789. [IV, 118.] Solomon Clark, of Canaan, Adm'r *cum Testamento annexo*, 15 Sep., 1789. [IV, 119.] Bryce McLellan and John White, both of Canaan, sureties. Inventory by Solomon Steward, Isaac Smith and Bryce McLellan, 10 Dec., 1789, £86 : 18 : 0. [IV, 120.]

Walter Meloney, of Cushing, *non compos*. Joseph Copeland, of Warren, guardian, 20 Ap., 1790. [IV, 122.] Inventory by Haunce Robinson, Robert McIntyer and Archibald Robinson, all of Cushing, £90 : 16 : 0. [IV, 258.]

Peleg Gardner, late of Bath. Mary Gardner, of Bath, widow, Adm'x, 14 June, 1790. [IV, 125.] William Marshal and Edward Pettingill, both of Bath, sureties. Inventory by Edward Pettingill, David Trufant and John Robinson, all of Bath, 15 July, 1790, £168 : 7 : 7. [IV, 178-9.] Mary, widow, guardian unto Ruth, minor daughter, 27 Nov., 1795. [VI, 124.]

Samuel Palmer, late of Pittston. Anna, widow, relinquished right to administer to son Edward 14 June, 1790; Edward Palmer, of Pittston, Adm'r, 21 June, 1790. [IV, 128.] Leonard Cooper, of Pittson, and Richard Bayley, of Pownalborough, sureties. Inventory by Carr Barker, Jonathan Morrison and John Woodman, Jr., 16 July, 1790, £137 : 9 : 2. [IV, 176-7.]

Thomas Sanders, late of Deer Isle. Hephzibah, widow, renounced right of administration, 5 Dec., 1789; James Sanders, of Deer Isle, Adm'r, 8 Dec., 1789. [IV, 129.] Timothy Sanders and Nathan Johnson, both of Deer Isle, sureties. Inventory by John Hooper, James Jordan and Ignastius Haskell, all of Deer Isle, 20 Feb., 1790, £82 : 19 : 10. [V, 70.] Ignatius Haskell and James Jordan, commissioners to examine claims. [V, 71.] Account filed and distribution ordered, 18 Sep., 1792. [V, 72 to 74.]

Benjamin Brainerd, late of Winthrop. Ruth Brainerd, of Winthrop, widow, Adm'x, 25 May, 1790. [IV, 131.] Jonathan Whiting and Reuben Brainerd, both of Winthrop, sureties. Inventory by Jonathan Whiting, Nathaniel Floyd and John Comings, 11 June, 1790, £295 : 12 : 0. [IV, 275.] Account filed 17 Jan., 1792. [IV, 275-6.] Ruth, widow, guardian unto Sarah, Mary, James and Orrin, minor children, 3 Mar., 1795. Benjamin, minor son, chose Ruth, widow, to be his guardian, 20 Mar., 1795. [VI, 124-5.] Guardian's accounts filed 9 Sep., 1796. [VII, 229 to 231.] Widow's dower set off and estate divided by Samuel Wood, Elijah Snell and John Kezer, all of Winthrop, 3 Dec., 1802. [X, 106-111.]

Philip Godfrid Hoyt, late of Topsham, physician. Elizabeth Hoyt, of Topsham, widow, Adm'x, 20 July, 1790. [IV, 144.] William Malcom and William Hunter, both of Topsham, sureties. Inventory by Gideon Owen, Joseph Foster and Ebenezer Emerson, all of Topsham, 2 Aug., 1790, £150 : 5 : 9. [IV, 172.] Gideon Owen and Joseph Foster, commissioners to examine claims. Account filed 8 Aug., 1791. [IV, 196-7.] Distribution ordered 15 Sep., 1791. [IV, 198.]

The Last will and testament of Obed Hussey of Hollawell in the County of Lincoln in the Common welth of Massachusets Esqr— I the Said Obed Hussey being of Sound and Disposing minde and memory and Considering the mortality of the body, Knowing that it is appointed unto all men once to Die, Do make and ordain this my Last will and testament in manner and form following—

And first I Recomend my Soul into the hands of God that Gave it and my body to the Earth to be Desently Buried-

And as touching Such worldly Estate wherewith it hath pleased God to Bless me with in this Life, I Do Give Devise and Dispose of the Same in maner and form following, *Imprimis* I Do will and order that all the Just Debts that I Shall owe to aney Person or persons at the time of my Decease Shall be well & truly paid and Discharged out of my Estate By my Executrix herein after mentioned or named. Item I Give to my Son Obed Hussey Ten Shillings Lawfull money and the Hous he now Lives In and the land it Stands upon, to him & to his heirs & assigns forever Item I Give to my Son Samuel Hussey a Certain Hous Called awerehous Standing on the Edg of the Land on the East Side kenebeck River & is to the Southward & Eastward of my dweling hous In Said kenebeck, with half an achor of Land Joyning Said hous the most Conveniant for both Houses, to him & to his heirs & assigns forever. Item I Give to my Grand daughter Polley Hussey Perkins Daughter to Ebenezer Perkins Ten Shillings lawfull money to be paid to her by my Executrix. Item I Give to my Daughter Elizebeth Delano wife to Thomas Delano Junr : ten Shillings Lawfull money to be paid her by my Executrix. Item I Give to my Daughter Ann Norcross wife to Phillip Norcross ten Shillings lawfull money to be paid her by my Executrix. Item I Give to my Daughter Sarah Hussey ten Shillings lawfull money to be paid her by my Executrix. Item I give to my Son in law Natthaniel Coffin ten Shillings lawfull money to be paid him by my Executrix Item I Give to my Son in law Ebenezer Perkins ten Shillings lawfull money to be paid him by my Executrix. Item I Give and Bequeath unto my Loveing wife Mary Hussey all my Real and Personal Estate which I Shall be Siezed of at the time of my Decease wheresoever the Same Shall or may be found to her Use and Disposall for Ever, and Likewise I appoint Constetute and ordan my Beloved wife Mary Hussey to be my Sole Executrix of all this my Last will and Testament   In witnes whereof I the Said Obed Hussey have to these presents Set my hand and Seal the Eith day of September *anoque Domini* 1789

Signed Sealled Published Pronounced
and declared by the Said Obed Hussey
to be his Last will and testament
in presence of us the Subscribers   Obed Hussey   [seal]
   Ezra Taylor
   John Johnson
   Samuel Twycross Goodwin

Probated 6 Aug., 1790. [IV, 145.] Inventory by Lazarus Goodwin, Samuel Bullin and James Hinkley, all of Hallowell, 28 Ap., 1791, £918 : 14 : 2. [Unrecorded.] Inventory of real estate in Nantucket by Christopher Starbuck, Richard

Mitchell and William Hammatt, all of Nantucket, 25th 10mo, 1790, £502 : 10. [Unrecorded.]

Ebenezer Preble, late of Woolwich. Samuel Preble, of Woolwich, Adm'r, 31 July, 1790. [IV, 147.] Thomas Motherwill and Ebenezer Smith, both of Woolwich, sureties. Inventory by Samuel Stinson, David Gilmore and Abner Wade, all of Woolwich, 19 Aug., 1790, £234 : 3 : 4. [IV, 173-4.] Dower set off to Martha, widow, 1 July, 1791. [IV, 227.] Nathaniel Thwing and David Gilmore, both of Woolwich, commissioners to examine claims. Account filed 27 Dec., 1791. [IV, 228-9.] Distribution ordered 6 Jan., 1792. [IV, 229-230.]

Joseph Mains, late of Woolwich. Beatris Mains, of Woolwich, widow, Adm'x, 24 July, 1790. [IV, 148.] Robert White and Joel Reed, both of Woolwich, sureties. Inventory by Samuel Harnden, Thomas Motherwill and David Gilmore, all of Woolwich, 20 Aug., 1790, £521 : 15 : 2. [IV, 175.] Nathaniel Thwing and David Gilmore, both of Woolwich, commissioners to examine claims. Bettrice, widow, guardian unto Sarah, minor daughter, 31 May, 1799. [IX, 180.] James Cobb, minor son, chose Robert White, of Woolwich, to be his guardian, 31 May, 1799. [IX, 229.] Bettrice and Anna, minor daughters, chose Bettrice, widow, to be their guardian, 31 May, 1799. [IX, 230-1.] Division of real estate by Nathaniel Thwing, David Gilmore and Jacob Eames, all of Woolwich, 5 June, 1801, among Susanna, wife of William Partridge, Anna, Beatrice, James, Sarah and Abigail Mains. [XIII, 453-4.]

Oliver Colburn, late of Hallowell. Margaret Colburn, of Hallowell, widow, Adm'x, 4 May, 1790. [IV, 148.] David Jackson and Benjamin White, both of Hallowell, sureties. Inventories by Lazarus Goodwin, Jonathan Davenport and Samuel Bullen, all of Hallowell, 22 June, 1790, £44 : 19 : 10. [IV, 164-5.] 4 June, 1791, £45. 11 May, 1792, £4 : 15 : 6. [V, 124.] Lazarus Goodwin and William Brooks, both of Hallowell, commissioners to examine claims. [V, 124.] Account filed and distribution ordered, 15 Jan., 1793. [V, 125 to 127.]

In the Name of God Amen. I Robert Barker of Pownalborough in the County of Lincoln Cooper, calling to mind the Brevity & uncertainty of Life, but being of a sound and disposing Mind & Memory, for which I thank God, do make and ordain this my last Will & Testament in manner following. In the first place I bequeathe my Soul into the Hand of God, whenever he may please to call for it, and my Body to the Earth, to be decently buried at the Discretion of my Executors hereafter named. And as to my worldly Estate, my Will is that my Executors pay all my just Debts with my personal Estate, excepting what I owe for the Farm I own in partnership with Timothy Folgier, and my Will is, that my Executors sell so much of said Farm, as will pay what is due therefor

Item. I give and bequeathe to my beloved Son Francis so much Money as will purchase a Yoke of Oxen and two Cows at the Time when he shall come to the Age of Twenty-one years, and to be paid to him at that Time.

Item. I give and bequeathe to my Son James a pair of three year old Steers which I now own, to be delivered to him in two Months after my decease.

Item. I give and bequeathe to my beloved Wife Sarah Barker all the rest and residue of my Estate both real and personal, for her to hold during the Time she continues to be my Widow, for her support and for the maintain and and bringing up my Children born or that may be born of her Body, and when my said Children shall arrive at full Age, and my said Wife shall decease or marry again, my Will is, that what of my Estate shall then remain whether real or personal, that it be equally divided amongst all my Children.

And I do hereby appoint my said Wife & my beloved Brother Josiah Barker my Executors of this my last Will and Testament, and hereby revoke all former Will & declare this to be my last

In witness whereof I hereunto set my hand & Seal the twenty fifth Day of Octr. A D 1779

Signed sealed published & declared by   Robert Barker (seal)
Testator to be his last Will and Testament
in presence of
William Wyman Tho. Rice
Prince Coffin—

Widow renounced executorship 27 Sep., 1790. Probated 18 Oct., 1790. [IV, 151.] Inventory by Shubael Barnard, Zaccheus Macy and Richard Mitchel, all of Sherburne, Nantucket County, 16 July, 1791, £276 : 9 : 1. [V, 188-9.] Nathaniel Thwing, of Woolwich, and Elihu Getchel, of Bowdoinham, commissioners to examine claims. [V, 231.] Distribution of estate ordered 7 May, 1802. [VIII, 132.]

Solomon Walker, late of Woolwich. Meriam, widow relinquished right of administration to son Solomon. [IV, 165.] Solomon Walker, of Woolwich, Adm'r, 13 Sep. 1790. [IV, 166.] Andrew Walker and Nathaniel Tibbets, both of Woolwich, sureties. Inventory by Elijah Grant, John Bailey and Nathaniel Tibbets, all of Woolwich, 9 Mar., 1791, £43 : 3 : 6. [IV, 231.] Nathaniel Thwing and David Gilmore, both of Woolwich, commissioners to examine claims. Account filed 27 Dec., 1791. [IV, 233.] Distribution ordered, 6 Jan., 1792. [IV, 234.]

Cornelius Bradford, late of Medumcook, mariner. Patience, widow, relinquished right of administration to son Joshua. [IV, 166.] Joshua Bradford, Jr., of Medumcook, Adm'r, 15 Sep., 1790. [IV, 167.] Joshua Collamore and Joshua Bradford, both of Medumcook, sureties. Inventory by Paul Jameson, Ebenezer Morton, Jr., and Elijah Cook, all of Medumcook, 15 June, 1791, £362 : 14 : 6. [IV, 270-1.] Dunbar Henderson and Eleazer Gay, both of Cushing, commissioners to examine claims. [V, 215.] Widow's dower set off by Paul Jameson, Elijah Cook and Ebenezer Morton, Jr., 8 Dec., 1794. [V, 217-218.] Advertisement of sale of real estate 10 Oct., 1794. [V, 218.] Appraisal of annual rent of real estate by Charles Samson, Joseph Simmons and Nathan Sprague, 11 Feb., 1795. [V, 219.] Account filed 11 Feb., 1795. [V, 219-220.] Distribution ordered, 13 Feb., 1795. [V, 220-1.]

In the name of God Amen
I Sherebiah Town of Winslow in the County of Lincoln & Commonwelth of Massachusetts husbandman being in a poore State of helth But of perfect mind and memory thanks be given to God Calling unto mind the mortality of my Body and knowing that it is apointed for all men once to Die Do make and ordain this my last will and testement that is to Say as touching Such worldly Estate wherewith it has pleased God to bless me with in this Life I Give and Demise and Dispose of the Same in the following mannar and forme
first I give and Bequath to my Honad : Fathar Thomas Town the Sum of fourty Shilling Lawfull mony of Massachusetts to be Raised and Levied out of my Estate
Also I Give to my Beloved Brothar Ephm : Town the Sum of five Shilling to be Raised and Levied out of my Estate
Also I Give to my Beloved Sister Hannah McCasland the Sum of ten Shillings to be Raised and Levied out of my Estate
Also I Give to my Beloved Sister Betty Barton the Sum of five Shillings

to be Raised and Levied out of my Estate

Also I Give and Bequath the Remainder of my Estate Lands Goods and Chattels for the Support of a School in a Plantation Lying to the Eastward of Winslow known by the name of Freetown at this time.

Also I Constitute and Apoint the Sellectt Men of the Towns of Vassalborough and Winslow to be the trustees of the Estate that is Left for Schooling

Also I Constitute make and Ordain William Howard of Hallowill in the County of Lincoln and Commonwelth of Massachusetts Esqr: the Sole Excutor of this my Last will and testement and I Do hereby utterly Disallow Revoke and Disanuel all and Every othar former testements wills Legices Bequeaths and Excuetors by me in any wise before named willied and Bequathed Ratifying and Confirming this and no othar to be my Last will and testement in witness whereof I have hereunto Set my hand and Seal this twentySixth Day of Febuary in the year of our Lord one thousand Seven hundred and Eighty Eight

            Sherebiah Town   (seal)

Sign'd Seal'd published pronounced and Declared
by the sd : Sherebiah Town as his Last will and
testement in the presents of us who in his presants
and in the presants of Each othar have hereunto Subscribed our Names
James Stackpole
Samuel Stackpole
Jonathan Ballard

        Probated 10 Sep., 1790. [IV, 167-8.] William Howard renounced executorship 10 Sep., 1790; Thomas Town refused to administer, 10 Sep., 1790. [IV, 168.] Ephraim Town, of Winslow, Adm'r *cum Testamento annexo*, 10 Sep, 1790. [IV, 169.] Samuel Stackpole, of Winslow, and Jonathan Ballard, of Hallowell, sureties. Inventory by James Stackpole, William Richardson and Enoch Fuller, all of Winslow, 18 Nov., 1790, £17 : 14 : 9. [IV, 170-1.] Josiah Hayden and James Stackpole, both of Winslow, commissioners to examine claims. [V, 117.] Advertisement of sale of real estate, 20 Oct., 1793. [V, 118.] Account filed 15 Jan., 1793. [V, 118-119.] Account filed 15 Ap., 1794. [V, 252-3.]

 John Weaver, late of Waldoborough. Molly Weaver, of Waldoborough, widow, Adm'x, 16 Nov., 1790. [IV, 180.] Cornelius Hyer and Henry Overlock, both of Waldoborough, sureties. Inventory by Caleb Turner, of Bristol, George Hebner and Francis Miller, both of Waldoborough, 3 Mar., 1791, £51 : 8 : 3. [IV, 219-220.]

John Trask, late of Vassalborough. Sarah Trask, of Vassalborough, widow, Adm'x, 14 Jan., 1790. [IV, 180-1.] Asa Wilber and Elijah Balkam, both of Vassalborough, sureties. Inventory by Nathan Sawtell, John Ward and James Stedman, all of Vassalborough, 17 Jan., 1792, £129 : 14 : 0. [V, 43-44.] Henry Sewall and Nathan Wesson both of Hallowell, commissioners to examine claims. [V, 112.] Account filed 15 Jan., 1793, at which date administratrix had become wife of David Wildbur. [V, 113-114.] John Woodcock, of Sidney, guardian unto Samuel, Sylvia and John, minor children, 21 Ap., 1794. [VI, 58-59.]

Calvin Edson, late of Sandy River. Elizabeth Edson, of Sandy River, widow, Adm'x, 17 Jan., 1790. [IV, 181.] Robert Kennady and Benjamin Wade, both of Hallowell, sureties. Inventory by Enoch Crage, Moses Starling and Jacob Eaton, 23 Feb., 1791, £29 : 0 : 2; inventory by Supply Belcher, John Church and Enoch Crage, all of Sandy River, 16 Jan., 1792, £12. [V, 48.] Supply Belcher and John Church, commissioners to examine claims. [V, 114.] Account filed 15 Jan., 1793. [V, 116.] Distribution ordered, 16 Jan., 1793. [V, 154.]

in the Name of God Amen—
I, John Walch of Waldoborough in the County of Lincoln and Common Wealth of Massachusetts yeoman : Being inferme in Body But in Berfect Memmory, Do make and ordain this my Last will and testament, in order following, that is to Say : I Give and Recomment my Soul into the hand of Almighty God that Gave it and my body I Recommend to the Earth to be Decently intered at the Discretion of my Executors, touching Such Worldly Estate Which it hath Pleased God to Bless me With, I will and bequeath in the following manner and form-

I Bequeath to Anna Elbet my Well be Loved Wife all My Real and Personal Estate, by her freely to be Posessed and injoyed Turing her Natural Life, or other ways as Long as She Shall Remain my widow : if my well beloved wife Should marry again, then my Estate is to be Equel Dividet among my Children and also if my well beloved wife Shall keep my Estate in her hand During Life, and after her Decease my Estate is then to be Equelly Dividet among my Children

Also I Lickwise Constitute make and ordain my well beloved wife the

Sole Executor of this my Last will and Testament   And I Do here by utterly Disallow Revoke and Disannul all and Every other former testaments and wills by me in any ways before named willed and Bequeathed, Ratifying and Confirming this and no other to be my Last will and testament.

In witness whereof, I have hereunto Set my hand and Seal this Twenty third Day of December, in the year of our Lord one thousand Seven hundred and Eighty nine.

his
John X Walch   (seal)
mark

Signed Sealed Published and Pronounced by the said John Walch as his Last will and testament in the Presence of us, who in his Presence and in the Presence of Each other have here unto Subscribed our Names.

Jacob Ludwig
Friederik Arnold
Johannes Werner

Probated 22 Nov., 1790. [IV, 187.] Peter Walch and Johannes Werner, both of Waldoborough, sureties. Inventory by Jacob Winchenback, Godfrey Bornheimer and George Heabner, all of Waldoborough, 14 Jan., 1791, £55 : 9 : 8. [IV, 244-5.]

Luke Barton, late of Hancock. Betty Barton, widow, Adm'x, 26 June, 1790. [IV, 192. V, 81-82.] Ephraim Town, of Winslow, and Jonathan Ballard, of Hallowell, sureties. Inventory by Zimri Heywood, James Stackpole and William Richardson, all of Winslow, 6 Sep., 1790. [IV, 191.] Josiah Hayden and James Stackpole, both of Winslow, commisioners to examine claims. [V, 82.] Account filed, 15 Jan., 1793. [V, 237-8.]

In the Name of GOD, Amen. The Thirty-first Day of December, in the Year of our Lord One Thousand, seven Hundred & ninety, I Matthew Hastings, of Vassalborough, in the County of Lincoln and Commonwealth of Massachusetts, Gentleman, being weak in Body, but of sound and disposing Mind and Memory, and knowing that I must shortly leave this earthly Tabernacle, do commit my Soul into the Hands of the all-merciful Author of it, firmly trusting, through the Merits of my most beneficent Saviour, in a glorious Resurrection to Eternal Life ; and my Body to be interred at the Discretion of my Executors. And with Regard to that earthly Substance with which it hath pleased God to endow me, I will and dispose of it in the following Manner, viz.

First. I will that all my just Debts and Funeral Charges shall be paid.
Secondly. I give devize and bequeath unto Mary, my beloved Wife, all my Live Stock and In-Door Moveables, forever, and the West Room in my Dwelling-House, during her natural Life.
Thirdly. I give, devize and bequeath unto my Son-in Law, Dodivah Townsend & Sarah his Wife, my Homestead Farm, with the Buildings & Appurtenances thereof, except my Wife's Living in the said West Room, together with all my Carpenter's Tools and farming Utensils, he paying what I am indebted to William Howard Esqr- and also Ten Bushels Indian corn & eight Bushels English Grain to my said Wife, *p Annum*, during her Natural Life and keeping two Cows & one Horse for her, during the same Term: and also supply her with Wood enough for one Fire during said Term.
Fourthly. I give, devize and bequeath unto my Son Moses Hastings, my Lot of Land at Sandy River, together with my Right in the Lot lately improved by Reuben Page, to the Westward of the West Pond, near said Vassalboro' with the Privileges & Appurtenances thereof- To have and to hold the same unto him the said Moses, his Heirs and Assigns forever.
Fifthly. I give, devise and bequeath unto the Heirs of Mary Brooks, Twenty Pounds, to be paid out of a Note of William Brooks's now in my possession.
Sixthly. I give devize & bequeath unto my Daughter Abigail Butterfield, Twenty Pounds, to be paid out of a Note payable to the late John Rogers, decd. on whose Estate I was Administrator.
Seventhly. I give devize and bequeath unto my Daughter Hannah Evens, Twenty Pounds, out of a Note in my Possession against her Husband Nathaniel Evens—This Legacy to be paid as soon as possible after my Decease.
Eighthly. I give, devize and bequeath unto my Daughter, Mercy Page, the Debt her Husband Reuben Page owes me.
Ninthly. I give, devize and bequeath unto my Daughter Susanna Greely, Fifteen Pounds, to be paid out of the Debt her Husband, Joseph Greely, owes me.
Tenthly. I give devize and bequeath unto the Children of Joseph Kelly, by my Daughter Rebecca, viz. To William Kelly Ten pounds, to be paid when he comes of age- To Sarah Kelly, Six pounds, to be paid when she comes of age- These Legacies to be paid by Jonathan Combs out of the Legacy hereinafter bequeathed to him.

Eleventhly. I give and bequeath unto Mary Combs & Elizabeth Rogers, all my Interest in a certain Saw-Mill, Dam & Privilege at the Outlet of the West Pond in Winslow, they paying the Legacy to Kelly's Children above bequeathed, and fully discharging me and my Heirs from all Claims on the Estate of their late Father John Rogers, decd. on which I was Administrator.

Twelfthly. I make, Ordain, constitute and appoint the said Moses Hastings and Dodivah Townsend, joint Executors of this my last Will and Testament, hereby revoking and annulling all former or other Wills by me heretofore made. In Witness whereof I do hereunto set my Hand and Seal the Day and Year herein first before written.

  N. B. The following Words were interlined before sealing &c viz- "and bequeath"—"and farming Utensils"—"said"—"The Heirs of"

          his
        Matthew ⋈ Hastings (seal)
Signed, sealed and declared   Mark
by the said Matthew Hastings,
the Testator, to be his last
Will and Testament, in
presence of us

W. WILKINS
Moses Hastings Jun
  her
Thankful X Robins
  Mark
Witness to Thankful Robins's Mark
  W. WILKINS

  Probated 18 Jan., 1791. [IV, 192-3.] Noah Woodward, of Hallowell, and Philip Snow, of a place called Washington, sureties. Inventory by Nathaniel Reynolds and Ephraim Butterfield, both of Vassalborough, and Noah Woodward, of Hallowell, 14 Ap., 1791. [IV, 218.] Henry Sewall and Samuel Colman, both of Hallowell, commissioners to examine claims. [V, 179.] Advertisement of sale of real estate 14 May, 1793. [V, 181.] Account filed 29 Ap., 1794. [V, 182-3.]

  David Woodcock, late of Union. Abigail Woodcock, of Union, widow, Adm'x, 12 Ap., 1791. [IV, 194-5.] Joseph Guild and Samuel Hill, both of Union, sureties. Inventory by Josiah Robbins, David Robbins and Moses Hawes, all of Union, 14 May, 1791, £76 : 14 : 0. [IV, 220-1.] Josiah Robbins and Joel Adams, both of

Union, commissioners to examine claims. [V, 156.] Account filed and distribution ordered, 17 Sep, 1793. [V, 158-9.]

James Campbell, late of Newcastle. Sarah Campbell, of Newcastle, widow, Adm'x, 15 June, 1791. [IV, 199-200.] Inventory by Samuel Nickels and Charles Chase, both of Newcastle, and Samuel Waters, of Balltown, 7 July, 1791. [IV, 201-2.] Account filed 31 May, 1792; division of estate by Samuel Nickels and Samuel Kennedy, both of Newcastle, and Thomas Boyd, of Boothbay, 31 Oct., 1792, heirs named: Joseph Campbell, Sally Borland, Betsey Campbell, Daniel Campbell, Michael Campbell, Thomas Campbell, Robert Campbell, James Campbell and Rachel Campbell. [Unrecorded.]

Thomas McCobb, late of Georgetown, trader. Upon petition of Ezekiel Cushing, Francis Cushing, Isabella Parker, Margaret Lee, Ann McCobb and Betras Mains, "Brethren & Sisters," dated July 2d., 1791, [V, 29], William Lee, Jr., of Georgetown, was appointed Adm'r, 17 Oct., 1791. [IV, 200-1.] Alexander Drummond and Elijah Drummond, both of Georgetown, sureties.

James Nickels, late of Newcastle, mariner. John Nickels, of Newcastle, tailor, Adm'r, 12 Sep., 1791. [IV, 209] Samuel Nickels and Samuel Kennedy, both of Newcastle, sureties.

Solomon Hearsey, late of Pownalborough. Betty Hearsey, of Pownalborough, widow, Adm'x, 26 May, 1791. [IV, 210.] Inventory by Daniel Scott, Isaac Prince and James Clark, all of Pownalborough, 7 June, 1791, £80 : 7 : 5. [IV, 269.] Advertisement of sale of real estate 2 June, 1794. [VI, 254.] Ebenezer Whittier and Thomas Fairservice, both of Pownalborough, commissioners to examine claims. [VI, 254-5.]

Andrew Reed the 2d :, late of Boothbay, mariner. Hannah Reed, of Pownalborough, widow, Adm'x, 10 June 1791. [IV, 210-211.] Inventory by Joseph Decker and Stephen Clough, both of Pownalborough, and Moses Davis, of Edgecomb, 19 July, 1791, £22 : 9 : 0. [IV, 222-3.] Moses Davis, of Edgecomb, and Ebenezer Whittier, of Pownalborough, commissioners to examine claims. [V, 25.] Account filed and distribution ordered 25 May, 1792, at which date administratrix had become the wife of Nathaniel Stevens, of Woolwich. [V, 26.]

Zachary Davis, late of Medumcook. Ephraim Davis, of Medumcook, Adm'r, 15 Sep., 1791. [IV, 211.] William Young and John Hathhorn, both of Cushing, sureties. Inventory by Eleazer Gay, of

Cushing, Robert Jameson and Paul Jameson, both of Medumcook, 6 Oct., 1791, £44 : 2 : 7. [V, 93.] Robert Jameson and Ebenezer Morton, both of Medumcook, commissioners to examine claims. [VI, 74.] Widow's dower set off by Wellington Gay, James Sweetland and William Bradford, all of Medumcook, in March, 1796. [VI, 218-219.] Account filed 20 Sep., 1796. [VI, 219.] Distribution ordered, 6 Jan., 1797. [VI, 255-6.]

John Thompson, late of Barretstown. Jane Thompson, of Barretstown, widow, Adm'x, 13 Sep., 1791. [IV, 212.] Robert Thompson and Winzer Jones, both of Barretstown, sureties. Inventory by Barnard Case, Prince Pease and Robert McLintock, 21 Sep., 1791, £141 : 1 : 1. [VI, 185-6.]

Comfort Barrows, late of Thomaston. Sabra Barrows, of Thomaston, widow, Adm'x, 26 July, 1791. [IV, 213-214.] Constant Rankin and Samuel Tolman, both of Thomaston, sureties. Inventory by William Spear, Jeremiah Tolman and Daniel Palmer, all of Thomaston, 5 Jan., 1792, £309 : 5 : 0. [V, 242-3.] Inventory by Oliver Nash, Peter Collamore and John McClain, all of Bristol, 14 Oct., 1794, £188 : 19 : 0. [V, 249.] Sabra, widow, guardian unto Sabra, minor daughter, 4 Nov., 1799. [IX, 184.]

William Martin, late of Bristol. Mary Martin, of Bristol, widow, Adm'x, 20 Sep., 1791. [IV, 214.] Thomas Johnston and Jacob Dockendorff, both of Bristol, sureties.

George Kellsy, or Kellsa, late of Bristol, Agnes Kellsy, of Bristol, widow, Adm'x, 20 Sep., 1791. [IV, 215.] Thomas Johnston and Jacob Dockendorff, both of Bristol, sureties. Inventory by Amos Goudy, Henry Fossett and William Sproul, all of Bristol, 7 Nov., 1791, £40 : 8 : 6. [V, 192.] Thomas Johnston and William Sproul, commissioners to examine claims. [V, 193.]

Samuel White, late of Pownalborough. Samuel White, of Pownalborough, Adm'r, 25 Jan., 1791. [IV, 215-216.] William Patterson and Joseph McFarland, Jr., both of Pownalborough, sureties. Inventory by William Lewis, Obadiah Call and Philip Theobald, all of Pownalborough, 1792, £32 : 0 : 8. [V, 30.]

Benjamin Maxey, late of Union. Amy Maxey, of Union, widow, Adm'x, 19 Sep., 1791. [IV, 216-217.] Philip Robbins and Josiah Robbins, both of Union, sureties. Amy Maxey guardian unto Sarah,

Lydia, Harvy and Amy, minor children, 20 Sep., 1791. [IV, 217.] Josiah Robbins, of Union, guardian unto Benjamin, minor son, 2 Jan., 1792. [V, 28.] Inventory by Joseph Guild, Joel Adams and William Hart, all of Union, 9 Nov., 1891, £635 : 17 : 11. [V, 76 to 78.] Sarah chose Matthias Hawes, of Union, to be her guardian, 30 May, 1793. [V, 128.] Josiah Maxey, of Union, guardian unto Harvey, 28 Aug., 1793. [V, 129.] Division of real estate by Joel Adams, Moses Hawes and Amariah Mero, all of Union, 23 May, 1794, among Benjamin, Joseph, Josiah and Harvey, and order of Court thereon, 16 Sep., 1794. [VI, 70 to 74.]

Christopher Blasdell, late of Georgetown. Sarah, widow, declined right of administration, 19 May, 1791. [IV, 242.] Daniel Blasdell, Adm'r; Timothy Blaisdell and Moses Morrison, both of Georgetown, sureties. Inventory by Elijah Drummond, Charles Bisbee and Theophilus Batchelder, all of Georgetown, 1 June, 1791, £15 : 16 : 3. [IV, 243.] Account filed 3 June, 1791. [IV, 244.]

John Parsons, late of Edgecomb, mariner. William Allbee, of Edgecomb, Adm'r, 17 Mar., 1790. [IV, 256.] Benjamin Allbee and Samuel Greenleaf, both of Edgecomb, sureties. Inventory by Barnabas Sears, William Cunningham and Samuel Greenleaf, all of Edgecomb, 6 Ap., 1790, £237 : 2 : 6. [IV, 255.] Yearly value of real estate appraised at $20, 20 Mar., 1798; account filed 4 June, 1798. [VIII, 66.] Widow's dower set off by Samuel Greenleaf, Spencer Decker and William Cunningham, all of Edgecomb, 21 June, 1798. [VIII, 67.] Advertisement of sale of real estate, 1798. [VIII, 67.] Account of William Albee, guardian unto William, John, Elihu and Patty, minor children, filed 4 June, 1798. [VIII, 75.]

I Nathniel Meigges of Vassalborough in the County of Lincoln yeoman seriously Considering the uncertainty of human Life in the best, and more particularly of my own in my Declining state of Health, Do while in a sound state of mind, make this my last Will, and Testament, intending to Dispose of all my worldly affairs, not as humour may prompt, but as Justice and equiety seem to Direct, I most humbly recommend my sole to the extensive mercy of that Suprem Eternal Intelligent Being who gave it me, most earnstly, at the same time Deprecating his Justice viz I give and bequeth to my two sones Nathniel and Ebenezer Meigges all my real Estat that I have in Vassalborough I give and bequeth to my Dear and loving wife Mary all my personel Estate after my Debts is paid out I likewise appont hir the Exutter to the estate which she is to bring up the Children out of the emprovements of my Estate untill tha Com of age I give to my Dafter Mary a Cow and Calf to be paid to hir after my estate is settled I give to my four other Dafters Hannhh Abigal Rebach Keziah fife shillings each to be paid out of my personal Estate when tha Com of age

Whereunto I have set my hand and seal this twenty first Day of December 1790

sined sealed by the said   Nathl Meiggs   (seal)
Nathniel Meiggs as for his last
will and testament in the presence
of us who ware present at the
sining and sealing thereof
William Wing
Silvanus Hatch
Lot Chadwick

Probated 2 June, 1791. [IV, 256.] Inventory by Jethro Gardiner, Richard Warren and Reuben Fairfield, all of Vassalborough, 9 July, 1791, £218 : 14 : 6. [V, 122.]

In the name of God amen I William McPhetres of Georgetown in the County of Lincoln & commonwealth of Massachusetts yeoman being sick & weak in Body but of perfect mind & memory, thanks be given to God, calling unto mind the mortality of my Body and knowing it is appointed for all men once to die do make & ordain this my last will and testament, that is to say principally and first of all I Give my Soul into the hand of Almighty God and my Body I recommend to be buried at the discretion of my Executors hoping that at the general resurrection I shall receive the same again by the mighty power of God. And as touching such worldly Estate wherewith it has pleased God to bless me I give demise and dispose of the same in the following manner & form -first- I give and bequeath to Abigail my dearly beloved wife the use and improvement of one third of all my Real Estate during her natural Life. And I give her all my personal Estate (except my stock in Cattle) during the time she shall continue my Widow—I also give to my only Son William all & singular my Lands and Tenements by him freely to be possessed & enjoyed saving and it is to be understood that my two Daughters Rachel & Betsy are to be supported and maintained of and on my said Lands until they shall be eighteen years of Age. And it is likewise my Will that my Brother James should during his natural Life be supported on and from the Farm I now live on Likewise I give to my Daughter Rachel two milch Cows and six sheep- I also give to my Daughter Betsey the same number of Cows & sheep and I give to each of my said Daughters a feather Bed & bedding to be possessed by them after my said Wife shall cease to be my Widow or cease to Live—Likewise I give to my Sister Betsey one good Cow— Also I give to my Nephew George Ring one pair of Calves. And I do constitute, make and ordain John White of Georgetown, Gentleman, and John Snipe of said Georgetown, yeoman Executors of this my last will & testament—And I do hereby utterly disallow revoke & disannul all and every other former testaments wills Legacies bequests and Executors by me in any wise before named willed & bequeathed ratifying & confirming this & no other to be my last will & testament

In Witness whereof I have hereunto set my hand & Seal this twenty seventh day of April in the year of our LORD one thousand seven hundred & ninety

Signed sealed published pronounced & declared by the said William McPhetres in the presence of us who in his Presence and in the presence of each other have hereto subscribed our Names—

William Mcphetres (seal)

Galen Otis
James Stinson
John Stinson

Probated 3 June, 1791. [IV, 259.]
John White and John Snipe renounced executorship 3 June, 1791. [IV, 260.]

In the Name of God, Amen. I Samuel Jameson of the Town of Topsham, Yeoman, being very sick, and weak in body, but of Perfect mind and memory, Thanks be Given to God: realising the mortality of my body, & knowing that is appointed unto all Men once to die, do make and ordain this my last Will and Testament, that is to say, first of all I give and recommend my Soul into the hand of God who gave it, and my body to the Earth to be buried in decent Christian Burial at the discretion of my Executors; nothing doubting, but at the general resurrection I shall receive the same again by the mighty Power of God. And as touching such Worldly Estate with which it hath pleased God to bless me in this Life I give, demise & dispose of the same, in the following manner and form. First. I give and bequeath to Mary my dearly beloved wife the improvement of one third part of my Real and Personal Estate during her Natural Life, or while she Continues my Widow, but if the said Mary marries again before all the Children are of Lawfull Age, then she is to quit all claim to the real and Personal Estate and to receive in lieu thereof, thirty five pounds lawfull money to be paid her out of my personal Estate in Articles which she may choose at their apprizement. Also I give unto my beloved sons Samuel and John, all my real estate to be equally divided between them, according to Quantity and Quality, excepting only the improvement of one third part during the Natural Life of their mother, or while she continues my Lawfull Widow.

Also, I give to my beloved Children, Samuel, John, Polly, Hannah, Peggy, Jenny, Dorcas, Sally, Eleanor & Susannah, all my Personal Estate not before disposed of, to be enjoyed by them equally, when they come of Lawful Age, the said Personal Estate to be improved by the said Samuel and John and by them to be paid to the other Children as they successively come of Lawfull Age. Also, My Will is That Mary my Wife, together with my two sons Samuel and John be Equal sharers in the expence which shall accrue in supporting and maintaining the Children untill they Come of Lawfull Age. Also I do hereby Appoint & Constitute Mary my Wife and Samuel my son to be the Executors of this my last Will and Testament. And I do hereby utterly disallow revoke and disannul all and every other former Testaments and wills by me in any wise before named, ratifying and Confirming this & no other to be my last Will and Testament. In Witness whereof I have hereunto set my hand & seal this 24th day of December in the year of our LORD one thousand seven hundred and ninety

           Saml: Jameson (seal)

Signed, sealed, published, pronounced & declared by the said Samuel Jameson as his Last Will & Testament in the Presence of us, who in his Presence, and in the Presence of each other, have hereto subscribed our Names

 John Fulton
 Abrm Whittemore
 James Fulton

Probated 27 May, 1791. [IV, 260.] Inventory by James Fulton and Alexander Rogers, both of Topsham, and Stephen Whitmore, of Bowdoinham, 28 Nov., 1791, £642 : 15 : 2. [V, 54-55.]

John Cochran, late of Newcastle. Agnes Cochran, of Newcastle, widow, Adm'x, 26 May, 1791; Samuel Kennedy and Robert Cochran, both of Newcastle, sureties. Inventory by Samuel Nickels, Peter Patterson and Samuel Groves, all of Newcastle, 3 June, 1791, £52 : 9 : 4. [IV, 266-7.] Samuel Nickels and Peter Patterson, commissioners to examine claims. [V, 228.] Advertisement of sale of real estate, 12 June, 1794. [V, 229.] Account filed 8 Sep., 1794. [V, 230.]

In the Name of God, Amen. I Katharine Gragg of Thomaston in the County of Lincoln and Commonwealth of Missachusetts Spinster being Sick and Weak in Body, but of perfect Mind and Memory, Thanks be given unto God; calling unto mind the Mortality of my Body and knowing that it is appointed for all Men once to die, do make and ordain this my last Will and Testament, That is to say, principally and first of all, I give and recommend my Soul into the Hand of Almighty God that give it, and my Body I recommend to the Earth, to be buried in decent Christian Burial, at the Discretion of my Executors; nothing douting, but at the general Resurrection, I shall receive the same again by the mighty Power of God. And as touching such worldly Estate wherewith it has pleased God to bless me in this Life, I give, demise and dispose of the same in the following Manner and Form:

Imprimis. I give and bequeath unto my well beloved Son William, commonly called and known by the Name of William Farnsworth, a Bible which with what I have already done for him, & he has already had is his full Part or Share out of my Estate.

Item. I give and bequeath unto my well beloved Daughter Sarah, commonly called and known by the Name of Sarah Farnsworth, my dark coloured callico Gown, black callimanco Skirt and Stone Sleeve Buttons to be delivered to her when she arrives at the Age of Eighteen years or in one Year after my decease, which with what She has already had is in full of her part or Share out of my Estate

Item. I give and bequeath to my well beloved Daughter Mehitabel commonly called and known by the Name of Mehitabel Dodge, my Silver Shoe-Buckles.

Item. I give and bequeath unto my well beloved Son and Daughter, to wit, Barnabas, commonly called and known by the Name of Barnabas Webb, Mary commonly called and known by the Name of Mary Webb, and the above named Mehitabel Dodge the whole remainder of my Estate of what Name or Nature soever (except what is herein otherwise particularly disposed of) to be equally divided to and amonst them, and each of them, or their or either of their legal Representatives in equal Shares, and Proportion.

Item I give unto my trusty Friend Ezekiel Goddard Dodge of Thomaston aforesaid Physician (in consideration of his Trouble and Care of me, and Expences laid out for me in my Present Sickness) The one half part of a certain Note of Hand for the Sum of twenty Seven Pounds with Interest due to me from him the said Ezekiel G. Dodge. which is now lodged in the Hands of Moses Copeland. And I do also constitute make and ordain him the said Ezekiel Goddard Dodge the Sole Executor of this my last Will and Testament. And I do hereby utterly disallow, revoke and disannul all and every other former Wills, Testaments, Legacies, Bequests, and Executors whatsoever in any ways before by me named, willed and bequeathed ratifying and confirming this and no other to be my last Will and Testament.

In Witness whereof I the said Katherine Gragg do hereunto set my Hand and Seal, this twenty first Day of September in the Year of our Lord One Thousand Seven Hundred and Ninety

Signed, Sealed, published pronounced and Declared by the said Katherine Gragg as her last Will and Testament in presence of us, who, in her presence, and in the Presence of each other have hereunto subscribed our Names, (The Words "and the above-"named Mehitabel Dodge" were interlined before signing and Sealing)
Deidamia Preist
Isaac Bernard
David Fales

Katherine X Gragg (seal)
her Mark

[Unrecorded.]

In the Name of God Amen, I William Butler of Georgetown in the County of Lincoln Yeoman being weak in body, but of sound and perfect mind and memory (blessed be God) do this eighteenth day of

February *Anno Domini* one Thousand seven hundred and ninety, make and publish this my last Will and Testament in manner following, Vizt.

Imprimis—I give and bequeath to my beloved Son William Butler all my Lands on Arrowsick Island in said Georgetown including the Farm whereon I now dwell with the buildings and appurtenances, excepting the House my said Son William now lives in, which, I give unto my beloved Daughters Sarah and Abigail during Their and each of Them remaining single and unmarried, to hold the same to him the said William Butler and the Heirs of his Body forever.—

2
Item—I give and bequeath to my beloved Son Thomas Butler and to the Heirs of his body forever Two hundred and seventeen Acres of Land fronting on Kennebec River being the easterly part of Three hundred and seventeen Acres which I own in Georgetown aforesaid on the west side of said River on a part of which the said Thomas Butler now lives, with the priviledges and appurtenances thereunto belonging together with a certain tract of Marsh on Parkers Island which I purchased of the Heirs of Edward Hutchinson Esquire.—

3
Item—I give and bequeath to my beloved Grand Son William Butler, Son of the said Thomas Butler all the residue and remainder of the said last mentioned tract of Land containing one hundred Acres and fronting in the whole width of said Tract of Land on Casco Bay to the Southward of Winnogance carrying place, to hold the same to him the said William Butler Son of the said Thomas and the Heirs of his body forever.—

4
Item—I will and order that the said Thomas Butler, Father of the said William Butler shall take care of and manage the same Lands to the use of the said William Butler and to his best profit and advantage during his Minority.—

5
Item—I will and ordain that in case my said Son William should die without Issue of his Body begotten, that then from and after his Death the Estate herein before devised to him shall enure to my said Son Thomas Butler, and the Male Heirs of his body forever.—

6
Item—I will and ordain that my beloved Wife Martha and my Daughter Sarah and Abigail Shall have the exclusive use and improvement of my Mansion House during the life of my said Wife, and I further will

and ordain that my said beloved Wife during her natural life shall have the use and improvement of all my personal Estate now upon and unto my homestead Estate on Arrowsick Island appertaining belonging and being; excepting Two Cows, Twelve Sheep and all my Farming Utensils and the use of my Oxen and all the Manure of the Cattle upon the Farm, which, I give to my said Son William during the natural life of my said Wife, for the better improvement of the said Farm which, the said William is to superintend oversee and manage and the annual profits thereof to be annually divided in equal Shares between the said William on the one part and my said Daughters and Wife on the other part, excepting the annual profits of the Cows and Sheep, which profits shall Accrue to the respective owners thereof for the time being.—

7
Item—I will and bequeath to my said Son William Butler at and after my Wife's decease all my said Farming Utensils, one Yoak of Oxen and Two Cows.—

8
Item—I also give to my said Son Thomas Butler, my Silver Watch, which he is to take into his possession immediately upon my decease.

9
Item—I give and bequeath to my said Sons, William and Thomas in common between Them my Share of the Fishing Boat and my Gundelow.—

10
Item—I also leave my Yawl Boat in common between my said Wife and Daughters & my said Son William and his family.—

11
Item—I will ordain and order that my said Son William his heirs executors or administrators as a consideration for the Estate I have herein before given him, shall within Two Years after the Death of me and my said Wife and of the longest liver of Us, pay unto my said Daughters Sarah and Abigail Twenty Pounds Lawful Money each, provided They or either of Them shall so long live.—

12
Item—I will ordain and order that my said Son Thomas his heirs executors or administrators as a consideration for the Estate which I have herein before given him, shall within Two Years after the decease of me and my Wife and of the longest liver of Us, pay unto my said Daughters Sarah and Abigail Ten pounds each, provided—They shall so long live.—

13
Item—I give and bequeath unto William Preble Son of Joseph Preble of said Georgetown to be immediately paid at my decease, Sixty Pounds Lawful money four Cows, Six Sheep, a Yoak of three Year old Stears, and a Bed and Beding together with half my Share in a certain lot of Marsh on Parkers Island which I purchased jointly with John Stinson esquire from Nathaniel Johnson Robbins, being in full for his services and dutiful behaviour towards me.

14
Item—I will and order that Forty pounds shall be paid to my Daughter Martha Soaper in the proportion of Six pounds annually untill the whole shall be paid up, provided my said Daughter shall so long live, said payments to commence within one Year after my decease being in full for her services and dutiful behavior towards me.

15
Item—I will and bequeath to each of my Daughters Sarah and Abigail a Bed and Beding to be paid and delivered to Them immediately upon the decease of my said Wife.

16
Item—I give and bequeath unto my beloved Grand Son William Butler Drummond Twenty pounds to be paid him at the age of Twenty one Years, also my other part of that certain lot of Marsh which I purchased with John Stinson esquire from Nathaniel Johnson Robbins.—

17
Item—I further will and order that the residue of my personal Estate not herein particularly disposed of, shall upon the decease of my said wife be equally divided between my Daughters Sarah, Abigail, Ann Drummond and Mary Preble wife of Joseph Preble aforesaid.—

18
Item—I will and ordain my said Son William Butler, Joseph Preble and Elijah Drummond all of said Georgetown Executors of this my last Will and Testament. In Witness whereof, I have hereunto set my hand and Seal the day and Year above and before mentioned.

William Butler   (seal)

Signed sealed published & declared by
the said William Butler the Testator as
& for his last Will and Testament in the
presence of Us, who were present at the
signing and Sealing thereof.
   Jas. Davidson
   Benj'n Pattee
   John Fisher

A Codicil to be added to and taken as a part of the last Will and Testiment of me William Butler to which this is a part. I do hereby confirm my said last Will in all Things not in and by this Codicil altered or revoked.—

I do in addition to what I have devised and bequeathed to my Two Daughters Sarah and Abigail in and by my said Will further give devise and bequeath to my said Daughters full and free liberty to cut and haul or cause to be cut & hauled for Their own use from the Homestead or Farm I live upon as much wood as They may find necessary for Their own Fires and House Use.

I also do in addition to what I have devised and bequeathed to my two Daughters Sarah and Abigail give devise and bequeath to my said Daughters Grass and Pasturage to be cut and fed from my Homestead Farm as much as may be necessary for Two Cows. Also Land proper and Sufficient for a Garden to be held by Them during Their and each of Them remaining single and unmarried.—

I do also give and bequeath to my Son Thomas Butler his Heirs and Assigns forever Two Acres of Land, bounded as follows, Viz.- easterly to the back River so called from Great Bald Head, from thence south westerly to the front or Kennebec River, on my Homestead farm, and northerly till the Two Acres is compleat.—

I do also give devise and bequeath unto my Son in law Elijah Drummond his Heirs and Assigns forever The Land property & Privileges which he now enjoys and improves in a Saw Mill in which my said Son in law concerned, now stands, it being my meaning and intention that he and his Heirs shall hold the same forever free from the disturbance hindrence or molestation of my Son Thomas or any other Person claiming by, from, or Under me.

                                              William Butler.   (seal)

Signed sealed, published and declared
by the said William Butler The Testator as
for a Codicil to his last Will and Testament
in the presence of Us who were present at
the Signing and Sealing thereof.

    Jas. Davidson
    Benj'n Pattee
    John Fisher

                        Probated 3 June, 1791. [V, 6 to 8.]
Inventory by John Fisher, Benjamin Pattee and James Williams, all of Georgetown, 7 July, 1791. [V, 51-52.]

In the name of God Amen- - - -

The twentyeth day of April in the Year of our Lord one thousand seven hundred and seventy six I James Nickels of New Castle in the County of Lincoln Gentn. being very Sick and Weak in Body but of perfect mind and memory thanks be given to God for the same, and Calling to mind the mortality of my Body, and knowing that it is appointed for all men once to Die do make and ordain this my last Will and Testament that is to say principally and first of all I give and Recommend my Soul in to the hands of God that gave it and for my Body I Recommend it to the Earth, to be buried in a Christian like and Decent manner at The Discretion of my Executors, nothing doubting but at the General Resurection I shall Receive the Same again by the mighty power of God, and as touching such Worldly Estate wherewith it hath pleased God to bless me in this life, I give and Devise and dispose of the same in manner and form following that is to Say—

In the first place I give and bequeth to Ruth Nickels my Dearly beloved Wife my Whole personal Estate to be at her disposal to be disposed of at her Death in the way and manner She sall think proper and also the third part of my Real Estate, I give and bequeth to my beloved son John Nickels Eighty Acres of Land in the middle of the Great mash With a piece of mash adjoining to it, also I give and bequeth to Alexander Nickels my beloved Son, Eighty Acres of Laud on the south side of fresh Water Cove on Kennedy's River, also I give and bequeth to my beloved Children, James Nickels William Nickels Ruth Fasset, Hanah Nickels Jann Nickels Fanny Nickels & Margaret Nickels the Whole Remainder of my Real Estate to be divided Equally among them after the youngest Child is of Age— also I appoint my Dearly beloved Wife Ruth Nickels, Thomas Rice Esqr. and Captain William Nickels Executors of this my last and Testament, and I also Will that no part of my Real Estate shall be sold Except to pay a lawful Debt.

Also I Revoke and Disannul all and every other Wills and Legacies or power of Attorney given to any person or persons Whatsoever before this date this being my last will and Testament in Witness Whereof I have here unto set my hand and Seal the Day and Year above Written—

James Nickels
(seal)

Signed Sealed published pronounced and declared by the said James Nickels as his last Will and Testament in the presence of us the Subscribers—

Archd: Robinson
John Robinson
Michael Ryan

Thomas Rice declined executorship, 9 July, 1776. Probated 12 Sep., 1792. John Nickels, Adm'r *cum Testamento annexo.* [V, 10.]

Be it Remembered, that I Dennis Getchell of Vassalborough, in the County of Lincoln and State of Massachusetts-Bay Yeoman, being of Sound Mind, & Memory, Do make and Ordain, this my last Will & Testament in manner Following-vizt—

1st- I will that all my Just Debts, & Funeral Charges be paid out of my Estate

2d- I give unto my beloved Wife Margaret my Best Bed & Sufficient furniture therewith—

3d I give unto my Son Dennis The whole of the Lot of Land I now Live on, being the front Division of Lott No. 85 East Side of Kennebec River in Vassalboro' save what I sold to Amos Child- with about ——Acres purchased of my Brother Nehemiah as pr Deed bearing date—— ninth month Seventeen hundred Ninety, will appear, together with all the Previleges & Appurtenances to the same belonging or in anywise appertaining—also all the remainder of my Estate, I die possessed of, Both real & personal & of what name or Nature soever except the Reserves hithertofore, and hereafter made, He the said Dennis on His part & in Consideration thereof, paying all my Just Debts, & legacies herein mentioned— and also Support & Maintain in a Comfortable Manner my Wife Margaret during her living in a State of Widowhood—or untill she may see Cause to Marry again—she yielding what Assistance she can towards her own & the Families Support—& also He the said Dennis is to Maintain, Support, bring up, & Educate according to Reasonable Expectation my Six Children here named vizt. Margaret, David, Anstrus, Lidia, Fanney & Mary, untill they the Girls shall come to the Age of Eighteen Years, & my Son David to the Age of Twenty One Years-at which periods of Time I will that He my Son Dennis shall give each of my Daughters aforesaid a Cow each. They the said Daughters—& the said David during their State of Minority yielding all Reasonable Aid & Help in & for Their own Support.

4ly. I give unto my Son Elihu five shillings—
5ly. I give unto my Son Edmund five shillings
6ly. I give unto my Daughter Abigail five shillings

7ly. I give unto my Son Remington the Eastern half of the Back Division of Lott No 84, East Side Kennebek River in Vassallboro.

8ly. I give unto my Son David the Western half of the aforesaid Back Division of Lott No 84.

9ly. It is my Will that when my Youngest Daughter shall arrive to the Age of Eighteen Years, that an equal Distribution be made of the remainder of my Household Goods, to my Daughters Margaret, Anstrus, Lidia, Fanney, and Mary.

10ly. I Nominate my Friend John Taber Guardian to my Son David, & to all my Daughters under age

11ly. I Nominate & appoint my Friend John Taber Executor to this my last Will & Testament Desireing His assistance in Executeing the same according to the True Intent & meaning thereof Disallowing, and Disannulling, all other Wills by me Hithertofore made. In Witness whereof I Hereunto Set my hand & Seal this Second day of the Ninth Month Seventeen hundred Ninety.

Sign'd, Seald, & Published, by the Testator, as, and for, His last Will & Testament in presence of us the Subscribers
Remington Hobby,
David Dickey
William Getchell

NB the Name *"Margaret"* & words *"& Testament"* were Interlined before signing &c also the word Ninth.—
Dennis Getchel (seal)

Probated 6 Jan., 1792. [V, 14-15.]

Samuel Silvester, late of Pownalborough. Mary Silvester, of Pownalborough, widow, Adm'x, 27 Dec., 1791. [V, 19-20.] David Silvester and Timothy Parsons, both of Pownalborough, sureties. Inventory by Jonathan Williamson, William Sevey and Ebenezer Whittier, all of Pownalborough, 3 Mar., 1792, £320 : 19 : 8. [V, 90.]

George Bradford, late of Winslow. William Bradford, of Winslow, Adm'r, 17 Jan., 1792. [V, 20-21.] Samuel Grant and Jeremiah Fairfield, both of Vassalborough, sureties.

Isaac Boney, late of Winthrop. Hannah Boney, of Winthrop, widow, Adm'x, 17 Jan., 1792. [V, 21.] Samuel Wood and Reuben Brainerd, both of Winthrop, sureties. Inventory by Amos Stevens, Nathaniel Fairbanks and William Pullen, all of Winthrop, 12 Feb., 1792. [V, 56.] Additional inventory 10 Jan., 1793. [VII, 226-227.] Nathaniel Fairbanks and Samuel Wood, commissioners to examine claims. [VII, 227.] Widow's dower set off by Nathaniel Fairbanks, Samuel Wood and William Pullen, 22 Sep., 1794. [VII, 228.] Advertisement of sale of real estate, 24 Sep., 1794. [VII, 228.]

David Jackson, late of Hallowell. Rebeckah Jackson, widow, and Benjamin Stickney, both of Hallowell, Adm'rs, 17 Jan., 1792. [V, 22.] James Page and Jason Livermore, both of Hallowell, sureties. Inventory by Nathaniel Dummer, Samuel Dutton and James Carr, all of Hallowell, 10 May, 1792, £505 : 0 : 2. [V, 101-102.] Daniel Cony and William Brooks, both of Hallowell, commissioners to examine claims. [V, 207-208.] Inventory of real estate at Sandy river by James Carr and Isaac Savage, both of Hallowell, and John Blunt, of Winthrop, 21 Jan., 1794, £ 21 : 7. 0. [V, 210.] Advertisement of sale of real estate, 13 Feb., 1794. [V, 211.] Account filed, 5 Sep., 1794. [V, 212-213.] Distribution ordered 6 Nov., 1794. [V, 213-214.] Advertisement of sale of real estate, 10 Feb., 1794. [V, 253.]

Nathaniel Foster, late of Woolwich, shipwright. Dorothy Foster, of Woolwich, widow, Adm'x, 6 Feb., 1792. [V, 22-23.] Aaron Abbot and Thomas Snell, both of Woolwich, sureties. Inventory by David Gilmore, Abner Wade and Richard Harnden, all of Woolwich, 14 Feb., 1792, £207 : 7 : 6. [V, 52-53.] Samuel Harnden and David Gilmore, both of Woolwich, commissioners to examine claims. [V, 184.] Widow's dower set off by David Gilmore, Richard Harnden and Abner Wade, 8 Ap., 1794. [V, 186.] Advertisement of sale of real estate 17 Mar., 1794. [V, 186-7.] Account filed and distribution ordered 30 May, 1794. [V, 187 and 200-201.]

Hatherly Foster, late of Bath. Hatherly Foster, of Bath, Adm'r, 15 Mar., 1792. [V, 23.] Consider Turner and Caleb Marsh, both of Bath, sureties. Inventory by Joshua Philbrook, Ephraim Fitts and Joseph Lambard, all of Bath, 2 June, 1792, £190 : 19 : 0. [V, 94.] John, minor son, and Martha, minor daughter, chose Dummer Sewall, of Bath, to be their guardian, 26 May, 1797. [VII, 55.] Dummer Sewall, guardian unto Benjamin, Alexander and Thomas, minor sons, 26 May, 1797. [VII, 55-56.] Yearly value of real estate appraised at $42- by Joshua Philbrook, Christopher Cushing and Laban Loring, all of Bath, 8 Sep., 1797. [VII, 157.] Account filed 19 Sep., 1797. [VII, 157.] Division of personal estate among Charles, Hatherly, William, John, Benjamin, Martha, Alexander and Thomas, 19 Sep., 1797. [VII, 211-212.] Division of real estate among same by Joshua Philbrook, Christopher Cushing and Joseph Sewall, all of Bath, 19 Ap., 1798. [VII,70.] Account of Dummer Sewall, guardian of Alexander, filed 24 Aug., 1804. [Unrecorded.]

John Winchell, late of Topsham. Samuel Winchell, of Topsham, Adm'r, 28 May, 1792. [V, 30-31.] Inventory by John Patten, James Fulton, and Joseph Graves, all of Topsham, 4 July, 1792, £313 : 2 : 4. [V, 97.] John Fulton and Ezekiel Thompson, both of Topsham, commissioners to examine claims. [V, 176.] Advertisement of sale of real estate, 23 Sep., 1793. [V, 178.] Account filed 29 Ap., 1794. [V, 179.] Distribution ordered 29 May, 1794. [V, 174-5.]

Timothy Foster, late of Winthrop. Sibella Foster, widow, Adm'x. Inventory by Josiah French, Benjamin Brainerd and Benjamin Fairbanks, all of Winthrop, 13 June, 1785, £565 : 18 : 10. [V, 31 to 33.] Division of real estate by John Page, Josiah French and Benjamin White, all of Winthrop, 2 June, 1786 ; dower to widow, remainder to Timothy Foster, David Foster, Stewart Foster, Stephen Foster, Micajah Dudley and Ephraim Stevens. [V, 34.]

Francis Perry, late a resident of Pownalborough. Ezra Taylor, of Pownalborough, Adm'r, 31 May, 1792. [V, 34-35.] Samuel Goodwin, of Pownalborough, and William Haley, of Pittston, sureties. Inventory by Philip Theobald, Samuel Goodwin, Jr., and Louis Houdelette, all of Pownalborough, 2 July, 1792, £6 : 8 : 2, to which Adm'r adds a sum of money, £7 : 16 : 0. [VI, 62-63.] Account filed 29 Ap., 1794. [VI, 64.]

In the Name of GOD. Amen. I Oliver Robins of Thomaston in the County of Lincoln and Commonwealth of Massachusetts yeoman, being sick and weak in Body, but of perfect Mind and Memory, Thanks be given unto GOD ; calling to Mind the Mortality of my Body, and knowing that it is appointed for all Men once to die ; do make and ordain this my last Will and Testament ; That is to say, principally and first of all, I give and recommend my Soul into the Hand of Almighty God, that gave it, and my Body I recommend to the Earth, to be buried in decent Christian Burial, at the Discretion of my Executors ; nothing doubting but at the general Resurrection I shall receive the same again by the mighty Power of God. And as touching such worldly Estate wherewith it has pleased God, to bless me in this Life, I give, demise, and dispose of the same in the following Manner and Form

Imprimis, I give and bequeath unto my well beloved Son Oliver

Robins junior the Sum of Five Shillings to be paid to him by my Executors, which together with what he has already received is his full part or Share out of my Estate.

Item. I give and bequeath unto my well beloved Son Otis Robins the Sum of Five Shillings to be paid to him by my Executors which together with what he has already received is his full part or Share out of my Estate.

Item. I give, devise, and bequeath unto my well beloved Sons Sheppard Robins and Rufus Robins, whom I likewise constitue, make and ordain joint Executors of this my last Will and Testament, all my Lands, Messuages, and Tenements of what name or nature soever, together with all my wearing Apparel, Husbandry Tools, and Cattle of all kinds, and all my other Estate of what name or nature soever, excepting what is herein otherwise particularly disposed of, by them freely to be possessed and enjoyed, and to be equally divided, for Quantity and, Quality, between them or their legal Representatives, they paying my just Debts, Funeral Expences, and the Legacies hereby otherwise given ; but if either of them shall not arrive at the Age of twenty and One Year, nor have Children of his own, or marry, the surviver to possess and enjoy the whole.

Item. I give and bequeath unto my well-beloved Daughter Elioenai Crocket the Sum of Five Shillings to be paid to her by My Executors, which together with what she has already received is her full Part or Share out of my Estate.

Item. I give and bequeath unto my well-beloved Daughter Sybel Fales the Sum of Five Shillings to be paid to her by my Executors, which, with what she has already received is her full Part or Share out of my Estate.

Item. I give and bequeath unto my well beloved Daughter Lois Killsa the Sum of Five Shillings to be paid to her by my Executors, which, with what she has already received is her full Part or Share out of my Estate.

Item. I give and bequeath unto my well beloved Daughter Lucy Butler the Sum of Five Shillings to be paid to her by my Executors, which, with what she has already received is her full Part or Share out of my Estate.

Item. I give and bequeath unto my well beloved Daughter Sabra Barrows the Sum of Five Shillings to be paid to her by my Executors, which, with what she has already received is her full Part or Share out of my Estate.

Item. I give and bequeath unto my well beloved Daughter Mella Butler the Sum of Five Shillings to be paid to her by my Executors, which with what she has already received is her full part or Share out of my Estate.

Item. I give and bequeath unto my well beloved Daughter Betsey Robins, my Feather-Beds, Case of Drawers, Tables, Chares, and Pewter with all my other Household Furniture to be by her free possessed and enjoyed; together with two Cows to be paid and delivered to her by my Executors when she arrives at the Age of twenty and one Years or on her Marriage. And I do hereby utterly disallow, revoke, and disannul all and every other former Testaments, Wills, Legacies, Bequests, and Executors by me in any ways before-named, willed and bequeathed; ratifying and confirming this and no other to be my last Will and Testament. In Witness whereof I have hereunto set my Hand and Seal this twenty Second Day of March, in the Year of LORD One Thousand Seven Hundred and Nine Two

Signed, Sealed, published pronounced and declared by the said Oliver Robins as his last Will and Testament in the Presence of us
James Stackpole
Saml Jennison
David Fales

        his
Oliver X Robins (seal)
      Mark

Probated 31 May, 1792. Oliver Robins, Adm'r *cum Testamento annexo*, 31 May, 1792. [V, 35-36.] Inventory by Mason Wheaton, James Weed and Samuel Brown, all of Thomaston, 2 July, 1792, £655 : 13 : 0. [V, 99-100.] Oliver Robins, guardian unto Rufus, minor son, 22 June, 1799. [IX, 180.]

Peter LeMercier, late of Pownalborough, merchant. Polly LeMercier, of Pownalborough, widow, Adm'x, 26 Dec., 1791; Jaque Goud, of Pownalborough, and Nicholas Gaubert, of Bowdoinham, sureties. Inventory by Daniel Spring, William Lewis and Samuel Goodwin, Jr., all of Pownalborough, 29 Dec., 1791, £230 : 14 : 3. [V, 41-42.] Edmund Bridge and Samuel Woodward, both of Pownalborough, commissioners to examine claims. [VI, 65.] Widow's dower set off by Daniel Spring, Samuel Woodward and Carr Barker, all of Pownalborough, 7 Nov., 1792. [VI, 67.] Advertisement of sale of real estate, 25 Jan., 1793. [VI, 68.] Account filed and distribution ordered 9 Jan., 1795. [VI, 111 to 113.] Advertisement of sale of real estate, 10 Mar., 1795. [VI, 113-114.] Account filed 28 May, 1785. [VI, 115.]

Mary Jennison, late of Cambden, spinster. William Gregory, of Cambden, Adm'r, 14 Jan., 1792: Moses Copeland, of Warren, and Samuel Tolman, of Thomaston, sureties. [V, 45.]

Mehitabel Grover, of Georgetown, widow, *non compos*. John White, of Georgetown, guardian, 5 June, 1792. [V, 47.]

John Orr, late of Bristol. Rosanna McMillen, of Boothbay, widow, Adm'x, 24 July, 1792. [V, 84-85.] Samuel Montgomery and John Murray, both of Boothbay, sureties. Inventory by Jonas Fitch and James Huston, both of Bristol, and James Little, of Newcastle, 15 Aug., 1792, £155 : 10 : 0. [V, 85.] Thomas McClure and James Little, commissioners to examine claims. [VI, 53.] Account filed 8 Sep., 1794. [VI, 54.]

Samuel Brown, late of Boothbay. Mary Brown, widow, declined administration, 15 June, 1792. John Murray, of Boothbay, Adm'r, 25 July, 1792. [V, 86.] Samuel Montgomery and Thomas Boyd, both of Boothbay, sureties.

Martha, Alexander and Samuel, minor children of Samuel Wylis, late of Boothbay, chose Hugh Rogers, of Georgetown, to be their guardian, 5 Oct., 1792. Robert, minor son of said Samuel Wylie, chose David Ring, of Bath, to be his guardian, 29 Sep., 1792. [V, 87-88.]

James McCobb, Jr., late of Georgetown. Mary McCobb, of Georgetown, widow, Adm'x, 7 Sep., 1792. [V, 88.] Jordan Parker and Joseph Bowker, both of Georgetown, sureties. Inventory by Jordan Parker, Elijah Drummond and Joseph Bowker, all of Georgetown 5 Nov., 1792, £10 : 16 : 0. [VI, 223.]

Nathaniel Leeman, late of Edgecomb. Betty Leeman, of Edgecomb, widow, Adm'x, 7 Aug., 1792. [V, 89.] Henry Leeman and William Foye, both of Pownalborough, sureties. Inventory by William Patterson, Ebenezer Gove and Isaac Clifford, 22 Aug., 1792, £208 : 11 : 3. [VI, 229-230.]

In the Name of God Amen. I John McCarter of a place called St, Georges, in the County of Lincoln and State of Massachusetts Bay in New England Yeoman, Being tho' weak in body yet of perfect mind and memory, thanks be given unto God; calling into mind the mortality of my body, and knowing that it is appointed for all men Once to die, Do make and ordain this my last Will and Testament. That is to say Principally and first of all, I give and recommend my Soul into the Hand of Almighty God that gave it, and my body I recommend to the Earth, to be buried in decent Christian burial at the Discretion of my of my Executor, nothing doubting but at the General Resurrection I shall receive the same again by the mighty power of God. And as touching such worldly Estate wherewith it hath pleased God to bless me in this Life, I give, demise, and dispose of the same in the following manner and form.

Imprimis I give and bequeath to my well beloved Daughter Jane, Ten Acres of Land, beginning at the Extremity of a point of Land, Commonly Called Winslow's point, bounded between St Georges River and a Cove Called Thomsons Cove, and running North Easterly along Said River; untill a Line running West North West, from said River to the Cove afore said includes the Ten Acres aforesaid: Also a Cow and three Sheep within Six months after my Decease.

Item. I Give unto my well beloved Daughter Mary Ten Acres of Land (adjoining to that bequeathed to my Daughter Jean) and running North Easterly along said River untill a West North West Line as afore said Shall include Ten Acres, Also Two Cows and three Sheep, to be delivered as afore said, together with the priviledge of the North westerly front room as long as she may require it.

Item I Give unto my well beloved Daughter Margaret Ten Acres of Land nex adjoining to that bequethed to my Daughter Mary, and running up along said river North Easterly untill a Line running West North west as aforesaid Shall include ten Acres, also a Cow and three Sheep to be delivered as aforesaid by my Executor

Item I Give to my well beloved Daughter Elizabeth Ten Acres of Land next adjoining to that bequeathed to my Daughter Margaret and running up along said River North Easterly untill a Line running West North west, includes ten acres, also a Cow and three Sheep to be delivered as afore Said by my Executor

Item I give unto my well beloved and Only Son James, the whole of my Land (except what is already bequeathed as is above Specified) together with all the Buildings thereon, together with all my personal Estate, Excepting what is herein bequeathed

Item I give unto the Children of my well beloved Daughter Martha Deceased each one a Guinea to be paid them as Soon as the Oldest of them Comes of Age

Lastly I do Constitute, make, and ordain my Son James McCarter Sole Executor of this my last Will and Testament. And do hereby utterly disallow, revoke, and disannul all, and every other former Testaments, Wills, Legacies, Bequests, and Executors, by me in any ways before named, Willed, and Bequeathed, Ratifying and Confirming this and no other to be my Last Will and Testament.

In Witness whereof I do hereunto Set my hand and Seal this fifth day of February *Annoque Domini* One thousand Seven hundred and Eighty nine

his
John X McCarter (seal)
Mark

Signed, Sealed, published, pronounced, and Declared, by the Said John McCarter as his last Will and Testament, in the presence of us, who in his presence, and in the presence of each other, have hereunto Subscribed our Names
John Nicholls, D. M
Jona. Nutting
John McKellar

Probated 18 Sep., 1792. [V, 94-95.] Inventory by Moses Copeland, of Warren, Seth Vose and Marlboro Packard, both of Cushing, 12 Dec., 1792, £897 : 8 : 3. [V, 195-6.]

Martin Sidelinger, late of Waldoborough. Agreement among heirs, viz : Peter Sidelinger, George Sidelinger, Daniel Sidelinger, Charles Sidelinger, Andrew Storer, Charles Brodman, who in their agreement mentioned as an heir one Jacob Rominger then living in North Carolina, and Mary Sidelinger, widow of deceased. [V, 102-103.] Peter Sidelinger, of Waldoborough, Adm'r, 12 Mar., 1793. [V, 130-1.] Peter Light, of Waldoborough, and Benjamin Kinsel, of Nobleborough, sureties.

Jesse Davis, late of Bowdoin. Hannah Davis, of Bowdoin, widow. and Joshua Davis, of Sidney, Adm'rs, 2 Oct., 1795. [V, 106.] Ezekiel Thompson, of Topsham, and James Curtis, of Brunswick, sureties. Inventory by Isaac Hinkley and Samuel Tibbets, both of Bowdoin, and James Wilson, of Topsham, 30 Oct., 1792, £359 : 4 : 3. [VI, 116.] John Merrill, of Topsham, and Samuel Tibbets, of Bowdoin, commissioners to examine claims. [VI, 117.] Widow's dower set off by Isaac Hinkley, John Merrill and Samuel Tibbets, 15 July, 1795.

[VI, 120.] Advertisement of sale of real estate 16 Sep., 1795. [VI, 139.] Account filed 27 May, 1796. [VI, 140.] Distribution ordered 30 May, 1796. [VI, 149-151.] Seth Hinkley, of Bowdoin, guardian unto Jonathan and Rebecca, minor children, 10 Jan., 1799. [IX, 178.] Rachel, minor daughter, chose Seth Hinckley, of Lisbon, to be her guardian, 25 Aug., 1804. [IX, 252.]

Joseph Stevens, late of Winthrop. Jonas Stevens, of Winthrop, Adm'r, 20 Dec., 1792. [V, 107.] Joel Chandler and Cyrus Baldwin, both of Winthrop, sureties. Inventory by Paul Lambert and Ebenezer Davenport, both of Winthrop, and John Gray, of Readfield, 26 Dec., 1792, £128 : 12 : 7. [V, 120.]

John Conely, of Bristol, *non compos*. Joshua Cross, of Bristol, guardian, 1 Jan., 1793. [V, 108.] Inventory by Thomas Thompson, Henry Fosset and James Drummond, all of Bristol, 31 May, 1793, £211 : 5 : 8. [VI, 165-6.] Account filed 9 Jan., 1795 and 27 May, 1795. [VI, 166 to 169.] Advertisement of sale of real estate 22 Jan., 1796. [VI, 250.] Account filed 8 Sep., 1797. [VI, 252.] Joshua Cross, Adm'r, 11 Sep., 1797. [VII, 153-4.] Inventory by Thomas Thompson, Andrew Parsons and Alexander Robinson, all of Bristol, 24 Oct., 1797, $537. 33; account filed 4 June, 1798. [VIII, 98.]

Peter Parker, minor son, and Prudence Parker, minor daughter, of Peter Parker, Jr., late of Groton, Middlesex County, chose John French Woods, of a place called Sandy River, to be their guardian, 10 Jan., 1793. [V, 120-121.]

Moses Dudley, of Sandy-river, *non compos*. William Reed, of Sandy-river, guardian, 9 Jan., 1793. [V, 123.]

Elizabeth Jewett, of Edgecomb, lately the wife of James Jewett, of Edgecomb, *non compos*. Moses Davis, of Edgecomb, guardian, 4 Oct., 1792. [V, 128.] Account filed 6 Jan., 1808. [XII, 377-8.]

Josiah Butterfield, late of Vassalborough. George Warren, of Winslow, Adm'r, 10 June, 1793. [V, 131.] James Bridge, of Hallowell, and John Peirce, of Winslow, sureties. Inventory by William Pattee and Solomon Parker, both of Winslow, and David Smiley, of Sidney, 12 Aug., 1793, £100 : 0 : 0. [VII, 88.] Account filed, 19 Jan., 1796. [VII, 89.]

Benjamin Hussey, late of Nobleborough. Hannah Hussey, of Nobleborough, widow, Adm'x, 3 Ap., 1793. [V, 132.] James Hall and David Dennis, both of Nobleborough, sureties. Inventory by

Joseph Rust, Thomas Merrill and John Clark, all of Nobleborough, 6 Ap., 1793, [VI, 60-61.] Hannah, widow, guardian unto Elsa, minor daughter, 17 Sep., 1793. [VI, 61-62.] Account filed 20 Sep., 1796, at which date the administratrix had become the wife of John Austin. [VI, 240.] Widow's dower set off by David Dennis, Joseph Rust and John Winslow, all of Nobleborough, 10 Ap., 1795. [VI, 241-2.] John Austin, of Nobleborough, Adm'r, *de bonis non*, 27 June, 1805. [IX, 86.] Else, minor daughter, chose Joseph Hussey, of Nobleborough, to be her guardian, 9 May, 1807. [IX, 277.] Accounts filed 27 Sep., 1806, and 9 May, 1807. [XII, 45 and 173.] Advertisement of sale of real estate 16 May, 1807. [XII, 348.]

Robert Miller, late of Bristol. Nancy Miller, of Bristol, widow, Adm'x, 14 June, 1793. [V, 133.] Samuel Nickels, of Newcastle, and Benjamin Rackliff, of Edgecomb, sureties. Inventory by Thomas Boyd, of Boothbay, Samuel Clark and Henry Hunter, both of Bristol, 30 July, 1793, £32 : 14 : 4. [V, 204.] Henry Hunter and Thomas Boyd, commissioners to examine claims. [V, 205.] Account filed, 16 Sep., 1794. [V, 206.] Distribution ordered, 10 Dec., 1794. [V, 207.]

Henry McKenney, Jr., late of a place called Seven mile brook. John Gray, of Seven mile brook, Adm'r, 6 June, 1793. [V, 133-4.] Oliver Wood, of Norridgewalk, and William Gray, of Pownalborough, sureties. Inventory by James Waugh, of Sandy river, Silas Wood, of Norridgewalk, and Jonathan Ames, of Seven mile brook, £246 : 10 : 2, to which Adm'r adds bricks valued at £11 : 3 : 0. [VI, 76-77.] Widow's dower set off by James Jones, John Hilton and John Moore, Jr., all of Seven mile brook, 21 Aug., 1797. [VI, 236.] Account filed 8 Sep., 1797. [VI, 236-7.]

Anna Bradbury, of Pownalborough, widow, *non compos*. John Sevey, of Pownalborough, guardian, 23 Jan,, 1793. [V, 134-5.] Inventory by Thomas Rice, Ebenezer Whittier and Jeremiah Dalton, all of Pownalborough, 12 Mar., 1793, £42 : 8 : 0. [V, 236-7.] Wyman Bradbury Sevey, of Pownalborough, guardian, 15 Mar., 1796. [VI, 133.]

Samuel Kennedy, late of Newcastle. Mary Kennedy declined administration, 15 Aug., 1793. Robert Kennedy, of Newcastle, Adm'r, 16 Aug., 1793. [135-6.] David Kennedy, of Newcastle, and Briggs Turner, of Pownalborough, sureties. Inventory by Charles Chase, Thomas Cunningham and Abernathy Cargill, all of Newcastle, 13 Nov.,

1793, £144 : 0 : 0. [Unrecorded.]

William Kennedy, late of Newcastle, mariner. Robert Kennedy, of Newcastle, Adm'r, 16 Aug., 1793. [V, 136.] David Kennedy, of Newcastle, and Briggs Turner, of Pownalborough, sureties. Sarah Kennedy, of Newcastle, widow, Adm'x *de bonis non*, 8 Dec., 1795. [VII, 209-210.] Samuel Kennedy and Thomas Cunningham, both of Newcastle, sureties. Inventory by Charles Chase, Thomas Cunningham and Abernathy Cargill, all of Newcastle, 21 Dec., 1795, $267. 33. [VII, 210-211.] Advertisement of sale of real estate 28 July, 1797. [VIII, 49.] Report of Samuel Nickels and Charles Chase, commissioners to examine claims. [VIII, 50.] Account filed 7 Jan., 1798, at which date the administratrix had become the wife of Stephen Jewett. [VIII, 50.] Distribution ordered 15 Jan., 1799. [VIII, 51.]

Abraham Whittemore, Jr., late of Bowdoinham, mariner. Hezekiah Purrinton, of Bowdoinham, Adm'r, 8 May, 1793. [V, 137.] Elihu Getchel and James Purrinton, both of Bowdoinham, sureties. Inventory by George Maxwell, Stephen Whitmore and George Thomas, all of Bowdoinham, 14 May, 1793, £13 : 2 : 9. [V, 196-7.] Elihu Getchel and Stephen Whitmore, commissioners to examine claims. [V, 197.] Distribution of estate ordered 30 May, 1794. [V, 199.]

Benjamin Thompson, late of Topsham. Rhoda Thompson, of Topsham, widow, Adm'x, 29 July, 1793. [V, 137-8.] Ezekiel Thompson, of Topsham, and Benjamin Ham, of Bath, sureties.

Robert Clarke, late of Topsham. Samuel Thompson, of Topsham, Adm'r, 29 July, 1793. [V, 138.] Ezekiel Thompson, of Topsham, and Benjamin Ham, of Bath, sureties. Elenor, widow, declined administration 3 May, 1791. Samuel, oldest son, declined administration 18 Aug., 1791. Inventory by John Merrill, Actor Patten and James Wilson, all of Topsham, 26 Mar., 1794, £149 : 19 : 9. [VI, 239.]

Jacob Eaton, late of a place called Sandy-river. Elizabeth Eaton, of Sandy-river, widow, Adm'x, 15 Jan., 1793. [V, 139.] Supply Belcher and John French Woods, both of Sandy-river, sureties. Inventory by Robert Gore, William Reed and Samuel Sewall, all of Sandy river, £617 : 2 : 11. [VI, 183-4.]

Rachel, reputed daughter of Seth Delano, of Winthrop, chose Abiel Walton, of Winthrop, to be her guardian. 26 Oct., 1793. [V, 139-140.]

Boyes Cooper Jameson, late of Warren, a minor. Katey Cox, of

Warren, widow Adm'x, 17 Sep., 1793. [V, 140.] Moses Copeland and William Bogs, both of Warren, sureties.

Joseph Decker, late of Edgecomb, mariner. Sarah Decker, of Edgecomb, widow, Adm'x, 4 Jan., 1793. [V, 141.] Moses Davis, of Edgecomb, and Ebenezer Whittier of Pownalborough, sureties. Inventory by Francis Cook and John Huse, both of Pownalborough, and Ebenezer Gove, of Edgecomb, 27 Mar., 1793, £574 : 2 : 9. [V, 142.] Francis Cook, of Pownalborough, and Barnabas Sears, of Edgecomb, commissioners to examine claims. [V, 225.] Distribution of estate 26 Aug., 1795. [VI, 91 to 93.] Widow's dower set off by Moses Davis, of Edgecomb, John Huse and Francis Cook, both of Pownalborough, 2 Jan., 1795. [VI, 127-8.] Advertisement of sale of real estate 18 Feb., 1795. [VI, 128.] Account filed 28 May, 1795. [VI, 129-130.]

Thomas Bowers Hurrup, late of a place called Barretts-town. Betsey Hurrup, of Barretts-town, widow, Adm'x, 11 July, 1793. [V, 145.] William Thompson, of Thomaston, and John Gordon, Jr., of Camden, sureties. Inventory by William Hewitt, John Hilt and Samuel Bartlett, all of Barrettstown, 7 Sep., 1793, £217 : 15 : 5. [V, 146.] William Gregory and Peter Ott, both of Camden, commissioners to examine claims. [V, 222.] Widow's dower set off by William Hewitt and John Hilt, both of Barrettstown, and John McKellar, of Cushing, 10 Oct., 1793. [V, 224.] Advertisement of sale of real estate 23 Sep., 1794. [V, 224-5.] Sale of reversion of widow's dower advertised 10 June, 1795; account filed and distribution ordered 10 Dec., 1795. [VI, 109 to 111.]

In the Name of God, Amen. I William Bogs of Warren in the County of Lincoln and Commonwealth of Massachusetts, Yeoman, being sick and weak in Body but of perfect Mind and Memory, Thanks be given unto GOD; calling to Mind the Mortality of my Body and knowing that it appointed unto all Men one to die; do make and ordain this my last Will and Testament; That is to say, principally and first of all, I give and recommend my Soul into the Hand of almighty God, that gave it, and my Body I recommend unto the Earth, to be buried in decent Christian Burial, at the Discretion of my Executors, nothing doubting but at the general Resurrection, I shall receive the same again by the mighty Power of God. And as touching such worldly Estate wherewith it hath pleased God to bless me in this Life,

I give, demise, and dispose of the same in the following manner and Form.

Imprimis. I give and bequeath unto my dearly beloved Wife Mary Bogs the improvement, use and Occupation of one third part of all my real Estate to be by her freely used and enjoyed during her natural Life; together with one third part of all my moveables and personal Estate (after the Payment of my just Debts and Settlement of the Estate) to be by her freely possessed and enjoyed.

Item. I give, devise, and bequeath unto my well beloved Sons and Daughters, Joseph Bogs, Ephraim Bogs, Alexander Bogs, Isabel Bogs, Lucy Bogs, and Rachel Bogs, the whole of my Homestead, with the out Meadows thereunto belonging containing One Hundred Acres in the whole, with the House Barn and other Buildings thereon, to be equally divided to and amongst them, or their legal Representatives; (but the Sons respective according to their age to have the Right of Redemption) and also the whole of my personal Estate, not herein otherwise particularly disposed of, to be equally divided to and amongst them and each of them

Item. I give, devise, and bequeath unto my said well beloved Sons Joseph, Ephraim and Alexander all my out Lands and other real Estate to be equally divide to and amongst them, and each of them.

Item I give and bequeath unto my true and loving Neice Elizabeth Bogs, one Cow, two Sheep, and two Lambs to be levied and paid for out of the whole of my Estate.

My further Wills that my Sons Ephraim and Alexander, and my said Daughter Rachel be properly taught and instructed in School learning suitable for Persons of their Station to be paid for out of the whole of my Estate.

I do likewise constitute make and ordain my said dearly beloved Wife, together with my said Son Joseph Bogs joint Executors of this my last Will and Testament. And I do hereby utterly disallow revoke and disannul all and every other former Testaments, Legacies, Bequests and Executors by me in any wise before named, willed and bequeathed; ratifying confirming this and no other to be my last Will and Testament.

In Witness whereof I have hereunto set my Hand and Seal this twentieth Day of June in the Year of our LORD One Thousand Seven Hundred and ninety two.

         William Bogs   (seal)

Signed sealed published pronounced
and declared by the said William
Bogs as his last Will and Testament
in the Presence of us
William Bogs junr
Robert Bogs
David Fales

Probated 18 Sep., 1792. [V, 147-8]
Moses Copeland and Thomas Kirkpatrick, both of Warren, sureties. Inventory by David Fales, of Thomaston, Thomas Starret and John Watt, both of Warren, 24 Oct., 1792, £618 : 19 : 8, to which executors added debts due the estate, £57 : 19 : 2. [V, 239 to 241.] Account filed, 13 Sep., 1794. [V, 241-2.] Ephraim, minor son, chose Thurston Whiting, of Warren, to be his guardian, 11 Feb., 1795. [VI, 27.] Joseph Bogs, of Warren, guardian unto Alexander and Rachel, minor children, 11 Feb., 1795. [VI, 28.] Lucy, minor daughter, chose William Bogs, of Warren, to be her guardian, 11 Feb., 1795. [VI, 29.] Division of estate by Rufus Crane, Joseph Copeland and Thomas Kirkpatrick, all of Warren, among Joseph, Ephraim and Alexander, sons of deceased, accepted 17 Sep., 1798. [VIII, 51-52.] Account filed, 17 Sep., 1798. [VIII, 52-53.]

In the Name of God Amen
the thirty first Day of December in the year of our Lord one thousand Seven Hundred Ninety & two. I Robert Sproul of Bristol in the County of Lincoln & Commonwealth of Massachusetts Gentleman Being Very Sick & weak in Body : But of Perfect mind and Memory : thanks be given unto God, therefore. Calling unto mind the Mortallity of my Body, and knowing that it is appointed for all men once to Dye Do make and ordain this my Last will & testament that is to Say first of all I give & Recommend my Soul into the hands of God that gave it; for my Body I Recommend it to the Earth, to Be Buried in a Christian Like & Decent Manner att the Descretion of my Executors—
and as touching Such worldly Estate wherewith it hath Pleased God to Bless me in this Life, I give Devise & Dispose of the Same in the following Manner and form—

first : it is my will & I Do order : that all my just Debts and fueral Charges, be Paid & Satisfyed.—

Item I give & Bequeath unto Sarah My Dearly Beloved wife the Place that I Now Live on togeather with the house & Barn togeather with all my Personal Estate During her widowhood to be Dis-Possed of in Manner followaring—I Likewise Constitute & appoint Sarah my wife my Sole Exetor & Administratrix of this my Last will & testament

Item: I give to my Beloved Son Robert Sproul five Shillings Lawfull money.

Item   Catherine Sproul My Daughter I give five Shillings.

Item   I give to my Beloved Son William Sproul five Shillings

item   I give to my Beloved Son John Sproul five Shillings.

Item   I give to my Beloved Daughter Margret Clark five Shillings.

Item   I give to my Beloved Daughter Sarah Sproul one Cow & one feather bed Bed & Beding Sutable for a Bed att her marrage if not married to Paid to her when My Son James Sproul is one & twenty years of age

Item—I give to my Beloved Daughter Jean Sproul the Same as is mentioned to my Daughter Sarah Sproul when married or att James Sproul Being one & twenty

Item—I give to my Beloved Daughter Susanna Sproul the Same as to the above mentioned Sarah & Jean Sproul & att the Same time.

Item, I give to my Beloved Son Thomas Sproul the whole of that Lot of Land joyning to William Sproul my Son att Orr Meadow and one Pair of Steer three years old and one heffer of three years old all the above to Be given to him att the time of his Being one & twenty years of Age to him & his heirs

Item.   I give to my Beloved Daughter Mary Sproul one Cow & one Bed & Beding att marridge or att James Sproul a Riveing to the years of one & twenty as is mentioned to Sarah, Jean, Susanna & Mary all a Like

Item—I give to my Beloved Son James Sproul the Place or fairm that I now Live on one third of the Place att his comeing of Lawfull age Viz—one & twenty & the other two third to his mother My Beloved wife During hir widowhood, & att her Disseas to him the Said James to have the whole Place to him his heirs and assigns for Ever—that is to Say—if the above Named Sarah, Jean, Susanna & Mary Should Remain Single & unmarried att the Disseas of my Beloved wife to have three Pounds Lawfull money Paid yearly by the Said James or his heirs During their Remaining Single to Each or ither of them as the Case may be.

Ratifying & Confirming this & no other to be my Last will & testement In Witness whereof I have hereunto Set my hand and Seal the

Day and year above written.

             Robert Sproul (Seal)
Signed: Sealed: Published. Pronounced, & Declared by the Said Robert Sproul as his Last will & testament in the Presence of us the Subscribers viz— the word, hood, Interlined before the Signing hereof

Thos. Johnston
Richd. Meagher
William McIntyer

           Probated 9 Sep., 1793. [V, 149-150.]
Thomas Johnston and William McIntyer, both of Bristol, sureties.

Ezekiel Linscott, son of John Linscott, late of a place called Balltown, chose John Linscott, of Nobleboro, to be his guardian, 28 Aug., 1793. [V, 151-2.]

Edward Young, late of Bristol. Jane Young, of Bristol, widow, Adm'x, 9 Sep., 1793. [V. 152-3.] Lemuel Doe and James Young, Jr., both of Bristol, sureties. Inventory by James Houston, Thomas Johnston and William McIntyer, all of Bristol, 6 Sep., 1794, £602 : 14 : 1, to which administrator added sundry notes of hand, £55 : 10 : 6. [VI, 190-1.] Inventory by Thomas Johnston, William McIntyer and Henry Fossat, all of Bristol, 1 Dec., 1795, £81 : 13 : 3. [VI, 192.]

Gideon Owen, late of Topsham. Jane, widow, Thomas and Hugh, oldest sons, desired that adm'n be granted to John, third son, 18 Oct., 1793. John Owen, of Topsham, Adm'r, 21 Oct., 1793. [V, 153-4.] William Burke and Samuel Winchell, both of Topsham, sureties. Inventory of real estate in Portland, Cumberland County, by Thomas Bradbury, Samuel Butts and Joseph McLellan, all of Portland, 31 Oct., 1793, £72 : 10 : 0. [VI, 176.] Inventory by John Patten, James Fulton and Joseph Graves, all of Topsham. [VI, 177 to 178.]

John Gardiner, late of Pownalborough. John Silvester John Gardiner, of Boston, Adm'r, 6 Jan., 1794. [V, 155.] Robert Hallowell, of Boston, and William Gardiner, of Pownalborough, sureties. Inventory by Caleb Blanchard, Edward Davis and John Erving, all of Boston, 11 July, 1794, £1625 : 2 : 5. [VII, 232-3.] Inventory by James Tupper, Jonathan Reed and William Patterson, all of Pownalborough, 5 June, 1794, £2501 : 13 : 7½. [VII, 234 to 238.]

Consider Thomas, late of Topsham, blacksmith. Sarah, widow, declined administration 5 Sep., 1793. Ezekiel Thompson, of Topsham,

Adm'r, 6 Sep., 1793. [V, 156.] James Wilson, of Topsham, and John Herrick, of a place called Lewiston, sureties.

In the Name of God, Amen. I James Killsa of the Town of Thomaston in the County of Lincoln yeoman being Very Sick and weak in Body but of perfect mind and Memory, thanks be Given unto God; Calling unto Mind the Mortality of my Body, and Knowing that it is Appointed for all Men once to die, Do Make and Ordain this my Last Will and Testament: That is to Say Principally and first of All I Give and Recommend my Soul into the Hand of Almighty God that gave it, and my Body I Recommend to the Earth to be Buried in decent Christian Burial at the Discretion of my Executors: Nothing Doubting but at the General Resurrection I shall receiv the Same again by the mighty Power of God and as touching Such Worldly Estate where with it has Pleased God to bless me in this life I Give Demise and dispose of the Same in the Following Manner and form—First I Give and bequeath to Lydia Killsa my Dearly beloved Wife, Whome I Constitute Make and ordain the Sole Executrix of this my last will and Testament, one half of my Possessions Adjoining to Oliver Robbins to gether with the Hous and Barn there on by hur to be Possesed and Injoied Dureing hur Natural life, and at hur Desase to be Eaqually Dividded Betwen my Children the other half to be Equally Divided betwen my Children the Children to have theire Maintainanc out of the whole place untill they Com of Age— and I do hereby utterly Disallow Revoke and Disannul all and Every Other former Testaments wills legacis Bequest and Executors by me in any wise before Named willed and bequeathed. Ratifying and Confirming this and No Other to be my Last will and Testament in Witness whereof I have hereunto Set my hand and Seal this the twenty third Day of May in the year of Our Lord one thousand seven hundred and Ninty two

        his
     James X Killsa (seal)
       Mark

Sighned Sealed published pronounced
and Delivered by the said Killsa as
his last will and Testament in presents
of us who in his presents and in the presents
of Each other have here unto Subscribed our Names
Jacob Keen
Lavinia Lewis
Elisha Keen

[Unrecorded.] Executrix gave notice of her appointment 24 Mar., 1794. Oliver Robins and Benjamin Blackinton, both of Thomaston, sureties. Inventory by David Fales, Oliver Robins and Benjamin Blackinton, all of Thomaston, 22 Ap., 1795, £254 : 19 : 4. [XIII, 380-1.]

In the Name of God Amen the Twentieth Day of November 1787 I George Varner of Waldoborough in the County of Lincoln and State of Massachusttas Bay in Newengland Yeoman Being Verey Weake and Low in Bodey But in parficit Mind and Memory Thanks be given unto God Tharefor Calling unto Mind the Mortalety of My Body and knowing that it is apointed for all Men once to Die Do Make and ordain this My Last Will and Testament That is to Say princalely and first of all I give and Recomend My Soul into the hands of God that gave it. and My Body I Recomend unto the Earth to Be Buried in Decant Cristeen Bureal at the Derection of My Exacuter Nothing Doubting But at the General Resurection I Shall Resive the Same again By the Mighty power of God. and as Touching Such worldly Estate wharewith haith pleased God to Bless Me in this Life I Give Demise and Dispose of in the following Manner and Form Viz I give and Bequath unto Sadoney Varner My Beloved wife the one Third of the use or incom of My Grist Mill and Land Now posessed By Me with the use of one third parte of all the Cattle Sheep & Hogs and all other Stock with the use of all the Buldings and Housald Goods During her Life— Item I give and Bequath unto My Soninlaw John Kinsel of Walldowborough in s'd County Whome I Likewis Constetute Make and ordain My Sole Exacuter of this My Last Will and Testement and Daniel Achorn of the Same Town and County My Son in law My Grist Mill and all and Singalur My Lands and Tenements of Evrey kind whatsoever With all the Cattle & Stock Housal Goods Moneys and Estat of Evrey kind whatsoever By Them Equaly to Be Devided and peacebaly to Be posessed By them the S'd John an Daniel their Heirs and asigns Exepting the one Third of the use of the Sevral Things above Mentioned to My Wife During her Life and I Do hearby uterly Disalow Revoke and Disanul all and Evry other former Testament Will Legisey and Bequaiths and Exacutors By Me in any wise Before Named Willed and Bequaithed Ratifying and Confirming this and no other to Be My Last will and Testament. in Wittness whareof I have hearunto Set My hand and Seal the Day and year above Written

George Varner

Signed Sealed published ⎫ (seal)
and Declared and pronounced ⎪
By the S'd George Varnor ⎬
as his Last Will and Testament ⎪
in the preasence of us the Subscribers, ⎭
  John Paine
  Thomas Rhoads
  David Vinall

Probated 25 Ap., 1794. [VI, 2-3.] Joseph Ludwig and Daniel Eichhorn both of Waldoboro, sureties. Inventory by Joseph Ludwig, Peter Procht and John Weaver, all of Waldoborough, 25 Ap., 1794, £159 : 9 : 11. [VI, 253.] Account filed 19 Sep., 1797. [VI, 254.]

    In the Name of God Amen I William Foset of Bristol in the County of Lincoln jun'r being weak of Body but of Perfect mind and memory Calling to mind the mortallity of my Body knowing it is ordained for all men once to die do make and ordain this my Last will and testament Viz I give my Soul into the hands of allmighty God that gave it my Body I Commit to the earth to be buried in decent and Christian burial and as touching such worly Estate as it has pleased God to Bless me with I give and bequeath in the following manner Viz I give to my Sister Mrs Jenny Gevin the Improvement of all my Estate real and Personal during her life after my Just debts and Funeral Charges are paid Except my Bed and Beding Which I Give to My Neice Ruth Foset Daughter to Henry Foset Sen'r and my young mare and six sheep which I Give and bequeath to my Apprentice boy Henry Light who is to be Decently Cloathed and sent to his mother if it should pleas almighty God to call me out of this world before he becomes of Age and all my Estate as aforesaid after my Sisters Decease I give and bequeath to my Nephew Henry Foset son to my Brother Henry Foset sen'r I also appoint William Rogers the sole Executor of this my last will and testament and it is further my Desire that a pair of tomb stones be procured and set up at my grave and I declare this and no other to be my last will and testament.

    Published pronounced and Declared by the said William Foset to be his last will and testament in the Presence of us this fourteenth day of Sep'r 1793

Robert Randall   N. B. the words all-sen'r- and pleas
Alexr Fossett Jun'r   were interlined before the signing
James Sproull   hereof

William U Foset (seal)
his mark

Probated 25 Ap., 1794. [VI, 4-5.] William Rodgers renounced executorship 10 Mar., 1794. [VI, 5-6.] Henry Fossat, of Bristol, Adm'r with will annexed, 25 Ap., 1794. [VI, 6.] Robert Randall and Alexander Fossett, both of Bristol, sureties. Inventory by Robert Randall, Robert Given and James Sproul, all of Bristol, 4 July, 1794, £200 : 1 : 2

I give to my wife the income of the Sloop till she thinks best to Sell her and then to be Devided between her and the Children as the rest of my Estate likewise one Hundred Dollars in Cash. Likewise I give to Polly Haupt Fifty Dollars and Thomas Waterman Fifty Dollars and Deborah Waterman Fifty Dollars, and I likewise give to my Sister Sarah Simmons a Note of Hand against my Brother Stephen for Twenty four Pounds. I Likewise give the Income of my Place to my wife and Children one third to my wife and the other two thirds to my Children till they come of age and then to be Eaqualy Devided between them after the Charges and Debts are paid. I likewise give the Debts due to me to my wife and Children to be Eaqualy Devided between them Except the Note of Hand and the Other Legacies that I have bequeathed above Likewise I would give Thomas Waterman my part of the Timber that I own in a Vessel frame but not as a gift but for him to have the Refusal of it towards what I owe him; Likewise I give my Mare to my wife to be Disposed of according to her Desire exclusive of what I have above given And all the Rest I have not Mentioned to my wife and Children to be Divided Eaqualy between them; Likewise appoint my Brother Stephen Simmons Thomas Waterman and my Brother Joseph Simmons Exicutors to this my will

In presence of
Ezekiel G. Dodge
Robt. Farnsworth

Zebedee Simmons
Given under my hand and seal this Sixteenth Day of October in the Year of our Lord one Thousand Seven Hundred and Ninetythree I Likewise appointe my wife Gaurdein to my Children till Thomas Waterman comes of Age and then I appoint him their Guardian

Probated 25 Ap., 1794. Letters testamentary issued to Stephen Simmons and Joseph Simmons, both of Waldoborough, 25 Ap., 1794. [VI, 7 to 9.] Mary Simmons, of Waldoborough, widow, guardian unto Zebedee, minor son, 26 Ap., 1794. [VI, 26.] Inventory by William Farnsworth, Peleg Oldham and Nathaniel Pitcher, all of Waldoborough. [VI, 161 to 165.] Account filed 25 June, 1806. [XI, 213-214.]

John Potter, late of Georgetown. Sarah Potter, of Georgetown, widow, Adm'x, 13 Feb., 1794. [VI, 10,] Benjamin Pattee, of Georgetown, and Samuel Stinson, of Woolwich, sureties. Inventory by Charles Couilliard and William Lee, Jr., both of Georgetown, and David Gilmore, of Woolwich, 1 May, 1794, £181 : 7 : 4. [VI, 158.] Samuel Stinson and David Gilmore, commissioners to examine claims. Account filed 31 May, 1796. [VI, 160.] Advertisement of real estate, 1796. [VIII, 45.] Account filed 7 Sep., 1798. [VIII, 46.] Widow's dower set off by David Gilmore, Denny McCobb and John Fisher, 23 July, 1798. [Unrecorded.]

In the name of God amen This the 10th day of February *Anno Domini* one thousand seven hundred and Ninety fore I John White of George Town in the County of Lincoln Gentleman being in perfict sound mind and memory thanks be given unto God, tharefore Calling to mind the Mortality of my body and knowing that it is Appointed for all men once to dy, do make and ordain this my last Will and Testament that is to say principally and first of all I give and recommend my soul into the hands of God who gave it, and my body I recommend to the Earth to be buried in a deasont mannor, not doubting but at the General Reserrection I shall receive the same again by the mighty powr of God, And as touching such worldly Interest wharewith it has pleased God to bless me in this life I do make and ordain this my last Will and Testament in manner Following Vz

Firstly I give and bequeath to my beloved wife Abigal White one third part of all my real and parsonal Estate with the improvement of my homestead farm during hir natrol life for the Suppoart and bringing up the young childrin or untill the youngist Surviving Mail Heir Shall arive to the Age of twenty one Years when said Estate shall be divided as is hereaftor divised.

Sec'dly I give and bequeath to my beloved Son John White the Eastrin end of Lot No 11 it beeing the northrin part of my Land to Contain forty Acres and likewise a Lot of Marsh lying in Joneses Marsh so col'd it being Lot No 18 Containing fore acres all which is to be Sot of to him for to improve when he Shall Arive to the age of twenty one Years as a Consideration for his Attention and Obediance to me and assisting his good sepmothor in bringing up the family and improving the farm aftor my decease.

thirdly I give and bequeath unto my two beloved eldest daughtors to wit, Rachel Drummand and Jane Fisher one Cow each to be paid by my Executors within twelve months aftor my deceas.

Forthly I give and bequeath unto my othor beloved daughtors to Wit Anmoriah White Margrat White Mary White Elisabeath White and Susanah White to be paid or delivered unto Each one when married or arving to the age of twenty one years, one good Cow to be paid by my Executors out of my Estate.

Fifthly I give and bequeath all my Real Estate to be eaqueally divided betwen my beloved surviving Sons to Wit John White, Jam's White and William White when they shall arive to the age of twnty one years or to aney one of them surviving and thair Heirs and Assigns for eavour including what has been sot of to John White which Shall be considred as a part of his Share

Sixthly I give and bequeath unto my beloved wife Abigal during hir nartol life all and the remaindor of my personal Estate aftor debts and leagasies is paid and Necessary Charges for the Suppoart of the family and at the deceas of my beloved Wife Abigal if my Youngist Surviving Child Should have arived to the Age of twnty one Years by that time the remainder of said personal Estate that may be found Shall be divided among my beloved above named Children.

Lastly I Will and ordain my beloved Wife Abigal White and my Estemed Neafew Denny McCobb Executors of this my last Will and Testament In witness whareof I have here unto Set my hand and Seal the tenth day of February in the Year of our Lord one thousand sevin hundread and ninety fore

February 10 AD 1794 Then John White the within named Testator signed seald published and declared the within writting Instroment as and for his last will and Testament in presence of us the Subscribors Witnesses who in presence of the said testator and of each othor at his request saw and heard him the said testator signe seale publish and declare the same Instroment as and for his last Will and Testament In mannor afore said In witness whareof we have here unto set our hands the day and Year aforesaid

    Joseph Preble   John White
    Benjamin Swett
    Ann Drummond

Probated 30 May, 1794. [VI, 11 to 13.] William Butler and Charles Couillard, both of Georgetown, sureties. Inventory by Benjamin Swett, Benjamin Pattee and John Fisher, all of Georgetown, 15 Aug., 1794, £615 : 17 : 6. [VI, 225-6.] Account filed 31 May, 1796. [VI, 226-7.]

In the Name of God Amen I Samuel McCobb of Georgetown in the County of Lincoln Esq., being sound in mind and memory : but calling to mind the uncertainty of all human events and more especially the fleeting and transitory life of Man; as touching the worldly property wherewith God has been pleased to bless me, I do make and ordain this my last Will and Testament in manner following Vizt.

Imprimis. I give bequeath and devise to my beloved Son Parker McCobb his heirs and assigns forever a certain Island near the entrance of Kennebec River, commonly called Stage Island, with the Previledges and appurtenances thereunto belonging

Secondly. I will and ordain that my beloved Wife Rachell shall have the sole use and improvement of the said Island to her own use and benefit, untill the said Parker McCobb shall have attained the age of twenty one years, in case my said Wife shall so long live.

Thirdly. I give and bequeath to my faithful servant Peter Cary one Pair of Steers and one pair of Heifars to be paid and delivered to him by my Executors hereafter-named, when he shall have attained the age of twentyone years, provided the said Peter shall in the meantime live with and faithfully serve in the capacity of a servant, my said beloved Wife in case she shall so long live.

Fourthly. I bequeath and devise to my said beloved Wife her Heirs and Assigns forever, all the rest and residue of my Estate both real and personal, wherever the same may be found at the time of my decease.

Lastly. I will and ordain my beloved Wife Rachell McCobb, my much esteemed Friend William Lithgow Jun'r and my beloved Son Denny McCobb, Executors of this my last Will and Testament. In Witness whereof, I have hereunto set my hand and seal the seventeenth day of March in the year of our Lord one thousand seven hundred and Ninety one.

Saml. McCobb (seal)

March 17th 1791 then Samuel McCobb Esq'r the within named Testator signed sealed published and declared the within within written Instrument as and for his last Will and Testament, in presence of us the subscribing Witnesses who in the presence of the said Testator and of each other at his request, saw and heared him the said Testator sign seal publish and declare the same Instrument as and for his last Will and Testament in manner aforesaid. In Witness whereof we have hereunto set our hands the day and year aforesaid

Saml. Howard
Jas. Davidson
Charlotte Lithgow
Mary Lithgow

I the before named Samuel McCobb being weak in body but of perfect mind and sound memory do make and publish this present writing as a Codicil to the before mentioned last Will and Testament in manner following Vizt. I will and ordain that each of my children towit Denny McCobb, Beatrice McCobb, Rachell McCobb, John McCobb, Jenny McCobb, Sally McCobb, and Nancy McCobb shall each of them be paid by my Executors the sum of five shillings after my decease. In Witness whereof I have hereunto set my hand and seal the twenty sixth day of July *Anno Domini* 1791.

Sam. McCobb (seal)

July 26th 1791 then the above named Samuel McCobb signed sealed published and declared the writing last above mentioned as and for a Codicil to his last Will and Testament aforesaid in presence of us the subscribing Witnesses who in presence of the said Testator and of each other at his request saw and heared him the said Testator sign seal publish and declare the same writing as and for his Codicil to the said last Will and Testament   In Witness whereof we have hereunto set our hands the twentysixth day of July *Anno Domini* 1791

Benjn Pattee
Anna McCobb
Isabel Cartter

Probated 18 Ap., 1793. [VI, 14-15.] William Lithgow, Jr., renounced executorship. Inventory by Benjamin Pattee, William Butler and Charles Couillard, all of Georgetown, 30 Ap., 1793. [VII, 57 to 59.]

In the name of God Amen I Joseph Johnson of Winthrop In the County of Lincoln & Common wealth of Massachusets Tanner Being of a Sound & Peesfull Mind & Memmory But Calling To mind the Mortallety of My Boddy Do Make and ordain this My Last will & Testament hereby Recomending My Soul to God who Gave it and My

Boddy to the Earth from whence it Came to be buryed in Such Decent Christain Manner as My Executers hereafter named Shall think propper and as to Such worldy Estate as it hath Pleesed God to bless me with in this Life I Do Give Devise & Despose of the Same in the following Manner Viz—

Imprimis My will is that My Just Debts Legacies & funeral Charges be paid & Descharged by My Sons Joshua Johnson & Joseph Johnson out of what I Shall give them of My Estate in this My Last will & Testament.

Item I give and bequeath to My wife Dinah Johnson all the household Stuff She brought me when I married her allso two Cowes & one year old heffer & five Sheep all the above articles are to be at her Desposel the hol of the articels following are to be for My Said wife for her Comfortable Support & Convenyense & for keeping what Stok She has to keep Duerring the time of her Remaning My widow.

Item I give and Bequeeath to My wife afore Said the use of a parte of My hom place to be twenty Six Rods in wedth from end to End of My said Land leving Eight Rods in wedth out of what I bought of Robert Page Esqr on th Southerly Side of Said Land with one thord of My orchard & half of My Dwelling house I now Live in with one quarter of My oldest Barn & one half of My Corn house with all My hogghouse & well my children to have the use threof allso allso Leving out of fore Said Land half an acor for Joshua for Convenyency for the tan yard & barke house & Drift way to the Same I allso give to My wife afore Said the use of My hors one thord of the time She peeping the the hors the Same part of time allso 30lb of Sollather & one Side of neets upperlather & four Midlin Calf Skins Curied allso ten Pound of Sheeps woll & 7lb of old flax allso provisons of all Sorts for her Self & the keepin of the Creters until Such times as She can have the first Crop off her own Emproved Land, allso the use of Every parttecelr artacel housold Stuf that She has not of her own as May aper by her & my agrement My Clock & grate Bibel is to be kept in this My Dwellin house During the above term of time the above Leather woll & flax is to be Recevid by My wife Emedetly after my Desese oute of what I Leve I allso give to My afore Said wife 30 pounds L Money to be paid to her by My Son Joshua Johnson for her Support when She Stands in need of the Same In Stock or Corn or grain

I give and Bequeath to My Daughter Elizabath Lyford the Improvement of a pece of Land Eleven Rods in wedth from End to End on the notherly Side of the Land My wife is to Improve & one quarter of My orchard for the Support of her Self and Childrin So Long as Shee Remains Oliver Lyfords widow also one quarter of My oldest barn I allso I give My fore Said Daughter one Cow & two Sheep Shee to have Said Cow & Sheep out of what I Shall Leve Emedatly after My Desece & to have them well kept until Shee can have keeping of her own Said Cow & Sheep are to be at her Desposal the above Land & barn after she Marries or Dies I give and bequeeath to her & her heirs for Ever

I Give & Bequeath to my Son Joshua Johnson the hol of the Land I bought of Joseph Greely Jur which he had of Henry Wyman with the house on the Same & a barn frame with all the Pertickerals which I have provided to finish Said Barn allso I give Said Joshua Eight Rods of Land in wedth on the Sotherly side of what My wife is to Improve & the hol Length of the Land I bought of Robert Page Esqr allso My Barke house barke Ston & Tanyard with the hol of My Stock in Trade allso all My Tools for farming & Trade one half of My Book Debts & half My Noats of hand one Ster Calf half the Remainder of My Sheep one yearling hefer the hol of the above perteckelrs I Give to My Son Joshua Johnson his heirs & assigns for Ever

My Son Joshua Johnson is to pay Benjamin Dudley Sexty pounds L M and to My wife 30 pounds L M as hertofore Spessiphied also 30 lb of Sollather & one Side of nets upperlather & four midling Calf Skins Curried

I Give & Bequeath to My Son Joseph Johnson his heirs and assigns for Ever the Remainder of My Land which I bouht of Robert Page Esqr not heretofore Dessposed of Lyeng one the Notherly Side of what My Daugter Elizabeth is to Emprove being about thirty three Rods in wedth and the hol Length of foreSaid Land with that part of My ochard not here to fore Dessposed of allso one half of My oldes Barn & one half of My Corn house & half of My Book Debts allso one half of My Notes of hand and I give to My foersaid Son Joseph as afore Said one two year old hefer givin Melk and two oxon Six year old and two thords of My hors Joshua having Said hors to Grind what barke he Shall have need of for two year Joshuas keepin Said hors a proper Space of time allso My Clock after his Mother has Don with it & two Sheep & two one year old Steers Joshua Johnson is to have So much out of Josephs Imprved Land as to make his Eqel to Josephs untel he Shall have as much Clerd Land Joseph has when thay first take posseshon of fore Said Land My Son Joseph Johnson is to pay the Remainder of the Debt Due to Benjamin Dudley which Joshua is not to pay

I Give and Bequeath to My Son Levi Johnson his heirs and assigns for Ever one half of My Land in Hollowell in fore Said County joining on kenebeck River to be the hol Length & half the wedth one the notherly Side of Said Land to be put in possesson of the Same at twenty one years of age also I give My Said Son Levi one Cow & two Stears Coming in three years old and three Sheep to be Delivered to him in two years after my Deceas by My Son Joshua

I Give and Bequeath to my Son Elisha Johnson his heirs and assigns for Ever the other part of My Land in Hollowell afore Said to be one half of the wedth & hol Length of Said Land on the Sotherly Side to be put in possesshon of the Same at twenty one years of age also I give to my Said Son Elisha one Cow and two Steers Coming In three years of age & three Sheep to be Delivered to him in Six Months after twenty one years of age by My Son Joshua

I Give and Bequeath to My Daughter Mary Lyford & Nathaniel Lyford her husband ten Dollars to be paid in neet Stoock or Corn or grain in one year after My Desece also I give to the Said Nathanil Lyford Aand Mary Lyford twenty two pounds ten Shillings L M to be paid by My Son Joseph Johnson in neet Live Stock or grain or Corn Stoock after the the Rate of Corn at fou Shillings pr bushel if in Corn or grain the Same Rate in Eightteen Months after my Desece to be Laid out in buying good unclered Land Land whaer it Shall Sute them best Said Joseph Johnson is to pay the hol of afoore Said ten Dollars & twenty two pounds L M to whomsoever Said Land Shall be purchesed of and to Receve a Deed in the following Manner first to the afore Said Nathaniel & Mary for their use in Improving the Same for their Suport During Life then to My grand Son Joseph Lyford Son of Nathaniel & Mary to him andhis heirs & assigns for Ever.

I give & Bequeath to My Daughter Bath Shebe Morrill ten Dollars to be paid by My Son Joseph Johnson in neet Live Stock or Corn or grain after the Rate of Corn at four Shillings pr bushel in two years after My Desece

I give & Bequeath to the Congrigashonal Church of Christ in Winthrop In fore Said County two Selver Cups Equel to two pounds Eight Shillings L M for Each Cup or Ef the Church Chueses the hol to be in one Cup thay are to Let It be knone these Cups or Cup are to be bougt by My Son Joseph oute of the Money Due from Capt James Robinson of Brintwood in New Hampshir and Delevered to the fore Said Church Commety in one year after My Desece by my Son Joseph Johnson to be Said Churches for Ever

My Will is that My thre fether Bedds with the hol Belongin to Said Beds with all My Real & personal Estate not herein Dsposed of togeather with what My widow Shall Leve to My Childrin be Devided EquiLy Betwen My four Sons Exsept thirty pound L M to be paid to My Daughter BathShebe Morril to be hers & her heirs for Ever

finally I Do Constitute ordain & apoint My Son Joshua Johnson & My Son Joseph Johnson Sol Executers of this My Last will & Testament

In witness whereof I Do hereunto Set my hand & Seal this thirt Day of July *Anno Domini* 1790.

Signed Sealed and published and
Deeclared by the fore Said
Joseph Johnson to be his Last will &
Testament in Presence of
Levi Morrill
Henry Wyman   Joseph Johnson   (seal)
Robert Page

Probated 4 Nov., 1794. Joseph Johnson renounced executorship; letters testamentary issued to Joshua Johnson, of Reedfield, 4 Nov., 1794. [VI, 17 to 21.] Inventory by Robert Page, of Reedfield, Jedediah Prescott and Nathaniel Fairbanks, both of Winthrop, 10 Jan., 1795. [VI, 171 to 173.] Widow's dower set off by Robert Page, Henry Wyman and Ichabod Simmons, all of Readfield, 1795. [VI, 174.] Account filed 19 Jan., 1796. [VI, 174 to 176.]

In The Name of Holy Thrinety Father uoŋ and Holy Ghost.—

Know all men by these Presents that I John Martin Shaffer of a Place called Broad Bay with out the bounds of any Town but in the County of Lincoln and Provinz of the Massachusetts Bay in New England Clarke am and be in Right, full and Good Senses and State of Health and being resolved to go to Europa to Germany my Native Country. and not Knowing when it shall please my Creator to call me out of this World I therefore make this my last Will and Testament disannulling all former Wills and Testaments or other Writings of any Kind of the like, Onely acknowledge this to be my onely and last Will to be observed

First. I Committ my Soul in to the Hands of Allmighty God and Crave His mercies and forgiveness.

Secondly I Comitt unto the Allmightys Protection my Wife Margett and my Daughter Mary which both I hereby Declare acknowledge Order and Appoint to be my onely and Lawfull Heirs to my Estate or Estates real or personall it may be or have Name what so ever and Order them hereby to administer to the same after my decease jointly and them to Devide all and every Estat's Effects, Goods and Things whatsoever equally amongst them, (Except the Bed which I intirely bequeathe to the Said Margett my Wife for her Sole Use and Propperty In Witness that this is my true, firm and Last Will and Testament to be observed, have hereunto Sett my Hand and Seal this Sixth Day of August *Anno Domini* one Thousand Seven Hundred and Sixty Seven and in the Seventh Year of His Majestys Reign.

John Martin Schaeffer (seal)

Signed Sealed & Delivred
in the presence of
Chars. Leissner
Andrew Storer
———— Miller

Lincoln sc. Broad Bay August 6th 1767 Then the Revd John Martin Schaeffer above named appearing personally Acknowledged published pronounced and Declared the above written Instrument to be his last Will and Testament.

Coram David Fales *Just Pacis*.

Probated 13 Sep., 1794. [VI, 21-22.] Margaret Schaeffer renounced executorship 13 Sep., 1794, and Mary Schaeffer being dead, Moses Copeland, of Warren, was appointed Adm'r *cum testamento annexo*, 13 Sep., 1794. [VI, 23.] Daniel Dunbar, of Warren, and Marlboro Packard, of Cushing, sureties. Inventory by Patrick Pepbles, Benjamin Webb and John Spear, all of Warren, 11 July, 1795, £656:2:11. [VI, 154 to 157.] Account filed 1 Nov., 1800. [VIII, 236.]

Edward Emerson, late of Edgecomb. Elizabeth Emerson, of Edgecomb, widow, Adm'x, 6 May, 1794. [VI, 24.] John Murray and John Emerson, both of Boothbay, sureties. Inventory by Thomas Boyd and John Leishman, both of Boothbay, and Daniel Webster, of Edgecomb, 2 Jan., 1795. [VI, 146.] Edward Emerson, of Edgecomb, Adm'r *de bonis non*, 11 Sep., 1797. [VII, 170-1.] John Murray and John Emerson, sureties.

John Searles, Junior, late of Hallowell, mariner, son of John Searl, of Winslow, who declined administration. Samuel Metcalf, of Hallowell, trader, Adm'r, 2 Jan., 1795. [VI, 25.] Joseph Smith and Samuel Lovejoy, both of Hallowell, sureties.

Stephen Simmons, late of Waldoborough. Betsey Simmons, of Waldoborough, widow, Adm'x, 11 Feb., 1795. [VI, 30.] Inventory by Jacob Ludwig, Peleg Oldham and Nathaniel Pitcher, all of Waldoborough, 20 Feb., 1795, £110 : 5 : 6. [VI, 169-170.] Abigail, minor daughter, chose Spooner Sprague, of Waldoborough, to be her guardian 20 Sep., 1796. [VII, 53-54.] Joseph Simmons, of Waldoborough, guardian unto Peabody, Stephen and Urainy Sprague, minor children, 20 Sep., 1796. [VII, 54.] Account filed 17 Sep., 1798, at which date the administratrix had become the wife of Ephraim Patch. [VIII, 4.] Division of personal estate among widow, Abigail, Peabody, Stephen, Urany Sprague, Nancy, Betsey, and Rachel, 5 Ap., 1799. [VIII, 4-5.] Account of Joseph Simmons, guardian, filed 11 Jan., 1805. [X, 327.] Account of Ezekiel Vinal, guardian of Nancy Simmons, filed 21 June, 1809. [XIII, 470-1.] Account of Nathan Sprague, guardian unto Urania Simmons, filed 21 June, 1809. [XIII, 471.]

John Montgomery, late of a place called Smithfield. Benjamin Shaw, of Pittston, Adm'r, 30 Ap., 1794. [VI, 31.] Reuben Colburn, of Pittston, and Samuel Goodwin, of Pownalborough, sureties. Inventory by William Barker, Ebenezer Byram and Reuben Colburn, all of Pittston, 23 Oct., 1794, £87 : 0 : 3. [VI, 81-82.]

Jason Robbins, late of Union. Jenny Robbins, of Union, widow, Adm'x, 13 Sep., 1794. [VI, 32.] David Robbins, of Union, and Moses Copeland, of Warren, sureties. Inventory by Moses Hawes, Amariah Mero and Rufus Gilmore, all of Union, 25 Dec., 1794, £68 : 6 : 9. [VI, 152-3.] Account filed 2 Mar., 1796. [VI, 153.]

David Mustard, late of Bowdoinham. Hatherly Randall, of Bowdoinham, Adm'r, 9 May, 1794. [VI, 33.] James Rogers and Joseph Randall, both of Bowdoin, sureties. Inventory by David Haynes and Nathaniel Purington, both of Bowdoinham, and Thomas Morgridge, of a place called Fairfield, 30 May, 1794, £92 : 5 : 0. [VI, 148.] Account filed 28 Oct., 1800. [VIII, 235.] Hatherly Randall, guardian unto James and Charity, minor children, 28 Oct., 1800. [IX, 192.] James and William, minor sons, chose James Rogers to be their guardian, 8 Feb., 1803. [IX, 241.]

Jonathan Williams, late of Bowdoin, mariner. John Starbird, of Bowdoin, Adm'r, 9 May, 1794. [VI, 34.] David Haynes and James Rogers, both of Bowdoin, sureties. Inventory by Joseph Randall, Benjamin Jaques and Daniel Cunningham, all of Bowdoin, 30 May, 1794, £212 : 2 : 9. [VI, 179-180.] Account filed 30 May, 1799. [VIII, 236.] George Ridley, of Bowdoin, guardian unto Samuel, James and Jonathan, minor sons, 7 Sep., 1798. [XI, 178.] Guardian's account filed 26 Jan., 1805. [X, 339.]

David Ring, late of Cambden, son of Thomas Ring, of Edgecomb. Eleanor, widow, declined administration. David Blodget, of Cambden, Adm'r, 5 June, 1794. [VI, 35.] Simon Barrett and Joseph Eaton, Jr., both of Cambden, sureties. Inventory by Joseph Eaton, Samuel Jacobs and Elisha Gibbs, all of Cambden, 19 June, 1794, £221 : 11 : 10. [VI, 80-81.] Samuel Jacobs and Charles Demorse, both of Camden, commissioners to examine claims. [VI, 250.] Account filed 12 Aug., 1803. [X, 206.]

Jonathan Bartlett, late of a place called Balltown. Jonathan Bartlett, of a place called Sheepscut great pond, Adm'r, 13 Nov., 1794. [VI, 35-36.] Joshua Little and Oliver Peasley, both of Balltown, sureties. Inventory by Solomon Potter, Oliver Peasley and Jonathan Heath, all of Balltown, $527. 31. [VIII, 58.] Account filed 4 Jan., 1799. [VIII, 63-64.]

Isaac Russell, late of Canaan. Betty Russell, of Canaan, widow, Adm'x, 31 May 1794. [VI, 36-37.] Solomon Steward, Jr., of Canaan, and Obadiah Witherell, of Norridgwalk, sureties. Inventory by Daniel Steward, of Norridgewalk, John Weston and Bryce McLellan, both of Canaan, 6 Aug., 1794, £259 : 16 : 4. [VI, 199.] Account filed, 26 May, 1796. [VI, 200.] Betty, widow, guardian unto Betsey, James, John, Polly, Ichabod, Nathaniel and Joseph, minor children, 26 May, 1796. [VI, 201,] Account filed 11 May, 1804. [X, 162.]

William Moore, late of Pownalborough. Elizabeth Moore, of Boston, widow, Adm'x, 10 Ap., 1794. [VI, 37-38.] Elizabeth Moore, of Boston, singlewoman, and Solomon Blanchard, of Pownalborough, sureties.

Jesse Eaton, late of Mount Vernon. Sarah Eaton, of Mount Vernon, widow, Adm'x, 16 Jan., 1795. [VI, 38-39.] Nathaniel Dudley and Benjamin Eastman, both of Mount Vernon, sureties. Inventory by Daniel Dudley, John Dudley and Joses Ladd, all of Mount Vernon,

29 Jan., 1795, £224 : 11 : 6. [VII, 80-81.] Account filed 19 Jan., 1796. [VII, 81-82.] Nathaniel Dudley, of Mount Vernon, guardian unto Polly, Relief, William and Sarah, minor children, 16 Jan., 1798. [IX, 177.] Widow's dower set off by Jedediah Prescott, Benjamin Philbrook and Joses Ladd, all of Mount Vernon, 23 June, 1803. [X, 75.]

In the Name of God Amen I James Mustard of Topsham in the County of Lincoln & Commonwealth of Massachusetts Gentln being week in body but of perfect mind & memory Blessd be God therefor. Calling unto mind the Mortality of my body and Knowing that it is appointed for all men once to die Do therefore make and ordain this my Last will and testament that is to Say princably and first of all I Give and Recommend my Soul in to the hands of Almighty God that gave it me and my body I Recommend to the Earth to be buried in Decent Christain Burial at the Discression of my Executors nothing Doubting but at the General Resurection I shall Recive the Same again by the Mighty power of God and as touching Such worldly Estate wherewith it has plesed God to Bless me in this Life I give Devise and Dispose of the Same in the following manner & form

first I Give to well beloved Son Charles Mustard the one half of all my Real and personal Estate of what name or nature So ever whome I Likewise Constitute make and ordain the Sole Executor of this my Last will and testement he to pay out Such Sum or Sums as is herein after mentioned that is to Say to Charity Mustard Daughter of my Son James Mustard Decesd one Wosted gound that was her grandmothers and also one Lining Spining wheel, and also that he the Said Charles pay to my Beloved Daughter Charity Mustard fifteen pounds in money or Stock at money price and that he also pay to the Heirs of my Son David Mustard Deceas'd twenty Seven pounds in money or Stock at money price, to be equally Devided between the three Children that my Son David Left.

Also I give to my Beloved Son Joseph Mustard the other half of all my Estate both Real and personal he to pay out Such Sums as is herein after mention'd that is to Say to my Beloved Daughter Mary Rogers twenty Seven pounds in Money or Stock at mony price and also that he the Said Joseph pay to my Beloved Daughter Charity Mustard fifteen pounds in money or Stock at money price.

Be it Known to all Men that there is nothing in this my Last will and testament to Deprive my Daughter Charity of a high Chist of Draws and one bed and Beding that was given her by her mother Charity Mustard Deceas'd and I Do hereby utterly Disallow Revook and Disanul all and every other former testements wills Legesayes Bequests Executors by me in any ways before named willed and bequeathed ratifying and Confirming this and no other to be my Last will and testament

In witnes whereof I have hereunto Set my hand and Seal this twenty fifth Day of May in the year of our Lord one thousand Seven Hundred and ninety two and the Sixteenth year of the Independence of the United States of America—

Signed Sealed published
pronounced and Declaired
by the Said James Mustard   James Mustard   (seal)
as his Last will and testament
in the presence of us who in
his presence and in the presence
of each other have hereunto
Subscribed our names
Nathll Larrabee
George Headdean
James Hunter Jun'r

Probated 12 May, 1794. [VI, 39-40.] John Reed, Jr., and Steal Foster, both of Topsham, sureties. Inventory by Ezekiel Thompson, Arthur Hunter and James Wilson, all of Topsham, 12 Aug., 1794, £602 : 15 : 1. [VI, 141-2.]

Joel Chandler, late of Winthrop. John Chandler, of Winthrop, Adm'r, 2 Feb., 1795. Samuel Goodwin, Jr., and James Currier, both of Dresden, sureties. Inventory by William Pullen, Samuel Wood and Nathaniel Fairbanks, all of Winthrop, 14 Mar., 1795, £507 : 7 : 4. [VI, 187 to 189.]

Asa Commings, late of Hallowell, blacksmith. Eleanor Commings relinquished right of administration. Samuel Commings, of Hallowell, Adm'r, 2 Feb., 1795. [VI, 43-44.] William Briggs and Aaron Page, both of Hallowell, sureties.

In the Name of God amen. I James Turner of Canaan in the county of Lincoln and State of Massachsetts bay husbandman being sick and weak but in Perfect mind and memory thanks be given unto God, calling unto mind the mortality of my body, and knowing that it is appointed for all men once to die, Do make ordain this my last Will and Testament, that is to say, principlely and first of all I give and recommend my Soul into the hands of Almighty God, that gave it, and my body to the Earth to be buried in decent christian burial at the discretion of my Executrix nothing doubting but at the general Resurection I shall receive the same again by the Mighty Power of God, and as touching such worldly Estate wherewith it has pleased God to bless me in this life, I give, demise, and dispose of the same in the following manner and form; I give and bequeath to Elizabeth my dearly beloved Wife Whom I likewise Constitute make and ordain the sole Executrix of this my last Will and Testament all and singular my Real and Personal Estate by her freely to be Possesed and Enjoyed and to dispose of at Pleasure—Ratifying and confirming this to be my last Will and Testament.

In Witness whereof I have hereunto set my hand and seal this twenty first day of February in the year of our Lord Seventeen hundred and ninety four.

Signed Sealed Published
pronounced and delivered by the said
James Turner as his last Will and
testament in his presence and
in the Presence of each other have
hereunto Subscribed our Names

mark
James (X) Turner (seal)
his

John Fowler
William Prudens
Timothy Brown

Probated 5 Sep., 1794. [VI, 44.]
John Fowler and Timothy Brown, both of Canaan, sureties.

In the Name of God Amen; I Barnard Case of Union in the County of Lincoln & Commonwealth of Massachusetts—Being weak of Body but (Blessed be God) of a Sound disposing Mind; Do make & Declare this my last will & Testament in following that is to say   First

I committ my Body to the Dust & my Soul to God who gave it—

I give to my Loving wife Thankfull Case the Sum of Sixty-five Pounds—And the Remainder of my Estate I give to my Brothers Wm and James Case & my Sister Rebeckah Foster to be Equaly Divided among them—After the payment of my Just Debts & my Funeral Charges which are to be paid by my Executor—And I hereby Apoint Capt George West of the same Union Sole Executor to this my last Will & Testament—In Confirmation whereof I have hereunto Set my Hand & Seal. Dated at Union this Nineteenth day of April in The

Year of Our Lord one thousand seven Hundred & Ninety-four.
Signed & Sealed
in presence of   Barnard Case   (seal)
Edward Jones
Mary West
George W. West

Probated 16 Sep., 1794.   [VI, 45-46.]
Edward Jones, of Union, and Benjamin Mesarve, of Barrettstown, sureties. Inventory by Joel Adams, Josiah Robbins and Rufus Gilmore, all of Union, 21 Jan., 1795, £95 : 4 : 7.   [VI, 123.]

in the Name of God Amen

I Henry Kaler of Waldoborough in the County of Lincoln and CommonWealth of Massachusetts: yeoman: Being infirm in Body, but in Perfect Health and Memmory: Do Make and ordain this my Last will and Testament in order following—That is to Say: I Give and Recomment my Soul into the hand of Almighty God that Gave it, and my body I Recomment to the Earth, to be decently intered at the Discretion of my Executors. And Touching Such worldly Estate which it hath Pleased God to Bless me with—I will and Bequeath in the following manner and form—

Firstly: I Give and Bequeath to my well be Loved Son Jacob Kaler whom I Lickwise Constitute Make and ordain my only and Soul Executor of this my last will and Testament, all and Singular My Lands Messuages and Tenements, also all my Personal Estate by him freely to be Possessed and Enjoyed for Ever—

2 :ly it is also my will that my Son Jacob Kaler Shall Keep my Dearly beloved wife Elizabeth in Vicktuals and trink and in all Necessarys During her Natural Life; and if Neglected, then my Dearly beloved wife is to have the incom of one third of my Real and Personal Estate During her Natural Life.

3 :ly: it is also my will that my Son Jacob Kaler Shall Pay to my well beloved Children Viz: Charls Kaler, Doredeah Kaler, Eva Kaler, Catherina Kaler, Margret Kaler, Anna Mariah Kaler, Mary Catharina Kaler Each one three Pound Six Shillings & 8d: Lawfull money of this Commonwealth. The afore Said Sumes of money to be Paid as followeth Viz: one Quarter Part of the afore Said Sums is to be Paid, twelve months after the Decease of my Dearly beloved wife Elizabeth, and one Quarter Part twelve months after the first Quarter, and one Quarter Part twelve months after the Second Quarter, and one Quarter

Part twelve months after the third Quarter: So to make in the whole four Quarterly Payments, as afore menṭioned—

And I Do hereby utterly Disallow Revoke Disannul all and every other former testaments and wills, by me in any ways before named willed and bequeathed Ratifying and Confirming this and no other to be my Last will and testament, in witness whereof I have here unto Set my hand and Seal this fourteenth Day of January in the year of of our Lord 1790.

Signed Sealed Published and Pronounced by the Said Henry Kaler as his Last will and testament in the Presence of us who in his Presence and in the Presence of Each other have here unto Subscribed our Names— —

Henry Kaler (seal)

Jacob Ludwig
Frederik Arnold
Jacob Winchenbach

Probated 25 Ap., 1794. [VI, 47-48.] Jacob Ludwig and Jacob Winchenbach, both of Waldoborough, sureties. Inventory by Jacob Bornheimer, Joseph Ludwig and Nathan Sprague, all of Waldoborough, 8 Sep., 1794, £84 : 6 : 2. [VI, 50.]

Benjamin Branch, late of Sidney. Benjamin Branch, of Sidney, Adm'r, 10 Jan., 1795. [VI, 51.] Daniel Branch, of a place called West ponds, and John Hamilton, of Sidney, sureties. Inventory by Edmund Matthews and Reuben Pinkham, both of Sidney, and Abisha Cowen, of Hallowell, 17 Jan., 1795. [VI, 244.] Account filed 19 Jan., 1796. [VI, 245.]

John Bridge, late of Pownalborough, trader. Rachel Bridge, of Pownalborough, widow, Adm'x, 3 Mar., 1795. [VI, 52.] Inventory by Thomas Rice, Joseph Christophers and David Silvester, all of Pownalborough, 20 Mar., 1795, £1069 : 10 : 5¾. [VI, 194-5.] William Bowman, of Wiscasset, guardian unto Rachel, minor daughter, 16 Aug., 1806. [IX, 214.] Fanny, minor daughter, chose Joshua Danforth, of Wiscasset, to be her guardian, 12 Aug., 1806. [IX, 268.] Account filed 7 Jan., 1807. [XII, 137-8.] Distribution ordered 7 Jan., 1807. [XII, 153.]

John Howard, of Hallowell, *non compos*. Ebenezer Farwell, of Vassalborough, guardian. Inventory by Joseph North, Henry Sewall and Samuel Colman, all of Hallowell, 30 May, 1792, £1967 : 6 : 5½. [VI, 55-56.]

James Blanchard, late of Woolwich. Susanna Blanchard, of Woolwich, widow, Adm'x, 10 Mar., 1795. [VI, 57.] James Blanchard and Samuel Blanchard, both of Woolwich, sureties. Inventory by Samuel Stinson, David Gilmore and Abner Wade, all of Woolwich, 25 Mar., 1796. [VI, 228.] Yearly value of real estate appraised at $80., 28 Mar., 1798. Accouut filed 4 June, 1798. [VIII, 44.] Robert Hanson, of Woolwich, guardian unto Sheppard and Patty, minor children, 4 June, 1798. [IX, 221.] Jane and Polly, minor daughters chose Robert Hanson to be their guardian, 16 Mar., 1798. [IX, 222.]

Jedediah Hammond, late of Bristol, mariner. Isaac Tirrill, of Bristol, Adm'r, 16 Sep., 1794. [VI, 58.] Timothy Farrow and Joseph Shaw Tirrill, both of Bristol, sureties. Inventory by Thomas Johnston, George Rhoads and Oliver Nash, all of Bristol, 15 Sep., 1798, $402. [VIII, 43.] Benjamin Brown, of Waldoborough, Adm'r *de bonis non*, 9 Jan., 1807. [IX, 112.] Account filed 8 Jan., 1808. [XII, 349.]

Robert Kennedy, late of Newcastle, mariner. Sarah Kennedy, of Newcastle, widow, Adm'x, 10 Nov., 1794. [VI, 84-85.] Robert Simpson and William Clark, both of Newcastle, sureties. Inventory by John Huse, Francis Cook and David Payson, all ot Pownalborough, 29 Feb., 1795. [VI, 237-8.] Account filed 7 Sep., 1798, at which date the administratrix had become the wife of Stephen Jewett. [VIII, 234-5.]

Israel Jordan, late of Thomaston, mariner. Susanna Jordan, of Thomaston, widow, Adm'x, 17 Sep., 1793. [VI, 86-87.] Israel Loveitt and Ephraim Snow, both of Thomaston, sureties. Inventory by Moses Copeland, of Warren, Samuel Brown and Joseph Coombs, both of Thomaston, 22 Oct., 1793, £197 : 6 : 0. [VI, 143-4.] Susanna, widow, guardian unto John and Hannah, minor children, 4 Nov., 1799. [IX, 190.]

John Patten, late of Topsham. David Patten, of Topsham, son, Adm'r, 17 Ap., 1795, [VI, 88-89,] upon petition of Mary, widow, Robert, Thomas, Joseph and Actor, children, dated 14 Ap., 1794. John Fulton and John Reed, both of Topsham, sureties. Inventory by John Merrill, James Wilson and Benjamin Jones Porter, all of Topsham, 27 May, 1795, £2004 : 12 : 11. [VI, 210-211.] Account filed 9 Sep., 1796. [VI, 245-6.]

Francis Whitmore, late of Bowdoinham. Stephen Whitmore, of

Bowdoinham, Adm'r, 22 Ap., 1795. [VI, 89.] Zacheus Beal and John Springer, both of Bowdoinham, sureties. Inventory by Zacheus Beal, William Denham and James Purrington, all of Bowdoinham, 20 June, 1795, £74 : 8 : 1. [VII, 85.] James Maxwell and Elihu Getchel, both of Bowdoinham, commissioners to examine claims. [VII, 86.] Advertisement of sale of real estate 27 Dec., 1796. [VII, 87.] Account filed 8 Sep., 1797. [VII, 136-7.] Distribution of estate to Stephen, Francis, John, William, Andrew, Elizabeth Sevens, and Susanna Dinsmore, children of deceased, and Nathan Blodget, son of Mary Blodget, who was a daughter of deceased. 8 Sep., 1797. [VII, 189-190.]

John Nelson, late of the Island of Grenada. Thomas Lindall Winthrop, of Boston, Adm'r, 17 Ap., 1795. [VI, 90.] James Bowdoin, of Dorchester, and Charles Coffin, of Boston, sureties. Inventory by Joseph North, William Howard and Samuel Colman, all of Hallowell, 29 July, 1795, $52,073.00. [VII, 194 to 196.] Account filed 1796. [VII, 197.] Caleb Blanchard, Jacob Rowe and Edward Davis, all of Boston, commissioners to examine claims. [VII, 198.] Account filed 19 Sep., 1797. [VII, 198-9.] Advertisements of sale of real estate 17 Ap., 1797. [VII, 199 to 201.] Account filed 24 Sep., 1806. [XII, 210-211.] Advertisements of sale of real estate 18 Ap., 1804, and 12 Mar., 1805. [XII, 276 to 280.] Account filed 5 Jan., 1820. [XXII, 376.]

In the Name of GOD. Amen.

I William Lee Senr of Georgetown in the County of Lincoln and Commonwealth of Massachusetts, yeoman, being Advanced in Age, tho of sound disposing mind & memory, and calling to mind my Mortality, Do make, ordain and publish this my last Will & testament in the manner following.— In the first place I Commit my soul to GOD, who gave it, & my body to the earth, hopeing at the last day I shell Obtain a happy resurrection to an Immortal life, thiough the merits of *Christ* my saviour.

And as touching such Estate as it hath pleased God to bestow upon me, I will and dispose of it in manner following Viz. *Imprimis.* I will and order that all my Just debts & Funeral Charges be paid by my herein after named Executors within a reasonable time after my decease.

Item. I give and bequeathe unto my well beloved wife Elizabeth & my Son John all my real Estate of what name or nature soever, (except what is hereinafter set off to my Son James) to be equally divided between them two, and after the decease of my said wife, her part of the whole to Accrue to my son John to him & his heirs forever. Item, I give and bequeath to my son James One hundred Acres of land lying at the Northeastern part of my farm, to be fifty rods in wedth on Kenebeck river, & to extend Northwesterly so far as that a parrellel Course with my Northeastern line (with the wedth Aforesaid) Compleate the said Hundred Acres of Upland, and Also I give to my son James ten Acres of Marsh, & six Acres of thatch, lying at Winnogance Creek, to be set off to him from the northern part of my marsh there as Convenient to all Concern'd as may be. And Also, I give and bequeath to my said son James the sum of fourty pounds L. money which my hereafter named executors is Order'd to pay in money or Articles suitable to build an house when my son James calls therefor, which sum, together with the hundred acres of Upland, ten Acres of marsh & six of thatch beforementioned, is to be given to him & his heirs forever, in full for all his Services, & to be consider'd as his full Share of my estate. Item. I will & bequeath to my Son William, ten Shillings L. money as his full Share of my estate.

Item I give & bequeath to my Daughter Ann ten Shillings L Money as her full Share of my Estate.—Item I give & bequeath to my Daughter Rebecca One hundred pounds Lawfull Money to be paid in two payments. One half at the End of the first year, & one half at the End of the second year after my decease which is to be in full for her Share of my Estate.

Item, I give & bequeath to my daughter Elizabeth One hundred pounds L money to be paid by my after named Executors in the same way & manner that my daughter Rebecca's is to be paid, & further Will that my daughter Elizabeth is to live in my house, with my said Wife Elizabeth & son John, so long as she lives single & unmarried. I further will & devise that after the Afore mentioned Legacys be paid & Also my debts, that all the personal Estate then remaining, shell be equally divided between my said Wife Elizabeth & son John. And Lastly I do hereby Constitute & Appoint my well beloved wife Elizabeth & my son John Executors, to this my last Will, hereby revoking & disannulling all former wills & testaments by me in any manner made. Confirming this, & no other to be my last Will & testament. In Witness whereof I have hereunto Set my hand & Seal the twenty sixth day of

June, *Anno Domini*, One thousand, seven hundred, & ninety four.

Sign'd, Seal'd, puplished & declar'd by the said Testator, to be his last Will in presence of us, who have Subscrib'd hereto as Witnesses, in the presence of the testator & of each other.—

Witnesses.
Charles Coullard Wm Lee (seal)
Iseballa Manson
Mark L. Hill

Probated 29 May, 1795. [VI, 93-94.]
Inventory by Mark Langdon Hill, John Rogers and Joseph Bowker, all of Georgetown, 14 June, 1795, £976 : 13 : 2. [VI, 181-2.]

In the Name of God Amen. I John Reed of Topsham in the County of Lincoln being of Sound Mind and Memory (blessed be God therefor) do this twenty first day of April *Anno Domini* 1781 Make and publish this My last Will and Testament, in Manner following (that is to Say).—

Imprimis I give and bequeath unto my Loving Wife Susanna Reed the improvement of all My Estate both Real and Personal as long as She remains My Widdow.—

Item. I Give to my Son John Reed Six Shillings to be paid by my Executor.—

Item. I Give to my Son David Reed one hundred and forty-five acres of land described as followeth viz. all the front of the lots Number five and six between Merimeeting Bay and Muddy River that I have not before disposed of by Deed, and forty five acres of Land out of the aforesaid lots on the North Side of Muddy River together with all my Personal Estate of every Sort.—

Item I give to My Daughter Mary the wife of Samuel Wilson Six Shillings to be paid by my Executor.

Item I give to my Daughter Jane the wife of Joseph Foster Six Shillings to be paid by My Executor.—

Item I give to my Daughter Susanna Reed Six Shillings to be paid by My Executor.—

Item I give to my Daughter Martha the wife of Joseph Randall Six Shillings to be paid by my Executor.—

Item I give to my Daughter Elizebeth Reed one Milch Cow, one Feather bed and bed Cloaths.—

Item I give to my Daughter Margaret Reed one milch Cow, one Feather bed and bed Cloaths.—

Item   I give to my Daughter Charity Reed one Milch Cow one feather bed and bed Cloaths.—
Item   I give to my Daughter Hannah Reed one Milch Cow one Feather bed and bed Cloaths—
Item   I give to My Grand Daughter Susanna Reed twenty pounds to be paid by my Executor.
Item   I make and ordain my Said Wife Susanna Reed My Sole Executrix of this my Will; and my loveing brother William Reed overseer thereof, to take Care and See the Same performed according to my true intent and meaning;—in witness whereof I have here unto Set my hand and Seal this 21st Day of April *Anno Domini* 1781.
Signed Sealed Delivered published
Pronounced and declared by the
Said John Reed to be his last
Will and Testament in Presence   John Reed   (seal)
of us.—
John Merrill
James Hewey
Samuel Akley

       Probated 29 May, 1795.   [VI, 95-96.] John Merrill and James Hewey, both of Topsham, sureties.   Inventory by William Randall, James Fulton and John Merrill, 25 Aug., 1795, £87 : 17 : 10.   [Unrecorded.]   Samuel Wilson, Adm'r *de bonis non*, 29 Oct., 1799.

 John Given, Jr., late of Newcastle.   James Given, of Newcastle, Adm'r, 16 June, 1795.   [VI, 97-98.]   James Simpson, of Newcastle, and Edmund Bridge, of Dresden, sureties.   Inventory by Samuel Nickels, John Farley and Alexander Little, all of Newcastle, 11 Sep., 1795, $180.42.   [VI, 213.]   Samuel Nickels and John Farley, commissioners to examine claims.   [VI, 214.]   Account filed 12 Sep., 1796.   [VI, 215.]   Distribution ordered 6 Jan., 1797.   [VI, 256-7.]

 Stephen Bartlett, late of Sheepscut great pond.   Jonathan Bartlett, of Sheepscut great pond, Adm'r, 15 May, 1795.   [VI, 98-99.]   Caleb Bartlett and James Peaslee, both of Balltown, sureties.

 Daniel Savage, late of Hallowell.   Ann Savage, of Hallowell, widow, Adm'x, 23 Ap., 1795.   [VI, 99.]   Samuel Howard and William Howard, both of Hallowell, sureties.   Inventory by Samuel Colman, David Thomas and Benjamin Pettingill, Jr., all of Hallowell, 25 May,

1795, £783 : 18 : 11. [VII, 70.] Widow's dower set off by William Howard, Seth Williams and Ephraim Ballard, all of Hallowell. [VII, 71-72.] Account filed, 12 Jan., 1797. [VII, 72-73.]

Peter Walch, late of Waldoborough. Jane Walch, widow, and John Walch, both of Waldoborough, Adm'rs, 10 Sep., 1795. [VI, 100.] Cornelius Burns and Joseph Henry Ludwig, both of Waldoborough, sureties. Inventory by Jacob Ludwig, Jacob Bornheimer and Charles Kaler, all of Waldoborough, 21 Sep., 1795. [VI, 198.]

Henry Sewall, late of Bath. Sarah Sewall, widow, and James Sewall, both of Bath, Adm'rs, 29 May, 1795. [VI, 101.] John Minot Moody and Thomas Clapp, both of Bath, sureties. Inventory by Joshua Philbrook, Joshua Raynes and Benjamin Ham, all of Bath, 19 Aug., 1795. [VII, 212-213.] Division of estate among Samuel Sewall, Jenny Sewall, Betsey Davenport, James Sewall, Henry Sewall, David Sewall, Joshua Sewall, Nancy Sewall, Hannah Sewall, Polly Sewall and Charles Sewall, children of deceased, by Edward Hall Page and Christopher Cushing, both of Bath, and William Bradbury, of a place called Chester, Kennebec County, 19 Sep., 1801. [VIII, 173-4.] Widow's dower set off by Edward Hall Page, Christopher Cushing and William Bradbury, 19 Sep., 1801. [Unrecorded.]

Frederick Hammond, late of Pownalborough, mariner. Anne Hammond, of Pownalborough, widow, Adm'x, 20 June, 1795. [VI, 102.] James Eveleth, of Pittston, and Benjamin Rackleff, of Edgecomb, sureties. Inventory by Thomas Rice, David Silvester and Levi Beal, all of Pownalborough, 29 Aug., 1795, £28 : 7 : 0. [VI, 193.] Thomas Rice and David Silvester, commissioners to examine claims. [VI, 231.] Account filed 5 June, 1797. [VI, 232.] Distribution of estate ordered 5 June, 1797. [VIII, 125.]

Joel Reed, late of Woolwich. Eunice Reed, of Woolwich, widow, Adm'x, 17 July, 1795, [VI, 102-103.] Robert Reed and Lemuel Trott, both of Woolwich, sureties. Inventory by Samuel Harnden, Jacob Eames and Lemuel Trott, all of Woolwich, 23 July, 1795, £213 : 1 : 0. [VI, 196-7.] Nathaniel Thwing and Samuel Harnden, commissioners to examine claims. [VI, 233.] Account filed 8 Sep., 1797. [VI, 234-5.]

Paul Jameson, late of Cushing. Sally Jameson, of Cushing, widow, Adm'x, 10 Dec., 1795. [VI, 103-104.] Moses Copeland and James Waller Head, both of Warren, sureties.

Church Nash, late of Waldoborough. Eve Nash, of Waldoborough, widow, Adm'x, 10 Dec., 1795. [VI, 104.] Joseph Simmons, of Waldoborough, and Benjamin Palmer, of Bristol, sureties. Inventory by Thomas Johnston and Benjamin Palmer, both of Bristol, and Joseph Simmons, of Waldoborough, 16 Dec., 1795, $2750.88. [VII, 143-4.] Account filed 17 Sep., 1798. [VIII, 99.] Eve, widow, guardian unto Lydia, Jane and Oliver, minor children, 17 Sep., 1798. [IX, 192.] Church and Samuel, minor sons, chose Eve, widow, to be their guardian, 17 Sep., 1798. [IX, 247-8.]

David Reed late of Topsham. Jane, widow, relinquished administration, 19 Oct., 1795. Samuel Dunlap, of Brunswick, Adm'r, 20 Oct., 1795. [VI, 105.] John Fulton and John Jameson, both of Topsham, sureties. Inventory by John Merrill, William Randall and James Fulton, all of Topsham, 22 Oct., 1795, $1333.33; additional inventory 8 Mar., 1796, $56.36. [VIII, 7-8.] Accounts filed 5 Jan., 1798, and 4 Jan., 1799. [VIII, 8 to 10.] Division of personal estate among widow, mother, Jane, wife of Joseph Foster, Martha, wife of Joseph Randall, Hannah, wife of Robert Potter, Margaret, wife of Robert Jack, Elizabeth, wife of John Soule, Charlotte, wife of John Herrin, the representatives of Samuel Wilson and wife, deceased, and the representatives of John Reed, deceased, 4 Jan., 1799. [VIII, 10-11.]

In the Name of God Amen. I James Yeats of Bristol in the County of Lincoln Yeoman being through the Goodness of God, tho weak in Body, yet of a Sound and perfect understanding and Memory, do Constitute this My last will and Testament, and Desire it may be recived by all as Such: first I most Humbly bequeath my Soul to God my Maker, beseeching his most Gracious Acceptance of it through the all Sufficient Merits and Mediation of my most Compassionate Redeemer Jesus Christ who gave himself to be an Atonement for my Sins, and is able to save to the uttermost all that come unto God by him, Seeing he ever liveth to make Intercession for them, and who, I trust will not reject me a returning penetent Sinner; when I come to him for Mercy; in this hope and Confidence I render up my Soul with Comfort, humbly beseeching the most blessed and Glorious Trinity, one God most holy, most Mercyfull, and Gracious, to prepare me for the time of my Dissolution, and then to take me to himself into that peace and rest, and incomparable felicity, which he has prepared for all that love and fear his holy Name, Amen, Blessed be God.—

I give my Body to the Earth, from whence it came, in full assurance of its Resurrection from thence at the last day. As for my Burial I Desire it may be Decent at the Discretion of my Executers. As to the worldly Estate that God has put into my hand, I have Divided the most of it among my Children many years ago, and what Little I am now Possessed of I Dispose in the following Manner. (Viz) To each of my Children To Elizabeth Rhoads, Sarah Hilton, Jean Poor, George Yeats, Mary Braint, Margret Nash, Sameul Yeats, Rachal Fuller, & Liddia Macker, I give Six Shillings to each and every one—what remains of my Estate Both real & personal I give and demise to my Beloved wife Jean Yeats her heirs and Assigns for ever, I Likewise Constitute and Appoint Sam'l Yeats & Oliver Nash Executers of this my last will and Testament, I do hereby revoke all former wills made by me, and Declare this only to be my last will and Testament, in Wittness whereof I the Said James Yeats have to this my last will Set my hand and Seal, this third day of August 1789 and in the thirteen year of the Independence of America

Signed Sealed and Declared by the
Said testator to be his last will and   his
Testament in the Presence of us   James ○ Yeats (seal)
have Subscribed our Names as   Mark
Wittnesses thereto

  Thos: Johnston   Lincoln ss   Personaly Appeared
  Thomas Johnston Ju'r   the Above Named James Yeats and
  Sarah Johnston   Acknowledged the Above will to be
                                his free act and Deed before me
                                 Thos: Johnston, Justice Peace.

Probated 10 Dec., 1795. [VI, 105-106.] Thomas Johnston, of Bristol, and Waterman Thomas, of Waldoborough, sureties.

Isaiah Crooker, late of Bath, blacksmith. Hannah Crooker, of Bath, widow, Adm'x, 30 Oct., 1795. [VI, 107-108.] Isaiah Crooker, of Bath, and Ezra Tubbs, of Dresden, sureties. Inventory by Francis Winter, Joseph White and Edward Hall Page, all of Bath, Dec., 1795, $8928.99. [VII, 45 to 49.] Widow's dower set off by Francis Winter, Joshua Shaw and Edward Hall Page, 12 May, 1797. [VII, 50.] Account filed 26 May, 1797. [VII, 51.] Hannah, minor daughter, and Zacheus, minor son, chose Hannah, widow, to be their guardian, 17 Nov., 1796. [VII, 51-52.]

Christopher Marson, late of Pittston, calker. Elizabeth Marson, of Pittston, widow, Adm'x, 4 Nov., 1795. [VI, 108-109.] Peter Pochard and James Bugnon, both of Dresden, sureties. Inventory by Louis Houdlette, John Polereczky and Ezra Taylor, all of Dresden, 16 Nov., 1795, $559.59. [VII, 90-91.] Elizabeth, widow, guardian unto James and Christopher, minor sons, 6 Sep., 1799. [IX, 191.]

Mary Shaw, of Woolwich, widow, guardian unto Benjamin, Jesse and Joseph, minor children of Benjamin Shaw, late of Woolwich, 29 May, 1795. [VI, 121.]

Francis Lovejoy, of Sidney, *non compos.* Abiel Lovejoy, Jr., of Sidney, guardian, 5 Ap., 1796. [VI, 131-2.]

Hallowell May 7. 1793
In the name of God amen. I Benjamin Pettingill Esqr., of Hallowell, in the county of Lincoln, and State of the Massachusetts Bay. Calling to mind the mortality of my Body; knowing that it is appointed for all men once to die, being through the goodness of God, of perfect mind and memory do make, and ordain, this my last Will and Testament, that is to say, principally and first of all. I give I give and recommend my Soul into the hands of God that gave it, and my Body I recommend to the earth, to be buried in decent christian burial at the discretion of my Executor, nothing doubting but at the general resurection I shall receive the same by the mighty power of God. And as touching such worldly estate wherewith it hath pleased God to bless me in this life I give Demise and dispose of the same in the following manner and form.

Imprimis. I give and bequeath to Judith my beloved Wife one third part of what Estate I die possess'd of after my just Debts and Funeral charges are paid during her natural life.

Item. I give to my well beloved Daughter Mary Allen nothing, having heretofore given her her full share of my Estate.

Item. I give to my well beloved Son Benjamin Pettingill one fourth part of my Mechanical and Husbandry Utensels & no more, having heretofore given him an Hundred Acres of Land.

Item. I give to my well beloved Daughter, Anna Badcok the sumn of five pounds in addition to what she has already received to be paid in three years after my decease.

Item. I give to my well beloved Daughter Amy Fletcher the sumn of two pounds, in addition to what she has already received, to be paid in three years after my decease.

Item. I give to my well beloved Daughter Rhoda Palmer, the sumn of three pounds, in addition to what she has already received, to be paid in three years after my decease.

Item. I give to my well beloved Daughter Rubie Church the sumn of seven pounds in addition to what she has already received, to be paid in three years after my decease.

Item. I give to my well beloved Daughter Rachel Wade the sumn of six pounds in addition to what she has already received to be paid in three years after my decease.

Item. I give to my well beloved Daughter Filena Foster the sumn of Fourteen pounds, in things provided and providing.

Item, I give to my well beloved Son Ziba Pettingill three fourths of my Mechanical and Husbandry utensils, together with all my real and personal estate, not herein otherwise disposed of after my just debts and Funeral charges are paid, whom I likewise constitute make and ordain, my sole Executor of this my last Will and Testament, by him freely to be possessed and enjoyed, and I do hereby utterly disannul revoke and disallow, all and every other former Testaments, Wills, Legacies and bequests, and Executors; by me in any way before named, will'd or bequeathed, ratifying and confirming this and no other to be my last will and Testament. In witness whereof, I have hereunto set my hand and Seal, the day and year above written.

Signed, Sealed, published, pronounced and declared, by the said Benjamin Pettingill as his last will and testament in presence of us, the Subscribers.

Obadiah Harris   Benjamin Pettingill   (seal)
Lois Harris
Harlowe Harris

Probated 14 Mar., 1796. [VI, 134.] James Bridge and Harlowe Harris, both of Hallowell, sureties. Inventory by Henry Sewall, Seth Williams and David Thomas, all of Hallowell, 21 May, 1796, $1292.5. [VII, 65.]

Thomas Moore, late of Pownalborough, clerk. Anna Moore, of Pownalborough, widow, Adm'x, 26 Aug., 1795. [VI, 136.] Ebenezer Whittier, of Pownalborough, and James Hodge, of New-Milford, sureties. Inventory by John Sutton Foye, Rogers Smith and Joseph Burr, all of Pownalborough, 16 Mar., 1796, $971.73, to which administratrix added notes of hand, $355. [VI, 216.] Account filed 5 June, 1797. [VI, 217.] Jeremiah Dalton, of Pownalborough, guardian unto Sally and Thomas, minor children, 27 Mar., 1798. [IX, 176 and 226.]

John Linscot, late of Balltown. Alexander Fairbanks, of Balltown, Adm'r, 1 Mar., 1790. [VI, 136-7.] Jonathan Hawks, of Balltown, and Nathaniel Bryant, of Newcastle, sureties.

Stephen Sewall, late of Bath, merchant. Moses Sewall, of Hallowell, merchant, Adm'r, 23 Ap., 1796. [VI, 139.] Thomas Fillebrown and David Sewall, both of Hallowell, sureties. Inventory by William Webb, Joshua Shaw and Edward H. Page, all of Bath, 24 June, 1796, $4,337.94. [VII, 182 to 184.] David Sewall, of Hallowell, Adm'r *de bonis non*, 18 July, 1798. [IX, 24.] Christopher Cushing, of Bath, guardian unto Dorcas, William, Meriam and Stephen, minor children, 11 Feb., 1799. [IX, 181.]

Peter Jones, late of Hallowell, trader, Eunice Jones, widow, and John Jones, both of Hallowell, Adm'rs, 26 May, 1796. [VI, 149.] Thomas Dickman and Samuel Colman, both of Hallowell, sureties. Inventory by Samuel Colman, Elias Craigg and William Pitt, all of Hallowell, 5 July, 1796, $440.21½. [VII, 60 to 62.] Samuel Colman and Elias Craig, commissioners to examine claims. [VIII, 11.] Account filed and distribution ordered 5 Ap., 1799. [VIII, 13-14.]

In the name of God amen. I Philip Higgins of Bath in the County of Lincoln & Commonwealth of Massachusetts, yeoman, being of sound mind & memory, calling to mind the mortality of my Body and knowing it is appointed for all Men once to die Do make & ordain this my last will and testament—that is to say—first of all I give & recommend my Soul into the hand of Almighty GOD—and my Body to the Earth to be buried decently according to the discretion of my Executor beleiving that at the general resurrection I shall receive the same again by the mighty power of GOD. And as touching such worldly Estate wherewith it hath pleased God to bless me in this Life, I give demise & dispose of the same in the following manner & form—first I give and bequeath to Mary my dearly beloved wife the use and improvement of my homestead farm on which we now live with all the Stock of Cattle & farming utensils thereon, during her natural life.—And all the House furniture to her use & disposal forever.

secondly. I give & bequeath to my Son Benjamin Higgins the sum of Ten Dollars and no more, I having formerly given him as much as I esteem his proportion.

3dly I give to my Son Reuben Higgins the Farm on which he now lives containing about eighty five Acres situate in said Bath

4"ly I give to my Daughter Ruth Marriner Ten Dollars, She having formerly had from me as much as I esteem her proportion.

5"ly—I give to my Daughter Abigail Williams the sum of Fifty Dollars.
6ly. I give to my Son Simeon Higgins the Land to the eastward of the road leading to Foster's point containing about eighty Acres adjoining to his own Land—

7 I give to my Son Philip Higgins the Homestead farm aforementioned with the Stock of Cattle and all the farming Utensils to his use & improvement after the dicease of his Mother my said wife Mary— until his Sons Isaiah & Jeremiah shall be twenty one years of Age— when it is my will & I bequeath accordingly that the said Isaiah and the said Jeremiah each have & hold forever to themselves their Heirs & Assigns one fourth part to each of them, of the said Homestead farm and the said Philip to Have & to Hold to himself & to his heirs & assigns forever the remaining half of the said Homestead farm.

8 I Give to my Daughter Mary Mathes ten dollars—she having received her proportion some time ago—

9 I Give to my Daughter Sarah Holbrook the sum of Fifty Dollars, also the Money due to me from her Husband

10 I Give to my Daughter Thankful Huffe of Bowdoin, all the right title & possession which I have to the Land on which she & her Husband now live in said Bowdoin- I likewise give to my said Daughter all the Money due to me from her said Husband.

11 I likewise Give to my Sons Reuben, Simeon, & Philip aforenamed my Saw-Mill, with the Mill privilege & all the privileges to the Mill Pond belonging—

12 I Give to my Son Philip aforesaid all other my Personal Estate not before particularly bequeathed except debts due to me which Debts my Executor hereafter named is to collect and with the Money so collected discharge my just debts and pay the Legacies & sums in this instrument mentioned & bequeathed and the remainder if any there should be I give & bequeath to my Daughter Thankful Huffe aforesaid—And the Legacies afore mentioned I will to be paid within two years after my Decease and I do hereby appoint my said Son Reuben Higgins sole Executor of this my last will & testament—And I do hereby utterly disallow revoke and disannull all & every former testaments wills Legacies & bequests by me in any wise before willed & bequeathed; ratifying & confirming this & no other to be my last will & testament—In witness whereof I have hereunto set my hand and seal this sixteenth day of December in the Year of LORD one thousand seven hundred & ninety five

signed sealed published
pronounced & declared by the
said Philip Higgins, as his last
will & testament, in the presence
of us, who in his presence & in the
presence of each other have here
to subscribed our names. The words
and I do hereby appoint my said Son Reuben
Higgins sole Executor of this my last will
& testament were interlined before
signing or sealing—

    Philip Higgins (seal)

  Arthur Bradman
  John Sprague
  Fra. Winter

                Probated 27 May, 1796. [VI, 202-203.] Inventory by Francis Winter, David Ring and Stephen Coombs, all of Bath, 17 June, 1796, $3,307.67. [VII, 83-84.]

Be it Remembered that I Caleb Barker of the Plantation of Lewiston in the County of Lincoln and Commonwealth of the Massachusetts yeoman
Being weak of Body yet through Divine Mercy of Sound mind and Memory do make and ordain this my Last will and testament in Manner following

1st   that all my Honest Debts be Paid

2ly I give to Hannah my trusty and well Beloved Wife the use and improvement of all my Real Estate So Long as She Remains unmaried to another Man and also all my Live Stock of Cattle Horses Sheep and Swine togather with all the Provision that is in the house at my decease all the above mentiond Stock She is to have the use income and improvement of So Long as she Remains unmarried also I give her all my Household Furniture Forever I also give her the use of all my Part of the Dwelling House and Barn

3ly I give to my Son William all my wearing apparyell

4ly I Give to my Son Jacob all my Real Estate when his mother hath done with it his paying my Son William thirty Pounds within two years after the dceeas of their mother and also to Pay my Daughters Kezia and Rhoda forty Shillings to Each within one year after their mother's Decease or marriage and I also Give my Son Jacob all my Live Stock which is Left at his mothers decease his paying the Funeral Charge and also my House and barn Reserving the fore Room for the use of my Daughter Rhoda for her use and benefit So Long as She Remains unmaried after her mother decease.

Lastly I do Nominate and appoint my Beloved Wife Executrix togather with trusty and well beloved Friend Joel Thompson Executor to this my Last will and testament to See it Executed according to the true intent and meaning thereof disannulling al other wills by me made Heretofore.

In witness whereof I have hereunto set my Hand and Seal this twenty third day of February in this year of our Lord one Thousand Seven hundred and Ninety

Signed Sealed and Published
by the Testator as his Last will
and testament In Presents   Caleb Barker   (seal)
of us
    Daniel Davis
    Samuel Tuck
    Andrew Coombes

Probated 19 Jan., 1796. [VI, 204-205.] Daniel Davis and Jacob Barker, Jr., both of Lewiston, sureties. Inventory by John Herrick, Josiah Mitchell and Abner Harris, all of Lewiston, 1 Feb., 1796, $880.14. [VI, 220.]

In the name of God Amen the twenty first Day of January in the year of our LORD one thousand Seven hundred and ninety five I Stephen Norton of Readfield in the County of Lincoln and Commonwealth of Massachusetts yeoman being far advanced in years though of perfect mind and memory Calling to mind the mortality of my Body and knowing that it is appointed for all men once to Die Do make and ordain this as my last will and Testament that is to Say Principally and first of all I Give and Recommend my Soul into the hands of God who Gave it and my Body I Commit to the Earth to be decently Buryed in a Christian manner at the Discression of my Executors hereafter named and as touching Such worldly estate as God hath Blessed me with in this life I Give and Dispose of the Same in the following manner and form

Imprimis I will that all my Just Debts and funeral Charges be well and truly paid in Some Convenient time after my Decease

Item I Give and Bequeath unto my wife Sarah Norton all my estate Real and personal lying and being on the Island of Nantuckit also all my live Stock farming utensils houshold furniture and every other article of personal estate

Item I Give and Bequeath to my Son Constant Norton five Shillings having before Given him his proportion of my estate
Item I Give and Bequeath to my Son Peter Norton five Shillings having before Given him his proportion of my estate
Item I Give and Bequeath to my Daughter Sarah Bean five Shillings having before Given hur a portion of my estate
Item I Give and Bequeath to my Daughter Kathariene Norton five Shillings having before Given hur a portion of my estate
Lastly I Constitute and appoint my Sons Constant Norton and Peter Norton to be my Executors of this my last will and Testament Ratifying and Confirming this for my last will and testament
In witness whereof I hereunto Set my hand and Seal the Day and year first above written
Signed Sealed and Declared
by the Said Stephen Norton
to be his last will and
Testament in presence of
Robert Page   Stephen Norton   (seal)
Benjamin Savage
William Wyman

    Probated 19 Jan., 1796. [VI, 206-207.] Robert Page and Benjamin Savage, both of Readfield, sureties. Inventory by Matthias Smith, Jr., Daniel Wing and Samuel Stevens, all of Readfield, 7 Jan., 1797. [Unrecorded.]

                     In the name of God—Amen—
I Prudence Chapman of Waldoborough in the County of Lincoln and Commonwealth of Massachusetts Widdow Being sick and weak in Body but of Perfect and Sound mind and Memory (Blessed be god for it) and Taking into Consideration that is appointed for all mortals once to die do make and ordain this my Last will and testament in form and manner following that Is to Say in the first Place I recomend my Soul to god who Gave it and my Body to the Earth to be Burried after the Manner of A Decent Cristian Burril not at all doupting of A Future resurection and as to what worldly goods god in his Providence hath been Pleased to bless me with in this world I Dispose of Will and bequeath them in the Manner following Viz
    Imprimus I will that all my Just Depts shall be first Paid and I will and Bequeth to My Beloved Daughter Prudence Loring three Pounds
Item. I will and Bequeth to my Beloved Daughter Sarah Cole three Pounds—

Item—I Will and Bequeth to my Beloved Daughter Deborah Chapman A Bed and A Cow together with A Room and her living in My House As long as She lives or So long as She Remeigns unmarried

Item I Will and bequeth unto My Beloved Daughter Mary Vinall three Pounds—

Item I Will and bequeth unto My Beloved Son Abraham Chapman (Whom I also make my Sole Executor to this my last will and Testement) all my Real and Personal Estate after taking or his Paying out the Above Leagecies and bequethments and it is my Will that After my Desscease he should have full Posesion of all My Lands Cattle Buildings Depts Due me moneys I leave and All & every Part of my Said real and Personal estate of what name or nature soever and I hereby make and ordain him my Sole Executor To this my Last will and testement As Aforesaid

And I herby Revoke and make null and Void all other wills By me heretofore ever made

In testimony Whereof I have hereunto Subscribed my name and affixed my Seal at Said Waldoborough this Seventh day of November in the year of our Lord one Thousand Seven hundred and Eighty eight

Signed Sealed and Declared by the said
Prudence Chapman to be her last
Will and testament in Presence of us
George Demuth   Prudence Chapman   (seal)
Paul Lash
Thos. McGuyer

Probated 26 May, 1796. [VI, 208.]

Jonathan Davis, late of Bath. Jonathan Davis, of Bath, Adm'r, 9 Sep., 1796. [VI, 211-212.]

In the Name of God amen
I William Hathorn Farmer in St Georges River Bing in bodilay helth and of sound and disposing mind and meomry Considring the unsertantes of this transitory life do for avoiding Controversies after my desease make and publesh and declare this my last Will and testament in manner following that is to Say First I recomend my Soul to God that gave it and my Body I Commit to the Earth and as for my Worldly Estate I give Bequath and dispose thereof as follouth first I Give and Bequeath to my Son Alexander Hathorn to the Valo of three

pounds laful money of Now Eangland and all my wearing apparell All the Rest and residue & Remainder of my Real & personal Estats of money lands & tenements Goods Chattels whatsover as Shall be aney ways due owing or belonging unto me at my decease I do Give devise and Bequeath the Same unto my Grand daughter Jean Hathorn only Encluding my Lawful and Endustres wifes thirdes Jean Hathorn while She lives I do hireby appoint them whole & Sole Executers of this my last will testament hireby Revoking all former & other Willes testaments & deeds of Gift by me at any time heretofore made And I do ordain & Ratify these presents to Stand & be for and as my Only Last Will and tesament in Wittness Whereof to this my Said will I have Set my hand & Seal the twenty third Day of November in the year of our Lord one thousand Seven Hundred and fifty Fave and in ye twenty Sevent year of the Reing of his Majesty King George over Great Britian &c

Sined Sealed & declared William hathorn
as my last Will & testament (seal)
In the Presence of mathusets
bay in new ingland Daniel Lewis
  William Smith
  Moses Robinson Jun'r

Jane Hathorn, widow, renounced executorship, 24 Feb., 1764. Jane, wife of Andrew Bird, of St. Georges, renounced executorship, 6 Mar., 1764. [Unrecorded.]

I William Kennedy of Boothbay in the county of Lincoln & Commonwealth of Massachusetts yeoman Calling to mind the Mortalaty of my Body, and the uncertainty of my Life, and not knowing how soon I may be called away by Death, and being at this present time weak in body, but of sound disposing mind & memory, do make and ordain this this my last Will and Testament—That is to say Principally and in the first place, I recomend my soul into the hands of God who gave it—and my Body I commit to the Earth to be buried at the Discration of my Executor, hereafter named, not Doughting but that I shall receive the same again at the General Resurrection; by the mighty Power of God—And as to my Worldly Estate I give Devise and dispose of the same in the following manner and form (viz.)—

Imps I order that all my just debts and funeral Expenses be first paid out of my personal Estate, immeadiatly after my Decese. Item I give and bequeath unto my two youngest sisters Ruth and Ann

Kennedy, the whole rest and Residue of my Estate Real & personal, to be Equaly Divided between them and to them and their heirs and asigns forever—

Lastly I do hereby apoint my Beloved Nephu Benjamin Kelley Juner my Sole Executor of this my last Will and Testement and do Revoak all and Every former Wills or Testements by me heretofore made, and declare this & no other to be my last Will and Testement. In Wittness whereof I do hereunto set my hand and seal this third day of August in the year of our Lord one Thousand seven hundred and Ninety Six—

Signed sealed published and Declared by the Testator, to be his last Will and Testement in presence of us—

Wm McCobb William Kennedy (seal)
Ichabod Pinkham
Mercy Pinkham

Probated 20 Sep., 1796. [VII, 1-2.] Benjamin Kelley and Adam Boyd, both of Boothbay, sureties. Inventory by William McCobb, John Murray and John Emerson, all of Boothbay, 7 Nov., 1796, $953.84. [VII, 120-121.] Account filed 3 June, 1799. [VIII, 88-89.]

Jacob Pressey, late Pownalborough. Elizabeth Pressey, of Pownalborough, widow, Adm'x, 29 Feb., 1796. [VII, 3-4.] Benjamin Pressey and Paul Nute, both of Pownalborough, sureties. Inventory by Ebenezer Whittier, Joseph Lowell and Samuel Groves, all of Pownalborough, 27 May, 1796, $501.55. [VII, 124.] Yearly rent of real estate appraised at $40, 4 June, 1798. [VIII, 72.] Account filed 4 June, 1798. [VIII, 72-73.] Widow's dower set off by Seth Tinkham, William Taylor and Rogers Smith, all of Pownalborough, 26 Ap., 1799. [XII, 29.]

Samuel Parce, late of Boothbay, mariner. Elizabeth Parce, of Boothbay, widow, Adm'x, 10 June, 1796. [VII, 4-5.] Samuel Nellson and Ezekiel Pearce, both of Boothbay, sureties. Inventory by Jonathan Sawyer, Edward Creamer and Robert Reed, all of Boothbay, 1796, $495. [VII, 135.] Account filed 5 June, 1797. [VII, 136.]

Samuel Chandler, late of Farmington. Rebecca Chandler, of Farmington, widow, Adm'x 14 July, 1796. [VII, 5.] Supply Belcher and Ebenezer Norton, both of Farmington, sureties. Phebe, minor daughter, chose Solomon Adams, of Farmington, to be her guardian, 13 Dec., 1797. [VII, 239.] Jacob, Moses and Samuel, minor sons, chose Solomon Adams to be their guardian, 13 Jan., 1797. [VII, 240-241.] Solomon Adams, guardian unto Rebecca and Sally, minor daughters, 16 Jan., 1798. [VII, 244.] Inventory by Moses Starling, Supply Belcher and Moses Sewall, all of Farmington, 1796, $1185. [VII, 245.] Accourt filed 16 Jan., 1798, at which date the administratrix, had become the wife of Jonas Green. [VII, 246.]

Benjamin Dudley, late of Readfield. Samuel Stevens Gilman, of Mount Vernon, Adm'r, 14 July, 1796. [VII, 5-6.] John Dudley and John Gilman, both of Mount Vernon, sureties. Inventory by Timothy Bartlett, of Mount Vernon, Joseph Hutchins and Thomas Whittier, both of Readfield, 25 Aug., 1796, $662.04. [Unrecorded.]

Elisha Bisbee, late of Hallowell. Desire Bisbee, of Hallowell, widow, Adm'x, 19 Jan., 1796. [VII, 6-7.] Elisha Matthews, of Sidney, and Ebenezer Moore, of Vassalborough, sureties. Inventory by Asa Williams, James Springer and Noah Woodward, all of Hallowell, 27 Jan., 1796, $565.50. [VII, 79-80.] Samuel Colman and John Jones, commissioners to examine claims. [VIII, 65.]

Samuel Bailey, late of Bristol. Sarah Richards, widow, declined to administer, 30 Ap., 1796, and requested that her brother John McMurphy be appointed. John McMurphy, of Bristol, Adm'r, 5 May, 1796. [VII, 7.] Samuel Yeates and Simon Eliot, Jr., both of Bristol, sureties. Inventory by Simon Eliot, George James Yeates and Zenas Fuller, all of Bristol, 16 May, 1796, $519.63. [VIII, 93.]

Jacob Day, late of Georgetown. Bethany Day, of Georgetown, widow, Adm'x, 19 Jan., 1796. [VII, 8.] Isaiah Wyman and Jonathan Morse, both of Georgetown, sureties. Inventory by Mark Langdon Hill, Daniel Morse and Daniel Campbell, all of Georgetown, 9 July, 1796. [Unrecorded.]

Timothy Reirdon, late of Georgetown. Elizabeth Reirdon, of Georgetown, widow, Adm'x, 16 June, 1796. [VII, 8-9.] Abel Keen and James Jewett, both of Edgecomb, sureties. Inventory by Bryant Linnen, Benjamin Riggs and John Hall, all of Georgetown, 4 Aug., 1796. [VII, 66-67.] Division of real estate by Lewis Thorp, Thomas Lennan and John Hall, all of Georgetown, 5 Oct., 1803, into nine shares, viz: heirs of John Radden, late of Georgetown, deceased; Robert Clary, (by his wife;) Allen Clary, (by his wife;) heirs of John Chisham, (which he had by his first wife;) William Sullivan, (by his wife;) David Poor, (by his wife;) Benjamin McKinney, (by his wife;) David Radden, and James Radden. [X, 215-216.] Widow's dower set off by Lewis Thorp, Benjamin Riggs and Joseph Tarr, all of Georgetown, 1800. [XIII, 414.]

John Given, late of Newcastle. Agnes Given, of Newcastle, widow, Adm'x, 13 May, 1796. [VII, 9-10.] Seth Curtis and Samuel Kennedy, both of Newcastle, sureties. Inventory by John Farley, Thomas Cunningham and Henry Kennedy, all of Newcastle, 2 June, 1796, $2010.61. [VII, 113-114.] David and Sarah, minor children, chose David Kennedy, of Newcastle, to be their guardian, 11 Sep., 1797. [VII, 159-160.]

Stephen Goodwin, late of Fairfield. Stephen Goodwin, of Clinton, Adm'r, 17 Mar., 1796. [VII, 10-11.] William Lewis and Charles Call, both of Dresden, sureties. Inventory by William Kendall, David Pearson and Nymphas Bodfish, all of Fairfield, 1 Ap., 1796, $728.47. [VII, 78.]

Francis Whitmore, Jr., late of Bowdoinham, mariner. Francis Whitmore, of Bowdoinham, Adm'r, 4 Feb., 1796. [VII, 11.] Samuel and William Whitmore, both of Bowdoinham, sureties.

Joseph Richardson, late of Winslow. Jerusha Richardson, of Winslow, widow, Adm'x, 19 Jan., 1796. [VII, 12.] Solomon Parker, of Winslow, and Silas Barrows, of Clinton, sureties. Inventory by Josiah Hayden, Emanuel Smith and Stephen Tobey, all of Winslow, 24 May, 1796, $1094.75. [VII, 76-77.] Ezekiel Pattee and Josiah Hayden, both of Winslow, commissioners to examine claims. [VII, 217.] Distribution of estate ordered 25 Nov., 1800, at which date the administratrix had become the wife of Solomon Parker. [VIII, 127-8.] Account filed 26 Aug., 1800. [VIII, 238-9.] Widow's dower set off by Ezekiel Pattee, Josiah Hayden and Manuel Smith, all of Winslow, 10 Sep., 1799. [Unrecorded.]

John Cox, late of Hallowell. Gershom Cox, of Hallowell, Adm'r, 20 Jan., 1796. [VII, 12-13.] Elisha Craig and Gershom North, both of Hallowell, sureties.

Joseph Webber, late of Vassalborough. Sarah Webber, widow, and Asa Webber, both of Vassalborough, Adm'rs, 9 Sep., 1796. [VII, 13-14.] Josiah Crowell and Rufus Ballard, both of Vassalborough, sureties. Joseph and Lewis, sons of deceased. Inventory by John Getchell, John Robinson and Ebenezer Moore, all of Vassalborough, 24 Nov., 1796, $1869.74. [VII, 128-9.]

Daniel Gardner late of Bowdoinham, mariner. Ruth Gardner, of Bowdoinham, widow, Adm'x, 8 Feb., 1796. [VII, 14.] Isaiah Gardner and Stephen Whitmore, both of Bowdoinham, sureties.

Moses Brown, late of Greene, mariner. Enoch Anderson, of Greene, Adm'r, 2 July, 1796. [VII, 15.] Robert Anderson and William Golder, both of Lewiston, sureties. Inventory by Benjamin Merrill, John Daggett and Luther Robbins, all of Greene, 29 Aug., 1796, $248.53. [VII, 116.] Benjamin Merrill and Luther Robbins, commissioners to examine claims. [VII, 117.]

Robert Light, late of Pownalborough, blacksmith. Elizabeth Light, of Pownalborough, widow, Adm'x, 14 Mar., 1796. [VII, 15-16.] David Silvester and Nymphas Stacy, both of Pownalborough, sureties. Inventory by Joseph Tinkham, Francis Cook and John Hues, all of Pownalborough, 2 Aug., 1796, $764.77. [VII, 126.]

David Dunham, late of Pittston, mariner. Hannah Dunham, of Pittston, widow, Adm'x, 23 Aug., 1796. [VII, 16.] David Moores and Levi Shepard, both of Pittston, sureties. Inventory by Christopher Jakins, Edward Fuller and Nathaniel Bailey, all of Pittston, 29 Nov., 1796, $112.75. [VII, 122.]

Ebenezer Gove, late of Edgecomb. Mary Gove, of Edgecomb, widow, Adm'x, 12 Sep., 1796. [VII, 17.] Ebenezer Gove, of Edgecomb, and William McCobb, of Boothbay, sureties. Inventory by William Cunningham, John Farley and James Little, all of Newcastle, 1797, $7769.35. [VII, 140-2.]

Samuel Parsons, late of Georgetown, mariner. John Parsons, of Georgetown, Adm'r, 1 June, 1796. [VII, 17-18.] Josiah Hinkley aud William Flitner, both of Georgetown, sureties. Inventory by John Rogers, Joseph Bowker & Elijah Drummond, all of Georgetown, 31 Mar., 1797, $55.55, to which the administrator added a debt of thirty dollars received. [VII, 114-115.]

Samuel Marson, late of Pittston, mariner. Abner Marson, of Pittston, Adm'r, 17 Feb., 1796. [VII, 18-19.] James Dumaresq, of Dresden, and Francis Stilfin, of Pittston, sureties.

William Jackson, late of Newcastle, mariner. James Jackson, of Pownalborough, Adm'r, 9 Jan., 1796. [VII, 19.] Benjamin Jackson and Samuel Jackson, both of Pownalborough, sureties. Inventory by Samuel Nickels, Nathaniel Bryant and Samuel Kennedy, all of Newcastle, 20 Feb., 1796, $159.58. [VII, 68-69.]

James Jackson, late of Pownalborough. Rebecca Jackson, of Pownalborough, widow, Adm'x, 12 Sep., 1796. [VII, 19-20.] Joseph Lambert, of Pownalborough, and James Hodge, of New Milford, sureties. Inventory by Thomas Rice, Rogers Smith and John Sutton Foye, all of Pownalborough, 7 Ap., 1797. [Unrecorded.]

Edmund Grover Rowe, late of Georgetown, mariner. Ebenezer Rowe, of Georgetown, Adm'r, 15 Ap., 1796. [VII, 20-21.] Noah Bradford, and Ebenezer Rowe, Jr., both of Georgetown, sureties. Inventory by Thomas Stevens, James McFaden and Lewis Thorp, 29 Aug., 1796, $130.25. [VII, 125.]

Sarah Soule, late of Waldoborough, widow. Waterman Thomas, of Waldoborough, Adm'r, 20 Sep., 1796. [VII, 21.] John Trowbridge and Joshua Howard, Jr., both of Waldoborough, sureties. John and Sarah Trowbridge, Alexander and Anna Turner, and Joshua Howard, Jr., heirs, requested appointment of administrator. Inventory by William Farnsworth, William Fish and Joseph Simmons, all of Waldoborough, 19 Sep., 1797, $527.92. [VII, 158.] Account filed 10 Jan., 1806. [XI, 152.]

James Buswell, late of Waldoborough. Jacob Ludwig, of Waldoborough, Adm'r, 20 Sep., 1796. [VII, 22.] Cornelius Turner and Lorinz Sides, both of Waldoborough, sureties. Jane, widow of deceased, resident in Hopkinton, N. H., requested appointment of administrator, 12 Aug., 1795, Inventory by Jacob Winchenbach, Samuel Angier and John Christopher Walliser, all of Waldoborough, $98.22. [VII, 179 to 181.]

William Pattee, late of Winslow. Sibyl Pattee, of Winslow, widow, Adm'x, 12 Jan., 1797. [VII, 22-23.] Solomon Parker and Stephen Tobey, both of Winslow, sureties. Inventory by Charles Hayden, Manuel Smith and Amos Childs, all of Winslow, 2 June, 1797, $577. [VII, 92.] Distribution of estate ordered 25 Nov., 1800. [VIII, 128-9.] Advertisement of sale of real estate 8 Ap., 1800. [VIII, 240.] Account filed 29 Aug., 1800. [Unrecorded.]

Perley Dow, late of Readfield, mariner. Dorothy Dow, of Readfield, widow, Adm'x, 19 Jan., 1797. [VII, 23-24.] John Blunt and William Stevens, both of Winthrop, sureties.

Daniel McFaden, late of Georgetown. James McFaden, of Georgetown, Adm'r, 3 Feb., 1797. [VII, 24.] James Maxwell and George Maxwell, both of Bowdoinham, sureties. Margrat, widow of deceased, and Daniel, John and Thomas, sons, requested appointment of James, eldest surviving heir, as administrator, 3 Feb., 1797. Inventory by Alexander Drummond and Denny McCobb, both of Georgetown, and David Gilmore, of Woolwich, 3 Mar., 1797, $519.25. [VII, 63.]

Samuel Tilton, late of Edgecomb, mariner. Benjamin Tilton, of Edgecomb, mariner, Adm'r, 9 Feb., 1797. [VII, 24-25.] Moses Davis, of Edgecomb, and Mariner Pearson, of Pownalborough, sureties. Inventory by Daniel Webster and Thomas Ring, both of Edgecomb, and Job Day, of Newcastle, 1797, $531.78. [VII, 119.]

Lemuel Doe, late of Bristol. Elizabeth Doe, of Bristol, widow, Adm'x, 20 Feb., 1797. [VII, 25-26.] John Boyd and Phillips Hatch, both of Bristol, sureties. Inventory by George Rodgers, William McIntyre and Samuel Boyd, all of Bristol, 23 May, 1797, $1828.46, and two notes of hand amounting to $147.21. [VII, 171-2.] Elizabeth and Thomas, minor children, chose Elizabeth, widow, to be their guardian, 9 Ap., 1805. [IX, 259.] Elizabeth, widow, guardian unto John, *non compos* son, 27 June, 1805. [X, 4 to 6.] Real estate valued at $1360- by William McIntyre, Henry Fosset and Samuel Boyd, all of Bristol, 25 June, 1805; assignment of real estate to Samuel, eldest son, 27 June, 1805; account filed 27 June, 1805. [XI, 96 to 98.]

Thomas Taylor, Jr., late of Winthrop, mariner. Squier Bishop, of Winthrop, Adm'r, 25 May, 1797. [VII, 26.] Squier Bishop, Jr., of Mount Vernon, and Robert Randall, of Hallowell, sureties.

Ephraim Fitz, late of Woolwich. Sarah Fitz, of Bath, widow, Adm'x, 26 May, 1797. [VII, 27.] Dummer Sewall and Edward Hall Page, both of Bath, sureties.

Hezekiah Eggleston, late of Bristol, mariner. Hannah Eggleston, of Bristol, widow, Adm'x, 5 June, 1797. [VII, 27-28.] William McIntyre and Robert McLintock both of Bristol, sureties.

Samuel Waters, Jr., late of a place called the great pond settlement. Samuel Waters, of Balltown, Adm'r, 5 June, 1797. [VII, 28-29.] Moses Davis, of Edgecomb, and Wyman Bradbury Sevey, of Pownalborough, sureties. Inventory by Samuel Longfellow, Amos Dennis and George Carr, all of the great pond settlement, 25 Aug., 1797, $434.20. [VII, 155-6.]

John Fulton, Jr., late of Topsham, mariner. Sarah Fulton, of Topsham, widow, Adm'x, 20 June, 1797. [VII, 29.] Jonathan Ellis and Samuel Winchel, both of Topsham, sureties. Inventory by John

Rogers, Alexander Rogers and James Sampson, all of Topsham, 3 July, 1797, $802.82. [Unrecorded.]

Samuel Graves, late of Topsham. Jacob Graves, of Topsham, Adm'r, 29 June, 1797. [VII, 29-30.] John Graves, Jr., and Charles Gowell, both of Topsham, sureties. Mary, widow, declined administration in favor of son Jacob. Inventory by Alexander Rogers, John Rogers and William Wilson, all of Topsham, 11 July, 1797, $1999.70. [Unrecorded.]

William Lithgow, Jr., late of Georgetown. William Lithgow, of Georgetown, Adm'r, 1 Aug., 1797. [VII, 30-31.] Denny McCobb and George Ring, both of Georgetown, sureties. Inventory by William Howard, of Augusta, Mark Langdon Hill and Denny McCobb, both of Georgetown, 22 Sep., 1797, $2417.87. [VIII, 25 to 28.] Arthur Lithgow, of Winslow, Adm'r *de bonis non*, 15 Jan., 1799. [IX, 16.] William Howard, of Augusta, and Ebenezer Farwell, of Vassalborough, commissioners to examine claims, 21 Jan., 1801. [XIII, 89-90.]

Ezra Dingley, late of Georgetown, cordwainer. Joseph Bowker, of Georgetown, Adm'r, 1 Aug., 1797. [VII, 31.] Denny McCobb and William Lee, both of Georgetown, sureties. Nabby, widow, requested appointment of administrator. Inventory by Mark Langdon Hill, Elijah Drummond and Thomas Butler, all of Georgetown, 13 Oct., 1797, $52.17, [VIII, 68,] to which administrator added sundry articles amounting to $39.38. [VIII, 69.] Account filed 31 May, 1799. [VIII, 69.]

Joseph Whalen, late of Georgetown. Patience Whalen, of Georgetown, widow, Adm'x, 1 Aug., 1797. [VII, 32.] William Sprague and William Sprague, Jr., both of Georgetown, sureties. Inventory by Mark Langdon Hill, Joseph Bowker and Elijah Drummond, all of Georgetown, 28 Oct., 1797, $992.70. [Unrecorded.]

James Linnan, late of Georgetown, mariner. Bryant Linnan, of Georgetown, Adm'r, 1 Aug., 1797. [VII, 32-33.] Denny McCobb and James McFadden, both of Georgetown, sureties.

William Balcom, late of Pittston, mariner. Abner Marson, of Pittston, Adm'r, 6 July, 1797. [VII, 33.] Ezra Taylor, of Dresden, and Christopher Jackins, of Pittston, sureties. Inventory by Christopher Jackins, Nathaniel Bailey and Edward Fuller, all of Pittston, 7 Oct., 1797, $355. [VIII, 64.] Account filed 7 Feb., 1804. [X, 154.]

Eliphalet Pierce, late of Augusta. Samuel Pierce, of Sidney, Adm'r,

10 Aug., 1797. [VII, 67-68.] Jacob Goodwin and Seth Pitts, both of Sidney, sureties. Inventory by Henry Sewall, Jeremiah Ingraham and Seth Williams, all of Augusta, 26 Sep., 1797, $840.30. [VIII, 31-32.]

Daniel Coss, minor son of John Coss, late of Portsmouth, N. H., chose Thomas Coss, of Dresden, to be his guardian, 22 Aug., 1797. [VII, 68.]

In the name of GOD amen !

I Robert Govan of Bristol in the County of Lincoln Gentleman, considering the uncertainty of this mortal life, and being of sound and perfect mind and memory, blessed be Almighty GOD for the same. Do make this my last Will and testament in manner and form following, that is to say.

I Give and bequeath to my beloved Wife Jane if she should survive me, My one quarter part of the Grist Mill at the Falls of Pemequid in Bristol and One third part of all my other Real estate of lands tenements and buildings with the priviledges and appurtenances on both sides of the same falls. To have and to hold the same to her and her assigns for and during the term of her Natural life. And I further give and bequeath to my said beloved Wife One third part of all my Personal Estate, Goods and Chattels of what kind or nature soever to Have and to hold the same to her, and her Assigns for ever, in equivalent to her right of Dower. I also give and bequeath to my son Robert, at my said Wifes Decease, My above mentioned One quarter part of the Grist mill then to have and to hold the same to him his heirs and assigns forever. And to my said son Robert and my son Alexander I give and bequeath all the Rest, residue and remainder of my real and personal estate in equal proportion between them as they may devide under the burthens before and afterwards mentioned, to have and to hold the same to them their Heirs and Assigns for ever. To the Children of my Daughter Sally, deceased, late the Wife of Alexander Maclean I Give and bequeath the sum of One hundred pounds lawful money, and to my Daughters Jenny the Wife of Israel Cox, Betsey the Wife of John Nickels and Hannah the Wife of Thomas Miller, their Heirs and Assigns the sum of One hundred pounds each, Which sums together making four hundred pounds I Will and ordain to be raised out of that part of my Estate bequeathed to my sons, or by them to be paid to the respective legatees the One half thereof in one Year and the other half in two Years after my Decease.

I also hereby appoint my said Wife Jane the Reverend Alexander Maclean before named and Major William McIntyre of said Bristol Gentleman to be my Executors of this my last Will and testament. In Witness Whereof I have hereunto set my hand and seal the twenty eighth day of May in the Year of our Lord one thousand seven hundred and Ninety six

            Robert Giveen (seal')

Signed, sealed, published and
declared by the above named
Robert Govan to be his last Will
and testament, in the presence of
us who have hereunto
subscribed our Names as Witnesses
in presence of the testator
 Hannah Child
 James Nickels
 Robert McLintock

 Probated 5 June, 1797. [VII, 93-94.] William McIntyer and James Nickels, both of Bristol, and Samuel Nickels, of Newcastle, sureties. Inventory by Phillips Hatch, John Boyd and Henry Fosset, all of Bristol, 5 Sep., 1797. [VII, 164-5.]

In The Name of God Amen This tenth day of October in the year of our Lord seventeen hundred and ninety two I Zebulon Coffin of Pownalboro in the County of Lincoln in the Commonwealth of Massachusetts Mariner, being of sound mind and memory, knowing the frailty of my body and that it is appointed for all men once to Dye, do make and ordain this my last will and testament; and first of all I recommend my Soul into the hands of God who gave it, and as touching such worldly goods and Estate as God has been pleased to favour me with in this life I do hereby dispose of in manner following Viz. First of all I order that all my Just debts and funeral charges be paid out of my Estate by my Executrix hereafter named—*Imprimies* I give and bequeath unto my beloved Wife Betsy Coffin of Pownalboro in the County aforesaid, all my goods and Estate of every kind and denomination whatsoever, which I shall dye seized or posssesed of or oweing to me at the time of my death wheresoever the same shall or may be found to her own use and disposal for ever And I do hereby Constitute and appoint my Wife the aforesaid Betsy Coffin the Sole Executrix of this my last will and Testament, hereby Ratifying and confirming this and no other to be my last will. In witness whereof I the s'd Zebulon Coffin have hereunto set my name and affix'd my Seal the day and year first mentioned

Signed, Sealed, published, pronounced
and declared by the Testator to be his   Zebulon Coffin   (seal)
last will and testament in the   James Atkins
presence of us wittnesses   Hannah Atkins
    David N. Brown.

Probated 26 May, 1796. [VII, 95.] Jacob Brown and Loyalist Brown, both of Dresden, sureties. Jacob Brown, of Bowdoinham, guardian unto David Newell, minor son, 31 Dec., 1804. [IX, 194.]

In the name of God Amen.

I John McIntyer of Warren in the County of Lincoln Gentleman—being old and weak in body, but of sound mind memory and understanding—taking into consideration the uncertainty of this transitory life—do make and publish this my last Will and Testament in manner and form following (to wit)—

First of all—I give and bequeath unto my son Robert McIntyer in addition to what I have heretofore given him by Deed & otherwise—the sum of twenty shillings to be paid him by my Executors within one year from my decease—

Also. I give and bequeath unto my son William the like sum of twenty shillings in addition to what I have heretofore given by Deed & otherwise to be paid him by my Executors within one year from my decease—

Also I give and bequeath unto my son John McIntyer the like sum of twenty shillings in addition to what I have heretofore given him by Deed and otherwise to be paid him by my Executors within one year from my decease. Also—I give and bequeath unto my daughter Jane Pembleton the sum of sixty dollars—to be paid her by my said Executors within one year from my decease—provided neverthless—that should I at any time, betwen the date of this my last will & Testament & my decease—give to my said daughter Jane any sum or sums of money it is my Will & intention that the same should be deducted from and considered as part payment of the above mentioned Legacy—and should I give to my said daughter Jane the above mentioned sum of sixty dollars at any time before my decease—then the said Jane is to receive from my Executors only the sum of twenty shillings, to be paid by them within one year from my decease.

Also I give and bequeath unto my daughter Mary Olcott the sum of one hundred dollars—to be paid her by my Executors within one year from my decease provided nevertheless that any sum or sums of money by me hereafter given her of goods or personal estate hereafter delivered her in my lifetime shall be deducted from and considered as part payment of the said legacy—and should I hereafter during my lifetime pay to my said daughter Mary the whole sum above mentioned then the said Mary is to receive from my Executors only the sum of twenty shillings to be by them paid within one year from my decease.

Also I give and bequeath unto my daughter Catharine McCarter the sum of Seventy dollars to be paid her by my Executors within one year from my decease—provided nevertheless that any sum or sums of money by me hereafter given her the said Catharine or any goods or personal estate hereafter delivered her in my lifetime shall be deducted from & considered as part payment of the said legacy—and should I hereafter during my lifetime pay to my said daughter Catharine the whole sum above mentioned then the said Catharine is to receive from my Executors only the sum of twenty shillings to be by them paid within one year from my decease.

And all the rest, residue and remainder of my estate, wordly goods or effects what soever I do hereby give devise and bequeath to my dearly beloved wife Jane McIntyer to be by her used, occupied, improved and enjoyed during the Term of her natural life—and afterwards to descend—ain over to the aforesaid Jane, Mary & Catharine our Children & Elizabeth Lermond daughter to my said Wife Jane & to their heirs forever to be equally divided between them—

And I do hereby nominate & appoint my said Wife Jane together with Thurston Whiting Executors of this my last Will & Testament hereby revoking all former Will or Wills by me heretofore made—In testimony whereof I have hereunto set my hand & seal this fifteenth day of August in the year of our Lord seventeen hundred & ninety five.
Note the interlineations in the twenty third
line of the first page—& the word seventy in
the 18th line of the second page—the word
hereafter in the 22nd line of the second
page—the arasure in the first & second
lines of the third page & the interlineation
in the third line of the third page were
all made before the signing & publishing of this Will & Testament—

            John McIntyer. (seal)

Signed sealed published and declared
by the above named John McIntyer
as and for his last Will and Testament in presence of us who have
hereunto subscribed our names as
Witnesses to the same—in presence
of the said Testator—and in presence of each other
  Eli Bosworth
  Timothy Pearson
  Sam'l S. Wilde

Probated 5 June, 1797. [VII, 96 to 98.]
Jane McIntyer renounced executorship 1 June, 1797. Letters testa-
mentary issued to Thurston Whiting, 5 June, 1797. [VII, 98-99.]
Samuel S. Wilde, of Warren, and William McIntyer, of Bristol, sureties.

In the name of God amen.—
I Joseph Philbrick of Mountvernon, in the County of Lincoln, & CommonWealth of Massachusetts Joiner. being very sick & weak in body,
but of sane mind, & memory, thanks to God for that.—Calling to
mind that I am mortal, & must sooner, or, later die; under this consideration, I do make & ordain this my last Will, & Testiment, in the
following manner. First I recommend my immortal part to God that
gave it, and my Body to be buried in a decent manner, as my Executors see fit.—
Respecting the worldly interest it has pleased God to bless me with, I
give & dispose of it in the following manner.—
firstly I give to my beloved Wife Mary Philbrick, the use and improvement of all my real Estate, during the term she shall remain my Widdow, with all the privileges, belonging thereto, together with all my
stock of Cattle, & husbandry tools, likewise all my household furnature
for & during the aforesaid term, her paying the Legacies herein after
mentioned. But in consideration she shall marry again, from &
after that time, she is to have the use & improvement of only one third
part of my real Estate in quantity & quality, and all my household
furniture during her natural life—
secondly—I give unto my Daughter Anna Philbrick fifty Dollars to be
paid her by her Mother on the day of her marriage or at her ariving to
twenty one years of Age.—
Thirdly I give to my Daughter Amay Filbrick fifty Dollars, to be

paid her by her Mother at her marriage day, or at her arival at twenty one years of age.—

fourthly I give my Apprentice Thomas Twist, one Hundred Dollars including what his Indentures specify, providing he shall faithfully fulfill his said Indentures, said one Hundred Dollars to be paid him, in neat stock, six feet Oxen to be estimated at fifty Dollars a yoke, to be paid by my Executors one half when he becomes of age the other half in three years from that time.

fifthly I give unto my beloved Daughters Anna & Amay Philbrick two thirds of all my real Estate to be divided between them equally, and all my Personal Estate to be equally divided between them, they to take possession thereof, at their Mothers death, or on the day she shall marry again, & likewise I give all my real & personal Estate to my aforesaid Daughters & to their heirs, Executors or Administrators, after their Mothers disease.—

sixthly I ordain, constitute & appoint my beloved Wife Mary Philbrick, my beloved Brother Benjamin Philbrick, and my honoured Father Squire Bishop Executors, of this my last will & testament—Iin testimony whereof I do hereunto set my hand & seal to this my last Will & Testament, this Eighth day of March in the year of our Lord seventeen Hundred & Ninety six—

Signed, & Sealed in presents of
us   Joseph Philbrick (seal)
 Samuel Quimby
 Squier Bishop
 Samuel Gilman

        Probated 25 May, 1797. [VII, 99-100.] Squier Bishop, Jr., and Samuel Gilman, both of Mount Vernon, sureties. Inventory by William Whittier, John Hovey and Samuel Brown, all of Mountvernon, 4 Jan., 1798, $1275.93. [VIII, 59.] Account filed 31 May, 1798. [VIII, 60.]

In the Name of God, Amen. I, Mary Ford of Woolwich in the County of Lincoln, Widow, Being Sick & Weak in Body, but of Perfect mind & Memory, for which I desire to Bless God, and knowing that it is appointed for all Men once to die, do make and Ordain this my last Will and Testament in manner following, Vizt—

Imprimis. I Bequeath my Soul into the hands of Almighty God who gave it, and my Body to the Earth to be buried with a decent Christian Burial at the discretion of my Executor hereafter named, not doubting

but that I shall receive the same again at the General Resurrection thro the merits & Mediation of Jesus Christ my Saviour. And as to such Worldly estate as it hath Pleased God to Bless me with me with. I Give & Bequeath in the following manner Vizt. I will that all my just debts and funeral Charges be paid in the first Place.
secondly I give and Bequeath unto my Nephew John Perkins a Feather Bed, bolster & Pillows, with a Coverlid and a pair of Blankets. Item. I give to my Nephew John Perkins's daughter Mary my Gold Necklace.
Item. I give to my Neice Mary Perkins, daughter of my Brother Robert my Red Grogram Gownd, Item. I give to my Neice Sally Perkins my black Silk Gownd, Item. I give to Lydia Kelley, to Nathan Webb and to Peter Bitum a Lad that now lives with me each of them a Bible, all the rest and Residue of my Estate whatever I give & Bequeath unto my Nephew Robert Perkins to be Enjoyed by him and his heirs forever. lastly I Nominate & Appoint my s'd Nephew Robert Perkins sole Executor of this my last Will & Testament hereby revoking all former Wills & Testaments by me heretofore made. In Testimony whereof I have hereunto set my hand & seal this first day of September in the Year of our Lord One thousand seven hundred & Eighty nine Signed Sealed Published and declared by the Testatrix as & for her last Will & Testament in presence of us who at her request in her presence & in presence of each other have subscribed our names as Witnesses thereto.

Nathl: Thwing   Mary Ford   (seal)
Ebenr: Emerson
Seth Hathorn

Probated 25 May, 1797. [VII, 101-102.] Nathaniel Thwing and Seth Hathorn, both of Woolwich, sureties.

In the Name of God Amen

I Daniel Stevens of Hallowell in the County of Lincoln, being very sick and weak in body, but of sound disposing mind and memory, thanks be given unto God therefor, calling to mind the mortality of my body, and that it is appointed unto all Men once die, do make and ordain this my last Will & Testament.

Imprimis.—I give and recommend my soul into the hands of Almity God who gave it, and my Body to the Grave—to be intered in a desent and christian manner, under the directions of my Executor hereafter named; and as touching such worldly Estate as it hath pleased God to bestow on me, I give and dispose thereof as follows, viz.

Item. I order and direct that all my Debts and funeral charges be first paid out of my personal Estate by my Executor.

Item. I give and bequeath unto my beloved Wife Mehitable Stevens all my household furniture to do and Dispose of as she shall think Best, and the use of one third part of my Real Estate as long as she may live.

Item. I give and bequeath unto my two beloved Son's Samuel Stevens and Daniel Stevens, the whole of my real Estate to be Equally divided between them—the same Daniel to have his moiety or one half part when he shall arive to the age of twenty one years.

Item. I give and bequeath unto my same son Samuel, all my personaly Estate which may be left after paying my just Debts funeral Charges and household furniture is taken out as aforesaid—it is my will and I hereby order and direct that my Beloved Daughters, Mary, Abigail Hannah Sarah Betsey Nancy Olive and Sophia, be severally supported in a decent manner out of the income and profit of my real Estat divided to my same two son's Samuel & Daniel till they respectively arive to the age of twenty one years or be respectively married, which ever shall first happen—and on thier ariveing to the age of twenty one years, or being severally married, whichever shall first happen I hereby order and direct my son Samuel to pay them Sixty Dollars Each out of my real Estate divided to my same sons Samuel & Daniel, by this my last will and Testament.

Item. I hereby give and devise to my daughter Mehitable Carr ten Dollars to be paid her by my Executor when Called for.

I hereby revoke and nulify all former wills and Testaments by me made—and hereby declare this and this only to be my last will & Testament—and I hereby appoint my son Samuel Stevens sole Executor thereof. In witness whereof I have hereto set my hand & seal this ninth day of January in the year of our Lord 1796.

Signed Sealed published and
pronounced and declared by the
said Testator as his last will and
Testament in the presents of us,   D Stevens (seal)
who in his presents and in the
presents of Each other, at his request,
have hereto subscribed our Nams
as witnesses

Stephen Scribner

Moses Carr
Jonathan Sewall
  I Do publish and declare this my last will and Testament.

                      Probated 9 Sep., 1796. [VII, 103-104.]
Stephen Scribner, of Mount Vernon, and Moses Carr, of Hallowell, sureties. Inventory by Nathaniel Dummer, James Page and John Haines, all of Hallowell, 24 Nov., 1796, $3922. [VII, 242-243.]

         IN, THE, NAME, OF, GOD, AMEN

I Abraham Tilton, being of Sound mind & memory, tho weak in body, and Considering the frailty of humane nature and the uncertainty of the time when I shall die, do make Publish & declare this to be my last will & testament.—

Imprimis. I Resign my Soul to him who is the Supreme Governour of the Universe, hoping for Salvation through the merits of our Lord & Saviour Jesus Christ, and my body to the dust from whence it came—as to my worldly Estate I dispose of it in the following manner, Vizt—After my Just Debts and funeral Charges are paid I give unto my Daughter Susannah Sevey one Dollar She haveing her Share of my Estate at the time of her Marriage, also I give unto my Son Samuel one Dollar, he also haveing his full Share of my Estate at his Freedom, the remainder of all my Estate both real & personal is to divided in equal Shares among & between the residue of my Children. Vizt. Benjamin, Daniel, Abraham, Charles, Andrew, John, Mary & Sarah, except as is hereafter Excepted—Mary is to have the one half of her own Mothers household furniture, and Sarah is to have the other half of her said Mothers houshold furniture together with all her said Mothers wearing apparrel, also the said Sarah is to have all her Stepmothers houshold furniture, and wearing apparrel—bed & beding inclusively—Lastly I make constitute and appoint my Son Benjamin Tilton Executor to this my last will & testament hereby revoking all other wills by me heretofore made. In witness whereof I have hereunto set my hand and Seal this twenty first day of February in the year of our Lord one thousand seven hundred & ninety six—

Signed sealed published & declared
to be the last will and Testament
of the above named Abraham Tilton   The words Dollar &
in Presence of us—   houshold were
                                              interlined before
                                              Signing & witnessing—

Tho's Ring
Benja Rackleff   Abraham Tilton   (seal)
Abner Hood

Probated 6 Jan., 1797. [VII, 105-106.] Moses Davis and Benjamin Rackleff, both of Edgecomb, sureties. Inventory by Thomas Ring and Daniel Webster, both of Edgecomb, and Job Day, of Newcastle, $801.49. [VII, 108.]

In the Name and fear of God Amen. I Stephen Sevey of Pownalborough in the County of Lincoln yeoman calling to mind the brevity & uncertainty of humane Life & feeling my Body decaying, tho' of sound & disposing mind & memory, do make this my last Will & Testament, in manner following viz I commend my Body to the Earth at my death to be decently buried at the discretion of my Executrix, & my Soul into the hands of God who gave it, and as to my worldly Estate with which God hath been pleased to bless me, I dispose of it as follows, viz

I give & bequeath to my beloved wife, Mary Sevey, (who I herein after name my Executrix,) all the Estate of every kind both real & personal, that I may die seized and possessed of after paying all my just Debts, all my real Estate in fee to her & her heirs forever & all my personal Estate to be her absolute property. And I hereby ordain & appoint my said beloved Wife Mary Sevey the sole Executrix of this my last Will & Testament, & hereby revoke and disannul all former Wills, & declare this to be my last Will & Testament.

In Witness whereof I hereto set my hand & Seal the fourteenth day of May in the year of our Lord one thousand seven hundred & Ninety six.

Signed Sealed, publishing   Stephen   (seal)
& declared by the Testator   Sevey
to be his last Will & testament
in presence of
Tho. Rice
Abraham Nason
James Honeywill

Probated 5 June, 1797. [VII, 108-109.] Abraham Nason and James Honeywell, both of Pownalborough, sureties.

John Plumer, of New-Milford, *non compos*. Daniel Plummer, of a place called Balltown, guardian, 1 Sep., 1797. [VII, 111-112.]

In the Name of God, Amen. I John Sevey of the Town of

Pownalborough in the state of Massachusetts, Trader, being very Sick and Weak of Body, but of Perfect Mind & Memory, thanks be given unto God, calling unto Mind the Mortality of my Body, and knowing that it is Appointed for all Men Once to die, do make and Ordain this my last Will and Testament, that is to say principally and first of all I give and recommend my Soul into the Hand of Almighty God, that gave it, And my Body I recommend to the Earth to be Buried in a decent Christian Burial at the Discretion of my Executors Nothing doubting but at the General Resurrection I shall receive the same Again by the Mighty Power of God, and as touching such Worldly Estate wherewith it has pleased God to bless me in this Life, I give, demise and dispose of the same in the following Manner and form—

First—I give and bequeath unto my Well beloved son Wyman Bradbury Sevey, One quarter of the Dwelling in which I now live with One quarter of the Lot on which it stands being a quarter of an Acre Lot also One half the store standing on the same also give unto the said Wyman the store and Wharfe on which it stands. Reserving unto my well Beloved Daughter Moriah Sevey the undisturbed Priviledge of Landing Wood or any other Commodity whatever on said Wharfe during her Natural Life free & clear of any expense of Wharfage or Dockage I also give him all my Right, Title & Intress with every priviledge thereunto belonging, to all the Land and Flatts lying below Fore street and between the Wharfe & store aforesaid and Zenas Stutsons line, also give him One half the Lot on which the Barn stands together with One half of the Barn—I also give him the said Wyman the Whole of the Lot on Which the Widow of Robert Light deceased Now lives together with Betty Elmes, the same Adjoining the Lands of Zenas Studson and the Heirs of John Bridge on the One side and the lands of Alexander Cuningham & Josiah Goddard on the other side being the same I purchased from Nathaniel Rundlet deceased—I also give to him the said Wyman all my Right, Title or Intress to a Lott or parcell of Land, lying between the Land & Dwelling House of Mr. Silas Lee and Fifth Street, being in Front of Lotts Number Five and Six, being the same I purchased from Samuel Williamson, Nathaniel Rundlet Junr. & Charles Rundlet. I also give unto the said Wyman all the Lands I own lying on the Easterly side of Thomas Follensbeys North line so called lying in Pownalborough to include all the Lands on said East side down to the Road by Robert Greenoughs—Reserving to my Daughter Moriah during her Natural Life the priviledge of

Pasturing two Cows free & Clear of any expense in such Grounds as shall commonly be Used as a Pasture by him his Heirs or Assigns I also give unto him the said Wyman One Pair of Steers Now kept by Nathaniel Rundlet, together with One half of all my remaining Cattle at Home and abroad after taking out such Ones as will be here after Mentioned which I give to my Daughter Moriah—I also give unto him my Cart & Wheels, together with One Quarter of all & singular my House hold furniture and Farming Utentials excepting such as shall be hereafter Mentioned which I give to my Son Samuel Sevey—

I Also give and bequeath unto my Well beloved son Samuel Sevey the Quarter Acre Lot on which Messrs. Roby & Crufts Store Now stands together with the North Easterly half of the quarter Acre Lot on which Mr. Mannassah Smiths Office & Messrs. Thompson & Tinkham's Store stands also the quarter Acre Lot I purchased from John Erskine Adjoining Lands of Abiel Wood Esqr. also I give him the said Samuel all my Right & Title which I have unto the Marsh and Lands lying in the Township of Newcastle which I purchased from Benjamin Woodbridge—also I give unto him the said Samuel all the Lands which I claim lying to the Westward of Thomas Follensbeys North line commonly so called being in the Township of Pownalborough and Adjoining the Lands of William Groves. I also give him the said Samuel One half the Lott Adjoining the Road leading from Henry Hodge's Esqr. to the Goal being the Northern half of said Lott, which to be divided by a North East & South West Course—I also give unto him the said Samuel, One half of all and singular my Cattle at Home or aBroad except such as has been particularly Mentioned which I have given my Son Wyman & also excepting such hereafter to be Mentioned which I give my Daughter Moriah Also I give him One good Feather Bed, Stead, & Beding Sufficient for the same, likewise One Looking Glass Now kept in the Front Chamber, also One Desk commonly Called Mrs. Sevey's Desk—

Also I give and bequeath unto my well beloved Daughter Moriah Sevey three Quarters of my Dwelling House with three Quarters of the Lot it stands upon with One half the store standing on the same also I give her the Southwesterly half of the quarter Acre Lot on which Mr. Mannassah Smith's Office & Messrs. Thompson & Tinkham store stands also I give unto the said Moriah the Whole of the Lott on which Messrs. Tinkham's & Savage's store stands except the Piece of said Lott which I leased unto the said Tinkham's & Savage being twenty Four feet fronting on Fore street & runing back on said Lott the same Width forty four feet the said Lott extending from Fore Street to Middle Street—also One half the Lott on which the Barn stands with One half the Barn—Also I give unto her the said Moriah One half the Lott by the Meeting House adjoining the Road leading from Henry Hodge's, Esqr. to the Goal, being the Southern half of the same to be divided by a North East and South West Course—also I give unto the said Moriah One Cow which is Now at Home also One Cow & Heffer Now at George Erskins likewise One Cow & Heffer Now at Thomas Woodbridge's together with One Colt—also I give her three Quarters of all and Singular the House hold Furniture & farming Utentials except such as have been particularly Mentioned before and given to my Sons Wyman & Samuel—also I give and bequeath unto my good Friend Joseph Tinkham of Pownalborough Merchant the piece of Land on which the Store stands Owned & improved by him Seth Tinkham & John Savage on the following Conditions, Vizt he the said Joseph Tinkham paying to my Daughter Moriah Sevey, the Anual Rent Agreed upon by Lease during the Remainder of the time yet unexpir'd of the Lease, the said Piece of Land buting on Fore Street twenty four feet in Width and runing back on said Lot keeping the same Width Forty four feet, and at the expiration of the aforesaid Lease the said Joseph Tinkham paying unto my said Daughter Moriah Sevey the Sum of One hundred Dollars—and then the said Joseph Tinkham to hold and enjoy the said Piece of Land him his Heirs or Assigns forever—I also give unto my said Daughter Moriah Sevey, all the Cloaths & Wairing Apperal of what Name or Nature soever which my late beloved Wife died Posessed off—And I also order give and bequeath that whatever Estate shall Remain of what Name or Nature soever after my Just Debts, Funeral charges, & expenses of settling my Estate are paid which has Not allready been given and bequeath'd away shall be equaly divided between my two sons Wyman Bradbury Sevey and Samuel Sevey—

And lastly I do Constitute make, Ordain and Appoint, Joseph Tinkham Esqr. & my son Wyman Bradbury Sevey Joint & Sole Executors of of this my last Will and Testament. And I do hereby utterly disallow revoke and disannul all & every other former Testaments, Wills legacies Bequests and Executors by me in any Wise before Named Willed and bequeathed Ratifying and Confirming this and No other to be my last Will & Testament—In Witness whereof I have hereunto set my hand and seal this fifth day of January in the Year of our Lord One thousand seven hundred and ninety six—

John Sevey (seal)

Sign'd Seal'd & Published pronounced and Declar'd by the said John Sevey as his last Will and Testament in the presence of us, who in his presence & in the presence of each other have hereunto Subscribed our Names—
David Silvester
Ezekiel Cutter
John Glidden

Probated 14 Mar., 1796. Samuel Sevey appealed 15 Mar., 1796. [VII, 129 to 134.] Executors authorized to take goods into custody during pendency of appeal, 14 Ap., 1796. [VI, 138.] Mariah, minor daughter, chose Silas Lee, of Pownalborough, to be her guardian, 14 Mar., 1796. [VI, 132.] Account of Silas Lee, guardian of Maria Sevey, filed 27 Mar., 1798. [VIII, 70-71.] Guardian's advertisement of sale of real estate, 28 Mar., 1798. [VIII, 72.] Inventory by Ebenezer Whittier, David Payson and Nymphas Stacy, all of Pownalborough, 18 Sep., 1798, $6423.28 [VIII, 83 to 85.]

Lemuel Hall, late of Bowdoin. John Hall of Bowdoin, Adm'r, 14 Sep., 1797. [VII, 139 to 140.] John Merrill, of Topsham, and Samuel Dunlap, of Brunswick, sureties. Mary, widow, declined administration 13 Sep., 1797. Inventory by Samuel Tibbets, James Potter and Daniel Cunningham, all of Bowdoin, 5 Oct., 1797, $2002.21. [VIII, 18-19.]

In the Name of GOD Amen this Twenty Twenty Forth day of February in the year of our Lord one Thousand Seven hundred and Ninety Seven—
I Stephen Call of Dresden in the County of Lincoln Yeoman Being Now in a weak and Low State of Body; but of perfect mind and Memory, blessed be God therefor, but Calling to mind the mortallity of my body Knowing That it is appointed to all men once to die, Do hereby make and ordain this my Last will and Testament Namely; First of all I humblely recommend my Soul into into the hands of allmighty God who gave it; and my Body I Submit to the Earth to be Decently buried at the Discretion of my Executrix hereafter Named, nothing doubting but at the Generall Ressurrection I shall receive the the Same again by the power of allmighty God and as to such worldly Goods and Estate as God has been pleased to bless me with in this Life; I hereby Give demise and dispose of in maner and form following Vizt— — —

Imprimis I Give and bequeathe unto my True and Loveing Wife Keziah Call the Income and Improvemen of all my Reall Estate untill my Son Stephen Call arives to the age of Twenty one years, and The Improvement and use of one Third part of my Real Estate afterwards dureing her Naturall Life, and as Touching my personall Estate I order my Executrix to pay all my Just debts and funerall Charges out of the same, and the remainder thereof Togather with all my moveables To remain in her hands and She to have the use and Improvement thereof for her Support and the Support of my Chldren under her Care and Direction So Long as She remains my Widow: and in Case my said wife Should marry an other man Then my said personall Estate Shall be Equally divided among my six Children—Item and as to my Real Estate my will is and I order the same To be divided as followeth Vizt. My homestead Farm with The buildings thereon I Give and bequeath to my four Sons Vizt Moses Call: Stephen Call, Nathaniel Call and Jonathan Call, and when my Son Stephen Call Shall arive at the age of Twenty one years then the share and parts of the said Moses Call and Stephen Call Shall be Set off to them to hold in Severallty: and the shares and parts of the said Nathaniel Call and Jonathan Call to be Set of to them Respectively as they arive at the age of Twenty one years: and I order that the said Moses Call, Stephen Call, Nathaniel Call, & Jonathan Call pay out of the said bequeathed Lands to my Daughter Polly Call four hundred and Eighty dollars to be paid by them in Equall Quarter parts vizt. one hundred and Twenty dollars Each to be paid when they Severally arive at the age of Twenty one years— — —

Item I Give and bequeathe unto my son Nathan Call My other farm which Lyeth on the East side of Eastern River about Eighty five acres of Land with the buildings thereon out of which he is to pay unto my Daughter Polly Call one hundred and Twenty Dollars to be Paid when the said Nathan Shall arive at the age of Twenty one years being the Time when the said Nathan Shall Come into Possesion of the aforesaid Farm; which Severall afore said Sums to be paid unto my said Daughter Polly to make up the sum of Six hundred Dollars which I have Given her for her full Share out of my Real Estate.

And I do hereby Constitute and appoint my beloved Wife Keziah Call Sole Executrix of this my Last will and Testament and disannulling and makeing Void all other wills and Testaments in anywise by me made, I do hereby Ratifye and Confirm this and no other to be Last

will and Testament which is to Stand and remain in full force In Wittness whereof I the said Stephen Call have here unto Set my hand and afixed my Seal the day and year First above written
Signed Sealed pronounced and
Declared by the Testator to be his
Last will and Testament in Witnes
where of we have hereunto Set our
names as Wittneses in his presence   Stephen Call   (seal)
   Jona. Reed
   James Connors
   Ezra Taylor

                       Probated 8 Sep., 1797. [VII, 145-146.] Executrix being dead at probate of will, Jonathan Reed, of Dresden, was appointed administrator *cum testamento annexo*, 8 Sep., 1797. [VII, 147.] Elihu Getchel, of Bowdoinham, and Jaque Goud, of Dresden, sureties. Jonathan Reed, guardian unto Mary, Nathan, Nathaniel and Jonathan, 8 Sep., 1797. [VII, 137-138.] Moses and Stephen chose Elihu Getchel to be their guardian, 8 Sep., 1797. [VII, 138-139.] Inventory by Ezra Taylor, Samuel Tubbs and William Lewis, all of Dresden, 26 Sep., 1797, $3851.66. [VIII, 21.] Accounts filed 30 May, 1799, and 30 Jan., 1800. [VIII, 237-8.] Division of real estate by Louis Houdlette, James H. Patterson and William Lewis, all of Dresden, 27 Ap., 1803. [X, 68-69.]

I Elizebath Emerson of Edgecomb in the County of Lincoln and Commonwealth of Massechusetts widow ; Calling to mind the mortality of my body and the uncertainty of my life, and not knowing how soon I may be Called away by Death and being at this present time weak in body but of Sound disposing mind and memory : do make and ordain this my last Will and Testament : That is to say, principally and in the first place, I Recomend my Soul into the hands of God who gave it : and my Body I commit to the Earth to buried at the Discration of my Executor hereafter named, not doughting but that I shall receive the same again at the General Resserection by the mighty Power of God— And as to my Worldly Estate—I give divise and dispose of the same in the following manner and form Viz.—

Imps. I order that all my just Debts and funeral Expences be paid by my sons imeadatly after my Decese—

Item I give and bequeath unto my son William Emerson the field or lot of Land which I purchased of Roger Handley Discribed in his

Deed he paying unto my son Edward within two years after my Decese thirty pounds and within that term thirty pounds unto my other Children—And the Rest & Residue of the home farm my will is that it be Equaly Devided between my son William and my son Joseph Emerson, and at my son Josephs ariving at twenty one years of age, that he then should com in for, and have one Equal share or half of the above mentioned field or Lot, then to be made Equal in the Division of the whole farm, he the said Joseph paying unto my son William thirty pounds within two years after he shall arive to said age of twenty one years—

I likewise give the whole of the account of Money I have paid and money Expended in Administration of my late husbands Estate unto my sons Edward William and Joseph who my will is that they pay all Debts Due from me and my said late Husband Edward Emerson Esqr. and my Will is that the money Received or to be Received from Joseph Campbell in pay of the Whitcher place so called, be applied to pay a debt Due to Wells Gardner upon a Bond signed by my late Husband and all Docter Bills against my famely unpaid, and the Remainder be the same more or Less to be Equaly Devided between my four sons, John, Edward, William, and Joseph, Josephs part to be Resarved and kept in the hands of my son William untill said Joseph arives at twenty one years of age, then to be paid to him or his order—and further my Will is that the stock now upon the farm be and Remain the property of my son William Except two Cows which I alow and bequeath to my son Edward as soon as they can be conveanently spared from the farm—My Will further is that my sons John and Edward Devide and have the Land and buildings they now Emprove agreable to the Division proposed by their late Father Decesed—I give and bequeath unto my Daughter Elizebath Kenney provided she aquits hir Brothers from any Demands she may Claim in hir own Right of any part of hir late Fathers Estate—One high Chist of Drawers one large square Table one green Chair three fraimed chairs with flag Bottoms—one purpel Brulio gound one Dark patch gound one long Broad cloth cloak, one dark crape gound with an apron and also my wearing linning such as caps hankirchefs aprons &c and also my Gould necklace and one large puter plater, and also my will is that twenty Dollars be paid my said Daughter Elizebath at the setelment of my Honoured Mothers thirds of my late Father William Shilebers Estate she complying with and aquiting as aforesaid.—

I give to my son John my largest Looking Glass also a scarlet coat and a light westcoat which ware his late Fathers—The Books which may be found in the house my will is that they be Equaly Devided amongst all my children.—

To my son Edward I give an Ovel Table and three framed chairs, also one large puter platter—Also one good fether Bead with a white Ravens Duck Tick, said bead to be filled up with fethers so as to make a good Bead—

I give to my Daughter in Law Anni Emerson one China gound now at hir house also one other China gound at my house, the two gounds which I proposed to hir to make hir a Bead Quilt—

I likewise give to my grand Daughter Susannah Emerson my gould Ring—I also give to my Daughter in Law Anney my Lambskin Cloak and black Calimenco skirt—I likewise give to my Grandaughter Elizebath Emerson my brown Tafety gound—I likewise give to my Daughter Elizebeth Kenney my black Quilted petecote and all my other wearing close not before Disposed off, upon hir aquitance as aforesaid—and to Rebeca Emerson I give my black mode Cloak and silk Bunnet and large furr muff—

I also give to my son William the whole of the yarn spun in the house and one good bead & beading togather with all the rist and residue of my housel furniture not before Disposed off Except one large silver Table spoon and two silver Teaspoons which I give to my son Edward—and one Table silver spoon and one silver Teaspoon I give to my grand son Pratt Emerson also one silver Table spoon and three silver Teaspoons I give Equaly between my sons William & Joseph to be sold or Disposed of to Each the other as they shall agree—

And my Will futher is that the whole part of my part of my Honoured Mothers Dower or thirds of my late Honoured Father William Shilebers Estate when settled—be Devided Equaly between my three sons Edward William and Joseph, Except the twenty Dollars before mentioned—

Lastly. I do hereby appoint my son William Emerson my sole Executor of this my last Will and Testement, and do revoak all and Every former wills or Testements by me heretofore made and Declare this & no other to be my last Will and Testement—In Wittness whereof I do hereto set my hand and seal this twenty sixth Day of July in the year of our Lord one thousand seven hundred and Ninty seven—

Signed sealed published & Declared by the Testator to be hir last Will and Testement in presence of us—
   Wm McCobb

Before signing my will is that my son Joseph have one Bead and Beading—

Abner Hood   Elizabeth Emerson   (seal)
Suky Williams

Probated 11 Sep., 1797. [VII, 147 to 150.] John Emerson, of Boothbay, and Edward Emerson, of Edgecomb, sureties.

In the name of GOD. Amen—

I Patrick Rodgers of Bristol in the County of Lincoln Gentleman, being weak in body but of sound and perfect mind and memory, blessed be Almighty GOD for the same ; Considering the uncertainty of this mortal life Do make and publish this my last will and testament in manner and form following, that is to say—First 1 give and bequeath unto my eldest Son George Rodgers All my wearing apparel at the time of my decease—I also give and bequeath to the Heirs of my eldest Daughter Francis, late the Wife of James Houston Gentleman, the sum of Six Shillings—I also give and bequeath to my Daughter Jane the widow of Edward Young deceased the sum of Six Shillings, which said several legacies I will and ordain shall be paid and delivered to the said respective Legatees within Three months after my decease. And lastly, as to all the rest, residue and remainder of Real and personal estate, goods and Chattels of what kind or nature soever to me belonging I give and bequeath the same to My Son William Rodgers, My Daughter Elizabeth Rodgers and my Daughter Mary Rodgers equally to be devided between them. And I hereby appoint my said son William Rodgers to be the Sole Executor of this my last will and testament—

In witness whereof I have hereunto set my hand and seal the Second day of October in the year of our Lord one thousand seven hundred Ninety four—

Signed, Sealed, published and   Patrick Rodgers   (seal)
declared by the above named
Patrick Rodgers the testator
to be his last will & testament
in the presence of us who have
hereunto subscribed our names
as witnesses in the presence of
the testator—

                                                William McIntyer
                                                Jonathan Grelee
                                                Robert McLintock

Probated 11 Sep., 1797. [VII, 151-2.] William McIntyer and Robert McLintock, both of Bristol, sureties. Inventory by William McIntyer, Robert McLintock and Robert McFarland, all of Bristol, 25 Sep., 1797, $1292. [VIII, 96.]

George Gillchrist, late of Cushing. Elizabeth Gillchrist, of Cushing, widow, Adm'x, 9 June, 1797. [VII, 161-2.] Samuel Gillchrist and Samuel Otis, both of Cushing, sureties. Inventory by Samuel Gillchrist, Dennis Fogerty and Samuel Otis, all of Cushing, 12 Sep., 1797, $1279.92. [VII, 162-3.]

Thomas Morrison, late of Warren, millwright. Rusha Morrison, of Warren, widow, Adm'x, 19 Sep., 1797. [VII, 165-166.] Rufus Crane, of Warren, and Jonathan Morrison, of New Milford, sureties. Inventory by Benjamin Brackett, Joseph Copeland and John Watt, 23 Feb., 1797, $110.99. [VII, 167.] Joseph Copeland and John Watt, commissioners to examine claims. [VIII, 2.] Account filed 17 Sep., 1798. [VIII, 2-3.] Distribution ordered 4 Jan., 1799. [VIII, 3.]

Joseph Winslow, late of Waldoborough, joiner. Mercy Winslow, of Waldoborough, widow, Adm'x, 19 Sep., 1797. [VII, 168-9.] George Reed and Barnabas Simmons, both of Waldoborough, sureties. Inventory by Peleg Oldham and Nathaniel Pitcher, both of Waldoborough, and Seth Hall, of Nobleborough, 26 Oct., 1797, $727.27. [VIII, 226-7.] Account filed 10 Sep., 1799. [VIII, 228.] Mercy, widow, guardian unto Bethiah and Esther, minor daughters, 10 Sep., 1799. [IX, 191.]

Charles Martin, late of Cushing, mariner. Lucy Martin, of Bristol, widow, Adm'x, 19 Sep., 1797. [VII, 169-170.] John Morton and Joshua Webber, both of Bristol, sureties. Inventory by Ezekiel Farrow, Samuel Tucker and Thomas Arnold, all of Bristol, 5 Oct., 1797, $13.92. [VII, 247-8.]

In the Name of God, Amen.
I George Roth of a place called Broad Bay in the County of Lincoln and Province of Massachusetts Bay in New England yeoman, being in health of Body and of perfect Mind and Memory Thanks be given to God ; calling to Mind the Mortality of my Body and knowing that it is appointed for all Men once to die, do make & ordain this my last Will & Testament ; That is to say, principally and first of all, I give and recommend my Soul into the Hand of Almighty God that gave it,

and my Body I recommend to the Earth, to be buried in decent Christian Burial, at the discretion of my Executors; nothing doubting but at the general Resurrection I shall receive the same again, by the mighty Power of God. And as touching such worldly Estate wherewith it has pleased God to bless me in this life, I give, demise, and dispose of the same in the following Manner & Form.

Imprimis, I give and Bequeath to Rosanna, my dearly beloved Wife, whom I likewise constitute, make and ordain the sole Executrix of this my last Will and Testament, all my Estate, both Real, Personal and mixt, of what name or Nature soever by her freely to be possessed and enjoyed. But my further Will is, that in Case I shall leave any Child or Children begotten of the Body of my said Wife, all the Estate hereby given to her shall descend to it, or them, in such Manner and wise as the Law directs.

Item I give unto my well-beloved Son Conrad Roth the Sum of One pound Six Shillings & eight pence, to be paid to him or his legal Representative in one year after my decease, which together with what he has already received is his full part or Share out of my Estate.

And I do hereby utterly disallow, revoke, and disannul all & every other former Testaments, Wills, Legacies, Bequests, & Executors, by me in any ways before-named, willed and bequeathed; ratifying and confirming this and no other, to be my last Will and Testament. In witness whereof, I have hereunto set my Hand & Seal this Second Day of July in the Year of our Lord One Thousand seven Hundred and seventy two

Signed, Sealed, published, pronounced and declared by the said George Roth as his last Will & Testament in the presence of us
John Martin Schaffer.
Moses Copeland
David Fales

George G R Roth (seal)
his mark

Probated 19 Sep., 1797. Letters testamentary issued to Rosanna Hute, of Waldoborough, widow, 19 Sep., 1797. [VII, 172 to 175.] Michael Sprague, of Waldoborough, and Moses Copeland, of Warren, sureties. Inventory by Waterman Thomas, Nathan Sprague and Jacob Ludwig, all of Waldoborough, 30 Sep., 1797, $602. [VIII, 61.] Account filed 17 Sep., 1798. [VIII, 61-62.]

In the Name of God Amen I Richard Adams of Cushing in the County of Lincoln & Commonwealth of Massachusetts Gentleman feeling the

Infirmities of Age though of sound mind & memory praised be God) & Knowing that it is appointed unto men to die do make Ordain & Constitute this my last Will and Testament hereby Revoking & disannulling all former Wills & testaments in any manner or form heretofore made by me

First I give & commend my Soul into the Hands of God who gave it & my Body I Recommend to the Earth to be Buried in decent Christian Burial at the discretion of my Executors hereafter named and as touching such Worldly Estate as it has pleased God to bless me I give demise & dispose of it in manner following

Imprimis, I give and bequeath to my well-beloved wife Mary during her natural Life the South East front Room in my Dwelling House together with the privilege of the Kitchen, Cellar, Oven, Well, item the Best feather bed I Leave with all necessary appurtenances to the same—Item all necessary Furniture for one Room & necessary Kitchen utensils. Item One good Cow to Be kept both Summer & Winter. Item Fire wood brot to her Door & Cut fit for the chimney during her Life Item Fifteen Bushels of Bread Corn of different kinds annually. Item flax & Wool annually sufficient to Keep her Bedding & Cloathing in Repair. Item a Sufficient annual supply of Potatoes & other kinds of Same & Vegetables & of Tea Coffee and Sweetning & other necessaries all the above articles to be provided by my Executors hereafter named and out of the Income of my Estate

Item I Give and Bequeath to my beloved Daughter Sela Baker one Cow to be delivered by my Executors within Six months after my Decease

Item I Give and Bequeath to my beloved Daughter Ruby Cook a Cow to be delivered by my Executors within six months after my Decease

Item I give and bequeath to my beloved Daughter Margaret Gray one Cow to be delivered by my Executors within six months after my Decease

Item I Give & bequeath to my beloved Daughter Hope Davis Six Shillings

Item I give & bequeath to my beloved Daughter Lucy Graffam Six Shillings

Item I give & bequeath to my before named daughters Sela, Ruby, Margaret, Hope and Lucy after the Decease of my Wife all my Houshold furniture to be Equally divided amongst them.—

Item I give to my Grand daughters Polly Baker Polly Bradford and Polly Adams the Daughters of my Son Richard Adams One Silver

Table Spoon apiece to be delivered after my wife's Decease

Item I give to my beloved Son Richard Adams all my wearing apparel

Item I give to my Grandson Richard Adams the Son of my said Son Richard my largest pair of Gold Sleeve Buttons

Item I give to my Grandson Robert Davis son of my Daughter Hope my Smallest pair of Gold Sleeve Buttons to be delivered after my Wifes Decease

Item To my three Sons Richard, Thomas & George after paying all the above Bequests & Legacies & all my Just Debts & funeral Charges I Give & bequeath the farm I Live on with the Buildings thereon, all my Stock, farming Tools & Implements Together with a certain Island nearly adjoining said Farm commonly called Crotch Island and in general all my Estate Real & personal to be Equally divided amongst them

And I do hereby appoint & constitute my said three Sons Richard, Thomas & George Executors of this my last Will and Testament

In Witness whereof I have hereunto set my Hand and Seal this twenty seventh day of August in the year of our Lord One Thousand seven hundred & Ninety Two and in the seventeenth year of American Independence.

Richard Adams (seal)

Signed Sealed published
& declared by the said
Richard Adams as his
last Will & Testament
in presence of us, who
in his presence & in
presence of Each other
have hereunto set our hands.
Thurston Whiting
Jacob Graffam
John Short

Probated 19 Sep., 1797. Thomas Adams being dead letters testamentary issued to Richard Adams and George Adams, both of Cushing, mariners, 19 Sep., 1797. [VII, 175 to 178.] Moses Copeland, and Joseph Copeland, both of Warren, sureties.

I Benjamin Linneken of Boothbay in the County of Lincoln yeoman, Calling to mind the mortalety of my Body and the uncertainty of my Life, and not knowing how soon I may be Called away by Death, and being at this present time of sound disposing mind & memory do make and ordain this my last Will and Testament, That is to say, princepelly and in the first place I Recommend my soul into the hands of God who gave it, and my Body I Commit to the Earth to be buried at the Discration of my Executor or Executrax hereafter named and as to my Worldly Estate I give devise and dispose of the same in the following manner & form (Viz)—

Imps. firstly I order that all my just Debts and funeral Expenses be paid out of my Estate Emeadeatly after my decese—

Item I give and bequeath unto my son Benjamin the sum of six shillings if Living to be paid him by my Executor and Executrax hereafter named, to be paid him in full of his share or part of my Estate—

Item I also give & bequeath to my son David the sum of six shillings in full of his share of said Estate—

Item I give also to my son Ephraim the sum of six shillings to be paid him in full of his part or share of my said Estate—

Item I give and Bequeath to my oldest Daughter Abigail Jonston the sum of six shillings to be paid hir by my said Executor & Executrax in full of hir share in my said Estate—

Item I also give my Daughter Elizebath Sawyer the sum of six shillings to be paid hir in full of hir share or part as aforesaid—

Item I give also to my Daughter Susannah Linneken the sum of six shillings to be paid hir in full of hir share or part of my said Estate—

Item I give and bequath unto my Daughter Mary Wall six shillings to be paid hir by my said Executor & Executrax in full of hir share or part of my said Estate—

Item I also give and bequath to my Daughter Sarah Alley the sum of six shillings to be paid hir in full of hir share or part of my said Estate—

Item I give also to my Daughter Phebe Wheeler the sum of six shillings to be paid hir in full of hir part or share of said Estate—

Item I also give to my Daughter Lydia Langdon the sum of six shillings to be paid hir in full of hir part or share in my said Estate—

Item I give also to my Daughter Martha the sum of six shillings in full of hir part of said Estate—

Item I give and bequeath to my Daughter Lucy six shillings to be paid hir in full of hir part of my said Estate—

Item All the rest and residue of my said Estate real and personal wheresoever the same is or may be found, I give devise & bequath to my Beloved Wife Mary Linneken and to hir heirs & asigns forever to hir & their sole use and benefit forever—

Lastly   I do hereby Appoint my said Beloved wife Mary Linneken with my son Epheraim Linneken Sole Executrax and Executor of this my last Will and Testement, and do revoke all & Every former Wills or Testements by me heretofore made and Declare this & no other to be my last Will and Testement—In Wittness whereof I do hereunto sett my hand and seal this fourth Day of March A D 1796
Signed sealed published & Declared by the
Testator to be his last Will & Testement in
presence of us—   his
Wm McCobb   Benjamin (X) Linneken   (seal)
Sam'l Bush   mark
     his
Ezekiel (X) Holbrook
     mark

                         Probated 12 Sep., 1796.   Jacob Sawyer and Samuel Alley appealed from decree 12 Sep., 1796.   [VII, 184 to 186.]

Thomas Woodman, late of Pownalborough, hatter.   Lucy Woodman, of Pownalborough, widow, Adm'x, 23 Oct., 1797.   [VII, 187-8.] William Sevey and Ebenezer Whittier, both of Pownalborough, sureties.   Inventory by Joseph Tinkham, David Payson, Jr., and Samuel Sevey, all of Pownalborough, 6 Nov., 1797, $391.52.   [VII, 248-9.]

Ebenezer Blunt, Jr., late of Farmington.   Ebenezer Blunt, of Bristol, Adm'r, 23 Oct., 1797.   [VII, 188.]   Samuel Miller, of Bristol, and Arthur Blunt, of Pownalborough, sureties.   Ebenezer, guardian unto Robert, minor son, 13 Sep., 1797.   [VII, 178.]   Inventory by Thomas Johnston, William McIntyer and William Jones, all of Bristol, 21 Dec., 1797, $170.29.   [VIII, 73-74.]   Account filed 4 June, 1798.] [VIII, 74.]

In the Name of God Amen, The Eight Day of October. in the year of our Lord, one thousand Seven hundred Ninety & four.   I Ebenezer Blunt Juner of Bristol, in the County of Lincoln and Commonwealth of Massachusetts yeoman Being Very Sick in body but of perfect mind & memory : thanks be given unto God therefore calling unto mind the mortality of my body, knowing that it is appointed for all men Once to Die, do make & ordain this my Last will & testament, that is to Say=First of all I give & Recommend my Soul into the hands of God that Gave it, for my Body I Recommend it to the Earth to be buried in a Deacent Christian Like maner at the Discretion of my Executors. And as touching Such worldly estate wherewith it hath pleased God to Bless me in this life : I give : Devise & dispose of the same in the following manner & form

First, it is my will : & I Do order : that all my just debts & funeral charges be paid & Satisfied

Item I give & bequeath unto Jean my Dearly beloved wife all my Personal Estate, Excepting my wareing appearil; and to have the in come of my Real Estate untill my Son Robert Blunt is one & twenty years of age (for the use of my wife & to Supor & Edicate my son Robert) if Said Robert Should Live untill Said time ; if not to be in the following manner that is my wife to have two thirds of my Real Estate, & my honered father the other third as is here in after more fully Expressed

Item = I give to my be loved Son Robert Blunt two Lots of Land Laying in farmington No fourty Six & fourty Seven Lay'd Down by Joseph North Plan : on the East Side of Sandy River; to come into full Possistion of Said Land att the age of one & twenty years or other ways as is before mentioned I likewise give all my wareing apperall to Said Robert for his use att the Discretion of my Executors

Item I give to my honered father on these Conditions that is to Say, if my Son Robert Should not Live untill one & twenty that my father Should have one third of my Real Estate otherways to go to said Robert as is Exprest before

I Likewise Desier Constitute & appoint Jean my wife & Ebenezer blunt My Honer'd father my Executors & administrators of this my Last will & Testament Ratifying & Confirming this & no other to be my last Will & testament : In Witness whereof I have here unto Set my hand & Seal the Day and year above written

Signed Sealed published pronounced & Declared by the Said Ebenezer Blunt Jur as his last will & testament in the Presence of us the Subscribers Viz the words (ways) & (for the use of my wife & to Suport & Edicate my Son Robert) interLined Before Signing hereof

            Ebenezer Blunt Junr (seal)

William McIntyer
John Sproul
Samuel Blunt

 Probated 5 Ap., 1799; Jane, executrix being dead, letters testamentary issued to Ebenezer Blunt 5 Ap., 1799; inventory by William McIntyer, Samuel Clark and James Drummond, all of Bristol, 31 May, 1799, $155.75. [VIII, 99 to 102.] Account filed 10 Sep., 1799. [XIII, 450-1.]

Valentine Nutter, late of Pownalborough, mariner. Hannah Nutter, of Pownalborough, widow, Adm'x, 9 Mar., 1796. [VII,190-191.] Azariah Pottle and Isaac Hedge, both of Pownalborough, sureties. Inventory by Moses Davis, of Edgecomb, and Francis Cook and Ebenezer Whittier, both of Pownalborough, 27 Ap., 1796, $125.20. [VII, 191.] Moses Davis and Ebenezer Whittier, commissioners to examine claims. [VII, 192.] Advertisement of sale of real estate, 4 Mar., 1797. [VII,193.] Account filed 5 June, 1797, at which date the administratrix had become the wife of Kenelam Cushman, of Pownalborough. [VII, 194.]

Robert Randall, Jr., late of Pownalborough, trader. Robert Randall, of Hallowell, Adm'r, 23 June, 1796. [VII, 207-8.] Moses Sewall and Amos Stoddard, both of Hallowell, sureties. Inventory by Nathaniel Dummer, David Sewall and John Beman, all of Hallowell, 8 Sep., 1796, $238.37. [VII, 208-9.]

Josiah Warren, late of Norridgewalk. Sarah Warren, of Norridgewalk, widow, Adm'x, 19 Jan., 1796. [VII,214-215.] John Moor and Charles Witherell, both of Norridgewalk, sureties. Inventory by John Moore, James Thompson and Daniel Steward, all of Norridgewalk, 10 May, 1796. [VII,216.] Bryce McLellan, of Canaan, and Daniel Steward of Norridgewalk, commissioners to examine claims. [VIII,35.] Widow's dower set off by Daniel Steward, Bryce McLellan and John Clark, 29 July, 1799. [VIII, 239-240.] Account filed 26 Aug., 1800. [VIII, 240.]

I Francis Rittal of Pownalborough in the County of Lincoln and Commonwealth of Massachusetts Tailor, being in health of Body and of sound Mind and Memory, and knowing that I must shortly put off this earthly Tabernacle, do make this my last Will and Testament; that is to say, in the first Place I commend my Soul into the hands of God who gave it, and my Body to the Earth to decently buried at the discretion of my Executrix hereafter named, in Expectation that I shall receive the same again glorious & immortal at the Resurrection of the Just.

And as touching such worldly Estate as it hath pleased God to bestow upon me in this Life, I give devise and dispose of the same in manner following,

Imprimis—I will and order that all my just Debts and funeral Expenses be paid out of my Estate as soon as may be after my Decease.

Item. I give and bequeath to my beloved Wife Lucy the Improvement of all my Estate real & personal till my youngest Child shall arrive to full age; she to take care of & provide for all my Children under age out of the Income & profits of my said Estate until they shall respectively arrive to full Age; and when the youngest Child shall arrive to full Age, then my said Wife to have one Third of all the Personal Estate, & a third Part of the real Estate, during her Life—
Item I give to my Daughter Sally Theobald twenty shillings to be paid her out of my Estate, by my Executrix, after my youngest Child arrives to full Age—
Item, I give & devise to my Children Molly Stilfinn, Francis, John, Louis, Lucy, Nancy, Betsey & Charlotta all the rest and Residue of my Estate, real personal & mixed, wheresoever the same is or may be found, equally to be divided among them, when my said youngest Child shall attain to the age of twenty one years.
Lastly, I do hereby constitute and appoint my said Wife Lucy sole Executrix of this my last Will and Testament. In Testimony whereof I the said Francis Rittal do hereto set my hand & seal the twenty fifth day of April in the year of our Lord 1789—

      Memo. The words, all my Children under Age, were interlin'd before seal'g.

        Francis Rittal   (seal)

The above Instrument was signed, sealed, and declared by the Testator to be his last Will & Testament in presence of us—

    Edmd Bridge
    Phebe Bridge jun
    Edmund Bridge juneor
    Jon. Bowman

  Probated 8 Jan., 1796. [VII, 219-220.] Inventory by Ezra Taylor, John Polereczky, and Jonathan Reed, all of Dresden, 13 Feb., 1796. [VII, 221 to 223.]

Robert Ridlon, of Newcastle, blacksmith, a spendthrift. Ebenezer Clarke, of Newcastle, guardian, 1 Nov., 1794. [VII, 224.]

John Mallet, of Bowdoin, a spendthrift. James Rogers and Hugh Molloy, both of Bowdoin, guardians, 9 Jan., 1796. [VII, 224.] Inventory by James Rogers, Samuel Tebbets and Nathaniel Jellison, all of Bowdoin, 23 July, 1799, $961.74. [VIII, 153-4.] Account of William Mallet and Benjamin Jaques, guardians, filed 21 Aug., 1802.

[VIII, 156.] Jesse, minor son, chose Joseph Potter, of Bowdoin, to be his guardain, 11 Sep., 1805. [IX, 261.] Inventory by James Rogers, William Gowell and David Willson, all of Bowdoin, 4 Dec., 1802, $1102.77. [X, 225.] Account of Joseph Potter and William Alexander, guardians, filed 28 Mar., 1809. [XIII, 485 to 490.]

Samuel Stinson, Jr., late of Woolwich, mariner. Samuel Stinson, of Woolwich, Adm'r, 26 Dec., 1797. [VII, 238-9.]

James Pattee, late of Winslow, mariner. David Pattee, of Winslow, Adm'r, 14 Feb., 1798. [VII, 250.] John McKechnie, of Winslow, and William Bowman, of Dresden, sureties.

David Huseton, son of John Huseton, late of Farmington, chose Abiel Sweet, late of Farmington, to be his guardian, 5 Ap., 1797. [VIII, 6-7.]

In the Name of God Amen. I David Silvester of Pownalborough in the County of Lincoln Esquire calling to mide the uncertainty & brevity of Life & feeling my Body decaying, tho' in perfect soundness of Mind and memory, do make & ordain this my last Will & testament, in manner following In the first place I will & bequeath my soul into the hands of God who gave it & my Body to the Earth to be decently buryed under the direction of my Executors hereafter named, in sure hope of a Joyfull resurrection & reunion of Soul & body at the great Day of Account.
As to my worldly Estate with which God has blessed me I will & dispose of it in the following manner I will & direct my Executors hereafter named that they pay all my Just Debts in the first place out of my personal Estate & Credits.
I give & bequeath unto my beloved Wife Martha my dwelling house & Stable with all the Land they stand upon & all the Lot appertaining thereto which lies between Water Street & Middle Street & the land of Zenas Stetson & the heirs of John Sevey decd. except the store & the Land on which it stands with the passage way into said Store as now improved with all the furniture of said House, except one Clock. To hold to her during her natural Life & at her decease, my will is that the same premises both real & personal descend to my two Sons David & Joshua & their heirs to be equally divided between them. I also give & bequeath to my said Wife the rents that may become due from time to Time for the Land on which the Houses of Alexr. Troup & —— Hilton now stand, together with the Rents of the Store in all its

parts above excepted & all the rents of the Ground on which the Rope walk stands leased to Messrs. Wigglesworth's to be enjoyed by her during her Life as aforesaid, also $200 to be paid of the Personal Estate.

I give & bequeath to my honored mother Mary Silvester the rents of Sheepscut River Bridge due on my Share in said Bridge from year to year after deducting the repairs, during her natural Life, after her decease to go to my beloved Wife Martha during her natural Life & after her decease to descend to my two Sons in equal Shares & their heirs forever

I give & bequeath to my beloved Son Joshua one Quarter part of my Ship called the Wiscasset, with one Quarter part of her Tackle & Appurtenances. Also my Brewhouse with all the implements & brewing Utensels belonging to the same with three Quarters of an Acre of Land to be so laid out as to include said house & priviledge & to extend to the Town road. To hold to him & his heirs forever, also one of my Clocks to be his absolute property

I give & bequeath to each of my Sisters Mary Lydia Sarah Jane Betsey & Rachael a black Lutestring Gown to be given to them by my Executors out of my Estate I give & bequeath to Elizabeth Light, in token of my gratefull remembrance of her great & painfull Care & Attention in my sickness, a Lutestring Gown to be paid for out of my Estate.

I give & bequeath to the rev'd Alden Bradford fifteen Dollars, for the purpose of purchasing a piece of Linnen in token of my gratefull remembrance of his kind attention to me in my sickness

I give & bequeath to each of my Executors hereafter named a Guinea each to purchase a remembrance Ring. Also to Joseph Tinkham Esq'r the same sum for the same purpose I give & bequeath all the rest & residue of my Estate both real & personal not before disposed of, to my two Sons David & Joshua to be divided between them in equal shares to hold to them & their heirs forever And I do hereby constitute & appoint Tho. Rice Esqr Silas Lee Gentleman & my Son David Silvester my Executors of this my last Will & Testament & hereby revoke & annul all former Wills & Testaments by me made & pronounce & declare this to be my last Will & Testament.

Tis my further will that my said Sons shall take care of & provide for Cynthya Young untill she is of the Age of fifteen years & then that she, by them, be put to learn the Trade of a mantua maker or Taylor at their Expence

In witness whereof I hereunto set my hand & seal the sixth day of February in the year of our Lord one thousand seven hundred & ninety eight
David Silvester (seal)
Signed sealed published
pronounced & declared
by the Testator to be his last
Will & Testament in presence
of us
John Hues
Thomas McCrate
Alexander Troup

Probated 27 Mar., 1798. [VIII, 77-78.] John Hues, Abiel Wood, Jr., Joshua Hilton, Ebenezer Whittier, Ezekiel Cutter and Nymphas Stacy, all of Pownalborough, sureties. Inventory by Henry Hodge, Joseph Tinkham and David Payson, all of Pownalborough, 11 Ap., 1798, $17,529.38. [VIII, 79 to 82.] Joshua, minor son, chose David Payson, of Pownalborough, to be his guardian, 4 June, 1798. [IX, 221.] Joseph Tinkham and Joseph Christophers, both of Pownalborough, commissioners to examine claims, 10 June, 1799. Account filed 17 Nov., 1801. [Unrecorded.]

Be it remembered that I Nathaniel Whittier of Readfield in the County of Lincoln and Commonwealth of Massachusetts Husbandman being weak in Body but of sound mind and memory do this tenth day of March *Anno Domini* one thousand seven hundred and ninty-eight make and publish this my last Will and Testament in the following manner that is to say—
In the first place I give to my beloved Wife all my Household furniture exclusive of her Lawfull right of Dower in my Estate excepting my Clock
Also I give to my Daughter Mary Page forty Dollars to be paid in Household Furniture by my Executor hereafter to be named to be paid in one year after my Decease.
Also I give to my Son Jedediah Whittier fifty acres of Land lying in a place called Wyman Plantation in the County of Lincoln aforesaid it being the northwesterly End of Lot No. forty seven also one undivided third of Lot No. eighty two in said Plantation
Also I give to my Daughter Ruth Cochran ten Dollars to be paid by my said Executor within one year after my Decease
Also I give to my Son Thomas Whittier all my Stock Including my

neet Cattle Horses Sheep and Swine and my Clock together with all my Implements of Husbandry—

Also I give to my Daughter Dorothy Johnson a Lot of Land lying in the aforesaid Plantation and numbered one hundred and four

Also I give to my Daughter Ruhamah Whittier a Lot of Land lying in the aforesaid Plantation and numbered ninty two also one hundred and fifty Dollars to be paid in household Furniture by my said Exector within one year after my Decease

Also I give to my Son Abel Whittier the northerly half of Lot No. fifty eight to be divided in the middle lengthways of said Lot also one undivided third of Lot No. eighty two said Lots lying in the aforesaid Plantation also one pair of Oxen measuring six feet and a good Cow and a good Suit of Cloaths to be Delivered to him by my Executor when he shall arrive to the age of twenty one Years until which time he said Abel shall work with my said Executor

Also I give to my Son Nathaniel Whittier the southerly half of Lot No. fifty eight excepting four Acres which I have sold off the Southeast Corner of said Lot also one undivided third of Lot No. eighty two said Lots lying in the aforesaid Plantation also a pair of Oxen measuring six feet and a Cow and a good Suit of Cloaths to be delivered to him by my said Executor when he shall arrive to the age of twenty one years untill which time he said Nathaniel shall work for said Executor

Also I give to my Son Levi Whittier a Lot of Land lying in the aforesaid Plantation and numbered one hundred and seven also a pair of Oxen measuring six feet and a good Cow and a good Suit of Cloaths to be delivered to him by my said Executor when he shall arrive to the age of twenty one Years untill which time he said Levi shall work for my said Executor

Also I give to my Daughter Hannah Whittier a Lot of Land lying in the aforesaid Plantation and numbred ninty four also one hundred and fifty Dollars to be paid her in household Furniture to be Delivered to her by my said Executor when She shall arrive to the age of eighteen years untill which time she said Hannah is to be maintained by my said Executor including her Labour

Also I give to my Grandson Nathaniel Cochran a Lot of Land lying in the aforesaid Plantation and numbered ninty eight

Also I give to my Grandson Cyrus Whittier a Lot of Land lying in the aforesaid Plantation and numbered ninty six

Also I give to the Methodist Society in said Wyman Plantation two hundred Dollars to be applyed towards Building a Methodist Meetinghouse in said Plantation and to be paid by my said Executor. To the Committee who shall be appointed by said Society to Superintend said Building whenever it shall be needed for that use

Also I give to my Son Thomas Whittier all the Debts that may be owing to me at my Decease he paying to my Children and to the Methodist Society as before named also I give to my said Son Thomas Whittier all my Estate Real and Personal not herein before Bequeathed and Devised wherever the same may be found And lastly I do Constitute and Ordain my said Son Thomas Whittier sole Executor of this my last Will and Testament

In Testamony whereof I do hereunto set my hand and Seal the day and Year above Written

Nathaniel Whittier (seal)

Signed Sealed Published Pronounced
and Declared by the said Nathaniel
Whittier as and for his last Will and
Testament in the Presents of us who at
his request and in his presents hereunto
set our names as Witneses to the same
  John Hubbard
  John Evens
  Samuel Judkins

Probated 31 May, 1798. [VIII, 91.] John Hubbard and Samuel Judkins, both of Readfield, sureties.

Israel Smith, late of Woolwich, blacksmith. Jane Smith, of Woolwich, widow, Adm'x, 4 June, 1798. [IX, 6.] Ebenezer Delano and Robert Hanson, both of Woolwich, sureties. Inventory by Abner Wade and Thomas Snell, both of Woolwich, and Moses Hilton, of Pownalborough, 26 June, 1798, $314.31. [VIII, 95.] Account filed 10 Aug., 1800. [VIII, 233.]

In the Name of God Amen, I John Campbell of Bath in the County of Lincoln and Commonwealth of Massachusetts Yeoman, being weak in Body but of sound and perfect Mind and Memory (blessed be God) do this twentyfirst day of December A D. One thousand seven hundred and Eighty six make and publish this my last Will and Testament in manner following Vizt.—

Imprimis. I give and devise to my beloved Son John Campbell Jun'r a certain tract of land, to hold to him his heirs and assigns forever, situate in Bath aforesaid containing One hundred Acres by estimation, with the buildings thereon and appurtenances to the same belonging, and which is bounded as followeth Vizt. beginning at a birch Tree standing on the West side of Winnegance Creek, thence running West by North half North to a Pile of Stones upon a Hill, thence continuing the same Course to a pine Stump on the west side of the Country Road and between that and Campbells Pond so called: Then beginning again at the northern End of said Pond at a hemlock Stump standing on the Western side of the same Pond thence running West by North half North to New-meadow's River to a spruce Stump standing a little to the Northward of certain Salt Works, thence southerly by the shore of said River so far as to make forty five Rods on a Direct line, to a large white Rock: thence East by South half South to a white Oak Tree marked on two Sides and standing on a Hill in sight of said Pond, thence continuing the same Course across said Pond to said Winnegance Creek, thence northerly by said Creek to the first mentioned Bounds.

Item—I give and devise to my said Son his heirs and assigns forever the undivided half part of a certain piece of Marsh lying on the western side of a certain Point called Cord Wood Point, containing about twelve Acres more or less and is commonly known by the name of the back Marsh the same being owned in common between me and my Brother Alexander Campbell: Also the half part of another piece of Marsh owned in common as aforesaid containing about three Acres more or less, bounded northerly by certain Marsh owned by Thomas Williams of Bath aforesaid and southerly by a small Creek called Williams's Creek

Item—I give and bequeath to my said Son John his Ex'ors and Adm'ors one yoak of Oxen, two Cows one Mare, one horse and one Mare Colt, four Sheep all the Swine now on my Farm aforesaid, my Bed and bedding, all my wearing apparrell of which I may die possessed, my Chest all my Sea Books and great Bible six Chairs, two Tables together with all my farming Utensils, and also my Armour & apparatus & the great Chair.

Item—I give and bequeath to my beloved Daughter Margaret Campbell two Cows one Sheep two Tables six Chairs, & two beds which are commonly called her own.

Item—I give and bequeath to my beloved Daughter Elizabeth Campbell one Cow one Sheep a Bed commonly called my Son John's Bed and bedding belonging to the same, one large square white Table and a brass Sieve

Item—It is my Will and desire that Mrs. Elizabeth Burnam Wife of Mr. Francis Burnam and Mrs. Margaret Williams shall distribute as I hereafter direct them among my Children the household Utensils and Furniture not herein before bequeathed.

Item—I make and ordain Mr. David Ring of Bath aforesaid Gentleman the Sole Executor of this my last Will and Testament to see the same performed according to my true intent and meaning; and I also ordain and appoint him the said David Ring the Guardian of my said Son John untill he shall attain the age of Twenty one years. In Testiment whereof I have hereunto affixed my hand and Seal the day and year abovewritten

NB. the words "Bath, AD., a, by, &" were interlined before Signing
Signed sealed published & declared by the said
the Testator, as & for his last Will & Testament
in the presence of us who were present at the
signing and sealing thereof
Elizabeth Burnham   John Campbell   (seal)
Francis Burnam
Wm Lithgow Jun'r

Probated 5 Jan., 1798.
David Ring declined executorship; letters testamentary issued to John Campbell, of Bath, 5 Jan., 1798. [VIII, 102 to 104.] Francis Burnham, of Georgetown, and Benjamin Raymond, of Bowdoinham, sureties. Inventory by Francis Winter, Thomas Williams and David Ring, all of Bath, 10 Dec., 1798, $534.61. [VIII, 104-105.]

Be it remembered that I Moses Whittier of Readfield in the County of Lincoln and Commonwealth of Massachusetts Husbandman Being weak of Body but sound in minde and memory Do this fourteenth day of August A D 1798 Constitute ordain and declare this my last will and testament in the following maner that is to say

Firstly I do give and bequeath unto my beloved wife Anna Whittier one third third part of all my Real Estate during her life and one third part of all my personal Estate during her life

Also I give and bequeath unto my beloved Son Moses Whittier one dollar to be paid by my Executrix hereafter to be named

Also I give and bequeath to my beloved Daughter Anna Taylor one dollar to be paid by my said Executrix

Also I give to my beloved Daughter Mary Melven one Dollar to be paid by my said Executrix

Also I give to my beloved daughter Abigail Jose a likely Heifer three years old to be paid by my said Executrix within three months after my Decease

Also I give and bequeath to my beloved Daughter Releaf Bean a likely heifer three Years old to be paid by my said Executrix within six Months after my Decease

Also I give to my beloved Son Josiah Whittier one third of all my Real Estate to be in his possession when he shall arrive to the age of twenty one Years and half of one other third at the Decease of my said Widow

And one third of my Personal Estate which shall remain after dischargin all my Debts and Funeral Charges (which are to be discharged out of my personal Estat before a division is made)

Also I give unto my beloved Son Benaiah Whittier one third of all my Real Estate to be in his possession when he shall arive to the age of twenty one Years and one half of an other third of my Real Estate at the decease of my said Widow also one third of all. my Personal Estate which shall remain after discharging all my debts and funeral Charges

Also I give to my grandaughter Betsy Sleeper Taylor a good Cow and heifer three Years old to be delivered to her by my said Executrix when she shall arive to the age of eighteen Years

Also I give to my beloved Wife all the Debts that may be owing to me at my Decease and all my Estate Real and Personal not herein before bequeathed and devised wherever the same may be found and lastly I do constitute and ordain my my said Wife Anna Whittier Sole Executrix to this my last will and Testament

In testimony whereof I do hereunto set my hand and Seal the day and year within Written

NB the words (to & half of an other) were interlined before Signing

           his
        Moses X Whittier (seal)
           mark

Signed Sealed published pronounced and declared by the said Moses Whittier as and for his last Will and Testament in the Presents of us who at his request and in his presents hereunto set our names as Witnesses to the same

           Joshua Bean
           John Hubbard
           Daniel Wing

Probated 15 Jan., 1799. [VIII,105-106.] Joshua Bean and Daniel Wing, both of Readfield, sureties.

In the name God Amen I James Craigue of Reedfield in the County of Lincoln being of sound disposing mind and memory but Knowing the uncertainty of life and the certainty of death ordain this my last will and Testament—

1st. Item I give and bequeath unto my son Thomas Craigue my house barn mills and fifteen acres of land on which I now live on the condition following (viz) on his maintaining Anna Craigue my wife handsomely during her natural life and to pay to Freeman Craigue the son of Nancy Goud the sum of three hundred dollars to be paid to him on his arriving at the age of twenty one years and to give the said Freeman Craigue a good common school education and to furnish him with all necessary books and further to maintain him to the age of fourteen years—out of my estate—and further to pay to Mary Craigue the daughter of Mary Allen the sum of one hundred dollars and to give her a good common school education as far as she can arrive at the age of ten years and that she be maintained untill she arrives at the age of ten years out of my estate and I hereby appoint my son Thomas Craigue Guardian of the said Freeman and Mary Craigue and if the said Thomas Craigue should decease before one or both arrive at the periods above mentioned I appoint John and Christopher Turner Guardians to the deceased one And if the said Freeman or Mary should die before they arrive at the age of twenty one years the sums bequeathed to the deceased shall revert and be equally divided amoungst my sons

2nd Item I give and bequeath to my three sons Thomas James and William Craigue equally to be divided amoungst them a certain lot of Land No 94 situated in Reedfield—

3rd Item I give and bequeath to Orison Craigue and Peter Craigue the sons of my son Thomas Craigue fifty dollars each to be paid out of my estate after my decease at their arriving at the age of twenty one years and if the said Peter or Orison shall die before the age of twenty one years their propotion of my estate to be equally divided amoungst the children now living of my son Thomas Craigue—

4th Item I give and bequeath to Elenor Anna and Delia the daughters of my son Thomas Craigue thirty dollars each to be paid out of my estate after my decease on their arrival at the age of twenty one if one either or all should die before the age of twenty one their propotion to be equally divided amoungst the children now living of my son Thomas Craigue.

5th Item I give and bequeath to my Grandson James Craigue the sum of fifty dollars. Item to Sally and Margarett Craigue daughters of my son James thirty dollars each to be paid them at the age of twenty one years likewise the said sum of fifty before mentioned dollars to be paid my Grandson at the age of twenty one years and if one or either of them should die before that age their proportion of my estate to be divided equally amoungst the children now living of my son James—

I order all my just debts and funeral charges to be paid out of my personal estate and all the residue of my personal estate if any I will that my son Thomas receive—

And I hereby appoint Thomas and James Craigue my Executors In testimony whereof I have hereunto set my hand and seal to this my last will and testament This twenty eighth August *Anno Domini* seventeen hundred and ninety seven in presents of—

    Eben'r Bradish   James Craigg   (seal)
    John Turner
    Christopher Turner

The Codicil underwritten I order as fully to be executed as any part of the foregoing—

I give and bequeath to John and George Craigue sons of my son William Craigue the sum of thirty dollars each and to each of the three daughters of my son William Craigue twenty dollars each to be paid out of my estate after my decease and if either of them should die before the age of twenty one years their propotion of my estate to be equally divided amongst the children of my son William now living—

In testomy whereof I have hereunto set my hand and seal to this my codicil of my last will and testament this twenty eigth August *Anno Domini* seventeen hundred and ninety seven

In presents of—   James Craigg   (seal)
Christopher Turner
John Turner
Eben'r Bradish
NB. all erasures and interlineations made before signing—

    Probated 16 Jan., 1798. [VIII, 107-108.] James Cragg declined executorship. Thomas Smith, of Readfield, and John Jones, of Augusta, sureties. Inventory by John Turner, of Winthrop, Elihu

Alden and Mathias Smith, both of Readfield, 22 Jan., 1798, $1347.30. [Unrecorded.]

In the name of god amen I Frances Alleen of Geogetown Within the County of Linclon an Province of the Massahesats bay in newengland widow being in good bodily health and allso of sound mind and memory thanks be gieven to god for it and nowing it is appointed for all once to die do therefore take this oppertunity to make and ordain this my Last will and testament in maner and form folowing Viz. In the first Place I give and Recomend my Soul into the hands of god who gave it me and my body I Recomend to the earth to be buried in decent Christain burial at the discreation of my Excetatrix beliving that I Shall receive the Same again by the mighty power of god at the Genarel resurection and as to Such worly estate werewith it hath Pleasd god to bless me with in this Life I Give and dispose of the Same in the following maner

Itum I Give and bequath unt my daughter Isabale Malcom my lead colord Silk gownd and black velvet Cloak one Cambelet Rideine hood and Part of my Common wearing apparel and one Gold Ring

Itum I Give and bequath unto my Son Thomas Alen Heirs five Shillings

Itum I Give and beqeth unto my daughter Anna Allen my best gownd and Cloth riding wood and my Gold necklace one gold ring and my black Cloaths and my best lining my best bed and beding and all my right to the plate as mention in the deed of Sail and all the dets that is due to me

Itum I give and bequeth unto my grand daughter Fransis Rogers my darck tably gownd and Part of my Linen

Itum I Give and bequath to my grand dafter Fransis Malcom my Silver Show buckels one gold ring one Callaco gownd black Callaco mico Coat

I do Ratify and confirm this and no other to be my last will and testament in witness whereof I have hereuto Set my hand and Seal this twenty third day of September one thousand Seven hundred and Eigty Eight Singed Sealed Published and declared by the Said Frances Allen to be hur last will and testament in Presents of us the Subscribers and before Singine and Sealing I do hereby appoint ordain my daughter Anna Allen to be my Soul Excutatrix of this my Last will and testament

Witness   Frances Allen   (seal)
Jordan Parker
Margaret wylie
John Parker

Probated 25 May, 1798. [VIII, 109.]
Joseph Bowker and Elijah Drummond, both of Georgetown, sureties. Inventory by Jordan Parker, Mark Langdon Hill and Andrew Reed, all of Georgetown, 14 Sep., 1798, $108.65, to which the executrix added sundry articles, $104. [VIII, 111-112.] Account filed 31 May, 1799. [VIII, 112.]

In the Name of God Amen This Ninteenth Day of April in the year of our Lord one Thousand Seven hundred and Ninty Seven I Edward Bean of Mount Vernon in the County of Lincoln and Common Wealth of Massachusetts Husbandman Being of Sound mind and Memory but weak in Body, and Calling to mind the Mortallity of the Same, Do make and Ordain this my Last will and Testement First of all Commiting my Soul to God who Gave It and my body to the Earth from whence It proceeded to be Buried in Such Deecant Christian manner as my Executors hereafter mentioned Shall see fit.

And as Touching Such Worldly Estate as It hath Pleased God to Bless me with in this life I hereby Give Divise and Dispose of in the following manner Viz

Impr's I will that all my Just Debts and furnal Charges be paid in Convenent time after my Decase by my Executors hereafter mentioned

Item I Give and Divise unto my Beloved Wife Eloner Bean two Cow togather with all my household Goods and moveables of that kind

Item I Give and Divise to my Beloved Daughter Sarah Brown Three Dollars

Item I Give and Divise to my Son John Bean and Josiah Bean all my Estate in Mount Vernon, Both Real and Personal, Not other ways Disposed of, with their paying out Such Leageces as Directed to be Eaquelly Divided Between them

Item I Give and Divise to my Daughter Margret Bean one year old heifer

Item I Give and Divise to my Daughter Phebe Perll Five Dollars

Item I Give and Divise to my Daugher Mary Creasy Five Dollars—

Item I Give and Divise to my Grand Son Neal Bean one hundred Dollars to be paid to him by my Executors when he Shall Come to the age of Twenty one years provided he Shall live so long—

and Lastly I Give and Bequeath to my Said Sons John and Josiah Bean all the Debts Due to me by any Lawfull way or meins whatsoever and I Do hereby Give unto them all those things that may Be forgotten or not Disposed of If If any such there be and order them to pay all my Debts and Leageces and Furnal Charges.

And I Do hereby Nominate and appoint my said Sons John & Josiah Bean Sole Executors of this my Last will and Testament hereby making Null and Void all other former wills and Testements by me heretofore made

In witness whereof I Do hereunto Set my hand and Seal—
Signed Sealed Published and Declared
by the Said Edward Bean to be his
Last will and Testement in the
presence of us—

Nath'l Dudley
Caleb Creasy

      his
Edward X Bean   (seal)
    mark

  her
Submit X Carl
   mark

Probated 16 Jan., 1798. [VIII, 112-113.] Nathaniel Dudley and Stephen Scribner, both of Mount Vernon, sureties. Inventory by William Whittier, Solomon Leighton and John Hovey, all of Mount Vernon, 1798, $280.01; account filed 15 Jan., 1799. [Unrecorded.]

In the Name of God, Amen. I Martha Butler of Georgetown in the county of Lincoln Widow being much advanced in years, and considering the uncertainty of this mortal life, though of sound and disposing mind & memory blessed be God therefor, do make and publish this my last will & testament, in manner & form following, that is to say. First, I give and bequeath unto my beloved son William Butler, of said Georgetown, the sum of one Dollar, in full for his share of my property or estate, of which I may die possessed.

Item—I do also give and bequeath to my beloved son Thomas Butler, of said Georgetown, the sum of one Dollar, in full for his share of my property & estate as aforesaid—

Item—I do also give and bequeath to my beloved Daughter Sarah Butler, of Georgetown Single woman all the provisions of eatables and drinkables of every kind, and description, which may be in my house, or in any manner belong to me at my decease.

Item—I do also give and bequeath to my beloved Daughters, Mary Preble, wife of Joseph Preble of said Town, Anne Drummond, wife of Elijah Drummond of said Town, Martha Soper, wife of Samuel Soper, Sarah Butler above named, and Abigail White, widow of John White, late of said Georgetown deceased, all my wearing apparell, of what nature and description soever, of which I may die possessed, or owner of at the time of my death, to be equally divided in quantity and quality among them my said Daughters; and if any or either of my said Daughters, should die before me, then, and in such case, I will & ordain, that her fifth part of my said wearing apparell, shall go to, and be equally divided between my grand Daughters, the Daughters, of such my deceased Daughter, as may be living at the time of my death; and if such deceased daughter shall then have no Daughter living then the same to go her son or sons, then living.

Item—I do also give and bequeath to my said Daughter Martha Soper, *one Cow*.

Item. I do also give and bequeath to my Grandson, Willam Butler son Son of Thomas Butler aforesaid, *One Cow*.

Item. And as to all the rest, and residue of my property and estate, of what name, nature and description soever, of which I may die the owner, I will and ordain, that, the same shall be equally divided in quantity and quality among my said Daughters, Mary Preble, Anne Drummond, Sarah Butler and Abigail White, their heirs executors & administrators forever: And in case either of my Daughters last mentioned, should die before me, then in such case, I will & ordain, that, the full share and proportion of such my deceased Daughter, shall be equally divided as aforesaid, between such Daughters of her's, as may be living at my death; And in case such deceased Daughter, should have no Daughter living, at the time of my death, then 1 will & ordain that, her full proportion as aforesaid of my estate, shall go to such son, or sons, of my said deceased Daughter equally to be divided between them, as may be living at the time of my death, and to their heirs and assigns forever. And if such my deceased Daughter, should have neither Son or Daughter living at the time of my decease, then in such case, I will and ordain, that, her full share of my said estate, shall be equally divided to & among the remainder of my said last mentioned Daughters, who may be living at the time of my death, and their heirs and assigns forever— And I do by these presents appoint Elijah Drummond & Jeams Williams executor of this my last Will and Testament: Hereby revoking all former Wills by me made. In witness whereof, I do hereunto set my hand & Seal the fifth day of September in the year of our Lord 1796.

Signed, sealed, published & declared
by the above named Martha Butler,   Martha Butler (seal)

to be her last will & testament, in the
presence of us, who have hereunto
subscribed our Names, as Witnesses, in
the presence of the Testatrix—
    John Fisher
    Thomas Williams

Probated 25 May, 1798. [VIII, 114-115.] Joseph Bowker and Mark Langdon Hill, both of Georgetown, sureties. Inventory by Thomas Williams, of Bath, Andrew Mcfaden and Brooks Mckinney, both of Georgetown, 28 May, 1799, $165.85. [Unrecorded.]

In the Name of God. Amen. The seventeen day of February in the year of our Lord one thousand seven hundred & ninety eight—I Thomas Sproul of Bristol, in the County of Lincoln, & Commonwealth of Massachusetts yeoman being sick and weak in Body but of perfect mind and memory, thanks be given unto God therefor calling unto mind the mortality of my Body & knowing that it is appointed for all men once to die, do make and ordain this my last will and Testament; that is to say.—
First of all I give & recommend my Soul into the hands of God that gave it, for my Body I recommend it to the earth to be buried in a Christian like & decent manner, at the discretion of my Executor.— And as touching such wordly estate wherwith it hath pleased God to bless me in this life, I give demise & dispose of the same in the following manner & form.
First It is my will, & I do order, that all my Just debts and funeral charges be paid & satisfied.
Item—I give & bequath my Honored & beloved mother sixty six Dollars & sixty six Cents. Likewise I constitute and appoint my said mother my sole Executor and administrator of this my last will & Testament—
Item—I give & bequeath unto my loving Sister Sarah Sproul Sixty six Dollars & Sixty six Cents—
Item—I give and bequeath unto my loving Sister Mary Sproul Sixty six Dollars & Sixty six Cents—
Item—I give & bequeath to my beloved Brother James Sproul the one half of my Land, and when said land is divided his half to be the eastren side—
Item—I give and bequath to my loving Brother John Sproul the

other half of my land it being the westren side—he paying to my said Mother and my two sisters aforesaid that is to each of them the sum of Sixty six Dollars & Sixty six Cents

Item—I give & Bequeath unto my loving sister Susan Sproul the sum of fifteen Dollars.

Item—I give & Bequeath unto my Brothers Robert Sproul & Wm. Sproul Likewise my Sisters Catherane Silvester & Margret Clark, to each of them fifty Cents—

Item—I Likewise give & Bequeath to my said Brother James Sproul all my Clothing & appearl, one Horse Saddel and Bridel one yoke of Steer and one Chest,—said horse to be keept on the place for the use of my said Mother as long as She lives—he the said James to pay to the above named Susan Sproul fifteen Dollars, and fifty Cents to be paid to each of the above Named Robt. Wm Catherane & Margret Likewise to pay what charges may arise at my Funeral

In Testimoney I the said Thomas Sproul do hereunto in the Presence of these Witnesses set my hand and seal

Signed Sealed Published and declared in presence of

Thomas Sproul (seal)

 Thos. Johnston
 William Johnston
 Thomas Johnston Jun'r

 Probated 17 Sep., 1798. VIII, 116.] Thomas Johnston and William McIntyer, both of Bristol, sureties. Inventory by William McIntyer, Samuel Clark and Joseph Clark, all of Bristol, 29 Dec., 1798, $558.10. [Unrecorded.]

In the Name of God Amen I David Persons of Fairfield in the County of Lincoln & Common wealth of Massachussetts Yeoman being Very Sick & weak in Body but of sound & Disposing minde & memory Do make & ordain this my last will & testament principally & first of all I Give & Recommend my Soul into the hand of all mighty God that Give it & my Body I Recommend to the Earth to Be Buried In Decent Buril at the Discretion of my Executors: And as touching my worldy Estate wherewith it hath pleased God to Bless me in this life First I will that all my Just Debts be paid Secondly I Give & Bequeath unto my Son David: all my Real Estate he paying to Each of my other Children the Severrall Sums in manner & form following (Vizt) to my Daughter Jane the Sum of Eighty Dollars when she arievs to the age of twenty four years & to Each of my other Children (vit) to my Daughters Melende Rachel & Diodami & to my Son William the Sum of twenty Dollars Each to be paid unto them when the youngest (of them) vit my Daughter Diodamia Shall arive to the age of twenty one years & whereas my wife Thankfull is now pregnant I will that the Child or Children whereof She is now pregnant Should be Conceded in this my last will & testament to be made Equal with my other Children through my Estate I Give bequethe my Personall Estate unt my wife thankfull & unto my Children to be Distributed In Equal Shares among them Reserving to my wife Thankfull the use & Improvement of all my Estate Both Real & personal During the tearm of time She Shall Remain my widdow & the use & Improvement of one third part of the whole of my Estate both Real & personal During her natural life & I do hereby Constitute & appoint my true & Loving wife Thankfull Executrix together with George Hobbs of Fairfield Yeoman and Ezekiel Brown Ju'r of Clinton Physician Executors of this my last will and Testament Revoking all former wills And I do hereby Ratify & Confirm this & no other to be my last will & Testament In witness whereof I have hereunto Set my hand & Seal this Eighteenth Day of October in the year of our Lord Seventeen hundred & Ninety Eight the words Revoking all former wills was Interlined before Signing—

David Pearson (seal)

Signed Sealed published pronounced and Declared by the Said David persons as his last will and testam't In the presence of us who in his presence & In the presence of Each other have hereunto Subscribed our names

  Jonathan Emery
  Ruth Lamb
  Rachel Perral

Probated 15 Jan., 1799. [VIII, 117-118.] Elnathan Sherwin, of Winslow, and Jonathan Emery, of Fairfield, sureties. Inventory by William Kendal, Jonas Dutton and James Lamb, all of Fairfield, 1799, $981.39. [XIII, 370-1.] Account filed 26 Aug., 1800. [XIII, 371-2.]

In the Name of God Amen. I Michael Sevey of Pownalborough in the County of Lincoln Gent'n being far advanced in Life & calling to mind the uncertainty of humane Life, & being thro' the goodness of God of sound & disposing Mind & Memory, do make this my last

Will & testament, & disposition of what personal Estate I may leave in manner following That is to say.

First I give & bequeath unto my beloved Wife Hannah all the household Goods & personal Estate, that she brought to me at the Time I married her

Secondly I give & bequeath to my beloved Children named in this bequest viz William John Hannah Stephen & Marcy five shillings apiece (they having received their share of my Estate,) to be paid by my Executor hereafter named

Thirdly I give & bequeath to my beloved Son Solomon all the rest & residue of my personal Estate of what nature soever, to enable him to pay the aforesaid Legacies & my just Debts, (having otherwise provided for my decent burial,) and I do make & constitute my said Son Solomon the Executor of this my last will & testament & hereby revoke & disannul all former Wills & declare this to be my last Will and Testament. In witness whereof I hereto set my hand & Seal the twentieth day of May in the year of our Lord one thousand seven hundred & ninety five.

Signed sealed prounced & declared   Michael Sevey (seal)
by the Testator to be his last Will
in Testament in presence of
  Joseph Lowell Junr.
  Samuel Young
  Tho. Rice

Probated 3 June, 1799. [VIII, 119.] Paul Nute and Solomon Sevey, Jr., both of Pownalborough, sureties. Inventory by Abraham Nason, Seth Tinkham and Josiah Goddard, all of Pownalborough,— June, 1799, $153.71. [Unrecorded.]

In the name of God Amen, I Stephen Stapel of Topsham in the County of Lincoln & CommonWealth of Massachusetts Yeoman, considering the uncertainty of this mortal life, and being of sound mind & memory, Blessed be Almighty God for the same, do make and publish this my last will & testament, in manner & form following that is to say. First I give and Bequeath unto my beloved Wife Susanna one third part of my Estate both Real & personal. I do also give and bequeath unto my eldest son Joseph six shillings, Lawf. money. I do also give and bequeath unto my son Ephraim a Cow or the Value thereof I do also give and bequeath unto my son John six shillings L money. I do also give and bequeath unto my Daughter Lucy a Cow. I do also give and bequeath unto my Daughter Anna a Cow. I do also give and bequeath unto my two Grand Children by the name of Potter, one year old Heiffer each, my three sons Josiah Daniel & James I give & bequeathe the remainder of my Estate, both Real & personal each one an Equal share It is my will that my son Robert shall be put to some trade which he may chose and untill he is of age to chuse a trade I put him in Care of my Son Josiah if my said Son Robert should not go to any trade it is my will that he be paid half a share of one of my three last mentioned sons

I appoint my Son Josiah sole Executor of this my last will & testament; hereby revoking all former wills by me made. In Witness Whereof, I have hereunto set my hand & Seal this Seventeenth day of November One thousand seven hundred & Ninety-Eight.

his
Stephen X Stapel (seal)
mark

Signed, seal'd, publish'd
and declared by the above
named Stephen Stapel
to be his last will & testament
in the presence of us who have
hereunto subscribed our names
as Witnesses in the presence
of the Testator.—

Alexander Rogers
Samuel Winchell
William Doggett

Probated 4 Jan., 1799. [VIII, 121-2.] Alexander Rogers and Samuel Winchell, both of Topsham, sureties. Inventory by John Rogers, John Sanford and Joseph Berry, all of Topsham, 9 Jan., 1799, $775.78. [VIII, 32.]

In the Name of God Amen. I David McKenney of Pownalborough in the County of Lincoln yeoman, being in a decaying state of health & calling to mind that I must soon die, but of sound & disposing mind & memory, do make this my last will & testament in manner following.—
In the first place I recommend my Soul to the hands of God who gave it, & my Body to the Earth to be decently buried by my Executor hereafter named, in full confidence that it will, at the general Resurrection be raised & reunited to my Soul, & enter upon an eternal Existance of happiness thro' the Atonement of the great Redeemer.

And as to my worldly Estate with which God has blessed me I will & dispose of it in manner following

First I will & direct that all my just debts be paid out of my personal Estate by my Executor.

Seconlyly. I give & bequeath to my Son Jonathan thirty Acres of Land lying on Jewanka Neck so called to hold to him & his Heirs forever

Thirdly. I give & bequeath to my Sons Daniel & David seven Acres of Land lying at the northwest Corner of the Land I have herein bequeathed to my Son Jonathan. Also my home place, also one Acre & half of Thatch beds with one Acre of upland lying at Monsweeg so called to hold to them & their heirs forever in equal moietys or shares

Fourthly. I give & bequeath to my four youngest Children viz Jonathan Martha Daniel & David my Pew in the Meeting house at Wiscasset to be possessed by them in equal shares.

Fifthly. I give & bequeath to my five Daughters viz Molly Honewell Katherine Hilton Keziah Gatchel Sarah Hilton and Martha McKenney thirteen Dollars & thirty three Cents each to be paid out of my personal Estate, by my Executor, if it should prove sufficient, if not, then & in that case any deficiency to be paid & made up by my said Sons in equal share out of what I have willed to them as they severally come of Age

Sixthly. I give & bequeath to the heirs of my Son James dec'd three Dollars & thirty three Cents to be equally divided between them, & to be paid out of my personal Estate

Seventhly. If after paying Debts, Legacies & expences of probate any thing should be left of my personal Estate my will is, that the same be equally divided among my aforesaid Sons

And I do hereby nominate & appoint Abraham Nason of said Pownalboro' yeoman Executor of this my last Will & testament & hereby revoke & disannul all former Wills & declare this to be my last will & testament

Signed sealed published & declared by
the Testator to be his last will & testament

in presence of	The word Daughters	David McKenney (seal)
Tho. Rice	erased & Sons inserted	
Rebecca Rice	in presence & by desire	
William Rice	of the Testator	

Probated 5 Ap., 1799. [VIII, 123-4.]

Israel Hunnewell and John Getchel, Jr., both of Pownalborough, sureties. Inventory by Seth Tinkham, Jesse White & Moses Hilton, all of Pownalborough, 1799, $948. [VIII, 82-3.] Abraham Nason of Pownalborough, guardian unto David, minor son, 5 Ap., 1799. [IX, 177.] Jesse White, of Wiscasset, guardian unto David, minor son, 5 Jan., 1803. [IX, 193.] Jonathan and Daniel, minor sons, chose Abraham Nason, to be their guardian, 5 Ap., 1799. [IX, 228.]

I Benjamin Swett of Georgetown and County of Lincoln and Common Welth of Massachusetts Shipwight now being of Sound mind and memery but Suposing I am Drawing near the hour of Death make this my last Will and testement as foloeth in the first place I Will and bequath my praches and imortal Soul to God from home I Recived it in Hoapes of Reciving the Same at the Reaseraction of the Just to life Eternal and my tempral intrest I Dispose of in the foloing manner Viz first I Will and bequath to my Son John a Sartean note against Rachel MCobb for the Sume of forty two Dollers Which he has Recived in the Second place I Will and bequath to my Son Benjamin the one half of my homested farm together With the one half of my Stock bulding and privileges their to belong in the Second place I Will and bequath to my two sons William and James the other half of my farme in the Same manner as before mentioned in third place I Will and bequath to my only and Dutifull Daughter Sarah one fether bed and beding in prepotion to the Rest of my Beds one Cow Six Sheep the bed and Cow She is to Recive at my Death and I Do ordain and order that she Shall have one Room in my house During her living Single and on married and to have the profits of the Cow and half the Wool of the Sheep yearly and if She Shold marrey my Son Benjamin is to Give her one other Cow and the Six Sheep is to be given her out of the Stock and I Do ordan and order that Said Cow Shall be maintained on the farm at the Expence of my Son or Sons that live on the farm and if She marrey the other Cow and Six Sheep is to be Delivered to her on Demand Item and I Do ordain and order that my Son Benjamin pay to my Son John one hundred Dollers fifty Dollers to be paid in the term of one year the other fifty in the term of two years and I Do ordain and order that my two Sons William and James pay to my Son John fifty Dollers Dollers Each in the Same manner as Benjamin is to pay and I Do ordain and order that if my Daughter Sarah Should marrey that my two Sons William and James Shall pay to her twenty five Dollers Each Within the term of two years and it is to be under Stood that her Room in the house is to be a Comforable Room and that is not to be Distrubed in it Without her Consent it is also to be under Stood that the other half of my Stock is to pay Charges and Debets if their be any arise and the Remand if any the be is for my Son Benjamin

and I Do Constitute and apointe Benjamin Pattee and my Son Benjamin to be my Executors to this my laste Will and testement NB all the Words araced and Counter lined Was Don before this Was Signed in Witnis hereof I have Sett my hand and Seal this 10th Day of June in the year of our lord one thousand Seven hundred and Ninty nine

Sealed Signed and Develard
in pracence of   Benjamin Swett   (seal)
William Stinson
Nathaniel Morse
Jain Power

Probated 30 Oct., 1799. [VIII, 142.] Jordan Parker and Denny McCobb, both of Georgetown, sureties. Inventory by Mark Langdon Hill, William Butler and Charles Couillard, all of Georgetown, gentlemen, 28 Mar., 1800, $1045. [VIII, 161-2.]

In the name of God Amen, I Thomas Rodbird of New Milford in the County of Lincoln and Common-wealth of Massachusets being in sound mind memmory and understanding do make and publish this my last will and testament in manner and form following that is to say I order and direct that all my just debts and funeral expences shall be paid out of my personal Estate by my executrix hereafter named :—I give and bequeath unto my Wife Martha Rodbird all Possession right title and interest that I have of and in all that land and Buildings which I purchased from Samuel Soul situated in New-milford and being the same on which I now live,—the same to be to her use and disposal and to her heirs Administrators or Assigns forever I also give and bequeath unto my said Wife Martha Rodbird the whole of my personal Estate let the same be in money, money at interest, notes, bonds, goods, or Chattels, or whatever else to her sole Use and benefit forever.—Except as hereafter is excepted Viz I give and bequeath unto my son Thomas Rodbird one Dollar only, to be paid to him by my Executrix hereafter named I also give and bequeath unto my son William Rodbird one Dollar only to be paid to him by my Executrix hereafter named.—I also give and bequeath one guinea unto my two Brothers Absolam and John Rodbird and Mary Hall my Sister the same to be divided in equal shares betwixt them and to be paid them by my Executrix hereafter named.

I also give and bequeath one guinea to my Mother Jane Rodbird to be paid to her by my Executrix hereafter named.

I also give and bequeath all residue and remainder of my Estate either real or personal be it whatever or wheresoever that I am or ever shall have rights to or Possession of unto my said Wife Martha Rodbird to her heirs Executors Administrators or Assigns for her or their sole Use or Benefit forever.

Lastly I do hereby Nominate and appoint my said Wife Martha Rodbird sole Executrix of this my last will and testament and do hereby revoke all former Wills by me made.—In witness whereof I the said Thomas Rodbird have hereunto sign'd my name and fix'd my Seal this Eleventh Day of October in the Year of our Lord one thousand seven hundred and ninety nine—

Sign'd seal'd and delivered in the presence of us who have sign'd our names as witnesses hereto being in one Room and in the presence of each other and in the presence of him the said Thomas Rodbird the testator Amos Soule John Jones and John Stuart

Thomas Rodbard (seal)
X
his Mark

Probated 29 Ap., 1800. [VIII, 145-6.]
Alexander Troup and William Taylor, both of Wiscasset, sureties.

In the Name of God Amen

I Andrew Schenck of Waldoborough, in the County of Lincoln and Commonwealth of Masachusets Gentleman—being in Perfect health and of Sound Memory and understanding, but—Considering the uncertainty of this Transitory Life, Do make publish and Declare this my last will and Testament, in Manner and form Following (to wit)

first of all, I Give and Commend my Soul to Almighty God my Creator, hoping through his Mercy and the Merits of my Savour Jesus Christ, I shall injoy Eternal Life my Body I Commit to the Earth, to be Decently Buried at the Discretion of my Executors hear after named, and as for what Worldly Estate which it hath Pleased God to bless me with I Give and Dispose hereof as followeth.

Imprimis. After payment of my Just Debts, and funeral Charges—I Give and bequeath unto my beloved Wife Sarah Schenck—one third part of all my Real Estate During her Life—to Gather with one third of my Personal Estate—

Item—I Give and bequeath unto my Eldest Daughter Sofiah Fitzgerald Two hundred Pounds Lawful money unto my Daughter Sofiah, Payable twelve months after after my Decease to and for her use During her Natural Life, and after here Decease, then, I Give and Devise the Same to My Grant Children, the Heirs of her Body Lawfully to be, be Gotten, Equally to be Devited betwixt them

Item—I Give and bequeath unto my other Daughter Catherina Cole, Two hundred Pounds Lawfull money, unto my Daughter Catharina Payable Twelve months after my Decease, to and for her use, During her Natural Life, and after her Decease, then I Give and bequeath the Same to my Grant Children the Heirs of her Body Lawfully to be begotten, Equally to be Devited betwixt them

Also: I Give and bequeath to my two Daughters, Sofiah Fitzgerald and Catharina Cole Two Thirds of my House Hold Furniture at my Decease to be Delivered them by my Executors—Also: I order my Executors to pay the Legacy before mentioned out of my Personal Estate at the time before Mentioned—

Item: I Give and bequeath unto my three Grand Sons:—James—John: and Andrew: being Children and heirs of my beloved Son George Schenck Deceased—one half of my Real Estate, to Gather with one half of my Personal Estate, not hear to fore Disposed of, they Paying to their three Sisters, Mary: Chrischana: & Lucy: Sixty Pounds to be Equally Devited and paid them, twelve months after my Decease by my Executors out of my Personal Estate

Item: I Give and bequeath unto my beloved Son James Shenck, and the heirs of his Body to be Lawfully to be begotten, the Remaining half of my Real and Personal Estate—and for Default of Such Issue, then to my three Grand Sons Viz James; John & Andrew above mentioned

Also: I order my Executors to Let my three Grand Sons above Named James: John: & Andrew improve the Estate of James Schenck above Devise, untill he Shall Legally Demand the Same, and if no Legal Demand be made within ten years after my Decease the Property to be Delivered them to and for their own use

And I make and Appoint Waterman Thomas Esqr: Jacob Ludwig Gentleman Both of Waldoborough in the County of Lincoln; Executors of this my Last will and Testament, and Do here by revoke all other and former wills, by me at any time hereto fore made, and Do Make and Declare this only to be my Last will and Testament—in

Witness whereof I Do hereunto Set my hand and Seal this Eighteenth Day of June, in the year of our Lord one thousand Seven hundred & Eighty eight—

Andrew Schenck (seal)

Signed Sealed Published and Pronounced by the Said Andrew Schenck as his Last will and Testament in the Presence of us, who in his Presence, and in the Presence of Each other, have here unto Subscribed our Names
Joseph Ludwig
Jacob Winchenbach
Godfrey Bornheimer

Probated 5 Ap., 1799. [VIII, 162-3.]
Waterman Thomas renounced executorship 5 Ap., 1799. William McIntyer and Ebenezer Blunt, both of Bristol, sureties. Inventory by John Farley, of Newcastle, Joseph Ludwig and Jacob Winchenbach, both of Waldoborough, 22 Ap., 1800, $4014.61. Widow's dower set off by Charles Samson, Jacob Winchenbach and Joseph Ludwig, all of Waldoborough, 27 June, 1800. Account filed 10 Aug., 1803. [Unrecorded.]

In the name of God Amen—I Henry Hunter of Bristol in the County of Lincoln, State of Massachusetts Bay being in Health of Body & of a Sound Mind, but sensible of my liableness to be removed from time to Eternity, do make this my last Will & testament

First I bequeath my Soul to God who gave it, looking for Salvation in & thro the merits & Mediation of the Lord Jesus Christ—

I give my Body to the Earth from whence it sprung in full assurance of its Resurrection from thence at the great day As to my burial I desire that it may be done decently, at the Discretion of my Wife & Executor hereafter mentioned—

As to my Worldly Estate, I order that any debts I owe may be paid— I give my dear Wife Sarah the whole of my Furniture & Stock of Cattle, to dispose of as she pleases, besides one half of my dwelling House & one half of the Farm I occupy & improve, call'd the home farm, during the Term of her life—

I give to my Daughter Nancy McClure the sum of ten dollars or a Garden spot to the Southward of her House which is now plowed, at her Option—

To my son Henry I give one half of the home farm formerly mentioned, during his Mothers life time, & the whole at her death with fifty Acres Land more or less lying back of Robert Thompsons Lot—To my Son John I give as his part two hundred Acres of the Land I have at Sandy River of which I propose to give him a deed hereafter—To my Son David I give another Lot of Land at Sandy River, which my Son Henry purchas'd of Ephraim Rollands of Nobleborough, of which the foresaid David has receiv'd a deed already—

To my Daughter Sarah Chamberlain, I give ten Dollars

To my Son William I give one hundred Acres Land at Sandy River, also the back Lot where Boston Miller some time ago lived, he paying to his Brother James when of Age the Sum of two hundred Dollars

I give to my Son James also two hundred Acres of Land at Sandy River

To my Son Thomas I give two hundred Acres Land at Sandy River, besides the Sum of two hundred Dollars to be paid him when he is of Age by his Brother Henry & I appoint the Rev'd Alex'r MacLean of Bristol & my beloved Wife Sarah Hunter Executors of this my last Will & testament—

Sign'd & sealed before these Witnesses   Henry Hunter (seal)
this twentieth day of February one thousand
seven hundred & ninety eight years—

  John Huston
  Robert Huston
  William Huston

  Probated 3 June, 1799. [VIII, 167-8.] Robert Huston and John Huston, sureties. Inventory by Thomas Johnston, Richard Hiscock and Samuel Woodward, all of Bristol, 20 June, 1799, $2893.65

In the name of GOD amen

  I Alexander Nickels of Bristol in the County of Lincoln Esquire, considering the uncertainty of this mortal life, and being of sound and perfect mind, blessed be almighty GOD for the same—Do make and publish this my last Will and testament in manner and form following that is to say, First. I Give and bequeath unto my beloved Wife Margaret the Sum of Two hundred pounds lawful Money, to be raised in manner following and paid to her—the one half in twelve months from the time of my Decease and the other half in twelve months thereafter, with Interest from those periods untill paid, subject to her own proper will as she then in her discretion may see cause to Dispose of, in full of her right of Dower

I also give and bequeath to my eldest son James his Heirs and Assigns All that my one half of the Island of land called Green Island situate lying & being in Penobscot bay in the County of Hancock: to hold the same to him and his Heirs and Assigns for Ever—
I also Give and bequeath to my Son Alexander the sum of six shillings, Considering that much with the Gifts in my life time to him in full of All that he ought to receive—
I also give and bequeath to my Youngest son John his Heirs and Assigns, All that my Mansion house, barn, buildings and tenements situate lying & being at Pemequid Old Fort in Bristol aforesaid, with all my other lands in lots or parcels situate lying & being thereat or thereabouts; And to him my said son John I also give and bequeath all those my two Islands of land, the one known by the name of fishermans Island situate lying and being in Boothbay in the County of Lincoln the other known by the Name of Ragged Arse situate lying and being near unto Metinicus Island in Penobscot bay aforesaid. To Hold the said House barn buildings, tenements and lots or parcels of land, now in my use and occupation or in the use and occupation of my said son John, to him his Heirs and Assigns for Ever Under the burthen of paying the aforesaid Sum of two hundred pounds to my beloved Wife Margaret in manner as hereinbefore mentioned
And lastly as to all the Rest, residue and remainder of My Estate both Real and personal whether Rights, debts Goods or Chattels of what kind or Nature soever, After that all Demands against Me or my Estate are satisfied, I Do give and bequeath the same to my sons James, William and John and to my Daughter Hannah the Wife of George Rogers, that is to each of them in severalty their Heirs and Assigns One equal fifth part thereof, and to the children of my son Alexander I give and bequeath the other equal fifth part of the same, under the management and direction of my Executors as trustees in that behalf to the use of the said children untill they arrive at Mature age—
And I Do hereby nominate and appoint my said sons James and John to be the Executors of this my last Will and testament

In witness whereof I have hereunto set my hand and seal the twenty seventh day of May in the year of our Lord One thousand seven hundred ninety six—

      Alexander Nickels   (seal)

Signed, sealed, published and declared
by the above named Alexander Nickels

Esquire to be his last Will & testament in the presence of us who have hereunto subscribed our names as Witnesses, in presence of the testator

Sally Simonton
Ezra Poland
Robert McLintock

Probated 2 July, 1799. [VIII, 169-170.] William McIntyer and Ebenezer Blunt, both of Bristol, sureties.

In the name of God, Amen. I Ichabod Pinkham of Boothbay in the County of Lincoln & Commonwealth of Massachusetts, gentleman, being weak in body but of sound & perfect mind and memory, blessed be Almighty God for the same; do make & publish this my last will & testament, in manner and form following that is to say

1st. I give & bequeath unto my oldest son Benjamin Pinkham forty-seven acres of land, where he now dwells.

2dly. I give unto my son Ichabod Pinkham the farm where he now dwells, which formerly belonged to my late father Benjamin Pinkham, with the buildings thereon, reserving however a road from the highway to the saw & grist mills, where the same will be most convenient, he the said Ichabod paying unto my oldest daughter Mary Adams or her order two hundred dollars, within two years after my decease.

3dly. I give unto my son Nathaniel Pinkham, the whole of the land known by the name of the Kennedy farm, which land I purchased of Ruth & Ann Kennedy, he the said Nathaniel paying, within two years after my decease, one hundred dollars unto my beloved wife Marcy Pinkham: The above devises of lands to my said sons, the above conditions being performed, to be to them their heirs & assigns forever.

4thly. I give & order unto my oldest daughter Mary Adams, one hundred dollars to be paid her within one year after my decease.

5thly. I give to my daughter Sally one hundred dollars to be paid her within one year after my decease.

6thly. I give to my daughter Polly one hundred dollars to be paid her within two years after my decease.

7thly. I give to my daughter Patty one hundred dollars to be paid her within four years after my decease.

8thly. My will is that my youngest daughter Betsey be maintained and supported out of the remainder of my Estate, during her natural life.

9thly. I also give & bequeath to my sons Benjamin & Nathaniel one half of my salt marsh & upland adjoining the same, laying on Wild cat meadow creek, so called, equally between them, they the said Benjamin and Nathaniel or either of them, keeping in good repair the fence around the whole marsh, during the natural life of my said wife, their mother.

10thly. I give and bequeath unto my beloved wife Marcey Pinkham the whole, rest and residue of my whole estate, real and personal, let the same be found where it may, during her natural life, she paying my just debts, and providing for my said youngest daughter Betsey as aforesaid, and at the decease of my said wife, my will is that the whole estate then remaining, after making provision for Betsey, as aforesaid, be equally divided amongst my surviving children.

11thly and lastly. I appoint my son Benjamin Pinkham and my beloved wife Marcey Pinkham, to be my sole executor & executrix of this my last will & testament, hereby revoking all former wills by me made. In witness whereof I have hereunto set my hand & seal, this fifteenth day of October, in the year of our Lord, one thousand eight hundred.

            Ichabod Pinkham (seal)

Signed, sealed, published & declared by the
above named Ichabod Pinkham to
be his last will & testament in the
presence of us who have hereunto subscribed our names as witnesses in the
presence of the Testator.
      Wm McCobb
      Nath'l Pinkham
      Martha Pinkham
       Probated 25 Nov., 1800. [VIII, 171-2]
Inventory by John Leishman, John Emerson and Jonathan Sawyer, all of Boothbay, 1801, $5260.55. [VIII, 183-4.]

Richard Tucker, late of Pownalborough, mariner. Joanna Tucker, of Pownalborough, widow, Adm'x, 19 Feb., 1798. [IX, 1.] David Silvester, Jr., and Ezekiel Cutter, both of Pownalborough, sureties. Inventory by Joseph Tinkham, John Hues and Ezekiel Cutter, all of Pownalborough, 26 Mar., 1798, $620.85. [VIII, 34.] Joanna, widow, guardian unto Richard Hawley, minor son, 3 Jan., 1799. [IX, 179.]

John Hues, Jr., late of Pownalborough, merchant. Elizabeth Hues, of Pownalborough, widow, Adm'x, 7 Mar., 1798. [IX, 2.] Ebenezer Whittier and David Silvester, both of Pownalborough, sureties. Inventory by Thomas Rice, Joseph Tinkham and William Pike, all of Pownalborough, 2 June, 1798, $305.01. [VIII, 30-31.]

Thomas Winch, late of Pownalborough, mariner. Priscilla Winch, of Pownalborough, widow, Adm'x, 2 May, 1798. [IX, 2.] Joseph Tinkham and Joseph Christophers, both of Pownalborough, sureties. Inventory by Joseph Tinkham, Seth Tinkham and Abiel Wood, Jr., all of Pownalborough, 4 June, 1798, $86.60. [VIII, 62-63.] Account filed 19 Dec., 1800, at which date the administratrix had become the wife of James Lowell. [Unrecorded.]

Benjamin Shaw, late of Woolwich. Josiah Shaw, of Woolwich, mariner, Adm'r, 22 Jan., 1798. [IX, 3.] James Fullerton, of Woolwich, and Samuel Goodwin, Jr., of Dresden, sureties. Inventory by James Fullerton, Benjamin Trott and David Gilmore, all of Woolwich, 14 Mar., 1798, $706.58. [VIII, 68.]

Arnold Sweet, late of Winthrop. Polly Sweet, of Winthrop, widow, Adm'x, 31 May, 1798. [IX, 3.] Inventory by Nathaniel Fairbanks, William Pullen and Silas Lambert, all of Winthrop, 5 Oct., 1798, $1215.28. [VIII, 15.]

Daniel Morse, late of Georgetown. Jonathan Morse, of Georgetown, Adm'r, 25 May, 1798. [IX, 4.] Mark Langdon Hill and Joseph Bowker, both of Georgetown, sureties.

William Dodge, late of Newcastle. Nancy Dodge, of Newcastle, widow, Adm'x, 1 May, 1798. [IX, 4.] David Somes, of Newcastle, and William Nickels, of Pownalborough, sureties.

Bunker Farwell, late of Augusta. Mary Farwell, of Augusta, widow, and Ebenezer Farwell, of Vassalborough, Adm'rs, 16 Jan., 1798. [IX, 5.] John Jones, of Augusta, and Ichabod Thomas, of Sidney, sureties. Inventory by William Howard, John Jones and Samuel Colman, all of Augusta, 9 Ap., 1798, $2449.66. [VIII, 54-55.]

Ichabod Reed, late of Lewiston, joiner. And Reed, of Lewiston, widow, Adm'x, 25 May, 1798. [IX, 5.] Robert Anderson, of Lewiston, and Richard Skolfield, of Brunswick, sureties. Inventory by Joel Thompson, Robert Anderson and Daniel Davis, all of Lewiston, 22 Mar., 1798, $513.43. [VIII, 56-57.] Robert Anderson and Daniel

Davis, commissioners to examine claims. [VIII, 213.] Widow's dower set off by Joel Thompson, Robert Anderson and Daniel Davis, 17 Mar., 1800. [VIII, 214.] Advertisement of sale of real estate 2 Jan., 1810. [VIII, 215.] Accounts filed 29 Oct., 1799, and 27 May, 1800. [VIII, 215-216.]

Samuel Thompson, late of Topsham. Ezekiel Thompson, of a place called Little river, and James Purinton, of Topsham, Admr's, 19 June, 1798. [IX, 6.] Benjamin Ham, of Bath, and James Purinton, of a place called Little river, sureties. Samuel, minor son, chose John Merrill, of Topsham, to be his guardian, 27 May, 1800. [IX, 250.] Inventory of real estate by Joseph Kilgore, Aaron Dwinel and Acter Patten, Jr., all of Topsham, 19 Dec., 1803, $17,833.73 and division of the same 25 Ap., 1806, among James Thompson; Mary, widow of Humphrey Thompson, and heirs of Humphrey Thompson, deceased; Aaron Thompson; Samuel Thompson; Samuel Thompson Mallet; John Wilson and Rachel, his wife; William Wise and Thankful, his wife. [XII, 95 to 104.]

Joseph Merrill, late of Topsham. John Merrill, of Topsham, Adm'r, 6 June, 1798. [IX, 7.] Benjamin Hasey, of Topsham, and John Merrill, Jr., of Pownalborough, sureties.

Zimri Heywood, late of Winslow. Jane Heywood, widow, and Samuel Heywood, both of Winslow, Adm'rs, 25 July, 1798. [IX, 8.] Josiah Crosby, of Winslow, and Samuel Grant, of Clinton, sureties. Inventory by Ezekiel Pattee, Josiah Hayden and Edmund Freeman, all of Winslow, 29 Sep., 1798. [VIII, 36 to 39.] Account filed 2 Feb., 1802. [XIII, 432-3.]

William Reed, late of Boothbay. Martha, widow, declined administration 7 Sep., 1798. John Leishman, of Boothbay, Adm'r, 10 Sep., 1798. [IX, 9.] William McCobb and David Kinnaston, both of Boothbay, sureties. Inventory by John Murray McFarland, Samuel Montgomery and John Dows, all of Boothbay, 15 Sep., 1798, $363.18. [VIII, 41.] William McCobb and Samuel Montgomery, both of Boothbay, commissioners to examine claims. [VIII, 42.] Account filed 3 June, 1799. [VIII, 90.] Distribution of real estate ordered 25 Nov., 1800. [VIII, 129.] Account filed 2 June, 1800. [VIII, 238.] Widow's dower set off by Jonathan Sawyer, John Murray McFarland and Samuel Montgomery, all of Boothbay, 1799. [Unrecorded.]

Samuel Day, late of Boothbay. David Kinnaston, of Boothbay, Adm'r, 10 Sep., 1798. [IX, 10.] William McCobb and John Leishman, both of Boothbay, sureties. Inventory by John Murray McFarland, Samuel Montgomery and John Daws, all of Boothbay, 15 Sep., 1798, $637. William McCobb and Samuel Montgomery, both of Boothbay, commissioners to examine claims. [VIII, 40.] Account filed 3 June, 1799. [VIII, 89.] Account filed and distribution ordered 2 June, 1800. [VIII, 125-6.] Widow's dower set off by Jonathan Sawyer, John Murray McFarland and Samuel Montgomery, all of Boothbay, 1799, at which date the widow had become the wife of the administrator. [XIII, 423.]

James Bird, late of Warren, mariner. Alexander Bird, of Warren, Adm'r, 17 Sep., 1798. [IX, 11.] Samuel Sumner Wilde and James Standish, both of Warren, sureties. Inventory by James Waller Head, Thurston Whiting and Benjamin Brackett, all of Warren, 8 Ap., 1799, $351.50. [Unrecorded.]

Daniel Knights, late of Boothbay. William Knights, of Boothbay, Adm'r, 20 Feb., 1798. [IX, 12.] Daniel Knights and Nathaniel Knights, both of Boothbay, sureties. Inventory by Thomas Ring, John Leishman and Solomon Burnham, all of Boothbay, 18 Ap., 1798, $5275. [VIII, 22-23.]

William Lackey, late of Thomaston, mariner, Olive Lackey, of Thomaston, widow, Adm'x, 17 Sep., 1798. [IX, 12.] Samuel Sumner Wilde, of Warren, and Josiah Keith, of Thomaston, sureties. Inventory by Samuel Brown, David Fales, Jr., and David Jenks, all of Thomaston, 6 Feb., 1799, $719.51; inventory of wine in Boston by Caleb Blanchard, Edward Davis and Jacob Rowe, all of Boston, 29 Oct., 1798, $735.90; account filed 12 Jan., 1802. [Unrecorded.] Distribution of estate ordered 7 May, 1802. [VIII, 132-3,]

Henry Hodge, late of Pownalborough. Sarah Hodge, of Pownalborough, widow, Adm'x, 3 Sep., 1798. [IX, 13.] Thomas Rice, Abiel Wood, Silas Lee and Abiel Wood, Jr., all of Pownalborough, sureties. Inventory by John Hues, Joseph Christophers and David Payson, all of Pownalborough, 3 Nov., 1798, $17,107.15. [XI,123 to 125.] Account filed 29 Jan., 1806. [XI, 126-7.] John Hodge and James Hodge, both of Wiscasset, Admr's *de bonis non*, 20 Sep., 1806. [IX, 108.] Division of dower among Henry Hodge; Joseph Carleton and Margaret, his wife in her right; Orchard

Cook and Mary, his wife in her right; John Hodge; James Hodge; heirs of William Hodge, deceased, 9 July, 1807, by Dummer Sewall, of Bath, William Patterson, of Edgecomb, and Thomas Fairservice of New Milford. [XII, 270 to 272.] Widow's dower set off by Thomas Rice, of Pownalborough, Dummer Sewall, of Bath, and William Patterson, of Edgecomb, 30 Nov., 1800. [Unrecorded.]

William Dinsmore, late of Bowdoinham. Lucinda Dinsmore, of Bowdoinham, widow, Adm'x, 18 July, 1798. [IX, 13.] James Maxwell and Zebulon Preble both of Bowdoinham, sureties. Inventory by Zacheus Beal, George Maxwell and James Bowker, all of Bowdoinham, 1798, $496.67. [VIII, 24-25.] Elihu Getchell, of Bowdoinham, guardian unto Prince and Judith, minor children, 11 Sep., 1805. [IX, 204.] Judith, minor daughter, chose Israel Jones, of Durham, Cunberland County, to be her guardian, 10 Sep., 1806. [IX, 269.]

Bartholomew Kimball, late of Winslow. Nathaniel Kimball, of Pittston, Adm'r, 29 Aug., 1798. [IX, 14.] Henry Smith and John Smith, both of Pittston, sureties. Inventory by William Springer, James Parker and Hugh Cox, all of Hallowell, $152.62, to which the administrator added sundry articles and money $353.56. [Unrecorded.]

John Reed, late of Topsham. Rachel Reed, of Topsham, widow, Adm'x, 18 Aug., 1798. [IX, 14.] David Patten, of Thomaston, and Levi Peterson, of Bath, sureties. Inventory by Alexander Rogers, Arthur Hunter and Benjamin Jones Porter, all of Topsham, 1 Feb., 1799, $3599.58. [VIII, 17-18.]

Joseph Crowell, late of Belgrade. Zadock Crowell, of Belgrade, Adm'r, 16 Aug., 1798. [IX, 15.] Levi Crowell, of Winslow, and Ezekiel Crowell, of Belgrade, sureties. Inventory by Samuel Tiffany and Moses Sawtell, both of Sidney, and Samuel Linnet, of Belgrade, 27 Aug., 1798, $1807.67, to which administrator added sundry articles amounting to $46.41. [VIII, 76-77.]

Daniel Stevens, late of Thomaston. Jerusha Stevens, of Thomaston, widow, Adm'x, 19 Sep., 1797. [IX, 15.] William Rowell and Ephraim Snow, both of Thomaston, sureties.

Joseph White, late of Hallowell. Sally White, widow, and Benjamin Prescott, both of Hallowell, Adm'rs, 15 Jan., 1799. [IX, 16.] Abner Lowell and William Palmer, Jr., both of Hallowell, sureties.

Moses Sewall, late of Hallowell, trader. Ruthy Sewall, of Hallowell, widow, Adm'x, 15 Jan., 1799. [IX, 17.] David Sewall and Nathaniel Perley, both of Hallowell, sureties.

John Braley, late of Sidney. Alice Braley declined administration. John Savage, of Readfield, Adm'r, 15 Jan., 1799. [IX, 17.] Aaron Seekins, of Augusta, and Moses Pollard, of Sidney, sureties.

Joseph Battle, late of Farmington. David Davis, of a place called the New-Vineyard, Adm'r, 15 Jan., 1799, [IX, 18.] Ebenezer Farwell, of Vassalboro, and Heartson Cony, of Farmington, sureties. Inventory by John Holly and Thomas Wendell, both of Farmington, and William Allen, of a place called still water pond, 11 Mar., 1800, $1038.82. [Unrecorded.]

Nathaniel Barstow, late of Bristol, shipcarpenter. Elizabeth Barstow, of Bristol, widow, Adm'x, 11 Feb., 1799. [IX, 18.] Benjamin Cushing, of Camden, and George Barstow, of Newcastle, sureties. Inventory by John Farley, of Newcastle, Elisha Hatch and Richard Hiscock, both of Bristol, $1449.98. [VIII, 217-218.] John Farley and Elisha Hatch, commissioners to examine claims. [VIII, 218.] Widow's dower set off by John Farley, of Newcastle, Benjamin Day, of Bristol, and Jesse Flint, of Nobleboro, 10 May, 1800. [VIII, 220.] Account filed 30 July, 1800. [VIII, 220-1.]

Ebenezer Emerson, late of Topsham, physician. Rebecca Emerson, of Topsham, widow, Adm'x, 4 Mar., 1799. [IX, 19.] George Whitefield Sawyer, of Topsham, and Ebenezer Nickels, of Brunswick, sureties. Inventory by George Whitfield Sawyer, William Wilson and Alexander Rogers, all of Topsham, 22 Mar., 1799, $744.89. [VIII, 29-30.] Distribution of estate ordered 9 Aug., 1802 [VIII, 136-7.] Jonathan R. Parker and William Wilson, both of Topsham, commissioners to examine claims. [VIII, 208-9.] Widow's dower set off by John Merrill, William Wilson and Alexander Rogers, 1800. [VIII, 210.] Advertisement of sale of real estate 5 Feb., 1802. [VIII,211.] Account filed 7 May, 1802. [VIII, 212] Sarah, minor daughter, chose Samuel Stinson, of Woolwich, to be her guardian, 2 Ap., 1807. [IX, 277.]

Hugh Wilson, late of Topsham. Mary Wilson, of Topsham, widow, Adm'x, 6 Mar., 1799. [IX, 19.] George Whitefield Sawyer and Joseph Haley, both of Topsham, sureties. Inventory by John Merrill, Joseph Hayley and James Wilson, all of Topsham, 12 Ap., 1799, $1712.14. [VIII, 20.]

John McKenney, late of Pownalborough. Sarah McKenney, of Pownalborough, widow, Adm'x, 9 Mar., 1799. [IX, 20.] Solomon Walker and Nathaniel Tibbetts, both of Woolwich, sureties. Inventory by Abner Wade, of Woolwich, Jesse White and Moses Hilton, both of Pownalborough, 30 May, 1799, $3260.98. [VIII, 86-87.] George and Catharine, minor children, chose Jesse White to be their guardian, 1800. [IX, 250-1.] Widow's dower set off and estate divided by Abner Wade and Richard Harnden, both of Woolwich, and Abraham Nason, of Pownalborough, 5 Dec., 1800, heirs named: Daniel McKenney, John McKenney, Charles McKenney, Lydia Hunewill, Sarah Walker, Nancy Potter, and Alexander, George, Catharine and Betsey McKenney. [Unrecorded.]

Thomas Burr, late of Bath, cooper. Matthew Burr, of Hingham, Suffolk County, cooper, Adm'r, 23 May, 1799. [IX, 20.] Christopher Cushing and Martin Cushing, both of Bath, sureties. Inventory by Laban Loring, Thomas Clap and Caleb Marsh, all of Bath, 30 May, 1799, $457.31. [VIII, 16.]

William S. McIntyer, late of Bristol, mariner. William McIntyer, of Bristol, Adm'r, 5 Ap., 1799. [IX, 21.] Jacob Ludwig, of Waldoborough, and Ebenezer Blunt, of Bristol, sureties.

James Cook, late of Meduncook, mariner. Else, widow, declined administration. Melzer Thomas, of Meduncook, Adm'r, 19 Ap., 1799. [IX, 21.] Elijah Cook, of Meduncook, and Howland Rogers, of Cushing, sureties. Elsey Cook, of Meduncook, widow, guardian unto Cornelius, Bethiah, James, Francis and Winslow Bradford, minor children, 31 Oct., 1800. [IX, 189.] Nancy and Elsy, minor daughters, chose Elsey, widow, to be their guardian, 31 Oct. 1800. [IX, 240.] Distribution of personal estate 11 Aug., 1803. [X, 15.] Account filed 11 Aug., 1803. [X, 201-2.] Inventory by Benjamin Burton, Paul Jameson and Wellington Gay, all of Meduncook. [Unrecorded.]

Paul Reed, late of Boothbay. Margery, widow, declined administration, 8 Ap., 1799. Andrew Reed, of Georgetown, Adm'r, 24 Ap., 1799. [IX, 22.] Mark Langdon Hill and Joseph Trott, both of Georgetown, sureties. Dower set off to widow, Margery, by John Leishman, William McCobb and Samuel Montgomery, all of Boothbay, 25 Mar., 1801. [XIII, 334-5.] Inventory by John Leishman, Jonathan Sawyer and Samuel Montgomery, all of Boothbay, 1799. [Unrecorded.]

Francis Wyman, late of Georgetown. William Wyman and John Wyman, both of Georgetown, Adm'rs, 31 May, 1799. [IX, 22.] Isaiah Wyman and Jordan Parker, both of Georgetown, sureties.

John Kingsbury, late of Pownalborough. Miriam Kingsbury, of Pownalborough, widow, Adm'x, 22 July, 1799. [IX, 23.] William Stinson and Robert Greenough, both of Pownalborough, sureties. Inventory by Joseph Christophers, Daniel Scott and Reuben Young, all of Pownalborough, Oct., 1799, $471.66. [VIII, 144.] Account filed 10 May, 1805. [XI, 77.]

Solomon Hutchens, late of Edgecomb, mariner. Elijah Brown, of Edgecomb, Adm'r, 3 June, 1799. [IX, 23.] John Bray Dearing and Stephen Adams, both of Edgecomb, sureties. Inventory by Moses Davis, William Patterson and David Trask, all of Edgecomb, 24 Aug., 1799, $240.24. [VIII, 175.]

James Auld, late of Boothbay. James Auld, of Boothbay, Adm'r, 3 June, 1799. [IX, 24.] David Kinnaston and Benjamin Kelley, Jr., both of Boothbay, sureties James Auld, guardian unto Peggy and Jenny, minor daughters, 11 May, 1804. [IX, 184.] Samuel, Rachel, Sally and William, minor children, chose James Auld to be their guardian 13 Nov., 1802. [X, 231.] Inventory by William McCobb, Jonathan Sawyer and John Leishman, all of Boothbay, $1202.98; dower of Frances Auld, widow, set off by Jonathan Sawyer, John Leishman and Thomas Boyd, all of Boothbay, 1802. [Unrecorded.]

Susanna Reed, late of Topsham, widow. Samuel Wilson, Adm'r, 29 Oct., 1799. Inventory by Jonathan Ellis and William Randall, both of Topsham, and Samuel Tibbets, of Bowdoinham, 1 Nov., 1799, $128. William Randall and Arthur Hunter, both of Topsham, commissioners to examine claims, 28 Jan., 1800. [Unrecorded.] Distribution ordered 9 Aug., 1802. [VIII, 131.]

Thomas Denham, late of Bowdoinham. Catherine Denham, widow, declined to administer, 27 Jan., 1800. William Denham, of Bowdoinham, Adm'r, 29 Jan., 1800. [IX, 30.] Zacheus Beal and Ziba Eaton, both of Bowdoinham, sureties. Inventory by Thomas Reed, of Bowdoinham, Joseph Sprague and William Fairfield, both of Topsham, 1800, $850.35, to which Adm'r added sundry notes of hand, etc., $371.33. Nathaniel Thwing, of Woolwich, and Stephen Whitmore, of Bowdoinham, commissioners to examine claims, 27 May, 1800. [VIII, 194 to 196.] Distribution ordered 2 Feb., 1802. [VIII, 130.]

Samuel Ball, late of Boothbay. Mary Ball, of Boothbay, widow, Adm'x, 10 Dec., 1800. [IX, 30.] Levi Ball and Solomon Pinkham, Jun'r, both of Boothbay, sureties. Inventory by William McCobb, Jonathan Sawyer and John Leishman, all of Boothbay, 26 Mar., 1801, $378.41. [VIII, 204.] Account of Solomon Pinkham, Jr., Adm'r *de bonis non*, filed 9 Aug., 1802. [VIII, 205-206.] Widow's dower set off by William McCobb, John Leishman and John McFarland, all of Boothbay, 11 Oct., 1802. [X, 60-61.] William McCobb and Jonathan Sawyer, commissioners to examine claims, 11 May, 1803. [X, 161-162.]

John Hathaway, late of Cambden. Benjamin Cushing, of Cambden, Adm'r, 7 Nov., 1799. [IX, 31.] William Gregory, Jr., and Edward Payson, both of Cambden, sureties. Inventory by Samuel Jacobs, Ephraim Wood and Joshua Dillingham, all of Cambden, 22 Jan., 1800, $2125.26. [XIII, 318-319.]

Thomas Stevens, (Stephens,) late of Georgetown. Charles Stephens, of Georgetown, Adm'r, 4 Dec., 1800. [IX, 31.] Benjamin Tarr and David Hunt, both of Georgetown, sureties. Inventory by Denny McCobb, David Hunt and James McFadden, all of Georgetown, 17 Jan., 1801, $322. [Unrecorded.] Account filed 16 Nov., 1802. [Unrecorded.] Division of real estate by Lewis Thorp, Thomas Lennan and John Campbell, all of Georgetown, 15 Jan., 1807, among Charles; Thomas; Mary, wife of Henry Mellus; Drusilla, wife Shubael Seallye; Charity, wife of Aaron Belden. [Unrecorded.]

Solomon Potter, late of a place called Balltown. Aaron Potter, of Balltown, Adm'r, 1 July, 1800. [IX, 58.] John Philbrook and William Fowles, both of Balltown, sureties. Account filed 8 Jan., 1806. [XI, 134-135.] Dower set off to Rachel, widow, by Samuel Waters and Thomas Trask, Jun'r, both of Balltown, and James Jewett, of New Milford, 5 Nov., 1800. [Unrecorded.] Daniel Clough, of New Milford, guardian unto Polly and Jane, minor daughters, 5 Jan., 1803. [IX, 190.]

Richard Martin, late of Cushing. Mary Martin, of Cushing, widow, Adm'x, 2 Nov., 1799. [IX, 31.] Moses Copeland, of Warren, and Richard Young, of Cushing, sureties. Inventory by James Malcom, Nathan Foster and Paul Crocker, all of Cushing, 6 Feb., 1800, $2211.99. [VIII, 231-232.] Richard, minor son, chose Robert Lovett, of Thomaston, to be his guardian, 11 Jan., 1800. [IX, 245.] Widow's dower set off by James Malcom, Patrick Wall and Ebenezer Otis, all of St. George, 27 Ap., 1804. [X, 255-256.] Division of real estate by James Malcom, Ebenezer Otis and Patrick Wall, all of St. George, between Thomas and Stephen Martin, elder sons, 27 Ap., 1804. [XI, 104-105.]

Edward Payson, late of Cambden, trader. Eunice Payson, of Cambden, widow, Adm'x, 27 Dec., 1800. [IX, 60.] David Payson, of Pownalborough, and James Payson, of Trenton, Hancock County, sureties. Inventory by Erastus Foote, Benjamin Cushing and Isaac Barnard, all of Cambden, 7 Jan., 1801, $59.17. [Unrecorded.] Erastus Foote and Benjamin Cushing, commissioners to examine claims, 4 Mar., 1801. Account filed 15 Jan., 1802. [Unrecorded.]

Mark Dexter, late of Thomaston, mariner. William Porterfield, of Cambden, Adm'r, 19 Mar., 1800. [IX, 61.] Josiah Reed and Robert Porterfield, both of Thomaston, sureties. Account filed 23 June, 1806. [XII, 32-33.] Inventory by Josiah Reed, of Thomaston, and William Lermond, of Warren, 21 Mar., 1800, $579.16. Josiah Reed and William Spear, both of Thomaston, commissioners to examine claims, 13 Aug., 1802. [XIII, 374 to 379.]

Patrick Porterfield, late of Thomaston. Robert Porterfield, of Thomaston, Adm'r, 4 Nov., 1799. [IX, 61.] Josiah Reed and David Fales, Jr., both of Thomaston, sureties. Inventory by Josiah Reed, John Dillaway and Nathaniel Woodcock, all of Thomaston, 30 May, 1800, $387.97. [VIII, 229-230.]

Ebenezer Philbrook, late of Balltown. Sarah Phibrook, of Balltown, widow, Adm'x, 25 Nov., 1800. [IX, 62.] Daniel Peaslee, of Balltown, and Daniel Rose, of New Milford, sureties. Inventory by John Woodman, of Balltown, Daniel Clough and Moses Jewett, both of New Milford, 22 Dec., 1800, $25.13. [VIII, 176.] Account filed 17 Nov., 1801. [VIII, 176-177.]

William Cunningham, late of Georgetown, mariner. Hannah Cunningham, of Georgetown, widow, Adm'x, 28 May, 1800. [IX, 63.] Inventory by Mark Langdon Hill, William Stinson and William Potter, all of Georgetown, 21 Oct., 1800, $437,51. [VIII, 151-152.] Account filed 27 May, 1801. [VIII, 152.]

Michael Howland, late of Bowdoinham, physician. Abigail Howland, of Bowdoinham, widow, Adm'x, 28 Oct., 1800. [IX, 63.] Samuel Blake, of Turner, Cumberland County, Adm'r *de bonis non*, 18 Jan., 1802. [IX, 51.] George Thomas and James McLelan, both of Bowdoinham, sureties. Distribution ordered 17 May, 1802. [VIII, 134 to 136.] Inventory by Joseph Sprague and James Cushman, both of Topsham, and Jacob Brown, of Dresden, 30 Oct., 1800, $835.38. [Unrecorded.] Inventory by Luther Cary, of Turner, David Millet and John Woodman, both of Poland, Cumberland County, 16 Jan., 1801, $331.10. [Unrecorded.] Ezekiel Thompson, of Thompsonborough, and Luther Cary, of Turner, commissioners to examine claims, 27 Jan., 1801. Account filed May, 1804. [Unrecorded.]

John Rittal, late of Dresden. Margaret Rittal, of Dresden, widow, Adm'x, 16 June, 1800. [IX, 64.] Distribution ordered 11 Nov., 1801. [VIII, 131.]

Walden Stone, late of Union, blacksmith. Daniel Stone, of Union, Adm'r, 7 Nov., 1799. [IX. 64.] Josiah Robbins and Moses Hawes, both of Union, sureties. Account filed 7 Feb., 1804. [X, 171-172.] Account filed 13 Aug., 1804. [X, 237.] Account filed 28 Jan., 1805. [X, 301.] Widow's dower set off by Rufus Gilmore, Amariah Mero and Thomas Mitchell, all of Union, 11 Jan., 1805. [XI, 110.] Division of estate by Joseph Maxey, Nathaniel Robbins and Joseph Morse, all of Union, 27 June, 1806. Heirs: Daniel Stone, Ebenezer Stone, Jonas Stone, John Stone, Sally Weatherly, Samuel Stone, Polly Parks, Betsey Stone and Nancy Stone. [XII, 132.] Inventory by Amariah Mero, Rufus Gilmore and Thomas Mitchell, all of Union, 20 Nov., 1799, $2866.16. [XIII, 440 to 443.]

Simon McLellan, late of Thomaston, mariner. Elizabeth McLellan, of Thomaston, widow, Adm'x, 3 Nov., 1800. [IX, 65.] Inventory by Josiah Reed, Benjamin Small and Benjamin Williams, all of Thomaston, 11 Nov., 1800, $317.63. Josiah Reed and Samuel Brown, both of Thomaston, commissioners to examine claims, 13 Jan., 1802. Account filed 12 Jan., 1805. [X, 241 to 245.] Advertisement of sale of real estate 4 May, 1805. [XI, 83.] Account filed 24 June, 1806. [XI, 215-216.] Elizabeth, guardian unto Nancy, Isaac and Simon, minor children, 25 June, 1805. [IX, 200.]

Henry Young, late of Cushing, mariner. Hannah Young, of Cushing, widow, Adm'x, 31 May, 1800. [IX, 65.] Thurston Whiting, of Warren, and James Malcom, of Cushing, sureties. Inventory by Moses Copeland, of Warren, James Malcom and John McKellar, both of Cushing, 11 Sep., 1800, $1764.61. [VIII, 186.] Account filed 11 Aug., 1803, at which date the administratrix had become the wife of Isaac Wylie, Jr. [X, 192.] Children named in order of distribution of estate 11 Aug., 1803: James, Gideon, Catherine and Jane. [X, 194.] Widow's dower set off by Moses Copeland, of Warren, John McKellar, of St. George, and Lawrence Parsons, of Cushing, 7 Sep., 1803. [X, 256-257.] James Malcom, guardian unto Catherine and Jane, minor daughters; Robert Henderson, of Cushing, guardian unto James and Gideon, minor sons, 12 Aug., 1802. [IX, 187.]

Joseph Haley, late of Topsham, housewright. Mary Haley, of Topsham, widow, Adm'x, 27 May, 1800. [IX, 66.] Inventory by John Merrill, Acter Patten and James Wilson, all of Topsham, 27 Oct., 1800, $2114.05. [VIII, 200.] Account filed 25 Aug., 1804. [X, 295.]

Godfrey Hofses, late of Waldoborough. Jacob Winchenbach, of Waldoborough, Adm'r, 30 May, 1800. [IX, 67.] George Hofses and Anthony Hofses, both of Waldoborough, sureties. Inventory by Joseph Ludwig, Henry Buckhart and Nathan Sprague, all of Waldoborough, 11 June, 1800, $1948.99. [VIII, 224.] Account filed 12 Jan., 1805. [XI, 55-56.] Mary, widow, guardian unto Mary, Barbary, Margaret, Andrew, William and Elizabeth, minor children. 29 Ap., 1805. [IX, 202-203.]

Daniel Mellus, late of Georgetown, mariner. Priscilla Mellus, of Georgetown, widow, Adm'x, 11 Sep., 1799. [IX, 67.] Daniel Fegan and Jeremiah W. Noyes, both of Pownalborough, sureties. Inventory by Thomas Stevens, Daniel McMahon and Thomas Linnan, all of Georgetown, 30 Oct., 1800, £10 : 2 : 0. [VIII, 191.]

Isaac Jameson, late of Meduncook, mariner. Paul Jameson, of Meduncook, Adm'r, 30 May, 1800. [IX, 68.] Jeremiah Jameson, of Meduncook, and Jacob Ludwig, of Waldoborough, sureties.

Robert Malcom, late of Topsham. Susanna Malcom, of Topsham, widow, Adm'x, 28 Oct., 1800. [IX, 68.] Inventory by Arthur Hunter, James Purrington and William Randall, all of Topsham, 26 Dec., 1800, $208.27. [XIII, 341.] Arthur Hunter and William Randall, commissioners to examine claims, 10 Aug., 1801. [XIII, 342.] Distribution ordered 19 Aug., 1802. [X, 13.]

Consider Turner, late of Georgetown, mariner. Sarah Turner, of Georgetown, widow, Adm'x, 30 Oct., 1799. [IX, 69.] Caleb Marsh, of Bath, guardian unto Bethiah, Betsey, Sally, George and William Hodgkins Turner, minor children, 28 May, 1800. [IX, 188.] Joanna, minor daughter, chose Caleb Marsh to be her guardian, 28 May, 1800. [IX, 246.] Inventory by Mark Langdon Hill, Parker Oliver and Josiah Hinkley, all of Georgetown, 14 Mar., 1800, $1157.75. [VIII, 148-149.] Account filed 20 Aug., 1802. [VIII, 150-151.]

John Chase, late of Edgecumbe. Solomon Trask, of Edgecumbe, Adm'r, 6 Nov., 1800. [IX, 69.] Moses Davis and David Trask, both of Edgecumbe, sureties.

John Kelsey, late of Bristol. William Kelsey, of Bristol, Adm'r, 20 Dec., 1800. [IX, 70.] John Ryan, of Edgecumbe, and Ebenezer Perkins, of Bristol, sureties. John Farley and Nathaniel Bryant, both of Newcastle, commissioners to examine claims, 10 Aug., 1801; advertisements of sale of real estate 25 Jan., 1803; account filed 7 May, 1803. [X, 53 to 57.] Inventory by John Farley, of Newcastle, John Ryan and Thomas Ring, both of Edgecumbe, $358.64. [Unrecorded.] Inventory by William Boyd, and Silas Hathorn, both of Bangor, and Isaac Hopkins, of Sourdabscock, Hancock County, 23 Jan., 1801, $1363.50. [Unrecorded.] William Kelsey, guardian unto John and Hannah, minor children, 28 Feb., 1807. [IX, 219.] William Wenworth, of Bristol, guardian unto Enoch and James, minor sons, 28 Feb., 1807. [IX, 220.]

William Patterson, of Edgecomb, mariner, guardian unto William, minor son of William Gove, late of Edgecomb, mariner, 4 June, 1798. [IX, 175.]

Jane, minor daughter of Pelatiah Allen, late of Topsham, chose Josiah Mitchel, of Readfield, to be her guardian, 14 Jan., 1799. [IX, 227.]

Thomas Mace, late of Camden. Hannah Mace, of Cambden, widow, Adm'x, 18 Sep., 1799. Briant Morton and Nathaniel Simmons, both Cambden, sureties. Inventory by Briant Morton, Waterman Hewet and Benaiah Bowers, all of Cambden, 24 Sep., 1799. [Unrecorded.]

Padshall Knights, late of Boothbay, mariner. Susanna Knights, of Boothbay, widow, Adm'x, 20 June, 1799. Edward Emerson and William Emerson, both of Edgecomb, sureties. Inventory by Thomas Boyd, Benjamin McFarland and David Webber, all of Boothbay, $453. William McCobb and John Leishman, both of Boothbay, commissioners to examine claims. Account filed 6 May, 1803, at which date the administratrix had become the wife of George Gilbert. [X. 11-12.] Widow's dower set off by John Leishman and Alfred Wadsworth, both of Boothbay, and Edward Emerson, of Edgecomb, 1803. [X, 277.]

William Lithgow, late of Georgetown. Sarah Lithgow, of Georgetown, widow, Adm'x, 2 May, 1799. James Noble Lithgow, of Dresden, and Thomas Butler, of Georgetown, sureties. Inventory by Dummer Sewall, Joseph Bowker and Elijah Drummond, 31 Mar., 1800, $15,605.47. [Unrecorded.] Division of estate 27 Oct., 1801, by Mark Langdon Hill, Joseph Bowker and Elijah Drummond, all of Georgetown. [Unrecorded.]

Nathaniel McClellan, late of Bowdoinham. Jean McClellan of Bowdoinham, widow, Adm'x, 2 May, 1799. Stephen Whitmore and James Purinton, both of Bowdoinham, sureties. Inventory by Elihu Getchel, James Maxwell and Hezekiah Purrinton, all of Bowdoinham, 9 May, 1799, $662.46. [Unrecorded.]

Samuel Goodwin, Jr., late of Dresden. George Goodwin, of Dresden, Adm'r. Inventory by Edmund Bridge, Jonathan Reed and George Ramsdell, all of Dresden, 9 Aug, 1798. Ezra Taylor and Samuel Woodward, both of Dresden, commissioners to examine claims, 28 Sep., 1799. [No papers recorded.]

Francis Choate, late of Balltown. Susannah Choate, Adm'x, 25 Mar., 1800. Inventory by Samuel Waters, Samuel Kincade and Benjamin King, 26 May, 1800. [VIII, 197-198.] Account filed 25 June, 1807, at which date the administratrix had become the wife of Samuel Hilton, Jr. [XII, 261.]

In the name of God Amen I Richard Knowls of Tosham in the County of Lincoln and Comon Welh of masachutt—Considring the unserenty of this mortal Life and being of Sound and perfect mind and memory blased be almighty god for it to make and Publish this my Last Will and testemant in manner and form foloing that is to say first I gave to my Son Richard Knowls Ju'r the Land that I Bout of Mr. Wm. Bourk about fifty Eackers as will apear by the dead Reference therunto being had and all the privleges and appurtenaces therunto beloning all the farming tools theron and all the neet Stock that I now Stock that I now have: and I also gave and bequath to my Dafter Margret Skolfield one Cow in one year after my desase—

and I also give and bequath to my Dafter mary Le Roys heirs the Some of one dollor.

and I also give and bequath to Dafter Susanah Hot the Sum of one dollor.

and I give and bequath to my Dafter Rebeca Blair four Sheep two Ewes and two Lambs—

and Lastly as to all the Rest of my goods and Cattels of whatsoever name or nature soever I give and bequath————Richard Knowls Ju'r whom I appoint Sole Executer of this my Last will and testament hearby Revoking all formor Wills by me made—

in Witness Whearof I have hear unto set my hand and Seal the fortheenth day September in the year of our Lord Seventeen hundred and Ninty Six—Sin'd Seal'd Published and Declared by the above named Richard Knowls to be his Last will and testament in the presants of us Who have hearunto Sel Subscribed

our mames as wittness }
in the presents of testator } Richard Knowles   (seal)

Charles Perry
David Owen
Gideon Owen

Probated 6 Mar., 1798. [Unrecorded.] Executor neglected to qualify. Thomas Rice, of Wiscasset, Adm'r *cum testamento annexo*, 5 Jan., 1803. [X, 8.] Ebenezer Whittier and Jeremiah Bailey both of Wiscasset, sureties. Inventory by John Rogers, John Fulton and Alexander Rogers, 7 Feb., 1803, $824.75 [X, 9.] John Merrill, Jr., and Nymphas Stacy, both of Wiscasset, commissioners to examine claims, 6 May 1803. [X, 173.] Account filed and distribution ordered 15 May, 1804. [X, 116 and 175.]

In the name of God Amen. I Joseph Withom of the plantation of Balltown in the County of Lincoln Yeoman being weak in body but of a sound mind and memory, do this twenty fourth day of May *Anno Domini* one Thousand seven hundred and ninety Eight, make and publish this my last will and testament in manner following that is to say first I give to my Beloved wife one third part of my Real Estate Dureing her life. I also give to my s'd wife the Use of one third part of my Real Estate Dureing the term of seven years I give to my wife the Use of the other third part to ocupy untill my youngest son Josiah shall arive at the age of twenty one years. I give to my son Isaac Withom one third part of my Real Estate to come into possession of in seven years from the date hereof I give to my son Josiah one third part of my Real estate when he shall arrive the age of twenty one years I give to my three Daughters Jane, Lydia and Sally one Cow each to be paid by my sons equally, when they the said Daughters shall arive at the age of Eighteen years. I give to the Child with wich my above said wife is pregnat, if it should live to the age of Eighteen years, one Cow to be paid by my two sons Isaac & Josiah Withom I give to my wife all my personal Estate for which, and the Use of the Real estate above mentioned, she is to maintain and bring up My Children untill they come of lawful age to maintain themselves I give to my sons Isaac and Josiah all the rest and residue of my estate after my wifs decease and lastly I do constitute and appoint my wife sole Executrix of this my last will and testament In Testimony Whereof I do hereunto Set my hand and seal the day and year above written

Joseph Withom (seal)

Signed Sealed published and declared by the said Joseph Withom for his last will and testament in the presants of us who at his request have hereunto set our hands as witnesses to the same

David Dennis
Elkanah Trague
her
Jane X Withom
mark

Probated 31 Oct., 1799 ; Sarah Withom, executrix, [XIII, 320.321.] Inventory by Samuel Waters, Joseph Jackson and Thomas Kenedy, all of a place called Balltown, 1? May, 1800. [XIII, 324-324.]

In the Name of God—Amen—I John Getchel of Pownalborough in the County of Lincoln yeoman being aged & infirm of Body, but of a Sound disposing Mind & Memory, for which I desire to give thanks to God, My Creator—Calling to Mind the uncertainty of this Life, & the certainty of Death, and wishing to settle all My affairs so that there may be no difficulty after My Death, do make publish pronounce & declare this to be My last Will & Testament hereby revoking all former Wills & Testaments—

Imprimis—I give & bequeath My Soul to God My Creator, & My Body I commit to the grave in hopes a Joyful resurrection through the Merits of our Blessed Redeemer—

Item. I give & bequeath to My beloved Wife Marcy, the use & improvement of all My Estate of every kind, wherewith it has pleased God to bless me, for & during her natural life, with full power and authority to dispose of so much thereof at any time as shall be necessary to for her comfortable Support—and after her death, I hereby give and bequeath to My good & worthy Friends Abraham Nason, Anna Nason his wife, all the rest & residue of my Estate afore mentioned, and to their heirs forever to be disposed of them the said Abraham and Anna as they shall chuse—And I do hereby nominate & appoint My said Friend Abraham Nason to be My Executor to this My last Will & Testament—I further will that all My Just debts be paid by My said Executor—and that he see that My Body, & the Body of said beloved wife, be decently buried after our Deaths—

In Testamony whereof I the said John Getchel have hereto Set My hand & affixed My Seal this twenty second day of October *Anno Domini* One thousand Seven hundred and Ninety four—

Signed sealed published pronounced
and declared by the
said John Getchel to be
his last Will & Testament
in the presence of us
who in his presence &
the presence of each
other subscribed our
names as witnesses—
Silas Lee
Nathan Dole
  her
Abigail X Slowman
  Mark
  her
Abigail X Nason
  Mark

    John
    Getchel (seal)

    Probated 2 June, 1800. [XIII, 325-326.]

In the Name of God Amen, the Second Day of April *Anno Domini* 1800 I John Choat of a Place Called Balltown in the County of Lincoln and Commonwelth of Massachusetts yeoman being in a Low State of health but of perfect Mind and Memory thro the goodness of God to me ; do make and ordain this my last will and testament ;

Principally and first of all I Give my Soul to God that Gave it me hoping thro the Grace of God & Merits of my Lord and Saviour, Jesus Christ to obtain free Pardon of all my Sins and to inherit Eternal Life ; My Body I Commit to the Earth to be buried in Christian Like Manner at the Disgression of my Executor hereafter Named; and as touching Such temporal Estate as it has pleased God to Bestow on me I Give and bequeath and dispose of the same in the folowing Manner and form—

Imprimis My Will is that all my just Depts and funural Charges be paid by my Executor hereafter Named

Item I Give to my Sister Sally after my Just Depts are Paid all my Real and Personal Estate my Sister Sally Providing a Comfortable Maintainence for my father and Mother Dureing there Life and a Decent Burael after Death—

Item I do hereby constitute and appoint my Brother Abraham Choat to be my Sole Executor of this my Last will and testament and do hereby Rattify and confirm this and no Other to be my Last will and testament In Witness whereof I the said John Choat have heareunto set my hand and seal the Day and year first Mentioned

Sign Sealed puplished Pronounced
and Declared as my Last will and
testament in Presents of Us
Abraham Choat Jr.
Moses Choat
Jeramiah Norris Jr

              his
John X Choat (seal)
        Mark

Probated 29 July, 1800. [XIII, 336-337.] Inventory by Samuel Waters, Jonathan Heath and Samuel Kincaid, Jun'r, all of Balltown, 1 Nov., 1800. [Unrecorded.]

In the Name of God, amen. I Jonathan Morrison of New Milford in the County of Lincoln, Gentleman, do make and publish this my last will and testament, in manner following, viz. :

Imprimis. It is my will and direction that my messuage or tenement in said New Milford where I now reside, and all my goods and chattels whatever, be sold in a reasonable time, for, and consistently with, the purposes hereafter mentioned

Item. It is my will and direction that, as speedily as may be convenient, all just demands against my estate be satisfied.

Item. It is my will and direction that, without delay, my whole property, excepting what is applied to the payment of all just claims against my estate as above mentioned, iucluding the avails of my messuage, goods and chattels aforesaid, when sold as afore directed, be, if practicable, placed at interest on good security; and the said property, so to be placed, I give and bequeath to Thomas Wallace Morrison, William Jackson Morrison, Rusha Field Morrison, and Jonathan Morrison, all Minors and children of my late brother Thomas Morrison, formerly of Warren in the County aforesaid, now deceased, in manner following :— One fourth part thereof to be paid to the said Thomas Wallace when he shall arrive to the age of twenty one years, with interest if any shall have arisen :— One fourth part thereof to be paid to the said William when he shall arrive to the age of twenty one years, with interest, if any shall have arisen ;— One fourth part thereof to be paid to the said Rusha, when she shall arrive to the age of twenty one years, or when she shall be married, whichever shall first happen, with interest if any shall have arisen ;— One fourth part thereof to be paid to the said Jonathan when he shall arrive to the age of twenty one years with interest if any shall have arisen ; Deducting in each case necessary & extraordinary expences, if any such there should be ; and providential losses, should any happen without default of the Executor of this will and testament.

Item. It is my further will, anything above written not withstanding, that should either of the aforesaid Minors decease before the time when, according to the terms of the foregoing paragraph, his or her fourth part aforesaid is to become payable, then the fourth part, to which the minor so deceased would, if he or she had lived, have been entitled, shall be paid in equal shares to the three survivors; payment to be made to each severally at such time as the minor so deceased would, had he or she lived, been entitled to receive the same or the survivors severally shall become entitled to receive their several fourth parts, whichever shall last happen.— And should more than one of said Minors decease not having become entitled to receive their several fourth parts aforesaid, then the survivors or survivor shall in like manner succeed to the whole right or rights of the several minors so deceased given by this will ; and payment shall accordingly be made to the survivors or survivor in time and manner above appointed and described. And I hereby constitute and appoint Josiah Stebbins of said New Milford Esquire Executor of this my last will and testament, and authorize and request him to do all matters and things which ought to be done for carrying this my last will and testament into faithful and full and complete execution according to the true intent and meaning thereof.—

In witness whereof I have hereunto set my hand and seal this seventeenth day of April in the year of our Lord one thousand eight hundred.

Signed, sealed, published and declared by the abovenamed Jonathan Morrison to be his last will and testament in the presence of us, who have hereunto subscribed our names as witnesses in the presence of the testator: the word *"eight* in the last line but one written on an erasure before signing.—
Pitt Dillingham
Nicholas Cooper
    her
Sally X Cooper
    mark

          his   (seal)
Jonathan ⊢ Morrison
    mark

Probated 29 Ap., 1800. [XIII, 344 to 346.] Inventory by Richard Bailey, John Plumer and Christopher Erskine, all of New Milford, 24 July, 1800, $501.79, to which the administrator added sundry votes amounting to $389.30. [XIII, 348 to 351.]

In the Name of God Amen. I Nathaniel Williams of Woolwich in the County of Lincoln Tanner, being a decaying & weak state of Body, & apprehending I cannot long continue but of a sound & disposing mind & Memory for which God be thanked, do make this my last & Testament as follows.

In the first place I bequeath my Soul to God who gave it when he shall call for it, & my Body to its parent Earth to be decently buried at the discretion of my Executors, with a comfortable hop that at the resurrection of the Dead Soul & Body will again be united & enter into the rest that remains to the Righteous, purchased by the great Redeemer.

And as to the worldly interest with which God has blessed me I will & bequeath the same in manner following.

In the first place

I give & bequeath to my beloved wife Mehetable one half of the Lot No 62 in the second Division on which I now live, not hereafter disposed of to my Son Timothy, with one third part of the house & Barn standing on the same Lot, to hold to her during the time remains by widow.

I also give & bequeath to my said Wife one sixth part of my Stock of Leather now on hand ready for sale, one Cow, one fifth part of the Sheep, fifty Dollars in Money and all the household furniture she brough to me when I married her, to be her absolute property forever. Secondly. I give & bequeath to my son Timothy, the western End of my Lot No. 22 first division, bounded beginning where my Sheep pasture fence adjoins the Land of Solomon Walker, thence northerly & easterly as the fence runs excluding the sheep pasture, till it comes to a large rock out of Ground standing close to the fence in the field, thence northerly by two large rocks till it comes to the Brook that runs from the Tan yard, thence westerly by the Brook till it comes to the Bridge, then westerly up the hill leaving the Cart road on the right hand, still westerly on the north side of the plowed field till it comes to the fence between the field & the pasture then north till it stiks the Line between Lot No. 22 first division & sixty two second Division, then westward as far as my Deed extends. Also my Tan yard with all implement for Tanning and all priviledges thereto belonging with half an Acre of Land so located as best to contain & accommodate the Tan yard, Pitts & building, with a priviledge of a convenient road from the house I now live in to said Tan yard & also the piece of Land before bequeathed to him. Also all that part of Lot No. 62 second Division which lies between the Town road & Monsweeg Brook, together with that small piece that lies before his house in the field westerly side of the Town road & easterly of a now Lot fence, reserving to my heirs & Assigns a convenient road frome the Town road, to the house where I now live also that part of Lot No. 58 second Division which lies between the Town road & the head of the Lot, all the above described real Estate to hold to him & his heirs forever in fee simple.

Also one Quarter part of my Stock now in the woks when the Tanning and currying is finished, he performing all the Labour at his expence, & my Estate to find the necessary materials to compleat the same, also forty Dollars out of the remaining three Quarters of said Stock to his absolute property forever.

I give to my two Daughters Abigail & Olive all that part of Lot No 58 second Division which lies between the Town road & Monsweeg brook in equal shares to hold to them & their heirs forever.

Also two yoke of oxen, two Cows & two fifth part of my flock of Sheep, to be equally divided between them also one hundred & fifty Dollars each, all to be their absolute property. also one half of the house hold furniture not before bequeathed, also one third part of the dwelling house & barn in equal Shares in fee forever.

I give & bequeath to my two Daughters Anne & Susanna the one half of the Lot I now live on being Lot No. 62 second division with my sheep pasture and Field not bequeathed in Lot No. 22 with one third part of my dwelling house & Barn in equal Shares between them to hold in fee forever. Also fifty Dollars each in Money, also one half of my house hold furniture not herein given to my wife in equal shares & one Cow each & two fifth of my flock of sheep in equal parts.

I give & bequeath to my said Wife one half the horse with the Side Saddle, while she lives in the house, the other half of the Horse to my Son Timothy All the rest & residue of my Estate not before disposed of, after my honest Debts are paid, I give & bequeath to my said Wife and my said four Daughters to be equally divided between them. And I do hereby constitute & appoint my said Wife Mehetable & my Son Timothy Executors of this my last will and testament & hereby revoke all other wills & declare this to be my last will & Testament

In witness whereof I hereto set my hand and Seal the thirteenth day of May A D. 1799

Signed sealed published
& declared by the testator
to be his last will & Testa
ment in presence of   Nathaniel Williams (seal)
   Robert Cushman
   Simeon Williams
   Betsey Grant

Probated 26 Nov., 1799. [XIII, 362 to 364.] Timothy Williams 2d, Robert Cushman and Ebenezer Savage, all of Woolwich, sureties. Inventory by Abner Wade, David Gilmore and Benjamin Bailey, all of Woolwich, 3 Dec., 1799. [XIII, 367-368.]

John O'Dee, late of Pownalborough, merchant. Thomas McCrate, of Pownalborough, Executor. [No record of will and no papers found.] Inventory by Seth Tinkham, Francis Anderson and William Pike, all of Pownalborough, 22 Jan., 1800, $505.21. [XIII, 373-374.]

In the name of GOD. Amen.

I John Elliot of Bristol in the County of Lincoln Mariner, considering the uncertainty of this mortal life, and being weak in body but of sound and perfect mind & memory, blessed be Almighty GOD for the same, DO made and publish this my last will & testament in manner and form following, that is to say—

First. I Considder my beloved wife Sabrah Elliot in her own right entitled to all the Real Estate and right of Dower therein comming from her former husbands estate, and instead, lieu or place of Dower from Me or my Estate to her comming I now Give and bequeath unto her the said Sabrah—my beloved wife, The Sum of Five hundred Dollars, including the demand I have of about One hundred dollars more or less, against her former husbands Estate for the maintainance & bringing up hitherto of their daughter Nancey Davis; which demand is to be at the disposal of my said Wife, after my decease; and the residue of the said five hundred dollars to be paid her from time to time as herein afterwards provided, in time not exceeding three years after my decease, for the last payment—

I also give to my said beloved Wife One good Cow to be furnished her immediately after my decease. I also give and bequeath to her All my Household linens, Beds, Bedding furniture; and all my Weiring Apparel, saving only my two best Suits of Cloths, the best of which suits I give and bequeath to my Youngest brother Daniel Elliot, and the other Suit I give and bequeath to my elder brother Simon Elliot Jun'r.

To my Sister Jenny the Wife of Enos Baxter I give and bequeath One Eighth part of the Schooner Two friends, with her Appurtenances, and Earnings in that proportion, and likewise my demand of Eighty Dollars which I have against her said husband—

To my Sister Isabella the widow of Peter Murphy Jun'r I give and bequeath One Sixteenth part of the Schooner Two friends with her Appurtenances and earnings in that same proportion—

To my Sister Anna, to be at her Sole disposal and at the disposal of no other person whatever I give and bequeath the remaining One Sixteenth part which I own of the said Schooner Two friends, with her Appurtenances, and earnings in the same proportion—

To my Sister Peggy Elliot I give and bequeath all the Money that is due me or in anywise comming to me from my honoured father Simon Elliot the Elder

To Jenny the daughter of Judith Polland as it is said to be the Child of my brother Peter deceased, I Give and bequeath One Cow, or the Value thereof in Money at my decease—

And as to all the rest residue & remainder of my Real & personal Estate, Goods, Chattels Rights and Credits of what kind or nature soever I Give and bequeath the Same to my said Brothers, Simon and Daniel, in equal proportion to be divided between them, they paying off in the same proportion, to my said beloved Wife and other the legatees as before entitled, the legacies & Sums of Money in manner as aforesaid, My funeral expences, One hundred dollars I Owe to Moses Davis, and all other Just Demands against Me or my Estate—

Lastly I Appoint my said Brother Simon Elliot Jun'r and Mr. William Rogers of Bristol aforesaid the Executors of this my last will & testament, to Carry the same into effect. In Witness whereof I the said John Elliot have hereunto Set my hand and Seal the Eighteenth day of August in the Year of our Lord One thousand Seven hundred Ninety Seven—

John Eliot (seal)

The aforegoing written Instrument was Signed, Sealed, published and declared by the afore Named John Elliot, to be his last Will and testament, in the presence of Us who have hereunto subscribed our Names as Witnesses, in the presence of the testator—

Samuel Yeates
Alex'r Fossett Jun } Witnesses
Robert McLintock

And afterwards on the same day before written I the said John Elliot being still of sound & perfect mind & memory Do make this Codicil to my will & testament aforesaid, that is to say I take back from my Sister Jenny the One half of the One eighth part of the Schooner Two friends with her appurtenances and earnings as aforesaid, which part so taken back being One Sixteenth part of the Said Vessel, with her appurtenances and Earnings due in that proportion I Now give & bequeath to my Sister Mary, Otherwise named Polly Elliot—

In Witness Whereof I have hereunto Set my hand & Seal the same day & Year aforesaid in my will & testament before written—

John Eliot (seal)

Signed Sealed published & declared
by the above named John Elliot
to be a Codicil to his last will and
testament, in presence of us, who
have hereunto subscribed our names
as witnesses in the presence of the
testator

Samuel Yeates
Alex'r Fossett Jun } Witnesses
Robert McLintock

Bond of Simon Eliot, Ju'r., Executor, dated 4 June, 1798. Samuel Yates and Robert McLintock, both of Bristol, sureties.

In the Name of God. Amen. I William Patterson of Dresden in the County of Lincoln, considering the uncertainty of this mortal life, and being weak in body, but of sound and perfect mind and memory, blessed be allmighty God for the same, do make and publish this my last Will and Testament in manner and form following, that is to Say. I give unto my beloved Wife Elisabeth Patterson the use and improvement of all the Real Estate I am now seased and possessed of as long as she remaines my Widow, and after her death it Shall be equally divided among my Children. But in case She Should marry again, She Shall have no more but the improvement of one third part of it, during her natural life. I also give and bequeath unto her all my Personal Estate to her own disposal for the Support of the family. And I give her full power to Sell and dispose at privat Sale of those Sixty acres of land I lately purchased of Christopher Turner of Reedfield, to pay the debt I owe him. Lastly I appoint the Said Elisabeth Patterson, the Sole Executrix of this my last will and Testament. In witness whereof I have hereunto Set my Hand and Seal this Sixth day of November A. D. one Thousand Seven hundred and ninety Seven.

Signed, Seal'd, publish'd and declared by the above named William Patterson, to be his last will & testament. in presence of us. who Signed our names as witnesses in the presence of the Testator.
  William Patterson (seal)

  Obadiah Call
  Sam'l White
  David Clancy

Probated 5 Jan., 1798. [XIII, 424.]

William Lewis and Philip Call, both of Dresden, sureties.

In the Name of God Amen.—The Twenty fourth day of March 1795 I James Hilton, of Bristol in the County of Lincoln yeoman being very Sick and weak in Body, but of perfect mind & Memory, thanks be given to God; Therefore calling to mind the Mortality of my Body, and knowing that it is appointed for all men once to die, do make and ordain this my last will and Testament; that is to say principally and first of all, I give and recomend my Soul into the hands of Allmighty God that gave it, and my Body I recomend to the earth, to buried in decent Christain

Burial at the Discretion of my Executor, nothing doubting but at the general Resurrection I shall receive the same again, by the mighty Power of God.—And as touching such Worldly Estate wherewith it has pleased God to bless me in this Life, I give demise, and dispose of the same in the following Manner & form.

first I give and bequeath to my son William Hilton the sum of four Dollars—

Itom I give & bequeath to my Daughter Mary Mirrit Twenty Dollars—

Itom I give & bequeath to my Daughter Jane Hilton one Dollar—

Itom I give & bequeath to my Son James Hilton Fifty Dollars—

Itom I give & bequeath to my Son John Hilton one Dollar

Itom I give & bequeath to my Daughter Margret Hilton Twenty Dollars

Itom I give & bequeath to my Daughter Sarah Hilton four Dollars

Itom I give & bequeath to my Daughter Susan Hilton Twenty Dollars

Itom I give & bequeath to my Daughter Elizebeth Hilton Twenty Dollars

Itom I give & bequeath to my Daughter Nancy Hilton Twenty Dollars

Itom I give and bequeath to my Daughter Liddia Hilton Twenty Dollars

Itom I also give Jointly & Severaly to my two Sons Joshua Hilton & Joseph Hilton whom I likewise constitute, make and ordain my sole Executers of this my last will and Testament all and Singular of my Personal Estate that is to say all my Stock of Cattle Sheep Horses & Swine with all my Farming Utencels of every kind or Nature, and I do hereby ratify and Confirm this & no other to be my last will and Testament—In Witness whereof I have hereunto Set my hand and Seal, the day and year Above-written———

James Hilton (seal)

Signed, Sealed, Published, Pronounced,
and Declared, by the said James
Hilton as his last will & Testament
in the Presence of us the Subscribers

    Thos Johnston
    Cornelius Rhoads
    Elizabeth Rhoads

Probated 2 July, 1799. [XIII, 433 to 435.] Inventory by John Paine, John McLain and Henry Little, all of Bristol, 2 Sep., 1799, $313.17. [XIII, 437-438.]

In the Name of God, Amen.—The Twelfth Day of August 1796, I Morris Fling of a place called Brookfield in the county of Lincoln and

Commonwealth of Massachusetts, yeoman—being very sick and Weak in body, but of perfect mind and memory, Thanks be Given to God ;—Therefore calling to mind the Mortality of my Body, and knowing that it is appointed for all men once to Die,— Do make and Ordain this my last Will and Testament,—That is to say ;—Principally, and first of all, I Give and recommend my soul into the hands of God that gave it and my Body I recommend to the Earth, to be buried in Decent Christian burial at the discretion of my Exeecutors ; nothing Doubting but at the General resurection I shall receive the same again by the mighty Power of God :—And as touching such Worldly Estate wherewith it has pleased God to bless me in this life I Give, Demise, and dispose of the same in the following manner and form—   *Imprimis,*
I Give and bequeath to Esther my Dearly beloved wife one third part of the income, and profits of all my Estate, so long as she the said Esther Shall continue to be my widow, and no longer—
Item,—I Give to my well beloved son, John Fling, one Dollar—
Item,—I Give to my well beloved Daughter, Elisabeth Farley, one Dollar
Item,—I Give to my well beloved Daughter, Mary Huntoon, one Dollar—
Item,—I Give to my well beloved Daughter, Sarah Perry, one Dollar—
Item,—I Give to my well beloved Son, Samuel Fling, one Dollar—
Item,—I Give to my well beloved Daughter, Eunice Fling, Sixty Dollars—
Item, I Give to my well beloved Daughter, Susanna Fling, Sixty Dollars—
Item,—The remainder of my Estate, I Give to my well beloved Daughters, Hannah Moor, Eunice Fling and Susanna Fling and is to be equally Divided between them
Item. I Constitute make & ordain Esther my Dearly Beloved wife, my Sole Exeecutrix of this my last will and Testament.—
Item,—And I do hereby disallow, revoke, and disanul all, and every other former Testaments, Wills, Legacies, and bequests and Executors, by me in any ways before named, Willed and bequeathed,—ratifying and confirming this and no other to be my last Will and Testament,—
   In Witness whereof I have hereunto set my hand and Seal the day and
   year above written—
Signed, Sealed, Published, Pronounced
and Declared by the said Morris Fling,
as his last Will and Testament, in the
presence of us the Subscribers—

            Moris fling (seal)

Samuel Titcomb
Joseph Cleveland
Nancy Titcomb
     Probated 16 Jan., 1798. [XIII, 438-9]

In the Name of God Amen—

I Arthur Percy of Georgetown in the County of Lincoln and State of Massathusets, Yeoman, being thro' the abundant Mercy and goodness of God, tho Weak in body, Yet of a sound and perfect Understanding and Memory, do Constitute this my Last will and Testament, and Desire it may be received by all as Such,—First I most humbly Bequeth my soul to God my maker, Beseeching his most Gracious Acceptance of it, thro the all sufficient Merrits and Mediation of my most Compassionate Redeemer jesus christ, Who gave himself to be an attonement for my sins, and is able to save, to the uttermost, all that come unto god by him, Seeing he Ever liveth to make Intercession for them, and who I trust will not Reject me a Returning Sinner, when I Come to him for Mercy; in this hope and Confidence I Render up my soul with Comfort, humbly, Beseeching the most blessed and Glorious trinity one god most holy, most Mercifull and gracious to Prepare me for the Time of Disolution, and then to take me to himself into that Peace and Rest, and incomparable felicity which he has Prepared for all that fear and love his Holy Name, Amen, blessed be god I Give my Body to the earth, from whence it was taken, in full assurance of its Resurrection from thence at the last day, as for my Burial I Desire it may be Decent without Pomp or State, at the Discretion of my dear wife and my Executors hereafter Named who I Doubt will Manage it with all Requisite Prudence,—

As to my worldly Estate, I will and Positively Order it in the manner and form following= *Imprimus* Or first I give and bequeth Unto my son David Percy my farm Situate at the head of Sheeps Gut River in Balt town so called Containing one hundred and fifty Acres of land to him and his heirs forever= Item I Give and Bequeth Unto my son Francis Percy fifty Acres adjoining the same farm, Or Nine pound Lawfull money to be Paid him by Joseph Rogers for the s'd fifty Acres= Item I Give and Bequeth Unto my Dear Wife the One third of my Real and Personal Estate Dureing her Natural life if She Remains a Widdow, & I Order that after her Decease or if she should alter her condition by Marriage my Youngest son, Arthur percy shall Inherit his mothers thirds; Item I Give and Bequeth unto my son John and James the Other two thirds of my Real and personal Estate to be Equally divided Between them, my Dear wife I appoint to be my Executor untill my son John Comes to age, I Order her to Bring my Children up to a Common Education Item I Give and Bequeth

Unto my Dear Wife my Case of Drawers to be hers Dureing her Natural life. Item I Give and Bequeth Unto my son Arthur percy junner, my Gold Sleeve Buttons, Unto my son James I Give and Bequeth my Silver Shoe Buceles, to my son John, I Give and Bequeth my Silver watch I order my Debts to be Paid with out fail by my Executors out of my Personal Estate Item I Give and Bequeth Unto my Dugters Polly and Betsey five shillings, Lawfull Money.—As to my Wareing Apparell I lave them to the Discretion of my Dr. Wife whom I appoint my Exc'r to Distribute them among the Children, in Witness Whereof I have hereunto Set my hand and Seal the 15 Day of July in the Year of Our lord One thousand Seven hundred and Eighty Eight.

Witness   Arthur Percei   (seal)
Jeremiah Daisy
John Whelen
Henry wright Blethen   [Not probated.]

I William Kennedy of Boothbay in the County of Lincoln yeoman. Calling to mind the mortality of my Body and the uncertainty of my life, and not knowing how soon I may be Called away by Death—and being at this present time of sound mind & memory do make and ordain this my last Will and Testement—that is to say principally and in the first place I Recomend my soul into the hands of God who gave it, and my Body I commit to the Earth to be Buried at the Discration of my Executor, hereafter named—And as to my Worldly Estate I give devise and dispose of the same in the following manner & form Viz—

Imps.

firstly I order that all my just Debts and funeral Expences be paid out of my personal Estate—

Item I give & bequeath to my son Thomas one Dollar and also my half of a Pew No Five in the meeting house in Boothbay in full of his part or share in my Estate—

Item I give & bequeath to my son James two Dollars to be paid him by my Executor hereafter named in full of his part or share in my said Estate—

Item I give & bequeath to my youngest son William one Dollar in Cash and my best Coat to be paid and Delivered him in full of his share or part of my Estate aforesaid—

Item I give & bequeath to my Daughter Sarah Kelley one Dollar to be paid hir in Cash in full of hir share or part in my said Estate—

Item   I give and bequath to my Daughter Elizebath Corbat two Dollars to be paid hir in Cash in full of hir share or part in my said Estate.

Item   I also give & bequeath to my Daughter Mary Mylie one Cow or the Value thereof in Cash in full of hir share or part of my said Estate—

Item   And also to my Daughter Hannah Wylie I give & bequeath one Cow or the Value thereof in Money in full of hir part or share in my said Estate—

Item   I also give and bequeath to my two youngest Daughters Anne and Ruth the whole Rest & Residue of my said Estate Real and personal of Every name or Nature whatsoever let the same be found where it may, to be to them Equaly, and to there Heirs and asigns forever

Lastly   I do hereby appoint my said son Thomas Kennedy my Sole Executor of this my last Will and Testement, and do revoke all & Every former Wills or Testements by me heretofore made and Declare this & no other to be my last Will and Testement —In Wittness whereof I do hereunto set my hand & seal this twenty second day of April in the year of our Lord one thousand seven hundred & Ninty six—

Signed sealed published & Declared by the Testator to be his last Will & Testement in   his
presence of us—   William O Kennedy   (seal)
   Wm McCobb   mark
   Ichabod Pinkham
   John Crommett

Probated 12 Sep., 1796. [Unrecorded.]

In the name of God Amen——

I Ebenezer Bacon of Sidney in the County of Lincoln & Commonwealth of Massachusetts Esq being weak in body, but of sound disposing mind & memory & calling to mind the shortness & uncertainty of life do make publish & declare this my last will & testament in manner following that is to say in the first place I give and bequeath my saw & grist mill in the town of Winslow on the river Kennebeck at the foot of teeconic falls the one third part to my wife Abigail Bacon during her natural life, the other two thirds to my children Ebenezer Bacon Jun William Bacon both of said Sidney gentlemen & Frances Thomas wife of Joseph Thomas of said Sidney yeoman and Abigail Sherwin wife of Elnathan Sherwin of Winslow in said County Esq in the following divisions to wit to the said Ebenezer Bacon Junr & William Bacon each one equal third part of said two thirds & the said Frances Thomas and Abigail Sherwin each one equal sixth part of said two thirds, and the said third part given to my said wife, after her deceas to be divided among my aforementioned children in the aforementioned proportion

Secondly I give and bequeath to my wife Abigail Bacon all my household furniture during her natural life & at her deceas to be equally divided between my children Frances Thomas & Abigail Sherwin aforesaid

Thirdly I give and bequeath to my daughter Abigail Sherwin twenty eight dollars & fifty cents to be paid out of my estate by my executor in one month after my deceas

Fourthly I give and bequeath to my daughter Frances Thomas one hundred & twenty five dollars & ninety three cents to be paid out of my estate in one month after my deceas

Fifthly I give and bequeath to my wife Abigail Bacon one third part of all the rest and residue of my personal estate during her natural life

Sixth I give and bequeath two third parts of all the rest and residue of my personal estate to my children Ebenezer Bacon Jun William Bacon Francis Thomas & Abigail Sherwin in the following division towit to the said Ebenezer Bacon Jr & William Bacon each one Just third part of said two thirds, and to the said Frances Thomas and Abigail Sherwin each one Just sixth part of said two third parts

Seventhly I give and bequeath to my said children the aforementioned third part given my wife after her decease, in the same proportion as the aforementioned two thirds are divided

Lastly I hereby constitute and appoint Ebenezer Farwell of Vassalboro in said County Esq my sole executor of this my last will & testament hereby revoking all former wills by me made

In testimony whereof I have hereto set my hand & seal this twelfth day of February in the year of our Lord one thousand seven hundred & ninety eight

Signed sealed published
and declared to be the last

will & testament of the said   Eben'r Bacon   (seal)
Ebenezer Bacon in presence
of us whose names are
hereunto subscribed
  Thomas Rice
  Moses Appleton
  Wm Heywood

[Unrecorded.]

Elnathan Sherwin, of Winslow, Adm'r *cum Testamento annexo*, 2 Aug., 1798. Benjamin Chase and Nehemiah A. Parker, both of Winslow, sureties.

In the Name of GOD. Amen! I John Parker of Georgetown in the County of Lincoln & Commonwealth of Massachusetts, Gentleman, being in Usual health but of sound disposeing mind & memory; calling to mind my Mortality and the Uncertainty of my Existance here do make & Ordain this my last Will & testament. And first of All I Chearfully give my soul to GOD, Through Jesus Christ and my body to the dust in hopes of Obtaining a happy resurrection to an Immortal Life thro' the merits of Christ my saviour. And as touching such worldly Estate, as it hath Pleased GOD to bless me with in this life, I dispose of the Same in manner following (that is to say) First. I Give & bequeath Unto Jordan Parker his heirs and assigns forever a Certain part of my homestead farm discribed & bounded as follows Viz. begining at the Mouth of the Cove on Kenebeck river in front of my dwelling house thence South-West to a small Apple Tree, standing on the Edge of the bank, thence Westerly & Southerly to ye first ledge of Rocks, thence Northerly on a Straight line to the head of the great cove, thence 'round by the Shore Easterly & Southerly to the first mentioned bounds: Also another piece of land, begining Ten rods North North East from humphries head bounds so called, thence North Easterly on a straight line to a great Stone in my Upper Corn field & thence the same Course to Kenebeck river, thence Northerly & Westerly by the Same to my Northern bounds in Wizzel's Cove, thence Southerly by the Same to the first mentioned bounds. (Excepting & reserveing out of the Same Eight Acres of land on the Point where Samuel Goodwin now lives, Only that the said Jordan Shell Improve One half of the Previledge of Fishing thereunto belonging; Excepting Also Five Acres of land, to be laid out on the Same point we Usually land at in Comeing from meeting at the time of low water; these two last mentioned pieces of land is to bound on the river, and laid out as Convenient to all

Parties Concern'd as may be, so that the said Jordan Shell have a Convenient road by or near my Northern bounds leading from Humphries head bounds to the river, Also that there shell be convenient roads to & from the two Points Aforesaid through the said Jordan's land Aforesaid.) I give, devise & bequeath to the said Jordan One third Part of the were Previledge, whenever he or his heirs, helps build to Improve it. Also a piece of marsh Marsh within my dikemarsh, begining at the most westerly Creek in Said Marsh, thence running Northerly along said Creek to the first ledge by the Side of Said Creek, thence Northerly & Easterly to the nearest part of the next Creek, thence Northerly & Westerly along the Western branch of Said Creek to the Upland at a Cove, near my wood road, thence Southerly Along by the Edge of said Marsh to the first mentioned bounds, with liberty to haul his hay home from Said marsh. Also I give & bequeath to the Said Jordan his heirs & Assigns, the whole Amount of his four notes of hand, payable to me with Interest thereon, and a book Account, which Amounts in the whole to two hundred & eighty pounds or thereabouts. Provided & On Condition that the Said Jordan shell not bring Any Account against my Estate after my decease; Otherwise I Order that all the Gifts made in this my last Will & testament Shell become forfeited & Shell become the Property of my well beloved Wife Elizabeth & Andrew Reed their heirs & Assigns, & that the Said Jordan Shell pay my said wife & Andrew Reed, the Amount due me on the Aforementioned notes and accounts, anything in this will & testament to the Contrary Notwithstanding.

Item. I give devise & bequeath to Andrew Reed his heirs And Assigns forever, in Consideration of his takeing care of me during my natural life, The One half of all my homestead farm, remaining after Jordan Parkers land is Sett off & a piece, I have Given to Alex'r Wilie by deed, Also One Quarter part of Five Stack marsh, together with One third part of all my Cows, horses, Sheep & Swine, One half of the barn on my homestead farm, with Onehalf of both the points of land Excepted Out of Capt. Jordan Parkers bounds with half of the fishing previledges adjoining the five Acres, & One Quart part of the fishing Previledges Adjoining the Eight Acres & One third of the ware Priveledge, to him the said Andrew Reed & his heirs forever, & for a part of which I have given him a deed off; heretofore.

Item. I give & bequeath and devise to David Oliver who liv'd with me, One fourth part of Five Stack Marsh & One fourth part of little river Marsh, Also the neck of land of Which he has a deed from me. Said land lying on Parkers Island in Georgetown as Also the Marsh; to him the Said David & his heirs forever

Item. I give & bequeath to Alexander Wilie Jun'r One half of the land I lately Purchas'd of William Lithgow Esq'r & of which I have Convey'd to the Said Alexander by Deed.

Item. I Order & Will that all my Just Debts & Funeral Charges be paid by my Executors out of my Personal Estate & Appoint the residue as followeth.

Item. I give devise & bequeath to my well beloved wife Elizabeth, her heirs & Assigns forever, in token of Gratitude for her tender care & regard, the whole of my dwelling house & Store & One half of my barn Situated on my homestead farm, together with One half of Said farm Exclusive of what I have given to Jordan Parker & Alex'r Wilie Jun'r. Also One Quarter part of my Saw Mill, Standing on my Mill Stream in Georgetown near & Adjoining my homestead farm. Also One half of the two points of land, excepted out of Jordan Parkers bounds, with a part of the fishing Priveledges equal to Andrew Reed as herein before express'd. And One third part of the ware Priveledge, adjoining my home farm, & my Pew in the Meeting house in said Georgetown. And One Quarter part of five Stack marsh & One half of little river marsh Situate on Parkers Island Aforesaid, Also two thirds of all my Cattle & all my farming Implements, together with all the rest, residue & remainder of my Estate of what name or nature Soever, wheresoever the Same is or may be found, (not before herein Particularly devised). I Give devise & bequeath to my said wife Elizabeth & her heirs forever, for her to dispose off as She thinks best.

Lastly, I do hereby Constitute and Appoint my said wife Elizabeth, And Andrew Reed to be Executors to this my last Will & testament, hereby revokeing & disannulling all former wills & Testaments by me heretofore in in Any manner made, ratifying & Confirming this & no Other to be my last Will & testament. In Witness wherof I have hereunto Set my hand & Seal this fourteenth Day of March *Anno Domini* One thousand Seven hundred & ninety Seven.

NB. the words a Ten rods North North East from, North, & thence the Same course" in the first Page was made before Signing hereof.

Sign'd, Seal'd, Publish'd, and declared by him
the said John Parker, to be his last Will
& testament in Presence of us, who have   John Parker (seal)
Subscribed our names as witnesses, in
the Presence of the Testator & of each Other.

   Mark Langdon Hill.
   George Todd
   Hugh Rogers
   Denny McCobb   [Unrecorded.]

Executors appointed by Court, 28 May, 1800. Thomas Percy, of Georgetown, and John Murray McFarland, of Boothbay, sureties. [No papers recorded.]

Index of Names.

Pages marked with a * are Wills; those marked with a † are Estates.

Abbott, Aaron, 220.
Achorn, (Eichorn) Daniel, 236.
Adams, Amos, 164.
    George, 301.
    Hope, 300.
    Joel, 193, 204, 207, 253.
    Lucy, 300.
    Margaret, 300.
    Mary, 300, 334.
    Polly, 300.
    Richard, 88, 109, *299, 300, 301.
    Ruby, 300.
    Samuel, 44.
    Sela, 300.
    Solomon, 272, 273.
    Stephen, 342.
    Thomas, 301.
Agry, Anna, 136.
    Thomas, 87, †136.
Akley, Samuel, 259.
Alden, Briggs, 129.
    Elihu, 317.
Alexander, John, 141.
    Priscilla, 141.
    William, 22, 23, 307.
All, John, †52.
Allbee, Benjamin, 207.
    William, 207.
Allen, Anna, 317.
    Daniel, 138.
    Frances, *317.
    Hannah, 119.
    Isabel, 317.
    Jane, 347.
    John, †188.
    Keturah, 188.

    Levina, 93.
    Mary, 263, 315.
    Olive, 162.
    Oliver, †93.
    Pelatiah, 347.
    Philip, 130.
    Thomas, 16, 17, 20, 25, 317.
    William, †11, 340.
Alley, Samuel, 303.
    Sarah, 302.
Ames, Jonathan, 228.
Anderson, Daniel, †12.
    Enoch, 275.
    Francis, 356.
    Robert, 275, 336, 337.
    Samuel, 12, 82.
Andrews, Asa, 137.
    Elizabeth, 64.
    George, 64, 140.
    John, 39.
Angier, Samuel, 276.
Appleton, Moses, 366.
Archibald, Francis, Jr., 87.
    James, †119.
Armstrong, Hannah, 83.
    William, *83.
Arnold, Frederick, 202, 254.
    Thomas, 163, 298.
    William, 164.
Askins, Alexander, †178.
    John, †162.
    Mary, 162.
    Robert, 178.
Atkins, Hannah, 281.
    Thomas, 164, 281.
Aubens, Philip, 1.

AULD, Frances, 342.
    James, 72, 145, †342.
    Jenny, 342.
    Peggy, 342.
    Rachel, 342.
    Sally, 342.
    Samuel, 342.
    William, 342.
AUSTIN, John, 228.
AVERELL, Daniel, 163.
    David, †163, †177.
    Enoch, 92, 93, †145.
    Israel, †92.
    Job, 92, 137.
    John, 93, 163.
    Ruth, 145.
    Samuel, 92, 93.
    Simeon, 163.
    William, 163.
AVERY, James, 119.
    Mary, 113.
AYER, James, 92.
BABBAGE, Courtney, †133.
BACON, Abigail, 364, 365.
    Ebenezer, *364, 365.
    James, 29, 177.
    William, 20, 364, 365.
BABCOCK, Anna, 263.
    Henry, 87.
    Samuel, 87.
BAILEY, Benjamin, 356.
    David, 55, †90.
    Hannah, 90.
    Jacob, 17.
    James, 24.
    Jeremiah, 349.
    John, 199.
    Joshua, 54.
    Nathaniel, 55, 275, 278.
    Richard, 354.
    Samuel, †273.
BAKER, George, 153.
    Joseph, 148.
    Polly, 300.
    Sela, 300.
    Susanna, 153, 154.
    Thomas, 153.
    Walter, 13.

    Zebulon, Jr., *153.
BALDWIN, Cyrus, 227.
BALCOM, William, †278.
BALKAM, Elijah, 201.
BALL, Levi, 343.
    Mary, 343.
    Samuel, †342.
BALLANTINE, John, †6, 7.
    Mary, 6, 7.
BALLARD, Alice, 90.
    Calvin, 90.
    Darius, 90.
    Ephraim, 90, 111, 260.
    Jonathan, †90, 200, 202.
    Rufus, 274.
BARD, Sarah, 62.
BARKER, Caleb, 161, *267.
    Carr, 67, 192, 194, 223.
    Francis, 198.
    Hannah, 119, 267.
    Jacob, 267, 268.
    James, 198.
    Jeremiah, 54.
    John, 17, †51.
    Josiah, 197.
    Keziah, 267.
    Prince, †119.
    Rhoda, 267, 268.
    Robert, 138, *197.
    Sarah, 198.
    Susanna, 51.
    William, 147, 248, 267.
BARNARD, Isaac, 147, 344.
    Shubael, 198.
    William, 105.
BARRETT, Simon, 249.
BARRON, Ceasar, *171.
BARROWS, Comfort, †206.
    Sabra, 206, 222.
    Silas, 274.
BARSTOW, Elizabeth, 340.
    George, 167, 340.
    Nathaniel, †340.
BARTER, John, 188.
    Samuel, Jr., 116.
BARTLETT, Caleb, 259.
    Christopher, 183.
    David, 183.
    Eleanor, 163.

INDEX OF NAMES.   3

  Jonathan, †249, 259.
  Samuel, 163, 230.
  Stephen, †259.
  Timothy, 273.
BARTON, Betty, 199, 202.
  Flint, 162.
  Luke, †202.
  Stephen, 172.
BASSETT, Barna, 176.
  Samuel, 78, 175, 176.
BATCHELDER, Hezekiah, 132.
   Theophilus, 207.
BATTLE, Joseph, †340.
BAXTER, Enos, 357.
BAYLEY, Richard, 194.
  Sarah, 193.
BEAL, Abigail, 54.
 Dorcas, 55.
 Eleanor, 54.
 Joshua, 55.
 Josiah, 55.
 Levi, 260.
 Mary, 54.
 Samuel, 124.
 Zaccheus, *54, 55, 124, 141, 166, 185, 256, 339, 342.
BEAN, Edward, *318, 319.
 Eleanor, 318,
 John, 318, 319.
 Joshua, 148, 314, 315.
 Josiah, 318, 319.
 Margaret, 318.
 Neal, 318.
 Phebe, 318.
 Releaf, 314.
 Sarah, 269, 318.
BEATH, Jeremiah, 52, 72.
 Joseph, 89.
BECKLER, Daniel, 68.
BELCHER, Supply, 201, 229, 272, 273.
BELDEN, Aaron, 343.
  Charity, 343.
BEMAN, John, 305.
BENNER, Charles, 178.
 Henry, *177, 178.
 Jacob, 178.
 John, 143, 177, 178.
 Keaty, 177.

 Matice, 177.
 Molly, 178.
 Sally, 178.
 Sedony, 177.
BERNARD, Isaac, 212.
BERRY, Jane, 73.
 John, 160.
BERREY, Joseph, 21, 73, 325.
  Westbrook, †52.
BICKFORD, Abigail, 35.
BILLINGS, Joseph, 154.
BIRD, Alexander, 338.
 Andrew, †101, 271.
 Edward, 189.
 James, †338.
 Jane, 271.
BISBEE, Charles, 207.
 Desire, 273.
 Elisha, 158, †273.
BISHOP, James, 24.
 Squier, 124, 129, 277, 284.
BITUM, Peter, 285.
BLACKINTON, Benjamin, 236.
BLAIR, Hannah, 156.
 John, 156.
 Rebecca, 349.
BLAISDELL, Christopher, †207.
  Daniel, 207.
  Enoch, 163.
  Sarah, 207.
  Timothy, 207.
BLAKE, Paul, 123.
 Samuel, 344, 345.
BLANCHARD, Anna, 173.
  Caleb, 234, 256, 338.
  Edward, *172, 173.
  Ellena, 173.
  James, †255.
  Jane, 255.
  Mary, 173.
  Patty, 255.
  Polly, 255.
  Rachel, 173.
  Samuel, 255.
  Sarah, 173.
  Sheppard, 255.
  Solomon, 249.
  Susanna, 255.

INDEX OF NAMES.

    Sybill, 173.
BLEN, James, 137.
BLETHEN, } Hannah, 1.
BLITHEN,
    Henry Wright, 363.
    John, †1.
    Welthey, 100.
BLODGET, David, 249.
    Mary, 256.
    Nathan, 256.
BLUNT, Arthur, 303.
    Ebenezer, †303, *303, 304, 331, 334, 341.
    Jean, 304.
    John, 130, 220, 276.
    Robert, 303, 304.
    Samuel, 304.
BODFISH, Nymphas, 109, 145, 160, 161, 274.
BOGS, Alexander, 231, 232.
    (Rax) Anne, 33.
    Elizabeth, 231
    Ephraim, 231, 232.
    Isabel, 231.
    (Motley) Jane, 33.
    John, 33, 34, *79.
    Joseph, 231, 232.
    Lucy, 231, 232.
    Mary, 34, 79, 111, 232.
    Rachel, 231, 232.
    Robert, 232.
    Samuel, 7, 20, *33, 34, †111.
    William, 33, 34, 80, 111, 148, *230, 231, 232.
BOIES, James, 11.
BOLTON, Daniel, 148.
BONNEY, Andrew, 152.
    Bariah, 152.
    Daniel, 152.
    Deborah, 152.
    Hannah, 219.
    Isaac, 149, 152, †219.
    James, 152.
    Joseph, 152.
    Lucy, 148.
    Rebecca, 152.
    Silva, 148, 149, 152.
    Simeon, 149, *151, 152.
    Solomon, 152.
    Thankful, 152.
    William, *148 152.
BOOKER, Joseph, 188.
BORLAND, John, 51, 64, 78.
    Sally, 205.
    Samuel, †64.
BORNHEIMER, Godfrey, 202, 331.
    Godfrid, 102, 152.
    Jacob, 254, 260.
BOSWORTH, Eli, 283.
BOURK, William, 112, 348.
BOWDOIN, James, 256.
BOWERMAN, David, 185.
    Pamelia, 192.
    Zacheus, 192.
BOWERS, Benaiah, 347.
BOWKER, James, 84, 124, 339.
    Joseph, 224, 258, 275, 278, 318, 321, 336, 348.
BOWMAN, Jonathan, 50, 306.
    Mary, 168.
    William, 254, 307.
BOYD, Adam, 272.
    John, 277, 280.
    Joseph, 176.
    Katharine, 51.
    Samuel, 38, 277.
    Thomas, 29, 45, 50, 51, 52, 65, 72, 101, 104, 205, 224, 228, 247, 342, 347.
    William. 347.
BOYINTON, }
BOYNTON,   } Amos, 140.
BOYINGTON, }
    (Delano) Anna, 69.
    Caleb, 153.
    Christian, *68.
    Daniel, 153.
    David, 108.
    Hannah, †153.
    (Hilton) Hepsebah, 69.
    Hester, 99.
    John, 69, 153.
    Joseph, 153.
    Joshua, 69, 153.
    (Decker) Rachel, 69.
    Sarah, 69, 153.
    Susanna, 153.

INDEX OF NAMES.

William, 69.
BRACHT, Peter, 45.
BRACKET, } Abraham, Jr., 64.
BRACKETT,
    Anthony, 64.
    Benjamin, 298, 338.
    James, 64.
    Joanna, 64.
    Nathaniel, 64.
    Sarah, 64.
    Thomas, 176.
BRADBURY, Anna, 70, 71, †228.
    Catharine, 60.
    Josiah, *69, 70, †104.
    (Sevey) Meriah, 70.
    Thomas, 234.
    William, 260.
BRADFORD, Alden, 308.
    Benjamin, 181.
    Cornelius, 83, †104, 166, †199.
    George, †219.
    Joshua, Jr., 199.
    Noah, 276.
    Patience, 199.
    Polly, 300.
    William, 206, 219.
BRADISH, Ebenezer, 316.
BRADLEY, } Thomas, 72.
BRADLEE,
BRADMAN, Arthur, 267.
BRAINERD, Benjamin, 99, 139, 140, 195, †195, 221.
    James, 195.
    Mary, 195.
    Orrin, 195.
    Reuben, 99, 195, 219.
    Ruth, 195.
    Sarah, 195.
BRAINT, } Mary, 262.
BRYANT,
BRALEY, Alice, 340.
    John, †340.
BRAMHALL, Cornelius, 162.
BRAN, Jeremiah, 60.
BRANCH, Abigail, 138.
    Benjamin, 138, †254.
    Daniel, 254.
BREWER, James, 51.

John, †51, 161.
Josiah, 86, 87, 141.
BRIAR, } Samuel, 89, 104, 135.
BRIER,
BRIDGDON, Sarah, 113.
    Timothy, 113.
BRIDGE, Edmund, 16, 19, 20, 34, 38, 39, 49, 52, 67, 87, 104, 108, 161, 162, 178, 180, 223, 259, 306, 348.
    Fanny, 254.
    James, 227, 264.
    John, 132, †254, 289.
    Phebe, 306.
    Rachel, 254.
BRIGGS, William, 251.
BRODMAN, Charles, 226.
BROEST, Joanne Peter, 45.
BROOKINS, Josiah, Jr., 138.
BROOKS, Mary, 203.
    Susanna, 111.
    William, 111, 158, 197, 203, 220.
BROWN, } Benjamin, 82, 83, 148, 183, 255.
BROWNE,
    David N., 281.
    Elijah, 342.
    Ezekiel, 323.
    Jacob, 192, 281, 345.
    James, 2, 50, †65, 76, 144, 167.
    Jane, 65, 76, 144, †167.
    John, 65, †144.
    Loyalist, 281
    Martha, 65, 144.
    Mary, 144, 224.
    Moses, 160, †275.
    Samuel, 75, 86, 193, 223, †224 255, 284, 338, 345.
    Sarah, 318.
    Stephen, 168.
    Timothy, 252.
    William, 183, 189.
BRYANT, } Charles, 115, 116.
BRIANT,
    David, Jr., 128.
    Hannah, 53, 54.
    Jonathan, 25, 41.
    Lemuel, 128.

Mary, 41, 262.
Nathaniel, †53, 54, 144, 160, 265, 275, 347.
Patience, 54.
BUCKHART, Henry, 346.
BUCKLEN, Nathan, 110, 170, 171.
BUCKNAM, William, 45.
BUDGE, James, 129.
BUGNON, James, 1, †49, 263.
Jane, 49.
Margaret, 49.
Susanna, 49.
BUKER, James, 84.
BULLIN, Samuel, 196.
BURKE, William, 234.
BURNHAM, } Abel, †82.
BURNAM, } Elizabeth, 313.
Francis, 313.
Mary, 103.
Solomon, 104, 338.
BURNS, Cornelius, 260.
James, 20, 66, 84.
Joseph, 20, 163, 191.
Mary, 34.
Robert, †20.
William, 38, 66, 128, 163.
BURR, Joseph, 264.
Matthew, 341.
Thomas, †341.
BURRELL, John, 75.
BURTON, Alice, 11.
Benjamin, †11, 53, 341.
John, 53.
BUSH, Samuel, 303.
BUSWELL, James, †276.
Jane, 276.
BUTLER, Abigail, 213, 214, 215, 216.
Ann, 215. 319.
Lucy, 222.
Martha, 213, 215, *319.
Mary, 215, 319.
Mella, 223.
Moses, 121.
Sarah, 213, 214, 215, 216, 319, 320.
Thomas, 185, 213, 214, 216, 278, 319, 320, 248.
William, 6, 84, *212, 213, 214, 215, 216, 241, 242, 319, 320, 328.
BUTTERFIELD, Abigail, 203.
Ephraim, 107, 204.
Josiah, 29, †227.
BUTTS, Samuel, 234.
BYRAM, Ebenezer, 248.
CALDERWOOD, Elizabeth, 59.
CALDWELL, George, 34.
CALL, Bethiah, 162.
Charles, 162, 274.
Deliverance, 35, 162.
Elizabeth, 162.
Experience, 161.
Hannah, 162.
James, 162.
John, 48, 162.
Jonathan, 293, 294.
Keziah, 293.
Lydia, 162.
Margaret, 162.
Moses, 293, 294.
Nathan, 293, 294.
Nathaniel, 293, 294.
Obadiah, 11, 36, 97, 108, 138, 140, †161, 162, 163, 206, 359.
Olive, 162.
Philip, †48, 87, 91, 108, 138, 140, †162, 359.
Polly, 293, 294.
Stephen, 108, *292, 293, 294.
William, 162.
CALLAHAN, Charles, †87.
CALLEY, Samuel, 65, 66.
CAMPBELL, Alexander, 2, 5, 6, 45, 312.
Betsey, 205.
Daniel, 205, 273.
Elizabeth, 76, 312.
James, †205.
Jane, 76.
John, 76, *311, 312, 313, 343.
Joseph, 205, 295.
Margaret, 312.
Martha, *75.
Mary, 76.
Michael, 205.
Rachel, 205.

INDEX OF NAMES. 7

Robert, 205.
Sarah, 205.
CANE, Walter, †16.
CARGILL, Abernethy, 228, 229.
　　　　　James, 7, 20, 24, 38, 45, 60, 90, 110.
CARL, } Nathaniel, 45.
CARLL,
　　　　　Submit, 319.
CARLTON, } John, †137.
CARLETON, } Joseph, 338.
　　　　　Margaret, 338.
CARLILE, } Abigail 134.
CARLISLE,
　　　　　David, 163.
　　　　　Elizabeth, 134.
　　　　　James, 134.
　　　　　Jane, 137.
　　　　　John, 92.
　　　　　Joseph, 101, 104, *133, 134.
　　　　　Mary, 135.
　　　　　Mirriam, 134.
　　　　　William 65.
CARNEY, Susannah, 50.
CARR, Elizabeth, 92.
　　　　George, 277.
　　　　James, 220.
　　　　Mecrus, (Meecres,) 4, †92.
　　　　Mehitable, 287.
　　　　Moses, 287.
CARTER, Isabel, 242.
　　　　Joseph, 77.
　　　　Nathaniel, 77.
CARY, Luther, 345.
　　　　Peter, 241.
CASE, Barnard, 206, *252, 253.
　　　　James, 252.
　　　　Rebeckah, 252.
　　　　Thankful, 252.
　　　　William, 252.
CASTNER, Anna, 142.
　　　　Baltas, †73.
　　　　Ludwig, 73, 142.
　　　　Ustana, 73.
CAVELEAR, Louis, †1.
　　　　John Louis, †38.
　　　　Mary 1, 38.
CAWLEY, Mary, 76, 77.

Samuel, 76.
CAZNEAU, Andrew, 10.
CHADWICK, Joseph, 87.
　　　　Lot, 208.
CHALMERS, William, 97.
CHAMBERLAIN, Sarah, 332.
CHANDLER, Jacob, 152, 272.
　　　　Joel, 227, †251.
　　　　John, 83, 129, 251.
　　　　John, Jr., 149.
　　　　Moses, 130, 152, 272.
　　　　Phebe, 272.
　　　　Rebecca, 272, 273.
　　　　Sally, 273.
　　　　Samuel, †272.
CHAPMAN, Abraham, 270.
　　　　Deborah, 270.
　　　　Nathaniel, 60.
　　　　Prudence, 38, *269.
　　　　Ralph, †38.
　　　　Sarah, 269.
CHASE, Abigail, 109.
　　　　Benjamin, 366.
　　　　Charles, 163, 205, 228, 229.
　　　　Ezekiel, 104, 109.
　　　　John †163, †347.
　　　　Mary, 109.
　　　　Mathew 48, 104, 109.
　　　　Rachel, 163.
　　　　Roger, 19, 25, 48, 104, *108.
　　　　Sarah, 109.
　　　　(Spear,) Mrs., 104.
　　　　Stephen, †19.
　　　　Tamor, 109.
　　　　Vernum, 109.
CHENEY, Elias, †17.
　　　　Sybyl, 17.
CHILD, Amos, 218, 276.
　　　　Hannah, 280.
CHISHAM, John, 273.
CHOATE, } Abraham, 352.
CHOAT,
　　　　Francis, †348.
　　　　John, *351.
　　　　Moses, 352.
　　　　Sally, 352.
　　　　Susannah, 348.
CHRISTOPHERS, Joseph, 254, 309, 336, 338, 342.

CHURCH, John, 201.
    Rubie, 264.
CLANCY, David, 359.
    Elizabeth, 49.
CLAP, Enos, 54.
    Hannah, (Barker,) 54.
    Thomas, 260, 341.
CLARK, Abigail, 94.
    Betty, 193.
    David, 88, 94, †122.
    Ebenezer, 306.
    Elenor, 229.
    Elisha, 79, 88.
    (Fling.) Hannah, 24.
    Isaac, 94.
    James, *23, †93, 205.
    John, 122. 164, 228, 305.
    Jonas, 88, 94.
    Jonathan, 161.
    Joseph, 64, 78, 84, *175, 322.
    Lois, 84, 175.
    Margaret, 93, 233, 322.
    Pease, *94.
    Peter, 95.
    Polly, 122.
    Robert, †229.
    Samuel, 79, 229, 304, 322.
    Sarah, 122, 155.
    Simeon, 94, 123.
    Solomon, 151, 194.
    Susanna, 94.
    Thomas, 23, 29, †84, †132, 175.
    Uriah, 88.
    William, 23, 155, 255.
CLARY, Allen, 273.
    Jane, 84.
    Michael, †163.
    Robert, 273.
CLEVELAND, Mrs. Jane, 181, *190.
    Joseph, 361.
    Rebeckah, 190.
CLIFFORD, Isaac, 224.
    Samuel, 110.
    William, 58, †110.
CLINE, Christian, †123.
    Elizabeth, 123.
    George, 123.
    John, 123.

CLOUGH, Abner, 159.
    Daniel, 343, 344.
    Stephen, 205.
CLOUSE, Cornelius, †68.
    George, 153.
    Mary, 68.
CLOUTMAN, Hezekiah, †24.
COCHRAN, Agnes, 211.
    John, †211.
    Martha, 125.
    Mary, 125.
    Nathaniel, 310.
    Robert, 2, †110, 125, 143, 211.
    Ruth, 309.
    Samuel, 125.
CODMAN, Richard, 45.
COFFIN, Betsey, 280.
    Charles, 256.
    David Newell, 281.
    Mary, 192.
    Nathaniel, 196.
    Prince, 105, †192, 198.
    Zebulon, †280, 281.
COGSWELL, Adam, †163.
COLBURN, Jonathan, 77.
    Margaret, 197.
    Oliver, †197.
    Reuben, 87, 136, 248.
COLBY, Ambros, *133.
    (Hoyt.) Annah, 133,
    Betty, 133.
    Hezekiah, †164.
    Joshua, 164.
COLE, Catherina, 330.
    Jabesh, 82, 126, 143, 170, 171, 178, 182.
    Joseph, 73.
    Sarah, 269.
COLLAMORE, Deborah, 20.
    Joshua, 83, 88, 101, 143, 170, 171, 199.
    Peter, 206.
    Sarah, 20.
    Samuel, †20.
    Susannah, 20.
COLMAN, Samuel, 148, 204, 254, 256, 259, 265, 273, 336.
CONLEY, John, †227.

INDEX OF NAMES.

CONNORS, James, 294.
CONY, CONEY, } Daniel, 111, 220.
    Heartson, 111, 340.
    Jason, 111.
    Samuel, 111.
    Susanna, 111.
COOK, Anna, 184.
    Bethiah, 341.
    Cornelius, 341.
    Crowell, 166.
    Elijah, 199, 341.
    Elsie, 341.
    Francis, 170, 230, 255, 275, 305, 341.
    Hannah, 189.
    James, 189, †341.
    John, 184.
    Joseph, 184.
    Mary, 339.
    Nancy, 341.
    Orchard, 338.
    Thomas, †183.
    Winslow Bradford, 341.
    Zenas, †189.
COOL, Hannah, 77.
    John Peter, †77.
COOLIDGE, Benjamin, 119.
COOMBS, Abigail, 161.
    Andrew, 268,
    Ebenezer, †161.
    George Fields, 183.
    Jacob, 183.
    Jonathan, 203.
    Joseph, 255.
    Joshua, †183.
    Mary, 204.
    Stephen, 267.
COOPER, Boyce, 11, 15.
    James, 93, 101.
    Leonard, 194.
    Nicholas, 354.
    Sally, 354.
COPELAND, Joseph, 148, 170, 171, 194, 232, 298, 301.
    Moses, 8, 11, 12, 20, 50, 51, 61, 67, 86, 90, 108, 110, 111, 119, 129, 132, 143, 144, 147, 163, 170, 171, 188, 189, 193, 212, 224, 226, 230, 232, 247, 248, 255, 260, 299, 301, 343, 345, 346.
CORBAT, Elizabeth, 364.
COSS, Daniel, †279.
    John, 279.
    Thomas, 279.
COSTELOW, John, 163, 179.
COUCH, Anna, 163.
    George, †164.
COUILLIARD, Charles, 239, 241, 242, 258, 328.
COUNCE, Samuel, 86, 144.
COUSENS, Samuel, 188.
    Thomas, 188.
COWAN, James, 107.
COWEN, Ephraim, 91.
COWIN, Abisha, 87, 148, 254.
    Isaac, 122.
COX, Ebenezer, †175, 176.
    Gershom, 274.
    Hugh, 339.
    Israel, 175, 279.
    John, †274.
    Katey, 229.
COYE, Abiah, 87, 93, †124.
    Daniel, 124.
    Judith, 124.
CRABTREE, Agreen, 36.
CRAGIN, Joseph, 79.
CRAIG, CRAIGUE, } Anna, 315.
    Delia, 315.
    Elenor, 315.
    Elias, 265.
    Elisha, 274.
    Enoch, 201.
    Freeman, 315.
    George, 316.
    Hannah, 141,
    James, *315, 316.
    John, 316.
    Margaret, 316.
    Mary, 315.
    Orison, 315.
    Peter, 315.
    Sally, 316.

Thomas, 315, 316.
William, 315, 316.
CRANE, Rufus, 232, 298.
    Samuel, 144.
CRAWFORD, Archibald, 148.
    James, 86, 161.
    John, 34.
    Joseph Brewer, 86.
    Margaret, 86.
    Mary, 86.
    William, *86.
CREAMER, Edward, 272.
CREIGHTON, James, 111.
    Jane, 111.
    Lucretia, 111.
    Samuel, 7, 34, 40, 51, 67, 80, 86, †111.
CREASY, } Caleb, †140, 319.
CRESSEY,
    Mary, 318.
    Meribah, 140.
CROOKER, Hannah, 262.
    Isaiah, 20, 25, 28, 50, 64, 77, 137, 140, †262.
    John, 52.
    Paul, 343.
    Zacheus, 262.
CROCKET, Elioenai, 222.
    John, †101.
    Jonathan, 101.
    Nathaniel, 101.
CROSBY, Hannah, 67.
    Joanna, 67.
    Joel, *67.
    John, 161.
    Jonah, 79.
    Josiah, 337.
    Rebeckah, 67.
    Robert, 183, 184.
    Ruth R., 67.
    Susannah, 126.
CROSS, Joshua, 227.
CROSSMAN, Jesse, †138.
    Sarah, 138.
CROWELL, Abner, 177.
    Ezekiel, 339.
    Jabez, *176.
    Joseph, †339.

    Josiah, 274.
    Levi, 339.
    Thankful, 176.
    Zadock, 339.
CUMMINGS, } Asa, †251.
COMINGS, } Eleanor, 251.
    John, 195.
    Samuel, 251.
CUNNINGHAM, Alexander, 289.
    Daniel, 249, 292.
    Hannah, 344.
    James, 7.
    John, 2, 6, 11, 12, 24, 29.
    Sarah, 7, 29.
    Thomas, 228, 229, 274.
    William, 110, 124, 136, 183, 207, 275, †344.
CURRIER, James, 251.
CURTIS, David, 1.
    James, 226.
    John, 18.
    Lot, †162.
    Seth, 274.
    Thomas, 130.
    William, 52.
CUSHING, Benjamin, 340, 343, 344.
    Charles, 4, 11, 16, 17, 19, 20, 25, 34, 38, 39, 48, 49, 50, 67, 87.
    Christopher, 220, 221, 260, 265, 341.
    Ezekiel, 205.
    Frances, 186, 188.
    Francis, 205.
    John, Jr., 54.
    Martin, 341.
    Roland, 87, †180.
    William, 36, 55.
CUSHMAN, James, 345.
    Kenelam, 305.
    Robert, 157, 356.
CUTTER, Ammi Ruhama, 99.
    Ezekiel, 292, 309, 335.
DAGGETT, Jesse, 180.
    John, 180, 275.
DAISY, Jeremiah, 363.
DALHEIM, George, 39.
DALTON, Jeremiah, 228, 364.

INDEX OF NAMES. 11

DANFORD, Enoch, 121.
DANFORTH, Joshua, 254.
DARLING, Jonathan, 166.
DAVENPORT, Betsey, 260.
        Ebenezer, 227.
DAVIDSON, James, 215, 216, 242.
DAVIS, Daniel, 268, 336, 337.
    David, 340.
    Ebenezer, 32.
    Edward, 234, 256, 338.
    Ephraim, 205.
    Hannah, 226.
    Hope, 300, 301.
    Israel, 50, 51, 52, 65, 143.
    Jacob, †130.
    Jesse, †226.
    John, 83, 135.
    Jonathan, 95, 227, †270.
    Joseph, †143.
    Joshua, 226.
    Mark, 143.
    Mary, 143.
    Moses, 47, 136, 143, 145, 183, 205, 227, 230, 277, 288, 305, 342, 347.
    Nancy, 357.
    Nathaniel, 175.
    Rachel, 227.
    Rebecca, 227.
    Robert, 301.
    Samuel, †47, 130.
    Zachary, †205.
DAWS, }
DAWES, } John, 63, 88, 101, 111, 338.
DAWSE, }
    Mary, 89.
DAY, Bethany, 273.
    Benjamin, 340.
    Daniel, *17.
    Jacob, †273.
    Job, 277, 288.
    Marthue, 103.
    Mary, 17.
    Samuel, †338.
    Sarah, 17, 29.
DEARBORN, Henry, 147.
DEARING, } John Bray, 342.
DEERING, }
DECKER, Anna, 70, 107.

    John, Jr., 53, †107.
    Joseph, †53, 110, 205, †230.
    Rachel, 69.
    Sarah, 230.
    Spencer, 207.
    William, 155.
DELANO, Amasa, 69.
    Anna, 69.
    Ebenezer, 311.
    Elizabeth, 196.
    Hopestill, 97.
    Rachel, †229.
    Seth, 229.
    Thomas, Jr., 196.
DEMORSE, Charles, 249.
    John, 130, 162, 189.
    John, Jr., 143.
    Samuel, †162.
DEMUTH, George, 45, 82, 143, 270.
DENHAM, Catharine, 342.
    Thomas, †342.
    William, 256, 342.
DENNIS, Amos, 277.
    David, 227, 228, 350.
DENNY, Catherin, 56, 57.
    Samuel, 8, 31, *55.
    (McCobb) Rachel, 57.
DEVENS, Samuel, 78.
DEXTER, Mark, †344.
DICKEY, David, 219.
    John, †64.
DICKMAN, Thomas, 265.
DIGBY, Abigail, 64.
DILLAWAY, John, 108, 344.
    Mary, 108.
DILLINGHAM, Joshua, 343.
    Pitt, 354.
DIMAN, Jacob, 141.
DINGLEY, Ezra, †278.
    Nabby, 278.
DINSMORE, Asa, 49, 161.
    Judith, 339.
    Lucinda, 339.
    Prince, 339.
    Samuel, 127.
    Susanna, 256.
    Thomas, 91.
    William, 192, †339.

DOCKENDORFF, Jacob, 47, 206.
DODGE, Abigail, 165.
    Abner, 165.
    Abraham, 165.
    Benjamin, 136, 165.
    Ezekiel Goddard, 212.
    Ezekiel G., 238.
    John, 140, 166.
    Jonah, *164, †164.
    Jonah, Jr., 165.
    Mehitable, 211, 212.
    Nancy, 336.
    Paul, 144.
    Rachel, 66.
    Reuben, 165, 166.
    Sarah, 164, 165, 166, 182.
    Simon, 165.
    William, †336.
    Zachariah, 136, 140, *182, 183.
DOE, Elizabeth, 277.
    John, 277.
    Lemuel, 234, †277.
    Samuel, 277.
    Thomas, 277.
DOGGETT, Samuel, 77.
DOLE, Nathan, 351.
    Nathaniel, †145.
DOLHEIM, George, 152.
DONNELL, Benjamin, 3.
    Elizabeth, 3.
    Nathaniel, *2, 3, 4.
    Thomas, 3.
Dow, Dorothy, 276.
Dows, John, 337, 338.
    Perley, †276.
DROWNE, David, 37.
    John, 179.
    Lucy, 179.
    Thomas, 64.
DRUMMOND, Alexander, 205, 277.
    Ann, 5, 215, 240, 319, 320.
    Elijah, 5, 6, 185, 205, 207, 215, 216, 224, 275, 278, 318, 319, 320, 348.
    Hannah, 106.
    James, 6, 47, 176, 227, 304.
    Jane, 6.
    John, 5, †63.
    Lutitia, 5.
    Margaret, 6.
    Mary, 63.
    Patrick, *4.
    Rachel, 240.
    Susannah, 4, 6.
    William Butler, 215.
DUDLEY, Benjamin, 244, 245, †273.
    Daniel, 249.
    John, 249, 273.
    Micajah, 221.
    Moses, †227.
    Nathaniel, 249, 250, 319.
DUMARESQ, James, 275.
DUMMER, Nathaniel, 220, 287, 305.
DUNBAR, Daniel, 247.
    Solomon, 144.
DUNHAM, David, †275.
    Hannah, 275.
DUNLAP, (Eaton), Jane, 51.
    John, 51.
    (Potter), Margaret, 51.
    Mary, 51.
    Robert, 51.
    Samuel, 261, 292.
DUNLOP, Jane, 42.
DUNNING, Andrew, 121.
    James, †166.
    Jean, 166.
DUTTON, Jonas, 123, 323.
    Samuel, 99, 220.
DWINEL, Aaron, 337.
DYER, Jonathan 84, 175.
EAMES, Jacob, 164, 197, 260.
EASTMAN, Benjamin, 249.
EATON, Abel, Jr., 82.
    Elizabeth, 229.
    George, 89.
    Jacob, 201, †227.
    Jane, 51.
    Jesse, †249.
    Joseph, 249.
    Joseph, Jr., 249,
    Polly, 250.
    Relief, 250.
    Sarah, 249, 250.
    Theophilus, 133, 163.
    William, 250.

INDEX OF NAMES. 13

Ziba, 342.
EDDY, Jonathan, 161.
EDSON, Calvin, 201.
    Elizabeth, 201.
EGGLESTON, Hannah, 277.
    Hezekiah, †277.
EICHORN, Daniel, 236, 237.
    Jacob, 51.
    Margaret Catharine Bane, 84, 167.
    Mathias, †84.
ELDER, James, †16.
ELLIOT, Anna, 357.
    Daniel, 357, 358.
    Isabella, 357.
    Jenny, 357, 358.
    John, *356.
    Mary, 358.
    Peggy, 357.
    Peter, 357.
    Sabrah, 357.
    Sarah, 178.
    Simon, 273, 357, 358, 359.
    William, †178.
ELLIS, Jonathan, 84, 277, 342.
ELLISON, Elizabeth, †125.
ELMES, Betty, 289.
ELWELL, Jacob, †82.
    William, 83.
    William, Jr., 88.
EMERSON, Anni, 296.
    Ebenezer, 195, 285, 340.
    Edward, 45, 118, 247, 295, 296, 297, 347, 348.
    Elizabeth, 247, *294, 295, 296.
    John, 247, 272, 295, 297, 335.
    Joseph, 295, 296.
    Philip, 185.
    Pratt, 296.
    Rebecca, 296, 340.
    Samuel, 38, 50, 87, 138, 140, 162, 180.
    Sarah, 340.
    Susannah, 296.
    William, 294, 295, 296, 347.
EMERY, Jonathan, 91, 104, 323.
ERSKINE, }
ERSKINES, } Alexander, 64.
ERSKIN, }

    Christopher, 138, 354.
    George, 93, 163, 177, 291.
    John, 290.
    Ninyin, 64.
ERVING, John, 234.
EVELETH, James, 260.
EVENS, } Hannah, 203.
EVANS, }
    John, 137, 311.
    Nathaniel, 203.
    Thomas, 172.
FAIRBANKS, Alexander, 264.
    Benjamin, 144, 221.
    Nathaniel, 129, 138, 219, 220, 246, 251, 336.
FAIRBROTHER, Lovel, 18.
    Thomas, 18.
FAIRFIELD, Daniel, Jr., †162.
    Elizabeth, 162.
    Jeremiah, 219.
    John, 7.
    Reuben, 208.
    William, 342.
FAIRSERVICE, Thomas, 205, 339.
FALES, David, 40, 51, 60, 67, 80, 108, 212, 223, 232, 236, 247, 299, 338, 344.
    Nathaniel, Jr., 80.
    Sybel, 222.
FALL, Richard, †20,
FARLEY, Elizabeth, 361.
    John, 54, 65, 144, 167, 170, 259, 274, 275, 331, 340, 347.
FARNAM, John, 110.
FARNHAM, Joshua, 97.
    Zebediah, 138.
FARNSWORTH, Abigail, 119.
    Jonas, 119.
    Robert, 238.
    Sarah, 211.
    William, 90, 118, 119, 145, 170, 171, 211, 239, 276.
FARRIN, John, 82.
FARROW, Ezekiel, 147, 298.
    Timothy, 255.
FARWELL, Bunker, †336.
    Ebenezer, 254, 278, 336, 340, 365.
    Mary, 336.

INDEX OF NAMES.

FASSET, Ruth, 217.
FEGAN, Daniel, 346.
FEILHUR, Daniel, 124.
FEILTREN, Daniel, 153.
FIELDS, James, 179.
Mary, 179.
FILLEBROWN, Thomas, 265.
FILLER, Godfrey, *126.
John, 126.
Regine, 126.
FISH, William, 276.
FISHER, Jane, 240.
John, 215, 216, 239, 241, 321.
FITCH, Jonas, 1, 15, 16, 17, 20, 34, 75, 144, 162, 176, 224.
FITTS, Elizabeth, 76, 77.
Ephraim, 159, 160, 220, †227.
Mark, 76.
Sarah, 277.
FITZGERALD, Daniel, 15.
Nicholas, 23.
Sophia, 330.
FLAGG, James, 16, 20, 24, 49.
FLETCHER, Amy, 263.
FLING, Esther, 361.
Eunice, 361.
Hannah, 24.
John, 361.
Morris,*360.
Samuel, 361.
Susanna, 361.
FLINT, Jesse, 54, 340.
Thomas, 65.
FLITNER, William, 275.
FLOYD, Joseph, †101.
Mary, 101.
Nathaniel, 99, 195.
FLY, Jonathan, †183.
Sarah, 183.
FOGERTY, Dennis, 298.
FOGG, Daniel, †68.
FOLGIER, Timothy, 198.
FOLLENSBEY, Thomas, 289, 290.
FOLLET, Abagail, 94.
Benjamin, 95.
FOOTE, Erastus, 344.
John, 137.
FORD, Francis, 61, 175.

Mary, 156. *284.
Robert, 285.
Samuel, 61, 92, 114, 132, 137, *156, 175.
FOSSET,
FOSET,   Alexander, 38, 237, 238, 358.
FOSSAT,

Henry, †34, 176, 179, 206, 227, 234, 237, 238, 277, 280.
Ruth, 237.
William, *237.
FOSTER, Alexander, 220, 221.
Benjamin, 220.
Charles, 220.
David, 144, 221.
Dorothy, 220.
Eliphalet, †130, †144.
Filena, 264.
Hatherly, 64, 124, 140, †164, †220.
Hatherly, Jr., 220.
Jane, 258, 261.
John, 220.
Joseph, 53, 195, 258, 261.
Martha, 220.
Mary, 164.
Nathan, 343.
Nathaniel, †220.
Rebeckah, 252.
Sibella, 221.
Steal, 251.
Stephen, †176, 221.
Stewart, 221.
Thomas, 220.
Timothy, 129, 130, 138, †176, †221.
William, †138, 220.
FOUGHT, Anthony, 174.
Frederick, 174.
Hannah, 174.
Jacob, 174.
Marget, 174.
Philip, 90, *173.
Rachel, 174.
FOUNTAIN, Barney, 120.
Elizabeth, 120.
Jacob, 120.
Rachel, 120.

INDEX OF NAMES.

FOWLE, Joshua, 146.
FOWLES, William, 343.
FOWLER, John, 151, 252.
    Simeon, 126.
FOYE, John Sutton, 264, 276.
    William, 224.
FRANCKFORT, Christian, 38.
FREEMAN, Edmund, 337.
FREES, George, 133.
    Isaac, 129.
FRENCH, Josiah, 138, 139, 140, 144, 221.
FRIEND, Benjamin, 163.
FULLER, Edward, 130, 275, 278.
    Enoch, 200.
    Francis, 137.
    Jonathan, 54, 95.
    Rachel, 262.
    William, 52.
    Zenas, 273.
FULLERTON, Ebenezer, 89.
    John, †140, †171.
    James, 118, 137, 336.
    William, 13.
FULLINGTON, James, 114.
    Martha, 113.
FULTON, James, 73, 75, 82, 121, 142, 210, 211, 221, 234, 259, 261.
    Jenny, 84.
    John, 73, 75, 82, 84, 107, 160, 210, 221, 255, 261, 349.
    John, Jr., 84, †277.
    Robert, †84.
    Sarah, 84, 277.
FURNALD, John, †144.
GAHAN, Bersheba, 193.
GAMBLE, Archibald, †110.
GARDINER, Benjamin, 84.
    Jethro, 208.
    John, 161, †234.
    John Silvester John, 234.
    William, 61, 161, †161, 234.
GARDNER, Abdial, 105.
    Benjamin, *105.
    Benjamin, Jr., 105.
    Daniel, 105, †275.
    Hannah, 105.
    Isaiah, 275.
    Mary, 105, 194.
    Parthena, 105.
    Peleg, †194.
    Rebeckah, 105.
    Richard, 105.
    Ruth, 105, 194, 275.
    Sabrina, 105.
    Wells, 295.
GATCHEL, John, 173.
    Nehemiah, 90, 162.
GAUBERT, Nicholas, 160, 223.
GAY, Eleazer, 188, 189, 199, 205.
    Jonah, †88.
    Seth, 147.
    Wellington, 88, 189, 206, 341.
GERRISH, Charles, 82.
    Joanna, 192.
    Thomas, †192.
GETCHEL, GETCHELL, } Abigail, 218.
    Anstrus, 218, 219.
    David, 218, 219.
    Dennis, 162, *218, 219.
    Dennis, Jr., 218.
    Edmund, 218.
    Elihu, 192, 198, 218, 229, 256, 294, 339, 348.
    Fanny, 218, 219.
    John, 274, *350.
    John, Jr., 326.
    Keziah, 326.
    Lydiah, 218, 219.
    Margaret, 218, 219.
    Mary, 218, 219, 350, 351.
    Nehemiah, 141, 161, 218.
    Remington, 219.
    William, 219.
GEVIN, Jenny, 237.
GEYER, Rudolph Frederick, 38.
GIBBS, Elisha, 249.
GILBERT, George, 348.
GILLCHRIST, Elizabeth, 298.
    George, †298.
    Samuel, 8, 11, 33, 298.
GILLINGHAM, John, †185.
GILMAN, John, 273.
    Peter, 130.
    Samuel, 284.
    Samuel Stevens, 273.

INDEX OF NAMES.

GILMORE, David, 36, 114, 118, 157, 197, 199, 220, 239, 255, 277, 336, 356.
 David, Jr., 54, 92.
 Rufus, 248, 253, 345.
GINN, James, 129, 161.
GIVEN,
GIVEEN, } Agnes, 274.
GOVAN,
 David, 2, 24, 82, 274.
 James, 259.
 John, †274.
 John, Jr., †259.
 Mary, 168.
 Robert, 80, 179, 238, 279, 280.
 Sarah, 274.
GLEASON, Abigail, 64.
GLIDDEN, Benjamin, 145.
 John, 292.
 Tobias, 15, 16.
GODDARD, Josiah, 289, 324.
GOLDER, William, 275.
GOLDTHWAIT, Thomas, 60.
GOOCH, Benjamin, †140.
GOODWIN, Benjamin, 114.
 Daniel, †19.
 George, 348.
 Jacob, 279.
 John, †67.
 Lazarus, 164, 167, 192, 196, 197.
 Olive, 35.
 Prudence, 35.
 Samuel, 25, 34, 39, 47, 48, 64, 65, 87, 91, 145, 221, 248, 366.
 Samuel, Jr., 19, 25, 38, 48, 52, 53, 67, 68, 107, 121, 221, 223, 251, 336, †348.
 Samuel Twycross, 196.
 Stephen, †274.
GOOLD, Hannah, 21.
 Joseph, 21.
GORDON, John Jr., 230.
GORE, Jeremiah, 40.
 Mary, 40.
 Robert, 229.
GOUD, Daniel, *49.
 (Clancey) Elizabeth, 49.
 George, 39, 50.
 { James, 162, 223, 294.
 { Jaque,
 Nancy, 315.
 (Carney) Susannah, 50.
GOUDY, Amos, †19, 144, 206.
 Betty, 19.
 Mercy, 19.
GOULD, Anstis, 81.
 Hannah, *81, 82.
 Joseph, *20, 81, 83.
 Mary, 81.
 Mercy, 81.
 Moriah, 183, 184.
 Moses, 81, *83.
 Robert, 17.
 Stephen, 81.
GOVAN, Alexander, 279.
(See GIVEN.)
 Betsey, 279.
 Hannah, 279.
 Jane, 279, 280.
 Jenny, 279.
 Robert, †279.
 Sally, 279.
GOVE, Asa, 124.
 Ebenezer, 143, 224, 230, †275.
 Mary, 275.
 Nathan, 47.
 Solomon, 110, 136.
 William, 347.
GOWELL, Charles, 278.
 William, 307.
GOWER, Robert, 45.
GRAFFAM, Jacob, 301.
 John, †147.
 Lydia, 147.
BRAGG, Barnabas, 212,
 Katherine, *211, 212.
 Mary, 212.
 Mehitable, 211.
 Samuel, 67, †145.
 Sarah, 145, 211.
 William, 211.
GRANT, Andrew, 126.
 Betsey, 356.
 Catharine, 18.
 Elijah, 199.

INDEX OF NAMES.

  Elisha, 126, 161.
  James, †18.
  Samuel, 161, 162, 173, 219, 337.
GRAVES, Calvin, 137.
  Jacob, 277, 278.
  Joseph, 23, 221, 234.
  Mary, 278.
  Samuel, 23, 121, †278.
GRAY, Abihail, 77.
  Alexander, 63, †77.
  Andrew, 183.
  Benjamin, 104.
  Ebenezer, 58, †92.
  Ebenezer, Jr., 92, 93.
  Elizabeth, 92.
  George, †7, 17.
  Jemima, 92, 93.
  John, 114, 227, 228.
  Levi, 92.
  Margaret, 300.
  Mary, 92, 102, 103.
  Reuben, 92, 93.
  Thomas, 92.
  William, 228.
GREELEY, Jonathan, 297.
  Joseph, 203.
  Joseph, Jr., 244.
  Moses, †48.
  Seth, 24.
  Susanna, 203.
GREEN, Jonas, 273.
GREENLEAF, Ebenezer, †15, 108.
  Mary, 108.
  Samuel, 207.
GREENOUGH, Robert, 289, 342.
GREGORY, William, 221, 232, 343.
GRIFFIN, Robert, 86.
GROSS, Anna Catharina, 102.
  John, 101.
  Mari Elizabeth, 102, 103.
  Peter, 102, 153.
GROVER, Ebenezer, 178.
  Mehitable, †224.
GROVES, Alice, 136.
  Annarh, 136, 146.
  Hannah, 136, 146.
  John, *135, 136, 146.

  Joseph, 169.
  Mary, 135, 136.
  Rebecca, 136.
  Samuel, 136, 211, 272.
  William, 136, *145, 290.
GUILD, Joseph, 204, 207.
GULLEFER, } Thomas, 172.
GUILLIVER, }
GUSTIN, David, †23.
HAINES, John, 287.
HALEY, } John, 192.
HAYLEY, }
  Joseph, 340, †346.
  Martin, †192.
  Mary, 346.
  William, 221.
HALL, Abigail, 98.
  Abijah, 129.
  Elizabeth, 129.
  James, 227.
  Jeremiah, 98, 124.
  John, 273, 292.
  Jonathan, 98.
  Josiah, 98.
  Lemuel, †292.
  Mary, 129, 292, 328.
  Nathan, †129.
  Oliver, 124.
  Preserved, *97.
  Reuben, 20, 86, 110, 111, 143, 144.
  Samuel, 124.
  Seth, 298.
  Timothy, 98.
HALLOWELL, Briggs, 105, †166.
  Eunice, 166.
  Robert, 234.
HALY, Pelathiah, 82.
HAM, Benjamin, 19, 137, 229, 260, 337.
  Tobias, 19.
HAMILTON, Gabriel, 77.
  John, 254.
HAMMATT, Joseph, 147.
  William, 197.
HAMMON, Seth, 126.
HAMMOND, Anne, 260.
  Frederick, 260.
  Jedediah, †255.
HANCOCK, David, †88, 94.

INDEX OF NAMES.

Susanna, 88, 94.
HANDLEY, Roger, 294.
HANKERSON, John, 19.
HANSON, Robert, 255, 331.
HARDING, Isaac, 21.
    Josiah, 21.
HARFORD, Joseph, 34, 75.
HARNDEN, Mary, 36.
    Richard, 220, 341.
    Samuel, 18, 32, †36, 54, 132, †175, 197, 220, 260.
HARRIS, Abner, 268.
    Harlowe, 264.
    Lois, 264.
    Obadiah, 264.
    Samuel, 75.
HART, William, 207.
HARWARD, George, †178.
    Thomas, 178.
HASEY, Benjamin, 337.
    Ebenezer, Jr., 97.
HASKELL, Ignatius, 162, 195.
    Mark, 133.
HASTINGS, Abigail, 203.
    Hannah, 203.
    Mary, 203.
    Matthew, 17 †18, 29, 72, 78, 84, 138, 174, 175, 176, *202, 204.
    Mercy, 203.
    Moses, 78, 203, 204.
    Moses, Jr., 204.
    Rebecca, 203.
    Sarah, 203.
    Susanna, 203.
HATCH, Elisha, 340.
    Phillips, 277, 280.
    Silvanus, 208.
HATHAWAY, John, †343.
HATHORN, Alexander, 101, 140, 270.
    Jane, 271.
    Jean, 271.
    John, 61, 157, 175, 205.
    Nathaniel, 164.
    Samuel, 101.
    Seth, 132, 157, 164, 192, 285.
    Silas, †129, †161, 166, 347.
    William, 270.

HAUPT, John, 182.
    Polly, 238.
HAWES, Matthias, 207.
    Moses, 193, 204, 207, 248, 345.
    Thomas, 177.
HAWKS, Jonathan, 264.
HAY, John, 114.
HAYDEN, Charles, 276.
    Joseph, 141.
    Josiah, 200, 204, 274, 337.
HAYES, John, 183.
    William, 192.
HAYNES, David, 248, 249.
    Ebenezer, 80.
HEABNER, George, 202.
HEAD, James Waller, 260, 338.
HEADDEAN, George, 251.
HEALD, Elizabeth, 141.
    Josiah, 142.
    Peter, †178.
    Timothy, 79, †141.
HEALY, Aaron, 78, 84.
HEARSEY, Betty, 205.
    Solomon, 108.
HEATH, Jonathan, 249, 352.
HEBNER, George, 201.
HEDDEAN, George, 94.
HEDGE, Isaac, 305.
HEIBNER, George, 153.
HEMBLY, (Hanbery) Christopher, †7.
HEMMENWAY, Daniel, 129.
    Mary, 129.
HENDERSON, Dunbar, 188, 199.
    Robert, 188, 346.
    Thomas, 162.
HENDLEY, Henry, 20.
    William, 20.
HENRY, James, 121, †142.
HENSHAW, Joseph, 38.
HERRICK, Ebenezer, 163.
    John, 235, 268.
HERRIN, Charlotte, 261.
    Daniel, 111, 162.
    John, 261.
    Betsey, 108,
    Jacob, †39.
    Solomon, †205.
HEWES, } Elihu, 126.
HUES,

Elizabeth, 336.
John, 275, 309, 335, 338.
John, Jr., †336.
HEWET, Deborah, 101.
    Solomon, †101.
    Waterman, 347.
    William, 230.
HEWEY, James, 259.
HEYARD, Zimri, 141.
HEYWOOD, Jane, 337.
    Peter, 110, 151.
    Peter, Jr., 151, 194.
    Samuel, 337.
    William, 366.
    Zimri, 68, 202, †337.
HIBBERT, Joseph, 160.
HIGGINS, Abigail, 266.
    Benjamin, 183, 265.
    Isaiah, 266.
    Jeremiah, 266.
    Mary, 265, 266.
    Philip, 21, 81, 83, *265, 266.
    Reuben, 265, 266, 267.
    Ruth, 265,
    Sarah, 266.
    Simeon, 266.
    Thankful, 266.
HIGH, George, †52.
HILL, Charles, 82.
    Japhet, 52.
    Mark L., 258.
    Mark Langdon, 186, 187, 258, 273, 278, 318, 321, 328, 336, 341, 344, 347, 348, 368.
    Samuel, 204.
    Thomas, 121.
    Tobias, 27.
HILT, John, 230.
    Mary, 153.
    Peter, 68, †153.
HILTON, Elizabeth, 360.
    Hepsebah, 69.
    James, †12, 177, 190, *359, 360.
    Jane, 360.
    John, †65, 228, 360.
    Joseph, 163, 360.
    Joshua, 191, 309, 360.
    Katherine, 326.
    Lydia, 360.
    Margaret, 360.
    Moses, 63, 77, 311, 327, 341.
    Nancy, 360.
    Rebecca, 65.
    Samuel, Jr., 348.
    Sarah, 262, 326, 360.
    Susan, 360.
    William, 69, 360.
HINKLEY, Aaron, 4, 19, 36, 53, 94.
    Edmund, 34.
    Hannah, 26, 118.
    Isaac, 226.
    James, 19, 123, 196.
    John, 79, †118.
    Josiah, 275, 347.
    Samuel, †34, 118.
    Sarah, 34.
    Seth, 227.
    Thomas, 88, 123.
HISCOCK, Richard, 332, 340.
HITCHCOCK, Richard, 190.
HOBBS, George, 323.
HOBBY, Remington, 162, 173, 185, 219.
    Wensly, 140.
HODGDON, Thomas, 50, 51.
HODGE, Hannah, 169, 170.
    Henry, 38, 92, 169, 170, 290, 291, 309, †338.
    James, 25, 137, 264, 276, 338, 339.
    Jane, 144, 169, 170.
    Jenny, 170.
    John, †90, 144, 338, 339.
    Margaret, 170.
    Mary, 90, 143, 144, 170.
    Polly, 170.
    Robert, 2, 7, 11, 12, 60, 66, 110, 130, *169, 170.
    Sally, 169, 170.
    Samuel, †38.
    Sarah, 169, 170, 338.
    William, †143, 144, 169, 339.
HODGKINS, Mary, 64.
    Moses, 19, 25, 28, 63.
HOETTENHEIM, John, 45.
HOFSES, Andrew, 346.
    Anthony, 346.
    Barbary, 346.

Elizabeth, 346.
George, 346.
Godfrey, †346.
Margaret, 346.
Mary, 346.
Mathias, 29.
William, 346.
HOLBROOK, Abiezer, 21, 82, 83.
    Ezekiel, 303.
    Richard, 49, 63.
    Sarah, 49, 266.
HOLDEN, Asa, 122.
HOLLAND, John, 66.
HOLLY, John, 340.
HOLMES, Hugh, 2, 11.
HOLT, Jedediah, 164, 166.
HOLTEN, John, 101.
    John, 118.
HONEYWELL, James, 288.
HOOD, Abner, 288, 297.
    Robert, 110.
HOOPER, John, 162, 195.
HOPKINS, Agnes, 2.
    Christopher, 140, 144, 167.
    David, 2, 11, 60, 82, 90, 145.
    Isaac, 347.
    Jane, 2.
    Jennet, 2.
    Martha, 2.
    Mary, 2.
    Mary, Jr., 2.
    Peter, 87, 93, 130.
    Ruth, 113.
    Solomon, †2.
    William, 2.
HOT, Susannah, 349.
HOUDLETTE, Louis, [Lewis,] 97, 162, 221, 263, 294.
HOURD, Mary, 96.
HOVEY, Ebenezer, 50.
    Ebenezer, Jr. †148.
    John, 284, 319.
    Samuel, 148.
    Jonathan, 144.
HOWARD, Abigail, 129.
HOW, HOWE, } Ichabod, 83, 137, 149, 152.
    Caleb, 39.
    Isabella, 158.

James, 41, 77, 111, *157, 158.
John, 157, †254.
Joshua Jr., 129, 276.
Margaret, 157, 158.
Samuel, 157, 158, 242, 259.
Squire, 109.
Susannah, 157, 158.
William, 72, 78, 107, 122, 157, 158, 167, 200, 203, 256, 259, 260, 278, 336.
William, Jr., 158.
HOWLAND, Abigail, 344.
    Benjamin, †75, †108.
    Michael, †344.
    Zebulon, 101, 144.
HOYT, Annah, 133.
    Elizabeth, 195.
    Philip, 160, 161, 169.
    Philip G., †195.
HUBBARD, John, 137, 311, 314.
HUFF, Thankful, 266.
HUES, HUGHES, HUSE, } James, 154.
    John, 107, 108, 155.
HUMPHREY, Richard, †130.
    Samuel, 130.
    William, 130.
    Joseph, 140.
    Sarah, 140.
    Thomas, 19, †140.
HUNNEWELL, Israel, 326.
    Lydia, 341.
    Molly, 326.
    Richard, Jr., 128.
HUNT, David, 343.
    John, 124, 181.
    Mary, 181.
    Stuart, 163, 177.
HUNTER, Adam, †73.
    Ann, 75.
    Arthur, 73, 121, 142, 168, 251, 339, 342, 346.
    David, 332.
    Elizabeth, 73.
    Henry, 51, 64, 144, 189, 228, *331, 332.
    James, 23, 73, 75, 82, 94, 112,

INDEX OF NAMES.

  332.
  James, Jr., 251.
  Jane, 73.
  John, 73, †75, 190, 332.
  Margaret, 73, 75.
  Mary, 73.
  Nancy, 331.
  Robert, 73, 94.
  Sarah, 168, 331, 332.
  Susanna, 73.
  Thomas, 332.
  William, 75, 195, 332.
HUNTOON, Mary, 361
HUPPER, Nathaniel, 121.
  Susanna, 121.
HURRUP, Betsey, 230.
  Thomas Bowers, †230.
HUSE, John, 92, 178, 230, 255.
HUSSEY, Ann, 196.
  Benjamin, †227.
  Elizabeth, 196.
  Elsa, 228.
  Hannah, 227, 228.
  John, 65, 77, 119.
  Joseph, 228.
  Mary, 196.
  Obed, *195, 196.
  Samuel, 196.
  Sarah, 196.
HUSTON, } Ann, 2.
HOUSTON,
  David, †307.
  Frances, 297.
  James, 2, 50, 66, 224, 234, 297.
  John, 24, 190, 307, 332.
  Robert, 2, 332.
  William, †2, †24, 332.
HUTCHINS, Hollis, 138.
  Joseph, 137, †138, 273.
  Solomon, †342.
HUTCHINSON, Edward, 213.
  Elizabeth, 113.
  Hannah, 113, 125.
  James, †138.
  Martha, 113.
  Mary, 113.

  Ruth, 113.
  Samuel, *113, 114.
  Sarah, 113.
  Susannah, 113.
HUTE, Rosanna, 299.
HYER, Cornelius, 200.
INGERSOLL, Benjamin, 45.
INGRAHAM, Beriah, 148.
  Catharine, 75.
  Jeremiah, 279.
  John, †75.
JACK, Margaret, 261.
  Robert, 261.
JACKSON, Benjamin, 275.
  Charles, 162.
  David, 197, †220.
  James, †275.
  Joseph, 350.
  Samuel, 275.
  Rebeckah, 220, 275.
  William, †275.
JACOBS, Samuel, 249, 343.
JACQUINS, } Christopher, 1, 11, 97, 275,
JACKINS,   } 278.
JAKINS,
  James Frederick, †1.
  Margaret, 1.
JAMES, Anne, 85.
  Frances, 85.
  Patrick, 85.
  Sarah, 86.
  William, 51, *84, 85, 86.
JAMESON, Alexander, 83.
  Boyes Cooper, †229.
  Brice, 32.
  Dorcas, 210.
  Eleanor, 210.
  George, 32.
  Hannah, 210.
  Isaac, †346.
  Jane, 32.
  Jenny, 210.
  Jeremiah, 346.
  John, 210, 261.
  Joseph, 32.
  Martin, 32.
  Mary, 32, 210.
  Paul, 32, 33, 88, 101, 130, 189,

INDEX OF NAMES.

    199, 206, †260, 341, 346.
    Peggy, 210.
    Polly, 210.
    Rachel, 32.
    Robert, 130, 206.
    Sally, 210, 260.
    Samuel, *32, 107, *209, 210.
    Sarah, 32.
    Susannah, 210.
    William, 189.
JAQUES, Benjamin, 110, 141, 249, 306.
JELLISON, Hannah, 162.
    Job, 166.
    Nathaniel, 124, †162, †166, †185, 306.
JENKS, David, 338.
JENNISON, Mary, †224.
    Samuel, 223.
JEWELL, James, 64.
    Susanna, 64.
JEWETT, David, *138, 139.
    Elizabeth, †227.
    Eunice, 139.
    James, 227, 273, 343.
    Jedediah, 147.
    John Winthrop, 139.
    Moses, 344.
    Nathan, 88, 153.
    Phebe, 139.
    Sarah, 139.
    Stephen, 229, 255.
JOHNSON, Bathsheba, 245.
    Dinah, 243.
    Dorothy, 310.
    Elisha, 245.
    Elizabeth, 243, 244.
    John, 68, 121, 140, 196.
    Joseph, *242, 243, 244, 245, 246.
    Joshua, 243, 244, 245, 246.
    Levi, 245.
    Mary, 245.
    Nathan, 162, 195.
JOHNSTON, Abigail, 302.
    Sarah, 262.
    Thomas, 47, 101, 147, 163, 191, 206, 234, 255, 261, 262, 303, 322, 332, 360.
    William, 322.
JONES, Apollos, 192.
    Avis, 192.
    Benjamin, 144.
    Edward, 253.
    Eunice, 265.
    Hannah, 74.
    Israel, 339.
    Jabez, 75.
    James, 228.
    John, 265, 273, 316, 329, 336.
    Jonas, *73.
    Jonathan, 65, 144.
    Joseph, 192.
    Lydia, 74.
    Meribah Allen, 192.
    Nathan, 128.
    Pamelia, 192.
    Paul, †192.
    Peter, †265.
    Phineas, 100.
    Richard, 178.
    Rosanna, 192.
    Stephen, 68.
    William, 50, 190, 303.
    Winzer, 206.
JORDAN, Hannah, 255.
    Israel, †255.
    James, 195.
    John, 255.
    Susanna, 255.
JOSE, Abigail, 314.
JOYCE, Elizabeth, 120.
    Isaac, 120.
    Jonathan, 120.
    Margaret, 120.
    Rachel, *120, 121.
    Seth, 120.
JUDKINS, Samuel, 311.
KALER, Anna Mariah, 253.
    Catherina, 253.
    Charles, 152, 253, 260.
    Doredeah, 253.
    Elizabeth, 253.
    Eva, 253.
    Henry, *253, 254.
    Jacob, 253.
    Margaret, 253.

INDEX OF NAMES. 23

Mary Catharina, 253.
William, †105.
KEEN, Abel, 273.
　Elisha, 235.
　Jacob, 235.
KEITH, Josiah, 338.
KELLEY, Alexander, 7.
　Benjamin, 272, 342.
　Ebenezer, 56.
　Findley, †7.
　Joseph, 203.
　Lydia, 285.
　Rebecca, 203.
　Sarah, 203.
　William, 203.
KELLOCH, Alexander, 8, 11, 12, 20.
KELSEY,　⎫
KELLSY,　⎬ Agnes, 206.
KILLSA,　 ⎭
　Enoch, 347.
　George, †206.
　Hannah, 347.
　James, *235, 347.
　John, †347.
　Lois, 222.
　Lydia, 235.
　William, 347.
KENDALL, Benjamin, 6.
　Jean, 9.
　William, 274, 323.
KENNEDY, Ann, 271, 334, 364.
　David, 228, 229, 264.
　Henry, 274.
　James, 363.
　Mary, 228.
　Nicholas, †136.
　Robert, 95, 111, 201, 228, 229, †255.
　Ruth, 271, 334, 364.
　Samuel, 205, 211, †228, 229, 274, 275.
　Samuel, Jr., 110.
　Sarah, 144, 229, 255, 363.
　Thomas, 163, 350, 363, 364.
　William, 170, †229, *271, *363.
KENNEY, Abijah, 51.
　Elizabeth, 295, 296.
　Esther, 51.

KENT, Benjamin, 10,
　John, 45.
KESLER, Johannes, 178.
KEYLER, Henry, 29.
KEZER, John, 195.
KIDDER, Richard, 38, 50, 52, 87, 137, 140, 161, 162, 163, 180.
　Samuel, 80.
KIER, John Henry, †25.
KILBERT, Sevilla Magdalene, 167.
KILGORE, Joseph, 337.
KILLERAN, Edward, 67, 189.
KILLPATRICK, Elizabeth, 59.
　Thomas, *58.
　William, 147.
KIMBALL, Anna, 184.
　Bartholomew, †339.
　Eleanor, 163.
　Hannah, 184.
　Molly, 184.
　Moses, *184.
　Nathaniel, 339.
　Ruth, 184.
　Solomon, 128.
　Timothy, †163.
KINCADE, Samuel, 348, 352.
KINDEL, Easter, 91.
KING, Benjamin, 348.
　Ezra, †163.
　Prudence, 163.
KINGSBURY, John, 15, †16, 133, †342.
　Miriam, 342.
　Patience, 16.
KINNASTON, David, 337, 338, 342.
KINSEL, Benjamin, 226.
　John, 236.
KIRKPATRICK, Ann, 147.
　John, †147.
　Thomas, 232.
KLINE, Christopher, 45.
　George, †170.
KNIGHT,　⎫
KNIGHTS,　⎬ Daniel, 87, *103, †338.
　Elizabeth, 103.
　Judeth, 103.
　Marthue, 103.
　Mary, 103.
　Nathaniel, 338.

INDEX OF NAMES.

Patishel, 103, †347.
Susanna, 103, 347.
William, 338.
KNOWLS, Mary, 349.
Richard, 2, *348, 349.
LACKEY, Olive, 338.
William, †338.
LADD, Joses, 249, 250.
LAITEN, Ezekiel, 60.
Hannah, 60.
Jean, 60, 164.
John, 60, †164.
Jonathan, 6, 7, *60.
Martha, 60.
Mary, 60.
Moses, 60.
Rebecca, 60.
Richard, 60.
Thomas, †17.
LAMB, James, 323.
Ruth, 323.
LAMBERD, Daniel, 151.
Gideon, 149.
Joseph, 64, 77, 124, 220.
Luke, 69.
LAMBERT, Gideon, 130.
Joseph, 276.
Paul, 227.
Silas, 336.
LANCESTER, Elihu, 92.
Joseph, 92.
LANCEY, William, †72.
LANGDON, Lydia, 302.
LARRABEE, Nathaniel, 1, 251.
LASH, Jacob, †82.
Mary, 82.
Paul, 270.
LEAVIT, Israel, 144.
LEE, Ann, 257.
Col. ———, 64.
Elizabeth, 256, 257.
James, 257.
John, †87, 256, 257.
Margaret, 186, 188, 205.
Rebecca, 257.
Silas, 170, 289, 292, 308, 338, 351.
William, 278.
William, sen'r., *256.

William, Jr., 185, 205, 239, 257.
LEEMAN, Betty, 224.
Henry, 224.
Nathaniel, 143, †224.
LEIGHTON, Solomon, 319.
LEISHMAN, John, 72, 118, 145, 192, 247, 335, 337, 338, 341, 342, 343, 347, 348.
LEISSNER, Charles, †38, 247.
Mary, 38.
LE MERCIER, Peter, †223.
Polly, 223.
LEMONT, Benjamin, 27, 28, 73, †137.
David, 28, 69.
Elizabeth, 27, 28.
Hannah, 28.
James, 20, 27, 28, 64, 73, 82, 83.
John, *27, 28.
Mary, 73.
Nancy, 28.
Robert, 28.
Samuel, 28.
Sarah, 28, 64.
Susanna, 73, 137.
Thomas, 28, 137.
LEPEAR, Andrew, †95.
Mary, 95.
LERMOND, Alexander, 7, 11, 12, 34, 41, 50, 51, 60, 66, 67, 80, 86, 108.
Elizabeth, 282.
John, †50.
William, 344.
LEROYS, Mary, 349.
LEWIS, Daniel, 271.
Jabez, 177.
Jane, 51.
John, 183.
Joseph, 51.
Lavinia, 235.
William, 46, 108, 144, 161, 162, 163, 179, 206, 223, 274, 294, 359.
Yardly 32.
LIBBEE, } Hatevil, 67, 108, 110, 111, 143.
LIBBY,
Jane, 40.
Joseph, 52, 140.
Samuel, 68.

INDEX OF NAMES. 25

LIESON, Edmund, 45.
LIGHT, Elizabeth, 275, 308.
    George, Jr., 29, †152.
    Henry, 237.
    Peter, 226.
    Robert, †275. 289.
LILLY, George, 11, 50, 140, 162.
LINCOLN, Benjamin, 144.
LENNAN, } Bryant, 84, 273, 278.
LINNEN, } James, †278.
LINNAN, }
    Thomas, 273, 343, 346.
LINNEKEN, Abigail, 302.
    Benjamin, *301, 302.
    David, 302.
    Elizabeth, 302.
    Ephraim, 302, 303.
    Lucy, 302.
    Martha, 302.
    Mary, 302, 303.
    Phebe, 302.
    Sarah, 302.
    Susannah, 302.
LINNET, Samuel, 339.
LINSCOTT, Ezekiel, †234.
    John, 234, †264.
LITHGOW, Arthur, 278.
    Charlotte, 242.
    James Noble, 348.
    Mary, 242.
    Sarah, 348.
    William, 105, 118, †278, 313,
      †348, 368.
    William, Jr., 180, 241, 242.
LITTLE, Alexander, 259.
    Henry, †45, 90, 360.
    James, 37, 45, 90, 140, 224, 275.
    Joshua, 249.
LIVERMORE, Jason, 220.
LOCKE, Abraham, 66.
    Daniel, †66.
LONGFELLOW, David, 140.
    Jonathan, 52.
    Samuel, 45, 277.
LONGLEY, Nehemiah, 121.
LORD, Nathan, 45.
LORING, Laban, 220, 341.
    Levi, 129.

    Perez, 129.
    Prudence, 269.
LOUD, William, 24, 121.
    Wm. Solomon, 130.
LOVEJOY, Abiel, 11, 17, 24, 25, 34, 36, 72,
      78, 90, 127, 138.
    Abiel, Jr., 127, 263.
    Francis, †263.
    Nathaniel, 127.
    Polley, 127.
    Sarah, 127.
    Samuel, 248.
LOVETT, Israel, 193, 255.
    Robert, 343.
LOW, Jonathan, 129, 173.
LOWDER, Jonathan, 128, 129, 160, 161,
      163, 166.
LOWELL, Abner, 339.
    Jacob, 108.
    James, 336.
    John, 75.
    Joseph, 272.
    Joseph, Jr., 324.
LUDWIG, Jacob, 29, 82, 84, 102, 152, 202,
      248, 254, 260, 276, 299, 330,
      341, 346.
    Joseph, 152, 237, 254, 331, 346.
    Joseph Henry, 260.
LUMBARD, } Samuel, 75.
LOMBARD, }
LYFORD, Elizabeth, 243.
    Joseph, 245.
    Mary, 245.
    Nathaniel, 245.
    Oliver, 244.
MCCAFFRY, Ann, 37.
    Frances, 37.
    James, 37.
    Jane, 37.
    John, 37.
    Margaret, 37.
    Mary, 37.
    Morgan, *36, 37.
MCCARTER, Catharine, 282.
    Elizabeth, 225.
    Jane, 225.
    James, 225, 226.

INDEX OF NAMES.

  John, 7, 41, *224.
  Margaret, 225.
  Martha, 225.
  Mary, 225.
McCARTY, John, 171.
McCASLAND, Hannah, 199.
McCAUSLAND, Elizabeth, 35.
McCLARY, Michael, *178.
McCLINTOCK, Margaret, 118.
  Robert, 206, 277, 280, 297, 298, 334, 358, 359.
  William, †118.
McCLURE, Nancy, 331.
  Thomas, 190, 224.
McCOBB, Ann, 205, 242.
  Beatrice, 242.
  ("Brother,") 8.
  Denny, 239, 240, 241, 242, 277, 278, 328, 343, 368.
  Elizabeth, 186.
  Frances, 186.
  George, 118.
  Isabel, 186, 188.
  James, 6, 9, 45, 105, 118, *185.
  James, Jr., †224.
  Jane, 188.
  Jenny, 186, 187, 188, 242.
  John, 145, 242.
  Margaret, 186.
  Mary, 185, 186, 187, 188, 224.
  Nancy, 186, 188, 242.
  Parker, 241.
  Polly, 186, 187.
  Rachel, 57, 188, 241, 242, 327.
  Sally, 242.
  Samuel, 13, 15, 52, 63, 72, 118, 186, *241-2.
  Thomas, †105, 186, 187, 188, †205.
  William, 51, 63, 72, 88, 101, 104, 111, 115, 135, 140, 192, 272, 275, 296, 303, 335, 337, 338, 341, 342, 343, 347.
McCORDY, James, 59.
  Martha, 59.
  Robert, 126.
McCRATE, Thomas, 309, 356.
McCULLOCH, Mr. ———, 44.

McCURDY, Daniel, *71, 72, 147.
McDANIEL, Ann, 34.
  James, 179.
McFADDEN, Andrew, 321.
  Daniel, 7, 47, 63, 107, †276.
  Daniel, Jr., 107.
  James, 63, 276, 278, 343.
  John, 276.
  Margaret, 276.
  Thomas, 276.
McFARLAND, Andrew, 44, 50, 52, 65, *114.
  Benjamin, 101, 104, 135, 347.
  Elizabeth, 114, 117.
  Ephraim, 19, 116.
  Jane, 117.
  John, 37, 38, †63, 115, 116, 117, 118, 124, 343.
  John Murray, 116, 337, 338, 368.
  Joseph, 140, 163.
  Joseph, Jun., 140, 206.
  Lydia, 63, 192.
  Margaret, 117.
  Mary, 117.
  Robert, 298.
  Rosanna, 117.
  Sarah, 117.
  Susannah, 117.
  Thomas, †192.
McGLATHRY, Alexander, 38.
  Margaret, 38.
  Robert, †38.
  Sarah, 38.
  William, 38.
McGOWN, John, 11, 39, 163, 179.
McGUIRE, Margaret, 72.
  Patrick, 72.
  Thomas, 152, 270.
McHONANE, James, 28, 100.
McINTIRE, Catharine, 282.
  Henry, 73.
  Jane, 281, 282, 283.
  John, 67, *281, 282, 283.
  Joseph, 1, †73.
  Robert, 194, 281.
  Sarah, 73.
  William, 73, 234, 277, 280, 281, 283, 297, 298, 303, 304, 322, 331, 334, 341.

INDEX OF NAMES. 27

    William S., †341.
MCKECHNIE, Alexander, 141.
    Jane, 141.
    John, 77, 116, †141, 307.
    Joseph, 141.
    Lydia, 141.
    (North,) Mary, 10, 141.
    (Tozer) Rebecca, 141.
    Sarah, 141.
    Thomas, 141.
    William, 141.
MACKER, Lydia, 262.
MCKELLAR, John, 192, 226, 230, 345, 346.
MCKELLY, John, 171.
MCKENNEY, Alexander, 341.
    Benjamin, 274.
    Betsey, 341.
    Brooks, 321.
    Catharine, 341.
    Charles, 341.
    David, *325, 326, 327.
    Daniel, 326, 327, 341.
    George, 341.
    Henry, Jun., †228.
    James, 326.
    Jonathan, 326, 327.
    John, †341.
    Martha, 326.
    Mathew, 34.
    Sarah, 341.
MCKIBB, James, 28.
MCKNIGHT, David, 107.
MCKOWN, John, 89, 169, 170.
    Margaret, 88.
    Nancy, 89.
    Patrick, *88.
    Robert, 64, †80, 89.
MCLANAKEN, Ann, 5.
    William, 5.
MCLEAN, MCCLAIN, } Alexander, 279, 280, 332.
    Fergus, 128.
    Hugh, 7, 11, 45, 171.
    James, 345.
    John, 206, 360.
    Lochran, †45.
    Samuel, 128.

    William, 38, 47, 101, 128, 190, 191.
MCCLELAN, MCCLELAND, MCLELLAN, } Alexander, 7, 11.
    Brice, 194.
    Bryce, 249, 305.
    Elizabeth, 11, 345.
    Isaac, 345.
    James, 7, 11.
    Jean, 348.
    John, 7, 11.
    Joseph, 234.
    Margaret, 7.
    Mary, 7, 11.
    Martha, 7, 11.
    Nancy, 345.
    Nathaniel, †148.
    Samuel, 7, 11.
    Sarah, 7.
    Simon, †345.
    William, 7, †11.
MCMAHON, Daniel, 346.
MCMILLEN, MCMOULLIN, } Rosanna, 224.
    Sarah, 190.
MCMURPHY, John, 273.
MCNEAR, John, 7, 11, 12, 16, 38.
MCPHETRES, Abigail, 208.
    Archibald, 161, 166.
    Betsey, 208, 209.
    James, 209.
    Rachel, 208, 209.
    William, †208.
    William, Jr., 208.
MACE, Hannah, 347.
    Thomas, †347.
MACY, Zaccheus, 198.
MADDIN, Owen, 171.
MAINS, Abigail, 197.
    Anna, 197.
    Beatrice, 188, 197, 205.
    Elizabeth, 186.
    James, 197.
    James Cobb, 197.
    Joseph, †197.
    Sarah, 197.
MALCOM, Abraham, 162.

Andrew, 20, 67, 171.
Andrew, Jr., 192.
Frances, 317.
Isabel, 317.
James, 144, 147, 189, 343, 344, 345, 346.
John, †12.
Joseph, 82, *112.
Robert, †346.
Sarah, 112.
Susanna, 346.
William, 7, 82, 125, 195.
MALLETT, Isaac, 114.
Jesse, 307.
John, †306.
Samuel Thompson, 337.
William, 306.
MANN, Oliver, 128.
MANSON, Isabella, 258.
MARRINER,
MARINER,   } Ruth, 265.
MARROW, Samuel, 29.
MARSH, Caleb, 220, 341, 346, 347.
John, 29, 72, 78, 84.
MARSHALL, William, 20, 194.
MARSON,
MARSTON,   } Abner, 1, 17, 130, 275, 278.
Christopher, †262, 263.
Elizabeth, 67, 262, 263.
Elizabeth Harris, 67.
George, 67.
James, 263.
Samuel, †275.
Sarah, 67.
Stephen, 17, †67.
Susanna, 67.
MARTIN, Charles, †298.
John, Jun., 38.
Lucy, 298.
Mary, 206, 343.
Richard, †343.
Stephen, 344.
Thomas, 344.
William, 47, †206.
MATCHLOFFE, Mary, 12.
Mathias, †12.
MATTHEWS, Edmund, 254.
Elisha, 273.
James, 176.

John, 101.
Mary, 266.
MAXEY, Amy, 206, 207.
Benjamin, †206, 207.
Harvey, 207.
Joseph, 207, 345.
Josiah, 207.
Lydia, 206, 207.
Sarah, 206, 207.
MAXWELL, George, 229, 276, 339.
James, 178, 256, 276, 339, 348.
MAYER,
MAYERS,   } Cassimier, 11.
MIER,
Catharine, 97.
Ludowick Cassemire, †104.
John, †11.
Mary Magdalene, *97.
Philip, 11.
Ulerick, †11.
MEAGHER, Richard, 234.
MEHANY, John, †84.
MEIGGES, Abigail, 208.
Ebenezer, 207.
Hannah, 208.
Keziah, 208.
Mary, 207, 208.
Nathaniel, *207.
Nathaniel, Jr., 207.
Rebecah, 208.
MELLUS, Daniel, †346.
Henry, 343.
Mary, 343.
Priscilla, 346.
MELOEY, Hannah, 113.
MELONY, James, †171.
Walter, †194.
MELVIN, Mary, 314.
MERIT, Daniel, 45.
MERRIT, Mary, 360.
MERO,
MERROW,   } Amariah, 207, 248, 345.
MERRILL, Benjamin, 275.
John, 23, 51, 82, 84, 112, 119, 121, 226, 229, 256, 259, 261, 292, 337, 340, 346, 349.
Joseph, †337.
Thomas, 228.
MERRY, Joseph, 136.
MESERVE, Benjamin, 253.

INDEX OF NAMES.

METCALF, Joseph, 192.
    Samuel, 248.
    Thomas, 192.
MICHELL, Noah, 45.
    James, 4, 6.
MIERS, } Catharine, 11.
MAYERS, } George, 11.
    Molly, 11.
MILLER, Alexander N., 66.
    Annas, 16.
    Ann Marey, 16.
    Boston, 332.
    Frances, 201.
    Francis, 102.
    Frank, 84.
    Hannah, 65, 66.
    Henry, †29.
    James, *15, 66.
    Jane, 66.
    Jeannet, 16.
    John, 16, 34, 66, 84.
    Mary, 16, 66.
    Nancy, 66, 228.
    Robert, 16, 65, 66, †228.
    Samuel, 66, 303.
    Sarah, 16.
    Thomas, 66, 279.
    William, 2, 13, †65.
MILLNER, Elizabeth, †127.
MILLET, David, 345.
MINK, Mary Lissabot, 103.
    Peter, 103.
MITCHEL, Christopher, 20.
    Jones, 192.
    Josiah, 161, 268, 347,
    Richard, 197, 198.
    Stephen, 100.
    Thomas, 345.
MOLLOY, (Hutchinson) Hannah, 125.
    Hugh, 306.
    John, *125.
MONTGOMERY, Anna, 12, 62.
    James, 12, †15.
    John, 12, 13, 15, 61, 89, 104, †145, †248.
    Lydia, 145.
    Robert, *12, †15.
    Samuel, 12, 61, 224, 337, 338, 341.
    Sarah, 12, 13, 15, *61.
MOODY, Amos, 88, †93.
    John, †88.
    John Minot, 260.
    Samuel, 22.
MOORE, }
MOOR, } Anna, 264.
MOORES, }
    David, 160, 275.
    Ebenezer, 72, 78, 175, 273, 274.
    Elizabeth, 249.
    Hannah, 361.
    John, †28, 142, 164, 183, 228, 305.
    Levi, 72, 90.
    Nathan, †72.
    Sally, 264.
    Sarah, 28, 72.
    Thomas, 126, †264.
    William, †249.
MOREY, Ezekiel, 162.
MORGRIDGE, Thomas, 248.
MORRILL, Bathsheba, 245, 246.
    Jedediah, 45.
    Levi, 246.
    Peter, |45.
MORRISON, Jonathan, 130, 194, 298, *352.
    Moses, 207.
    Rusha, 298, 353.
    Thomas, †298, 353.
    Thomas Wallace, 353.
    William Jackson, 353.
MORSE, Daniel, 273, †336.
    David, 73.
    Jonathan, 273, 336.
    Joseph, 345.
    Nathaniel, 328.
MORTON, Briant, 347.
    Cornelius, †104.
    Ebenezer, 206.
    Ebenezer, Jr., 199.
    James, 82, *127.
    Jean, 128.
    John, 128, 298.
    Joshua, 83.
    Margaret, 128.
    Robert, 128.
    Sarah, 128.

INDEX OF NAMES.

William, 128.
MOTHERWILL, Thomas, 197.
MOTLEY, Jane, 33.
MURPHY, Alexander, †184.
    Peter, Jr., 357.
    Priscilla, 166.
    Thomas, 184.
    Thomas, Jr., †166.
MURRAY, Anne, 62.
    David, 93, 110, 130.
    Elizabeth, 7.
    John, 43, 52, 62, 72, 88, 89, 111, 118, 145, 189, 224, 247, 272.
    Robert, 43.
    Robert Montgomery, 62.
MUSTARD, Abigail, 93.
    Charity, 248, 250, 251.
    Charles, 250.
    David, †248, 250.
    James, 73, 93, †141, 248, *250, 251.
    John, *93.
    Joseph, 250.
    Mary, 250.
    William, 248.
MYLIE, Mary, 364.
NARDEN, Zachariah, †25.
NASH, Church, †261.
    Eve, 261.
    Jane, 261.
    Lydia, 261.
    Margret, 262.
    Oliver, 101, 191, 206, 255, 261, 262.
    Samuel, 261.
NASON, Abigail, 351.
    Abraham, 288, 324, 326, 327, 341, 351.
    Anna, 351.
NELSON, John, †256.
    Samuel, 272.
NEVERS, Phinehas, 28, †161.
    Samuell, 28.
NEWBERT, Christopher, 73, 103, 126.
    Elizabeth, 177.
    John, 73.
    Mary, 103.
NEWCOMB, Reuben, 126.

NICKELS, Alexander, 38, 63, 80, 217, *332.
    Ebenezer, 340.
    Fanny, 217.
    Hannah, 217, 333.
    James, †205, *217, 280, 333.
    Jane, 169.
    Jann, 217.
    John, 205, 217, 218, 226, 279, 333.
    Margaret, 217, 332, 333.
    Ruth, 217.
    Samuel, 2, 6, 7, 11, 38, 53, 64, 80, 110, 169, 170, 187, 188, 205, 211, 228, 229, 259, 275, 280.
    William, 217, 333, 336.
NOBLE, Arthur, 38, 53, 54, 66.
    Benjamin, 24.
    Francis, 25.
    Jane, 76.
    John, 24.
    Lazarus, †24, 36.
    Tamor, 109.
NORCROSS, Ann, 196.
    Joanna, 64.
    Martha, 64.
    Philip, 64, 196.
NORRIS, Jeremiah, 352.
NORTH, Elizabeth, 10.
    Gershom, 274.
    John, *9, 13.
    Joseph, 10, 53, 87, 121, 122, 136, 141, 148, 158, 167, 180, 254, 256, 304.
    Mary, 10.
    William, 10.
NORTON, Ebenezer, 272.
    Constant, 269.
    Kathariene, 269.
    Peter, 269.
    Sarah, 268, 269.
    Stephen, *268.
NOYES, Jeremiah W., 346
NUTE, Paul, 272, 324.
NUTTER, Hannah, 305.
    Valentine, *305.
NUTTING, Ebenezer, 90.
    George, 90.

INDEX OF NAMES. 31

    Jonathan, 41, †90, 226.
    Oliver, 90.
NYE, Adino, 16, 17, 19, 24, 25, †34.
    Mary, 34, 50.
OAKMAN, Joseph, †77.
    Samuel, 77, 136.
OAKS, } Abel, 151.
OAK, }
    Daniel, 150.
    Elizabeth, 150.
    John, 150.
    Jonathan, *149.
    Jonathan, Jr., 150.
    Levi, 150, 151.
    Lois, 150.
    Lucy, 150, 151.
    Lydia, 150.
    Mary, 150.
    Mille, 150, 151.
    Rebeckah, 150.
    Sarah, 150.
    Sibbel, 150, 151.
    Solomon, 150, 151.
    William, 151.
O'BRIAN, John, †188.
O'DEE, John, †356.
OLCOTT, Mary, 281, 282.
OLDHAM, Peleg, 182, 239, 248, 298.
OLIVER, Daniel, *25.
    David, 118, 367, 368.
    Ephreim, 26.
    (Hinkley,) Hannah, 26.
    Henry, 26.
    Jacob, 26.
    John, 26.
    Parker, 347.
    Thomas, 26.
ORBETON, Jonathan, 132.
ORR, Elizabeth, 42.
    John, 13, 15, †224.
    John, 94.
OSBORN, Jennet, 144.
    Ephraim, 141.
OSGOOD, Daniel, 164, 166.
OTIS, Ebenezer, 344.
    Galen, 209.
    Samuel, 298.
OTT, Peter, 230.

OVERLOCK, Henry, 201.
OWEN, David, 349.
    Gideon, 160, 161, 195, †234, 349.
    Hugh, 234.
    James, 140.
    Jane, 234.
    John, 234.
    Thomas, 234.
PACKARD, Benjamin, 51.
    Marlboro, 226, 247.
    Micah, 90, 171.
PADDOCK, Barnabas, 105.
PAGE, Aaron, 251.
    Dorcas, 159.
    Dudley, 159.
    Edward Hall, 159, 160, 164, 260, 262, 265, 277.
    Enoch, 161.
    James, 148, 192, 220, 287.
    John, 71, 221.
    Jonas, 122.
    Judith, 159, 160.
    Mercy, 203.
    Nathan, 159.
    (Owen), 159.
    Reuben, 203.
    Robert, 148, 161, 243, 244, 246, 269.
    Ruth, 159.
    Simon, 159.
    Solomon, *158.
PAINE, Eunice, 64.
    Isabella, 96.
    John, 147, 237, 360.
    Simeon, 64.
    Thomas, 188.
PALMER, Anna, 194.
    Benjamin, 261.
    Daniel, 206.
    Edward, 194.
    Mary, 111.
    Nancy, 111.
    Rhoda, 263.
    Samuel, †194.
    William, †111.
    William, Jr., 339.
PARIS, Amos, †140.
    Margaret, 140.

INDEX OF NAMES.

PARKER, Elizabeth, 367, 368.
    Isabel, 186, 188, 205.
    James, 339.
    John, 1, 9, 28, 317, *366.
    Jonathan R., 340.
    Jordan, 118, 183, 224, 317, 318, 328, 342, 366, 367, 368.
    Nathan, 183.
    Nehemiah A., 366.
    Obadiah, 68.
    Oliver, 160.
    Peter, †227.
    Peter, Jr., 227.
    Prudence, 227.
    Robert, 166, 183.
    Solomon, 141, 173, 227, 274, 276.
PARKMAN, Betty, 193.
    Daniel, 193.
    Gideon, *193.
    Mary, 193, 194.
    Noah, 193, 194.
    Rhode, 193.
PARKS, Polly, 345.
PARLIN, Nathan, 183, 184.
PARSONS, Andrew, 227.
    Elihu, 207.
    John, †207, 275.
    Lawrence, 111, 171, 345.
    Patty, 207.
    Samuel, †275.
    Timothy, 219.
    William, 207.
PARTRIDGE, Elisha, †193.
    Elisha, Jr., 193.
    Sarah, 193.
    Susanna, 197.
    Thomas, †38.
    William, 197.
PATCH, Ephraim, 248.
PATTEE, Benjamin, 185, 215, 216, 239, 241, 242, 328.
    Benjamin, Jr., 57, 58, 84.
    David, 141, 307.
    Elizabeth, 57, 58.
    Ezekiel, 79, 141, 274, 337.
    James, †307.
    Mary, 141.
    Sibyl, 276.
    William, 227, †276.
PATTEN, Actor, 45, 82, 121, 229, 255, 337, 346.
    Charles, 107.
    David, 255, 339.
    Hannah, 107.
    James, 107.
    John, 107, 121, 126, 221, 234, †255.
    Joseph, 255.
    Margaret, 73.
    Mary, 255.
    Matthew, 107.
    Robert, 73, 107, 255.
    Sarah, 107.
    Thomas, 255.
    William, †107.
    William, Jr., 107.
PATTERSON, Abigail, 41.
    David, 7, 12, 51.
    David, Jr., †51.
    Elizabeth, 162, 359.
    James, *41, 110.
    James Howard, 41, 294.
    John, 144, 190.
    Margaret, 41, 157.
    Nancy, 51.
    Peter, 2, 211.
    Samuel, 64, †144.
    William, 41, 162, 163, 206, 224, 234, 339, 342, †347, *359.
PAYSON, David, 255, 292, 303, 309, 338, 344.
    Edward, 343, †344.
    Eunice, 344.
    James, 344.
PEARCE, Ann, 49.
    Elizabeth, 272.
    Ezekiel, 272.
    John, 49.
    Samuel, †272.
PEARL, Phebe, 318.
PEARSON, Amos, †130.
    Amos, Jr., 130.
    David, 274, *322.
    Diodami, 323.

INDEX OF NAMES.

Elizabeth. 130.
Jane, 322.
Marcy, 130.
Maria, 130.
Mariner, 277.
Melinda, 323.
Rachel, 323.
Thankful, 323.
Timothy, 283.
William, 323.
PEASE, Prince, 206.
PEASLEE, Anna, 108.
Daniel, 344.
Ezekiel, 108.
James, 259.
Jonathan, 178.
Oliver, 108, 249.
Sarah, 108.
PEIRCE, Jane, 189.
John, 227.
PEMBLETON, Jane, 281.
PEPBLES, Patrick, 247.
PERCY, Arthur, *362, †363.
Betsy, 363.
David, 362.
Febby, 85.
Francis, 362.
James, 362, 363.
John, 362, 363.
Polly, 363.
Thomas, 368.
PERKINS, Ebenezer, 196, 347.
Eunice, 138.
John, 156, 285.
Joseph, 104, 160.
Mary, 285.
Nathaniel, †138,
Polley Hussey, 196.
Robert, 285.
Sally, 285.
PERLEY, Nathaniel, 340.
PERRAL, Rachel, 323.
PRRRIN, Thomas, †48.
PERRY, Charles, 349.
Eli, 187, 188.
Francis, †221.
Jonathan, 107.
Martha, 187, 188.

Sarah, 361.
PETERS, John, 166.
PETERSON, Levi, 339.
PETTENGILL, Amy, 263.
Anna, 263.
Benjamin, 111, 158, 259, *263, 264.
Edward, 25, 194.
Filena, 264.
Judith, 263.
Mary, 263.
Rachel, 264.
Rhoda, 263.
Rubie, 264.
Ziba, 264.
PHILBRICK, Amy, 283, 284.
Anna, 283, 284.
Benjamin, 284.
Bishop, 284.
Joseph, †283.
Mary, 283, 284.
PHILBROOK, Benjamin, 250.
Ebenezer, †344.
John, 343.
Joshua, 24, 25, 64, 137, 220, 221, 260.
Sarah, 344.
William, 1.
PHILIPS, Asa, 141, 172.
Thomas, 128.
PIERCE, David, †189.
Eliphalet, †278.
Jane, 189.
John, 77.
Samuel, 278.
PIKE, William, 336, 356.
PINKHAM, Amos, †47.
Benjamin, 334, 335.
Betsey, 334, 335.
Ichabod, 272, *334, 335.
Martha, 335.
Mary, 334.
Mercy, 334, 335.
Nathaniel, 334, 335.
Patty, 334.
Polly, 334.
Reuben, 254.
Sally, 334,

Index of Names.

    Solomon, 343.
PITCHER, Nathaniel, 145, 182, 239, 248, 298.
    Reuben, †60.
PITT, William, 265.
    Seth, 279.
PLUMER, } Daniel, 288.
PLUMMER, }
    David, 65, 138.
    David, Jr., 130.
    John, 88, 138, †288, 354.
    Samuel, †88.
POCHARD, Peter, 262.
POLAND, Ezra, 334.
    Jenny, 357.
    Judith, 357.
POLERECZKY, John, 263, 306.
POLLARD, Moses, 340.
POOR, David, 274.
    Jean, 262.
    Richard, 178.
PORTER, Benjamin Jones, 255, 339.
PORTERFIELD, Patrick, 11, 33, 34, 59, 86, †344.
    Robert, 344.
    William, 344.
POTE, Jeremiah, 45.
POTTER, Aaron, 343.
    Hannah, 261.
    James, 22, 110, 292.
    Jane, 343.
    John, †239.
    Joseph, †166, 307.
    Margaret, 51, 166.
    Nancy, 341.
    Polly, 343.
    Rachel, 343.
    Robert, 261.
    Sarah, 106, 239.
    Solomon, 249, †343.
    William, †110, 344.
POTTLE, Azariah, 92, 305.
    David, 179.
POWEL, John, 99.
POWER, } Arad, 75.
POWERS, }
    Jane, 328.
    Levi, 17, 18.
    Mary, 109.
    Robert, 84.
PRATT, Asa, 109.
    David, 108.
    Elisha, 162, 166, 185.
    Elizabeth, 109.
    James, 109.
    Mary, 193.
    Sarah, 109.
    Seth, 170.
PREBLE, Abraham, 30, 31, 36, 105, †108, 124, 141.
    Ebenezer, 30, 31, 32, 161, †197.
    James, 108.
    Jedediah, 108.
    Jonathan, 7, *29, 31, 161.
    Joseph, 30, 31, 36, 107, 215, 240, 319.
    Martha, 197.
    Mary, 32, 108, 215, 319, 320.
    Mehitable, 29.
    Samuel, 31, 197.
    William, 215.
    Zebulon, 124, 339.
PREIST, Deidamia, 212.
PRESCOTT, Benjamin, 339.
    Jedediah, 246, 250.
PRESSEY, Benjamin, 272.
    Elizabeth, 272.
    Jacob, 133, †272.
PRINCE, Isaac, 205.
PROCHT, Peter, 237.
PRUDENS, William, 252.
PULLEN, Stephen, 83, 129, 138, 144.
    William, 149, 219, 220, 251, 336.
PURINGTON, David, †84.
    Hezekiah, †4, 229, 348.
    Humphrey, †1, 141.
    Isabella, 4.
    James, 229, 256, 337, 346, 348.
    James Scals, 74.
    Joshua, 4.
    Mary, 84.
    Nathaniel, 1, 248.
    Silence, 168.
QUIGG, Daniel, 177.
QUIMBY, Samuel, 284.
RACKLIFF, Benjamin, 228, 260, 288.

INDEX OF NAMES. 35

RADDEN, David, 274.
    James, 274.
    John, 274.
REMELY, RAMELEY, } Mathias, 38, 39, 178.
RAMSDELL, George, 348.
RANDAL, RANDALL, } Daniel, 119.
    Ezra, 2, 53.
    Hatherly, 248.
    Huldah, *119.
    John, 24.
    Joseph, 53, 248, 249, 258, 261.
    Martha, 258, 261.
    Robert, 237, 238, 277, 305.
    Robert, Jr., †305.
    William, 73, 84, 119, 125, 142, 160, 259, 261, 342, 346.
RANKIN, Constant, 206.
    Robert, †29.
RAX, Anne, 33.
RAYMOND, Benjamin, 313.
    Elnathan, 185,
RAYNES, Joshua, 64, 260.
REA, Benjamin, 162.
REARDON, Elizabeth, 273.
    Timothy, †273, †274.
REDINGTON, Asa, 162.
REED, Andrew, 43, 44, †51, †205, 318, 341, 367, 368.
    Ann, 9, 193, 336.
    Catharine, 97.
    Charity, 259.
    Charlotte, 261.
    David, 43, 44, 50, 51, 53, 65, 75, 121, 258, *261.
    Elizabeth, 50, 258, 261.
    Eunice, 260.
    Eve Christine Margaret, 167.
    George, 298.
    Hannah, 205, 259, 261.
    Henry, 44.
    Ichabod, †336.
    Jacob, 167.
    Jane, 117, 258, 261.
    Joel, 92, 193, 197, †260.
    John, *43, 44, †111, 118, 125, 255, *258, 259, 261, †339.
    John, Jr., 125, 251, 258, 259.
    John George, *167.
    Jonathan, 61, 87, 97, 162, 163, 193, 234, 294, 306, 348.
    Jonathan, Jr., 140.
    Joseph, 50, 51, 192.
    Josiah, 344, 345.
    Margaret, 258, 261.
    Margaret Catharine Bare, 167.
    Margery, 341.
    Martha, 51, 258, 261, 337.
    Mary, 117, 258.
    Mary Magdalene, 167.
    Michael, 84, 167.
    Paul, 19, 118, †341.
    Rachel, 339.
    Robert, 132, 189, 260, 272.
    Samuel, 39, 193.
    Sarah, 111.
    Sevilla Magdalene, 167.
    Susanna, 258, 259, †342.
    Thomas, 342.
    William, 44, 51, †65, 227, 229, 259, †337.
REYNOLDS, Nathaniel, 204.
RHOADS, Cornelius, 360.
    Elizabeth, 191, 262, 360.
    George, 255.
    Thomas, 237.
RICE, Joseph, 138.
    Rebecca, 326.
    Thomas, 28, 53, 63, 71, 92, 104, 107, 108, 133, 136, 170, 188, 198, 217, 228, 254, 260, 276, 288, 308, 324, 326, 336, 338, 339, 349, 366.
    William, 325.
RICH, Samuel, 68.
RICHARDS, Sarah, 273.
RICHARDSON, Abijah, 110.
    Jerusha, 274.
    Joseph, †274.
    William, 68, 200, 202.
RICHMOND, Thomas B. 189.
RICKER, Paul, †17.
RIDLON, Robert, †306.
RIDLEY, George, 249.
RIGGS, Benjamin, 273, 274.
RING, David, 224, †249, 267, 313.
    Eleanor, 249.
    George, 209, 278.

36 INDEX OF NAMES.

Thomas, 29, 183, 249, 277, 288, 338, 347.
RITTAL, Betsey, 306.
    Charlotte, 306.
    Francis, 1, 11, 16, 29, 38, 75, 97, 140, 168, *305.
    John, 306, †345.
    Louis, 306.
    Lucy, 306.
    Margaret, 345.
    Molly, 306.
    Sally, 306.
    Nancy, 306.
RIVERS, Mary, 14.
    Moses, 140.
ROBARTSON, Charity, 53.
    Charles, *52.
    David, 53, 119.
    (Savage) Elizabeth, 52.
    (Stinson) Jane, 53.
    Martha, 52.
    (Stinson) Mary, 53.
    William, 52.
ROBINS, ROBBINS, Betsey, 223.
    David, 204, 248.
    Ebenezer, 101.
    Elioenai, 222.
    Jason, †248.
    Jenny, 248.
    Josiah, 204, 206, 207, 253, 345.
    Lois, 222.
    Lucy, 222.
    Luther, 275.
    Mella, 223.
    Nathaniel, 345.
    Nathaniel Johnson, 215.
    Oliver, *221.
    Oliver, Jr., 221, 235, 236.
    Otis, 222.
    Philip, 111, 193, 206
    Rufus, 222, 223.
    Sabra, 222.
    Shephard, 222.
    Sybel, 222.
    Thankful, 204.
ROBERSON, Bryant, 20.
ROBINSON, Alexander, 227.

Archibald, 14, 16, 140, 143, 171, 194, 218.
    Haunce, 90, 108, 194.
    James, 88, 246.
    John, 14, †143, 194, 218, 274.
    Joseph, 14, 15, 40, 118.
    Levi, 95.
    Margaret, 1, 40.
    Mary, 14, 15.
    Moses, *13, 101, 271.
    Sarah, 143.
    Timothy, 285.
    William, †2, 14.
    Winthrop, 177.
ROBY, Henry, 170.
    Margaret, 170.
    & Cruft, 290.
RODBIRD, Absalom, 328.
    Jane, 328,
    John, 328.
    Martha, 328, 329.
    Thomas, *328.
    William, 328.
RODGERS, (Read) Ann, 9.
    Elizabeth, 297.
    Francis, 297.
    George, 6, 8, 9, 27, 34, 80, 277, 297.
    Hugh, 8.
    Jane, 297.
    (Kendall) Jean, 9.
    John, 9, 27.
    Margaret, 9.
    Mary, 297.
    Patrick, 35, 37, 38, *297.
    Robert, 9.
    Ruth, 8, 9.
    Thomas, 8.
    William, 9, 297.
ROGERS, Alexander, 211, 278, 325, 339, 340, 349.
    Elisha, 58.
    Elizabeth, 78, 204.
    Frances, 317.
    George, 333.
    Hannah, 333.
    Howland, 341.

INDEX OF NAMES.

Hugh, 224, 368.
James, 248, 249, 306, 307.
John, *77, 121, 160, 185, 203, 204, 258, 275, 278, 325, 349.
Joseph, 362.
Kata, 78.
Martha, 154.
Mary, 78, 250.
Moses, †58.
Peleg, 54.
Phebe, 179.
Sarah, 99, 100.
William, *8, 237, 238, 358.

ROLLANDS, } Ephraim, 332.
ROLLINS,
    Mary, 101.

ROMINGER, Jacob, 226.
    Philip, †39.

ROSE, Daniel, 344.
    Prince, 43, 51, 110, 141.

ROTH, Conrad, 299.
    George, *298.
    Rosanna, 299.

ROWE, Ebenezer, 276.
    Ebenezer, Jr., 276.
    Edmund G., †276.
    Jacob, 256, 338.

ROWELL, Jacob, 145.
    William, 339.

RUNDLET, Charles, 289.
    Nathaniel, 289, 290.

RUNELS, Benjamin, 141.

RUPERT, John Wolfe, †25.

RUSSELL, Betsey, 249.
    Ichabod, 249.
    Isaac, †249.
    James, 249.
    John, 249.
    Joseph, 249.
    Nathaniel, 249.
    Polly, 249.
    Thomas, 154.

RUST, Joseph, 228,

RYAN, Bryan, 50.
    John, 124, 347.
    Michael, 218.

SALLY, Daniel, 7.
    Elizabeth, 7.
    James, 17.
    John, †7.

SAMPSON, } Charles, 101, 110, 129, 199,
SAMSON,   331.
    James, 278.

SANDERS, Hephzibah, 195.
    James, 195.
    Thomas, †195.
    Timothy, 195.

SANFORD, John, 169, 325.
    Thomas, 138.

SAVAGE, Ann, 259.
    Benjamin, 269.
    Daniel, 87, 88, 107, †259.
    Ebenezer, 356.
    Edward, 17.
    Elizabeth, 52.
    Isaac, 18, 220.
    Isaac, Jr., 148.
    John, 178, 179, 291, 340.
    Thomas, 178, 179.

SAWTELL, Hezekiah, †121.
    Obadiah, 122.
    Moses, 122, 339.
    Nathan, 201.

SAWYER, Aaron, 136.
    Benjamin, 136.
    Elizabeth, 302.
    George Whitefield, 340.
    Jacob, 303.
    Jonathan, 189, 272, 335, 337, 338, 341, 342, 343.
    Joshua, †136.

SCHAEFFER, John Martin, 143, *246, 299.
    Margaret, 247,
    Mary, 247.

SCHENCK, } Andrew, 68, 82, 110, 129,
SHANK,   143, *329.
SCHANCKS,
    Catharina, 330.
    Chrischana, 330.
    George, 330.
    James, 330.
    John, 330.
    Lucy, 330.
    Mary, 330.
    Sarah, 329.
    Sophia, 330.

SCOTT, Daniel, 92, 93, 108, 156, 205, 342.

SCRIBNER, Stephen, 286, 287, 319.
SEALEY, Drusilla, 343.
    Shubael, 343.
SEARL, John, 248.
    John, Jr., †248.
SEARS, Barnabas, 183, 207, 230.
SEEKINS, Aaron, 340.
SEVENS, Elizabeth, 256.
SEVEY, Hannah, 324.
    John, 136, 146, 228, *288, 307, 324.
    Maria, (Moriah,) 70, 289, 290, 291, 292.
    Mary, 29, 288.
    Mercy, 324.
    Michael, 7, 16, 28, 53, 63, 92, 104, *323.
    Samuel, 290, 291, 292, 303.
    Solomon, 324.
    Stephen, 29, *288, 324.
    Susannah, 287.
    William, 219, 303, 324.
    Wyman Bradbury, 228, 277, 289, 290, 291.
SEWALL, Charles, 260.
    David, 260, 265, 305, 340.
    Dorcas, 265.
    Dummer, 19, 24, 64, 69, 75, 124, 137, 160, 164, 170, 183, 188, 220, 221, 277, 339, 348.
    H., 158.
    Hannah, 260.
    Henry, 111, 124, 201, 204, 254, †260, 264, 279.
    Jenny, 260.
    Jonathan, 287.
    Joseph, 221.
    Joshua, 260.
    Meriam, 265.
    Moses, 265, 273, 305, †340.
    Nancy, 260.
    Polly, 260.
    Ruthy, 340.
    Samuel, 229, 260.
    Sarah, 260.
    Stephen, †265.
    William, 265.
SHANNON, James Noble, 68.

SHAW, Benjamin, 114, 248, 263, †336.
    Elias, 4.
    Elisha, 19, 20, 24, †69, 75.
    Francis, 17.
    Jesse, 263.
    John, 4, †50, 87.
    Joseph, 263.
    Joshua, 262, 265.
    Josiah, 336.
    Mary, †263.
    Nathaniel, 192.
    Susanna, 69.
SHEEN, John, †23.
SHEPHERD, Abner, †161.
    Avis, 192.
    Daniel, 192.
    Levi, 275.
SHERBURNE, Abiel, 191.
    Jacob, 160.
    Nathan, *191.
    Polly, 191.
SHERWIN, Abigail, 365.
    Elnathan, 323, 365, 366.
SHIBLES, David, 108.
    James, 108.
    John, 59, †108.
    Mary, 108.
    Robert Killpatrick, 59, 108.
    Thomas, 59, 108.
SHILEBER, William, 295, 296.
SHORT, John, 301.
SHUMAN, John, 73.
SHURTLEFF, Dorcas, 159.
SHUTE, Benjamin, 87.
SIDELINGER, Charles, 226.
    Daniel, 226.
    George, 226.
    Martin, †226.
    Mary, 226.
    Peter, 226.
SIDENPARKER, Mathias, †143.
    Michael, 143.
    Susanna, 143.
SIDES, Lawrence, 143.
    Lorinz, 276.
    Michael, 39.
SILVESTER, Betsey, 308.
    Catherine, 322.

INDEX OF NAMES.

David, 136, 137, 145, 146, 219, 254, 260, 275, 292, *307, 335, 336.
Jane, 49, 69, 308.
Joshua, 307, 308, 309.
Lucy, 49.
Lydia, 308.
Martha, 307, 308.
Mary, 69, 71, 219, 308.
Rachel, 308.
Samuel, †219.
Sarah, 308.
William, 34, 48.
SIMMONS, Abigail, 248.
Barnabas, 145, 298.
Betsey, 248.
Dorothy, 181.
Ichabod, 246.
Joseph, 181, 182, 199, 238, 248, 261, 276.
Marcy, 181.
Mary, 181, 238.
Nancy, 248.
Nathaniel, 73, 129, *180, 347.
Peobody, 248.
Rachel, 181, 248.
Sarah, 181, 238.
Stephen, 181, 238, †248.
Urainy Sprague, 248.
Zebedee, 129, 181, 182, *238.
Zebedee, Jr., 239.
SIMONTON, Sally, 334.
SIMPSON, Elizabeth, 82, 124.
James, 259.
Paul, 121.
Robert, 255.
William, †82, †124.
SINKLER, Nathaniel, 52.
SKOLFIELD, Margaret, 348.
Richard, 336.
SLEEPER, John, 92.
Moses, 185.
SLOMAN, Lydia, 95.
Thomas, †95.
SLOSSES, Mr., 44.
SLOWMAN, Abigail, 351.
SMALL, Benjamin, 345.
Bethiah, 35.

John, 141.
SMALLY, Francis, 21.
SMART, Elizabeth, 80.
John, 80.
Joshua, 169.
Thomas, †80.
SMILEY, David, 227.
Hugh, 175.
Thomas, 122.
SMITH, Asa, 65, 93.
China, 137.
Daniel, 68.
Ebenezer, 138, 197.
Eliab, 173.
Emanuel, 274.
Henry, 136, 339.
Hugh, 138.
Isaac, 194.
Israel, 54, †311.
Jane, 311.
John, 339.
Joseph, 248.
Mannasseh, 290.
Manuel, 276.
Mathias, 48, 148, 269, 317.
Rogers, 155, 264, 272, 276.
Thomas, 316.
William, 271.
SMOUSE, John, †171.
SNELL, Elijah, 195.
Thomas, 54, 95, 138, 220, 311.
SNIPE, Ann, 106.
Charles, 7, 47, *105.
Gordon, 106.
Hannah, 106.
Jean, 106.
John, 106, 209.
Marthow (Martha,) 106.
Sarah, 106.
SNOW, Elisha, 132.
Ephraim, 255, 339.
Isaac, 1, 4, 75.
Philip, 204.
SOMES, David, 2, 336.
SOPER, Martha, 215, 319, 320.
Samuel, 319.
Seth, 87, 136.
SOULE, Abigail, 129.

Amos, 329.
Anna, 129.
Asa, 185.
Cornelius, 100.
Elizabeth, 261.
John, 73, 261.
Levi, †129.
Nathan, 101, †129.
Samuel, 328.
Sarah, 129, †276.
SPAFFORD, Jacob, 154.
    James, 155.
    John, 155.
    Jonathan, 108, †125, *154.
    Martha, 154, 155
    Mary, 154, 155.
    Phebe, 140.
    Robert, 155.
    Samuel, 155.
    William, 155.
SPAULDING, Eleazer, 164.
    Josiah, 164.
    William, 164.
SPEAR, John, 247.
    Jonathan, 60.
    Robert, †104.
    William, 206, 344.
SPENCER, Isaac, 24.
SPINNEY, Joanna, 79.
    John, †79.
SPRAGUE, Jethro, 100.
    John, 267.
    Joseph, 342, 345.
    Michael, 129, 299.
    Nathan, 124, 199, 248, 254, 299, 346.
    Spooner, 248.
    William, 73, 100, 278.
SPRING, Daniel, 223.
SPRINGER, Anna, 64.
    Betsey, 137.
    Edward, 64.
    Hannah, 64, 121.
    James, 16, 24, †63, 273.
    John, 25, 64, †121, 140, 256.
    Lucy, 137.
    Martha, 64.
    Mary, 64.
    Nathaniel, 63, 64, †137.
    Rachel, 24, 64.
    Samuel, 137.
    Sarah, 137.
    William, 121, 339.
SPROUL, James, 64, 80, 179, 233, 237, 238, 321, 322.
    Jean, 233.
    John, 233, 304, 321, 322.
    Margaret, 233.
    Mary, 233, 321, 322.
    Robert, 38, 78, *232, 322.
    Sarah, 232, 233, 321, 322.
    Susan, 322.
    Susanna, 233.
    Thomas, 233, *321.
    William, 35, 206, 233, 322.
STACKPOLE, James, 132, 141, 193, 200, 202, 223.
    Mary, 141.
    Samuel, 200.
STACY, Nymphas, 156, 178, 275, 292, 309, 349.
STAIN, John, 11, 38.
STANDISH, James, 338.
STANDLEY, David, 17.
STANLEY, Solomon, 130.
STANWOOD, Job, †188.
STAPEL, } Anna, 325.
STAPLE, }
    Daniel, 325.
    Ephraim, 324.
    James, 325.
    John, 324.
    Joseph, 324.
    Josiah, 325.
    Lucy, 324.
    Robert, 325.
    Samuel, 169.
    Stephen, *324.
    Susanna, 324.
STARBIRD, John, 249.
STARBUCK, Christopher, 196.
STARKEY, Thomas, 180.
STARLING, Joseph, †101.
    Moses, 101, 147, 201, 273.
STARRETT, Thomas, 66, 80, 108, 111, 148, 232.
STEBBINS, Josiah, 353.

INDEX OF NAMES.

STEDMAN, James, 201.
STEPHENS, Joseph, 173.
STEVENS, Abigail, 286.
    Amos, 219.
    Betsey, 286.
    Charity, 343.
    Charles, 343.
    Daniel, *285, 286, †339.
    Drusilla, 343.
    Ephraim, 221.
    Hannah, 286.
    Jacob, †124.
    Jerusha, 339.
    Jonas, 227.
    Joseph, †129, †227.
    Mary, 286, 343.
    Mehitable, 286.
    Nancy, 286.
    Nathaniel, 205.
    Olive, 286.
    Rachel, 129.
    Samuel, 269, 286.
    Sarah, 286.
    Sophia, 286.
    Thomas, 75, 276, †343, 346.
    William, 276.
STEWARD, Abraham, 141.
    Daniel, 249, 305.
    Sarah, 141.
    Solomon, 110, 194.
    Solomon, Jr., 249.
STICKNEY, Benjamin, 220.
STILFIN, Francis, 275.
    Margaret, 49.
    Michael, 49.
    Molly, 306.
STILKEY, John George, †188.
STINSON, Ann, 46, 47.
    Elizabeth, 46.
    Isabella, 96.
    James, 46, 66, 209.
    Jean, 46.
    John, 2, 7, 31, 36, 46, 47, 51, 63, 96, 106, 209, 215.
    Margaret, 46.
    Mary, 53, 96.
    Mercy, 46.
    Robert, 80, 96, 114.

    Samuel, 18, 96, 138, 157, 197, 239, 255, 307, 340.
    Samuel, Jr., †307.
    Sarah, 46.
    Thomas, 18, *95.
    William, *45, 107, 328, 342, 344.
STODDARD, Amos, 305.
STONE, Betsey, 345.
    Daniel, 140, 345.
    Ebenezer, 345
    John, 345.
    Jonas, 345.
    Nancy, 345.
    Samuel, 345.
    Walden, †345.
STORER, Andrew, 34, 126, 182, 226, 247.
    Ebenezer, 187, 188.
STORY, Jane, 189.
    Thomas, *189.
STUART, Abigail, 118.
    Charles, †118.
    John, 329.
STUTSON, STUDSON, } Zenas, 289, 307.
SULLIVAN, William, 47, 273.
SUMNER, Ezra, 143, 144.
    Hopestill, 90, 111, 171.
SUTTON, John, 276.
SWANTON, William, 64.
SWATZ, (Castner) Anna, 142.
    Catharine, 142.
    Christehana, 142.
    Fredrick, †142.
    Jacob, 142.
    Lucy, 142, †143.
    Margrate, 142.
    Mary, 142.
    Peter, 142.
    Susannah, 142.
SWASEY, Joseph, †124.
SWEET, Abiel, 307.
    Arnold, †336.
    Polly, 336.
SWEETLAND, James, 206.
    Samuel, 145, 162.
SWEETSER, Jane, 99, 100.
SWETT, Benjamin, 240, 241. *327, 328.

James, 327.
John, 327.
Sarah, 327.
William, 327.
SYLVESTER, Mary, 64, 140.
    William, 24, †140.
TABER, John, 219.
TALBUT, Samuel, 189.
TARR, Benjamin, 343.
    Joseph, 274.
TAYLOR, Anna, 313, 314.
    Betsey Sleeper, 314.
    Elias, †87.
    Ephraim, 160.
    Ezra, 196, 221, 263, 278, 294, 306, 348.
    Jerusha, †160.
    Joseph, 119, 160.
    Mary, 87.
    Thomas, Jr., †277.
    William, 272, 329.
TEMPLE, Elizabeth, 124.
    Richard, 84, 124.
TENNY, Thomas, †7.
THATCHER, Josiah, 177.
THAYER, Gideon, 10.
THEOBALD, Philip, 49, 137, 192, 206, 221.
    Sally, 306.
THOMAS, Consider, †234.
    David, 87, 88, 259, 264.
    Frances, 364, 365.
    George, 84, 124, 141, 229, 345.
    Ichabod, 336.
    Jesse, 88, 130.
    Joseph, 185, 365.
    Melzer, 341.
    Sarah, 234.
    Waterman, 90, 101, 129, 143, 145, 262, 276, 299, 330, 331.
THOMPSON, Aaron, 337.
    Abigail, 18.
    Benjamin, *18. †229.
    Cornelius, 188.
    Ebenezer, †144.
    Ezekiel, 221, 226, 229, 234, 251, 337, 345.
    Humphrey, 337.
    James, 1, 4, 143, 305, 337.
    Jane, 206.
    Joel, 268, 336, 337.
    John, 64, †206.
    Mary, 337.
    Rhoda, 229.
    Robert, 66, 206, 332.
    Samual, 44, 161, 229, †337.
    Story, 189.
    William, 144, 160, 230.
    & Tinkham, 290.
THORN, Elizabeth, 82.
    Lucy, 82.
    Martha, 82.
    Sarah, 82.
    Thomas, 82.
    William, 43, †82.
    William, Jr., 43.
THORNTON, James, 20, †124.
    John, 124.
    Joshua, 124.
    Susanna, 124.
    William, 124, 125.
THORP Lewis, 273, 274, 276, 343.
THWING, Nathaniel, 87, 92, 131, 137, 157, 158, 180, 185, 197, 198, 199, 260, 285, 342.
TIBBETTS, John, 28.
    Nathaniel, 63, 95, 192, 199, 341.
    Samuel, 226, 292, 306, 342.
TIFFANY, Daniel 339.
TILTON, Abraham, *287.
    Andrew, 287.
    Benjamin, 277, 287.
    Charles, 287.
    Daniel, 287.
    John, 287.
    Mary, 287.
    Samuel, 277, 287.
    Sarah, 287.
    Susannah, 287.
TINKHAM, Joseph, 275, 291, 303, 308, 309, 335, 336.
    Mary, 170.
    Polly, 170.
    Seth, 272, 291, 324, 327, 336, 356.
    Spencer, 170.
    & Savage, 290.
TIRRILL, Isaac, 255.

INDEX OF NAMES. 43

Joseph Shaw, 255.
TITCOMB, Nancy, 361.
 Samuel, 361.
TOBEY, Stephen, 274, 276.
TODD, George, 368.
 Samuel, 4.
TOLMAN, Jeremiah, 206.
 Mary, 17.
 Samuel, †17, 206, 224.
TOTMAN, Henry, 188.
TOWN, Ephraim, 199, 202.
 Sherebiah, *199,
 Thomas, 90, 199.
TOWNSEND, Daniel, †107, 138.
  Dodivah, 203, 204.
  Sarah, 107, 203.
TOWNSLEY, Jacob, 140.
TOZER, } Jeremiah, 57, 58.
TOZIER, } John, 68, 77.
 Rebecca, 141.
 Simon, 141.
TRAFTON, Zacheus, †20.
TRAGUE, Elkanah, 350.
TRASK, Allis, 144.
 David, 342, 347.
 Elizabeth, 144.
 John, 144, †201.
 Samuel, †87, 201.
 Sarah, 201.
 Solomon, 347.
 Sylvia, 201.
 Thomas, 343.
 William, 87.
TREAST, Catran, 85.
TROUP, } Alexander, 307, 309, 329.
TROOP, }
TROTT, Benjamin, 18, 31, 336.
 John, 31, 132.
 Joseph, 341.
 Lemuel, 31, 164, 260.
TROWBRIDGE, John, 129, 276.
  Sarah, 129, 276.
TRUFANT, David, 20, †25, 64, 69, 194.
 Mary, 25.
TUBBS, Ezra, 262.
 Samuel, 294.
TUCK, Samuel, 268, 298.
TUCKER, Joanna, 335.
 John, 189.

Josiah, 17,
 Richard, †335.
 Richard Hawley, 335.
TUCKERMAN, David, †137.
TULLY, Dorothy, 72.
TUPPER, James, 161, 180, 234.
 William, 140.
TURNER, Alexander, 129, 276.
 Anna, 276.
 Bethiah, 347.
 Betsey, 347.
 Briggs, 163, 228, 229.
 Caleb, 201.
 Christopher, 315, 316, 359.
 Consider, 220, †346.
 Cornelius, 129, 166, 182, 188, 276.
 Elisabeth, 113, 252.
 George, 347.
 James, 151, *251.
 Joanna, 347.
 John, 315, 316.
 Sarah, 346, 347.
 Simeon, 124.
 William Hodgkins, 347.
TWIST, Thomas, 284.
TWYCROSS, Robert, 48, 49.
TYLER, Belcher, 133.
 Ebenezer, 98.
ULMER, George, 166, 188.
 John, 38, 82, 143.
UMBEHIND, Jacob, 124.
UMPHRIZE, John, 125.
VARNER, George, *236.
 Sadoney, 236.
VAUGHAN, Eliot, 76.
 Jane, 76.
 Samuel, Jr., 167.
 William, 76.
VEERZ, Mary, 123.
VINALL, David, 129, 237.
 Ezekiel, 248.
 Mary, 270.
VINING, Benjamin, 82.
VOSE, Seth, 111, 171, 226.
WADE, Abner, 138, 197, 220, 255, 311, 341, 356.
 Benjamin, 201.
 Jacob, 181.

INDEX OF NAMES.

Joseph, 54, 92, 95, 132.
Rachel, 264.
WADSWORTH, Abiah, 32.
    Alfred, 348.
WALCH, Anna Elbet, 201.
    Jane, 260.
    John, *201, 260.
    Peter, 202, †260.
WALKER, Andrew, 199.
    Benjamin, 192.
    Charles, 164.
    Meriam, 198.
    Sarah, 341.
    Solomon, †198, 199, 341, 355.
WALL, Mary, 302.
    Patrick, 344.
WALLISER, John Christopher, 276.
WALTON, Abiel, 229.
WARD, John, 65, 77, 119, 138, 201.
WARNER, John, 45.
    Silas, 104.
WARREN, George, 141, 227.
    Josiah, 142, †305.
    Richard, 208.
    Sarah, 305.
WATERHOUSE, Samuel, 186.
WATERMAN, Abijah, 101, †110.
    Deborah, 110, 238.
    Joseph, 101.
    Mary, 110.
    Thomas, 110, 238.
WATERS, Patience, 54.
    Samuel, 65, 90, 130, 138, 143, 144, 145, 163, 177, 208, 277, 343, 348, 350, 352.
    Samuel, Jr., 277.
    William, 54.
WATSON, David, 39, 40.
    Elizabeth, 40.
    James, 39, 67, 108.
    (Libbee) Jane, 40.
    John, 40.
    (Robinson) Margaret, 40.
    (Gore) Mary, 40.
    Matthew, 39, 40.
    William, *39, 51, 108, 111.
WATT, John, 86, 232, 298.
WATTS, Samuel, 20, 28.

WAUGH, James, 164, 183, 228.
WEATHERLY, Sally, 345.
WEAVER, John, †200, 237.
    Joseph, 103.
    Molly, 200.
WEBB, Anne, 193.
    Barnabas, 212.
    Benjamin, 193, 247.
    Bersheba, 193.
    Ebenezer, †193.
    Jane, 54.
    John, 193.
    Luther, 54.
    Lydia, 54.
    Mary, 212.
    Nathan, 193, 285.
    Nathaniel, †54.
    Samuel, *91.
    Sarah, 54, 91, 92, 193.
    Seth, †128.
    William, 265.
WEBBER, Asa, 274.
    Charles, 29, 90.
    David, 347.
    Joseph, †274.
    Joshua, 298.
    Lewis, 274.
    Samuel, 124.
    Sarah 274.
    William, 160.
WEBSTER, Andrew, 129, 166.
    Andrew, Jr., 80.
    Daniel, 29, 247, 277, 288.
WEED, James, 223.
WEEKS, John, 88, 145.
WELLER, Andrew, †52, 105.
    John, 105.
    Lehn, 52.
WENDELL, Thomas, 340.
WENTWORTH, William, 347.
WERNER, Johannes, 202.
WESSON, Eunice, 79.
    Joseph, †79.
    Nathan, 201.
WEST, Capt. George, 252.
    George W., 253.
    Mary, 253.
WESTCUTT, Elizabeth, 160.

INDEX OF NAMES.

William, †160.
WESTON, Arunah, 163.
    John, 249.
    Joseph, 151, 194.
    Nathan, 61.
WEYMOUTH, Elizabeth, 45.
WHELEN, } John, 363.
WHALEN,
    Joseph, †278.
    Patience, 278.
WHEATON, Mason, 41, 51, 223.
WHEELER, Benjamin, †126.
    Elizabeth, 87, 103, 126.
    John, †87.
    Joseph, 185.
    Phebe, 302.
WHITAKER, Nathaniel, 194.
WHITE, Abigail, 239, 240, 319, 320.
    Abijah, 54.
    Anmoriah, 240.
    Benjamin, 95, 1 97, 221.
    Carpous, 120.
    Elizabeth, 240.
    George, 125.
    James, 240.
    Jane, 240.
    Jesse, 327, 341.
    John, 57, 79, 97, 110, 183, 194, 209, 224, *239, 240, 319.
    Joseph, 24, 63, 64, 95, 137, 160, 262, †339.
    Margaret, 240.
    Mary, 131, 240.
    Philip, *130.
    Rachel, 240.
    Robert, 130, 131, 197.
    Samuel, †206, 359.
    Sarah, 131, 339.
    Susannah, 240.
    William, 240.
WHITING, John, 95.
    Jonathan, 68, 95, 129, 139, 140, 176, 195.
    Solomon, 99.
    Thurston, 95, 232, 282, 283. 301, 338, 345.
WHITMAN, Rhode, 193.
WHITTEMORE, } Abraham, 84, 107, 210.
WHITIMORE,

    Abraham, Jr., †229.
    Andrew, 256.
    Elizabeth, 256.
    Francis, †255, 256, †274.
    John, 256.
    Joseph, 133.
    Mary, 256.
    Samuel, 274.
    Stephen, 211, 229, 255, 256, 275, 342, 348.
    Susanna, 256.
    William, 256, 274.
WHITTEN, John, 82.
WHITTIER, Abel, 310.
    Abigail, 314.
    Ann, 313, 314.
    Benaiah, 314.
    Cyrus, 310.
    Dorothy, 310.
    Ebenezer, 136, 137, 145, 146, 156, 205, 219, 228, 230, 264, 272, 292, 303, 305, 309, 336, 349.
    Hannah, 310.
    Jedediah, 309.
    Josiah, 314.
    Levi, 310.
    Mary, 314.
    Mary Page, 309.
    Moses, *313.
    Nathaniel, †137, *309.
    Ruhamah, 310.
    Ruth, 309.
    Thomas, 137, 273, 309, 311.
    William, 161, 284, 319.
WIGGLESWORTH, ———, 308.
WILBER, Asa, 201.
WILDBUR, David, 201.
WILDE, Samuel S., 283.
    Samuel Sumner, 338.
WILEY, Alexander, 51, 367, 368.
    Easther, 51.
    (Kenney) Esther, 51.
    Isaac, 118.
    (Lewis) Jane, 51.
    John, 50, 51.
    (Boyd) Katharine, 51.

Martha, 50.
Neal, 51.
(Wylie) Robart, *50.
Samuel, 51.
William, 51.
WILKINS, W., 78, 204.
William, 87.
WILLARD, Andrew, †45.
Margaret, 45.
WILLIAMS, Abigail, 266, 355.
Alice, 90.
Anne, 356.
Asa, 273.
Benjamin, 345.
Gardner, *146.
Henry, 135.
James, 216, 249, 320.
John, 82, 83.
Jonathan, †249.
Mehitable, 354, 356.
Nathaniel, *354.
Olive, 355.
Polley, 147.
Samuel, 249.
Seth, 260, 264, 279.
Simeon, 356.
Susana, 103, 356.
Sukey, 297.
Thomas, 312, 313, 321.
Timothy, 355, 356.
WILLIAMSON, Abigail, 153.
Anna, 153.
Hannah, 153.
Jonathan, 7, 16, 28, 49, 53, 69, 92, 104, 219.
Ruth, 153.
Samuel, 289.
Sarah, †153.
Thomas, 69, 153.
WILSON, David, 55, 307.
Dorcas, 55.
Elizabeth, 45.
Ephraim, 104.
Gowen, †45.
Hugh, †45, †340.
Isaac, 121.
Isabella, 22.
James, 226, 229, 235, 251, 255,
340, 346.
John, 22, 100, 337.
Mary, 22, 258, 340.
Rachel, 337.
Robert, †121.
Samuel, 22, 45, 121, 161, 258, 259, 261, 342.
Thomas, 22, 23, 45, 51, 107.
William, *21, 45, †160, 278, 340.
WINCH, Priscilla, 336.
Thomas, †336.
WINCHELL, Anne, 168.
Hannah, 168.
John, 23, †221.
Quash, *168.
Samuel, 23, †121, 168, 221, 234, 277, 325.
Sarah, 121.
WINCHENBACH,
WINCHENBAUGH, } Jacob, 68, 102, 202,
WINCHENBACK, } 254, 331, 346.
WING, Daniel, 148, 269, 314, 315.
Samuel, †148.
William, 208.
WINGEBOW, Jacob, 68.
WINN, Jonathan, †61.
Joseph, 61.
WINSHIP, Joseph, 114.
WINSLOW, Anna, 78.
Bethiah, 298.
Dorothy, 181.
Esther, 298.
John, 181, 228.
Joseph, †298.
Kenelm, 77, 119, 140.
Martha, 63.
Mercy, 298.
Nathaniel, 63, †78, 136, 178.
WINTER, Francis, 137, 262, 267, 313.
WISE, Thankful, 337.
William, 337.
WITHAM, Isaac, 349, 350.
Jane, 350.
Joseph, *349.
Josiah, 349, 350.
Lydia, 350.
Sally, 350.
WITHERELL, Charles, 305.
Obadiah, 142, 164, 249.

INDEX OF NAMES.

WINTHROP, Thomas Lindall, 256.
WOOD, Abiel, 16, 170, 290, 309, 336, 338.
    Ephraim, 343.
    Hannah, 170.
    John, 64, 77, 137.
    Joseph, 138, 163, 166, 183.
    Mary, 2.
    Oliver, 228.
    Samuel, 195, 219, 220, 251.
    Silas, 228.
WOODBRIDGE, Anna, 144.
    Benjamin, 2, 6, 16, 38, 45, 65, 119, 163, 290.
    David, 11.
    James, 144.
    Thomas, 291.
WOODCOCK, Abigail, 204.
    Benjamin, 180.
    David, 180, †204.
    John, 201.
    Lucy, 179.
    Mary (Fields,) 179.
    Nathaniel, 344.
    Submit, 179, 180.
    Phebe, 179.
    William, *179.
WOODMAN, Jacob, 137.
    John, 344.
    John, Jr., 194.
    Lucy, 303.
    Thomas, †303.
WOODS, Bennet, 24.
    John French, 227, 229.
WOODSIDE, Elizabeth, 73.
    William, 73.
WOODWARD, Noah, 148, 204, 273.
    Samuel, 164, 192, 223, 332, 348.
WORK, Ebenezer, 42, 51.
    (Orr) Elizabeth, 42.
    James, *41.
    (Dunlap) Jane, 42.
    Margaret, 42.
    William, 42.
WOSTAR, Moses, 45.
WYLIE, Hannah, 364.
    Isaac, Jr., 346.
    Margaret, 317.
    Robert, 13, 15.
WYLIS, Alexander, 224.
    Martha, 224.
    Robert, 224.
    Samuel †224.
WYMAN, (Bickford) Abigail, 35.
    Abram, 20.
    Bethiah, 35.
    Daniel, 36, 161.
    (Call) Deliverance, 35.
    (McCausland) Elizabeth, 35.
    Francis, 73, *99, 100, †342.
    Hannah, 35.
    Henry, 244, 246.
    Hester, 99.
    Isaiah, 183, 273, 342.
    James, *35.
    Jane, 99, 100.
    John, 342.
    Love, 141.
    Martha, 183.
    Molly, 35, 36.
    Nathaniel, 73, 79, 99, 100, 118, †183.
    Olive, 35.
    (Goodwin) Prudence, 35.
    Sarah, 99.
    Simeon, 84.
    William, 25, 35, 36, 141, 198, 269, 342.
YEATS, Elizabeth, 262.
    George, 262.
    George James, 273.
    James, *261.
    Jean, 262, 297.
    Lydia, 262.
    Margret, 262.
    Mary, 262.
    Rachel, 262.
    Samuel, 262, 273, 358, 359.
    Sarah, 262.
YOUNG, Abihail, 63.
    (Pearce) Ann, 49.
    Catharine, 345.
    Cyntha, 308.
    Edward, †234, 297.
    Ezra, 188.
    Francis, 35.
    Gideon, 345.

Hannah, 345.
Henry, †345.
Isaac, 48, 92.
Jacob, †171.
James, 234, 345.
Jane, 234, 297, 345.
Joseph, *48, †63.
Joshua, 48, 77.

Reuben, 342.
Richard, 20, 343.
Robert, 188.
Samuel, 324.
(Holbrook) Sarah, 49.
Thomas, 48, 49.
William, 53, 205.

Index of Places.

(Omitting "Lincoln County," "Massachusetts," "Maine," etc.)

ABAGADUSSET, 30, 55.
ALMSBURY, 88.
ANTEGO, Island of, 127.
ANTRIM, COUNTY, 89.
ARROWSICK, } 29, 46, 57, 106, 213,
ARROWSIC ISLAND, } 214.
ATTLEBOROUGH, 18, 179.
AUGUSTA, 278, 279, 316, 336, 340.
BACK RIVER, 46, 47.
BAGGADUCE, } 128.
BIGWADUCE, }
BALLTOWN, 92, 93, 130, 140, 145, 178, 205, 234, 249, 259, 264, 277, 288, 343, 344, 348, 349, 350, 351, 352, 362.
BANGOR, 347.
BARNSTABLE, 54, 192.
BARRETSTOWN, 206, 230, 253.
BARTERS ISLAND, (BOOTHBAY) 116.
BATH, 28, 64, 121, 124, 137, 140, 158, 159, 160, 164, 170, 183, 188, 194, 220, 221, 224, 229, 260, 262, 264, 267, 270, 277, 311, 312, 313, 321, 337, 339, 341, 347.
BELGRADE, 339.
BERWICK, 45.
BLUEHILL BAY, 164, 166, 183.
BAKERS POINT, 46, 47.
BOOTHBAY, 19, 29, 43, 45, 50, 51, 52, 54, 61, 63, 65, 71, 72, 75, 87, 88, 101, 103, 104, 111, 114, 115, 116, 118, 133, 135, 136, 140, 145, 178, 189, 192, 205, 224, 228, 247, 271, 272, 275, 297, 301, 333, 334, 335, 337, 338, 341, 342, 343, 347, 348, 363, 368.
BOSTON, 17, 20, 38, 64, 77, 95, 119, 167, 234, 249, 256, 338.
BOWDOIN, 141, 185, 226, 227, 248, 249, 266, 292, 306, 307.
BOWDOINHAM, 36, 54, 75, 84, 105, 107, 108, 110, 121, 124, 141, 160, 162, 166, 178, 185, 192, 198, 211, 223, 229, 248, 255, 256, 274, 275, 276, 281, 294, 313, 339, 342, 344, 348.
BRENTWOOD, N. H., 246.
BRISTOL, 23, 34, 35, 38, 45, 47, 50, 51, 64, 65, 78, 79, 80, 101, 127, 128, 144, 147, 162, 163, 169, 170, 175, 176, 178, 179, 184, 189, 190, 191, 201, 206, 224, 227, 228, 232, 234, 237, 238, 255, 261, 262, 273, 277, 279, 280, 283, 297, 298, 303, 304, 321, 322, 331, 332, 333, 334, 340, 341, 347, 356, 358, 359, 360.
BRISTOL COUNTY, MASS., 18, 179, 189.
BROAD BAY, 29, 38, 39, 45, 52, 105, 246, 298.
BROAD COVE, 12.
BROOKFIELD, 360.
BRUNSWICK, 1, 4, 45, 121, 161, 226, 261, 292, 336, 340.
CAMDEN, 192, 224, 230, 249, 340, 343, 344, 347.
CAMPBELL'S POND, 312.
CANAAN, 79, 110, 149, 193, 194, 249, 251, 252, 305.
CASCO BAY, 3, 213.
CHARLESTOWN, 113, 114.
CHESTER, 260.
CLINTON, 274, 323, 337.
COBBISECONTE, 16, 17, 20.
CORD WOOD POINT, 312.
COUSINS ISLAND, 30.

INDEX OF PLACES.

CROTCH ISLAND, 301.
CUMBERLAND, COUNTY, 69, 82, 99, 136, 183, 234, 339, 345.
CUSHING, 111, 188, 189, 192, 194, 199, 205, 206, 226, 230, 247, 260, 298, 299, 300, 301, 341, 343, 345, 346.
DAMARISCOTTA, 76.
DAMARISCOTTA POND, 88, 93.
DAMARISCOVE ISLAND, 103.
DEER ISLAND, 133, 162, 163, 164, 195.
DIGHTON, 189.
DORCHESTER, 256.
DRESDEN, 251, 259, 262, 263, 274, 275, 278, 279, 292, 294, 306, 307, 336, 345, 348, 359.
DUCK TRAP, 166, 188.
DUNSTABLE, N. H., 24.
DURHAM, 339.
DUXBOROUGH, 129.
DYER'S POND, 92.
DYER'S RIVER, 55, 90, 92.
EASTERN RIVER, 293.
EDGECOMB, 29, 110, 124, 136, 143, 145, 178, 182, 183, 205, 207, 224, 227, 228, 230, 247, 249, 260, 273, 275, 277, 288, 294, 297, 305, 339, 342, 347, 348.
ESSEX COUNTY, MASS., 88, 138, 164.
FAIRFIELD, 248, 274, 322, 323.
FAIRFIELD PLANTATION, 192.
FALMOUTH, 36, 45, 69.
FARMINGTON, 272, 273, 303, 304, 307, 340.
FISHERMAN'S ISLAND, 333.
FIVE STACK MARSH, 367.
FORT POWNALL, 61, 86.
FORT WESTERN, 17, 18.
FOXHOLE, (MARSHFIELD,) 120.
FOX ISLANDS, 101.
FRANKFORT, 126.
FREETOWN, 47, 200.
FRENCHMAN'S BAY, 64, 121, 128, 140.
FRESHWATER COVE, 217.
GARDINERSTON, 77, 87.
GEORGES ISLAND, 188.
GEORGES RIVER, 32.
GEORGETOWN, 1, 2, 4, 6, 7, 8, 17, 18, 20, 24, 25, 27, 28, 29, 31, 34, 45, 50, 51, 55, 63, 64, 69, 73, 75, 79, 81, 82, 83, 84, 95, 99, 105, 118, 137, 178, 183, 185, 188, 205, 207, 208, 209, 212, 213, 215, 216, 224, 239, 241, 242, 256, 258, 273, 274, 275, 276, 277, 278, 313, 317, 318, 319, 320, 321, 327, 328, 337, 341, 342, 343, 344, 346, 347, 348, 362, 366, 367, 368.
GIDNEY'S CLAIM, 99.
GLENARM, 89.
GOULDSBOROUGH, 17, 121.
GREAT BALD HEAD, 216.
GREAT LEDGE, 46.
GREAT MARSH, 217.
GREAT POND SETTLEMENT, 277.
GREEN ISLAND, 116, 333.
GREENE, 275.
GRENADA, Island of, 256.
GROTON, MASS., 227.
HALLOWELL, 54, 72, 78, 87, 88, 90, 92, 93, 94, 95, 98, 104, 105, 107, 111, 122, 123, 124, 136, 141, 148, 157, 158, 161, 166, 167, 180, 191, 192, 195, 196, 197, 200, 201, 202, 204, 220, 227, 244, 248, 251, 254, 256, 259, 261, 263, 264, 265, 273, 274, 277, 285, 287, 305, 339, 340.
HANCOCK, 202, 333.
HANCOCK COUNTY, 344.
HARPSWELL, 1, 75.
HARRINGTON, 10, 19.
HINGHAM, 341.
HOLTS ISLAND, 129.
HUNNEWELL'S POINT, 185.
HOPKINTON, N. H., 276.
HOWARDSTON, 151.
HUMPHREY'S HEAD, 356, 367.
IRELAND, 89.
JEREMY ISLAND, } 50, 53, 70.
JERRYMISQUAM, }
JEWANKA NECK, 326.
JEWELL'S ISLAND, 3.

INDEX OF PLACES.   51

JONES MARSH, 239.
KENNEBEC COUNTY, 260.
KENNEBEC RIVER, 17, 18, 19 24, 29, 34, 46, 47, 48, 90, 104, 108, 185, 196, 213, 216, 218, 219, 241, 245, 257, 364, 366.
KENNEDY'S RIVER, 217.
LEWISTON, 235, 267, 268, 265, 336.
LISBON, 227.
LITTLE RIVER, 121, 161, 337, 367.
LONG ISLAND, 162, 181.
MACHIAS, 52, 68, 119, 140.
MAJABAGADUCE, 128, 160.
MARBLEHEAD, 58.
MARSHFIELD, 54, 120.
MEDUMCOOK, 32, 82, 83, 88, 101, 104, 130, 143, 144, 162, 166, 170, 189, 199, 205, 206, 341, 346.
MERRYMEETING BAY, 29, 258.
MATINICUS ISLAND, 338.
MIDDLE NARROWS, 181.
MIDDLESEX COUNTY, 114, 122, 227.
MILL CREEK, 47.
MILTON, 45, 171.
MONSWEEG, 326.
MONSWEEG BROOK, 355.
MOUNT DESERT, 183, 188.
MOUNT VERNON, 249, 250, 273, 277, 283, 284, 287, 318, 319.
MUDDY RIVER, 258.
MUSCONGUS ISLAND, 120, 130.
NANTUCKET, 196, 197, 268.
NANTUCKET COUNTY, 198.
NASSKEEG, 188.
NEWBURYPORT, 47.
NEWCASTLE, 2, 6, 7, 11, 12, 19, 23, 24, 38, 45, 50, 53, 54, 60, 64, 65, 66, 75, 76, 77, 82, 90, 93, 110, 115, 119, 124, 125, 130, 136, 138, 140, 143, 144, 145, 160, 163, 167, 169, 177, 187, 188, 205, 211, 217, 224, 228, 229, 255, 259, 265, 274, 275, 277, 280, 288, 290, 306, 331, 336, 340, 347.
NEW HAMPSHIRE, 246.
NEW MEADOWS RIVER, 312.

NEW MILFORD, 130, 264, 276, 288, 298, 328, 339, 343, 344, 352, 354.
NEW ROWLEY, 164.
NEWTON, 56.
NEW VINEYARD, 340.
NOBLEBOROUGH, 226, 227, 228, 234, 298, 332, 340.
NORRIDGEWOCK, 141, 142, 164, 183, 228, 249, 305.
NORTH CAROLINA, 226.
NORTH YARMOUTH, 10, 30, 99, 100, 183.
ORR MEADOW, 233.
ORRINGTON, 126.
PARKER'S ISLAND, 3, 213, 215, 368.
PEARSONTOWN, 136.
PEMAQUID, 34, 279, 333.
PEMAQUID OLD FORT, 333.
PENOBSCOT, 45, 80, 160, 163, 166.
PENOBSCOT BAY, 116, 162, 333.
PENOBSCOT RIVER, 60, 118, 125, 129, 160, 161, 166.
PHILADELPHIA, 167.
PITTSTON, 130, 136, 146, 161, 192, 194, 221, 248, 260, 262, 275, 278, 339.
PLEASANT COVE, 173.
PLEASANT RIVER, 45.
PLYMOUTH COUNTY, 54, 129.
POCASSET, 144.
POLAND, 345.
PORTLAND, 234.
PORTSMOUTH, 279.
POWNALBOROUGH, 1, 7, 11, 15, 16, 17, 18, 19, 20, 23, 24, 25, 28, 34, 35, 36, 38, 39, 41, 48, 49, 51, 52, 63, 65, 67, 68, 69, 77, 78, 87, 90, 91, 92, 93, 97, 104, 105, 107, 108, 121, 125, 133, 135, 136, 137, 138, 140, 144, 145, 146, 153, 154, 156, 160, 161, 162, 163, 163, 166, 169, 177, 178, 179, 180, 188, 189, 192, 194, 197, 205, 206, 219, 221, 223, 224, 228, 229, 230, 234, 248, 249,

INDEX OF PLACES.

254, 255, 260, 264, 272, 275, 276, 277, 280, 288, 289, 290, 291, 292, 303, 305, 307, 309, 311, 323, 324, 325, 326, 327, 335, 336, 338, 339, 341, 342, 344, 346, 350, 356.
PREBLE'S LANDING, 4, 5.
RAGGED ISLAND, 333.
READFIELD, 227, 246, 268, 269, 273, 276, 309, 311, 314, 315, 316, 317, 340, 347, 359.
RESQUEAGHEAN ISLAND, 3.
RICHMOND, 90.
ROYALSBOROUGH, 82,
ROYAL'S RIVER, 99.
ST. GEORGES, 7, 8, 9, 11, 12, 13, 20, 33, 34, 39, 40, 41, 50, 51, 53, 58, 66, 67, 79, 80, 84, 86, 90, 101, 111, 118, 132, 140, 143, 144, 147, 162, 171, 224, 271, 344, 345.
ST. GEORGES LOWER TOWN, 108.
ST. GEORGES RIVER, 225, 270.
SALEM, MASS., 138.
SANDY RIVER, 183, 184, 201, 203, 220, 227, 228, 229, 304, 332.
SCITUATE, 54.
SEVEN MILE BROOK, 142, 228.
SHEEPSCOT GREAT POND, 138, 249, 259.
SHEEPSCOT RIVER, 3, 308, 362.
SHERBURNE, 198.
SHIRLEY, 122.
SIDNEY, 201, 226, 227, 254, 263, 273, 278, 279, 336, 339, 340, 364, 365.
SMITHFIELD, 248.
SOURDABSCOCK, 347.
SPRUCE POINT, (BOOTHBAY,) 116.
STAGE ISLAND, 241.
STEPHEN'S RIVER, 5.
STERLINGTON, 111.
STILL-WATER POND, 340.
SUFFOLK COUNTY, 171, 341.
SUNBURY, 166.
SWAN ISLAND, 36.
TABERWYNE STREET, (GLENARM, ANTRIM COUNTY, IRELAND,) 89.
THOMASTON, 86, 108, 132, 144, 160, 193, 206, 211, 212, 221, 223, 224, 230, 232, 235, 236, 255, 338, 339, 343, 344, 345.
THOMPSONBOROUGH, 345.
THOMSON'S COVE, 225.
TISBURY, 48.
TOPSHAM, 2, 21, 23, 31, 41, 45, 51, 52, 65, 73, 75, 82, 84, 93, 94, 107, 112, 119, 121, 125, 141, 142, 160, 161, 168, 169, 195, 209, 211, 211, 221, 226, 229, 234, 235, 250, 251, 255, 258, 259, 261, 277, 278, 292, 324, 325, 337, 339, 340, 342, 345, 346, 347, 348.
TOWNSEND, 12, 13, 15.
TOWNSHIP No. 4, 163.
TOWNSHIP No. 5, 163.
TRENTON, 344.
TURNER, 344.
UNION, 193, 204, 205, 206, 207, 248, 252, 253, 345.
UNION RIVER, 183.
VASSALBOROUGH, 72, 77, 78, 84, 90, 107, 121, 122, 124, 127, 129, 138, 141, 161, 162, 171, 172, 173, 174, 175, 176, 177, 184, 185, 200, 201, 202, 203, 204, 207, 208, 218, 219, 227, 254, 273, 274, 278, 340, 365.
WALDOBOROUGH, 51, 68, 73, 82, 84, 90, 101, 110, 118, 119, 123, 124, 126, 129, 142, 143, 145, 152, 153, 162, 166, 167, 170, 171, 177, 180, 181, 182, 188, 190, 200, 201, 202, 226, 236, 237, 238, 239, 248, 253, 254, 255, 260, 261, 262, 269, 270, 276, 298, 299, 329, 330, 331, 341, 346.
WALES, 130, 138.
WALPOLE, 2, 15, 38, 53, 54, 65, 66, 153.
WARREN, 90, 108, 110, 111, 119, 129, 143, 144, 147, 148, 163, 170, 171, 188, 189, 193, 194, 224, 226, 229, 230, 232, 247, 248, 255, 281, 282, 283, 298, 299, 301,

INDEX OF PLACES.

338, 343, 344, 345, 353.
WASHINGTON, 124, 204.
WESSERUNSETT, } 151.
WESSERUMSEET,
WEST BOWDOINHAM, 110, 141.
WEST POND, 203, 204, 254.
WILD-CAT MEADOW CREEK, 335.
WILLIAMS CREEK, 312.
WILMINGTON, 61.
WINIGANCE, 4, 5, 8, 213.
WINIGANCE CREEK, 257, 312.
WINSLOW, 67, 68, 77, 79, 104, 141, 173, 184, 199, 200, 202, 204, 219, 227, 248, 274, 276, 278, 307, 323, 337, 339, 364, 365, 366.
WINSLOW'S POINT, 225.
WINTHROP, 83, 87, 93, 124, 129, 130, 137, 138, 144, 148, 151, 152, 161, 173, 176, 195, 219, 220, 221, 227, 229, 242, 245, 246, 251, 276, 277, 316, 336.
WISCASSET, 7, 254, 326, 327, 329, 338, 349,
WISCASSET BAY, 2.
WIZZELL'S COVE, 366.
WOOLWICH, 15, 18, 32, 36, 54, 61, 77, 87, 91, 92, 95, 97, 113, 114, 118, 130, 131, 132, 137, 138, 156, 161, 164, 175, 180, 185, 192, 193, 197, 198, 199, 205, 220, 239, 255, 260, 263, 277, 284, 285, 307, 311, 336, 340, 341, 342, 354, 356.
WYMAN PLANTATION, 309, 310.
YARMOUTH, 177.
YORK COUNTY, 4, 12, 45.

www.ingramcontent.com/pod-product-compliance
Lightning Source LLC
Chambersburg PA
CBHW030539080526
44585CB00012B/204